T0213684

Lecture Notes in Computer Science   10610

Commenced Publication in 1973
Founding and Former Series Editors:
Gerhard Goos, Juris Hartmanis, and Jan van Leeuwen

More information about this series at http://www.springer.com/series/7408

Zhenhua Duan · Luke Ong (Eds.)

Formal Methods and Software Engineering

19th International Conference
on Formal Engineering Methods, ICFEM 2017
Xi'an, China, November 13–17, 2017
Proceedings

Springer

Editors
Zhenhua Duan
Xidian University
Xi'an
China

Luke Ong
University of Oxford
Oxford
UK

ISSN 0302-9743   ISSN 1611-3349 (electronic)
Lecture Notes in Computer Science
ISBN 978-3-319-68689-9   ISBN 978-3-319-68690-5 (eBook)
https://doi.org/10.1007/978-3-319-68690-5

Library of Congress Control Number: 2017955779

LNCS Sublibrary: SL2 – Programming and Software Engineering

Printed on acid-free paper

This Springer imprint is published by Springer Nature
The registered company is Springer International Publishing AG
The registered company address is: Gewerbestrasse 11, 6330 Cham, Switzerland

Preface

The International Conference on Formal Engineering Methods (ICFEM) is a forum for advances in formal engineering methods. Among other topics, ICFEM covers verification and validation, software engineering, formal specification and modeling, software security, and software reliability. Since its inception in 1997, ICFEM has served as a primary venue for formal methods theory that promises to bring practical and tangible benefits, as well as practical developments that have been incorporated into real production systems. In recent years, ICFEM has taken place in Tokyo (2016), Paris (2015), Luxembourg (2014), Queenstown (2013), Kyoto (2012), Durham (2011), and Shanghai (2010).

This volume contains the papers presented at 19th International Conference on Formal Engineering Methods (ICFEM 2017), held during November 13–15, 2017, in Xi'an, China. There were 80 submissions. Each submission was reviewed by three Program Committee (PC) members or external reviewers. The program consisted of 28 accepted papers and a paper and two abstracts from the three keynote speakers, David Rosenblum (National University of Singapore), Moshe Vardi (Rice University), and Wang Yi (Uppsala University). The conference was followed by four workshops: the 7th International Workshop SOFL+MSVL 2017, Workshop on Formal and Model-Driven Techniques for Developing Trustworthy Systems (FMMDD 2017), the First International Workshop on Handling Implicit and Explicit Knowledge in Formal System Development (IMPEX 2017), and the 11th NSFC-JSPS Joint Workshop on Formal Methods (NSFC-JSPS FM 2017).

ICFEM 2017 was organized and supported by Xidian University, Xi'an, China. The conference would not have been possible without the assistance of NSFC (grant No. 61420106004), Ministry of Education of the People's Republic of China, and the State Key Laboratory of Integrated Services Networks. Various people contributed to the success of ICFEM 2017: ICFEM Steering Committee members, the PC members and the external reviewers, the authors and the invited speakers, and the local Organizing Committee members; we thank them all for their help. Last but not least we thank Springer for their support in the production of this proceedings volume, and the EasyChair team for their excellent conference management system.

August 2017

Zhenhua Duan
Luke Ong

Organization

Program Committee

Bernhard Aichernig	TU Graz, Austria
Étienne André	Université Paris 13, France
Christian Attiogbe	University of Nantes, France
Richard Banach	University of Manchester, UK
Ezio Bartocci	TU Wien, Austria
Ana Cavalcanti	University of York, UK
Yuting Chen	Shanghai Jiaotong University, China
Sylvain Conchon	Université Paris-Sud, France
Frank De Boer	CWI, The Netherlands
Jinsong Dong	National University of Singapore, Singapore
Zhenhua Duan	Xidian University, China
Carlo Ghezzi	Politecnico di Milano, Italy
Jeremy Gibbons	University of Oxford, UK
Stefania Gnesi	ISTI-CNR, Italy
Lindsay Groves	Victoria University of Wellington, New Zealand
Ian J. Hayes	University of Queensland, Australia
Weiqiang Kong	Dalian University of Technology, China
Fabrice Kordon	LIP6/UPMC, France
Daniel Kroening	University of Oxford, UK
Guoqiang Li	Shanghai Jiaotong University, China
Yuto Lim	JAIST, Japan
Shaoying Liu	Hosei University, Japan
Yang Liu	Nanyang Technological University, Singapore
Larissa Meinicke	University of Queensland, Australia
Stephan Merz	Inria Nancy, France
Huaikou Miao	Shanghai University, China
Mohammadreza Mousavi	Halmstad University, Sweden
Shin Nakajima	National Institute of Informatics, Japan
Luke Ong	University of Oxford, UK
Jun Pang	University of Luxembourg, Luxembourg
Ion Petre	Åbo Akademi University, Finland
Mauro Pezzè	University of Lugano, Italy
Shengchao Qin	Teesside University, UK
Silvio Ranise	FBK-IRST, Italy
Adrian Riesco	Universidad Complutense de Madrid, Spain
Jing Sun	University of Auckland, New Zealand
Cong Tian	Xidian University, China
Jaco van de Pol	University of Twente, The Netherlands

Thomas Wahl	Northeastern University, USA
Xi Wang	Shanghai University, China
Alan Wassyng	McMaster University, Canada
Zijiang Yang	Western Michigan University, USA
Jian Zhang	Chinese Academy of Sciences, China
Hong Zhu	Oxford Brookes University, UK
Huibiao Zhu	East China Normal University, China

Additional Reviewers

Azimi, Sepinoud
Basile, Davide
Bezirgiannis, Nikolaos
Bijo, Shiji
Cheng, Zhuo
Colange, Maximilien
Colvin, Robert
Delahaye, Benoit
Dong, Xiaoju
Dos Santos, Daniel Ricardo
Fantechi, Alessandro
Fiterau-Brostean, Paul
Foster, Simon
Freitas, Leo
Ge, Cunjing
Gerhold, Marcus
He, Mengda
Jérôme, Rocheteau
Keiren, Jeroen
Klai, Kais
Le Gall, Pascale
Le, Quang Loc
Liu, Ailun
Liu, Shuang
Mazzanti, Franco
Menghi, Claudio
Miyazawa, Alvaro
Mostowski, Wojciech
Mu, Chunyan

Nguyen, Kim
Peroni, Marta
Poizat, Pascal
Qu, Hongyang
Renault, Etienne
Rogojin, Vladimir
Sampaio, Gabriela
Sanwal, Muhammad Usman
Schumi, Richard
Shi, Ling
Su, Wen
Sun, Youcheng
Tappler, Martin
Taromirad, Masoumeh
Ter Beek, Maurice H.
Varshosaz, Mahsa
Wang, Dongxia
Wu, Xi
Wu, Zhimin
Xu, Ming
Xu, Qingguo
Xu, Zhiwu
Xuan, Jifeng
Ye, Quanqi
Zeyda, Frank
Zhang, Haitao
Zhang, Lijun
Zhang, Xiaozhen
Zhu, Xiaoran

Abstracts of the Invited Presentations

The Challenges of Probabilistic Thinking: Keynote Talk

David S. Rosenblum

National University of Singapore, Singapore 117417, Singapore
david@comp.nus.edu.sg

Abstract. At ASE 2016, I gave a keynote talk entitled "The Power of Probabilistic Thinking", in which I argued the benefits of applying probabilistic modeling and reasoning to problems in software engineering, and the advantages of this approach over the more "absolutist" approach afforded by reasoning based solely on Boolean logic.

In this talk I will discuss some of the challenges in applying a probabilistic viewpoint. Where do the probabilities for a model come from? What if they're incorrect? What if the behavior of the system to be modeled is imprecise, approximate, noisy, or otherwise uncertain? These challenges, and others, have informed my research in probabilistic verification over the past dozen years, and I have applied a variety of techniques to model and reason about the complexities and "messiness" that arise in real-world software systems using a probabilistic viewpoint.

Keywords: Probabilistic model checking · Probabilistic reasoning · Software engineering · Stochastic behavior

Biography: David S. Rosenblum is Provost's Chair Professor of Computer Science at the National University of Singapore (NUS). He holds a Ph.D. from Stanford University and joined NUS in April 2011 after holding positions as Member of the Technical Staff at AT&T Bell Laboratories (Murray Hill); Associate Professor at the University of California, Irvine; Principal Architect and Chief Technology Officer of PreCache (a technology startup funded by Sony Music); and Professor of Software Systems at University College London.

David's research interests span many problems in software engineering, distributed systems and ubiquitous computing, and his current research focuses on probabilistic verification, uncertainty in software testing, and infrastructure support for the Internet-of-Things. He is a Fellow of the ACM and IEEE. He serves as Editor-in-Chief of the ACM Transactions on Software Engineering and Methodology (ACM TOSEM), and he was previously Chair of the ACM Special Interest Group in Software Engineering (ACM SIGSOFT). He has received two "test-of-time" awards for his research papers, including the ICSE 2002 Most Influential Paper Award for his ICSE 1992 paper on assertion checking, and the first ACM SIGSOFT Impact Paper Award in 2008 for his ESEC/FSE 1997 on Internet-scale event observation and notification (co-authored with Alexander L. Wolf). For more information please visit http://www.comp.nus.edu.sg/∼david/.

A Logical Revolution

Moshe Y. Vardi

Rice University

Abstract. Mathematical logic was developed in an effort to provide formal foundations for mathematics. In this quest, which ultimately failed, logic begat computer science, yielding both computers and theoretical computer science. But then logic turned out to be a disappointment as foundations for computer science, as almost all decision problems in logic are either unsolvable or intractable. Starting from the mid 1970s, however, there has been a quiet revolution in logic in computer science, and problems that are theoretically undecidable or intractable were shown to be quite feasible in practice. This talk describes the rise, fall, and rise of logic in computer science, describing several modern applications of logic to computing, include databases, hardware design, and software engineering.

References

1. Halpern, J.Y., Harper, R., Immerman, N., Kolaitis, P.G., Vardi, M.Y., Vianu, V.: On the unusual effectiveness of logic in computer science. Bull. Assoc. Symb. Logic **7**(2), 213–236 (2001)
2. Vardi, M.Y.: Solving the unsolvable. Commun. ACM **54**(7), 5 (2011)
3. Vardi, M.Y.: Boolean satisfiability: theory and engineering. Commun. ACM **57**(3), 5 (2014)

Towards Customizable CPS: Composability, Efficiency and Predictability

Wang Yi

Uppsala University, Sweden

Abstract. Today, many industrial products are defined by software, and therefore *customizable* by installing new applications on demand - their functionalities are implemented by software and can be modified and extended by software updates. This trend towards customizable products is extending into all domains of IT, including Cyber-Physical Systems (CPS) such as cars, robotics, and medical devices. However, these systems are often highly safety-critical. The current state-of-practice allows hardly any modifications once safety-critical systems are put in operation. This is due to the lack of techniques to preserve crucial safety conditions for the modified system, which severely restricts the benefits of software.

This work aims at new paradigms and technologies for the design and safe software updates of CPS at operation-time – subject to stringent timing constraints, dynamic workloads, and limited resources on complex computing platforms. Essentially there are three key challenges: *Composability*, *Resource-Efficiency* and *Predictability* to enable modular, incremental and safe software updates over system life-time in use. We present research directions to address these challenges: (1) Open architectures and implementation schemes for building composable systems, (2) Fundamental issues in real-time scheduling aiming at a theory of multi-resource (inc. multiprocessor) scheduling, and (3) New-generation techniques and tools for fully separated verification of timing and functional properties of real-time systems with significantly improved efficiency and scalability. The tools shall support not only verification, but also code generation tailored for both co-simulation (interfaced) with existing design tools such as Open Modelica (for modeling and simulation of physical components), and deployment on given computing platforms.

Contents

Invited Talk

Towards Customizable CPS: Composability, Efficiency and Predictability

Wang Yi[✉]

Uppsala University, Uppsala, Sweden
yi@it.uu.se

Abstract. Today, many industrial products are defined by software, and therefore *customizable* by installing new applications on demand - their functionalities are implemented by software and can be modified and extended by software updates. This trend towards customizable products is extending into all domains of IT, including Cyber-Physical Systems (CPS) such as cars, robotics, and medical devices. However, these systems are often highly safety-critical. The current state-of-practice allows hardly any modifications once safety-critical systems are put in operation. This is due to the lack of techniques to preserve crucial safety conditions for the modified system, which severely restricts the benefits of software.

This work aims at new paradigms and technologies for the design and safe software updates of CPS at operation-time – subject to stringent timing constraints, dynamic workloads, and limited resources on complex computing platforms. Essentially there are three key challenges: *Composability, Resource-Efficiency* and *Predictability* to enable modular, incremental and safe software updates over system life-time in use. We present research directions to address these challenges: (1) Open architectures and implementation schemes for building composable systems, (2) Fundamental issues in real-time scheduling aiming at a theory of multi-resource (inc. multiprocessor) scheduling, and (3) New-generation techniques and tools for fully separated verification of timing and functional properties of real-time systems with significantly improved efficiency and scalability. The tools shall support not only verification, but also code generation tailored for both co-simulation (interfaced) with existing design tools such as Open Modelica (for modeling and simulation of physical components), and deployment on given computing platforms.

1 Background

Our life is becoming increasingly dependent on software. Many industrial products are defined by software, thus *customizable* as smart phones: their functionalities, features and economical values are realized by software and can be changed on demand over their life-time through software update. Indeed these products often serve as an open platform through software to access numerous services provided by remote servers in the cloud thanks to the emerging technologies of Internet-of-Things (IoT), cloud storage, cloud computing, data centers etc. The

© Springer International Publishing AG 2017
Z. Duan and L. Ong (Eds.): ICFEM 2017, LNCS 10610, pp. 3–15, 2017.
https://doi.org/10.1007/978-3-319-68690-5_1

trend towards customizable products is extending into all application domains of IT including Cyber-Physical Systems (CPS) such as cars, robotics and medical devices. Today software in our cars may be updated in service workshops; Tesla even allows customers to upgrade remotely the software system of their electric vehicles. Even avionics, traditionally a very conservative area, is moving from functionally separated solutions on uniprocessors to integrated systems on multi-core platforms with the capability to re-configure during operations [10]. However, CPS are often highly safety-critical, thus utmost care must be taken to ensure crucial safety conditions.

Current design methodologies for CPS offer limited support for software updates on systems in operation. Although updates are possible in areas where certification is not mandatory, it is often restricted to updates either offered by professional service providers or software upgrading prepared (through intensive verification and test in the lab [23]) by the manufacturers e.g., Tesla. In general, the current state-of-practice allows hardly any modifications once safety-critical systems are put in operation due to the lack of technology to preserve the safety conditions of

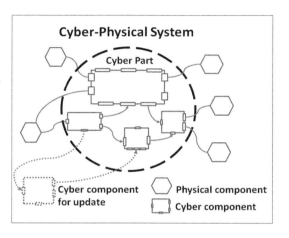

Fig. 1. Towards an open architecture for updatable CPS

the modified systems. A classic example is civil avionics [28]: once a passenger aircraft built by Boeing is certified for operation, it should fly for life-time (estimated 50 years) without modifications to its electronic system and for maintenance the company must purchase the original electronic control units and store them for 50 years. It is remarkable that in the era of IoT when everything is connected and everything is changing over time, we are flying in a machine running outdated software made decades ago. This largely restricts the benefits of software.

2 Why Update CPS in Operation?

In less safety-critical areas, software updates are widely adopted by users to increase system safety by software patches or extend system functionalities for better utilization of the computational resources by installing new applications on demand. Smart phones and notebooks are examples. Apart from the lack of technologies for safety preservation, there seems to be no reason why software for CPS in general should not be updated.

CPS may be small embedded devices or large-scale networked embedded systems often viewed as systems of (sub-)systems with underlining communication infrastructure; a (sub-)system may have the overall architecture as shown in Fig. 1, consisting of a collection of cyber components (software components) interacting with physical components in real time through sensors and actuators. At operation-time, the user or customer may want to update the software system by installing a new application (a software component) purchased from a software provider. The update should be done by herself, not a professional service provider or the manufacturer who has full access to the software system. For example, consider smart transportation. When travelling in North Europe in the winter with a future self-driving car, we may want to install *ourselves* applications for ice- and elk-detection for safe driving. Another example is medical device e.g., pacemaker. In a possible future scenario, for a patient carrying such a device, a new heart problem may manifest over time (e.g., due to aging of the patient). To treat the upcoming problem, a doctor may propose to install a new application instead of replacing the device.

3 The Challenges

Clearly, the examples illustrate that software updates may lead to more reliable and cost-efficient solutions. However, for both examples, we must make sure to preserve the following two basic conditions before the intended updates are realized:

Condition 1 the new application will not interfere with the existing system: they should not block each other due to synchronization and their input and output values should be compatible, satisfying required relationships – the functional correctness must be preserved.

Condition 2 the computing platforms have enough computational resources to run the new application without being overloaded or violating any timing constraints – non-functional correctness must be preserved.

These two safety conditions illustrate the following key challenges for the design and update of CPS:

Composability (The design challenge) to build systems that are updatable at operation-time, allowing for modular updates that should neither require re-designing the original system, nor interfere with the functionalities of the original system (Condition 1).

Efficiency (The run-time challenge)to optimize resource utilization for preserving Condition 2 such that incremental updates may be applied over the system's life-time.

Predictability (The verification challenge) to enable safe updates through verification of the two conditions (Condition 1 and 2) on demand before the intended updates are committed.

The three challenges are often contradicting. For example, to optimize resource utilization, a global solution may be preferred. However, globally dynamic resource sharing may result in unmanageable non-determinism leading to poor predictability. Similarly designing systems for predictability using monolithic-threading or time-triggered approaches may not be an advantage for achieving the composability because these approaches require all computation jobs and resource accesses must be scheduled at design-time, which leaves little possibility for updates after deployment. In fact, current design methodologies of embedded systems allow for systems that are either predictable or composable, and often resource in-efficient in many cases due to resource over-dimensioning. For instance, synchronous systems [22] designed for predictable and deterministic behavior are often hard to modify and difficult for integration of new functionalities without re-designing the whole system; whereas concurrent systems [6] with multi-threading can be extended easily by new threads for new functionalities, thus are better for composability, but poor for predictability as they are hard to verify due to non-determinism.

For the design of updatable systems, naturally we take a component-based approach, which allows for modular changes. Component-based software development has attracted a large amount of research; in the past decades, various component models have been developed e.g. [9] for a classification of software models in the context of software engineering. In the domain of embedded systems, considerable efforts have been investigated within the ARTIST initiatives on model-based design (see e.g. [5]). An interesting line of work is the theories of interfaces e.g. [12] for timed systems, [8,41] for resource modeling and scheduling and more recently, contract-based systems design [3,13]. However, all previous attempts address only issues on the design of systems. Our focus will be on updates after deployment. Conceptually the existing techniques are useful, but not applicable. For updates, we must address composability issues at run-time. First, we must build systems that are updatable. Second, we must make sure that the updates are safe before they are realized.

4   Objectives

We distinguish design-time, operation-time and run-time. Operation-time means when systems are in operation after deployment, which can be off-line or on-line but not necessarily run-time. Any requirement at operation-time is more demanding than design-time but less than run-time. Therefore for operation-time updates, we assume that the overall architecture of a system and also its components (or sub-systems) are all designed, verified and deployed at design-time and abstract models tailored for operation-time verification of the two conditions are available.

The overall objective of this work is three-fold. First we aim at new implementation schemes for building updatable systems. Second, we develop scheduling techniques to optimize resource utilization at run-time and thus enable incremental updates over system's life-time. Third, we develop verification techniques and tools to validate the safety of updates on demand. Now we outline our ideas to reach the goals.

Composability shall be achieved by (1) multi-threading and (2) non-blocking communication that preserves synchronous semantics for data exchange among components. The objective of this work is to develop open system architectures as illustrated in Fig. 1 offering open interfaces and new implementation schemes to build systems allowing for integration of new software components by simply creating new threads. The threads will be coordinated by a centralized run-time system to ensure that the synchronous semantics of data exchange among threads (by reading and writing requests) is preserved [7] and the timing constraints on computation jobs released by threads are satisfied. For updating such multi-threading systems with new software components under the described requirements, we need to solve optimization problems similar to retiming of synchronous circuits, a classic problem in circuits design [29].

Resource-efficiency will be addressed by static partitioning and run-time scheduling. The objective of this work is two-fold. First, we study fundamental issues in real-time scheduling, addressing the optimality and complexity of scheduling algorithms [15] in particular questions related to dynamic workloads with complex release patterns of computation jobs and parallel computing platforms such as multi- and many-cores with massive parallel and heterogeneous processing units. The goal is to develop a parallel version of the real-time calculus [40] aiming at a unified theory for characterization of parallel and heterogeneous resource demands and resource supplies, as well as optimal mapping between them, as a scientific foundation for multiprocessor scheduling, which is a hard open problem in the field of real-time systems. Second, a practical approach will be taken to achieve near-optimal solutions for applications under assumptions in systems building such as non-blocking data exchange.

Safety-conditions will be ensured by verification on demand before the intended updates are committed. The objective of this work is to develop a new generation of verification techniques and tools for CPS in particular a new version of UPPAAL with significant improvements on efficiency and scalability by fully separating the analysis of timing and functional correctness. Functional properties will be specified and verified in a contract-based framework supported with SMT-based verification techniques. Timing and non-functional properties will be specified on computation jobs and verified using scalable techniques developed for scheduling analysis [34,35]. For uniprocessor platforms, the existing techniques and tools e.g. [1] scale well with industrial size problems. The future focus will be on multicore platforms.

5   Work Directions

To address the challenges, we propose the following work directions.

5.1   Towards Open Architectures for Updates

We consider CPS that may be large-scale networked embedded systems of (sub-)systems. A (sub-)system with its own computing platform may have a set of software components (cyber part as shown in Fig. 1) deployed based on a data-flow-like diagram with basic blocks representing its components (which may have hierarchical structures) and (links representing the input and output relation among the components via interfaces. A sub-system may contain local network links for which extra blocks should be created, modelling the delays for data exchange if the delays are not ignorable. The diagram may also contain cycles; however a cycle should contain a delay block to avoid infeasible behaviors. For abstraction, each physical-component is assumed to have a set of data buffers (e.g., implemented by a driver) as its interface for data exchange with software components.

To enable updates at operation-time after deployment, we must build systems that enjoy the following properties (see e.g. [2]): (1) integrating a new component should not require re-designing the whole system, and (2) a newly integrated component should not interfere with the existing components. Apart from resource sharing that shall be addressed separately, there are essentially two sources for potential interferences:

- The outputs of a component are not needed by the others, violating the functional correctness and
- The Components may block each other due to synchronization mechanisms for keeping data coherence.

In the following we propose solutions to disable these potential interferences.

Components, Interfaces and Contracts. We do not restrict how a component is implemented inside but it must offer a well-defined interface containing a set of input and output data buffers open for updates allowing for integration of new components. The functional correctness of a component is specified by a contract on its interface consisting of a pre-condition on input buffers and a post-condition on output buffers. The contract is a local invariant satisfied by the computational behavior of the component, which should be verified at design-time.

Furthermore, a workload model specifying the timing constraints and resource requirement of each component should be available (created at design-time), which may be considered as part of the contract. The workload model (or task model) of a component specifies the release patterns of three types of requests: reading, writing and computing (jobs). At run-time, the computing jobs will be scheduled and executed according to the timing constraints. The reading and writing requests will be non-blocking and coordinated to preserve the synchronous semantics.

Non-blocking Data Exchange that Preserves Synchronous Semantics. To implement the components and the original system, any synchronization schemes may be adopted to keep data coherence. However for integration of new components at operation-time, we have to adopt non-blocking data exchange. For non-blocking writing on an input buffer, only one-writer is allowed; but an output buffer may allow arbitrary number of readers. Data items written should be considered as non-consumable. The rationale is that new integrated components may only read data from an open interface of the existing system for computing their own output. The computed values may be used for realizing new functionalities or write back to the existing system to improve the existing functionalities on input buffers that previously have default values before the integration.

Reading is enabled (non-blocking) at any time; it is only copying (but not consuming) the data; writing will over-write the previously written data; thus only the latest data (i.e., the most fresh) values are available in the input buffers if the buffer capacity is not enough and the readers are slower than the writer.

To keep data coherence, we will develop new synchronization protocols to preserve the synchronous semantics of data exchange [7], ensuring two conditions:

- Globally all readers should receive the same data if the reading requests are issued after the same writing request and
- Locally for each component, the writing of an output value should correspond to the input value by the preceding reading request.

Essentially the arrival order of reading and writing requests should be enforced by the centralized run-time system; whereas the computation jobs may be scheduled in any orders satisfying the timing constraints provided that the local order of reading (input), computing (jobs) and writing (output) is preserved for each component. For the simple case when computation jobs take no time, the the DBP protocol (Dynamic Buffering Protocols [7]) can be used to preserve the synchronous semantics. Here we have a challenging case where computation jobs will have non-zero computation times (specified by WCETs) and timing constraints such as deadlines. The computation jobs may be released according to any patterns e.g., specified using graph-based real-time task models e.g., [34]. Our goal is to develop scheduling algorithms and data buffering protocols to preserve both the timing constraints and also the synchronous semantics. The hard technical challenge is to design algorithms and protocols which can be re-configured at operation-time to handle software updates. This requires to solve non-trivial optimization problems similar to retiming of synchronous circuits [29]. We aim at techniques for near-optimal solutions. This work shall be driven and evaluated by case studies including a large-scale industrial application to build a solar-powered electric vehicle [31].

5.2   Towards Precise Workload Modelling and Optimal Scheduling

Product customization often refers to incremental modifications. For CPS, it is about (1) integrating a new software component for extensions with new functionalities or (2) updating an existing software component for improvements on the systems functionalities. Both cases may increase resource requirement incrementally and so incease the system workload. Eventually it will hit the limit of resource utilization (the ideal case is 100%) when the system is infeasible or when a timing constraint for a computation job is violated. Thus run-time resource management and scheduling is crucial for the customization of systems in operation if not for the original design where the ad hoc solution in practice is often by over-dimensioning the system resources with redundancy, which is not an option for customization. If system resources are not utilized in an optimal manner, the possibility for customization will not last long. There are two technical challenges. First, the workload (or resource requirement) of each software component (and the whole system) should be modelled and characterized as precisely as possible to reduce the pessimism of scheduling analysis, thus potentially allow for more applications to run concurrently on the platform. Second, the workload should be mapped and scheduled on the platform to achieve optimal resource utilization.

For a survey on real-time workload models, see e.g. [25, 36]. There is a full hierarchy of workloads models available of different expressive powers and degrees of analysis difficulty as shown in Fig. 2. In the context of real-time systems, often simplistic models such as periodic or sporadic models (e.g. the classic task model L&L due to Liu and Layland [30]) are adopted to over-approximate the workload generated by physical- and software-components, which in many applications may lead to pessimistic analysis and resource over-dimensioning. To faithfully describe the

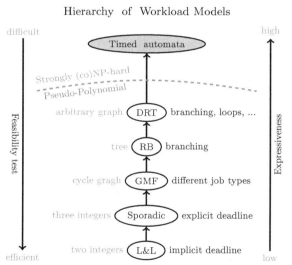

Fig. 2. Expressiveness vs. analysis efficiency

resource requirements and timing constraints of software components, as the basis for workload characterization, we will use the di-graph real-time task model [34] and further extend it within manageable complexity for automated analysis with features including parallel OpenMP like structures [37,38], synchronization [32] as well as mixed criticality workloads [14,18]. To capture the dynamic workload triggered by physical components, a new line of work has been proposed in [4,33] to compute faithful abstract models from hybrid models for precise schedulability analysis. The work will be further developed to compute the di-graph models from general hybrid automata based on the theory of optimal control and abstraction techniques [24].

Second, efficient scheduling algorithms and methods must be develop to optimize resource utilization at run-time. For uniprocessor platforms, the theoretical foundation of real-time scheduling has been established in the past decades with various scheduling and analysis techniques available. Several fundamental problems are solved recently [16,17,19]. However to implement the synchronous semantics of data exchange in a multi-threading setting, run-time scheduling must consider dependent tasks imposed by the input and output relations defined by a data-flow like diagram as shown in Fig. 1. It is a non-trivial technical challenge to design optimal scheduling algorithms for graph-based real-time models under precedence constraints even for uniprocessor platforms. To enforce the synchronous semantics, we foresee that memory consumption must be handled efficiently to make multiple local copies of the same data dynamically to serve the reading requests. Thus memory requirements must be considered in run-time scheduling, which brings another dimension of complexity in uniprocessor scheduling. On the theory side, there are still open issues in uniprocessor scheduling, including the complexity of uniprocessor scheduling of sporadic tasks with arbitrary deadlines and optimality of mixed-criticality scheduling [15].

For multicore platforms, the research community has produced a large number of insightful theoretical results [11], with the hope to extend the well-established theory for uniprocessor systems developed in the last three decades to the multiprocessor setting, e.g. our work on extending the classic result of Liu and Layland on rate-monotonic scheduling to multiprocessor setting [20]. We aim at obtaining such results also for heterogeneous platforms. In particular, we will study the application mapping problem on heterogeneous multiprocessor platforms that may have processor cores e.g. GPU, CPU with different processing speeds, and non-trivial interaction with I/O devices, as well as memory requirements, which is often the case in embedded applications in the context of CPS. The ultimate goal is to develop a parallel version of the real-time calculus [21,26,39,40], as a scientific foundation for multi-resource (including multiprocessor cores) scheduling, which is one of the challenging open problems in the field of real-time systems.

However, we will also take a practical approach to develop real-time applications for updatable systems on platforms with massive parallel processing units such as multi- and many-core, for which near-optimal solutions may be possible under the assumption in systems building such as non-blocking data-exchange.

5.3 Towards Fully Separated Verification of Timing and Functional Properties

To validate the safety of operation-time updates, we must developed powerful and scalable techniques for automated verification of the safety conditions as outlined earlier. Since the invention of model checking, the area of verification has advanced significantly with tremendous success in industrial applications.

Complex systems with millions of states and configurations may be verified today in seconds.

Model checking technology has been adopted to verify real-time systems where UPPAAL [27] is one of the leading tools. However, it is well-recognized that the technique suffers from the scalability problem, which is even more critical for real-time systems where the tool must handle not only functional properties but also timing constraints. We will take a different approach and fully separate the verification of functional and non-functional properties to improve the scalability of the tool. This is a lesson learnt from the development of UPPAAL. Mixing up functional and timing behaviors in modelling harms significantly the efficiency of the tool, which is the critical barrier for its scalability. In the implementation of UPPAAL, for verifying functional correctness e.g. deadlock-freeness or mutual exclusion properties, it demands a large amount of memory for keeping track of the timing constraints. Unfortunately UPPAAL had to treat these aspects in one unified framework which is not adequate for verification with manageable complexity. Major safety-critical properties should be guaranteed independently of timing. For example, a system should be deadlock-free independently of how fast a component is executed. There is room for great improvements.

The term *predictability* refers often to *easy-to-verify*. It concerns two parts. First, the system must be built *verifiable*. The model selected for design and verification should be as expressive as possible to express interesting system features; however it should not be too expressive with unnecessarily expressive power which may harm the analysis efficiency. The models for verification should be carefully selected for efficient analysis and fast termination. For many applications, timed automata are often too powerful. For example, to model real-time task release patterns, only lower bounds on clocks are needed to express the minimal release distances of computation jobs, mimicking the delay statements in real-time programming languages e.g. Ada. However for reasoning about timing constraints on computations, upper bounds on clocks are needed to express deadlines. Separating lower bounds on task releases and upper bounds on computation jobs leads to an adequate model for real-time systems [34] for which feasibility analysis can be verified efficiently in pseudo polynomial time [17]. This model will be the basis for our work on verification of timing and non-functional properties.

For non-functional correctness, as part of its interface to the computing platform, each component will have a workload model specifying its timing constraint and resource requirement within the tractable hierarchy as shown in Fig. 2 (see [36] for details) for efficient operation-time checks on demand. However, the demanding challenge is in the scheduling and analysis on complex platforms such as multi-cores. A partition-based approach is promising [20], which may reduce the analysis problems to the uniprocessor setting. In connection with the work on developing the theory of multiprocessor scheduling outlined earlier, different strategies will be evaluated for multiprocessor schedulability analysis.

To reason about functional correctness, a theory of contract-based interfaces will be developed based on first-order logic where a component interface will be specified using pre- and post-condition on input and output data as a local invariant of the component. Given contracts for each component, two essential properties have to be verified: (1) each component satisfies its own contract; and (2) the contracts of components combined in a system are compatible, i.e., each component produces the outputs needed by the other components. The first aspect (1) is essentially a problem of software verification, and will be addressed using techniques from abstract interpretation, software model checking, and SMT-based verification. A central concern in (1) will be the handling of real-valued quantities, which are today in software represented mainly as fixed-point or floating-point data, and supported by only few of the existing analysis tools (and usually with limited scalability). A technical challenge is to advance the state of the art in floating-point verification and develop improved SMT techniques for this theory. In (2), logical relationship between multiple contracts must be checked, a problem that is today primarily addressed with the help of SMT solving. Again, the main concern will be to scale up SMT methods to handle the relevant data-types and the extent of contracts needed for real-world systems.

Acknowledgement. For discussions on ideas presented in this document, the author wish to thank Jakaria Abdullah, David Black-Schaffer, Gaoyang Dai, Pontus Ekberg, Peter Fritzon, Nan Guan, Bengt Jonsson, Morteza Mohagheghy, Christer Nordström, Philipp Ruemmer, Joseph Sifakis, Martin Stigge, Janos Sztipanovits and Aleksandar Zeljic.

References

1. Abdullah, J., Dai, G., Guan, N., Mohaqeqi, M., Yi, W.: Towards a tool: times-pro for modeling, analysis, simulation and implementation of cyber-physical systems. In: Aceto, L., et al. (eds.) Larsen Festschrift. LNCS, vol. 10460, pp. 23–639. Springer, Heidelberg (2017). doi:10.1007/978-3-319-63121-9_31
2. Attie, P., Baranov, E., Bliudze, S., Jaber, M., Sifakis, J.: A general framework for architecture composability. Formal Aspects Comput. **28**(2), 207–231 (2016)
3. Benveniste, A., Caillaud, B., Nickovic, D., Passerone, R., Raclet, J., Reinkemeier, P., Vincentelli, A.S., Damm, W., Henzinger, T., Larsen, K.G.: Contracts for systems design: theory. INRIA report, France (2015)
4. Biondi, A., Buttazzo, G., Simoncelli, S.: Feasibility analysis of engine control tasks under edf scheduling. In: Proceedings of ECRTS15, pp. 139–148. IEEE (2015)
5. Bouyssounouse, B., Sifakis, J.: Embedded Systems Design: The ARTIST Roadmap for Research and Development, vol. 3436. Springer, Heidelberg (2005)
6. Burns, A., Wellings, A.: Concurrent and Real-Time Programming in Ada. Cambridge University Press, New York (2007)
7. Caspi, P., Scaife, N., Sofronis, C., Tripakis, S.: Semantics-preserving multitask implementation of synchronous programs. ACM Trans. Embed. Comput. Syst. **7**(2), 15:1–15:40 (2008)
8. Chakabarti, A., de Alfaro, L., Henzinger, T.A., Stoelinga, M.I.A.: Resource interfaces. In: Alur, R., Lee, I. (eds.) EMSOFT 2003 (2003)

9. Crnkovic, I., Sentilles, S., Vulgarakis, A., Chaudron, M.R.V.: A classification framework for software component models. IEEE Trans. Softw. Eng. **37**(5), 593–615 (2011)
10. Certainty (Deliverable D1.2): Certification of real time applications designed for mixed criticality (2014). www.certainty-project.eu/
11. Davis, R.I., Burns, A.: A survey of hard real-time scheduling for multiprocessor systems. ACM Comput. Surv. **43**(4), 35:1–35:44 (2011)
12. de Alfaro, L., Henzinger, T.A., Stoelinga, M.I.A.: Timed interfaces. In: EMSOFT 2002, pp. 108–122 (2002)
13. Derler, P., Lee, E.A., Tripakis, S., Törngren, M.: Cyber-physical system design contracts. In: Proceedings of the ACM/IEEE 4th International Conference on Cyber-Physical Systems, ICCPS 2013, pp. 109–118. ACM (2013)
14. Ekberg, P., Yi, W.: Bounding and shaping the demand of generalized mixed-criticality sporadic task systems. Real-Time Syst. **50**(1), 48–86 (2014)
15. Ekberg, P., Yi, W.: A note on some open problems in mixed-criticality scheduling. In: Proceedings of the 6th International Real-Time Scheduling Open Problems Seminar (RTSOPS) (2015)
16. Ekberg, P., Yi, W.: Uniprocessor feasibility of sporadic tasks remains conp-complete under bounded utilization. In: Proceedings of RTSS15, pp. 87–95 (2015)
17. Ekberg, P., Yi, W.: Uniprocessor feasibility of sporadic tasks with constrained deadlines is strongly conp-complete. In: ECRTS 2015, pp. 281–286 (2015)
18. Ekberg, P., Yi, W.: Schedulability analysis of a graph-based task model for mixed-criticality systems. Real-Time Syst. **52**(1), 1–37 (2016)
19. Ekberg, P., Yi, W.: Fixed-priority schedulability of sporadic tasks on uniprocessors is np-hard. In: Proceedings of RTSS17, Paris (2017)
20. Guan, N., Stigge, M., Yi, W., Yu, G.: Fixed-priority multiprocessor scheduling with liu and layland's utilization bound. In: Proceedings of RTAS 2010, Stockholm, pp. 165–174 (2010)
21. Guan, N., Yi, W.: Finitary real-time calculus: efficient performance analysis of distributed embedded systems. In: RTSS 2013, pp. 330–339, December 2013
22. Halbwachs, N.: Synchronous Programming of Reactive Systems. The Springer International Series in Engineering and Computer Science. Springer, New York (2013)
23. Holthusen, S., Quinton, S., Schaefer, I., Schlatow, J., Wegner, M.: Using multi-viewpoint contracts for negotiation of embedded software updates. In: Proceedings 1st Workshop on Pre- and Post-Deployment Verification Techniques, Iceland, pp. 31–45, June 2016
24. Krčál, P., Mokrushin, L., Thiagarajan, P.S., Yi, W.: Timed vs. time-triggered automata. In: Proceedings of CONCUR 2004, London, pp. 340–354 (2004)
25. Krcál, P., Yi, W.: Decidable and undecidable problems in schedulability analysis using timed automata. In: Proceedings of TACAS 2004, pp. 236–250 (2004)
26. Lampka, K., Bondorf, S., Schmitt, J., Guan, N., Yi, W.: Generalized finitary real-time calculus. In: Proceedings of IEEE INFOCOM 2017, Atlanta, GA, USA (2017)
27. Larsen, K.G., Pettersson, P., Yi, W.: Uppaal in a nutshell. STTT **1**(1), 134–152 (1997)
28. Lee, E.A.: Time for high-confidence cyber-physical systems. In: ICES workshop on Embedded and Cyber-physical Systems - Model-Based Design for Analysis and Synthesis, 6 February 2012, Stockholm, Sweden (2014)
29. Leiserson, C.E., Saxe, J.B.: Optimizing synchronous systems. In: FOCS 1981, the 22nd Annual Symposium on Foundations of Computer Science, pp. 23–36. IEEE (1981)

30. Liu, C.L., Layland, J.W.: Scheduling algorithms for multiprogramming in a hard-real-time environment. J. ACM **20**(1), 46–61 (1973)
31. Lv, M., Guan, N., Ma, Y., Ji, D., Knippel, E., Liu, X., Yi, W.: Speed planning for solar-powered electric vehicles. In: Proceedings of the Seventh International Conference on Future Energy Systems, Waterloo, ON, Canada, 21–24 June 2016, pp. 6:1–6:10 (2016)
32. Mohaqeqi, M., Abdullah, J., Guan, N., Yi, W.: Schedulability analysis of synchronous digraph real-time tasks. In: Proceedings of ECRTS 2016, France, pp. 176–186 (2016)
33. Mohaqeqi, M., Abdullah, S.M.J., Ekberg, P., Yi, W.: Refinement of workload models for engine controllers by state space partitioning. In: Proceedings of ECRTS 2017, Croatia, pp. 11:1–11:22 (2017)
34. Stigge, M., Ekberg, P., Guan, N., Yi, W.: The digraph real-time task model. In: Proceedings of RTAS 2011, Chicago, IL, USA (2011)
35. Stigge, M., Yi, W.: Combinatorial abstraction refinement for feasibility analysis. In: Proceedings of RTSS 2013 (2013)
36. Stigge, M., Yi, W.: Graph-based models for real-time workload: a survey. Real-Time Syst. **51**(5), 602–636 (2015)
37. Sun, J., Guan, N., Wang, Y., He, Q., Yi, W.: Scheduling and analysis of real-time openmp task systems with tied tasks. In: Proceedings of RTSS 2017, Paris (2017)
38. Sun, J., Guan, N., Wang, Y., Deng, Q., Zeng, P., Yi, W.: Feasibility of fork-join real-time task graph models: hardness and algorithms. ACM Trans. Embed. Comput. Syst. **15**(1), 14:1–14:28 (2016)
39. Tang, Y., Guan, N., Liu, W., Phan, L., Yi, W.: Revisiting gpc and and connector in real-time calculus. In: Proceedings of RTSS 2017, Paris (2017)
40. Thiele, L., Chakraborty, S., Naedele, M.: Real-time calculus for scheduling hard real-time systems. In: ISCAS 2000, vol. 4, pp. 101–104 (2000)
41. Thiele, L., Wandeler, E., Stoimenov, N.: Real-time interfaces for composing real-time systems. In: Proceedings of the 6th ACM & Amp; IEEE International Conference on Embedded Software, EMSOFT 2006, pp. 34–43. ACM (2006)

Contributed Papers

Modularization of Refinement Steps
for Agile Formal Methods

Fabian Benduhn[1(✉)], Thomas Thüm[2], Ina Schaefer[2], and Gunter Saake[1]

[1] University of Magdeburg, Magdeburg, Germany
fabian.benduhn@ovgu.de
[2] TU Braunschweig, Braunschweig, Germany

Abstract. The combination of agile methods and formal methods has been recognized as a promising field of research. However, many formal methods rely on a refinement-based development process which poses problems for their integration into agile processes. We consider redundancies within refinement hierarchies as a challenge for the practical application of stepwise refinement and propose superimposition-based modularization of refinement steps as a potential solution. While traditionally, each model in a refinement hierarchy must be developed and maintained separately, our concept allows developers to specify the refinement steps that transform a model into a refined one. We have developed tool support for the language AsmetaL and evaluated our approach by means of a case study. The results indicate a reduction of complexity for the development artifacts in terms of their overall size by 48.6% for the ground model and four refinements. Furthermore, the case study shows that superimposition-based refinement eases the development of alternative refinements for exploratory development and to cope with changing requirements. Thus, we consider this work as a step towards agile formal methods that are tailored to support iterative development, facilitating their incorporation into agile development processes.

Keywords: Formal methods · Agile methods · Refinement · Modularity · Superimposition · Abstract state machines

1 Introduction

Despite the potential benefits of applying formal methods to increase the quality of software and a growing number of success stories, facilitating their industrial adoption has been recognized as an important research challenge [46]. Traditional formal methods and techniques have mostly been developed assuming a waterfall-like development process in which all requirements are known from the beginning and do not change during the development process [36]. For decades, research has focused on developing techniques to prevent errors when transforming a set of well-known requirements into an implementation that faithfully fulfills them [19]. However, researchers and practitioners increasingly recognize the

© Springer International Publishing AG 2017
Z. Duan and L. Ong (Eds.): ICFEM 2017, LNCS 10610, pp. 19–35, 2017.
https://doi.org/10.1007/978-3-319-68690-5_2

need to adapt and develop formal methods to be incorporated into agile development processes in which requirements are expected to change frequently [13,24]. In this paper, we contribute to agile formal methods by investigating concepts to ease the integration of refinement-based formal methods into agile processes.

Stepwise refinement is an essential concept in formal methods and has been integrated into many popular methods such as Event-B, ASM, or Z [1,17,42]. The idea of stepwise refinement is that the developer starts by specifying a high-level model of the system that is derived from the requirements and easy to understand, but still accurate regarding all relevant system properties [16]. Such a high-level model can already be subject to verification and validation, which helps to prevent errors early in the development process [16]. Once the developer is satisfied with the initial model, it is refined by adding more details or additional functionality. This refinement process continues until a satisfying level of abstraction has been reached, eventually leading to executable code.

While the general idea of model-based refinement (i.e., to postpone design decisions as long as possible during the development process) seems to be compatible with agile processes such as iterative development, its practical application poses several challenges. Researchers have identified the development of reusable modules for model-based refinement as a challenge for their integration into agile processes [23]. In particular, iterative development becomes difficult because of the inherent redundancies between the different representations of the system in the refinement hierarchy. When requirements change, the model of the system needs to be adjusted on several levels of refinement. Every modification potentially needs to be performed on all succeeding levels, each typically maintained as a separate development artifact. This overhead is especially a problem for agile processes, in which changes are expected to occur frequently and must be synchronized between all levels of refinement.

We propose to apply superimposition-based modularization to refinement steps with the goal to avoid redundancies within refinement hierarchies and to ease the replacement and removal of design decisions, making it easier to cope with changing requirements. We exemplify superimposition-based refinement using the Abstract State Machine (ASM) method which includes a very general notion of refinement, subsuming other more restricted refinement concepts used in other formal methods [16]. That is, we do not aim to define a specific mathematical notion of refinement for ASMs - this has to be done by the engineer for each project - but to investigate how to describe the required development artifacts of a given refinement hierarchy. As such, we expect superimposition-based refinement to be applicable for other methods than ASM as well.

We have developed tool support based on FeatureHouse, a tool for compositional development of software based on language-independent superimposition [5]. We extended it to support modular refinement steps using the language AsmetaL [27,28]. To evaluate our approach, we have performed a case study based on the Landing Gear System [8,14]. In detail, we make the following contributions:

- We propose to apply **superimposition-based refinement**, allowing developers to specify modular refinement steps that can be automatically composed to derive a model of the system on the desired levels of abstraction, to facilitate flexibility.
- We exemplify the concept with an **extension of AsmetaL** that supports superimposition-based refinement.
- We developed **tool support** for our extension of AsmetaL. It is integrated into Eclipse and allows the direct application of the Asmeta toolset to perform various analyses to the model on each level of refinement.
- We provide **first empirical evidence** of the feasibility of our approach by means of its application to the landing gear case study which indicates a large reduction of system size due to removed redundancies in the models.

2 Modularization of Refinement Steps

We explain the basic concept of model-based refinement in formal methods and discuss some of its challenges for the application to agile development in Sect. 2.1. In Sect. 2.2, we propose to modularize refinement steps based on superimposition to reduce redundancies within development artifacts.

2.1 Refinement in Formal Methods

In model-based refinement, the developer starts with an abstract model that is refined stepwise to executable code or a sufficiently detailed model [16]. For the sake of clarity, we explicitly distinguish between refinements and refinement steps; A refinement step describes the changes that are applied to transform the initial model or one of its refinements into a more concrete refinement. The result of a refinement-based development process is a sequence of refinements.

In Fig. 1, we show a sequence of refinements for the Landing Gear System that we use as a running example. The Landing Gear System has been proposed by Boniol et al. as a benchmark for formal methods and behavioral verification [14]. It describes an airplane landing gear system consisting of three landing sets. The system controls opening and closing mechanisms of the landing sets and includes features such as sensors, cylinders, and a health monitoring system. For a more complete description of the system we refer to the literature [14].

The refinement sequence of the Landing Gear system, presented in Fig. 1, has been adapted from Arcaini et al. who exemplified its stepwise development from an abstract model to Java code [8]. Each refinement step can be applied to the model on a previous level of refinement. The initial model, here simply called *Landing Gear*, only includes behavior of a single landing set and its most basic elements, namely doors and gears, and describes their interaction. The first refinement step *Cylinders* adds the behavior of cylinders that extend and retract during the landing sequence. We depict the resulting refinement of the system model in terms of the involved refinement steps: {Landing Gear, Cylinders} describes the first refinement of the Landing Gear model. Similarly, the next

Fig. 1. Sequence of refinements for the Landing Gear System

refinement steps add details about the behavior of sensors to the landing set, the two additional landing sets, and a health monitoring system, respectively.

A sequence of refinements typically leads to development artifacts containing a high degree of redundancy. The reason is that typically each refinement is merely an extended version of the previous one and only differs in a specific aspect. In practice, refinements are typically created manually by duplicating the initial model and adapting it sequentially by applying refinement steps. This procedure is known as clone-and-own in the context of software variability and has been studied on the level of code [21,38].

Assuming a sequential development process in which all requirements are known a priori and are not subject to change, the clone-and-own approach would be feasible. However, it is not suitable for agile practices such as iterative development. In particular, the redundancies within the refinement sequence lead to practical problems, especially for the maintenance of development artifacts. In the Landing Gear System, changes to the cylinder sub-system may involve additional adjustments in three succeeding refinement levels. In general, each modification on a given level of refinement may affect lower levels as well. The high degree of redundancy makes it difficult to react flexibly to changing requirements.

2.2 Superimposition-Based Modularization

We have seen that redundancies between development artifacts in traditional refinement hierarchies pose several challenges for the integration of formal methods into iterative processes. To avoid those redundancies, we propose superimposition-based modularization of refinement steps, as illustrated in Fig. 2. One of the key ideas is to specify the refinement steps, as partial model representing the delta between the abstract and the refined model. Based on the concept of superimposition, the refinements for each level can be automatically derived from the modular refinement steps (e.g., for analysis purposes). Developers do not need to maintain the models on each level of refinement directly. Instead, only the modular refinement steps have to be maintained manually, allowing the developer to reduce the degree of redundancy in development artifacts. Thus, if we perform a change to a modular refinement step (e.g., Sensors) the change automatically applies to subsequent refinements.

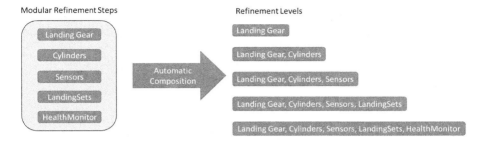

Fig. 2. Concept of modular refinement applied to the Landing Gear System

We propose to modularize refinement steps using hierarchical superimposition as proposed by Apel et al. [5]. As depicted in Fig. 3, the base model and each refinement step are considered as syntax trees, whose nodes represent syntactical elements of the model. When superimposing two trees, their nodes are merged recursively based on their names, types, and relative positions. Nodes are merged, if they have the same name and type and if their parents have been merged. Nodes that cannot be matched this way are added to the tree at the current position, as is the case for node $n4$ in the example. Corresponding nonterminal nodes are merged recursively, by merging their children. When merging terminal nodes (node $n2$ in the example), specific composition rules are to be defined. We propose such composition rules for AsmetaL in Sect. 3.2.

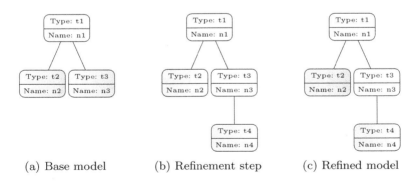

    (a) Base model   (b) Refinement step   (c) Refined model

Fig. 3. Superimposition-based refinement. The colors indicate that node $n2$ is merged using language-specific rules. (Color figure online)

By applying superimposition-based composition, the developer only needs to specify the parts of the model that are changed during a refinement step, the model can be generated automatically for each level of refinement. Thus, redundancies within the refinement hierarchy can be avoided to a large extent. As each refinement typically represents a design decision, the modularization facilitates flexibility by allowing developers to replace or modify functionality to reflect changing requirements by merely replacing a module. Thus, it may also become easier to adapt the system or create different variants of the system and respond to changing requirements quickly.

3   Modularization of ASM Refinement Steps

We exemplify superimposition-based refinement for the ASM method, and in particular for the language AsmetaL for which we provide composition rules. We introduce ASMs and the language AsmetaL in Sect. 3.1 and composition rules for AsmetaL in Sect. 3.2.

3.1   Abstract State Machines and the Language AsmetaL

Abstract State Machines (ASMs) have been proposed by Gurevich as a means to describe algorithms on arbitrary levels of abstraction, and made popular by Börger as the underlying formalism of the ASM method [15,30]. Besides the ASM formalism, the ASM method, comprises the idea to describe a system on any desired level of abstraction (ground model), and refine it stepwise. For a detailed description of the ASM method we refer to the literature [17].

In this work, we exemplify the proposed concepts using the ASM-language AsmetaL [28] and our running example. The ASM model for the Landing Gear System as used for illustration has been proposed by Arcaini et al. [8]. In AsmetaL, a model include domains, functions, and rules.

Domains represent a mathematical specification for named complex structures. Domains are thereby a combination of either simple predefined types such as integers or other domains. The type of the combination is defined by a set of keywords, such as *enum*, *Set*, or *Map*. Line 1–3 of Fig. 4 shows an example of domain definitions from the Landing Gear System.

Functions in ASMs, define the state of the system by their values at a given point of execution. We mainly distinguish between controlled functions, whose value is controlled by the system, and monitored functions, whose values are given by the environment. An exemplary declaration and definition of functions from the Landing Gear System is shown in Fig. 4, Lines 4–5. The type of function *doors* is *DoorStatus* (i.e., a door can be either closing, closed, opening, or open). The function definition uses a case term with the obvious semantics as known from switch statements in programming languages. The doors are open when cylinders are extended and closed when the cylinders are retracted. Thus, the value of function doors is determined by the value of other functions, thus it is considered as a derived function.

```
1  enum domain HandleStatus={UP|DOWN}
2  enum domain DoorStatus={CLOSED|OPENING|OPEN|CLOSING}
3  enum domain GearStatus={RETRACTED|EXTENDING|EXTENDED|RETRACTING}
4  derived doors: DoorStatus
5  function doors = switch cylindersDoors
6                      case CYLINDER_EXTENDED: OPEN
7                      case CYLINDER_RETRACTED: CLOSED
8                  endswitch
9
10  rule r_closeDoor = switch doors
11                      case OPEN: doors := CLOSING
12                      case CLOSING: doors := CLOSED
13                      case OPENING: doors := CLOSING
14                  endswitch
15
16 function doors = OPEN
```

Fig. 4. Domain, function and rule definition in AsmetaL

Rules in ASMs are sets of updates that, in its basic form, are controlled by conditional statements called guards. In each step, all rules of an ASM are executed
simultaneously and define the update set for the next state transition. Figure 4,
Line 10 shows the definition of rule r_closeDoor which handles the opening and
closing of the doors. In AsmetaL, the main rule marks the entry point of the
ASM's execution, from which further rules can be invoked.

3.2 Composition Rules for Refinement Steps in AsmetaL

We propose an extension of AsmetaL that allows to express refinement steps
modularly and to derive the desired refinement hierarchies automatically. The
composition mechanism is based on superimposition as explained in Sect. 2.2.
Each refinement step contains a syntactically correct, yet partial, ASM. However,
only those parts that are subject to change during a refinement step have to be
specified in the corresponding module. The developer can introduce new elements
in a refinement step or refine an existing element with the same type and name.
For the automated composition of terminal nodes, specific composition rules are
required, which we will explain in the following.

Refinement Steps in AsmetaL. A refinement step may introduce new functions or
refine existing ones. When refining a function, the default behavior is to replace
the previous definition of the function. Nevertheless, it is possible to include
the content of the function from the previous refinement level by using keyword
@original that we have adopted from method refinement in feature-oriented
programming [5]. Figure 5 shows an example of a function refinement and the
result of the composition. It is crucial, that the keyword *@original* does not
constitute an absolute reference to a particular previous refinement, facilitating
a notion of optional refinements providing more flexibility for agile development.

The refinement of rules and domains follows the same principle as the refinement of functions as depicted in Fig. 6. As our running example does not contain any refinements of domains, we do not show an example.

1 **function** flow_rate (valveSize, speed) =	**Ground Model**
2 valveSize * speed	

1 **function** flow_rate	**Refinement Step (Valves)**
2 (valveSize1, valveSize2, speed) =	
3 @original(valveSize1, speed) + @original(valveSize2, speed)	

1 **function** flow_rate	**Composed Refinement**
2 (valveSize1, valveSize2, speed) =	
3 (valveSize1 * speed) + (valveSize2 * speed)	

Fig. 5. Refinement of a function in our extension of AsmetaL

1 **Ground Model**	1 **Refinement Step (Valves)**
2 **rule** r_openValve =	2 **rule** r_openValve
3 valve := open	3 **if** (pipeFill = empty) **then**
4	4 @original()
5	5 **endif**

1 **rule** r_openValve =	**Composed Refinement**
2 **if** (pipeFill == empty) **then**	
3 valve := open	
4 **endif**	

Fig. 6. Refinement of a rule in our extension of AsmetaL

Granularity of Refinement. To prepare AsmetaL for superimposition-based composition, we had to define which language elements should serve as units of composition by representing them as terminal nodes during superimposition. A natural choice for rules are to consider rule definitions as non-terminals. However, our evaluation with the Landing Gear System showed that it might be useful to consider the possibility to refine specific cases of case rules. The reason is that it appeared as a common pattern to add cases or elements to a given case. Thus, we have introduced the keyword *extendable* that can be used to assign a unique identifier to a case rule. This identifier can be used during refinement by referencing it with the keyword *extend_original*. By means of both keywords, it is now possible to explicitly refine cases rules by adding new cases or modify existing ones as illustrated in Fig. 7.

```
1  Ground Model                          1  Refinement Step (Valves)
2                                        2  /*extend_original(pipe)*/
3  switch(pipeFill)                      3  switch(pipeFill)
4  /*extendable(pipe)*/                  4    case filled:
5    case empty:                         5    par
6      r_closeValve()                    6      @original
7    case filled:                        7      warnLight = yellow
8      r_openValve()                     8    endpar
9  endswitch                             9    case overflowing:
10                                       10     warnLight = red
11                                       11 endswitch
```

```
1  switch(pipeFill)                                     Composed Refinement
2    case empty:        r_closeValve()
3    case filled:       par
4                         r_openValve()
5                         warnLight = yellow
6                       endpar
7    case overflowing:  warnLight = red
8  endswitch
```

Fig. 7. Refinement of a switch statement in our extension of AsmetaL

4   Tool Support and Evaluation

In order to evaluate our concepts, we have developed tool support and performed
a case study based on the Landing Gear System, which already served as a running example in the previous sections. We give an overview about tool support
in Sect. 4.1 and present results of our case study in Sect. 4.2.

4.1   Tool Support for Superimposition-Based Refinement in Eclipse

The core of our tool support is an extension of FeatureHouse [5], a command-
line tool supporting different types of software composition including superimposition. We integrated support for the language AsmetaL [28], to enable
superimposition-based composition of refinement rules. It is necessary to decide
on a granularity for superimposition by choosing which elements should be considered as terminal nodes during superimposition. For each type of terminal
node, we implemented composition rules supporting the keyword *@original()* as
explained in Sect. 3.2. Our extension of FeatureHouse can be used to compose a
set of AsmetaL models representing different refinement steps.

Our extension of FeatureHouse is integrated into FeatureIDE [45], an Eclipse
plug-in integrating numerous tools to develop configurable software. We have
extended existing views to handle ASM models, so that they can be used to
maintain an overview about the refinement hierarchy. The general development
interface can be seen in Fig. 8. The Package Explorer, on the left, shows a FeatureIDE project with the Landing Gear System. The folder *refinement_steps*,

contains for each refinement step a sub-folder containing a set of AsmetaL models. A configuration describes a sequence of refinement steps and can be created using the Configuration Editor in the top-right window. The set of selectable refinement sequences can be defined in the model.xml file, for which also a graphical editor exists.

The composed models are automatically generated into the *refinement* folder and can be used as input for other tools. Our tool is developed as an Eclipse plugin, and thus, it easily integrates with the Asmeta toolset, which has been built around the Asmeta Framework and the language AsmetaL [28]. It incorporates several tools including support for simulation, model checking, and static analysis of ASM models. These existing editors, views and analysis tools can be used for the automatically generated ASM models on each level of refinement.

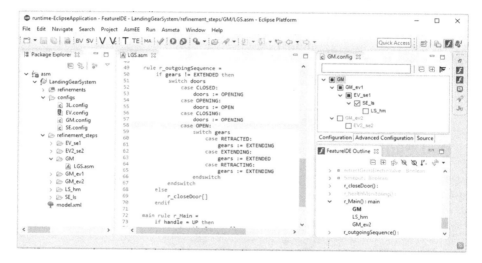

Fig. 8. Integration of our tool support into Eclipse including language-specific editor and views for ASMs in our extension of the language AsmetaL.

4.2   Modularizing Refinement Steps of the Landing Gear System

To evaluate the feasibility of superimposition-based refinement for ASMs, we have used our tool to perform a case study based on the Landing Gear System. Arcaini et al. provide an ASM implementation of the system that has been used as the foundation for our case study [7].

The existing refinement hierarchy by Arcaini et al. describes the AsmetaL model on each level of refinement in detail [8]. We derived the necessary refinement steps, which makes the differences between two subsequent refinement explicit and by modularizing them manually. We took care that the composed models for each level of refinement do not differ semantically from the original models. In addition to syntactical comparisons that were sufficient for large parts of the model, we applied the Asmeta Simulator, Validator, Model Adviser, and Refinement Prover of the Asmeta toolset[1] and compared the results to ensure the correctness of our modularization. After defining the refinement hierarchy and modularizing the refinement steps of the Landing Gear System, we were able to automatically derive the ASM model for each level of refinement.

As our goal is a reduction of redundancies, we compared the size of the model on each level of refinement with the size of the modularized refinement steps. Our results show that it is possible to remove large parts of the redundancy in the development artifacts. In Table 1, we present the size of the AsmetaL models in lines of code, i.e., non-empty lines excluding comments. The second column shows the lines of code of the original refinement step and the third column (the accumulated) size of the necessary refinement steps. In the third row, we present the percentage of the reduction in size.

Table 1. Reduction of system size achieved by modularization of refinement steps in the Landing Gear case study.

Refinement	Refinement (acc.) [loc]	Refinement step (acc.) [loc]	Reduction (acc.) [%]
Ground model	83 (83)	83 (83)	0.00 (0.00)
Cylinders	170 (253)	154 (237)	9.41 (6.3)
Sensors	187 (440)	131 (368)	29.94 (16.4)
LandingSets	199 (639)	23 (391)	88.44 (38.8)
HealthMonitor	250 (889)	66 (457)	73.60 (48.6)

The overall size of the refinement sequence has been reduced by decomposition into modular refinement steps by 48.6%. In general, it can be seen that the reduction increases with a growing number of refinement steps. In some cases, such as Cylinders, the reduction is relatively low while other refinement steps benefit from larger savings. These results suggest that a relevant reduction of redundancies is possible, in particular for large refinement hierarchies, but its degree also depends on the particular design of the modularization, such as the choice of granularity for superimposition, and possibly on the nature of the given refinement steps.

Despite being able to derive the original refinement hierarchy from the refinement modules automatically, the modularization of refinement steps allows us to derive even more variants of the system by composing different combinations of refinement steps. We considered the development of two alternative refinements (for Cylinders and Sensors) that have been created during exploratory phases of the original development. With superimposition-based refinement, it was possible to switch between alternative implementations of individual refinement steps. Changes are implicitly propagated to all generated refined models

---

[1] http://asmeta.sourceforge.net/.

by automatically rebuilding them after each change. This was especially helpful, when considering the impact of changes to subsequent refinements of the original sequence.

We have experienced that it is possible to omit certain refinement steps, allowing the generation of completely new variants of the system. For instance, it would be possible to derive a variant of the Landing Gear System without Sensors but with HealthMonitor. We explored the idea by considering different optional refinements. Our results show that it is generally possible, but may require non-trivial changes to the design of the involved refinement steps or modules to handle particular combinations of refinement steps. For instance, the refinement step *LandingSets* does not depend on a particular refinement, which means that it can be modified arbitrarily (e.g., by choosing a different number of landing sets). In contrast, the refinement step *HealthMonitor* contained syntactical dependencies to the previous refinement step and cannot be freely combined in other ways without major changes.

Furthermore, we observed that each iteration in agile development corresponds to identifying a set of desired refinements in the design space, and developing the necessary refinement steps to generate these refinements. For the sake of generality, we do not restrict the particular mapping between refinement steps and iterations. One the one hand, it is possible to decide on a set of features for the next iteration, extend the ground model of the previous iteration and adapt all refinements accordingly all the way to the implementation. On the other hand, each iteration could involve the development of a single refinement step only. In this case, the suitability of ASMs to model a system on arbitrary levels of abstraction enables early validation and can be used to get early feedback from the customer. In this case, the refinement sequence might involve an arbitrary combination of refinements.

5 Related Work

Researchers increasingly recognize the need to incorporate formal methods into agile development processes [13,24]. The use of light-weight formal techniques, such as static verification, in agile development processes has been shown to be applicable in practice [36]. However, researchers have identified the integration of more heavy-weight formal methods typically based on stepwise refinement, such as Event-B, ASM, and Z, as a promising way to develop safety-critical systems [36]. In particular, the need for concepts to facilitate reusability in model-based refinement has been identified as a major challenge [23]. We address this challenge by investigating the application of superimposition as a technique to achieve reuse between refined models. Furthermore, to our knowledge, we are the first to propose the integration of ASM and agile methods.

Formal refinement concepts have been studied intensively [9,16,25,35]. However, the main focus of this line of research are the theoretical underpinnings of refinement rather than on ways to facilitate flexibility. In contrast, we aim to ease development in the presence of refinement hierarchies independent of particular notions of refinement.

There exist other approaches to avoid redundancies in model-based refinement. In particular, the Rodin tool-suite for Event-B allows developers to express a refinement by defining only those parts that differ from the abstract model [2]. However, this merely corresponds to a static reference to previous models which does not facilitate the desired flexibility for agile methods. In contrast, the keyword *@original* in our approach facilitates more flexible extensions by omitting to specify a particular model to which it refers.

Various concepts to modularize features and cross-cutting concerns, such as feature-oriented programming [12,39], aspect-oriented programming [33] and delta-oriented programming [40], have been proposed [4,43]. In particular, these approaches build on superimposition (or similar concepts) which has been recognized as a general concept for software composition that can be applied uniformly to all kinds of software artifacts [5,10].

Historically, superimposition has been proposed as a concept to extend distributed programs with parrallel composition [18,32]. In general, the early work on superimposition focuses on semantic superimposition of particular models, typically with the goal to establish a set of desired properties [26].We adopt a more general approach from Apel et al., which merely operates on AST-like representations of development artifacts, facilitating a notion of uniform composition for all kind of development artifacts [5]. In this work, we consider this language-independent notion of superimposition.

Superimposition has already been applied to compose method contracts in JML [20,31,44,47], Alloy specifications [6], state machines and markov decision processes [22,37], and unit tests [3,34]. We build on this idea by investigating its application to refinement steps, showing that similar benefits such as reduction of redundancies and compositionality can be expected. However, we are the first to apply it to refinement hierarchies. Further, the focus of our work is to leverage the incorporation of refinement-based formal methods into agile processes.

In this work, we combine techniques from formal methods and software composition. Börger and Batory exemplified the modularization of programs, theorems, and correctness proofs from the JBook case study in a uniform compositional way [11]. In our work, we build on their observation that refinements can be modularized in the same way as features in the context of software product lines, but consider the modularization of refinement steps to achieve practical benefits for applying formal refinements. Gondal et al. have proposed a feature-oriented extension of Event-B to investigate to which extent the traditional Event-B composition mechanisms can be used to implement and compose features [29]. However, the focus is on enabling the correct development of several similar variants of a system, but not on the implications of the refinement hierarchies for the development process itself. Schaefer et al. consider modularizing software taxonomies which represent a family of different software variants in a refinement-based fashion [41]. The authors describe a process how a software taxonomy can be transformed into a software product line, but do not target the modularization of the refinement hierarchies themselves as done in this work.

6   Conclusion and Future Work

The introduction of refinement hierarchies to agile development processes poses several challenges. We have identified the inherent redundancies between refinements as particularly problematic for iterative development in which models on multiple levels of refinement may need to be changed frequently to respond to changing requirements. We have proposed superimposition-based modularization as a possible solution and exemplified it using ASMs. We have developed composition-rules and implemented tool support for the language AsmetaL.

To evaluate the concept, we have performed a case study using the well-known Landing Gear System. Our results indicate a significant reduction of redundancies, possibly reducing development and maintenance effort. Furthermore, we show that superimposition-based refinement enables a more flexible refinement hierarchy. While these results are promising, it remains to be seen to which extent developers benefit from this reduction in practice. Further empirical studies regarding comprehensibility and maintainability of the development artifacts would help to better understand the potential advantages.

The modularization of refinement steps may facilitate agile development by allowing developers to modify a design decision by merely replacing the corresponding module. In future work, we want to investigate the potential of modularization of refinement steps to serve as a basis for refinement-based development of software product lines and their efficient verification.

Acknowledgments. This work was partially supported by the DFG (German Research Foundation) under the Researcher Unit FOR1800: Controlling Concurrent Change (CCC) and project EXPLANT (DFG, grant SA 465). We thank Paolo Arcaini and Angelo Gargantini for their valuable support with the Asmeta framework and providing the original AsmetaL refinement sequence for the Landing Gear System case study.

References

1. Abrial, J.R.: Modeling in Event-B: System and Software Engineering, 1st edn. Cambridge University Press, New York (2010)
2. Abrial, J.-R., Butler, M., Hallerstede, S., Voisin, L.: An open extensible tool environment for event-B. In: Liu, Z., He, J. (eds.) ICFEM 2006. LNCS, vol. 4260, pp. 588–605. Springer, Heidelberg (2006). doi:10.1007/11901433_32
3. Al-Hajjaji, M., Meinicke, J., Krieter, S., Schröter, R., Thüm, T., Leich, T., Saake, G.: Tool demo: testing configurable systems with featureIDE. In: Proceedings of International Conference on Generative Programming: Concepts and Experiences (GPCE), pp. 173–177. ACM, New York (2016)
4. Apel, S., Batory, D., Kästner, C., Saake, G.: Feature-Oriented Software Product Lines: Concepts and Implementation. Springer, Berlin, Heidelberg (2013)
5. Apel, S., Kästner, C., Lengauer, C.: Language-independent and automated software composition: the featurehouse experience. IEEE Trans. Softw. Eng. (TSE) **39**(1), 63–79 (2013)

6. Apel, S., von Rhein, A., Thüm, T., Kästner, C.: Feature-interaction detection based on feature-based specifications. Comput. Netw. **57**(12), 2399–2409 (2013)
7. Boniol, F., Wiels, V.: The landing gear system case study. In: Boniol, F., Wiels, V., Ait Ameur, Y., Schewe, K.-D. (eds.) ABZ 2014. CCIS, vol. 433, pp. 1–18. Springer, Cham (2014). doi:10.1007/978-3-319-07512-9_1
8. Arcaini, P., Gargantini, A., Riccobene, E.: Rigorous development process of a safety-critical system: from asm models to java code. Int. J. Softw. Tools Technol. Transfer **19**(2), 247–269 (2017)
9. Banach, R.: Model based refinement and the tools of tomorrow. In: Börger, E., Butler, M., Bowen, J.P., Boca, P. (eds.) ABZ 2008. LNCS, vol. 5238, pp. 42–56. Springer, Heidelberg (2008). doi:10.1007/978-3-540-87603-8_5
10. Batory, D.: A tutorial on feature oriented programming and the AHEAD tool suite. In: Lämmel, R., Saraiva, J., Visser, J. (eds.) GTTSE 2005. LNCS, vol. 4143, pp. 3–35. Springer, Heidelberg (2006). doi:10.1007/11877028_1
11. Batory, D., Börger, E.: Modularizing theorems for software product lines: the Jbook case study. J. Univ. Comput. Sci. (J.UCS) **14**(12), 2059–2082 (2008)
12. Batory, D., Sarvela, J.N., Rauschmayer, A.: Scaling step-wise refinement. IEEE Trans. Softw. Eng. (TSE) **30**(6), 355–371 (2004)
13. Black, S., Boca, P.P., Bowen, J.P., Gorman, J., Hinchey, M.: Formal versus agile: survival of the fittest. Comput. **42**(9), 37–45 (2009)
14. Boniol, F., Wiels, V.: The landing gear system case study. In: Boniol, F., Wiels, V., Ait Ameur, Y., Schewe, K.-D. (eds.) ABZ 2014. CCIS, vol. 433, pp. 1–18. Springer, Cham (2014). doi:10.1007/978-3-319-07512-9_1
15. Börger, E.: High level system design and analysis using abstract state machines. In: Hutter, D., Stephan, W., Traverso, P., Ullmann, M. (eds.) FM-Trends 1998. LNCS, vol. 1641, pp. 1–43. Springer, Heidelberg (1999). doi:10.1007/3-540-48257-1_1
16. Börger, E.: The asm refinement method. Formal Aspects Comput. **15**(2), 237–257 (2003)
17. Börger, E., Stark, R.F.: Abstract State Machines: A Method for High-Level System Design and Analysis. Springer, Secaucus (2003)
18. Bougé, L., Francez, N.: A compositional approach to superimposition. In: Proceedings of the 15th ACM SIGPLAN-SIGACT Symposium on Principles of Programming Languages, pp. 240–249. ACM (1988)
19. Clarke, E.M., Wing, J.M.: Formal methods: state of the art and future directions. ACM Comput. Surv. (CSUR) **28**(4), 626–643 (1996)
20. Clifton, C., Leavens, G.T.: Observers and assistants: a proposal for modular aspect-oriented reasoning. In: Proceedings of Workshop Foundations of Aspect-Oriented Languages (FOAL), pp. 33–44. Iowa State University, Ames, April 2002
21. Dubinsky, Y., Rubin, J., Berger, T., Duszynski, S., Becker, M., Czarnecki, K.: An exploratory study of cloning in industrial software product lines. In: Proceedings of European Conference on Software Maintenance and Reengineering (CSMR), pp. 25–34. IEEE, Washington, DC (2013)
22. Dubslaff, C., Klüppelholz, S., Baier, C.: Probabilistic model checking for energy analysis in software product lines. In: Proceedings of International Conference on Aspect-Oriented Software Development (AOSD), pp. 169–180. ACM, New York (2014)
23. Edmunds, A., Olszewska, M., Waldén, M.: Using the event-b formal method for disciplined agile delivery of safety-critical systems (2015)
24. Eleftherakis, G., Cowling, A.J.: An agile formal development methodology. In: Proceedings of the 1st South-East European Workshop on Formal Methods, pp. 36–47 (2003)

25. Ernst, G., Pfähler, J., Schellhorn, G., Reif, W.: Modular refinement for submachines of asms. In: Ameur, Y.A., Schewe, K.D. (eds.) Abstract State Machines, Alloy, B, TLA, VDM, and Z. LNCS, vol. 8477, pp. 188–203. Springer, Heidelberg (2014). doi:10.1007/978-3-662-43652-3_16
26. Fiadeiro, J., Maibaum, T.: Categorical semantics of parallel program design. Sci. Comput. Program. **28**(2–3), 111–138 (1997)
27. Gargantini, A., Riccobene, E., Scandurra, P.: Deriving a textual notation from a metamodel: an experience on bridging modelware and grammarware. Milestones, Models and Mappings for Model-Driven Architecture, p. 33 (2006)
28. Gargantini, A., Riccobene, E., Scandurra, P.: A metamodel-based language and a simulation engine for abstract state machines. J. UCS **14**(12), 1949–1983 (2008)
29. Gondal, A., Poppleton, M., Butler, M.: Composing event-B specifications - case-study experience. In: Apel, S., Jackson, E. (eds.) SC 2011. LNCS, vol. 6708, pp. 100–115. Springer, Heidelberg (2011). doi:10.1007/978-3-642-22045-6_7
30. Gurevich, Y.: Sequential abstract-state machines capture sequential algorithms. ACM Trans. Comput. Logic (TOCL) **1**(1), 77–111 (2000)
31. Hähnle, R., Schaefer, I.: A Liskov principle for delta-oriented programming. In: Margaria, T., Steffen, B. (eds.) ISoLA 2012. LNCS, vol. 7609, pp. 32–46. Springer, Heidelberg (2012). doi:10.1007/978-3-642-34026-0_4
32. Katz, S.: A superimposition control construct for distributed systems. ACM Trans. Program. Lang. Syst. (TOPLAS) **15**(2), 337–356 (1993)
33. Kiczales, G., Lamping, J., Mendhekar, A., Maeda, C., Lopes, C., Loingtier, J.-M., Irwin, J.: Aspect-oriented programming. In: Akşit, M., Matsuoka, S. (eds.) ECOOP 1997. LNCS, vol. 1241, pp. 220–242. Springer, Heidelberg (1997). doi:10.1007/BFb0053381
34. Kim, C.H.P., Marinov, D., Khurshid, S., Batory, D., Souto, S., Barros, P., D'Amorim, M.: SPLat: lightweight dynamic analysis for reducing combinatorics in testing configurable systems. In: Proceedings of European Software Engineering Conference/Foundations of Software Engineering (ESEC/FSE), pp. 257–267. ACM, New York, August 2013
35. Kourie, D.G., Watson, B.W.: The Correctness-by-Construction Approach to Programming. Springer, Heidelberg (2012)
36. Larsen, P.G., Fitzgerald, J.S., Wolff, S.: Are formal methods ready for agility? a reality check. In: FM + AM, pp. 13–25. Citeseer (2010)
37. Li, H., Krishnamurthi, S., Fisler, K.: Modular verification of open features using three-valued model checking. Autom. Softw. Eng. **12**(3), 349–382 (2005)
38. Linsbauer, L., Lopez-Herrejon, R.E., Egyed, A.: Softw. Syst. Model (2016). https://doi.org/10.1007/s10270-015-0512-y
39. Prehofer, C.: Feature-oriented programming: a fresh look at objects. In: Akşit, M., Matsuoka, S. (eds.) ECOOP 1997. LNCS, vol. 1241, pp. 419–443. Springer, Heidelberg (1997). doi:10.1007/BFb0053389
40. Schaefer, I., Bettini, L., Bono, V., Damiani, F., Tanzarella, N.: Delta-oriented programming of software product lines. In: Bosch, J., Lee, J. (eds.) SPLC 2010. LNCS, vol. 6287, pp. 77–91. Springer, Heidelberg (2010). doi:10.1007/978-3-642-15579-6_6
41. Schaefer, I., Seidl, C., Cleophas, L.G., Watson, B.W.: Splicing TABASCO: custom-tailored software product line variants from taxonomy-based toolkits. In: SAICSIT 2015, p. 34:1–34:10 (2015)
42. Spivey, J.M.: Understanding Z: A Specification Language and Its Formal Semantics. Cambridge University Press, New York (1988)

43. Tarr, P., Ossher, H., Harrison, W., Sutton Jr., S.M.: N degrees of separation: multidimensional separation of concerns. In: Proceedings of International Conference on Software Engineering (ICSE), pp. 107–119. ACM, New York (1999)

44. Thüm, T.: Product-line specification and verification with feature-oriented contracts. Ph.D. thesis, University of Magdeburg, Germany, February 2015

45. Thüm, T., Kästner, C., Benduhn, F., Meinicke, J., Saake, G., Leich, T.: FeatureIDE: an extensible framework for feature-oriented software development. Sci. Comput. Program. (SCP) **79**, 70–85 (2014)

46. Woodcock, J., Larsen, P.G., Bicarregui, J., Fitzgerald, J.: Formal methods: practice and experience. ACM Comput. Surv. (CSUR) **41**(4), 19 (2009)

47. Zhao, J., Rinard, M.: Pipa: a behavioral interface specification language for aspect. In: Pezzè, M. (ed.) FASE 2003. LNCS, vol. 2621, pp. 150–165. Springer, Heidelberg (2003). doi:10.1007/3-540-36578-8_11

Model Checking Pushdown Epistemic Game Structures

Taolue Chen[1,4], Fu Song[2(✉)], and Zhilin Wu[3]

[1] Department of Computer Science and Information Systems,
Birkbeck, University of London, London, UK
[2] School of Information Science and Technology,
ShanghaiTech University, Shanghai, China
songfu@shanghaitech.edu.cn
[3] State Key Laboratory of Computer Science, Institute of Software,
Chinese Academy of Sciences, Beijing, China
[4] State Key Laboratory of Novel Software Technology,
Nanjing University, Nanjing, China

Abstract. In this paper, we investigate the problem of verifying pushdown multi-agent systems with imperfect information. As the formal model, we introduce *pushdown epistemic game structures* (PEGSs), an extension of pushdown game structures with *epistemic accessibility relations* (EARs). For the specification, we consider extensions of alternating-time temporal logics with epistemic modalities: ATEL, ATEL* and AEMC. We study the model checking problems for ATEL, ATEL* and AEMC over PEGSs under various imperfect information settings. For ATEL and ATEL*, we show that size-preserving EARs, a common definition of the accessibility relation in the literature of games over pushdown systems with imperfect information, will render the model checking problem undecidable under imperfect information and imperfect recall setting. We then propose *regular* EARs, and provide automata-theoretic model checking algorithms with matching low bounds, i.e., EXPTIME-complete for ATEL and 2EXPTIME-complete for ATEL*. In contrast, for AEMC, we show that the model checking problem is EXPTIME-complete even in the presence of size-preserving EARs.

1 Introduction

Model checking, a well-studied method for automatic formal verification of complex systems, has been successfully applied to verify communication protocols, hardware designs and software, etc. [15]. The key idea underlying the model checking method is to represent the system as a mathematical model, to express a desired property by a logic formula, and then to determine whether the formula is true in the model [15].

This work was partially supported by NSFC grant (61402179, 61532019, 61662035, 61572478, 61472474, 61100062, and 61272135), UK EPSRC grant (EP/P00430X/1), and European CHIST-ERA project SUCCESS.

Z. Duan and L. Ong (Eds.): ICFEM 2017, LNCS 10610, pp. 36–53, 2017.
https://doi.org/10.1007/978-3-319-68690-5_3

Recently, it has been extended to verify *multi-agent systems* (MASs), a novel paradigm which can be used to solve many complex tasks that might be difficult or inefficient for an individual agent to tackle. As a model of *finite-state* MASs, Alur et al. proposed *concurrent game structures* (CGSs), whilst alternating-time temporal logics (ATL, ATL*) and alternating-time μ-calculus (AMC) are employed as specification languages, for which model checking algorithms were also provided [1,2]. Since then, a number of model checking algorithms for MASs have been studied for various models and logics. For instance, [26] proposed a more expressive logic, called *strategy logic* (SL), which allows to express cooperation and enforcement of agents. However, the model checking problem for strategy logic on CGSs is NonElementarySpace-hard and the satisfiability problem is undecidable [23]. As a result, several fragments of strategy logic were investigated [10,23–25].

CGSs are usually determined by *Interpreted Systems* which are constructed via a Mealy-type or Moore-type synchronous composition of local transition systems of agents [18,22]. In the literature, local transition systems of each agent are usually *finite* (as, e.g., a finite Kripke structure), yielding a finite-state CGS only via the synchronous composition. However, in practice often there are scenarios of interest where agents *cannot* be represented by a finite-state system (e.g., pushdown scheduler [27]), or recourses shared between agents are unbounded [8], but can be rightly modeled by a *pushdown* system. Hence, it would be of great interest to study verification problems on the CGS obtained by a synchronous composition of local *pushdown* systems. Unfortunately, the verification of even the simplest property (e.g., reachability) for such a model is undecidable. To see this, one can easily reduce from the emptiness problem of the intersection of two pushdown automata which is known to be undecidable. To gain decidability while still capturing many interesting practical cases, *pushdown game structures* (PGSs) were proposed and investigated [13,14,27]. In PGSs, agents do not posses their own local stacks, but can be seen as sharing a global stack. As the stack is unbounded, PGSs represent a class of *infinite-state* MASs, a proper extension of the finite-state MASs. PGSs allow, among others, modeling of unbounded memory or a unbound shared resource of agents, which is of particular importance in MASs [8,27].

On the logic side, one considers alternating-time temporal *epistemic* logics (ATEL, ATEL*) [19,20,28,29,33], alternating-time *epistemic* μ-calculus (AEMC) [7], and SLK [9], which are respectively extensions of ATL, ATL*, AMC and SL with epistemic modalities for representing knowledge of individual agents, as well as "everyone knows" and common knowledge [18]. These logics are usually interpreted over *finite-state* concurrent *epistemic* game structures, which are an extension of CGSs with **epistemic accessibility relations** (EARs), giving rise to a model for representing finite-state MASs with *imperfect information*. Assuming agents only access imperfect information arises naturally in various real-world scenarios, typically in sensor networks, security, robotics, distributed systems, communication protocols, etc. In addition, the extension of logics with epistemic modalities allows one to succinctly express a range of (un)desirable properties of MASs, and has found a wide range of applications in AI, particularly for reasoning about MASs [18,34].

This paper investigates model checking problems for ATEL, ATEL* and AEMC over *infinite-state* MASs under *imperfect* information setting. To this end, we propose *pushdown epistemic game structures* (PEGSs), an extension of PGSs with EARs, as a mathematical model for infinite-state MASs with imperfect information. To the best of our knowledge, analogous models have not been considered in literature.

Model checking PEGSs depends crucially on how EARs are defined. A commonly adopted definition, called *size-preserving* EARs, was introduced for games over pushdown systems with imperfect information [3], where two configurations are deemed to be indistinguishable if the two stack contents are of the same size and, in addition, neither the pair of control states nor pairs of stack symbols in the same position of the two stack contents are distinguishable. While this sounds to be a very natural definition, we show, unfortunately, that the model checking problems for ATEL and ATEL* over PEGSs are undecidable in general, even when restricted to imperfect recall (memoryless) strategies. This result suggests that alternative definitions of EARs are needed.

As a solution, we propose EARs that are *regular* and *simple*. Simple EARs are defined over control states of PEGSs and the top symbol of the stack, while regular EARs are simple EARs extended with a finite set of deterministic finite-state automata (DFA), one for each agent, where the states of each DFA divide the set of stack contents into finitely many equivalence classes. We first provide an automata-theoretic algorithm that solves the model checking problem for ATEL (resp. ATEL*) over PEGSs with simple EARs, then present a reduction from the model checking problems over PEGSs with regular EARs to the one over PEGSs with simple one. The algorithm runs in EXPTIME for ATEL and 2EXPTIME for ATEL*, and we show that these algorithms are optimal by giving matching lower bounds. In contrast, for AEMC, we show that the model checking problem is EXPTIME-complete, even in the presence of size-preserving EARs.

Related Work. Model checking over finite-state CGSs under perfect information setting is well-studied in the literature [2,10,23–25]. The problem becomes undecidable for ATL on CGSs under imperfect information and perfect recall setting [16]. Therefore, many works restrict to imperfect information and imperfect recall strategies [7,9,19,20,28,29,33]. The model checking problem over PGSs under perfect information and perfect recall setting was studied in [13,14,27], but only with perfect information. Furthermore, timed (resp. probabilistic) ATLs and timed (resp. probabilistic) CGSs were proposed to verify timed (resp. probabilistic) MASs, e.g., [6,11,12]. These works are, however, orthogonal to the one reported in the current paper.

Structure of the Paper. In Sect. 2, we introduce pushdown epistemic game structures. In Sect. 3, we recall the definitions of ATEL, ATEL* and AEMC. In Sect. 4, we present the undecidable result for ATEL, ATEL* and propose model checking algorithms for decidable setting. The model checking algorithms for AEMC are presented in Sect. 5. Finally, we conclude in Sect. 6. Due to space restriction, all proofs are committed here which can be found in the accompanying technical report.

2   Pushdown Epistemic Game Structures

We fix a countable set $\mathbf{AP}$ of *atomic propositions* (also called observations). Let $[k]$ denote the set $\{1, ..., k\}$ for some natural number $k \in \mathbb{N}$.

Definition 1. *A* pushdown epistemic game structure *(PEGS) is a tuple* $\mathcal{P} = (Ag, Ac, P, \Gamma, \Delta, \lambda, \{\sim_i | \ i \in Ag\})$, *where*

- $Ag = \{1, ..., n\}$ *is a finite set of* agents *(a.k.a. players); we assume that n is bounded;*
- Ac *is a finite set of* actions *made by agents; we further define $\mathcal{D} = Ac^n$ to be the set of* decisions $\mathbf{d} = \langle a_1, ..., a_n \rangle$ *such that for all $i \in [n]$, $\mathbf{d}(i) := a_i \in Ac$;*
- P *is a finite set of* control states*;*
- Γ *is a finite* stack alphabet*;*
- $\Delta : P \times \Gamma \times \mathcal{D} \to P \times \Gamma^*$ *is a* transition function[1]*;*
- $\lambda : P \times \Gamma^* \to 2^{\mathbf{AP}}$ *is a* valuation *that assigns to each configuration (i.e., an element of $P \times \Gamma^*$) a set of atomic propositions (i.e., observations);*
- $\sim_i \subseteq (P \times \Gamma^*) \times (P \times \Gamma^*)$ *is an* epistemic accessibility relation *(EAR) which is an equivalence relation.*

A *concurrent epistemic game structure* (CEGS) is a tuple $\mathcal{P} = (Ag, Ac, P, \Delta, \lambda, \{\sim_i | \ i \in Ag\})$ where $\Delta : P \times \mathcal{D} \to P$, Ag, Ac, P are defined similarly as PEGS, whereas λ and $\sim_i$ are over P solely. A *pushdown game structure* (PGS) is a PEGS $\mathcal{P} = (Ag, Ac, P, \Gamma, \Delta, \lambda, \{\sim_i | \ i \in Ag\})$ in which $\sim_i$ is an identity for every agent $i \in Ag$. Hence, a PGS $\mathcal{P}$ is usually denoted as $(Ag, Ac, P, \Gamma, \Delta, \lambda)$.

A *configuration* of the PEGS $\mathcal{P}$ is a pair $\langle p, \omega \rangle$, where $p \in P$ and $\omega \in \Gamma^*$. We write $\mathcal{C}_\mathcal{P}$ to denote the set of configurations of $\mathcal{P}$. For every $(p, \gamma, \mathbf{d}) \in P \times \Gamma \times \mathcal{D}$ such that $\Delta(p, \gamma, \mathbf{d}) = (p', \omega)$, we write $\langle p, \gamma \rangle \overset{\mathbf{d}}{\hookrightarrow}_\mathcal{P} \langle p', \omega \rangle$ instead.

The transition relation $\Longrightarrow_\mathcal{P}: \mathcal{C}_\mathcal{P} \times \mathcal{D} \times \mathcal{C}_\mathcal{P}$ of the PEGS $\mathcal{P}$ is defined as follows: for every $\omega' \in \Gamma^*$, if $\langle p, \gamma \rangle \overset{\mathbf{d}}{\hookrightarrow}_\mathcal{P} \langle p', \omega \rangle$, then $\langle p, \gamma\omega' \rangle \overset{\mathbf{d}}{\Longrightarrow}_\mathcal{P} \langle p', \omega\omega' \rangle$. Intuitively, if the PEGS $\mathcal{P}$ is at the configuration $\langle p, \gamma\omega' \rangle$, by making the decision $\mathbf{d}$, $\mathcal{P}$ moves from the control state p to the control state p', pops γ from the stack and then pushes ω onto the stack.

Tracks and Paths. A *track* (resp. *path*) in the PEGS $\mathcal{P}$ is a *finite* (resp. *infinite*) sequence π of configurations $c_0...c_m$ (resp. $c_0 c_1...$) such that for every $i : 0 \le i < m$ (resp. $i \ge 0$), $c_i \overset{\mathbf{d}}{\Longrightarrow}_\mathcal{P} c_{i+1}$ for some $\mathbf{d}$. Given a track $\pi = c_0...c_m$ (resp. path $\pi = $

---

[1] One may notice that, in the definition of PEGSs, Δ is defined as a *complete* function $P \times \Gamma \times \mathcal{D} \to P \times \Gamma^*$, meaning that all actions are available to each agent. This does not restrict the expressiveness of PEGSs, as we can easily add transitions to some additional sink state to simulate the situation where some actions are unavailable to some agents.

$c_0 c_1 ...$), let $|\pi| = m$ (resp. $|\pi| = +\infty$), and for every $i : 0 \le i \le m$ (resp. $i \ge 0$), let π_i denote the configuration c_i, $\pi_{\le i}$ denote $c_0 \dots c_i$ and $\pi_{\ge i}$ denote $c_i c_{i+1} \dots$. Given two tracks π and π', π and π' are *indistinguishable* for an agent $i \in \mathsf{Ag}$, denoted by $\pi \sim_i \pi'$, if $|\pi| = |\pi'|$ and for all $k : 0 \le k \le |\pi|$, $\pi_k \sim_i \pi'_k$. Let $\mathsf{Trks}_\mathcal{P} \subseteq \mathcal{C}_\mathcal{P}^+$ denote the set of all tracks in $\mathcal{P}$, $\prod_\mathcal{P} \subseteq \mathcal{C}_\mathcal{P}^\omega$ denote the set of all paths in $\mathcal{P}$, $\mathsf{Trks}_\mathcal{P}(c) = \{\pi \in \mathsf{Trks}_\mathcal{P} \mid \pi_0 = c\}$ and $\prod_\mathcal{P}(c) = \{\pi \in \prod_\mathcal{P} \mid \pi_0 = c\}$ respectively denote the set of all the tracks and paths starting from the configuration c.

Strategies. Intuitively, a *strategy* of an agent $i \in \mathsf{Ag}$ specifies what i plans to do in each situation. In the literature, there are four types of strategies [7, 29] classified by whether the action chosen by an agent relies on the whole history of past configurations or the current configuration, and whether the whole information is visible or not. Formally, the four types of strategies are defined as follows: where **i** (resp. **I**) denotes imperfect (resp. perfect) information and **r** (resp. **R**) denotes imperfect (resp. perfect) recall,

- **Ir** strategy is a function $\theta_i : \mathcal{C}_\mathcal{P} \to \mathsf{Ac}$, i.e., the action made by the agent i depends on the current configuration;
- **IR** strategy is a function $\theta_i : \mathsf{Trks}_\mathcal{P} \to \mathsf{Ac}$, i.e., the action made by the agent i depends on the history, i.e. the sequence of configurations visited before;
- **ir** strategy is a function $\theta_i : \mathcal{C}_\mathcal{P} \to \mathsf{Ac}$ such that for all configurations $c, c' \in \mathcal{C}_\mathcal{P}$, if $c \sim_i c'$, then $\theta_i(c) = \theta_i(c')$, i.e., the agent i has to make the same action at the configurations that are indistinguishable from each other;
- **iR** strategy is a function $\theta_i : \mathsf{Trks}_\mathcal{P} \to \mathsf{Ac}$ such that for all tracks $\pi, \pi' \in \mathsf{Trks}_\mathcal{P}$, if $\pi \sim_i \pi'$, then $\theta_i(\pi) = \theta_i(\pi')$, i.e., the agent i has to make the same action on the tracks that are indistinguishable from each other.

Let Θ^σ for $\sigma \in \{\mathbf{Ir}, \mathbf{IR}, \mathbf{ir}, \mathbf{iR}\}$ denote the set of all σ-strategies. Given a set of agents $A \subseteq \mathsf{Ag}$, a *collective σ-strategy* of A is a function $\upsilon_A : A \to \Theta^\sigma$ that assigns to each agent $i \in A$ a σ-strategy. We write $\overline{A} = \mathsf{Ag} \setminus A$.

Outcomes. Let c be a configuration and υ_A be a collective σ-strategy for a set of agents A. A path π is *compatible* with respect to υ_A iff for every $k \ge 1$, there exists $\mathbf{d}_k \in \mathcal{D}$ such that $\pi_{k-1} \stackrel{\mathbf{d}_k}{\Longrightarrow}_\mathcal{P} \pi_k$ and $\mathbf{d}_k(i) = \upsilon_A(i)(\pi_{\le k-1})$ for all $i \in A$. The *outcome starting from c with respect to υ_A*, denoted by $\mathsf{out}^\sigma(c, \upsilon_A)$, is defined as the set of all the paths that start from c and are compatible with respect to υ_A, which rules out infeasible paths with respect to the collective σ-strategy υ_A.

Epistemic Accessibility Relations (EARs). An EAR $\sim_i$ for $i \in \mathsf{Ag}$ over PEGSs is defined as an equivalence relation over configurations. As the set of configurations is infinite in general, we need to represent each $\sim_i$ *finitely*.

A very natural definition of EARs, called *size-preserving* EARs and considered in [3], is formulated as follows: for each $i \in \mathsf{Ag}$, there is an equivalence relation $\simeq_i \subseteq (P \times P) \cup (\Gamma \times \Gamma)$, which captures the indistinguishability of control states and stack symbols. For two configurations $c = \langle p, \gamma_1 ... \gamma_m \rangle$ and $c' = \langle p', \gamma'_1 ... \gamma'_{m'} \rangle$, $c \sim_i c'$ iff $m = m'$, $p \simeq_i p'$, and for every $j \in [m] = [m']$, $\gamma_j \simeq_i \gamma'_j$. It turns out that the model checking problem for logic ATEL/ATEL* is undecidable under this type of EARs, even with imperfect recall (cf. Theorem 3). To gain decidability, in this paper, we introduce *regular EARs* and a special case thereof, i.e. *simple* EARs. We remark that regular EARs align to the regular valuations (see later in this section) of atomic propositions, can been seen as approximations of size-preserving EARs, and turn out to be useful in practice.

An EAR $\sim_i$ is *regular* if there is an equivalence relation $\approx_i$ over $P \times \Gamma$ and a complete deterministic finite-state automaton[2] (DFA) $\mathcal{A}_i = (S_i, \Gamma, \Delta_i, s_{i,0})$ such that for all $\langle p, \gamma\omega\rangle, \langle p_1, \gamma_1\omega_1\rangle \in \mathcal{C}_\mathcal{P}$, $\langle p, \gamma\omega\rangle \sim_i \langle p_1, \gamma_1\omega_1\rangle$ iff $(p, \gamma) \approx_i (p_1, \gamma_1)$ and $\Delta_i^*(s_{i,0}, \omega^R) = \Delta_i^*(s_{i,0}, \omega_1^R)$, where Δ_i^* denotes the reflexive and transitive closure of Δ_i, and ω^R, ω_1^R denote the reverse of ω, ω_1 (recall that the rightmost symbol of ω corresponds to the bottom symbol of the stack). Intuitively, two words ω, ω_1 which record the stack contents (excluding the tops), are equivalent with respect to $\sim_i$ if the two runs of $\mathcal{A}_i$ on ω^R and ω_1^R respectively reach the same state. Note that the purpose of the DFA $\mathcal{A}_i$ is to partition Γ^* into finitely many equivalence classes, hence we do *not* introduce the accepting states. A regular EAR is *simple* if for all words $\omega, \omega_1 \in \Gamma^*$, $\Delta_i^*(s_{i,0}, \omega^R) = \Delta_i^*(s_{i,0}, \omega_1^R)$, that is, $\mathcal{A}_i$ contains only one state. Therefore, a simple EAR can be expressed by an equivalence relation $\approx_i$ on $P \times \Gamma$.

Given a set of agents $A \subseteq \mathsf{Ag}$, let $\sim_A^E$ denote $\bigcup_{i \in A} \sim_i$, and $\sim_A^C$ denote the transitive closure of $\sim_A^E$. We use $|\mathcal{P}|$ to denote $|P| + |\Gamma| + |\Delta| + \prod_{i \in \mathsf{Ag}} |S_i|$.

Regular Valuations. The model checking problem for pushdown systems (hence for PEGSs as well) with general valuations λ, e.g., defined by a function l which assigns to each atomic proposition a context free language, is undecidable [21]. To gain decidability, we consider valuations specified by a function l which associates each pair $(p, q) \in P \times \mathbf{AP}$ with a DFA $\mathcal{A}_{p,q} = (S_{p,q}, \Gamma, \Delta_{p,q}, s_{p,q,0}, F_{p,q})$. This is usually referred to as a *regular valuation* [17]. The function l can be lifted to the valuation $\lambda_l : P \times \Gamma^* \to 2^{\mathbf{AP}}$: for every $\langle p, \omega\rangle \in \mathcal{C}_\mathcal{P}$, $\lambda_l(\langle p, \omega\rangle) = \{q \in \mathbf{AP} \mid \Delta_{p,q}^*(\omega^R) \in F_{p,q}\}$.

A *simple valuation* is a regular valuation l such that for every $q \in \mathbf{AP}$, $p \in P, \gamma \in \Gamma$, and $\omega \in \Gamma^*$, it holds that $\Delta_{p,q}^*(\omega^R\gamma) = \Delta_{p,q}^*(\gamma)$, i.e., the truth of an atomic proposition only depends on the control state and the top of the stack. Let $|\lambda|$ denote the number of states of the product automaton of all the DFA's that represents λ.

Alternating Multi-Automata. In order to represent potentially infinite sets of configurations finitely, we use alternating multi-automata (AMA) as the "data structure" of the model checking algorithms.

Definition 2 [4]. *An AMA is a tuple* $\mathcal{M} = (S, \Gamma, \delta, I, S_f)$, *where S is a finite set of states, Γ is the input alphabet, $\delta \subseteq S \times \Gamma \times 2^S$ is a transition relation, $I \subseteq S$ is a finite set of initial states, $S_f \subseteq S$ is a finite set of final states. An AMA is multi-automaton (MA) if for all $(s, S') \in \delta$, $|S'| \leq 1$.*

---

[2] "complete" means that $\Delta(q, \gamma)$ is defined for each $(q, \gamma) \in Q \times \Gamma$.

If $(s, \gamma, \{s_1, ..., s_m\}) \in \delta$, we will write $s \xrightarrow{\gamma} \{s_1, ..., s_m\}$ instead. We define the relation $\longrightarrow^* \subseteq S \times \Gamma^* \times 2^S$ as the least relation such that the following conditions hold:

- $s \xrightarrow{\epsilon}^* \{s\}$, for every $s \in S$;
- $s \xrightarrow{\gamma\omega}^* \bigcup_{i \in [m]} S_i$, if $s \xrightarrow{\gamma} \{s_1, ..., s_m\}$ and $s_i \xrightarrow{\omega}^* S_i$ for every $i \in [m]$.

$\mathcal{M}$ accepts a configuration $\langle p, \omega \rangle$ if $p \in I$ and there exists $S' \subseteq S_f$ such that $p \xrightarrow{\omega}^* S'$. Let $\mathcal{L}(\mathcal{M})$ denote the set of all configurations accepted by $\mathcal{M}$.

Proposition 1 [4]. *The membership problem of AMAs can be decided in polynomial time. AMAs are closed under all Boolean operations.*

Example 1. We illustrate our model by a modified example on the departmental travelling budget from [8]. Consider a department consisting of two professors 1, 2 and three lecturers 3, 4, and 5. The department's base budget (say 10 units) is allocated annually and can be spent to attend conferences or apply for grants, at most twice for each professor and at most once for each lecturer. Suppose there are two categories to request money to attend a conference: 1 unit or 2 units depending on whether it is *early* or *late* registration. Parts of a successful grant application will be credited to the department's budget. Suppose 3 units for each successful grant application will be added into the budget. A successful grant application from a member will immediately decrements 1 of his/her times using the budget. But, there is no a priori bound on the total budget, and no one can know how much or which way each of others has used budget. Therefore, all departmental members compete for the budget with imperfect information.

We can model this system as a PEGS $\mathcal{P}$ as follows. Each departmental member $i \in \{1, ..., 5\}$ is modeled as an agent which has actions $\{\mathsf{idle}, \mathsf{AG}, \mathsf{AC}\}$, where AG denotes "applying for a grant", AC denotes "attending a conference", and idle denotes other actions without any cost. There is an additional agent 6 denoting the environment which decides whether the application is granted or not by nondeterministically choosing an action from $\{\mathsf{award}_i, \mathsf{reject}_i \mid i \in \{1, ..., 5\}\}$. Each control state of $\mathcal{P}$ is a tuple of local states of all the agents, where the local states of each agent encode the number of times that the agent has used the budget, namely, the local state $p_{i,k}$ denotes that the number is k for agent i. The submitted grant applications are recorded into the local states of the environment agent. The available units of budget are encoded into the stack, where the length of the stack content denotes the number of available units. Each decision made by the agents determines the stack operation according to the total costs of actions in the decision. Pushing m symbols onto the stack denotes that m units are added into the budget. Similarly, popping m symbols from the stack denotes that m units are consumed from the budget[3]. Therefore, the length of stack content restricts the chosen of actions by agents. This means that we only need one stack symbol for the stack alphabet. The transition rules of $\mathcal{P}$ can be constructed accordingly.

---

[3] Since normal PEGS only pops one symbol from the stack at one step, in order to pop m symbols, we need to introduce some additional control states as done in [30].

For this system, we can use size-preserving EARs to represent the constraint that each departmental member chooses the same action at two different scenaria but its local states and the number of available units are identical. In particular, for each agent $i \in \{1, ..., 5\}$ and two configurations c, c' of $\mathcal{P}$, $c \sim_i c'$ iff the local states of i in c, c', as well as lengths of stack contents in c, c', are the same.

On the other hand, it is also natural to assume that each departmental member chooses the same action at two different scenaria when its local states are identical, and the numbers of available units are either equal, or both greater than some bound (e.g., 6 units). This assumption can be described using regular EARs.

3   Specification Logics: ATEL, ATEL* and AEMC

In this section, we recall the definition of alternating-time temporal epistemic logics: ATEL [33], ATEL* [19] and AEMC [7], which were introduced for reasoning about knowledge and cooperation of agents in multi-agent systems. Informally, ATEL, ATLE* and AEMC can be considered as extensions of ATL, ATL* and AMC respectively with *epistemic modalities* for representing knowledge. These include $\mathbf{K}_i$ for $i \in \mathsf{Ag}$ (agent i knows), $\mathbf{E}_A$ for $A \subseteq \mathsf{Ag}$ (every agent in A knows) and $\mathbf{C}_A$ (group modalities to characterise common knowledge).

3.1   ATEL$_\sigma$ and ATEL$_\sigma^*$ (where $\sigma \in \{\mathbf{Ir}, \mathbf{IR}, \mathbf{ir}, \mathbf{iR}\}$)

Definition 3 (ATEL$_\sigma^*$). *The syntax of ATEL$_\sigma^*$ is defined as follows, where ϕ denotes state formulae, ψ denotes path formulae,*

$$\phi ::= q \mid \neg q \mid \phi \vee \phi \mid \phi \wedge \phi \mid \mathbf{K}_i \phi \mid \mathbf{E}_A \phi \mid \mathbf{C}_A \phi \mid \overline{\mathbf{K}}_i \phi \mid \overline{\mathbf{E}}_A \phi \mid \overline{\mathbf{C}}_A \phi \mid \langle A \rangle \psi \mid [A] \psi$$
$$\psi ::= \phi \mid \psi \vee \psi \mid \psi \wedge \psi \mid \mathbf{X} \psi \mid \mathbf{G} \psi \mid \psi \mathbf{U} \psi$$

where $q \in \mathbf{AP}$, $i \in \mathsf{Ag}$ and $A \subseteq \mathsf{Ag}$.

We use $\mathbf{F}\, \psi$ to abbreviate *true* $\mathbf{U}\, \psi$. An LTL formula is an ATEL$_\sigma^*$ path formula ψ with ϕ being restricted to be atomic propositions and their negations.

The semantics of ATEL$_\sigma^*$ is defined over PEGSs. Let $\mathcal{P} = (\mathsf{Ag}, \mathsf{Ac}, P, \Gamma, \Delta, \lambda, \{\sim_i \mid i \in \mathsf{Ag}\})$ be a PEGS, ϕ be an ATEL$_\sigma^*$ state formula, and $c \in \mathcal{C}_{\mathcal{P}}$ be a configuration of $\mathcal{P}$. The satisfiability relation $\mathcal{P}, c \models_\sigma \phi$ is defined inductively on the structure of ϕ.

- $\mathcal{P}, c \models_\sigma q$ iff $q \in \lambda(c)$; $- \mathcal{P}, c \models_\sigma \neg q$ iff $q \notin \lambda(c)$;
- $\mathcal{P}, c \models_\sigma \phi_1 \vee \phi_2$ iff $\mathcal{P}, c \models_\sigma \phi_1$ or $\mathcal{P}, c \models_\sigma \phi_2$;
- $\mathcal{P}, c \models_\sigma \phi_1 \wedge \phi_2$ iff $\mathcal{P}, c \models_\sigma \phi_1$ and $\mathcal{P}, c \models_\sigma \phi_2$;
- $\mathcal{P}, c \models_\sigma \langle A \rangle \psi$ iff there exists a collective σ-strategy $\upsilon_A : A \to \Theta^\sigma$ s.t. for all paths $\pi \in \mathsf{out}^\sigma(c, \upsilon_A)$, $\mathcal{P}, \pi \models_\sigma \psi$;
- $\mathcal{P}, c \models_\sigma [A] \psi$ iff for all collective σ-strategies $\upsilon_A : A \to \Theta^\sigma$, there exists a path $\pi \in \mathsf{out}^\sigma(c, \upsilon_A)$ such that $\mathcal{P}, \pi \models_\sigma \psi$;
- $\mathcal{P}, c \models_\sigma \mathbf{K}_i \phi$ iff for all configurations $c' \in \mathcal{C}_{\mathcal{P}}$ such that $c \sim_i c'$, $\mathcal{P}, c' \models_\sigma \phi$;

- $\mathcal{P}, c \models_\sigma \overline{\mathbf{K}}_i \phi$ iff there is a configuration $c' \in \mathcal{C}_\mathcal{P}$ such that $c \sim_i c'$ and $\mathcal{P}, c' \models_\sigma \phi$;
- $\mathbf{E}_A \phi, \overline{\mathbf{E}}_A \phi, \mathbf{C}_A \phi$ and $\overline{\mathbf{C}}_A \phi$ are defined similar to $\mathbf{K}_i \phi$ and $\overline{\mathbf{K}}_i \phi$, but we use the relations $\sim_A^E$ and $\sim_A^C$.

The semantics of path formulae ψ is specified by a relation $\mathcal{P}, \pi \models_\sigma \psi$, where π is a path. Since the definition is essentially the one of LTL and standard, we refer the readers to, e.g., [15] for details. We denote by $\|\phi\|_\mathcal{P}^\sigma = \{c \in \mathcal{C}_\mathcal{P} \mid \mathcal{P}, c \models_\sigma \phi\}$ the set of configurations satisfying ϕ. The *model checking problem* is to decide whether $c \in \|\phi\|_\mathcal{P}^\sigma$ for a given configuration c.

ATEL$_\sigma$ is a syntactical fragment of ATEL$_\sigma^*$ with restricted path formulae of the form

$$\psi ::= \mathbf{X}\,\phi \mid \mathbf{G}\,\phi \mid \phi\,\mathbf{U}\,\phi.$$

An ATEL$_\sigma$ (resp. ATEL$_\sigma^*$) formula ϕ is *principal* if ϕ is in the form of $\langle A \rangle \psi$ or $[A]\psi$ such that ψ is a LTL formula. For instance, $\langle \{1\} \rangle \mathbf{F}\,q$ is a principal formula, while neither $\langle \{1\} \rangle \mathbf{F}(q \wedge \langle \{2\} \rangle \mathbf{G}\,q')$ nor $\langle \{1\} \rangle \mathbf{F}(\mathbf{K}_2\,q)$ is.

Example 2. Recall Example 1. Suppose that there are atomic propositions q_3, q_4, q_5 such that for each $i \in \{3, 4, 5\}$, $q_i \in \lambda(c)$ iff the configuration c contains the local state $p_{i,1}$, i.e., the agent i attends a conference. In addition, the atomic propositions g_i for $i \in \{1, 2\}$ denote that agent i has applied for some grants. Consider the formula: $\phi_1 \triangleq \langle \{3, 4, 5\} \rangle \mathbf{F}(q_3 \wedge q_4 \wedge q_5)$, $\phi_2 \triangleq \langle \{2, 3, 4, 5\} \rangle \mathbf{F}(q_3 \wedge q_4 \wedge q_5)$ and $\phi_3 \triangleq \mathbf{E}_{\{3,4,5\}} \langle \{3, 4, 5\} \rangle ((\mathbf{F}(g_1 \vee g_2)) \implies \mathbf{F}(q_3 \wedge q_4 \wedge q_5))$. ϕ_1 expresses that three lecturers have strategies such that all of them can attend some conferences. Obviously, ϕ_1 does not hold when both two professors attended conferences twice with late registrations, which costs 8 units. ϕ_2 expresses that three lecturers together with professor 2 have strategies such that all the lecturers can attend some conferences. ϕ_3 states that all three lecturers know that they have strategies such that if some professor applies for some grants, then all of them can attend some conferences. Obviously, ϕ_2 and ϕ_3 hold.

3.2   AEMC$_\sigma$ (where $\sigma \in \{\text{Ir, IR, ir, iR}\}$)

Definition 4 (Alternating-Time Epistemic μ-Calculus). *Given a finite set of propositional variables $\mathcal{Z}$, AEMC$_\sigma$ formulae are defined by the following grammar:*

$$\phi ::= q \mid \neg q \mid Z \mid \phi \vee \phi \mid \phi \wedge \phi \mid \langle A \rangle \mathbf{X}\phi \mid [A]\mathbf{X}\phi \mid$$
$$\mu Z.\phi \mid \nu Z.\phi \mid \mathbf{K}_i \phi \mid \mathbf{E}_A \phi \mid \mathbf{C}_A \phi \mid \overline{\mathbf{K}}_i \phi \mid \overline{\mathbf{E}}_A \phi \mid \overline{\mathbf{C}}_A \phi$$

where $q \in \mathbf{AP}$, $Z \in \mathcal{Z}$, $i \in Ag$ and $A \subseteq Ag$.

The variables $Z \in \mathcal{Z}$ in the definition of AEMC$_\sigma$ are monadic second-order variables with the intention to represent a set of configurations of PEGSs. An occurrence of a variable $Z \in \mathcal{Z}$ is said to be *closed* in an AEMC$_\sigma$ formula ϕ if the occurrence of Z is in ϕ_1 for some subformula $\mu Z.\,\phi_1$ or $\nu Z.\,\phi_1$ of ϕ. Otherwise, the occurrence of Z in ϕ is said to be *free*. An AEMC_σ formula ϕ is *closed* if it contains no free occurrences of variables from $\mathcal{Z}$.

The semantics of AEMC_σ can be defined in an obvious way, where temporal modalities $\langle A \rangle \mathbf{X}\phi$ and $[A]\mathbf{X}\phi$ and epistemic modaliteis can be interpreted as in ATEL^*_σ and the fixpoint modalities can be interpreted as in alternating mu-calculus [2]. Given a PEGS $\mathcal{P} = (\mathsf{Ag}, \mathsf{Ac}, P, \Gamma, \Delta, \lambda, \{\sim_i |\ i \in \mathsf{Ag}\})$, and a closed formula ϕ, the denotation function $\| \circ \|^\sigma_\mathcal{P}$ maps AEMC_σ formulae to sets of configurations. A configuration c satisfies ϕ iff $c \in \|\phi\|^\sigma_\mathcal{P}$.

For closed AEMC_σ formula ϕ, $\|\phi\|^\sigma_{\mathcal{P},\xi}$ is independent of ξ. Therefore, the superscript ξ will be dropped from $\|\phi\|^\sigma_{\mathcal{P},\xi}$, for closed AEMC_σ formula ϕ. In addition, the subscript $\mathcal{P}$ is also dropped from $\|\phi\|^\sigma_{\mathcal{P},\xi}$ and $\|\phi\|^\sigma_\mathcal{P}$ when it is clear.

We remark that, for AEMC_σ (where $\sigma \in \{\mathbf{Ir}, \mathbf{IR}, \mathbf{ir}, \mathbf{iR}\}$), it makes no difference whether the strategies are perfect recall or not, since each occurrence of the modalities $\langle A \rangle \mathbf{X}\phi$ and $[A]\mathbf{X}\phi$ will "reset" the strategies of agents. Therefore, we will ignore $\mathbf{R}$ and $\mathbf{r}$ and use $\mathrm{AEMC}_\mathbf{I}/\mathrm{AEMC}_\mathbf{i}$ to denote AEMC under perfect/imperfect information.

Proposition 2 [7]. *For any closed $AEMC_\sigma$ formula ϕ and a PEGS $\mathcal{P}$, $\|\phi\|^\mathbf{ir}_\mathcal{P} = \|\phi\|^\mathbf{iR}_\mathcal{P}$ and $\|\phi\|^\mathbf{Ir}_\mathcal{P} = \|\phi\|^\mathbf{IR}_\mathcal{P}$.*

We mention that, although $\mathrm{ATEL}_\mathbf{IR}$ and $\mathrm{ATEL}^*_\mathbf{IR}$ can be translated into $\mathrm{AEMC}_\mathbf{I}$, this is *not* the case for imperfect information. Namely, $\mathrm{ATEL}_\mathbf{iR}$, $\mathrm{ATEL}_\mathbf{ir}$, $\mathrm{ATEL}^*_\mathbf{iR}$, and $\mathrm{ATEL}^*_\mathbf{ir}$ cannot be translated into $\mathrm{AEMC}_\mathbf{i}$. The interested readers are referred to [7] for more discussions.

CTL, CTL* and μ-calculus are special cases of ATL_σ, ATL^*_σ and AMC in which all the modalities $\langle A \rangle \psi$ and $[A]\psi$ satisfy $A = \emptyset$[4], while ATL_σ, ATL^*_σ and AMC_σ are special cases of ATEL_σ, ATEL^*_σ and AEMC_σ in which no epistemic modalities occur.

The following results are known for model checking PEGSs with perfect information and perfect recall.

Theorem 1 ([13]). *The model checking problem for $ATEL_\mathbf{IR}/AEMC_\mathbf{IR}$ over PEGSs is EXPTIME-complete, and for $ATEL^*_\mathbf{IR}$ 3EXPTIME-complete .*

Remark 1. In [7], the outcome of a configuration c with respect to a given collective σ-strategy υ_A is defined differently from that in this paper. More specifically, the outcome in [7] corresponds to $\bigcup_{i \in A} \bigcup_{c \sim_i c'} \mathrm{out}^\sigma(c', \upsilon_A)$ in our notation. It is easy to see that for every ATEL_σ or ATEL^*_σ formula $\langle A \rangle \psi$ (resp. $[A]\psi$) and every configuration $c \in \mathcal{C}_\mathcal{P}$, $c \in \|\langle A \rangle \psi\|^\sigma_\mathcal{P}$ (resp. $c \in \|[A]\psi\|^\sigma_\mathcal{P}$) in [7] iff $c \in \|\mathbf{E}_A \langle A \rangle \psi\|^\sigma_\mathcal{P}$ (resp. $c \in \|\mathbf{E}_A[A]\psi\|^\sigma_\mathcal{P}$) in our notation. Similar differences exist for AEMC_σ. We decide to make the hidden epistemic modalities $\mathbf{E}_A$ explicit in this paper.

---

[4] $\langle \emptyset \rangle$ (resp. $[\emptyset]$) is the universal (resp. existential) path quantification A (resp. E).

4   ATEL and ATEL* Model Checking

We first recall the following undecidability result.

Theorem 2 ([16]). *The model checking problem for ATL_{iR} and ATL_{iR}^* over CEGSs is undecidable.*

In light of Theorems 1 and 2, in this section, we focus on the model checking problems for $ATEL_{ir}/ATEL_{ir}^*$.

We observe that, when the stack is available, the histories in CEGSs can be stored into the stack, so that we can reduce from the model checking problem for ATL_{iR} over CEGSs to the one for ATL_{ir} over PEGSs. From Theorem 2, we deduce the following result.

Theorem 3. *The model checking problems for ATL_{ir}/ATL_{ir}^* over PEGSs with size-preserving EARs are undecidable.*

Theorem 3 rules out model checking algorithms for $ATEL_{ir}/ATEL_{ir}^*$ when the PEGS is equipped with size-preserving EARs. As mentioned before, we therefore consider the case with regular/simple EARs. We first consider the model checking problem over PEGSs with simple EARs. This will be solved by a reduction to the model checking problem for CTL/CTL* over pushdown systems [17,31]. We then provide a reduction from the model checking problem over PEGSs with regular EARs to the one over PEGSs with simple EARs. The main idea of the reduction, which is inspired by the reduction of PDSs with regular valuations to PDSs with simple valuations in [17], is to store the runs of DFAs representing the regular EARs into the stack.

4.1   Pushdown Systems

Definition 5. *A* pushdown system *(PDS) is a tuple $\mathcal{P} = (P, \Gamma, \Delta, \lambda)$, where P, Γ, λ are defined as for PEGSs, and $\Delta \subseteq (P \times \Gamma) \times (P \times \Gamma^*)$ is a finite set of transition rules.*

A configuration of $\mathcal{P}$ is an element $\langle p, \omega \rangle$ of $P \times \Gamma^*$. We write $\langle p, \gamma \rangle \hookrightarrow \langle q, \omega \rangle$ instead of $((p, \gamma), (q, \omega)) \in \Delta$. If $\langle p, \gamma \rangle \hookrightarrow \langle q, \omega \rangle$, then for every $\omega' \in \Gamma^*$, $\langle q, \omega\omega' \rangle$ is a *successor* of $\langle p, \gamma\omega' \rangle$. Given a configuration c, a path π of $\mathcal{P}$ starting from c is a sequence of configurations $c_0 c_1 ...$ such that $c_0 = c$ and for all $i > 0$, c_i is a successor of c_{i-1}. Let $\prod_{\mathcal{P}}(c) \subseteq \mathcal{C}_{\mathcal{P}}^\omega$ denote the set of all paths in $\mathcal{P}$ starting from c onwards.

Given a configuration c and a CTL/CTL* formula ϕ, the satisfiability relation $\mathcal{P}, c \models \phi$ is defined in a standard way (cf. [17,31]). For instance, $\mathcal{P}, c \models \langle \emptyset \rangle \psi$ iff $\forall \pi \in \prod_{\mathcal{P}}(c)$, $\mathcal{P}, \pi \models \psi$, $\mathcal{P}, c \models [\emptyset] \psi$ iff $\exists \pi \in \prod_{\mathcal{P}}(c)$, $\mathcal{P}, \pi \models \psi$. Let $\|\phi\|_{\mathcal{P}} = \{c \in \mathcal{C}_{\mathcal{P}} \mid \mathcal{P}, c \models \phi\}$.

Theorem 4 [17]. *Given a PDS $\mathcal{P} = (P, \Gamma, \Delta, \lambda)$ and a CTL/CTL* formula ϕ such that all state subformulae in ϕ are atomic propositions, we can effectively compute a MA $\mathcal{M}$ with $\mathbf{O}(|\lambda| \cdot |P| \cdot |\Delta| \cdot k)$ states in $\mathbf{O}(|\lambda| \cdot |P|^2 \cdot |\Delta| \cdot k)$ time such that* *the MA exactly recognizes* $\|\phi\|_{\mathcal{P}}$, *where* k *is* $2^{\mathbf{O}(|\phi|)}$ *(resp.* $\mathbf{O}(|\phi|)$*) for CTL* (resp. CTL). Moreover, a DFA* $\mathcal{A} = (S, \Gamma, \Delta_1, s_0)$ *with* $\mathbf{O}(|\lambda| \cdot |\Delta| \cdot 2^{|P| \cdot k})$ *states and a tuple of sets of accepting states* $(F_p)_{p \in P}$ *can be constructed in* $\mathbf{O}(|\lambda| \cdot |\Delta| \cdot 2^{|P| \cdot k})$ *time such that for every configuration* $\langle p, \omega \rangle \in P \times \Gamma^*$, $\langle p, \omega \rangle \in \mathcal{L}(\mathcal{M})$ *iff* $\Delta_1^*(s_0, \omega^R) \in F_p$.

4.2   Model Checking for PEGSs with Simple EARs

In this subsection, we propose an automatic-theoretic approach for solving the model checking problems for ATEL$_{ir}$ and ATEL$_{ir}^*$ over PEGSs with simple EARs.

Let us fix the ATEL$_{ir}$/ATEL$_{ir}^*$ formula ϕ and a PEGS $\mathcal{P} = ($Ag, Ac, $P, \Gamma, \Delta, \lambda, \{\sim_i | \ i \ \in \ Ag\})$ with a regular valuation l represented by DFAs $(\mathcal{A}_{p,q})_{p \in P, q \in \mathbf{AP}}$ and $\sim_i$ is specified by an equivalence relation $\approx_i$ on $P \times \Gamma$ for $i \in $ Ag.

The idea of the algorithm is to construct, for each state subformula ϕ' of ϕ, an MA $\mathcal{M}_{\phi'}$ to represent the set of configurations satisfying ϕ'. We will first illustrate the construction in case that $\phi' = \langle A \rangle \psi$ (resp. $\phi' = [A]\psi$) is a principal formula, then extend the construction to the more general case.

Principal Formulae. Our approach will reduce the model checking problem over PEGSs to the model checking problem for CTL/CTL* over PDSs. Note that for $i \in A$, $\approx_i$ is defined over $P \times \Gamma$. It follows that the strategy of any agent $i \in A$ must respect $\approx_i$, namely, for all $(p, \gamma\omega)$ and $(p', \gamma'\omega')$ with $(p, \gamma) \approx_i (p', \gamma')$, $v_i(p, \gamma\omega) = v_i(p', \gamma'\omega')$ for any **ir**-strategy v_i of i. Therefore, any **ir**-strategy v_i with respect to $\approx_i$ can be regarded as a function over $P \times \Gamma$ (instead of configurations of $\mathcal{P}$), i.e., $v_i : P \times \Gamma \to $ Ac such that $v_i(p, \gamma) = v_i(p', \gamma')$ for all (p, γ) and (p', γ') with $(p, \gamma) \approx_i (p', \gamma')$.

Proposition 3. *Given a configuration* $c \in \mathcal{C}_{\mathcal{P}}$ *and a set of agents* $A \subseteq $ Ag, *the following statements hold:*

i. *for any collective* **ir**-*strategy* v_A *such that* $v_A(i)$ *respects to* $\approx_i$ *for* $i \in A$, *there exist functions* $v_i' : P \times \Gamma \to $ Ac *for* $i \in A$ *such that* $out^{ir}(c, v_A) = out(c, \bigcup_{i \in A} v_i')$ *and* $v_i'(p, \gamma) = v_i'(p', \gamma')$ *for all* (p, γ) *and* (p', γ') *with* $(p, \gamma) \approx_i (p', \gamma')$;

ii. *for any function* $v_i' : P \times \Gamma \to $ Ac *for* $i \in A$ *such that* $v_i'(p, \gamma) = v_i'(p', \gamma')$ *for all* (p, γ) *and* (p', γ') *with* $(p, \gamma) \approx_i (p', \gamma')$, *there exists a collective* **ir**-*strategy* v_A *such that* $v_A(i)$ *respects to* $\approx_i$ *for* $i \in A$ *and* $out^{ir}(c, v_A) = out(c, \bigcup_{i \in A} v_i')$;

where $out(c, \bigcup_{i \in A} v_i')$ *denotes the set of all paths* $\pi = \langle p_0, \gamma_0\omega_0 \rangle \langle p_1, \gamma_1\omega_1 \rangle \cdots$ *such that* $\langle p_0, \gamma_0\omega_0 \rangle = c$ *and for all* $k \geq 0$, *there exists* $\mathbf{d}_k \in \mathcal{D}$ *such that* $\langle p_k, \gamma_k\omega_k \rangle \overset{\mathbf{d}_k}{\Longrightarrow}_{\mathcal{P}} \langle p_{k+1}, \gamma_{k+1}\omega_{k+1} \rangle$ *and* $\mathbf{d}_k(i) = v_i'(p_k, \gamma_k)$ *for all* $i \in A$.

According to Proposition 3, we can check all the possible collective **ir**-strategies, as the number of possible functions from $P \times \Gamma \to $ Ac is finite. Let us now fix a specific collective **ir**-strategy $v_A = (v_i)_{i \in A}$ for A. For each $(p, \gamma) \in P \times \Gamma$, after applying a collective **ir**-strategy $v_A = (v_i)_{i \in A}$ for A, we define a PDS

$\mathcal{P}_{v_A} = (P, \Gamma, \Delta', \lambda)$, where Δ' is defined as follows: for every $p, p' \in P$, $\gamma \in \Gamma$ and $\omega \in \Gamma^*$,

$$((p, \gamma), (p', \omega)) \in \Delta' \text{ iff } \exists \mathbf{d} \in \mathcal{D} \text{ s.t. } \forall i \in A, \mathbf{d}(i) = v_i(p, \gamma) \text{ and } \Delta(p, \gamma, \mathbf{d}) = (p', \omega).$$

Lemma 1. $out^{\mathbf{ir}}(c, v_A) = \prod_{\mathcal{P}_{v_A}}(c)$.

Following from Lemma 1, for $\phi' = \langle A \rangle \psi$, $\mathcal{P}, c \models_{\mathbf{ir}} \phi'$ iff there exists a collective **ir**-strategy v_A such that for all paths $\pi \in \prod_{\mathcal{P}_{v_A}}(c)$, $\mathcal{P}, \pi \models_{\mathbf{ir}} \psi$. The latter holds iff there exists a collective **ir**-strategy v_A such that $\mathcal{P}_{v_A}, c \models \langle \emptyset \rangle \psi$. Similarly, for $\phi' = [A]\psi$, $\mathcal{P}, c \models_{\mathbf{ir}} \phi'$ iff for all collective **ir**-strategies v_A, there exists a path $\pi \in \prod_{\mathcal{P}_{v_A}}(c)$ such that $\mathcal{P}, \pi \models_{\mathbf{ir}} \psi$. The latter holds iff for all collective **ir**-strategies v_A, $\mathcal{P}_{v_A}, c \models [\emptyset]\psi$.

Fix a collective **ir**-strategy v_A with respect to $\approx_i$ for $i \in A$, by applying Theorem 4, we can construct a MA $\mathcal{M}_{v_A}$ such that $\mathcal{L}(\mathcal{M}_{v_A}) = \{c \in P \times \Gamma^* \mid \mathcal{P}_{v_A}, c \models \langle \emptyset \rangle \psi'\}$ (resp. $\mathcal{L}(\mathcal{M}_{v_A}) = \{c \in P \times \Gamma^* \mid \mathcal{P}_{v_A}, c \models [\emptyset]\psi'\}$). Since, there are at most $|Ac|^{|P| \cdot |\Gamma| \cdot |A|}$ collective **ir**-strategies with respect to $\approx_i$ for $i \in A$ and $|A| \le |Ag|$, we can construct a MA $\mathcal{M}_{\phi'}$ such that $\mathcal{L}(\mathcal{M}_{\phi'}) = \bigcup_{v_A} \mathcal{L}(\mathcal{M}_{v_A})$ (resp. $\mathcal{L}(\mathcal{M}_{\phi'}) = \bigcap_{v_A} \mathcal{L}(\mathcal{M}_{v_A}))$.

Lemma 2. *For every principal* $ATEL^*_{\mathbf{ir}}$ *(resp.* $ATEL_{\mathbf{ir}}$*) formula* ϕ'*, we can construct a MA* $\mathcal{M}_{\phi'}$ *with* $\mathbf{O}(|Ac|^{|P| \cdot |\Gamma| \cdot |Ag|} \cdot |\lambda| \cdot |P| \cdot |\Delta| \cdot k)$ *states in* $\mathbf{O}(|Ac|^{|P| \cdot |\Gamma| \cdot |Ag|} \cdot |\lambda| \cdot |P|^2 \cdot |\Delta| \cdot k)$ *time such that the MA exactly recognizes* $\|\phi'\|^{\mathbf{ir}}_{\mathcal{P}}$*, where* k *is* $2^{\mathbf{O}(|\phi|)}$ *(resp.* $\mathbf{O}(|\phi|))$*. Moreover, a DFA* $\mathcal{A} = (S, \Gamma, \Delta_1, s_0)$ *with* $\mathbf{O}(|Ac|^{|P| \cdot |\Gamma| \cdot |Ag|} \cdot |\lambda| \cdot |\Delta| \cdot 2^{|P| \cdot k})$ *states and a tuple of sets of accepting states* $(F_p)_{p \in P}$ *can be constructed in* $\mathbf{O}(|Ac|^{|P| \cdot |\Gamma| \cdot |Ag|} \cdot |\lambda| \cdot |\Delta| \cdot 2^{|P| \cdot k})$ *time such that for every configuration* $\langle p, \omega \rangle \in P \times \Gamma^*$*,* $\langle p, \omega \rangle \in \mathcal{L}(\mathcal{M}_{\phi'})$ *iff* $\Delta^*_1(s_0, \omega^R) \in F_p$*.*

General $ATEL_{\mathbf{ir}}/ATEL^*_{\mathbf{ir}}$ Formulae. We now present a model checking algorithm for general $ATEL_{\mathbf{ir}}/ATEL^*_{\mathbf{ir}}$ formulae. Given an $ATEL_{\mathbf{ir}}/ATEL^*_{\mathbf{ir}}$ formula ϕ, we inductively compute a MA $\mathcal{M}_{\phi'}$ from the state subformula ϕ' such that $\mathcal{L}(\mathcal{M}_{\phi'}) = \|\phi'\|^{\mathbf{ir}}_{\mathcal{P}}$. The base case for atomic propositions is trivial. For the induction step:

- For ϕ' of the form $\neg q$, $\phi_1 \wedge \phi_2$ or $\phi_1 \vee \phi_2$, $\mathcal{M}_{\phi'}$ can be computed by applying Boolean operations on $\mathcal{M}_{\phi_1}/\mathcal{M}_{\phi_2}$.
- For ϕ' of the form $\langle A \rangle \psi'$, we first compute a principal formula ϕ'' by replacing each state subformula ϕ''' in ψ' by a fresh atomic proposition $q_{\phi'''}$ and then compute a new regular valuation λ' by saturating λ which sets $q_{\phi'''} \in \lambda(c)$ for $c \in \mathcal{L}(\mathcal{M}_{\phi'''})$. To saturate λ, we use the DFA transformed from $\mathcal{M}_{\phi'''}$. Similar to the construction in [17], $|\lambda'| = |\lambda| \cdot |Ac|^{|P| \cdot |\Gamma| \cdot |Ag|} \cdot 2^{|P| \cdot k}$, where k is $2^{\mathbf{O}(|\phi|)}$ (resp. $\mathbf{O}(|\phi|)$) for $ATEL^*_{\mathbf{ir}}$ (resp. $ATEL_{\mathbf{ir}}$). By Lemma 2, we can construct a MA $\mathcal{M}_{\phi''}$ from ϕ'' which is the desired MA $\mathcal{M}_{\phi'}$. The construction for $\mathcal{M}_{[A]\psi'}$ is similar.
- For ϕ' of the form $\mathbf{K}_i \phi''$ (resp. $\mathbf{E}_A \phi''$ and $\mathbf{C}_A \phi''$), suppose that the MA $\mathcal{M}_{\phi''} = (S_1, \Gamma, \delta_1, I_1, S_f)$ recognizes $\|\phi''\|^{\mathbf{ir}}_{\mathcal{P}}$. Let $[p_1, \gamma_1], ..., [p_m, \gamma_m] \subseteq P \times \Gamma$ be the equivalence classes induced by the relation $\approx_i$ (resp. $\sim^E_A$ and $\sim^C_A$). We define

the MA $\mathcal{M}_{\phi'} = (P \cup \{s_f\}, \Gamma, \delta', P, \{s_f\})$, where for every $j \in [m]$, if $\{\langle p, \gamma\omega\rangle \mid (p, \gamma) \in [p_j, \gamma_j], \omega \in \Gamma^*\} \subseteq \mathcal{L}(\mathcal{M}_{\phi''})$, then for all $(p, \gamma) \in [p_j, \gamma_j]$ and $\gamma' \in \Gamma$, $\delta'(p, \gamma) = s_f$ and $\delta'(s_f, \gamma') = s_f$. The MA $\mathcal{M}_{\phi'}$ for formulae ϕ' of the form $\overline{\mathbf{K}}_i\phi''$ (resp. $\overline{\mathbf{E}}_A\phi''$ and $\overline{\mathbf{C}}_A\phi''$) can be constructed similarly as for $\mathbf{K}_i\phi''$, using the condition $\{\langle p, \gamma\omega\rangle \mid (p, \gamma) \in [p_j, \gamma_j], \omega \in \Gamma^*\} \cap \mathcal{L}(\mathcal{M}_{\phi''}) \neq \emptyset$, instead of $\{\langle p, \gamma\omega\rangle \mid (p, \gamma) \in [p_j, \gamma_j], \omega \in \Gamma^*\} \subseteq \mathcal{L}(\mathcal{M}_{\phi''})$.

In the above algorithm, MAs are transformed into DFAs at most $|\phi|$ times. Each transformation only introduces the factor $|\mathsf{Ac}|^{|P| \cdot |\Gamma| \cdot |\mathsf{Ag}|} \cdot 2^{|P| \cdot k}$ into $|\lambda|$ [17]. We then deduce the following result from Proposition 1 and Lemma 2.

Theorem 5. *The model checking problem for $ATEL_{\mathbf{ir}}^*$ over PEGSs with simple EARs is 2EXPTIME-complete, while the problem for $ATEL_{\mathbf{ir}}$ is EXPTIME-complete.*

Proof. The lower bound of the model checking problem for $ATEL_{\mathbf{ir}}^*$ follows from that the model checking problem for CTL* over PDSs with simple valuations [5] is 2EXPTIME-complete. Namely, even for PEGSs with a single agent, and simple valuations, the model checking problem is already 2EXPTIME-hard. The hardness for $ATEL_{\mathbf{ir}}$ follows from the fact that the model checking problem for CTL over PDSs is EXPTIME-complete [32,35]. □

4.3 Model Checking for PEGSs with Regular EARs

In this subsection, we present a reduction from the model checking problem over PEGSs with regular EARs to the problem over PEGSs with simple EARs. Assume a PEGS $\mathcal{P} = (\mathsf{Ag}, \mathsf{Ac}, P, \Gamma, \Delta, \lambda, \{\sim_i \mid i \in \mathsf{Ag}\})$ with regular EARs such that, for each $i \in \mathsf{Ag}$, $\sim_i$ is given as the pair $(\approx_i, \mathcal{A}_i)$, where $\approx_i \subseteq P \times \Gamma$ is an equivalence relation and $\mathcal{A}_i = (S_i, \Gamma, \delta_i, s_{i,0})$ is a DFA.

Let $\mathcal{A} = (\mathbf{S}, \Gamma, \boldsymbol{\delta}, \mathbf{s_0})$ be the product automaton of $\mathcal{A}_i$'s for $i \in \mathsf{Ag}$, such that $\mathbf{S} = S_1 \times ... \times S_n$, $\mathbf{s_0} = [s_{1,0}, ..., s_{n,0}]$, and $\boldsymbol{\delta}(\mathbf{s_1}, \gamma) = \mathbf{s_2}$ if for every $i \in [n]$, $\delta_i(s_{i,1}, \gamma) = s_{i,2}$, where $s_{i,j}$ denotes the state of $\mathcal{A}_i$ in $\mathbf{s_j}$.

We will construct a new PEGS $\mathcal{P}'$ with simple EARs such that the model checking problem over $\mathcal{P}$ is reduced to the problem over $\mathcal{P}'$. Intuitively, the PEGS $\mathcal{P}'$ with simple EARs to be constructed stores the state obtained by running $\mathcal{A}$ over the reverse of the partial stack content up to the current position (exclusive) into the stack. Formally, the PEGS $\mathcal{P}'$ is given by $(\mathsf{Ag}, \mathsf{Ac}, P, \Gamma', \Delta', \lambda', \{\sim_i' \mid i \in \mathsf{Ag}\})$, where

- $\Gamma' = \Gamma \times \mathbf{S}$;
- for each $i \in \mathsf{Ag}$, $\sim_i'$ is specified by an equivalence relation $\approx_i'$ on $P \times \Gamma'$ defined as follows: $(p, [\gamma, \mathbf{s}]) \approx_i' (p', [\gamma', \mathbf{s'}])$ iff $(p, \gamma) \approx_i (p', \gamma')$ and $\mathbf{s} = \mathbf{s'}$;
- Δ' is defined as follows: for every state $\mathbf{s} \in \mathbf{S}$,
  1. for every $\langle p, \gamma\rangle \overset{\mathbf{d}}{\hookrightarrow}_{\mathcal{P}} \langle p', \epsilon\rangle$, $\langle p, [\gamma, \mathbf{s}]\rangle \overset{\mathbf{d}}{\hookrightarrow}_{\mathcal{P}'} \langle p', \epsilon\rangle$,
  2. for every $\langle p, \gamma\rangle \overset{\mathbf{d}}{\hookrightarrow}_{\mathcal{P}} \langle p', \gamma_k...\gamma_1\rangle$ with $k \geq 1$ and $\boldsymbol{\delta}(\mathbf{s_j}, \gamma_j) = \mathbf{s_{j+1}}$ for every $j : 1 \leq j \leq k-1$ (where $\mathbf{s_1} = \mathbf{s}$), then $\langle p, [\gamma, \mathbf{s}]\rangle \overset{\mathbf{d}}{\hookrightarrow}_{\mathcal{P}'} \langle p', [\gamma_k, \mathbf{s_k}]...[\gamma_1, \mathbf{s_1}]\rangle$.

Finally, the valuation λ' is adjusted accordingly to λ, i.e., for every $\langle p', [\gamma_k, s_k]...[\gamma_0, s_0] \rangle \in \mathcal{C}_{\mathcal{P}'}$, $\lambda'(\langle p', [\gamma_k, s_k]...[\gamma_0, s_0] \rangle) = \lambda(\langle p', \gamma_k...\gamma_0 \rangle)$.

Lemma 3. *The model checking problem for $ATEL_{\mathbf{ir}}$ (resp. $ATEL_{\mathbf{ir}}^*$) over a PEGS $\mathcal{P}$, with stack alphabet Γ and regular EARs $\sim_i = (\approx_i, \mathcal{A}_i)$ for $i \in \mathsf{Ag}$, can be reduced to the problem over a PEGS $\mathcal{P}'$ with simple EARs $\sim_i'$, such that the state space of $\mathcal{P}'$ is the same as that of $\mathcal{P}$, and the stack alphabet of $\mathcal{P}'$ is $\Gamma \times S$, where S is the state space of the product of $\mathcal{A}_i$'s for $i \in \mathsf{Ag}$.*

Theorem 6. *The model checking problem for $ATEL_{\mathbf{ir}}^*$ (resp. $ATEL_{\mathbf{ir}}$) over PEGSs with regular EARs is 2EXPTIME-complete (resp. EXPTIME-complete).*

5   AEMC Model Checking

In this section, we propose algorithms for the model checking problems for $AEMC_{\mathbf{i}}$ over PEGSs with size-preserving/regular/simple EARs. At first, we remark that Theorem 3 does *not* hold for $AEMC_{\mathbf{i}}$ (recall that $AEMC_{\mathbf{i}} = AEMC_{\mathbf{ir}} = AEMC_{\mathbf{iR}}$). Indeed, we will show that the model checking problems for $AEMC_{\mathbf{i}}$ over PEGSs with size-preserving/regular/simple EARs are EXMPTIME-complete.

Fix a closed $AEMC_{\mathbf{i}}$ formula ϕ and a PEGS $\mathcal{P} = (\mathsf{Ag}, \mathsf{Ac}, P, \Gamma, \Delta, \lambda, \{\sim_i | i \in \mathsf{Ag}\})$ with size-preserving/regular/simple EARs. We will construct an AMA $\mathcal{A}_\phi$ to capture $\|\phi\|_{\mathcal{P}}^{\mathbf{i}}$ by induction on the syntax of $AEMC_{\mathbf{i}}$ formulae.

Atomic formulae, Boolean operators, formulae of the form $\langle A \rangle \mathbf{X} \phi'$ and $[A] \mathbf{X} \phi'$, and fixpoint operators can be handled as in [13], where the model checking problem for AMC over PGSs was considered, as imperfect information does not play a role for these operators. In the sequel, we illustrate how to deal with the epistemic modalities. Regular/simple EARs can be tackled in a very similar way to Sect. 4, we focus on the size-preserving one.

Suppose size-preserving EARs $\sim_i$ for $i \in \mathsf{Ag}$ are specified by equivalence relations $\simeq_i \subseteq (P \times P) \cup (\Gamma \times \Gamma)$. For the formula $\phi = \mathbf{K}_i \phi'$, suppose the AMA $\mathcal{A}_{\phi'} = (S', \Gamma, \delta', I', S_f')$ recognizing $\|\phi'\|_{\mathcal{P}}^{\mathbf{ir}}$ has been constructed. We construct $\mathcal{A}_\phi = (S', \Gamma, \delta, I, S_f')$ as follows.

- $I = \{p \in P \mid \exists p' \in I'.\, p \simeq_i p'\}$.
- For each $(p, \gamma) \in P \times \Gamma$, let $[p]_{\simeq_i}$ (resp. $[\gamma]_{\simeq_i}$) be the equivalence of p (resp. γ) under $\simeq_i$, and $\overline{S'_{p,\gamma}} := \{S'_{p,\gamma} \mid (p, \gamma, S'_{p,\gamma}) \in \delta'\}$. Then $(p, \gamma, S) \in \delta$ if (1) for all $p' \in [p]_{\simeq_i}$ and $\gamma' \in [\gamma]_{\simeq_i}$, $\overline{S'_{p',\gamma'}} \neq \emptyset$; and (2) $S = \bigcup_{p' \in [p]_{\simeq_i}, \gamma' \in [\gamma]_{\simeq_i}} S''_{p',\gamma'}$, where $S''_{p',\gamma'} \in \overline{S'_{p',\gamma'}}$.
- For every $(s, \gamma, S) \in \delta'$ such that $s \in S' \setminus P$, let $(s, \gamma', S) \in \delta$ for every $\gamma' \in \Gamma$ with $\gamma' \simeq_i \gamma$.

For the formula $\phi = \overline{\mathbf{K}}_i \phi'$, suppose the AMA $\mathcal{A}_{\phi'} = (S', \Gamma, \delta', I', S_f')$ recognizes $\|\phi'\|_{\mathcal{P}}^{\mathbf{ir}}$. We construct $\mathcal{A}_\phi = (S', \Gamma, \delta, I, S_f')$ as follows.

- $I = \{p \in P \mid \exists p' \in I'.\, p \sim_i p'\}$.
- For each $(p, \gamma) \in P \times \Gamma$, if there is $(p', \gamma', S_1') \in \delta'$ such that $p \simeq_i p'$ and $\gamma \simeq_i \gamma'$, let $(p, \gamma, S_1') \in \delta$.

– For every $(s, \gamma, S) \in \delta'$ such that $s \in S' \setminus P$, let $(s, \gamma', S) \in \delta$ for every $\gamma' \in \Gamma$ with $\gamma' \simeq_i \gamma$.

The AMA $\mathcal{A}_\phi$ for ϕ of the form $\mathbf{E}_A \phi'$, $\mathbf{C}_A \phi'$, $\overline{\mathbf{E}}_A \phi'$ or $\overline{\mathbf{C}}_A \phi'$ can be constructed in a very similar way, in which the relation $\simeq_i$ is replaced by the relation $\bigcup_{i \in A} \simeq_i$ (resp. the transitive closure of $\bigcup_{i \in A} \simeq_i$).

Lemma 4. *Given a PEGS $\mathcal{P}$ with regular valuations and size-preserving EARs , and a closed AEMC$_i$ formula ϕ, we can construct an AMA $\mathcal{A}_\phi$ recognizing $\|\phi\|_{\mathcal{P}}^i$ in exponential time with respect to $|\mathcal{P}|$, $|\lambda|$ and $|\phi|$.*

From Lemma 4 and Proposition 1, we have:

Theorem 7. *The model checking problem for AEMC$_i$ over PEGSs with regular/simple valuations and size-preserving/regular/simple EARs is EXPTIME-complete.*

The lower bound follows from fact that the model checking problem for AMC over PGSs with simple valuations is EXPTIME-complete [13].

6 Conclusion and Future Work

In this paper, we have shown that the model checking problem is undecidable for ATL$_{ir}$/ATL$_{ir}^*$ over PEGSs with size-preserving EARs, and provided optimal automata-theoretic model checking algorithms for ATEL$_{ir}$/ATEL$_{ir}^*$ over PEGSs with regular/simple EARs. We also have provided optimal model checking algorithms for AEMC$_i$ over PEGSs under size-preserving/regular/simple EARs with matching lower bounds.

The model checking problem for ATEL$_{Ir}$/ATEL$_{Ir}^*$ or ATL$_{Ir}$/ATL$_{Ir}^*$ over PEGSs is still open. We note that the problem for ATEL$_{Ir}$/ATEL$_{Ir}^*$ or ATL$_{Ir}$/ATL$_{Ir}^*$ over CEGSs can be solved by nondeterministically choosing a strategy via selecting a subset of the transition relation, as the strategies only depend on control states yielding a finite set of possible strategies [29]. However, similar techniques are no longer applicable in PEGSs, as the strategies depend on stack contents apart from control states, which may yield an infinite set of possible strategies.

References

1. Alur, R., Henzinger, T.A., Kupferman, O.: Alternating-time temporal logic. In: FOCS 1997, pp. 100–109 (1997)
2. Alur, R., Henzinger, T.A., Kupferman, O.: Alternating-time temporal logic. J. ACM **49**(5), 672–713 (2002)
3. Aminof, B., Legay, A., Murano, A., Serre, O., Vardi, M.Y.: Pushdown module checking with imperfect information. Inf. Comput. **223**, 1–17 (2013)

4. Bouajjani, A., Esparza, J., Maler, O.: Reachability analysis of pushdown automata: application to model-checking. In: Mazurkiewicz, A., Winkowski, J. (eds.) CONCUR 1997. LNCS, vol. 1243, pp. 135–150. Springer, Heidelberg (1997). doi:10.1007/3-540-63141-0_10

5. Bozzelli, L.: Complexity results on branching-time pushdown model checking. Theoret. Comput. Sci. **379**(1–2), 286–297 (2007)

6. Brihaye, T., Laroussinie, F., Markey, N., Oreiby, G.: Timed concurrent game structures. In: Caires, L., Vasconcelos, V.T. (eds.) CONCUR 2007. LNCS, vol. 4703, pp. 445–459. Springer, Heidelberg (2007). doi:10.1007/978-3-540-74407-8_30

7. Bulling, N., Jamroga, W.: Alternating epistemic mu-calculus. In: IJCAI 2011, pp. 109–114 (2011)

8. Bulling, N., Nguyen, H.N.: Model checking resource bounded systems with shared resources via alternating büchi pushdown systems. In: Chen, Q., Torroni, P., Villata, S., Hsu, J., Omicini, A. (eds.) PRIMA 2015. LNCS (LNAI), vol. 9387, pp. 640–649. Springer, Cham (2015). doi:10.1007/978-3-319-25524-8_47

9. Cermák, Petr: A model checker for strategy logic. Meng individual project, Department of Computing, Imperial College, London (2015)

10. Cermák, P., Lomuscio, A., Murano, A.: Verifying and synthesising multi-agent systems against one-goal strategy logic specifications. In: AAAI 2015, pp. 2038–2044 (2015)

11. Chen, T., Forejt, V., Kwiatkowska, M.Z., Parker, D., Simaitis, A.: Automatic verification of competitive stochastic systems. Formal Methods Syst. Des. **43**(1), 61–92 (2013)

12. Chen, T., Forejt, V., Kwiatkowska, M., Parker, D., Simaitis, A.: PRISM-games: a model checker for stochastic multi-player games. In: Piterman, N., Smolka, S.A. (eds.) TACAS 2013. LNCS, vol. 7795, pp. 185–191. Springer, Heidelberg (2013). doi:10.1007/978-3-642-36742-7_13

13. Chen, T., Song, F., Wu, Z.: Global model checking on pushdown multi-agent systems. In: AAAI 2016, pp. 2459–2465 (2016)

14. Chen, T., Song, F., Wu, Z.: Verifying pushdown multi-agent systems against strategy logics. In: IJCAI 2016, pp. 180–186 (2016)

15. Clarke, E.M., Grumberg, O., Peled, D.A.: Model Checking. MIT Press, Cambridge (2001)

16. Dima, C., Tiplea, F.L.: Model-checking ATL under imperfect information and perfect recall semantics is undecidable. CoRR, abs/1102.4225 (2011)

17. Esparza, J., Kucera, A., Schwoon, S.: Model checking LTL with regular valuations for pushdown systems. Inf. Comput. **186**(2), 355–376 (2003)

18. Fagin, R., Halpern, J.Y., Moses, Y., Vardi, M.Y.: Reasoning About Knowledge. MIT Press, Cambridge (1995)

19. Jamroga, W.: Some remarks on alternating temporal epistemic logic. In: FAMAS 2003, pp. 133–140 (2003)

20. Jamroga, W., Dix, J.: Model checking abilities under incomplete information is indeed Delta2-complete. In: EUMAS 2006 (2006)

21. Kupferman, O., Piterman, N., Vardi, M.Y.: Pushdown specifications. In: Baaz, M., Voronkov, A. (eds.) LPAR 2002. LNCS (LNAI), vol. 2514, pp. 262–277. Springer, Heidelberg (2002). doi:10.1007/3-540-36078-6_18

22. Lomuscio, A., Raimondi, F.: Model checking knowledge, strategies, and games in multi-agent systems. In: AAMAS 2006, pp. 161–168 (2006)

23. Mogavero, F., Murano, A., Perelli, G., Vardi, M.Y.: Reasoning about strategies: on the model-checking problem. ACM Trans. Comput. Logic **15**(4), 34:1–34:47 (2014)

24. Mogavero, F., Murano, A., Sauro, L.: On the boundary of behavioral strategies. In: LICS 2013, pp. 263–272 (2013)
25. Mogavero, F., Murano, A., Sauro, L.: A behavioral hierarchy of strategy logic. In: Bulling, N., Torre, L., Villata, S., Jamroga, W., Vasconcelos, W. (eds.) CLIMA 2014. LNCS (LNAI), vol. 8624, pp. 148–165. Springer, Cham (2014). doi:10.1007/978-3-319-09764-0_10
26. Mogavero, F., Murano, A., Vardi, M.Y.: Reasoning about strategies. In: FSTTCS 2010, pp. 133–144 (2010)
27. Murano, A., Perelli, G.: Pushdown multi-agent system verification. In: IJCAI 2015, pp. 1090–1097 (2015)
28. Pilecki, J., Bednarczyk, M.A., Jamroga, W.: Model checking properties of multi-agent systems with imperfect information and imperfect recall. In: IS 2014, pp. 415–426 (2014)
29. Schobbens, P.-Y.: Alternating-time logic with imperfect recall. Electron. Notes Theoret. Comput. Sci. **85**(2), 82–93 (2004)
30. Schwoon, S.: Model checking pushdown systems. Ph.D. thesis, Technical University Munich, Germany (2002)
31. Song, F., Touili, T.: Efficient CTL model-checking for pushdown systems. In: Katoen, J.-P., König, B. (eds.) CONCUR 2011. LNCS, vol. 6901, pp. 434–449. Springer, Heidelberg (2011). doi:10.1007/978-3-642-23217-6_29
32. Song, F., Touili, T.: Efficient CTL model-checking for pushdown systems. Theoret. Comput. Sci. **549**, 127–145 (2014)
33. van der Hoek, W., Wooldridge, M.: Tractable multiagent planning for epistemic goals. In: AAMAS 2002, pp. 1167–1174 (2002)
34. van der Hoek, W., Wooldridge, M.: Cooperation, knowledge, and time: alternating-time temporal epistemic logic and its applications. Stud. Logica **75**(1), 125–157 (2003)
35. Walukiewicz, I.: Model checking CTL properties of pushdown systems. In: Kapoor, S., Prasad, S. (eds.) FSTTCS 2000. LNCS, vol. 1974, pp. 127–138. Springer, Heidelberg (2000). doi:10.1007/3-540-44450-5_10
36. Hague, M., Ong, C.-H.L.: A saturation method for the modal μ-calculus over pushdown systems. Inf. Comput. **209**(5), 799–821 (2011)

Transforming Timing Requirements into CCSL Constraints to Verify Cyber-Physical Systems

Xiaohong Chen[1]([⊠]), Ling Yin[2], Yijun Yu[3], and Zhi Jin[4]

[1] Shanghai Key Laboratory of Trustworthy Computing,
East China Normal University, Shanghai, China
xhchen@sei.ecnu.edu.cn
[2] Shanghai University of Engineering Science, Shanghai, China
[3] School of Computing and Communications, The Open University,
Milton Keynes, UK
[4] Key Laboratory of High Confidence Software Technologies, Ministry of Education,
Institute of Software, School of EE & CS, Peking University, Beijing, China

Abstract. The timing requirements of embedded cyber-physical systems (CPS) constrain CPS behaviors made by scheduling analysis. Lack of physical entity properties modeling and the need of scheduling analysis require a systematic approach to specify timing requirements of CPS at the early phase of requirements engineering. In this work, we extend the Problem Frames notations to capture timing properties of both cyber and physical domain entities into Clock Constraint Specification Language (CCSL) constraints which is more explicit that LTL for scheduling analysis. Interpreting them using operational semantics as finite state machines, we are able to transform these timing requirements into CCSL scheduling constraints, and verify their consistency on NuSMV. Our TimePF tool-supported approach is illustrated through the verification of timing requirements for a representative problem in embedded CPS.

Keywords: Cyber-physical systems · Problem Frames · Timing requirements · CCSL constraints

1 Introduction

Mission-critical cyber-physical systems (CPS) [1] are widely used. With growing complexity, they are getting more expensive to develop and harder to verify without explicitly documented requirements. Unlike other software systems, CPS interconnect with many cyber and physical entities [2]. Typically, data must be collected from the physical world using *sensors*, fed into *controllers* of cyber entities which in turn make decisions for *actuators* to change the properties of physical world entities. All these decisions are constrained by timing requirements and made by scheduling analysis.

The timing requirements of CPS are especially important for real-time safety-critical systems, such as computer controlled trains. If they cannot stop within a

© Springer International Publishing AG 2017
Z. Duan and L. Ong (Eds.): ICFEM 2017, LNCS 10610, pp. 54–70, 2017.
https://doi.org/10.1007/978-3-319-68690-5_4

specific duration, serious accidents could happen. In such cases, timing requirements are as prominent as functional requirements. As the classical requirements derivation by Jackson and Zave [3], the timing requirements computation should consider the physical domain properties as well as evolution. However, there is no systematic approach to specify timing requirements of CPS early for lack of domain knowledge of physical domains which require explicit models.

Existing RE approaches provide some formalisms to express timing requirements. For example, goal-oriented approaches [4] use linear temporal logic (LTL) to describe requirements, e.g., a property will be achieved eventually, and they also extend temporal logic to specify real-time properties. Due to the prevailing interactions of software and physical entities in CPS, we argue that the Problem Frames (PF) approach [5], which models physical domains explicitly, is particularly suitable for modelling such requirements. However, current practice using PF focus mainly on the representation rather than the systematic derivation of timing requirements and formal verification. For example, Choppy et al. model time events [6]; Barroca et al. use Timer as a part of problem domain [7]. Little attention has been paid to deriving and verifying the timing specifications, i.e., scheduling specification.

Our previous work [8] relates the PF to timing constraints in terms of clock constraint specification language(CCSL) [9,10] uses CCSL constraints for scheduling analysis. But [8] does not support specification due to big modeling granularity-entity as the basic element. So further in this paper, we propose an approach to specify timing requirements in terms of interactions using CCSL and deriving scheduling specification from these requirements, with the following major contributions: (1) an extension to PF language is proposed to express timing requirements and define timing specification derivation. The extension includes basic CPS timing requirement concepts in syntax, timing behavioural model constraints in operational semantics, and formal compositional semantics; (2) a model-driven specification process is defined from the functional requirements on problem diagrams, and enriched by individual behaviours of physical entities and compositional behaviours of physical entities; and (3) the scheduling constraints can be translated into an input to a model checker, NuSMV [11], for checking consistency. The proposed processes are supported by TimePF tool.

The remainder of the paper is organised as follows. Section 2 illustrates a motivating example before introducing our approach (Sect. 3) and a case study (Sect. 4). Section 5 evaluates the approach and discusses its limitation. Section 6 compares to related work and Sect. 7 concludes.

2   A Motivating Example

To illustrate the problem and motivate our approach, we use a real example from the analysis of a critical accident involving an embedded CPS.

The class A accident happened to an on-board switch at Beijing railway station around the GongZhuFen (i.e., Tomb of Princess) stop on 18 May 2013 at 15:46. It caused 4 trains to delay by at least 5 min, 1 train to return to the original stop, 1 temporally train added into the schedule and changes of 13 scheduling tables[1]. The reason is that the switch was wrongly represented, which was not found out in time. The involved subsystem is the switch control system (SC). Here we simplify for illustration by describing basic problem domains.

SC monitors the states and actions of train and crossings to decide whether or not to let the train pass and control equipments to perform corresponding reactions. While a train is near the crossing, the on-board system of the train sends a Request to SC, asking for entry. SC then checks about the state (either Occupied or Unoccupied) of current Track, in order to respond to the Train. If the state is Unoccupied, SC shall accept; otherwise it shall reject the request. If SC does accept the request, it will notify the Light to turn into Green, and the Switch to turn into Forward position. If SC does reject the request, the train must wait. Only when the train sees the Green light and the Forward switch, it can enter the crossing. And only after the train has left, it will send a message to inform the SC. Then SC will notify the Light to turn into Red and the Switch to position Reverse.

The problem diagram (a basic model in the PF) of the SC system is shown in Fig. 1. It captures the problem domains and their interactions. The problem domains include *On-board System (OS), Track (TK), Light (LT)*, and *Switch (SH)*. As interfaces, requirement references and requirement constraints are modeling phenomena shared between problem domains and *SC*, we unifyly call them interactions. There are 17 interactions, in which '!' means 'control'. Detailed informations please refer to https://github.com/B214-ECNU/A_case_study/blob/master/Switch_Control_System.pdf. Figure 2 shows the state diagrams of the four problem domains, *On-board system, Track, Switch*, and *Light*.

However, it is clear that we cannot yet analyse the accident using the basic problem diagram information. In the next section, we show how we add such

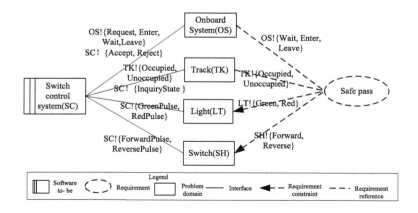

Fig. 1. Problem diagram of the SC

---

[1] www.ditiezu.com/thread-317756-1-1.html.

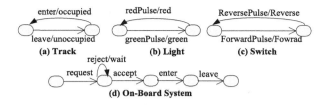

Fig. 2. State diagrams of physical entities in the SC systems

information that is sufficient to analyse the timing constraints and check for the violations which cause such accident.

3   Our Approach

Figure 3 shows our proposed framework, TimePF, for specifying and verifying timing requirements. TimePF has mainly three parts, i.e., models, specification, and the consistency verification of timing requirements.

The model part includes a conceptual model for providing basic concepts to describe timing requirements, an operational model interpreting timing constraints in operational semantics, and a compositional model composing physical entities to derive the timing specification for the whole CPS.

Driven by these models, we design a four level elicitation process to obtain the timing specification: (1) at the basic interaction level, we elicit temporal relations between interaction instances by borrowing the concepts of "clock"

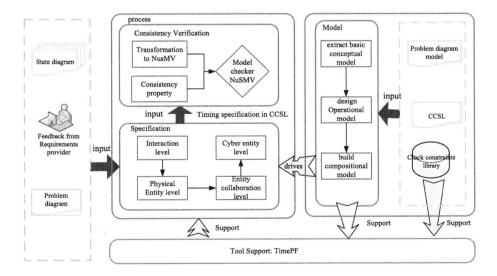

Fig. 3. An overview of our approach

from MARTE/CCSL [9]; (2) at the physical entity level, we reify the notion of "Entity Clock Specification" to gather causal and time constraints inferred from the physical properties of each physical entity; (3) at the physical entity collaboration level, we specify physical entity collaborations by composing the entity clock specifications; and (4) at the cyber entity level, we compose the specifications of all the physical entities that will share interactions with the cyber entity (i.e., problem domains) to form a specification for the timing requirement. Putting all the compositions of entity clock specifications together will results in an overall timing specification.

Finally, we use the model checker NuSMV to verify the consistency of the elicited timing requirements in the specification. To do so, we define the consistency properties and transform the timing specification into NuSMV input for checking these consistency properties.

3.1 Models

Conceptual Model. In our conceptual model, a CPS consists of the *cyber* and *physical entities*. These entities can be classified into *atomic* and *composite* ones. They interact with each other. We define *interactions* as shared phenomena between a cyber entity and some physical entities. They are observable.

Interactions can happen from time to time. According to Lamport [12], any thing in which a sequence of occurrences can be observed or produced can be defined as a logical clock. In MARTE/CCSL terminology, an event which may happen millions of time can be simply one logical clock. Therefore, in this work, we model each interaction with a *logical clock*. *This differs from* [8] *because it maps a problem domain to a* logical clock *instead of an interaction*. Each occurrence of the interaction will be an instant of the clock. When there are many interactions, we use multiple clocks.

Moreover, as an entity can be seen as the combination of many interactions from outside, each entity can also have a clock. In order to distinguish these two different kinds of clocks, we name the clock from interaction *interaction clock*, and the clock from entity the *entity clock*.

Borrowing the clock definition in CCSL [9], we also define each *clock* to be a totally ordered set of *instants*, i.e. time points. In our context, each time an interaction happens is an instant.

Definition 1. *Clock* $C \doteq < I, \prec, u >$ *where, I is a set of instants, $\prec$, named strict precedence, is a strict order relation on I: antisymmetric and transitive, and u is a symbol, standing for a unit.*

Here a clock is discrete. We let $C[k]$ denote the kth instant in I (here k is called index of I, denoted as $k = idx_C(C[k])$).

We use "clock constraints" to further constrain timing constraints between interactions. According to CCSL, the clock constraints are actually defined by *instants constraints*. The constraints usually used are *strictPre, cause, alternate, union, exclusion* and *coincides*. In this paper, we do not list the mathematical definition of these constraints. For details please refer to [9].

These clock constraints may come from one physical entity limited by its physical entity property, or come from different physical entities. In order to explicitly express constraints within a physical entity, we reify the notion of "Entity Clock Specification" to gather causal and time constraints inferred from the requirements on each physical entity (including composite entities). As the timing constraints on the interactions will fallen on constraints on clocks, the entity clock specification can be defined as a triple of entity clock, interaction clocks, and their clock constraints, in order to capture the various relationships amongst the interactions.

Definition 2. *An entity e's clock specification $e.CS$*

$$e.CS \doteq < EC, ICs, CCs >$$

where, EC is the entity clock of the entity e, ICs is a set of interaction clocks, and CCs is a set of clock constraints that EC and ICs clocks need to follow.

At the physical entity composition level, we define a composition operator $||$ for composing entity clock specifications to be a larger specification. The clock set of the big clock specification should be the union of the Clock set of each individual clock specification, and constraints should work in conjunction.

Definition 3. *Entity clock specification composition operator $||$*
Let $CS_i =< EC_i, ICs_i, CCs_i >$ for $i \in \zeta$, where $\zeta = \{1, ..., n\}$ is a finite index set, be a set of clock specifications, then their composition is

$$||\{CS_i\}_{i\in\zeta} =< EC, ICs, CCs >$$

where, $EC = C_{new}$, which is the new created entity clock, $ICs = ICs_1 \cup \cdots \cup ICs_n \cup EC_1 \cdots \cup EC_n$, and $CCs = CCs_1 \cup \cdots \cup CCs_n \cup CCs_{new}$ with CCs_{new} the constraints newly introduced.

Timing Constraints Operational Semantics. According to the possible interaction relations, we choose 7 types of clock constraints from the CCSL clock constraints library, i.e., *strictPre, union, cause, alternate, exclusion, coincidence, and boundedDiff.* Our previous work [10] has defined a state-based operational semantics interpretation called ccLTS to describe the behaviors that each clock constraint allows. The ccLTS is a special kind of labelled transition system. States in ccLTS represent the states of clock constraints, and each label in ccLTS represents the set of clocks that are due to tick in that transition.

As the ccLTS is the basis of semantics of entity clock specification composition model, we list the definition of ccLTS in the paper. For each clock constraint, we build a ccLTS. For details, please refer to [10].

Definition 4. *A ccLTS is a tuple $L =< S, Clocks, T, \hat{s} >$, where S is a set of states and $\hat{s} \in S$ is the initial state, Clocks is a finite set of clock names, whose powerset is denoted as ClockSets, $T \subseteq S \times ClockSets \times S$ defines the transition* *relation, each transition is labelled by a set of clocks that tick simultaneously in that transition. $(s, Cs, s') \in T$ is also denoted as $s \xrightarrow{Cs}_T s'$ simply or $s \xrightarrow{Cs} s'$ if clear from context.*

Entity Clock Specification Composition Semantics. Using $\|$, we present an entity clock specification composition model for specifying the behaviours. These behaviours underlie the clock specification composition operator constrained by multiple clock constraints. In fact, the composition of clock specifications requires the composed clock specification satisfy all the constraints from the two clock specifications and the ones newly introduced, through the conjunction of clock constraints. Based on the operational semantics of clock constraints, we define the semantics of "$\|$" as follows.

Definition 5. *Let $L_i = \{S_i, Clocks_i, T_i, \hat{s}_i\}$ for $i \in \zeta$, where $\zeta = \{1, ..., n\}$ is a finite index set, be a set of ccLTSs, their composition is a synchronized product,*

$$\|\{L_i\}_{i \in \zeta} = \{S, Clocks, T, \hat{s}\}$$

where, $S = S_1 \times \cdots \times S_n$; $\hat{s} = \hat{s}_1 \times \cdots \times \hat{s}_n$; $Clocks = Clocks_1 \cup \cdots \cup Clocks_n$; and $\forall i, j \in \zeta (i \neq j), s_i \xrightarrow{C_i}_{T_i} s'_i, s_j \xrightarrow{C_j}_{T_j} s'_j, \dfrac{\forall c \in Clocks_i \cap Clocks_j, c \in C_i \Leftrightarrow c \in C_j}{(s_1, ..., s_n) \xrightarrow{C_1 \cup \cdots \cup C_n} (s'_1, ..., s'_n)}$

We want to point out transitions from two ccLTSs can be composed only if there is no conflict; conflict here means violating the constraint conjunction: a common involved clock ticks in one transition while does not in the other.

According to the $\|$, the specification of a system is a composition result of all the entity clock specifications. Thus the semantics of a specification is given by the composed ccLTS from the ccLTS of its contained individual clock constrains. An execution of the specification is a run of the composed ccLTS, which is a sequence of steps; at each step, several clocks tick simultaneously with respect to all the clock constraints. So, based on the semantics of clock specification composition, the timing specification, i.e., scheduling specification, can be defined as a set of clocks and clock constraints.

3.2   Specification

This subsection presents a multi-step process for timing requirements specification. The initial inputs are problem diagrams for the functional requirements in terms of the PF and state diagrams for properties of each physical entity.

Step 1: Define Entity and Interaction Clocks. This step is to define all the interaction clocks and entity clocks from a problem diagram (constructed in our previous work [13]). From a problem diagram, we could get the following information for CPS requirements modelling: the cyber entity from the software-to be; physical entities from the problem domains; interactions from interfaces, requirement references and requirement constraints.

Suppose we get an physical entity set $EntS = \{ent_1, ent_2, \ldots, ent_n\}$ and an interaction set $IntS = \{int_1, int_2, \ldots, int_n\}$. For each physical entity $ent_i \in EntS$, define an entity clock C_{ent_i}: $C_{ent_i} = < I_{ent_i}, \prec_{ent_i}, 'u' >$, where 'u' can be ms, s or other measure unit. For each interaction $int_i \in IntS$, it defines a clock C_{int_i}: $C_{int_i} = < I_{int_i}, \prec_{int_i}, 'u' >$ (u is the same unit).

Step 2: Define a Clock Specification for Each Physical Entity. According to Definition 2, there are three sub-steps to finish a clock specification for each physical entity from the problem diagram:

(1) Getting entity and interaction clocks, i.e., for each problem domain pd in the problem diagram, we get its physical entity clock C_{pd}: $pd.CS.EC = C_{pd}$. Then we gather its involving interactions. These interactions are initiated or received by the domain pd. Then for each interaction int, we assert its corresponding clock to be an interaction clock of the entity clock specification: $pd.CS.ICs = pd.CS.ICs \cup \{C_{int}\}$.

(2) Identifying clock relations between the entity clocks and interaction clocks: The entity clock is defined for representing the problem domain. It can be constructed by its interaction clocks using constraint "union".

(3) Reasoning about clock relations among interaction clocks using physical entity property: The physical properties of physical entities will finally enforce clock constraints on the interaction clocks. The interactions are actually shared phenomena, which means some constrained private phenomena can not be observed. So, the clock relations among interaction clocks must be reasoned.

In the PF book [5], Jackson models the entity property with a state diagram. Here we propose to add the time related information based on the state diagram. From the state diagram, so as to get qualitative clock constrains of corresponding clocks transformed. Figure 4 presents a set of state diagram patterns that could be transformed to a set of clock constraints. In this figure, triggers are transformed to clocks, and transitions are transformed into clock constraints.

It is worth noticing that from the state diagram, one could only get qualitative information. If there exists quantitative information, we could add them by asking the time duration taken by each transition. For example, if we get transition 'tr' ($a \rightarrow b$) takes 2 s, we could use $a\ boundedDiff\_0\_20\ b$.

After getting these qualitative and quantitative constraints, we provide two reasoning rules to obtain relations among interaction clocks:

– Qualitative reasoning: $a\ X\ b, b\ X\ c \rightarrow a\ X\ c$, where X could be $strictPre$, $cause$, and $coincidence$.
– Quantitative reasoning: $a\ boundedDiff\_i\_j\ b, b\ boundedDiff\_m\_n\ c \rightarrow a$ boundedDiff $\_(i+m)\_(j+n)\ c$

After these sub-steps, we finish the construction of an entity clock specification. For each problem domain in the problem diagram, an entity clock specification can be obtained.

Fragment of state diagram	clocks	Clock constraints
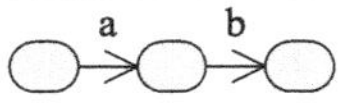 a → b (states)	a,b	a strictPre b
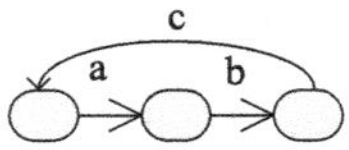 c / a → b (states)	a,b,c	a strictPre b a alternate c b strictPre c
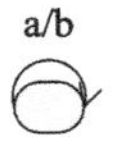 a/b (self loop)	a,b	a strictPre b
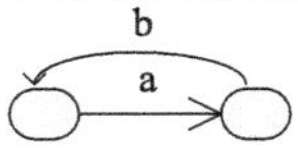 b / a (states)	a,b	a alternate b a exclude b

Fig. 4. Patterns for state diagram transformation

Step 3: Construct Clock Specification Compositions for Collaboration of Physical Entities. This step is to compose the entity clock specifications until only one clock specification exists. We could construct them one by one. They could be finished by repeating the following steps:

(1) Finding interaction clocks for the composed clock specification: suppose problem domain pd is composed by pd_1 and pd_2. Its interaction clocks of $pd.CS$ would be the union of pd_1's interaction clocks and pd_2's interaction clocks. $pd.CS.ICs = pd_1.CS.ICs \cup pd_2.CS.ICs$.

(2) Defining entity clock for the composed entity: define its entity clock C_{pd}, $pd.CS.OCk$ could be C_{pd}, i.e., $pd.CS.EC = C_{pd}$

(3) Finding entity clock and interaction clock relation: Actually, pd's entity clock is the union of C_{pd_1} and C_{pd_2}, i.e., $C_{pd} = C_{pd_1} \, union C_{pd_2}$. The relation between C_{pd_1} and its interaction clocks $pd_1.CS.ICs$ is already given in $pd_1.CS.CCs$, and the relation between C_{pd_2} and its interaction clocks $pd_2.CS.ICs$ is already given in $pd_2.CS.CCs$.

(4) Identifying clock relations among interaction clocks: When interactions from different entities meet, there may exist timing constraints. As the clock relations are actually deduced from instant relations, we could identify them by identifying instant relations. Assume there are two interactions, int_1 and int_2, and their corresponding clocks are C_{int1} and C_{int2}. We provide a questionnaire in Fig. 5 to guide the requirement providers. A 'Yes' answer to these questions will lead to the following constraints: Stakeholders need to provide additional input where one needs to specify clock relations between interactions. According to the semantics of entity clock specification and clock constraints, we designed a fairly simple questionnaire for the providers to choose. Figure 5 lists 6 questions for clock relation identification. Each answer (or choice) indicates a clock constraint in CCSL.

Questions for identifying clock relations between interaction int_1 and int_2. You can choose the following question to answer.

(1). Interaction int_1 and int_2 always happen together.

  Yes ○   No ○

(2). Each time int_1 happens strictly earlier than int_2.

  Yes ○   No ○

(3). Each time int_1 happens earlier than int_2.

  Yes ○   No ○

(4). Interactions int_1 and int_2 happens this way: int_1 happens, then int_2, then int_1 and so on.

  Yes ○   No ○

(5) Interactions int_1 and int_2 Can never happen Together.

  Yes ○   No ○

(6). Each time int_1 happens, within an interval [i,j],int_2 will happen.

  Yes ○   No ○

  If yes, please input i= , j= , i and j are measured by the same time unit.

Fig. 5. Questionnaire for providers

- 'Yes' to question (1), then we have: C_{int1} *coincidence* C_{int2}
- 'Yes' to question (2), then we have: C_{int1} *stricPre* C_{int2}
- 'Yes' to question (3), then we have: C_{int1} *cause* C_{int2}
- 'Yes' to question (4), then this could be: C_{int1} *alternate* C_{int2}
- 'Yes' to question (5), the description would be: C_{int1} *exclusion* C_{int2}
- 'Yes' to question (6), the description would be: C_1 *boundedDiff_i_j* C_2

After the above steps, we could get a composed entity clock specification. Then we replace pd_1 and pd_2 with pd in the problem diagram. Repeat these steps until the biggest clock specification $PD.CS$ is obtained.

Step 4: Derive Timing Specification for the Cyber Entity. We define the timing specification to be a set of clocks and related clock constraints. Then the timing specification derivation will be finished in two steps: (1) defining an entity clock specification for the cyber entity, and (2) extracting clocks and clock constraints from the entity clock specification to form the timing specification.

To define an entity clock specification $cyb.CS$, firstly define a clock for the cyber entity C_{cyb}. The clock C_{cyb} equals to the biggest composed problem domain clock C_{PD}. The interaction clocks are actually the interaction clocks in $PD.CS.ICs$. Then the clock specification $cyb.CS$ can be obtained by:

$$cyb.CS = < C_{cyb}, PD.CS.ICs, PD.CS.CCs \cup \{C_{cyb} = C_{PD}\} >$$

3.3   Consistency Checking

Once obtained, the timing specification must be checked before being used. For this purpose, we choose a model checker NuSMV [11] because it allows checking finite state systems against properties in CTL or LTL.

The process for consistency checking is usually three steps. Firstly, the timing specification in terms of clocks and clock constraints are transformed to NuSMV models by support of the clock constraints. Then consistency is expressed in CTL formula and finally checked against the transformed NuSMV model.

As our previous work [10] has done the transformation work from CCSL specification to NuSMV, in this paper, we only need to define the consistency property in CTL. The consistency checking determines whether the specifications are consistent. The most typical inconsistent scenario is "deadlock", in which the specification cannot fire all (or some) clocks anymore (since all clocks are assumed to be able to tick infinitely often in a reactive system). Usually, a deadlock is caused by inconsistency of used clock constraints, e.g., one constraint says that clock C_1 ticks after C_2 ticks while another constraint impose that C_2 ticks after C_1, the result is that none can tick. We want to point out that deadlocks could only be caused by inconsistency because redundancies in constraints are impossible by our construction. For a timing specification s, whose clock set is $\{C_1, C_2, \ldots, C_n\}$, we define it *consistent* if it is not a global deadlock and every clock C_i $(1 \preceq i \preceq n)$ will tick infinitely in future.

Definition 6. *If a specification s with clocks $\{C_1, C_2, \ldots, C_n\}$, satisfies AGp and AG AF C_i $(1 \preceq i \preceq n)$, where $p = !(C1|C2|...|Cn)$ (! and $|$ are CTL operators), then s is consistent.*

By putting the consistency property in the .smv file, we can run NuSMV to check whether the specification is consistent. A counter example showing a path that cannot go on can help locate the problem in the specification. Such diagnosis procedure is however out of the scope of this paper.

4   A Case Study

To support the techniques proposed in this paper, we have developed a prototype tool *timePF* using Java [14]. Our aim was to develop a tool to allow users to manipulate diagrammatic elements and transform them in a stepwise manner according to the process defined previously in this paper. Hence, we decided to develop a customised supporting tool, instead of using a generic graph editor such as Microsoft Visio.

We developed TimePF by extending a tool DPTool [15] which is an editor of the PF problem diagram. TimePF allows the user to graphically edit the interaction relations, the qualitative relations and quantitative relations. Moreover, the tool allows the user to follow the specification process, and aids the user with some automated timing requirements processing. Finally, it performs automated consistency checking for the resulting timing specification. In the following, we will still use the motivating example to show the feasibility of our approach. Due to limited space, the details are given in https://github.com/B214-ECNU/A_case_study/blob/master/Switch_Control_System.pdf.

Step 1: Define entity and interaction clocks. For each problem domain in the problem diagram (see Fig. 1), we define an entity clock for it. For example, for the domain *Light*, we define a clock C_{LT}: $C_{LT} =< I_{LT}, \prec_{LT}, \text{'}ms\text{'} >$.

For each interaction in the problem diagram, we construct an interaction clock for it. For example, interaction *Green*. Its corresponding clock is defined as C_{Gn}: $C_{Gn} =< I_{Gn}, \prec_{Gn}, \text{'}ms\text{'} >$, where $I_{Gn} = \{C_{Gn}[1], C_{Gn}[2], \dots, C_{Gn}[n]\}$. In order to simply the clock name, we pick the first and last characters of the one word interaction and first two characters for two word interactions to represent the whole interaction.

Step 2: Define entity clock specifications for physical entities. For each problem domain in the problem diagram, we define a clock specification for it. Take domain "Light" as an example.

(1) Find entity and interaction clocks. For domain "Light", its entity clock is C_{LT}. Then $LT.CS. EC=C_{LT}$. The domain LT has four interactions: int_{10} (GreenPulse, GP), int_{11} (RedPulse, RP), int_{12} (Green, Gn) and int_{13} (Red, Rd). Their corresponding clocks are: C_{GP}, C_{Rd}, C_{Gn} and C_{RP}. Then we have: $LT.CS.ICs = \{C_{GP}, C_{RP}, C_{Gn}, C_{Rd}\}$.

(2) Identify clock relations between the entity clocks and interaction clocks. The entity clock C_{Light} is constructed by union of its interaction clocks. That means: $C_{LT} = C_{GP}$ *union* C_{RP} *union* C_{Gn} *union* C_{Rd}

(3) Reason about the clock relations among interaction clocks using physical entity property. From the state diagram of Light in Fig. 2 and state diagram transformation patterns in Fig. 4, we know that int_{GP} and int_{Green} has *alternate* relation. As to the quantitative constraints, suppose the response time of turning red or green is less than 3 ms.

Step 3: Construct clock specification composition for problem domain collaboration. We combine On-board Systems (OS) and Track (TK) because after the OS requests, the SC asks the state of the track. If the state is occupied, then SC rejects the request, and if the state is unoccupied, then SC accepts the request. In this way, we get constraints $ct25, ct26$, and $ct27$.

Suppose the combine entity is called ComOSTK (CK), then the clock specification for the CK could be: $CK.CS = OS.CS\|TK.CS$. We define a clock called C_{CK} for the entity clock: $C_{CK} =< I_{CK}, \prec_{CK}, \text{'}ms\text{'} >$ where C_{CK} is actually the union of all the interaction clocks of OS and TK. Thus we get ct28. In the construction of CK.CS, the newly introduced constraints include ct25-ct28.

Similarly, as to the combination of ComOSRK and Light and Switch, they collaborate together as a domain *SCPD* to fulfil their requirements. So the composed clock specification would be: $SCPD.CS = CK.CS\|LT.CS\|SH.CS$. The newly introduced constraints are ct29-ct38.

Step 4: Derive timing specification for the cyber entity. The clock for the cyber entity C_{cyb} is the composed problem domain clock C_{SCPD}. So we have $C_{cyb} = C_{SCPD}$ (ct39). The interaction clocks are actually the interaction clocks in $SCPD.CS$. Then the *cyb.CS* eaquals to $SCPD.CS$.

Finally, all the 39 clock constraints in *cyb.CS* are extracted to form a timing specification. We also noted that the constraint "ct36" (C_{Le} *boundedDiff_0_5* C_{Re}) was not given from the accident description: the device was not reset in time after the train is left.

Step 5: Perform automated consistency verification. Our tool TimePF checks the specification against the consistency properties. It can detect a counter example on the specification without constraint "ct36". Figure 6 shows the main checking interfaces of TimePF. The left part is the menu for users to choose. The right part is the result of consistency checking for the switch control system. The verification only takes 1 s.

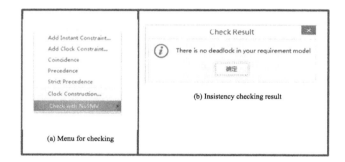

Fig. 6. A checking snapshot of the switch control system in TimePF

5   Empirical Evaluation

In order to evaluate our technique, we have conducted two kinds of evaluations. One is a laboratory-based evaluation supported by our prototype tool TimePF for computer-aided timing requirements elicitation and verification. The other one is conducted by a railway signaling company person.

In the laboratory-based evaluation, we enrolled 6 first-year postgraduate software engineering students studying at Shanghai in China. All were MSc students majoring in Software Engineering. Since PF and CCSL are relatively new in the software engineering curriculum, the students' knowledge about PF, CCSL and the tool was minimum before the first author's lectures.

In the industry evaluation, we asked a testing manager from one of the biggest railway companies in China. Since we have a long time collaboration with the company, the manager knows what we are doing exactly. He told us the timing constraints for the railway systems are given in the document written in natural language. These timing constraints are from the experts' mind. Each time a big accident happens, many constraints will be forced into the documents.

Before the experiments, all the participants including the students and manager were given several lectures on the basics of the PF approach as well as tutorials on timing requirements expression (CCSL). Because we wanted to see whether the approach is easy to be understood by the industry, a case from the railway control system is chosen. In order to be easily understood, it consists of only main functions of two subsystems, vehicle on-board controller (VOBC) and interlocking systems. As the problem description is internal and secret, we only provide functional steps in the problem description document.

At last, we extract problem diagrams for the systems, and build the state diagrams for the invloved physical entities. Unfortunately, it is not easy for us to understand the domain of railway systems. So it took us 2 weeks to get them even with the help of experts from the company.

To assess the feasibility of the approach through user studies, we designed the following two experiments. The first experiment investigates how easy it is to identify time constraints from the perspective of academy? We divide the 6 students into 2 groups. One group is provided with a fully described problem diagram and state diagrams of the problem domains in the problem diagram, while the other group is provided only with the problem description document. Both groups are asked to identify the timing constraints. The second experiment investigates how easy it is for participants to obtain timing specification following the guided process from the perspective of industry. We give the manager the same problem diagram and state diagrams.

In the first experiment, these 2 groups behaved differently. In 7 days, (each day 10 hours' work), the best person who use our approach gets 511 time constraints for the interlocking system, and 338 time constraints for the VOBC system, and the least gets 653 constraints for the two sub-systems. Among the 3 persons who do not use our approach, the best only obtains 552 constraints for the two subsystems. In this way, we can conclude that our approach is more easy to elicit more time constraints.

In the second experiment, it only took the manager 3 days (each day 8 hours' work) to get 1121 time constraints consisting of 623 for the interlocking systems and 498 for the VOBC system. Obviously, his domain knowledge helps him a lot. When we was asked about the GongZhu Fen switch accidents, the manager easily found we could add time constraints on the inquiry of switch state. He said through the approach, especially the PF to represent the functional requirements, it was more easier to master the relations of interactions.

Of course, the problem diagrams and state diagrams help the students to understand the domain. So it makes sense that the first group students get more constraints in the same time duration. But it still told us that our approach would work well with non-experienced ones. As to the experts experiment, the result may not be repeated because the manager knows formal methods well.

Another limitation of our consistency checking is that large systems with too many timing constraints may never gets verification results due to the state explosion problem in the formal methods.

6   Related Work

Related work representing timing requirements are broadly classified into UML-based and RE-based approaches. UML 1.0 Profile for Schedulability, Performance, and Time specification (SPT) [16] standardises time modelling extension. It is followed by UML 2.0 Profile for Modelling and Analysis of Real-Time and Embedded Systems (MARTE) [17], which defines on its companion language clock constraints specification language (CCSL). Although MARTE targets at real-time embedded systems, it does not provide specific means for RE. UML For Systems Engineers (SysML) [18] incorporates requirements diagram, however, it does not provide specific support for time. Selic et al. [19] have argued that complex time-sensitive systems like CPS could benefit from a joint use of SysML and MARTE, thereby addressing both requirement engineering and real-time systems issues. One attempt [20] also makes a specific argumentation for combining MARTE, CCSL and SysML. Our work also uses the same time model as with MARTE/CCSL, whilst further interpreting state-based operational semantics for their use on the early phase of RE through transformations, which enables the verification of consistency of timing requirements.

Knowledge Acquisition in Automated Specification (KAOS) [21] approaches view goals as the source of timing requirements, which are associated with temporal behaviours of the system-to-be in terms of typed first-order real-time logic. Agent-oriented RE approaches [22] use actors to identify requirements, which can be formalised through Formal Tropos, a language supplements i* [23] with a rich temporal specification language inspired by KAOS. Formal Tropos also uses a linear-time typed first-order temporal logic. Agent-Oriented Language for Building and Eliciting Real-Time Requirements (ALBERT-II) [24] is another agent-oriented framework for specifying distributed real-time systems based on temporal logic. Compared to existing RE-based time modelling approaches, TimePF has adopts PF as the descriptions of functional requirements, thus inherits the advantages of existing PF-based modelling such as [5, 7, 25–27]. As a consequence, our timing requirements are integrated tightly with the functional requirements, and are more expressive than temporal logics [28]. Although our previous work [8] also extends the PF with CCSL, it maps problem domains to clocks while this paper maps interactions to clocks. Moreover, this paper focuses on the specification process.

Another related work is CCSL based verfication and analysis. Many researchers work on this like [29–32]. Actually, Their contributions even make our work more important. Because our specification language is CCSL, their work can be used by our work although we use previous work [10] as further work, and even can help us to solve the state explosion problem in the verfication. Compared with them, this paper focuses on how to get the CCSL specification in the early requirement engineering phases instead of analysing it.

7   Conclusions and Future Work

In this paper, we propose an approach to derive timing specification from requirements, which contributes the following: (1) basic concepts for describing timing requirements and semantics of behaviour composition as a model integrated seamlessly with functional requirements on the problem diagrams; (2) a model-driven tool supported process for deriving timing requirements from the levels of interaction, physical entity, and their composition; and (3) automatic consistency checker for deadlocks by transforming them into NuSMV inputs. With the formal specification of timing requirements obtained, it is our next step to fully integrate it with the follow-on activities of CPS development.

Acknowledgments. This work was supported by the Natural Science Foundation of China under grant 61620106007 and 61472140, Microsoft Azure Award, British Council Researcher Links on Cybersecurity ERC Adaptive Security And Privacy 291652.

References

1. Lee, E.: Cyber physical systems: design challenges. In: International Symposium on Object/Component/Service-Oriented Real-Time Distributed Computing (ISORC2008), pp. 363–369 (2008)
2. Ying, T., Goddard, S., Perez, L.C.: A prototype architecture for cyber-physical systems. ACM SIGBED Rev. (2008)
3. Jackson, M.: The meaning of requirements. Ann. Softw. Eng. **3**, 5–21 (1997)
4. Lamsweerde, A.: Goal-oriented requirements engineering: a guided tour. In: Fm, T. (ed.) Proceedings of the 5th IEEE International Symposium on Requirements Engineering (RE 2001), pp. 249–263. IEEE Computer Society, Toronto (2001)
5. Jackson, M., Frames, P.: Analyzing and Structuring Software Development Problems. Addison-Wesley, New York (2001)
6. Choppy, C., Reggio, G.: A UML-based method for the commanded behaviour frame. In: Cox, K., Hall, J., Rapanotti, L. (eds.) Proceedings of the 1st International Workshop on Advances and Applications of Problem Frames (IWAAPF 2004), pp. 27–34 (2004)
7. Barroca, L., Fiadeiro, J., Jackson, M., Laney, R., Nuseibeh, B.: Problem frames: a case for coordination. In: Rocco, D.N., Gianluigi, F., Greg, M. (eds.) Proceedings of the 6th International Conference on Coordination Models and Languages, pp. 5–19 (2004)
8. Chen, X., Liu, J., Mallet, F., Jin, Z.: Modeling timing requirements in problem frames using CCSL. In: the 18th Asia-Pacific Software Engineering Conference (APSEC 2011), pp. 381–388 (2011)
9. Andre, C.: Syntax and semantics of the clock constraint speci?cation language (CCSL). INRIA, Research report (2009)
10. Yin, L., Liu, J., Ding, Z., Mallet, F., de Simone, R.: Schedulability analysis with CCSL specifications. In: APSEC, pp. 414–421 (2013)
11. Nusmv 2.5 tutorial (2014). http://nusmv.fbk.eu/NuSMV/tutorial/v25/tutorial.pdf
12. Lamport, L.: Time, clocks, and the ordering of events in a distributed system. Commun. ACM **7**, 558–565 (1978)
13. Chen, X., Jin, Z.: Capturing software requirements from the expected interactions between the software and its environment: an ontology based approach. Int. J. Software Eng. Knowl. Eng. **26**(1), 15–39 (2016)

14. Wang, Y., Chen, X., Yin, L.: TimePF: a tool for modeling and verifying timing requirements based on problem frames. Requirements Engineering in the Big Data Era. CCIS, vol. 558, pp. 149–154. Springer, Heidelberg (2015). doi:10.1007/978-3-662-48634-4_11

15. Chen, X., Yin, B., Jin, Z.: DPtool: a tool for guiding the problem description and the problem projection. In: The 18th IEEE International Requirements Engineering Conference, pp. 401–402 (2010)

16. OMG, UML Profile for Schedulability, Performance, and Time Specification, v1.1, Object Management Group, formal/05-01-02, January 2005

17. OMG, UML Profile for MARTE, v1.1, June 2011

18. Weilkiens, T.: Systems Engineering with SysML/UML: Modeling, Analysis, Design. The MK/OMG Press, Burlington (2008)

19. Selic, B., Gerard, S.: Modeling and Analysis of Real-Time and Embedded Systems with UML and MARTE. Elsevier, Amsterdam (2013)

20. Mallet, F.: MARTE/CCSL for modeling cyber-physical systems. In: Drechsler, R., Kühne, U. (eds.) Formal Modeling and Verification of Cyber-Physical Systems, pp. 26–49. Springer, Wiesbaden (2015). doi:10.1007/978-3-658-09994-7_2

21. Lamsweerde, A.: Formal refinement patterns for goal-driven requirements elaboration. In: Proceedings of the 4th ACM Symposium on the Foundations of Software Engineering (FSE4), San Francisco, USA, pp. 179–190 (1996)

22. Yu, E.: Agent orientation as a modeling paradigm. Wirtschaftsinformatik **43**(2), 123–132 (2001)

23. Yu, E.: Modelling organizations for information systems requirements engineering. In: Proceedings of First IEEE Symposium on Requirements Engineering, pp. 34–41 (1993)

24. Bois, P.: The albert ii language - on the design and the use of a formal specification language for requirements analysis. Ph.D. dissertation, Department of Computer Science, University of Namur, Namur, Belgium (1995)

25. Jackson, M., Zave, P.: Deriving specifications from requirements: an example. In: ICSE 1995, pp. 15–24 (1995)

26. Lavazza, L., Del Bianco, V.: Combining problem frames and UML in the description of software requirements. In: Baresi, L., Heckel, R. (eds.) FASE 2006. LNCS, vol. 3922, pp. 199–213. Springer, Heidelberg (2006). doi:10.1007/11693017_16

27. Li, Z., Hall, J.G., Rapanotti, L.: On the systematic transformation of requirements to specifications. Requirements Eng. J. **19**(4), 397–419 (2014)

28. Gascon, R., Mallet, F., DeAntoni, J.: Logical time and temporal logics: comparing UML MARTE/CCSL and PSL. In: TIME 2011, pp. 141–148 (2011)

29. Zhang, M., Mallet, F., Zhu, H.: An SMT-based approach to the formal analysis of MARTE/CCSL. In: Ogata, K., Lawford, M., Liu, S. (eds.) ICFEM 2016. LNCS, vol. 10009, pp. 433–449. Springer, Cham (2016). doi:10.1007/978-3-319-47846-3_27

30. Suryadevara, J., Seceleanu, C., Mallet, F., Pettersson, P.: Verifying MARTE/CCSL mode behaviors using UPPAAL. In: Hierons, R.M., Merayo, M.G., Bravetti, M. (eds.) SEFM 2013. LNCS, vol. 8137, pp. 1–15. Springer, Heidelberg (2013). doi:10.1007/978-3-642-40561-7_1

31. Khan, A.M., Rashid, M.: Generation of SystemVerilog observers from SysML and MARTE/CCSL. In: ISORC 2016, pp. 61–68 (2016)

32. Peters, J., Przigoda, N., Wille, R., Drechsler, R.: Clocks vs. instants relations: Verifying CCSL time constraints in uml/marte models. In: MEMOCODE 2016, pp. 78–84 (2016)

A Framework for Multi-view Reconciliation and for Medical Devices Personalization

Yihai Chen[1,2], Bofang Zhang[1,2], Ridha Khedri[1,3(✉)], and Huaikou Miao[1,2]

[1] School of Computer Engineering and Science,
Shanghai University, Shanghai, China
[2] Shanghai Key Laboratory of Computer Software Evaluating and Testing,
Shanghai, China
[3] Department of Computing and Software, McMaster University,
Hamilton, ON, Canada
khedri@mcmaster.ca

Abstract. Software product family approaches have found broad adoption in the embedded systems industry, where systems are modelled from several views such as the software view and the hardware view. A view uses the feature perceived only from the view's perspective. For example, from a hardware view we perceive only the hardware features. Generating the feasible products of the considered family from these views and the constraints imposed on them is called view reconciliation.

The paper presents a mathematical framework to reason on view reconciliation. It articulates this process as a product of sets of product families. We give the conditions under which the product forms a direct product. We also demonstrate that (multi-) view reconciliation is an operation that is indifferent to the order of integrating the views. Finally, we show that personalizing medical devices is a simple view reconciliation operation that gives a direct-product allowing, using projections, the retrieval of any of the involved views from the conciliated view.

Keywords: Medical devices · Software requirement · Multi-view reconciliation · Product family algebra · Personalized software development

1 Introduction

Over the last few decades, software has significantly revolutionised medical device industry. Many medical device functionalities and innovations are realized by software. Modern medical devices such as pacemakers, insulin pumps, and artificial pancreas are essentially sophisticated software-intensive embedded systems. As early as 2006, over half of the medical devices on the U.S.

This research is supported by the Natural Sciences and Engineering Research Council of Canada (NSERC) through the grant RGPIN 2014-06115, by the National Natural Science Foundation of China through the grants No. 61602293 and No. 61572306, and by the Science and Technology Commission of Shanghai Municipality through the grant No. 15YF1403900.

Z. Duan and L. Ong (Eds.): ICFEM 2017, LNCS 10610, pp. 71–87, 2017.
https://doi.org/10.1007/978-3-319-68690-5_5

market involved software [1]. The European Medical Device Directive MDD 93/42/EEC [2], one of the foundational council directives in medical devices, includes software as one type of medical devices. Also, the International Electrotechnical Commission (IEC) and the U.S. Food and Drug Administration (FDA) have included software as a category of medical devices. Software considered as a medical device is called Medical Device Software (MDS).

The development of medical devices is challenging [3] for several reasons. The first challenge is the size of the software embedded in them. For an idea about the software content in some critical medical devices, we find in [4] that state-of-the-art pacemakers may have up to 80,000 lines of code in them. Also, we find in [4] that infusion pumps may have over 170,000 lines of code. In addition to software size, the variability within a set of related medical devices is high. This is due to the fact that for a specific medical need, such controlling blood sugar level, patients have needs for several functional features due to age, pathological condition, cost of the device, etc. One might think of building a device with all the possible features parametrized; if one needs a special feature, we configure the device to activate the needed feature while all the not needed features remain deactivated. For safety reasons, this solution is not recommended. It involves the risk that one of these deactivated features gets triggered by a sequence of events and leads to unsafe or fatal behaviour of the device. Each medical devise has to be minimal in the software it contains; it contains exactly what is needed by the patient and noting more and nothing less. This leads us to the development of a family of medical devices that have a set of common features and each device has specific set of features that distinguishes it from all the rest of the devices. This diversity of patients and the diversity in the features that devices might include lead to a high number of product variants. At the same time, medical device companies are facing the pressure to deliver new devices to market on time, comply with strict regulatory guidelines, and make sure the devices are safe and secure.

This challenge usually leads to building families of products instead of single products. A product family approach is shown to be the most appropriate solution for this challenge [5]. A family of software-intensive systems sharing a common, managed set of features that satisfy the specific needs of a particular market segment or mission and that are developed from a common set of core assets in a prescribed way or place is commonly referred to as a product line [6]. A software product line is a set of software-intensive systems sharing a common, managed set of features that satisfy the specific needs of a particular market segment or mission and that are developed from a common set of core assets in a prescribed way in place [6]. When a software organization adopts software product family, it can bring the benefits of reducing development time and increasing productivity. There are many successful applications of software product family approach. In particular, they have found broad adoption in the embedded systems industry [5], where a platform that implements the common features to all devices is built then extended with features that are specific to products built on it. Also, the adoption of product families approaches is well documented in areas such as aerospace, automotive, or medical device [7,8].

Modelling MDS or any complex system requires modelling several views of the system. Then these views are integrated to form the general model of the system. This approach allows us to focus our attention on one view at the time. A view is a representation of a whole system or part of a system from the perspective of concer [9]. It is difficult to work out a model for a medical device in one shot. Modelling a family of MDS products as a single view leads to models that are hard to elaborate and involve a lot of features which makes them unreadable. Multi-view approach is commonly adopted in practice. For MDS, we advocate for the adoption of a multi-view approach for the feature modelling of familes of MDS. Using Product Family Algebra (PFA) [10], which is an idempotent semiring, we capture the specification of the MDS from each view. These views are usually related. We use constraints to capture these relationships among views. Then, should we need to have the model for the whole family, the global view that integrates all the views, is generated through algebraic calculations. This approach allows us to manage the models as it is easy to make changes to a system model from one view, then generate the new global view that encompasses the new changes and the other views. We use this approach to include patient's characteristics in one view. The aim is to derive through calculation the model of a personalized medical device that fits the needs of the patient. Suppose that the considered medical device has two views: hardware view and software view. The hardware view gives the hardware components (features) of the device, while the software view captures its software features. These two views are related with constraints such as a hardware component needs a specific software feature (e.g., module). The integration of these two views generates a family of possible products that only some of them can fit the patient. If we integrate these views with that of the patient, we get the products that fit the patient. The paper discusses this approach and its theoretical background.

As stated above, we adopt a view-based approach to model a family of medical devices. For instance, we give the family feature model from a hardware, software, and patient perspectives. Other views can be added. For instance, some medical devices can be affected by the environment of the patient. Therefore, in a such situation, a view capturing the possible environments in which the family of devices can operate are added to the set of essential view: software, hardware, and patient. Each one of them constitutes a view on the family of medical devices. The hardware view gives the hardware features either mandatory or optional that are encompassed in the family of medical devices. The software view gives the software features that can be identified in the family. The patient view describe the family of patients based on their attributes such as age or pathological characteristics (each constitutes a feature) that are relevant to the selection of an appropriate medical device for a patient. In general, a feature is a conceptual characteristic that is visible to stakeholders (e.g., users, doctors, customers, developers, managers, etc.). We use PFA to give the feature model of each view as a family of products constituted of homogenous (i.e., coming from features same view) features. The language of PFA is more expressive in articulating feature models in a concise way. Graphical representation of feature models can be straight forwardly generated from PFA feature models. In addition, calculations can be done on them as they are sets of algebraic terms. For more information on advantages of PFA related to these aspects, we refer the reader to [10–13].

Section 2 gives the basic concepts of product family algebra. In Sect. 3, we present the mathematical setting for the process of multi-view reconciliation and we derive several results linking it to the direct-product construction. Section 4 uses the mathematical language of the framework to present medical device personalization as a constrained product construction. We use a pacemaker family example to illustrate the usage of the framework for personalizing medical devices. In Sect. 5, we discuss the related work. Our concluding remarks and the direction of our future work are given in Sect. 6.

2 Mathematical Background: Product Family Algebra

Product Family Algebra is a simple algebraic structure. It is an idempotent semiring. A semiring is a quintuple $(S, +, 0, \cdot, 1)$ such as $(S, +, 0)$ is a commutative monoid and $(S, \cdot, 1)$ is a monoid such that $\cdot$ distribute over $+$ and 0 is an annihilator, (i.e., $0 \cdot a = 0 = a \cdot 0$). The semiring is commutative if $\cdot$ is commutative and it is idempotent if $+$ is idempotent (i.e., $a + a = a$). The relation $a \leq b \iff_{df} a + b = b$ is a partial order (i.e., a reflexive, antisymmetric and transitive relation), called the natural order on S. It has 0 as its least element. Moreover, $+$ and $\cdot$ are isotone with respect to $\leq$.

In the context of feature modelling, addition $+$ can be interpreted as a choice between two optional features. The multiplication operation $\cdot$ is interpreted as feature composition or their mandatory presence. The element 0 represents the empty family of products while 1 represents a product with no features; a pseudo family that is neutral to mandatory composition. More details about (idempotent) semirings and examples of their relevance to computer science and system's modelling can be found in [10,14,15]. A product family algebra is an idempotent and commutative semiring. Its elements are called product families. We find in [10], that a product is a family that is indivisible with regard to $+$ (i.e., does not contain optional features). A feature is therefore a product that is atomic (i.e., that is not dividable with regard to $\cdot$ operator). We refer the reader to [10] for the formal definition of a product. The above intuitive definition given above is enough for the paper. In particular, 0 is a product. A product a is proper if $a \neq 0$. When we want to express that a feature is optional, we simply write it as an alternative choice between 1 and the feature f. For example, let us consider a family F that has a feature a as mandatory and a feature f as optional. Then we write $F = a \cdot (1 + f)$, which can be rewritten as $= a + a \cdot f$ In this case, F is a family that contains two products: a and $a \cdot f$. If we look at product family algebras like the set-based or the bag-based ones discussed in [10], we can expresss determining the commonality of two families as finding the Greatest Common Divisor (GCD), or to factor out the features common to all given products. The classical Euclidean algorithm for finding the GCD is used to find commonalities. We can also define a divisibility relation among families that is given by $(a \mid b) \iff (\exists c \mid \cdot \quad b = a.c)$[1].

In the requirement of embedded systems, we need to express that a feature requires the existence of another feature and that within a family. The language of PFA has a *requirement* relation that is used to express this kind of requirements. We call this relation a *requirement* relation and it is defined using two other relations: *subfamily* $\leq$ and *refinement* $\sqsubseteq$. We say that a is a subfamily of b if and only if all of the products of a are also products of b. Formally, the subfamily relation ($\leq$) is defined as $a \leq b \stackrel{\text{def}}{\iff} a + b = b$ (note: the $\leq$ relation is the natural order of the semiring). The refinement relation indicates that, for two given product families a and b, a is a refinement of b if and only if every product in family a has at least all the features of some products in family b. In mathematical terms, $a \sqsubseteq b \stackrel{\text{def}}{\iff} (\exists c \mid \cdot \quad a \leq b \cdot c)$. For elements a, b, c, d and a product p in PFA, the requirement relation ($\rightarrow$) is defined in a family-induction style [10] as:

$$a \stackrel{p}{\rightarrow} b \stackrel{\text{def}}{\iff} p \sqsubseteq a \implies p \sqsubseteq b$$
$$a \stackrel{c+d}{\rightarrow} b \stackrel{\text{def}}{\iff} a \stackrel{c}{\rightarrow} b \wedge a \stackrel{d}{\rightarrow} b$$

For elements a, b and c, $a \stackrel{c}{\rightarrow} b$ reads as "a requires b within c". If we want to indicate that the combination of families/products/features a and b generates an empty family in the bigger family c, we write $a \cdot b \stackrel{c}{\rightarrow} 0$. It is to say that the combination of a and b is impossible. Features from several view can require each other. For instance, a pump in an insulin pump hardware view would require a controller in the software view. For these kind of relationships, we use the requirement relation ($\rightarrow$). We say that a family f satisfies a constraint $(a \stackrel{q}{\rightarrow} b)$, and we write $((a \stackrel{q}{\rightarrow} b) \vdash f)$, iff $(\forall p \mid p \leq f \wedge q \sqsubseteq p \cdot a \stackrel{p}{\rightarrow} b)$.

3   Multi-view Reconciliation Mathematical Framework

In this section, we present the mathematical foundation for the notion of family-view reconciliation. We also present some results related to the properties of view reconciliation.

Definition 1. *Let* $(S, +, \cdot, 0, 1)$ *be a product family algebra. Let* U, V, W *be subsets of* S. *Then* W *is said to be the product of* U *and* V, *written* $W = U \odot V$, *if* $(\forall w \mid w \in W \cdot (\exists u, v \mid u \in U \wedge v \in V \cdot w = u \cdot v))$. *We also say that* U *and* V *are family-views of* W. *If every element* w *of* W *has a unique expression*

---

[1] Throughout this paper, we adopt the uniform linear notation provided. The general form of the notation is $(\star x \mid R \cdot P)$ where $\star$ is the quantifier, x is the dummy or quantified variable, R is predicate representing the range, and P is an expression representing the body of the quantification. An empty range is taken to mean **true** and we write $(\star x \mid \cdot P)$; in this case the range is over all values of variable x.

$w = u \cdot v$, then W is the direct product of U and V. The family-views U and V are said to be independent or orthogonal if $U \cap V = \{1\}$.

Obviously, S and $\{1\}$ are two family-views of S as every element of S can be written as the product of itself and 1. The family-view given by $\{1\}$ is a neutral view that does not bring any new features. A family-view that is formed by $\{1\}$ is orthogonal to any other family-views. Another observation from the above definition is that a view is defined with regard to another; it means that a set of families W is given by at least two views (one of them could a neutral view $\{1\}$). Therefore, a view is a partial description of a set of families (very often in practice, it is a singleton set).

  In the remaining of the paper, we take S as the support set of a product family algebra, and we consider U and V are subsets of S. We also use *view* and *family-view* interchangeably.

Lemma 1. *If $0 \in U$, then U cannot be a family-view that contributes with V to the construction of a direct product.*

Proof. Let us assume $W = U \odot V$ form a direct product. It means that every element $w \in W$ has a unique expression $w = u \cdot v$ for $u \in U$ and $v \in V$. This statement is false as $w = 0 \cdot v = 0 \cdot v' = 0$, for any other $v' \in V$. ☐

The element 0 of S is a pseudo family used to capture the notion of impossible family. Lemma 1 states that 0 cannot be a part of any family-view. We recall that the mandatory combination of two incompatible features leads to 0. Any view of a product family needs to be free from impossible families, which requires that all the involved features are compatible with each other and do not present any feature-interactions that might lead to undesirable system behaviour.

  The product of two subsets of S cannot be a direct product if one of them contains 0. Conversely, a set that contains 0 cannot be written as the direct product of two subsets of S. Hence, S cannot be the direct product of two sets due to its inclusion of 0, while $S - \{0\}$ can be the direct product of two family-views.

Definition 2. *Let U and V be family-views of W. We say that U is a* proper view, *if it does not contain 0. Also, we say that the family-views are* minimal, *if each of U and V are formed by co-prime elements.*

Containing 0 in a set of product families indicates that one of the elements (which is 0) is an impossible family. The axioms of product families indicates that the product of 0 and any product family gives 0. So, having 0 in a family-view makes it not suitable for mandatory composition. The elements of U are co-prime iff $(\forall a, b \mid a, b \in U \cdot \neg(a \mid b)) \iff (\forall a, b \mid a, b \in U \cdot \neg(\exists c \mid c \in S \cdot a = b \cdot c)) \implies (\forall a, b \mid a, b \in U \cdot \neg(a \sqsubseteq b))$. If a family-view contains two elements that are not co-prime (i.e., one can divide the other), then the two elements express two related families and therefore we need to keep only one of them in the view. If we seek the minimality, we should keep only one of them; for example the one that is the refinement of the other.

Theorem 1. *Let U and V be two subsets of S that form two orthogonal, proper, and minimal family-views of W, then W is a direct product.*

Proof. Let U, V, W be subsets S, such that $W = U_\odot V$. The elements of U are co-prime iff $(\forall a, b \mid a, b \in U \cdot \neg(a \mid b)) \iff (\forall a, b \mid a, b \in U \cdot \neg(\exists c \mid c \in S \cdot a = b \cdot c)) \implies (\forall a, b \mid a, b \in U \cdot \neg(a \sqsubseteq b))$.

$(\implies)$ $0 \notin U \wedge 0 \notin V$ and we have $U \cap V = \{1\}$. Then, according to Lemma 1, every element $w \in W$ can possibly be written as a unique expression $w = u \cdot v$ where $u \in U$ and $v \in V$. We also have $W = U_\odot V$ (it means the $w = u \cdot v$ but not with unique expressions). If $w = 1$ then it has a unique expression $w = 1 \cdot 1$ as 1 is prime (can be divided only by itself).

Let us assume that $u \cdot v$ is not a unique expression for w. This means that there exists $u' \in U - \{1\} \wedge v' \in V - \{1\}$ such that $u \neq u' \wedge v \neq v' \wedge w = u' \cdot v' = u \cdot v$. Hence, there exists a $u'' \in U - \{1\}$ such that $v = u'' \cdot v'$. Therefore, the elements v and v' are not co-prime (an element can divide another), which is false due of our co-prime assumption. Similar argument can be made for the case where we $u = u'' \cdot u'$ for $u'' \in V - \{1\}$. Then $u \cdot v$ is a unique expression for w. Then the product $W \stackrel{\text{def}}{=} U_\odot V$ is a direct product.

$(\impliedby)$ Suppose that U is not proper. It means that $0 \in U$. Hence there should be an element $w \in W$ such that $w = 0 \cdot v = 0$, which can be written with another expression $w = 0 \cdot v'$ for any $v' \in V$. Hence, we have a product of U and V but not a direct one as 0 does not have a unique expression. Also, suppose that U and V are not orthogonal. It means that $(\exists c \mid c \in U \cap V \wedge c \neq 1 \cdot w = c \cdot c)$ or $U \cap V = \emptyset$. In the first case, if there exist an element $c_u \in U$ and $c_v \in V$ such that $c = c_u \cdot c_v$ and we have $t = c_u \cdot c \in V$, then $w = c_u \cdot t$. Hence, there is a w that has two expressions. Then the product is not direct. $\qquad\square$

Theorem 1 requires that the views U and V share no more than 1 and should not include 0. Also it requires that every element of U (respectively, V) is co-prime to the other elements of U (respectively, V). For example, if $U \stackrel{\text{def}}{=} \{a \cdot b + a \cdot c, a\}$, then its elements are not co-prime as the element a can divide the element $(a \cdot b + a \cdot c)$. In this case, one of the elements of U refines the other. Every information you get about the family a you can have it in the family $(a \cdot b + a \cdot c)$. If one is seeking minimality should keep one of them only.

We say that a family f satisfies a constraint $(a \stackrel{q}{\to} b)$, and we write $((a \stackrel{q}{\to} b) \vdash f)$, iff $(\forall p \mid p \leq f \wedge q \sqsubseteq p \cdot a \stackrel{p}{\to} b)$.

Definition 3 (Multi-view reconciliation). *Let U, V, W be subsets S, such that U and V are two family-views of W. Let C be a set of constraints on the views U and V. (Multi-) view reconciliation is the construction of the set $U_{\odot C} V \stackrel{\text{def}}{=} \{w \mid w \in U_\odot V \wedge c \vdash w \text{ for every } c \in C\}$. We call $U_{\odot C} V$ the concili-ated view obtained from the reconciliation of U and V with respect to the set of constraints C.*

View reconciliation is noting but the construction of a product (does not need to be direct) leading to elements that satisfy a set of constraints.

Lemma 2. *Let U and V be two subsets of S that form two orthogonal, proper, and minimal family-views of W. Given a set of constraints C. Then $U \odot_C V$ is a direct product of U and V.*

Proof. According to Theorem 1, U and V as characterised in the lemma give a direct product. The remaining issue is whether eliminating element of $W \stackrel{\text{def}}{=} U \odot V$ that do not satisfy any of the constraints alter or not the property of direct product. The answer is no as all the remaining elements of W still can be written in a unique way as the product of an element from U and another from V. $\square$

Lemma 3. *For U and V family-views and for C and D sets of constraints, we have:*

1. $(U \odot_C V) \odot_D T = (U \odot_{(C \cup D)} V) \odot_{(C \cup D)} T$

2. $U \odot_C V = V \odot_C U$
3. $U \odot_C (V \odot_D T) = ((U \odot_C V) \odot_D T)$

Proof.

1. The proof uses the definition of View reconciliation (applied twice), and basic set theory laws.
2. Obvious due to the commutativity of operation $\cdot$ on product families.
3. Using Lemma 3(1) and the commutativity of $\cup$, we have $U \odot_C (V \odot_D T) = U \odot_{(C \cup D)} (V \odot_{(C \cup D)} T) = ((U \odot_C V) \odot_D T)$.

   Lemma 3(1) states that progressive involvement of constraints leads to the same results as using all the constraints all through the view reconciliation process. This property is practically very important as we discover the constraints by considering the relationship between views two by two. With this result, combining views by taking the constraints that relate them two by two is the same as putting all the constraints together and then use them to integrate all the views.

   Lemma 3(2–3) indicate that view reconciliation is commutative and associative. It means that the order in which we integrate the views by reconciling them with the constraints does not matter at all. This is very important property from a practical perspective. Any rigidity in the order of reconciling views would lead to a lot of practical complications, which we do not have due to the above results.

4   Personalising Medical Devices as a Multi-view Reconciliation Construction

Medical devices are usually quite complex systems. They involve hundreds of features that are related together. Some of the features inhibit the behaviour or others. Also, these features are related to different concerns. For instance, some are from hardware concern while other are from software perspective. The appropriate medical device for a patient would require also involving the patient perspective or view that gives her features as a human patient. Also, one can think about the medical view that brings new features related to the patient pathology. So, each of this perspective gives a family-view as per Definition 1. However, in the case when we are considering only one medical device, the views are singleton sets.

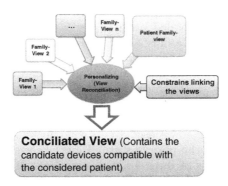

Fig. 1. Combining family-view through view reconciliation

Definition 3 indicates that, when we perform view reconciliation, we eliminate the members of the product view that do not satisfy the constraints. So the process of view reconciliation is a process that leads to shrinking the size (number of elements) of the families in the conciliated view as some element are eliminated since they do not satisfy the constraints. After integrating all the views, as illustrated by Fig. 1, the resulting view (or set of product family) contains only the products that satisfy a patient needs as modelled in the patient view. Therefore, personalizing medical devices is a simple view reconciliation operation.

With medical devices, the family views are very often singleton sets views that are proper. By adding the element 1 to these views, we obtains size 2 sets that additionally contain the element 1. Then we have proper and orthogonal views. Moreover, they are minimal. According to Theorem 1, view reconciliation is direct product operation. Therefore, we can project out the specific view from the conciliated view. In the following, we use the modelling of a pacemaker for a specific patient to illustrate the personalization process as a view reconciliation one.

A human heart has four chambers: left and right atrium and left and right ventricles. The primary function of the heart is to maintain the blood circulation of the body. Muscle contractions, and in particular the contraction of the atria and ventricles which are triggered by electrical signals, drive rhythmic and pump-like function of the heart [16]. During each heartbeat, an electrical signal travels through the heart along a specialized pathway called the conduction system, which consists of cells that are adept at carrying the electrical impulse. Therefore, without electrical signal goes through the conduction system is necessary for the heart to beat. Unfortunately, many factors such as disease, medication, or congenital heart defects can make the conduction system abnormal. It can suspend the heart, cause heart beat too slowly, or beat erratically. In these situations, the body may not receive enough blood, which causes several symptoms such as low blood pressure, weakness, and fatigue. To avoid these symptoms, a pacemaker can be used to regulate the heartbeat.

When there is a problem in getting the heart to beat naturally, doctor adopt pacemakers, which are embedded medical devices that monitor and regulate the heart to keep beating at a normal rate by assisting the natural conduction system. Pacemakers achieve this by monitoring the heart's electrical activity and intervening when the conduction system falters and delivers the electrical stimulation over leads with electrodes. The stimulation is called paces, and the monitoring of the heart's electrical stimuli by the pacemaker is called senses.

A pacemaker may have many modes, distinguished by which chambers of the heart are sensed and paced, how sensed events will affect pacing, and whether the pacing rate is adapted to the patient state. Table 1 shows the operating mode. Pacemaker system consists of three major components: Pulse Generator (PG), Device Controller-Monitor (DCM) and associated software, and *Leads* system.

Table 1. NBG-code of bradycardia operating modes

	I	II	III	IV (optional)
Category	Chambers paced	Chambers sensed	Response to sensing	Rate modulation
Letters	O-None	O-None	O-None	R-Rate
	A-Atrium	A-Atrium	T-Triggered	Modulation
	V-Ventricle	V-Ventricle	I-Inhibited	
	D-Dual	D-Dual	D-Tracked	

4.1   Pacemaker Views and Their Constraints

It is hard to describe a medical device system clearly by a single view. The example we are handling is a simplified version of that given by the system specification developed by Boston Scientific [17]. We start by presenting the views of the family of pacemakers. A state-of-the-art pacemaker is equivalent to a micro-computer.

Hardware View. The hardware view is built up from the following basic components (features):

Controller (*ctrl*)
Lead (*ld*)
Double leads (*d_lds*)
Pulse generator (*pls_gnrt*)
Storage (*strg*)
Accelerometer (*acclr*)
Defibrillator (*dfb*)

Leads system can be changed according to different requirement. Single chamber pacemakers need a lead, double chamber pacemaker need two leads:
$leads\_system = ld \cdot (1 + ld) = ld + ld \cdot ld$

More advanced pacemakers can be extended from the basic pacemaker models. For example, a rate-responsive pacemaker consists of an accelerometer (acclr) and a pacemaker may have a storage (strg).
$pulse\_generator\_device = opt[strg] \cdot pls\_gnrt$, where $opt[strg]$ is the abbreviation for $(1 + strg)$
$basic\_pacemaker = cntrl \cdot pulse\_generator\_device \cdot leads\_system$
$rate\_responsive\_pacemaker = basic\_pacemaker \cdot acclr$

When integrating a defibrillator with the basic pacemaker, we can get a defibrillative pacemaker:

$defibrillative\_pacemaker = basic\_pacemaker \cdot defibrillator$

The whole hardware family of pacemaker:

$hardware\_family = basic\_pacemaker \cdot opt[accelerometer, defibrillator]$

Then the hardware view is formed by the set $\{hardware\_family\}$. If we want the view to have the possibility to be orthogonal to the other views, we add the family 1 to it making it $hardware\_view = \{1, hardware\_family\}$. This view is therefore proper (as it does not contain 0) and minimal (all its members are co-prime).

Software View. From a software perspective, there are many pacing modes. We just consider three frequently used modes. We conceptually merge the other functions that we are omitting in a feature called "other auxiliary functions".

Set parameter function (*set_prmt_fnct*)
Default safe (*dflt_sf*)
Operation abnormalities buzzer warning (*op_abn_bzz*)
Operation abnormalities color warning (*op_abn_clr*)
Atrium-atrium-inhibited mode (*aai*)
Ventricle-ventricle-inhibited mode (*vvi*)
Dual-dual-tracked mode (*ddd*)

Rate modulation ($rate\_mod$)
Download data function ($dwnl$)
Other auxiliary functions ($other\_fnc$)

The advanced combinations:

$pacing\_mode = (aai + vvi + ddd) \cdot (1 + rate\_mod)$
$opration\_abnormalities\_warning = op\_abn\_bzz + op\_abn\_clr$

In particular, $(1+rate\_mod)$ is corresponding with the fourth letter in NBG-code as shown in Table 1. If we select feature $rate\_mod$, it means that there is the function of rate modulation in pacemaker. Finally, the whole family of the pacemaker's software is:

$$software\_family \stackrel{\text{def}}{=} opration\_abnormalities\_warning \cdot pacing\_mode \cdot$$
$$set\_prmt\_fnct \cdot default\_safe \cdot opt[dwnl, other\_fnc]$$

The software view is the set $\{software\_family\}$. Similar to the preview view, if we want the view to have the possibility to be orthogonal to the others views, we define the software view as $software\_view \stackrel{\text{def}}{=} \{1, software\_family\}$.

Patient View. This view describes the condition of the considered patient, and features of her physical condition that need a particular pacing mode. The "Heavy labor" feature, which we denote by hv_lbr, indicates whether a patient has to do a lot of physical activity in daily life or not. Also, we can have the following patient conditions:

- For patients with normal AV and ventricular conduction, AAI pacing mode is a feature that is recommended. Let us label this condition (i.e., having normal AV and ventricular conduction) cnd_nd_aai.
- In cases where frequent pacing is not expected or where the patient has significant comorbidities that are likely to influence survival and clinical outcomes, Single-chamber VVI pacing is recommended. We refer to this condition as cnd_nd_vvi.
- For patients with SND and intact AV conduction, doctors usually recommend Dual-chamber pacing (DDD) or single-chamber atrial pacing (AAI). We identify this condition with cnd_nd_ddd.

Assume these are all of information that we need to know about patients, and the whole patient family is $patient\_family \stackrel{\text{def}}{=} (cnd\_nd\_aai + cnd\_nd\_vvi + cnd\_nd\_vvi) \cdot (1 + hv\_lbr)$ and the patient view is the set

$$patient\_view \stackrel{\text{def}}{=} \{1, patient\_family\}.$$

Multi-view Reconciliation and Results. We have three views including a view that gives us the characteristics of the patient. The three views, which each obtain the family 1, are minimal, proper, and orthogonal. Their product is a direct product. It implies that once we integrated the views, we can get back each of the them using projections (we did not elaborate on this mathematical aspect in the Sect. 3, but it is a well established fact on direct products). We showed in Lemma 2 that applying constraints to eliminate unfit products preserve the direct product property. We also showed in Lemma 3 that the order in which we put together the views does not matter. Also, Lemma 3(1) indicates that we can apply the constraints all together or a subset of them at each combination of the views.

View reconciliation require a set of constraints. Without constraints, the pacemaker products in the views count 768 possible products. However, there are many unfeasible products. For example, if a product has a storage to store data, it is unreasonable that the product doesn't have the download date function. In addition, if a product includes an accelerometer, it should be able to modulate the pacing rate.

These constraints are on the pacemaker products elements of the product $\mathcal{P}$ of all the considered views that is defined as follows:

$$\mathcal{P} \stackrel{\text{def}}{=} hardware\_view \circ software\_view \circ patient\_view.$$

In the following, the notation $a \xrightarrow{F} b$, where F is a set of families and a and b product families denotes the set of constraints $a \xrightarrow{g} b$ for every $g \in F$. Let us consider the following constraints:

$$c_1 : \quad strg \xrightarrow{\mathcal{P}} dwnld \qquad\qquad c_2 : \quad acclr \xrightarrow{\mathcal{P}} rate\_mod$$

If we use these constraints as our set of Constraints Const $= \{c_1, c_2\}$, then $(hardware\_view \circ_{\text{Const}} software\_view) \circ_{\text{Const}} patient\_view$ leads to 432 products involving features from the three views from 768 possible products without constraints. It is a size reduction of 43.8%. Adding more detailed constraints, products will be fewer but more suitable for the patient.

Let us assume that a patient with a heart disease engages in heavy labor in daily life, and she needs to use a pacemaker with DDD mode. We should therefore add the following constraints:

$$c_3 : \quad cnd\_nd\_ddd \xrightarrow{\mathcal{P}} ddd \qquad\qquad c_4 : \quad hv\_lbr \xrightarrow{\mathcal{P}} acclr$$

The set of constraints is now Const $= \{c_1, c_2, c_3, c_4\}$ and the view reconciliation $(hardware\_view \circ_{\text{Const}} software\_view) \circ_{\text{Const}} patient\_view$ leads to only 48 products involving features from the three views. It is a size reduction of 93.8%. These 48 products are personalized for the patient. The Physician can select one of the 48 products to implant into the patient. For any of these products, we can obtain by simple projections the software (or hardware) features that they encompass. If software developers want to know the requirements for software, they can project $((patient\_hardware \circ_{\text{Const}} patient\_software) \circ_{\text{Const}} patient\_view)$ on the software dimension to get all the software products involved. In our case study, we obtain 8 software products. The conciliated software products are shown in Table 2. These products must have basic features like *Default safe*, *Set parameter function*. Due to

Table 2. The reconciled software products

Pacemaker product number	Product features
1	Default safe, download data function, dual-dual-tracked mode, operation abnormalities buzzer warning, other auxiliary function, rate modulation, set parameter function
2	Default safe, download data function, dual-dual-tracked mode, operation abnormalities buzzer warning, rate modulation, set parameter function
3	Default safe, download data function, dual-dual-tracked mode, operation abnormalities color warning, other auxiliary function, rate modulation, set parameter function
4	Default safe, download data function, dual-dual-tracked mode, operation abnormalities color warning, rate modulation, set parameter function
5	Default safe, dual-dual-tracked mode, operation abnormalities buzzer warning, other auxiliary function, rate modulation, set parameter function
6	Default safe, dual-dual-tracked mode, operation abnormalities buzzer warning, rate modulation, set parameter function
7	Default safe, dual-dual-tracked mode, operation abnormalities color warning, other auxiliary function, rate modulation, set parameter function
8	Default safe, dual-dual-tracked mode, operation abnormalities color warning, rate modulation, set parameter function

the patient's condition, each product has feature *Dual-dual-tracked mode* and feature *Rate modulation*. Other features such as the two kinds of operation abnormalities warning are optional. The 8 software products can match all of the hardware products to generate real and feasible products for the patient. For example, besides some basic or optional functions, the first product in the Table 1 includes *Download data function* to match the hardware *Storage*, *Dual-dual-tracked mode* and *Rate modulation* to satisfy the patient's condition.

5   Related Work

Although there is an abundant literature on software product family or software product line, only a few directly discuss multi-view reconciliation problem in software product family development. There are some literature about the reconciliation of non-functional requirements such as security and performance [18]. Also, there are approaches to resolving architectural mismatched resulting from integrating commercial off-the-shelf (COTS) components [19]. When merging views of database there is a similar problem called *view reconciliation problem* [20]. The above case is considering a single software system and not a product family at the initial phase of the software development.

Jose Proenca et al. [21] studied reconciliation of feature models via pullbacks. In their study, a view can be a feature view, a product view or a product line view. When reconciling two elements, they considered the compatibility of the two elements. If two features are compatible, one feature should abstract the other one. For example, "Internet" abstract "3g" or "wifi". If reconciliation of two products exists, every feature in one product should be compatible with a feature in the other product. Reconciliation of two product lines exists if every product in a line is compatible with one in the other line. Programmers in one team need not see the complete variability of the product line from the perspective of other teams. So they just need to refer to the abstraction of other teams. The reconciliation is the process that replaces the abstract features with specific features. For example, a product has feature "APPs", and the other product has feature "email". When reconciling the two product the reconciled product includes feature "email" instead of "APPs". The core issue of the method is to find the refined and abstract relations between different features. Our approach constructs view models from several perspectives of different domains or the same domain, and uses constraints to reconcile multiple views.

Yi Li et al. [22] list 6 kinds of merging of feature models, and a conceptual reconciliation framework of feature model was proposed and compared with the existing 6 methods. In their research, the merging of feature model is combining two feature models into one model. In the merging, they focused on solving the inconsistency of structural layer, equality of root feature, and constraint relations. The third focus is the problem we pay attention to, but the structural layer and the root feature is not. In our approach, we first construct several views using PFA, these view has structural layer at this moment while the generated products are shown as sets of features without considering the layer. In addition, they defined the refinement relation and a root feature. If two models can be merged, both of models should have the same root feature. In our approach, we may construct views from different domains. As shown in Sect. 4, software view and hardware view have different root feature, but we can reconcile them flexibly using our approach.

6   Conclusions and Future Work

The paper presents a mathematical setting for multi-view reconciliation. We precisely define a (family) view and how to reconcile views. (Multi-) view reconciliation is presented as a product construction. Under given conditions, the view reconciliation can lead to a direct product. We showed that desirable properties of the considered views such orthogonality, properness, and minimality are need for a practical approach to view reconciliations. Then, we present personalizing medical devices as a constraint view reconciliation operation. By including in the view reconciliation the patient's view, which is giving the person's pathological condition or any of her relevant physical/medical characteristics (features), leads to identifying the specific medical devices from the considered family that are more suitable for the patient. Our future work related to this topic include further development of the mathematical framework. Then we plan to build a plugin to Jory Tool, which is a tool supporting PFA, to carry all the calculation needed for view specification, verification, and reconciliation. Then we plan adopting a model-driven approach to generate the software specification of a personalized medical device from its PFA model and the Event-B specification of each of its features. Therefore, our approach will join the research efforts for model driven software development for medical device software.

References

1. Faris, T.H.: Safe and Sound Software: Creating an Efficient and Effective Quality System for Software Medical Device Organizations. Asq Quality Press, Milwaukee (2006)
2. The Council Of The European Communities: Council Directive 93/42/EEC concerning medical devices (1993)
3. Chen, Y., Lawford, M., Wang, H., Wassyng, A.: Insulin pump software certification. In: Gibbons, J., MacCaull, W. (eds.) FHIES 2013. Lecture Notes in Computer Science, vol. 8315. Springer, Heidelberg (2013). doi:10.1007/978-3-642-53956-5_7
4. Jones, P., Jetley, R., Abraham, J.: A formal methods-based verification approach to medical device software analysis. In: Embedded Systems Design (2010)
5. Bosch, J.: The challenges of broadening the scope of software product families. Commun. ACM **49**(12), 41–44 (2006)
6. Long, C.A.: Software Product Lines: Practices and Patterns. Addison-Wesley Longman Publishing Co., Inc., Boston (2001)
7. SPLC: Product line hall of fame (2017). http://splc.net/fame.html
8. Mcgregor, J.D., Muthig, D., Yoshimura, K., Jensen, P.: Successful software product line practices. IEEE Software (2010)
9. Software Engineering Standards Committee of the IEEE Computer Society: ISO/IEC Standard for Systems and Software Engineering - Recommended Practice for Architectural Description of Software-Intensive Systems (2007)
10. Höfner, P., Khedri, R., Möller, B.: An algebra of product families. Softw. Syst. Model. **10**(2), 161–182 (2011)
11. Höfner, P., Khedri, R., Möller, B.: Algebraic view reconciliation. In: 6th IEEE International Conferences on Software Engineering and Formal Methods, Cape Town, South Africa, pp. 85–94, 10–14 November 2008
12. Zhang, Q., Khedri, R.: On the weaving process of aspect-oriented product family algebra. J. Logic. Algebraic Methods Program. **85**(12), 146–172 (2016)
13. Zhang, Q., Khedri, R., Jaskolka, J.: An aspect-oriented language for feature-modeling. J. Ambient Intell. Humaniz. Comput. **5**, 343–356 (2014)
14. Hebisch, U., Weinert, H.J.: Semirings: Algebraic Theory and Applications in Computer Science. World Scientific, Singapore (1998)

15. Brear, M.: Modal kleene algebra and applications. In: Relational Methods in Computer Science, pp. 93–131 (2004)
16. Diciolla, M.: Quantitative verification of real-time properties with application to medical devices. Ph.D. thesis, University of Oxford (2014)
17. Scientific, B.: PACEMAKER System Specification (2007)
18. Cysneiros, L.M., do Prado Leite, J.C.S.: Nonfunctional requirements: from elicitation to conceptual models. IEEE Trans. Software Eng. 30(5), 328–350 (2004)
19. Avgeriou, P., Guelfi, N.: Resolving architectural mismatches of COTS through architectural reconciliation. In: Franch, X., Port, D. (eds.) ICCBSS 2005. LNCS, vol. 3412, pp. 248–257. Springer, Heidelberg (2005). doi:10.1007/978-3-540-30587-3_34
20. Jacobs, B.E.: Applied Database Logic. Volume I: Fundamental Database Issues. Prentice-Hall, Inc., Upper Saddle River (1985)
21. Proenca, J., Clarke, D.: Reconciliation of feature models via pullbacks. CS Reports Report CW601, Department of Computer Science, K.U.Leuven, January 2011
22. Yi, L., Haiyan, Z., Zhang, W., Jin, Z., Mei, H.: Research on the merging of feature models. Chin. J. Comput. 36(1), 1–9 (2014)

Compiling Parameterized X86-TSO Concurrent Programs to Cubicle-$\mathcal{W}$

Sylvain Conchon[1,2], David Declerck[1,2(✉)], and Fatiha Zaïdi[1]

[1] LRI (CNRS & Univ. Paris-Sud), Université Paris-Saclay, 91405 Orsay, France
{sylvain.conchon,fatiha.zaidi}@lri.fr, david.declerck@u-psud.fr
[2] Inria, Université Paris-Saclay, 91120 Palaiseau, France

Abstract. We present PMCx86, a compiler from x86 concurrent programs to Cubicle-$\mathcal{W}$, a model checker for parameterized weak memory array-based transition systems. Our tool handles x86 concurrent programs designed to be executed for an arbitrary number of threads and under the TSO weak memory model. The correctness of our approach relies on a simulation result to show that the translation preserves x86-TSO semantics. To show the effectiveness of our translation scheme, we prove the safety of parameterized critical primitives found in operating systems like mutexes and synchronization barriers. To our knowledge, this is the first approach to prove safety of such parameterized x86-TSO programs.

Keywords: Model checking · MCMT · SMT · Weak memory · x86 · TSO

1 Introduction

Optimizations found in modern multiprocessors architectures affect the order in which memory operations from different threads may take place. For instance, on Intel x86 processors [21], each hardware thread has a write buffer in which it temporarily stores values before they reach the main memory. This allows the processor to execute the next instruction immediately but delays the store.

From an x86 programmer's point of view, the main drawback of this new memory model, called x86-TSO [25], is that most concurrent algorithms, designed under a global time (sequential consistency – SC) assumption [23], are incorrect on weaker semantics. However, while concurrent programming is known to be difficult, it is even harder to design correct programs when one has to deal with memory reordering.

This situation is further complicated by the fact that critical concurrent primitives found (for instance) in operating systems are usually designed to be

---

The paper is supported by the French ANR project PARDI (DS0703).

Z. Duan and L. Ong (Eds.): ICFEM 2017, LNCS 10610, pp. 88–104, 2017.
https://doi.org/10.1007/978-3-319-68690-5_6

executed for an arbitrary number of processes. Mutual exclusion algorithms or synchronization barriers are typical examples of such *parameterized* programs.

As a consequence, the design and verification of parameterized x86-TSO programs is a very hard challenge due to the state explosion problem caused by the combination of both *unbouded writing buffers* and *unbounded number of threads*.

Checking safety of programs running under a relaxed memory model has been shown to be a (non-primitive recursive-)hard problem [9,11] and various verification techniques have been applied to handle it [3,10,12,13,17,22,24]. Among those techniques, model checking of systems under weak memory assumption has been investigated and several tools have been implemented. The list of state-of-the-art model checkers for weak memory includes CBMC [7], MEMORAX [4] and TRENCHER [10].

Model checking has also been applied to parameterized systems for a long time ago [8,14,18] and automatic tools for the analysis of such systems exist. The list of state-of-the-art parametric model checkers includes MCMT [19], Undip [6], PFS [5] and Cubicle [16]. But until now, there is no model checker for reasoning about both weak memory and parameterized models, except Cubicle which has been extended recently to a new version, Cubicle-$\mathcal{W}$ [1], to verify parameterized array-based systems with weak memories.

In this paper, we present PMCx86 [2], a compiler from x86 assembly language to Cubicle-$\mathcal{W}$. The main originality of PMCx86 is that it can handle x86 concurrent programs designed to be executed for an arbitrary number of threads and under the TSO weak memory model. Our contributions are as follows:

- A compilation scheme from x86 to array-based transition systems with weak memory assumptions
- A simulation result to show that our translation preserves the TSO semantics
- An end-to-end tool that allows the verification of real critical x86 primitives found in OS like mutex or synchronization barriers.

To our knowledge, this is the first framework to model check parameterized x86-TSO concurrent programs.

In the remainder, we present in Sect. 2 the syntax and semantics of Cubicle-$\mathcal{W}$. In Sect. 3, we present the x86-TSO fragment supported by our framework. Section 4 is about the translation to Cubicle-$\mathcal{W}$. Finally Sect. 5 exhibits the experiments and the obtained results and we conclude and give some lines for future work in Sect. 6.

2 Overview of Cubicle-$\mathcal{W}$

In this section, we present the syntax and semantics of Cubicle-$\mathcal{W}$'s input language. This language is the target of our compiler PMCx86.

To illustrate our presentation, we use the crafted example shown in Fig. 1. A Cubicle-$\mathcal{W}$ input file starts with enumerated type declarations (**type** keyword), followed by variables declarations. Thread-local (*i.e.* non shared) variables are declared as **proc**-indexed arrays. Those variables behave as *sequential consistent*

```
type loc = L1 | L2 | L3 | END          transition t1 (p)
                                       requires { PC[p] = L1 }
array PC[proc] : loc                   { p @ A[p] := 1; PC[p] := L2 }
weak var X : int
weak array A[proc] : int               transition t2 (p q)
                                       requires { PC[p] = L2 &&
init (p) {                               fence(p) && p @ A[q] <> 0 }
  PC[p] = L1 && X = 0 && A[p] = 0 }    { PC[p] := L3 }

unsafe (p q) {                         transition t3 (p)
  PC[p] = End && PC[q] = End }         requires { PC[p] = L3 }
                                       { p @ X := p @ X + 1; PC[p] := End }
```

Fig. 1. A crafted Cubicle-$\mathcal{W}$ example illustrating its syntactic features

(SC) memories. The **weak var** keyword is used to declare *shared* variables subject to weak memory effects. Similarly, shared weak arrays indexed by process
identifiers are defined using **weak array** declarations. The initial states of the
system are described by a (implicitly universally quantified) logical formula introduced by the **init** keyword. Similarly, the dangerous states are described by
logical formulas introduced by the **unsafe** keyword and implicitly existentially
quantified by process variables. Transitions are introduced by the **transition**
keyword and are parameterized by existentially quantified process variables.
Implicitly, the first parameter of each transition indicates which process performs
the action. Each transition is composed of two parts: the *guard* and the *actions*.
The *guard* is a logical formula that determines when the transition is enabled.
The *actions* part is a set of updates on SC and weak variable. The *guard* evaluation and *actions* are performed *atomically*, *i.e.* no other transition can occur
in between. In both parts, accesses to weak variables are performed using the
p @ X notation, indicating that process p accesses the variable X. Cubicle-$\mathcal{W}$
imposes one restriction: All weak variable accesses in the same transition (guard
and action) *must be* performed by the same process.

Cubicle-$\mathcal{W}$ simulates a write buffer semantics à la TSO for weak variables (or
weak arrays). This means that each process has an associated FIFO-like write
buffer, and when a transition performs writes to weak variables, all these writes
are enqueued as a single update in the buffer. In a non-deterministic manner, an
update may be dequeued from the buffer and committed to the weak variables.
A process always knows the most recent value it wrote to a weak variables: when
evaluating a read, a process first checks in its own buffer for the most recent write
to the weak variable and returns the associated value, if any, otherwise it just
returns the value from the variable itself. A transition *guard* may use a **fence(p)**
predicate (as in transition **t2** for instance) to indicate that the transition may
only be taken when process p's buffer is empty. When a transition contains both
a read and a write (transition **t3**), it is given a *lock* semantics: it may be taken
only when the buffer of the process performing the actions is empty (a **fence(p)**

predicate is syntactically added to the transition *guard*), and the writes to weak variables bypass the buffer.

Formal semantics of Cubicle-$\mathcal{W}$

To make the semantics more formal, we give the pseudo-code of an interpreter for Cubicle-$\mathcal{W}$'s input programs in Algorithm 1. This interpreter makes use of data structures for buffers and some functions that we briefly describe here.

Buffers. A buffer (type `buffer`) is a queue containing updates. An update is made up of several writes, which associate a variable to a value. The operations on these buffers are:

- `is_empty`: determines if a buffer is empty
- `enqueue`: add an update at the head of the buffer
- `dequeue`: get and remove the update at the tail of the buffer
- `peek`: inspect every update from head to tail in the buffer until a given variable is found; if it is, return the associated value, otherwise, return *None*

Auxiliary functions. The `upreg`(t) function returns the set of actions on local variables from a transition t. Similarly, the `upmem`(t) function returns the set of actions on weak variables. The `req`(t) function returns the whole transition *guard*. The `locked`(t) function determines if the transition has *lock* semantics. More importantly, the `eval`($\mathcal{S}, e$) function evaluates the expression e in state $\mathcal{S}$. It is trivial for most cases, except for reads and fences.

```
function eval(S, e) : begin
    match e with
        • i @ X →
            match peek(B[i], X) with
                • Some v → return v
                • None → return W[X]
            end
        • fence(i) → is_empty(B[i])
        • ... → ...
    end
end
```

The interpreter takes the form of an infinite loop that randomly chooses between executing a transition t ready to be triggered for some process arguments σ (*i.e.* `eval`($\mathcal{S}, \text{req}(t)\sigma = true$) or flushing a non-empty buffer $\mathcal{B}[i]$ of some process i. The execution of a transition first directly assigns local variables $R[i]$ in the (SC) memory. Then, it constructs an update value U with all pairs of (variable, value) corresponding to the weak assignments of t. If the transition has the *locked* semantics, this update value is enqueued in the buffer of the process which performs the action. Otherwise, its assignments are flushed in memory.

Algorithm 1: A Cubicle-$\mathcal{W}$ interpreter

Input: a number of processes n and a set of transitions τ
State: $\mathcal{S} = \{ \mathcal{R} : (\text{register} \mapsto \text{value}) \text{ map}$
$\qquad\qquad \mathcal{W} : (\text{variable} \mapsto \text{value}) \text{ map}$
$\qquad\qquad \mathcal{B} : (\text{proc} \mapsto \text{buffer}) \text{ map} \}$
procedure run(n, τ) : **begin**
$\quad$ **while** *true* **do**
$\qquad$ **non-deterministically choose**
$\qquad\quad$ • *a transition t and a substitution σ s.t* $eval(\mathcal{S}, \, req(t)\sigma) = true \rightarrow$
$\qquad\qquad$ **foreach** $R[i] := e$ *in* $upreg(t)$ **do** $\mathcal{R}[R[i\sigma] \leftarrow \text{eval}(\mathcal{S}, e\sigma)]$;
$\qquad\qquad$ $U := \emptyset$;
$\qquad\qquad$ **foreach** $X := e$ *in* $upmem(t)$ **do**
$\qquad\qquad$ $\mid$ $\quad U := (X, \text{eval}(\mathcal{S}, e\sigma)) + U$
$\qquad\qquad$ **end foreach**
$\qquad\qquad$ **if** *locked(t)* = *false* **then**
$\qquad\qquad$ $\mid$ $\quad$ enqueue($\mathcal{B}[i]$, U)
$\qquad\qquad$ **else**
$\qquad\qquad$ $\mid$ $\quad$ **foreach** *(X, v) in U* **do** $\mathcal{W}[X \leftarrow v]$
$\qquad\qquad$ **end if**
$\qquad\quad$ • *a process i s.t* $is\_empty(\mathcal{B}[i]) = false \rightarrow$
$\qquad\qquad$ **let** $U = $ dequeue($\mathcal{B}[i]$) **in**
$\qquad\qquad$ **foreach** *(X, v) in U* **do** $\mathcal{W}[X \leftarrow v]$
$\qquad$ **or exit if no choice possible**
$\quad$ **end while**
end

---

3   Supported X86-TSO Fragment

We present in this section the subset of 32-bit x86 assembly instructions supported by our tool. In order to guide (and prove correct) our translation to Cubicle-$\mathcal{W}$, we also give an operational semantics of this fragment.

Input programs are written in a NASM-like syntax. The six general purpose registers eax, ebx, ecx, edx, esi and edi are available. Instruction operands may be registers, immediate data, and direct memory references of the form [var]. Memory accesses occur under the TSO weak memory semantics. The supported instructions are:

- Load/store: mov
- Arithmetic: add, sub, inc, dec
- Exchange: xadd, xchg
- Compare: cmp
- Jump: jmp, jCC
- Memory ordering: mfence, lock prefix (on add, sub, inc, dec, xadd, xchg)

In order to write (and translate) parametric programs, we allow data declarations to be decorated with an annotation ! as counter which specifies a counter on the number of threads. These counters are still treated as regular integers on x86, but may only be manipulated by the inc, dec, cmp and mov instructions. Moreover, they will be translated differently in Cubicle-$\mathcal{W}$.

For the sake of simplicity, we only introduce in this section the most relevant aspects of our fragment, as shown in the grammar in Fig. 2. The interested reader may refer to [15] for a detailed grammar of the supported fragment.

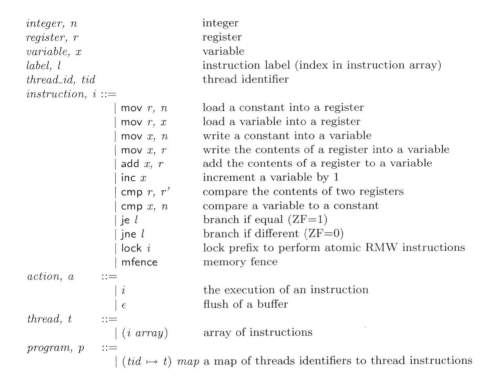

integer, n		integer
register, r		register
variable, x		variable
label, l		instruction label (index in instruction array)
thread_id, *tid*		thread identifier
instruction, $i ::=$		
	| mov r, n	load a constant into a register
	| mov r, x	load a variable into a register
	| mov x, n	write a constant into a variable
	| mov x, r	write the contents of a register into a variable
	| add x, r	add the contents of a register to a variable
	| inc x	increment a variable by 1
	| cmp r, r'	compare the contents of two registers
	| cmp x, n	compare a variable to a constant
	| je l	branch if equal (ZF=1)
	| jne l	branch if different (ZF=0)
	| lock i	lock prefix to perform atomic RMW instructions
	| mfence	memory fence
action, a $::=$		
	| i	the execution of an instruction
	| ϵ	flush of a buffer
thread, t $::=$		
	| (i *array*)	array of instructions
program, p $::=$		
	| ($tid \mapsto t$) *map*	a map of threads identifiers to thread instructions

Fig. 2. Abstract syntax tree of x86 program

In our abstract syntax, a *thread* is described by an array of instructions and a *program* is just a map from thread identifiers to threads. A thread executes an *action* which is either an instrucion or a flush of its buffer.

Representation of x86-TSO states

In order to give the semantics of this fragment, we need to define an x86-TSO memory state S. Such state is composed of two parts: the set of thread's local states LS and the shared memory M. Each thread local state ls is composed of its *instruction pointer* eip, its *zero flag* zf, its set of *registers* Q, and its *writing buffer* B.

$$
\begin{array}{ll}
S = (LS \times M) & \text{An x86-TSO machine state} \\
M = (var \mapsto int)\ map & \text{A memory: dictionary from variables to integers} \\
LS = (tid \mapsto ls)\ map & \text{The thread local states: dictionary from} \\
& \text{thread identifiers to their states} \\
ls = (\texttt{eip} \times \texttt{zf} \times Q \times B) & \text{A thread local state} \\
Q = (reg \mapsto int)\ map & \text{A thread's registers: dictionary from} \\
& \text{register names do integers} \\
B = (var \times int)\ queue & \text{A thread's TSO write buffer} \\
\texttt{eip} = int & \text{A thread's instruction pointer} \\
\texttt{zf} = int & \text{A thread's } zero\ flag \\
var & \text{The set of all variables} \\
tid & \text{The set of all thread identifiers} \\
reg & \text{The set of all register names}
\end{array}
$$

The $\texttt{eip}$ register represents a thread's *instruction pointer*, *i.e.* the threads's current program point. For simplicity, we choose to represent it using an integer type. The $\texttt{zf}$ is a boolean register, commonly used to store the result of the compare instruction, and more generally of any arithmetic instruction. It must be set to *true* if the result of the last instruction was 0, and *false* otherwise. We represent it using an integer, with the usual convention that $0 = false$ and $1 = true$. Writing buffers are represented as queues containing pairs of variables and integers. Initially, the x86-TSO machine is in a state S_{init} such that all thread's $\texttt{eip}$ are set to 0, all buffers are empty, and all registers and the shared memory are in an undetermined state.

Notations for manipulating TSO buffers

When describing the instruction semantics, we use the following notations to manipulate the buffers:

$$
\begin{array}{ll}
x \in B & \text{True if at least one pair in } B \text{ concerns variable } x \\
x \notin B & \text{True if no pair in } B \text{ concerns variable } x \\
B = \varnothing & \text{True if } B \text{ is empty} \\
B_1 +\!\!+ B_2 & \text{Concatenation of } B_1 \text{ and } B_2 \\
(x, n) +\!\!+ B & \text{Prepend } (x, n) \text{ to the head of } B \\
B +\!\!+ (x, n) & \text{Append } (x, n) \text{ to the tail of } B
\end{array}
$$

Semantics of programs

The semantics of a program is defined by the smallest relation $\xrightarrow{tid:a}$ on x86-TSO machine states that satisfies the rule SCHEDULING below.

We define a scheduling function $\pi_p(S)$ which given a program p and a state S chooses the next action to be executed by a thread.

$$
\frac{\pi_p(LS, M) = tid : a \quad LS(tid) = ls \quad (ls, M) \xrightarrow{a} (ls', M')}{(LS, M) \xrightarrow{tid:a} (LS[t \mapsto ls'], M')} \text{SCHEDULING}
$$

Semantics of instructions

The semantics of instructions is given by the smallest relation $\xrightarrow{i}$ that satisfies the rule below.

There are as many rules as required to cover the different combination of operand kinds (constant, register, memory). Here, for the sake of readability, we only present some rules that are TSO specific and explain the main principles of that relaxed memory semantics.

The rule MovVarCst assigns a shared variable x with a constant n. As assignments are delayed in TSO, a new pairs (x, n) is enqueued in buffer B.

$$\frac{a = \mathsf{mov}\ x, n}{((eip, zf, Q, B), M) \xrightarrow{a} ((eip + 1, zf, Q, (x, n) \mathbin{+\mkern-5mu+} B), M)}\ \text{MovVarCst}$$

The next two rules illustrate the TSO semantics of an instruction $\mathsf{mov}\ r, x$ that assigns to a register r the contents of a shared memory x. When the thread's buffer does not have a write on x, MovRegVarM applies and the value of x is directly read in memory.

$$\frac{a = \mathsf{mov}\ r, x \quad x \notin B \quad M(x) = n}{((eip, zf, Q, B), M) \xrightarrow{a} ((eip + 1, zf, Q[r \mapsto n], B), M)}\ \text{MovRegVarM}$$

On the contrary, when the thread's buffer contains a pair (x, n), rule MovRegVarB looks for the value of the most recent assignment to x in B.

$$\frac{a = \mathsf{mov}\ r, x \quad B = B_1 \mathbin{+\mkern-5mu+} (x, n) \mathbin{+\mkern-5mu+} B_2 \quad x \notin B_1}{((eip, zf, Q, B), M) \xrightarrow{a} ((eip + 1, zf, Q[r \mapsto n], B), M)}\ \text{MovRegVarB}$$

The semantics of non-atomic read-modify-write instructions like add is still given by a single rule. Indeed, since the write is buffered, it has the same effect as splitting the read and the write in two rules.

$$\frac{a = \mathsf{add}\ x, r \quad x \notin B \quad M(x) + Q(r) = n}{((eip, zf, Q, B), M) \xrightarrow{a} ((eip + 1, \mathsf{iszero}(n), Q, (x, n) \mathbin{+\mkern-5mu+} B), M)}\ \text{AddVarMReg}$$

$$\frac{a = \mathsf{add}\ x, r \quad B = B_1 \mathbin{+\mkern-5mu+} (x, m) \mathbin{+\mkern-5mu+} B_2 \quad x \notin B_1 \quad m + Q(r) = n}{((eip, zf, Q, B), M) \xrightarrow{a} ((eip + 1, \mathsf{iszero}(n), Q, (x, n) \mathbin{+\mkern-5mu+} B), M)}\ \text{AddVarBReg}$$

When the lock prefix is used on a read-modify-write instruction, we simply require the thread's buffer to be empty, and directly write to memory.

$$\frac{a = \mathsf{lock}\ \mathsf{add}\ x, r \quad x \notin B \quad M(x) + Q(r) = n}{((eip, zf, Q, B), M) \xrightarrow{a} ((eip + 1, \mathsf{iszero}(n), Q, B), M[x \mapsto n])}\ \text{LockAddVarReg}$$

Last, the rule MFENCE describes the effect of a memory fence which enforces a thread buffer to be flushed.

$$\frac{a = \mathsf{mfence} \quad B = \varnothing}{((eip, zf, Q, B), M) \xrightarrow{a} ((eip + 1, zf, Q, B), M)} \ \text{MFENCE}$$

Buffer / Memory synchronization

Buffers can flush their oldest writes to memory in an asynchronous manner. We express this using a rule that only involves the state of buffers, without involving the eip registers.

$$\frac{a = \epsilon \quad B = B_1 +\!\!+ (x, n)}{((eip, zf, Q, B), M) \xrightarrow{a} ((eip, zf, Q, B_1), M[x \mapsto n])} \ \text{WRITEMEM}$$

4   Translation to Cubicle-$\mathcal{W}$

We represent x86-TSO states in Cubicle-$\mathcal{W}$ by a set of variables corresponding to the shared variables and local states of each thread. Local registers are encoded as elements of an array indexed by process identifiers. The type of the array depends on the kind of values carried by the registers.

Instruction pointers. They are represented by a PC array. Program points are given an enumerated type *loc*, whose elements are of the form L_0, ... L_1. The number of these elements can be determined statically at compile time: it depends on the length of the longest instruction sequence.

Zero flags. They are represented by a ZF array of type int. We use the convention that $n = 0 \equiv true$ and $n \neq 0 \equiv false$. Note that this is the opposite of x86: this allows to compute this flag more easily, as we simply set it to the result of the last arithmetic operation. This allows to reduce the number of transitions, as we do not have to make any further operation to compute it.

Shared variables. Each shared variable X gives rise to an **weak X : int** declaration. Counters (see below) are mapped to **weak** arrays of type **bool**.

Translation of x86-TSO instructions

For the sake of readability, we only give the translation of the subset of instructions given in the previous section.

We define a compilation function $\mathcal{C}$ that takes as input a thread identifier, an instruction, and the instruction position in the array (this is equivalent to the *instruction pointer*). It returns a set of Cubicle-$\mathcal{W}$ transitions that simulates the instruction.

The first rule TMOVVARCST explains how to translate the write of a constant into a shared variable. It simply amounts to use Cubicle-$\mathcal{W}$'s write instruction on weak variables. This instruction imposes to prefix the operation with the thread identifier which performs the assignment.

$\mathcal{C}(\mathtt{t}\ ;\ \mathsf{mov}\ x, n\ ;\ i) =$ TMovVarCst

```
transition mov_var_cst_i(t)
requires { PC[t] = L_i }
{ t @ X := n; PC[t] = L_{i+1} }
```

The next rule is the opposite operation: the read of a variable into a register. To achieve it, we only rely on the *read* operation on shared variables. Similarly to write instructions, reads must be prefixed with a thread identifier.

$\mathcal{C}(t\ ;\ \mathsf{mov}\ r, x\ ;\ i) =$ TMovRegVar

```
transition mov_reg_var_i(t)
requires { PC[t] = L_i }
{ R[t] := t @ X; PC[t] = L_{i+1} }
```

Adding the contents of a register to a variable is a read-modify-write operation. As Cubicle-$\mathcal{W}$ makes everything inside a transition atomic, we need two transitions to translate this operation. The first one, TAddVarReg1, reads the shared variable X, sums it with the local register and stores the result into a temporary register T[t]. The second rule, TAddVarReg2, stores the contents of this temporary register into the variable X and updates the *zero flag* accordingly.

$\mathcal{C}(t\ ;\ \mathsf{add}\ x, r\ ;\ i) =$ TAddVarReg1

```
transition add_var_reg_1_i(t)
requires { PC[t] = L_i }
{ T[t] := t @ X + R[t]; PC[t] = L_{xi} }
```

                                                                 TAddVarReg2

```
transition add_var_reg_2_i(t)
requires { PC[t] = L_{xi} }
{ t @ X := R[t]; ZF[t] := T[t];
  PC[t] = L_{i+1} }
```

Translating the atomic counterpart of this operation is very simple, since Cubicle-$\mathcal{W}$ transitions are atomic. We just need a single transition, as given by rule TLockAddVarReg.

$\mathcal{C}(t\ ;\ \mathsf{add}\ x, r\ ;\ i) =$ TLockAddVarReg

```
transition lockadd_var_reg_i(t)
requires { PC[t] = L_i }
{ t @ X := t @ X + R[t];
  ZF[t] := t @ X + R[t];
  PC[t] = L_{i+1} }
```

The translation of a memory fence simply relies on the *fence* predicate of Cubicle-$\mathcal{W}$ to express that the transition may only be taken if the thread's buffer is empty.

$\mathcal{C}(t\ ;\ \mathsf{mfence}\ ;\ i) =$ TMFence

```
transition mfence_i(t)
requires { PC[t] = L_i & & fence(t) }
{ PC[t] = L_{i+1} }
```

Translation of operations on counters

Operations on counters are restricted and translated differently. When X is a variable declared with a ! as counter annotation, our tool only supports the following operations:

$$
\begin{array}{ll}
\texttt{mov X, 0} & \text{reset} \\
\texttt{inc X} & \text{incrementation} \\
\texttt{cmp X, } N & \text{comparison to } N \\
\texttt{cmp X, 0} &
\end{array}
$$

where N is an abstract value represented the (parameterized) number of threads.

At first sight, it would be tempting to translate counters directly as variables of type int. However, this solution makes it impossible to compare a counter with N as Cubicle does not explicitly provide this constant. To solve this issue, we represent counters by weak arrays of Booleans indexed by processes. Each operation is then encoded in a unary numeral system. In the rest of this section, we only describe the first three ones.

Reset. To reset a counter, we just need to apply the transition given by the rule below which writes the value False in all the array cells.

$$\mathcal{C}(t \;;\; \texttt{mov } x, n \;;\; i) = \hspace{3cm} \text{TMovCnt0}$$

```
transition mov_cnt0ᵢ(t)
requires { PC[t] = Lᵢ }
{ t @ X[k] := case | _ : False;
  PC[t] = L_{i+1} }
```

Incrementation. As for the incrementation of shared variables, a counter incrementation has to be performed in two steps. This first one for reading the contents of the variable and the second one adding one and assigning the new value. In our unary numeral system, adding one to a variable amounts to switch an array cell from False to True. The goal of the first transition is thus to find a cell equal to False and the second rule performs the assignment to True. The rules are duplicated as we may either switch the cell belonging to the running thread or to another thread.

$\mathcal{C}(t \;;\; \texttt{inc } x \;;\; i) = $ `transition inc_cntS_1ᵢ(t)` TINCCNTS1
```
requires { PC[t] = Lᵢ && t @ X[t] = False }
{ PC[t] = L_{xi} }
```

`transition inc_cntS_2ᵢ(t)` TINCCNTS2
```
requires { PC[t] = L_{xi} }
{ t @ X[t] := True; ZF[t] := 1;
  PC[t] = L_{i+1} }
```

`transition inc_cnt0_1ᵢ(t o)` TINCCNTO1
```
requires { PC[t] = Lᵢ && t @ X[o] = False}
{ PC[t] = L_{yi}; TP[t] = o }
```

`transition inc_cnt0_2ᵢ(t o)` TINCCNTO2
```
requires { PC[t] = L_{yi} & & TP[t] = o}
{ t @ X[o] := True; ZF[t] := 1;
  PC[t] = L_{i+1} }
```

Comparison. We design three transitions for comparing a counter with the (parametric) number N of threads. To check if a counter is equal to N, we just check whether all cell of the array are **True**, using a universally quantified process variable. If it is the case, then the counter has reached the total number of threads, and the *zero flag* is set to 0. To check the opposite, we check if there exists a cell with the value **False**. In that case, the counter has not reached the total number of threads yet, so the *zero flag* is set to 1. Note that we need two transitions to achieve this: one to compare the cell owned by the executing thread, and another to compare any other cell.

$\mathcal{C}(t \; ; \; \text{cmp } x, N \; ; \; i) =$ TCMPCNTEQN

```
transition cmp_cnt_eqN_i(t)
requires { PC[t] = L_i
    && t @ X[t] = True
    && forall_other o.
            t @ X[o] = True }
{ ZF[t] = 0; PC[t] = L_xi }
```

                                       TCMPCNTSNEQN

```
transition cmp_cntS_NeqN_i(t)
requires { PC[t] = L_xi
    && t @ X[t] = False }
{ ZF[t] := 1; PC[t] = L_{i+1} }
```

                                       TCMPCNTONEQN

```
transition cmp_cntO_NeqN_i(t o)
requires { PC[t] = L_xi
    && t @ X[o] = False }
{ ZF[t] := 1; PC[t] = L_{i+1} }
```

Translation of programs

In order to compile all instructions of a thread, we define a compilation function $\mathcal{C}_t$ that takes as input a thread identifier and an instruction array. This function returns the set of Cubicle-$\mathcal{W}$ transitions corresponding to the translation of every instruction in the array.

$$\mathcal{C}_t(tid \; ; \; t) = \bigcup_{i=1}^{|t|} \mathcal{C}(tid \; ; \; t(i) \; ; \; i)$$

Similarly, we define a compilation function $\mathcal{C}_p$ that takes as input an x86 program and returns the set of transitions corresponding to the translation of every instruction in every thread.

$$\mathcal{C}_p(p) = \bigcup_{tid \, \in \, dom(p)} \mathcal{C}_t(tid \; ; \; p(tid))$$

Correctness

In order to prove the correctness of our approach, we demonstrate a simulation lemma between x86 programs and weak array-based transition systems obtained by translation.

Let $S = (LS \times M)$ be an x86-TSO machine state. Translating S to a Cubicle-$\mathcal{W}$ state A is straightforward, except for the memory map M and the contents of each thread buffer. For that, we define a predicate $\mathcal{T}(S, A)$ on Cubicle-$\mathcal{W}$ states such that $\mathcal{T}(S, A)$ is true if and only if:

- Local thread registers, eip and flags in LS contain the same values as their array-based representation
- For each local buffer B of a thread `tid` and for all shared variable X
  if $(X \notin B$ and $M(X) = v)$ or $(B = B_1 \mathbin{+\!+} (X, v) \mathbin{+\!+} B_2$ and $X \notin B_1)$ then
  - if X is a counter, then `tid @ X[k] = True` is true for v thread identifiers in A
  - otherwise, `tid @ X = v` is true in A

Lemma 1 (Simulation). *For all program p and state S, if $S \xrightarrow{tid:a} S'$ then their exists a Cubicle-$\mathcal{W}$ state A such that $\mathcal{T}(S, A)$ is true and $\mathcal{C}_p(p)$ can move from A to A' and $\mathcal{T}(S', A')$ is true as well.*

Proof. By a simple inspection of each transition rule of x86 instructions. See [15] for more details.

Theorem 1. *Given a program p, if Cubicle-$\mathcal{W}$ returns* safe *on $\mathcal{C}_p(p)$ then p cannot reach an unsafe state (as described in the section* unsafe_prop *of p).*

Proof. By induction on the length of the reduction $p \xrightarrow{tid:a}^{+} \bot$ and by case on each step (using simulation lemma).

5   Experiments

We used our framework to translate and check the correctness of several mutual exclusion algorithms, as well as a sense reversing barrier algorithm. In this section, we only describe two of them. The source code and Cubicle-$\mathcal{W}$ translations of all the examples can be found on the tool page [2].

Figure 3 is a spinlock implementation found in the Linux kernel (version 2.6.24.7), and is an example used in [25]. It requires a single shared variable Lock, initialized to 1, and the use of the *lock dec* instruction. The lock prefix is required to make this algorithm correct. To enter the critical section, a thread t has to atomically decrement the contents of the Lock variable. It then checks the result of the operation, using a conditional branch instruction: if the result is not negative, it means that Lock was 1 before the decrement, so t performs the branch to enter the critical section. If the result is negative, it means that Lock was 0 or less before the decrement, so another thread is already in the critical

```
begin shared_data
    Lock   dd   1
end shared_data

begin unsafe_prop
    eip[$t1] = cs &&
    eip[$t2] = cs
end unsafe_prop

begin init_code
    start_threads
end init_code
```

```
begin thread_code
acquire: lock dec dword [Lock]
         jns cs
spin:    cmp dword [Lock], 0
         jle spin
         jmp acquire
cs:      ; critical section
exit:    mov dword [Lock], 1
         jmp acquire
end thread_code
```

Fig. 3. A Linux spinlock implementation

section: t enters a spinlock, waiting for Lock to be 1 before retrying to enter the critical section. To release the lock, the thread in critical section simply sets back Lock to 1.

Our next example shown in Fig. 4 is a Sense Reversing Barrier [20]. It allows a number of threads to synchronize their execution flow at a specific program point. It requires a process counter count and a boolean variable sense that gives the sense of the barrier. It locally uses the esi register to track the current value of the sense variable. Initially, count is set to N, and sense and esi are to 0. Threads start by reversing esi. Then, each thread atomically decrements the count variable. If, as a result of this operation, the count is not 0, then the thread enters a spinlock that waits for sense to be equal to esi (that is, for the barrier sense to be changed). If however the count reaches 0, then the thread resets count to N and copies esi into sense, which in effect reverses the sense of the barrier. At this point, threads that were waiting at the spinlock are released.

```
begin shared_data
    sense   dd   0
    count   dd   N ! as counter
end shared_data

begin unsafe_prop
    eip[$t1] = entr &&
    eip[$t2] = end
end unsafe_prop

begin init_code
    start_threads
end init_code
```

```
begin thread_code
      mov esi, 0 ; esi = local sense
entr: not esi
      lock dec dword [count]
      jne spin
last: mov dword [count], N
      mov dword [sense], esi
      jmp end
spin: cmp dword [sense], esi
      jne spin
end:  nop
end thread_code
```

Fig. 4. A sense reversing barrier algorithm in x86

The results of our experiments are given in the table below. As a measure of the problem's complexity, we give the number of Registers, Weak variable and Transitions of the corresponding Cubicle-$\mathcal{W}$ program. The CE Length column gives the length of the counter-example, where applicable. It is the smallest number of transitions that lead to a state that violates the safety property. The Time column is the total time to prove the safety property (or to exhibit a counter-example). We considered both correct (S) and incorrect (US) versions of program. Incorrect versions are obtained by removing the lock prefixes.

Case study	Regs	Weak vars	Trans	CE length	Time
naive mutex (dlock.) (US)	3	2	11	12	0,38 s
naive mutex (no dlock.) (US)	3	2	14	12	0,38 s
mutex w/ $xchg$ (US)	4	1	8	10	0,07 s
mutex w/ $xchg$ (S)	3	1	7	–	0,08 s
mutex w/ $cmpxchg$ (US)	4	1	10	10	0,12 s
mutex w/ $cmpxchg$ (S)	4	1	8	–	0,47 s
Linux spinlock (US)	4	1	10	6	0,06 s
Linux spinlock (S)	4	1	9	–	0,30 s
sense barrier (sing. ent.) (S)	3	2	15	–	0,27 s
sense barrier (mult. ent.) (S)	3	2	16	–	1min37 s

6   Conclusion and Future Work

We have presented in this paper a compilation scheme from parameterized x86-TSO programs to weak array-based transitions systems in Cubicle-$\mathcal{W}$. The subset of the 32-bit x86 assembly instructions supported allows us to express critical concurrent primitives like mutexes and synchronization barriers. Experiments are promising. To our knowledge, this is the first tool for proving automatically the safety of parameterized x86-TSO programs.

An immediate line of future work is to enhance the subset of x86 that is supported according to new experiments that will be conducted. These adding should also be proved correct regarding the preservation of the TSO semantics. Another line of work will be to consider others memory models as a given input to the model checker and to make change in its reachability analysis algorithm accordingly.

References

1. Cubicle-W. https://www.lri.fr/~declerck/cubiclew/
2. PMCX86. https://www.lri.fr/~declerck/pmcx86/

3. Abdulla, P.A., Atig, M.F., Chen, Y.-F., Leonardsson, C., Rezine, A.: Counter-example guided fence insertion under TSO. In: Flanagan, C., König, B. (eds.) TACAS 2012. LNCS, vol. 7214, pp. 204–219. Springer, Heidelberg (2012). doi:10.1007/978-3-642-28756-5_15

4. Abdulla, P.A., Atig, M.F., Chen, Y.-F., Leonardsson, C., Rezine, A.: MEMORAX, a precise and sound tool for automatic fence insertion under TSO. In: Piterman, N., Smolka, S.A. (eds.) TACAS 2013. LNCS, vol. 7795, pp. 530–536. Springer, Heidelberg (2013). doi:10.1007/978-3-642-36742-7_37

5. Abdulla, P.A., Delzanno, G., Henda, N.B., Rezine, A.: Regular model checking without transducers (on efficient verification of parameterized systems). In: Grumberg, O., Huth, M. (eds.) TACAS 2007. LNCS, vol. 4424, pp. 721–736. Springer, Heidelberg (2007). doi:10.1007/978-3-540-71209-1_56

6. Abdulla, P.A., Delzanno, G., Rezine, A.: Parameterized verification of infinite-state processes with global conditions. In: Damm, W., Hermanns, H. (eds.) CAV 2007. LNCS, vol. 4590, pp. 145–157. Springer, Heidelberg (2007). doi:10.1007/978-3-540-73368-3_17

7. Alglave, J., Kroening, D., Nimal, V., Tautschnig, M.: Software verification for weak memory via program transformation. In: Felleisen, M., Gardner, P. (eds.) ESOP 2013. LNCS, vol. 7792, pp. 512–532. Springer, Heidelberg (2013). doi:10.1007/978-3-642-37036-6_28

8. Apt, K.R., Kozen, D.C.: Limits for automatic verification of finite-state concurrent systems. Inf. Process. Lett. **22**(6), 307–309 (1986)

9. Atig, M.F., Bouajjani, A., Burckhardt, S., Musuvathi, M.: On the verification problem for weak memory models. In: POPL, pp. 7–18 (2010)

10. Bouajjani, A., Derevenetc, E., Meyer, R.: Checking and enforcing robustness against TSO. In: Felleisen, M., Gardner, P. (eds.) ESOP 2013. LNCS, vol. 7792, pp. 533–553. Springer, Heidelberg (2013). doi:10.1007/978-3-642-37036-6_29

11. Bouajjani, A., Meyer, R., Möhlmann, E.: Deciding robustness against total store ordering. In: Aceto, L., Henzinger, M., Sgall, J. (eds.) ICALP 2011. LNCS, vol. 6756, pp. 428–440. Springer, Heidelberg (2011). doi:10.1007/978-3-642-22012-8_34

12. Burckhardt, S., Musuvathi, M.: Effective program verification for relaxed memory models. In: Gupta, A., Malik, S. (eds.) CAV 2008. LNCS, vol. 5123, pp. 107–120. Springer, Heidelberg (2008). doi:10.1007/978-3-540-70545-1_12

13. Burnim, J., Sen, K., Stergiou, C.: Sound and complete monitoring of sequential consistency for relaxed memory models. In: Abdulla, P.A., Leino, K.R.M. (eds.) TACAS 2011. LNCS, vol. 6605, pp. 11–25. Springer, Heidelberg (2011). doi:10.1007/978-3-642-19835-9_3

14. Clarke, E.M., Grumberg, O., Browne, M.C.: Reasoning about networks with many identical finite-state processes. In: PODC 1986, NY, USA. ACM, New York (1986)

15. Conchon, S., Declerck, D., Zaïdi, F.: Compiling parameterized X86-TSO concurrent programs to cubicle-W. https://www.lri.fr/~declerck/pmcx86.pdf

16. Conchon, S., Goel, A., Krstić, S., Mebsout, A., Zaïdi, F.: Cubicle: a parallel SMT-based model checker for parameterized systems. In: Madhusudan, P., Seshia, S.A. (eds.) CAV 2012. LNCS, vol. 7358, pp. 718–724. Springer, Heidelberg (2012). doi:10.1007/978-3-642-31424-7_55

17. Dan, A., Meshman, Y., Vechev, M., Yahav, E.: Effective abstractions for verification under relaxed memory models. In: D'Souza, D., Lal, A., Larsen, K.G. (eds.) VMCAI 2015. LNCS, vol. 8931, pp. 449–466. Springer, Heidelberg (2015). doi:10.1007/978-3-662-46081-8_25

18. German, S.M., Sistla, A.P.: Reasoning about systems with many processes. J. ACM **39**(3), 675–735 (1992)

19. Ghilardi, S., Ranise, S.: MCMT: a model checker modulo theories. In: Giesl, J., Hähnle, R. (eds.) IJCAR 2010. LNCS, vol. 6173, pp. 22–29. Springer, Heidelberg (2010). doi:10.1007/978-3-642-14203-1_3
20. Herlihy, M., Shavit, N.: The Art of Multiprocessor Programming. Morgan Kaufmann Publishers Inc., San Francisco (2008)
21. Intel Corporation: Intel 64 and IA-32 Architectures SDM, December 2016
22. Kuperstein, M., Vechev, M.T., Yahav, E.: Partial-coherence abstractions for relaxed memory models. In: PLDI, pp. 187–198 (2011)
23. Lamport, L.: How to make a multiprocessor computer that correctly executes multiprocess programs. IEEE Trans. Comput. **28**(9), 690–691 (1979)
24. Linden, A., Wolper, P.: A verification-based approach to memory fence insertion in PSO memory systems. In: Piterman, N., Smolka, S.A. (eds.) TACAS 2013. LNCS, vol. 7795, pp. 339–353. Springer, Heidelberg (2013). doi:10.1007/978-3-642-36742-7_24
25. Sewell, P., Sarkar, S., Owens, S., Nardelli, F.Z., Myreen, M.O.: X86-TSO: a rigorous and usable programmer's model for x86 multiprocessors. Commun. ACM **53**(7), 89–97 (2010)

Improving the Scalability of Automatic Linearizability Checking in SPIN

Patrick Doolan[1], Graeme Smith[2], Chenyi Zhang[3(✉)],
and Padmanabhan Krishnan[1]

[1] Oracle Labs, Brisbane, Australia
[2] The University of Queensland, Brisbane, Australia
[3] Jinan University, Guangzhou, China
chenyi_zhang@jnu.edu.cn

Abstract. Concurrency in data structures is crucial to the performance of multithreaded programs in shared-memory multiprocessor environments. However, greater concurrency also increases the difficulty of verifying correctness of the data structure. Model checking has been used for verifying concurrent data structures satisfy the correctness condition 'linearizability'. In particular, 'automatic' tools achieve verification without requiring user-specified linearization points. This has several advantages, but is generally not scalable. We examine the automatic checking used by Vechev et al. in their 2009 work to understand the scalability issues of automatic checking in SPIN. We then describe a new, more scalable automatic technique based on these insights, and present the results of a proof-of-concept implementation.

1 Introduction

How efficiently data structures are shared is a crucial factor in the performance of multithreaded programs in shared-memory multiprocessor environments [14]. This motivates programmers to create objects with fewer safety mechanisms (such as locks) to achieve greater concurrency. However, as noted by [14], any enhancement in the performance of these objects also increases the difficulty of verifying they behave as expected. Several published concurrent data structures – often with manual proofs of correctness – have been shown to contain errors (e.g., [7,18]). This has resulted in a wealth of research on proving the safety of these objects with minimal input from programmers.

To verify concurrent data structures it is necessary to have a suitable definition of correctness. The general consensus of the literature is that linearizability, first introduced in [10], is the appropriate notion of correctness. The definition of linearizability given by Vechev et al. [24] is summarised below.

Definition 1. *A concurrent data structure is **linearizable** if every concurrent/overlapping history of the data structure's operations has an equivalent sequential history that*

The corresponding author was at Oracle Labs, Australia during the initial stages of this work.

© Springer International Publishing AG 2017
Z. Duan and L. Ong (Eds.): ICFEM 2017, LNCS 10610, pp. 105–121, 2017.
https://doi.org/10.1007/978-3-319-68690-5_7

1. *meets a sequential specification of the data structure, and*
2. *respects the ordering of non-overlapping operations.*

Note that condition (2) is also referred to as the *partial ordering condition*. When discussing linearizability the sequential specification is often referred to as the *abstract specification*, and the implementation of the concurrent data structure the *concrete implementation*. The equivalent sequential history generated from a concurrent history is referred to as the *linearization* or *sequential witness*.

Given a sequential specification, a history can be checked for a linearization. This requires examining permutations of the history to identify whether any one of them is a linearization. This process is called *linearization checking* (not to be confused with the overall process of linearizability checking).

Example 1. Figure 1 shows a history of operations for a concurrent queue. By enumerating all permutations, it can be seen that this history has the linearization [enqueue(1), dequeue() → 1, enqueue(2)].

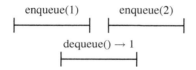

Fig. 1. A sample concurrent history with a linearization.   **Fig. 2.** A sample concurrent history with no linearization.

Conversely, consider Fig. 2, which is also a history of a concurrent queue. This does not have a linearization, because, by the partial ordering condition, enqueue(2) must linearize after enqueue(1). It follows that dequeue() can only correctly return 1 (if it linearizes after enqueue(1)) or 'empty' (if it linearizes before enqueue(1)). No sequential equivalent of this history will satisfy the sequential specification of a queue. This history is in fact a behaviour of the 'buggy queue' from [18].

Linearizability is useful for programmers because it allows them to view a concurrent data structure's operations as happening at a single point in time (called the *linearization point*) [14]. Furthermore, [9] proves that linearizability generally coincides with 'observational refinement', meaning that when a linearizable data structure replaces a correct but sub-optimal data structure, the new program produces a subset of its previous, acceptable behaviour.

In this paper we identify reasons why some of the techniques to verify linearizability are not scalable and present a technique that overcomes some of these hurdles. We also present experimental results to demonstrate the feasibility of our ideas.

1.1   Related Work

There are a wide variety of approaches used to verify linearizability of data structures. These range from manual proofs, possibly with the help of a theorem prover (see [16,22] respectively for examples with and without a theorem prover), to static and runtime analysis (e.g., [23,27], respectively) and model checking (e.g., [4,12,19,24]).

Model checkers give a high degree of automation because they work by exhaustive checking of behaviour, but are limited compared to other approaches because their verification is typically within bounds on the number of threads, arguments and other factors. We distinguish two approaches to model checking linearizability:

- *linearization point-based checking* requires the user to specify the linearization points (see [19] for an example), whereas
- *automatic checking* does not require user specification of linearization points (see [4,12,24]).

The latter has two advantages, viz., greater flexibility for data structures with non-fixed linearization points, and certainty that reported failures are from bugs in the data structure and not incorrectly identified linearization points.

There is a substantial literature on automatic checking which illustrates that many different model checkers and techniques have been used for this purpose. Vechev et al. [24] describe a tool for examining many potential versions of a data structure and determining which are linearizable. To this end they use both automatic and linearization point-based methods in SPIN [11]. They note, importantly, that automatic checking can be used to cull a large number of potential implementations but that its inherent scalability issues make it intractable for thorough checking.

Similarly, Liu et al. [12] use the model checker PAT [17,20] for automatic checking of linearizability. Both the implementation (the concurrent data structure) and the specification (the sequential behaviour) are modelled in the process algebra CSP, and the verification is carried out as checking observational refinement with certain optimizations. The verification process is, generally, automatic checking, though the results can be enhanced if linearization points are known. This result was further improved on by Zhang [28] by combining partial order reduction and symmetry reduction to narrow the potential state space, and in doing so they were able to verify concurrent data structures (albeit simple ones) for three to six threads. In contrast, automatic checking reported by Vechev et al. [24] only allows two threads, though the comparison may not be fair, as SPIN does not have built-in support for symmetry reduction.

Burckhardt et al. [4] describe the tool Line-Up, built on top of the model checker CHESS [15], for automatically checking linearizability of data structures. It is one of the most automated approaches to date; it does not require user-specified linearization points nor an abstract specification of the data structure (a specification is instead automatically extracted from the implementation). It also operates on actual code, as opposed to a model of the code.

The compromise for this convenience, as pointed out by [28], is that Line-Up is "only sound with respect to its inputs". Specifically, a user must specify which sequences of operations Line-Up checks, whereas other model checking techniques generate all possible sequences of operations (within bounds). Line-Up also requires that a specification be deterministic, as otherwise the extracted specification will misrepresent the actual abstract specification.

Regarding the complexities of linearizability checking, the problem has been shown decidable for a special class of concurrent linked-list, by a reduction to reachability of method automata [5]. As an observational refinement problem, checking linearizability is in general undecidable, and it is EXPSPACE-complete even with fixed linearization points [2]. More recently, Bouajjani et al. discovered that for a class of concurrent objects and data structures such as stacks and queues, the linearizability property can be reduced to the control state reachability problem [3].

1.2   Contributions

A notable theme in the related work is that automatic methods are considered to have inherent scalability issues for verification [12,24], though they can be used effectively when limits are placed on types or numbers of operations checked [4,24] or advanced state compression techniques are used [28]. However, the exact causes of the scalability issues are not discussed in detail, and there is some disagreement in the literature.

This paper explores in detail the causes of scalability issues in automatic checking, using the work of Vechev et al. [24] as our starting point. The insights derived are then used to describe a technique for improving the scalability of automatic checking methods using SPIN. Our solution, as currently implemented, is not sound and hence can only be used to find bugs. However, we describe how the technique can be extended to support verification.

The paper is structured as follows. In Sect. 2 we present our analysis of the scalability issues in the work of Vechev et al. [24]. A technique for overcoming these issues is presented in Sect. 3, and the results of applying an implementation of this technique to data structures from the literature with known bugs is described in Sect. 4. Also in Sect. 4 we discuss the main limitation of our technique which restricts it to bug finding, rather than full verification. Section 5 then describes how this limitation can be overcome and how the technique can be integrated into SPIN.

2   Scalability Issues of Automatic Checking with SPIN

To understand the scalability issues of automatic checking in [24], we first describe their methods. We will refer to their approach as using 'global internal recordings' since a (global) list of all invocations and responses of operations by any thread is recorded (internally) as part of the model checker's state.

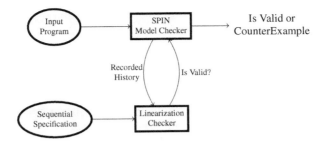

Fig. 3. Checking linearizability using global internal recordings.

Figure 3 depicts the process of checking with global internal recordings (based on the top right section of [24, Fig. 1]). In the input program, data structure models to be tested are instrumented so that client threads non-deterministically invoke operations on the data structure. Invocations and responses of operations are recorded during the state-space exploration. These recordings are then passed to an (external) linearization checker which searches for a valid linearization of the history. It searches by generating a permutation of the history, and then checking whether it satisfies conditions (1) and (2) of Definition 1. Note that condition (1) requires that the linearization checker has its own sequential specification of the data structure, separate from the model checker. If no such linearization can be found, the value returned by the linearization checker causes a local assertion to fail in the model checker.

2.1   Existing Explanations for the Scalability Issues of Automatic Checking

Though well-acknowledged in the literature, explanations for the scalability issues of automatic checking in [24] are not comprehensive. In [24], the authors assert that storing history recordings in the state during model checking limits the state space which can be explored, because "every time we append an element into [sic] the history, we introduce a new state".

In contrast, the authors of [12] consider linearization checking, not model checking, to be the performance-limiting factor of automatic checking in [24], stating that:

> "Their approach needs to find a linearizable sequence for each history . . . [and] may have to try all possible permutations of the history. As a result, the number of operations they can check is only 2 or 3."

Long and Zhang [13] describe heuristics for improving linearization checking. Their approach also suggests that linearization checking is a performance-limiting factor of automatic linearizability checking. Though their results show the effectiveness of their optimisations, they only test their methods on pre-generated traces; that is, without doing model checking to generate the traces.

As a result, the impact of these optimisations on overall linearizability checking is unclear.

2.2 Testing Explanations for the Scalability Issues of Automatic Checking

To test these different hypotheses, we conducted several preliminary experiments on a concurrent set provided as supplementary material by Vechev et al. [25]. All experiments were performed on a machine running Ubuntu 14.04.3 with 32 GB RAM and a 4-core Intel Core i7-4790 processor. The first compared the performance of automatic checking with and without the linearization checker; see Tables 1 and 2. Without the linearization checker, histories are explored by SPIN but not checked for linearizability. Checking with a linearization point-based approach is also shown for comparison.

In this experiment, two threads invoked operations on the data structure. For 6 operations, both automatic methods were given a moderate state compression setting (the built-in COLLAPSE flag in SPIN – see [11]) but failed to complete due to memory requirements. All times shown are the average of 10 executions. Note that SPIN was used with a single core to avoid time overhead for small tests and memory overhead for large tests.

The results clearly indicate model checking is the performance-limiting factor, since disabling linearization checking does not lead to performance comparable to checking with linearization points.

Table 1. Comparison of execution times for automatic and non-automatic checking methods of Vechev et al. [24]. All times in milliseconds.

Method	History length (# operations)		
	2	4	6
Linearization points	22	257	2160
Global internal recordings	33	10 590	Out of memory (30 GB)
Global internal recordings without linearization checker	33	10 240	Out of memory (30 GB)

Table 2. Comparison of memory use for automatic and non-automatic checking methods of Vechev et al. [24]. All measurements in MB.

Method	History length (# operations)		
	2	4	6
Linearization points	131.0	204.4	773.3
Global internal recordings	136.2	3780.80	Out of memory (30 GB)
Global internal recordings without linearization checker	136.2	3744.2	Out of memory (30 GB)

A second experiment investigated scalability issues in the model checking process. The number of states and histories explored in the same concurrent set were compared; see Tables 3, 4 and 5. For global internal recordings, histories were recorded by modifying the linearization checker. Each time the linearization checker was invoked, the history it was acting on was recorded. When checking with linearization points, the SPIN model was instrumented to output each operation as it was checked. The histories checked were then reconstructed from the output list of recordings.[1]

Note that states 'stored' refers to the number of distinct states in the state space, whereas states 'matched' refers to how many times a state was revisited [11]. Together they give an indication of how much state space exploration occurred.

Table 3. Comparison of states stored by global internal recordings and linearization points methods.

Method	History length (# operations)		
	2	4	6
Linearization points	21 198	1 215 501	12 899 275
Global internal recordings	25 740	12 693 435	Out of memory (30 GB)

Table 4. Comparison of states matched by global internal recordings and linearization points methods.

Method	History length (# operations)		
	2	4	6
Linearization points	4514	329 884	3 765 699
Global internal recordings	4699	2 570 412	Out of memory (30 GB)

Table 5. Comparison of histories checked by global internal recordings and linearization points methods.

Method	History length (# operations)		
	2	4	6
Linearization points	165	2876	9783
Global internal recordings	296	133 536	Out of memory (30 GB)

Tables 3 and 4 confirm the statement of [24] – many more states are explored using automatic checking. However, the magnitude of the difference suggests

---

[1] Note that reconstruction of histories required adding a global index variable which would not normally be used in checking with linearization points and inflates the state space for reasons explained later in this section. The number of states and number of histories listed for checking with linearization points are therefore over-estimates.

more than just one state is introduced by each recording. Table 5 also reveals some implications not immediately evident from previous explanations – that checking with global internal recordings generates and checks many more histories than checking with linearization points. Because this is not encoded manually by the different approaches, it suggests an optimisation by SPIN which allows checking with linearization points to shrink the state space and remove histories which are unnecessary for verifying linearizability.

An interesting trend from the results was the ratio of 'matched' (revisited) to 'stored' (total distinct) states, which was higher for checking done with linearization points. For example, in the case of 2 operations, even though checking with linearization points has 4000 fewer states, it revisits them almost as much as global internal recordings checking. This provides some insight as to why it checks many fewer histories and has vastly better performance.

It was found that the histories checked with linearization points are a strict subset of those checked using global internal recordings. The histories missing from linearization points checking were due to the model checker stopping and backtracking in the middle of a history. That is, SPIN would generate the start of the history but stop before generating some of the recordings for the end of the history. For example, Fig. 4 shows a history that is missed when checking a concurrent set using linearization points. The point 'X' shows where checking for this history stops.

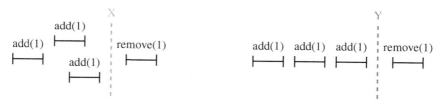

Fig. 4. A missing history when model checking with linearization points.

Fig. 5. A history that precedes the missing history.

After examining such histories and considering the algorithm applied by SPIN for model checking it became apparent that the reason SPIN stopped preemptively in some histories was the presence of repeated states. Explicit-state model checking algorithms optimise state space exploration by not returning to a state if all of the possibilities extending from that state have been previously checked (see, for example, [1]).

For example, when checking with global internal recordings, the history in Fig. 4 occurs (in the search process) after the history shown in Fig. 5. When checking with linearization points, at the point X the global state in the history of Fig. 4 matches the global state at point Y in Fig. 5, so the model checker does not proceed any further.

This explains the large number of states and histories generated by global internal recordings. Because of the recordings, states which would otherwise appear identical to SPIN are differentiated. SPIN therefore continues to search down the branch of the state space, whereas with linearization points it would backtrack.

3   A Technique for Improving Scalability of Automatic Checking

We now describe a new automatic checking technique. The key insight is to improve scalability by storing less global data, allowing SPIN to optimise state space exploration by backtracking. The technique is referred to as 'external checking' because it outputs recordings which are stored by the model checker in the automatic checking of [24].

The description provided in this section is for a proof-of-concept implementation using machinery built to work with SPIN. Unfortunately, subtle issues in the state space exploration technique make this implementation an unsound checking procedure for verification. In Sect. 5 we describe the reasons for this unsoundness and present a sound and complete checking procedure that extends the basic idea. Implementing the extension would require altering the SPIN source code and is left for future work.

3.1   External Checking: Preliminary Implementation

The general concept is similar to that of automatic checking with global internal recordings because each history is checked for a linearization. The implementation is also similar, viz., client threads non-deterministically invoke operations on the concurrent data structure to generate the histories. The key difference is that the external checking method outputs information about the operations to an external linearization checker as they occur, rather than keeping an internal list of recordings until the end of each history.

A simplistic approach was taken to outputting recordings externally. An embedded printf statement was included in the Promela model whenever an invocation or response occurred. For example,

```
c_code{printf("%d %d %d %d %d %d\n", now.gix,
    Pclient->par, Pclient->op, Pclient->retval,
    Pclient->arg, Pclient->type);}
```

outputs the index of the recording in the history (gix), the parent recording (i.e., invocation) of the operation if it was a response (par), the operation (op), argument (arg), return value (retval) and whether this was an invocation or response (type) for the thread 'client' (Pclient).

External checking requires that output recordings be assembled into complete histories, since the recordings are output in the order in which SPIN explores the state space. Since SPIN uses a depth-first search of the state space, this simply requires iterating over the list of recordings and outputting a history whenever the last recording (a complete history) is reached.[2] In pseudocode,

```
Recording current_history[history_length];
for (Recording recording : output_recordings) {
    current_history[recording.index] = recording;
    if (recording.index == history_length) {
        //leaf node in the search tree
        outputHistory(current_history);
    }
}
```

A process takes the output from SPIN and reconstructs the histories as shown above. It then passes the histories to the linearization checker which checks each history for a linearization. The entire external checking procedure is illustrated in Fig. 6. Compare this to Fig. 3 for checking with global recordings. Note that the external linearization checker runs concurrently with the model checker. If a failure (non-linearizable history) occurs, it notifies the model checker and both stop.

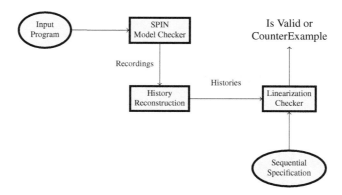

Fig. 6. The external checking procedure.

Note that at present external checking is only suitable for use with single-core SPIN checking. Using several cores changes how the state space is explored and therefore how recordings are output, so it requires understanding a different state space exploration algorithm and also the capacity to determine from which core the recordings originated. Further work could explore implementing these features.

---

[2] Note that histories are limited to a given length to make model checking feasible.

4   Results

Three popular data structures from the literature with known defects were used for testing the effectiveness of the external checking method. These data structures are summarised in Table 6. It is important to note that both the buggy queue and the Snark deque were originally published with proofs of correctness, and only later found to be defective. They therefore represent realistic examples of bugs in concurrent data structures. The ABA problem, tested for in both the Treiber Stack and Snark deque, is also a common problem with concurrent data structures which use the compare-and-swap primitive.

Table 6. Faulty data structures used for testing external checking.

Data structure	Source	Description of bug
Treiber stack	[21]	Suffers from the ABA problem in non-memory managed environments. Excellent explanation in [26, Sect. 1.2.4]
Buggy queue	[18]	When a dequeue is interrupted by two enqueues at critical sections, the dequeue returns a value not from front of the queue. See [6, Sect. 3.3]
Snark deque	[7]	Two bugs, the first of which can cause either popLeft or popRight to return empty when the queue is nonempty, and the second of which is an ABA-type error resulting in the return of an already popped value. See [8, Sect. 3] for detailed descriptions

Promela models of the data structures in Table 6 were created and instrumented to allow automatic checking both externally and via global internal recordings. In cases where more than one bug existed in a single data structure, each bug was repaired after being flagged so that others could be tested. Experiments were performed on a machine running Ubuntu 14.04.3 with 32 GB RAM and a 4-core Intel Core i7-4790 processor, with the exception of the final Snark deque bug. Its tests were executed on a machine running Oracle Linux 6 with two 22-core Intel Xeon CPU E5-2699 v4 processors and 378 GB RAM due to high memory requirements. SPIN was used with a single core to avoid time overhead for small tests and memory overhead for large tests. Also, external checking does not currently support checking with multiple cores.

External checking located all bugs. Global checking found all except the final Snark deque bug - after 2.87×10^7 ms (~ 8 h) the memory limit of 300000 MB was reached and SPIN exited without locating the bug. The results of testing for detected bugs are shown in Table 7. For the first 3 bugs, no state compression flags were needed, and only 2 threads and 4 operations were required for detection. Times shown are an average of 10 executions for both methods. For

Table 7. Bugs detected by external checking and global recordings checking.

Data structure	Bug number	External checking		Global recordings checking	
		Time (ms)	Memory (MB)	Time (ms)	Memory (MB)
Treiber stack	1/1	373	172	1346	342
Buggy queue	1/1	248	159	774	252
Snark deque	1/2	86	139	123	145
Snark deque	2/2	2.71×10^7	248227	–	–

the final snark deque bug, the COLLAPSE memory compression flag was used (see [11] for details), as the failure trace required 3 threads and 7 operations. Trials for this bug were run once due to resource constraints.

4.1 Discussion of External Checking Performance

The results in Table 7 illustrate the utility of the external checking method. It was able to locate all bugs, even without the improvements described in Sect. 5. This suggests it is uncommon in practice that a bug cannot be detected by the method.

In addition, external checking was both faster and used less memory than global checking in all cases. For the Treiber stack and buggy queue, memory use was roughly half that of global recordings checking, and checking was around three times faster.

In the case of the second Snark deque bug, there was sufficient memory for external checking to find the bug, but not enough for global recordings checking. Of course, global recordings checking would detect the bug if sufficient memory or time were available, since it is a verification technique. However, the results show it requires *at least* 50 GB more memory than external checking (or the equivalent amount of time with a stronger compression), which illustrates the benefit of a faster bug-finding technique for bugs with long failure traces.

For comparison, tests with linearization point-based checking show that this bug can be located in under 30 min with COLLAPSE state compression, illustrating that automatic methods are not as scalable as linearization points-based methods.

The two automatic methods are closest in performance for the first bug of the Snark deque. This is because the failing history occurs very early in the model checking process. External checking takes longer to check any individual history because it must be reconstructed and then passed to the linearization checker. Its performance benefit comes from checking far fewer histories. Therefore when a bug occurs after only very few histories, external checking does not have time to yield a significant performance benefit. Conversely, the deeper the execution required to locate a bug, the greater the improvement in performance compared to global internal recordings.

5   Potential Improvements: Integration with SPIN

The technique described in Sect. 3.1 is in fact unsound. Recall from Sect. 2.2 that checking with linearization points covers fewer histories due to SPIN optimisations that cause it to stop at repeated states. This is valid with linearization point-based checking because such approaches include an abstract specification that runs in parallel with the model of the concrete implementation. The state variables of the abstract specification ensure that the sub-history encountered before backtracking is truly equivalent to one checked earlier.

However, in external checking no abstract specification is kept by SPIN. This means there are cases where SPIN stops preemptively and this prevents it checking a history that could violate linearizability.

For example, consider the sequential specification of a data structure as shown in Fig. 7. Suppose this specification was incorrectly implemented as shown in Fig. 8. If checking on a single thread is used, the SPIN output (shown diagrammatically) is as in Fig. 9.

```
int x = 0;
atomic operation 1:
    x++;
    return x;
atomic operation 2:
    return True;
```

```
int x = 0;
operation 1:
    x++;
    return x;
operation 2:
    if (x == 0)
        x = 1;
    return True;
```

Fig. 7. Abstract specification.   **Fig. 8.** Incorrect implementation.

Checking stops before the end of the third (faulty) history, and therefore it is not checked and no error is raised. The model checker stops because of the repeated global state x = 1. It reaches this state after operation1 in the first two histories and from those histories has explored all states extending from that

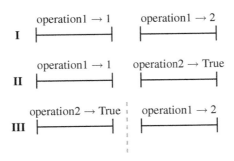

Fig. 9. Histories output by SPIN when using external checking on the data structure of Fig. 8. The dashed line indicates SPIN stopping.

point. When SPIN encounters the same state after `operation2` completes in the third history, it stops, despite the global state being incorrect for an execution of `operation2`.

Note that checking with linearization points, where an abstract specification is included, would prevent this error, since the abstract specification's `operation1` and `operation2` will alter the global data differently.

5.1   A Sound Verification Algorithm

We now describe a means of extending our technique for verification, which requires modifying the SPIN source. Doing this would also lead to a significant performance benefit.

Outputting recordings requires keeping track of a global index. As Sect. 2.2 showed, global variables tracked by SPIN can unnecessarily inflate the state space. If SPIN were modified it would not be necessary to keep a global index as a global variable in the model – it could be kept as metadata instead.

Likewise, the machinery of Sect. 3.1 could be implemented in a very similar fashion in SPIN. Instead of outputting recordings, it could be stored as metadata separate from the state vector and model checking process. Complete histories would still have to be passed to an external linearization checker, as was done in [24].

We now outline the extra checking necessary to prevent the missing histories described in the previous section, making the approach sound. It was noted that repeated global states cause the lack of soundness. This problem does not occur when checking with linearization points because the abstract specification is present in the global state and represents the expected behaviour of the implementation. Therefore a repeated state always indicates identical behaviour.

Incorrect backtracking in external checking could therefore be prevented by using the abstract specification to decide when a repeated global state represents correct behaviour of the implementation. We propose the following method: whenever a repeated global state is reached, ensure that the current sub-history has a linearization which leads to the same state in the abstract specification as the sub-history which originally created that global state. This would require keeping track of the valid linearizations for previously encountered histories.

For example, suppose during checking histories for a stack implementation, the model checker had explored all states extending from the global state G, as shown in Fig. 10. This implies every full history reached from G with the sub-history shown in Fig. 10 had a linearization. In verifying this, the linearization checker would have found that the operations before G have the valid linearization [push(1) $\rightarrow$ `True`, pop() $\rightarrow$ 1]. Therefore the abstract state at G was an empty stack in all of the checked histories represented by Fig. 10.

Suppose the sub-history shown in Fig. 11 then occurred, repeating the global state G. To determine whether backtracking is correct, it suffices to check that the sub-history up to G has a linearization which would lead to an empty stack in the abstract specification. In this case it is possible by the linearization [push(1) $\rightarrow$ `True`, pop() $\rightarrow$ 1, pop() $\rightarrow$ `empty`]. This means SPIN can backtrack safely.

Fig. 10. Example history.   **Fig. 11.** Second example history.

In contrast, recall the counter-example to verification from Fig. 9. In this example, the histories verified by the model checker (histories I and II) have linearizations [operation1 → 1, operation1 → 2] and [operation1 → 1, operation2 → True], respectively. That is, in both cases the linearization up to the repeated state is operation1 → 1, meaning the abstract specification state at that point is x = 1. When the same global state is reached in history III, there is no linearization of operation2 → True which leads to the abstract state x = 1. Only x = 0 is possible. Therefore in the proposed implementation SPIN cannot backtrack after operation2 → True and the entire history would be checked and found invalid.

Note that this extended approach requires checking for linearizations, metadata caching and the usual state exploration of model checking. Performance could be improved by a high degree of parallelism between these separate functions.

6 Conclusions

We have described in detail the scalability issues of automatic linearizability checking in [24]. The main cause is a lack of state space traversal optimisations due to a large amount of global data in the model checking state. This identified cause makes explicit a fact which is widely assumed in the literature but whose explanation is often omitted or unclear.

These observations motivated a new, more scalable technique for automatic checking with SPIN. The key insight is to *not store the recordings* in the model checker for checking at the end of each history, but instead to output them immediately. This allows the model checker to optimise the state space exploration. The algorithm we have implemented reconstructs the histories from the recordings and determines if these histories satisfy the linearization conditions. Our experiments show that the extra cost of generating the history from the recordings that are output directly is smaller than the speed-up gained from the more efficient execution of the model checker.

This external checking technique reduces the number of histories that need exploration and thus is able to explore longer traces. As a consequence bugs that occur on long traces are detected more efficiently than when using the global internal recordings technique in the literature. External checking does detect bugs that occur after a few histories but the performance benefits are not significant. In other words, the more states the model checker is required to explore before it can detect a bug, the more effective our technique will be.

We have also presented a limitation of the implemented external checking technique (namely, that it can be used for bug detection but not verification). We have developed an algorithm that overcomes this limitation, and intend to implement this in SPIN as future work. Note that if only an efficient bug detection technique is desired, the external checking algorithm described in Sect. 3 would suffice.

Acknowledgments. The authors would like to thank Martin Vechev for providing extra materials that allowed evaluation of the automatic checking in [24]. This work is partially supported by ARC Discovery Grant DP160102457.

References

1. Baier, C., Katoen, J.-P.: Principles of Model Checking. The MIT Press, Cambridge (2008)
2. Bouajjani, A., Emmi, M., Enea, C., Hamza, J.: Verifying concurrent programs against sequential specifications. In: Felleisen, M., Gardner, P. (eds.) ESOP 2013. LNCS, vol. 7792, pp. 290–309. Springer, Heidelberg (2013). doi:10.1007/978-3-642-37036-6_17
3. Bouajjani, A., Emmi, M., Enea, C., Hamza, J.: On reducing linearizability to state reachability. In: Halldórsson, M.M., Iwama, K., Kobayashi, N., Speckmann, B. (eds.) ICALP 2015. LNCS, vol. 9135, pp. 95–107. Springer, Heidelberg (2015). doi:10.1007/978-3-662-47666-6_8
4. Burckhardt, S., Dern, C., Musuvathi, M., Tan, R.: Line-up: a complete and automatic linearizability checker. In: PLDI 2010, Proceedings of 2010 ACM SIGPLAN Conference on Programming Language Design and Implementation, pp. 330–340. ACM, New York (2010)
5. Černý, P., Radhakrishna, A., Zufferey, D., Chaudhuri, S., Alur, R.: Model checking of linearizability of concurrent list implementations. In: Touili, T., Cook, B., Jackson, P. (eds.) CAV 2010. LNCS, vol. 6174, pp. 465–479. Springer, Heidelberg (2010). doi:10.1007/978-3-642-14295-6_41
6. Colvin, R., Groves, L.: Formal verification of an array-based nonblocking queue. In: ICECCS 2005, pp. 507–516. IEEE, Los Alamitos (2005)
7. Detlefs, D.L., Flood, C.H., Garthwaite, A.T., Martin, P.A., Shavit, N.N., Steele, G.L.: Even better DCAS-based concurrent deques. In: Herlihy, M. (ed.) DISC 2000. LNCS, vol. 1914, pp. 59–73. Springer, Heidelberg (2000). doi:10.1007/3-540-40026-5_4
8. Doherty, S., Detlefs, D.L., Groves, L., Flood, C.H., Luchangco, V., Martin, P.A., Moir, M., Shavit, N., Steele Jr., G.L.: DCAS is not a silver bullet for nonblocking algorithm design. In: Gibbons, P.B., Adler, M. (eds.) SPAA 2004, pp. 216–224. ACM, New York (2004)
9. Filipovic, I., O'Hearn, P.W., Rinetzky, N., Yang, H.: Abstraction for concurrent objects. Theor. Comput. Sci. **411**(51–52), 4379–4398 (2010)
10. Herlihy, M.P., Wing, J.M.: Linearizability: a correctness condition for concurrent objects. ACM Trans. Program. Lang. Syst. **12**(3), 463–492 (1990)
11. Holzmann, G.J.: The SPIN Model Checker: Primer and Reference Manual. Addison-Wesley, Reading (2003)

12. Liu, Y., Chen, W., Liu, Y.A., Sun, J.: Model checking linearizability via refinement. In: Cavalcanti, A., Dams, D.R. (eds.) FM 2009. LNCS, vol. 5850, pp. 321–337. Springer, Heidelberg (2009). doi:10.1007/978-3-642-05089-3_21

13. Long, Z., Zhang, Y.: Checking linearizability with fine-grained traces. In: SAC 2016, pp. 1394–1400. ACM, New York (2016)

14. Moir, M., Shavit, N.: Concurrent data structures. In: Mehta, D.P., Sahni, S. (eds.) Handbook of Data Structures and Applications, Chap. 47, pp. 1–30. Chapman and Hall, CRC Press (2004)

15. Research in Software Engineering Group (RiSE). http://chesstool.codeplex.com/

16. Schellhorn, G., Derrick, J., Wehrheim, H.: A sound and complete proof technique for linearizability of concurrent data structures. ACM Trans. Comput. Log. **15**(4), 31:1–31:37 (2014)

17. School of Computing, National University of Singapore. http://pat.comp.nus.edu. sg/

18. Shann, C.H., Huang, T.L., Chen, C.: A practical nonblocking queue algorithm using compare-and-swap. In: ICPADS 2000, pp. 470–475. IEEE, Los Alamitos (2000)

19. Smith, G.: Model checking simulation rules for linearizability. In: De Nicola, R., Kühn, E. (eds.) SEFM 2016. LNCS, vol. 9763, pp. 188–203. Springer, Cham (2016). doi:10.1007/978-3-319-41591-8_13

20. Sun, J., Liu, Y., Dong, J.S., Pang, J.: PAT: towards flexible verification under fairness. In: Bouajjani, A., Maler, O. (eds.) CAV 2009. LNCS, vol. 5643, pp. 709–714. Springer, Heidelberg (2009). doi:10.1007/978-3-642-02658-4_59

21. Treiber, R.K.: Systems Programming: Coping with Parallelism. International Business Machines Incorporated, Thomas J. Watson Research Center, New York (1986)

22. Vafeiadis, V., Parkinson, M.: A marriage of rely/guarantee and separation logic. In: Caires, L., Vasconcelos, V.T. (eds.) CONCUR 2007. LNCS, vol. 4703, pp. 256–271. Springer, Heidelberg (2007). doi:10.1007/978-3-540-74407-8_18

23. Vafeiadis, V.: Shape-value abstraction for verifying linearizability. In: Jones, N.D., Müller-Olm, M. (eds.) VMCAI 2009. LNCS, vol. 5403, pp. 335–348. Springer, Heidelberg (2008). doi:10.1007/978-3-540-93900-9_27

24. Vechev, M., Yahav, E., Yorsh, G.: Experience with model checking linearizability. In: Păsăreanu, C.S. (ed.) SPIN 2009. LNCS, vol. 5578, pp. 261–278. Springer, Heidelberg (2009). doi:10.1007/978-3-642-02652-2_21

25. Vechev, M., Yahav, E., Yorsh, G.: Paraglide: SPIN Models. http://researcher. watson.ibm.com/researcher/view_group_subpage.php?id=1290

26. Wolff, S.: Thread-modular reasoning for heap-manipulating programs: exploiting pointer race freedom. Master's thesis, University of Kaiserslautern (2015)

27. Zhang, L., Chattopadhyay, A., Wang, C.: Round-up: runtime checking quasi linearizability of concurrent data structures. In: Denney, E., Bultan, T., Zeller, A. (eds.) ASE 2013, pp. 4–14. IEEE, Los Alamitos (2013)

28. Zhang, S.J.: Scalable automatic linearizability checking. In: ICSE 2011, Proceedings of 33rd International Conference on Software Engineering, pp. 1185–1187. ACM, New York (2011)

Verifying Temporal Properties of C Programs via Lazy Abstraction

Zhao Duan, Cong Tian$^{(\boxtimes)}$, and Zhenhua Duan

ICTT and ISN Lab, Xidian University, Xi'an 710071, People's Republic of China
`ctian@mail.xidian.edu.cn`

Abstract. To verify both safety and liveness temporal properties of programs in practice, this paper investigates scalable Linear Temporal Logic (LTL) property verification approach of C programs. We show that the verification target can be accomplished as a scalable lazy abstraction supplemented Counter-Example Guided Abstraction Refinement (CEGAR) based program analysis task. As a result, the scalable lazy abstraction based safety property analysis approaches as well as their mature supporting tools can be reused to verify temporal properties of C programs. We have implemented the proposed approach in TPCHECKER to verify temporal properties of C programs. Experimental results on benchmark programs show that the proposed approach performs well when verifying non-safety temporal properties of C programs.

Keywords: Temporal property · Lazy abstraction · Linear temporal logic · Model checking · CEGAR

1 Introduction

Model checking [1,2] is an automatic approach for discovering flaws in programs. However, when it is applied in practice, most of the respective verification tools lack scalability due to the state-space explosion problem [18]. Abstraction technique is useful in reducing the state space of the system to be verified. It maps a concrete set of states to a smaller set of states that is actually an approximation of the concrete system. Predicate abstraction [19] is one of the most often used methods in software model checking for attaining a finite abstract model from a program. With predicate abstraction, a finite set of predicates, which determines the precision of the abstraction, is selected to keep track of certain facts about the program variables. The model obtained via predicate abstraction is an over-approximation of the original program. Thus, spurious paths may exist if an insufficient set of predicates is considered.

In order to eliminate spurious counterexamples (false alarms), predicate abstraction has been paired with Counter-Example Guided Abstraction Refinement (CEGAR) [3,21,22] where a reported counterexample is further analyzed

This research is supported by the NSFC Grant No. 61420106004.

Z. Duan and L. Ong (Eds.): ICFEM 2017, LNCS 10610, pp. 122–139, 2017.
https://doi.org/10.1007/978-3-319-68690-5_8

to check whether it is spurious. If the counterexample is spurious, additional predicates are required for eliminating it. Cooperating with CEGAR, Interpolation [20] is often used to discover new predicates. Currently, CEGAR has been popular in most of the software model checkers. To further enhance the efficiency, lazy abstraction [16] is introduced in CEGAR to reduce the cost of time used for refinement. As a result, different parts of the model may exhibit different degrees of precision, but it is enough for verifying the property. Lazy abstraction supplemented CEGAR has been implemented in software model checkers [3] such as BLAST, CPAChecker, SLAM, and so forth. Thanks to these efforts, software model checkers are able to work on software systems with industrial scale.

Most of the CEGAR based software model checkers available are typically used for verifying safety properties expressed as assertions in the code. But they can only be utilized to verify limited temporal properties of programs [23]. Many important properties of programs itself or requirements on the software behavior cannot, however, be expressed as safety properties. These properties have components that assert something must eventually happen. A common example of our daily life computer programs is: if a memory chunk is dynamically allocated for temporal use, it should eventually be released before it is unable to be released (not referenced by any pointer variables). This presents that memory leak is not permitted to occur in a program. Whenever this property is not valid on a program, the allocated memory chunk will be leaked. This is a typically simple but non-safety property which is often desired to be valid on programs. Therefore, how to support the verification of more temporal properties in software model checking is useful in ensuring the correctness of programs in practice. Furthermore, in case that the verification of rich temporal properties is supported, the scale of programs that can be verified is a key issue which directly decides whether the methods or tools are applicable for industrial designs.

Motivated by this, we present a lazy abstraction supplemented CEGAR based Linear Temporal Logic (LTL) [6,7] property verification approach of C programs in this paper. We choose LTL instead of Computing Tree Logic (CTL) [1] since it has been proved by the common wisdom amongst users and developers of tools that LTL is more intuitive than CTL. To further improve the efficiency, under the consideration that most of the programs in real world are terminable, we also provide an efficient approach for verifying temporal properties of C programs over finite traces by simplifing the general LTL to LTL interpreted over finite models. For programs whose executing traces are finite, utilizing LTL over finite models to specify properties will lose nothing but make the verification more efficient. This is mainly because to obtain a deterministic automaton from a formula in LTL over finite models is much more easier than obtaining one from a formula in LTL (over infinite models). We present an efficient algorithm for building Deterministic Finite Automata (DFA) from LTL formulas over finite models. By integrating the DFA construction process into the construction of Abstract Reachability Tree (ART) for creating counterexamples, we show that the temporal property verification task can be accomplished by the scalable lazy abstraction based program analyzing. As a result, the scalable lazy abstraction supplemented CEGAR based safety property analysis approaches as well as their mature supporting tools, such as BLAST, CPAChecker, and SLAM, etc., can be reused to verify temporal properties of programs. We have implemented the proposed approach in TPCHECKER to verify temporal properties of C programs. Experimental results on benchmark programs show that the proposed approach performs well in practice when it is used to verify non-safety properties of real world programs.

As a summary, we make the following main contributions: (1) We extend the scalable lazy abstraction supplemented CEGAR based safety property verification to LTL specified temporal property verification of C programs. (2) We formalize an efficient LTL model checking approach of C programs over finite traces. With this approach, path explosion problem is largely relieved in software model checking. (3) We provide a scalable software model checker with the ability of temporal property verification. As a result, temporal properties expressible in LTL can be verified.

The reminder of the paper is organized as follows. The next section introduces Linear Temporal Logic (LTL) and extends the existing lazy abstraction supplemented CEGAR based safety verification approach to verify temporal properties of programs and points out the challenge problem involved in the field. In Sect. 3, an efficient verification approach is presented for verifying temporal properties of programs over finite traces. Section 4 presents implementation of the supporting tool and Sect. 5 shows the experimental results. Finally, in Sect. 6, related work is discussed.

2   A General Approach

This section presents a general approach for verifying temporal properties of programs with CEGAR supplemented by lazy abstraction. We start by a short exposition of CEGAR supplemented by lazy abstraction based safety property verification of C programs. Then we show how it can be extended to temporal property verification and point out the challenging problem.

2.1   Safety Property Verification

With lazy abstraction based property verification approach, the data structures Control Flow Automaton (CFA) and Abstract Reachability Tree (ART) play important roles.

A CFA is a directed graph presented as a tuple (L, E, I) where L is the set of locations, E the set of edges between two locations, and I a function that maps an edge to an instruction that executes when control moves from the source to the destination. An instruction is either a basic block of assignments, an assume predicate corresponding to the condition that must hold for the control to proceed across the edge, a function call with call-by-value parameters, or a return instruction. For convenience, in a CFA, the set of succeeding locations of a location $l \in L$ is denoted as $Suc(l)$, and the set of predecessors of l is written as $Pre(l)$. Also, $I(e)$ indicates the instruction labeled on edge e.

An ART is a labeled tree that represents a portion of the reachable state space of a program. Each node of the ART is labeled with a location of the relative CFA, the current call stack (a sequence of CFA locations representing return addresses), and a set of predicates (called the reachable region) representing a set of data states. We denote a labeled tree node by $n : (q, s, p)$, where n is the tree node, q is the CFA location, s is a sequence of CFA locations, and p is a set of predicates denoting the reachable region of n. Similar to the CFA, each edge of the tree is also marked with a basic block of assignments, an assume predicate, a function call, or a return instruction in the program.

A path in the ART corresponds to a program execution. The reachable region of a node n describes an over-approximation of the reachable states of the program assuming execution follows the sequence of operations labeling the path from the root of the tree to n. Intuitively, a complete ART is a finite unfolding of a CFA. As a consequence, the less predicates are cared about, the smaller the complete ART will be, and the more efficient the verification on this ART will be. As a special case, a CFA can be seen as an ART with $p = \emptyset$ for each node. However, a reported path that violates the desired property, i.e. a path satisfies the undesired property, in the ART is possible to be spurious which does not exist in the concrete program. Thereby, lazy abstraction supplemented CEGAR approach is utilized to eliminate spurious counterexamples by considering more predicates discovered via interpolation [11].

2.2 Verifying Temporal Properties of General Programs

Different from the safety property verification approach discussed above, to verify temporal properties of programs, we do not need to instrument assertions in the code. Instead, we specify the undesired property as an LTL formula. Then, we unwind the CFA as an ART to check whether there exits a path that can satisfy the formula. The rest thing is nearly the same as in safety property verification. That is if no paths that violate the desired property are found, the program can be proved free of the specific error. Otherwise, CEGAR supplemented with lazy abstraction is utilized to eliminate spurious counterexamples. We now concentrate on how the second phase will be carried on to produce a candidate counterexample.

To verify whether a path in an ART satisfies the undesired property written as an LTL formula, we first transform the LTL specification to an equivalent Büchi automaton. About the transformation, lots of theoretical research have been done and several mature tools were developed in the past years [17,24,25]. Then we construct the ART under the guidance of the Büchi automaton until a complete path is formed. If the path formed can be accepted by the Büchi automaton, a candidate counterexample is found. To record the information about the state of the Büchi automaton whose successors should be traversed through the construction of ART, we further enrich the ART as enriched ART (eART).

Definition 1. *Enriched Abstract Reachability Tree (eART) is an ART with an extra state f in the relative Büchi automaton decorated on each node expressing that the Büchi automaton is running at state f. Precisely, a node in an eART is denoted by n : (q, s, p, f), where n, q, s, and p are the same as in ART, and f is a state in the relative Büchi automaton.*

An eART can be seen as the product of an ART of the program and the Büchi automaton equivalent to the LTL specification. Thus, a path (infinite) in the eART which can be accepted by the Büchi automaton presents a flaw that violates the desired property. Note that here all paths are infinite since LTL formulas are tranditionally interpreted over infinite models. This can be accomplished by adding a do-nothing self-loop at the last node of a finite path in the ART in case the program is terminable.

Algorithm 2.1. Producing a counterexamples under the guidance of Büchi automaton

---

Input: A CFA and a Büchi automaton
Output: A counterexample
1 Set $Node\_Set$;
2 Stack $Node\_Stack$;
3 Create the root node $n_0 : (q_0, s_0, p_0, f_0)$ with $n_0.q$ being the initial location in the CFA, $n_0.s$ empty, $n_0.p$ empty, and $n_0.f$ the initial state in the Büchi automaton;
4 push($Node\_Stack, n_0$);
5 **while** $Node\_Stack \neq \emptyset$ **do**
6 $\quad$ $n = pop(Node\_Stack)$;
7 $\quad$ **if** $n \in Node\_Set$ **then**
8 $\quad\quad$ **if** *The path is acceptable by the Büchi automaton* **then**
9 $\quad\quad\quad$ Return a candidate counterexample;
10 $\quad\quad$ **else**
11 $\quad\quad\quad$ Continue;
12 $\quad$ **else**
13 $\quad\quad$ put n in $Node\_Set$;
14 $\quad\quad$ Create the successors of n by going forward on the CFA and the Büchi automaton simultaneously;
15 $\quad\quad$ push all the created successors into $Node\_Stack$;
16 Return: no counterexamples are found;

Given the CFA of a program and a Büchi automaton obtained from an LTL specification, a candidate counterexample can be produced by Algorithm 2.1 where a set *node_set* and a stack *node_stack* are utilized to record all the visited nodes as well as the nodes whose descendants are still required to be checked, respectively. Initially, the root node n_0 of the eART is created with $n_0.q$ being the initial location in the CFA, $n_0.s$ an empty string, $n_0.p$ an empty set, and $n_0.f$ the initial state in the Büchi automaton. The root node is pushed into the stack as soon as it is created. Whenever the stack is not empty, the top node n is popped and put in *node_set* if n is not a member of *node_set* yet. Otherwise, if n is already in *node_set*, an infinite path is formed in the eART. If the path is a valid one which is acceptable by the Büchi automaton, a candidate counterexample is returned. Whenever a new member n joins in *node_set*, we create all of its successors by computing the production of all the direct successors of $n.q$ in the CFA and all the succeeding states of $n.f$ in the Büchi automaton. Precisely, the set of successors of n will be $Suc(n) = \{n' \mid n'.q \in Suc(n.q), n'.s$ depends on whether $I((n.q, n'.q))$ is a function call, $n'.f \in Suc(n.f)$, and $n'.p$ is the label of the transition from $n.f$ to $n'.f$ in the Büchi automaton.$\}$. All nodes in $Suc(n)$ are pushed into the stack *node_stack* immediately when they are created. Whenever the stack becomes empty, the desired property is valid on the program.

Similar to the safety verification, a candidate counterexample is possible a spurious path that is infeasible actually. To eliminate spurious counterexamples, the verification proceeds on the CEGAR loop. That is when a candidate counterexample is produced by Algorithm 3.2, its feasibility is checked by an SMT solver. If it is feasible, we return it as a real counterexample. Otherwise, new predicates are discovered by interpolant and added at a proper node n_a. Then the eARG is rebuilt from n_a in a lazy style by the same way in Algorithm 2.1.

2.3   Challenging Problem

Comparing the approach for verifying temporal properties with the original safety property verification approach, most of the work can be reused such as the ART construction process and the lazy abstraction supplemented CEGAR loop. The differences are (1) a Büchi automaton equivalent to the given LTL formula should be constructed; (2) the ART should be constructed under the guidance of the obtained automaton; and (3) whether the paths formed in an eART can be accepted by the Büchi automaton should be checked. The approach is a general LTL specified temporal property verification method. However, to construct the equivalent Büchi automaton from an LTL formula is expensive. It is already known as an PSPACE-Complete problem [24]. What makes matters worse is the resulting Büchi automaton is non-deterministic. This will exacerbate the path explosion problem since to create the ART under the guidance of a non-deterministic automata may bring in lots of useless attempts such that the scale of the ART will grow exponentially. Conversely, if the automaton is deterministic, the ART will be in a similar size with the one for verifying safety property. However, to obtain an equivalent deterministic automaton from a nondeterministic Büchi automaton is inherently expensive which notoriously resistant the efficiency of temporal property verification of programs.

3 Verifying Temporal Properties of Programs over Finite Traces

As a matter of fact, most of the programs in real-world are terminable. So, with the general LTL model checking approach proposed in the previous section, to work together with LTL which is interpreted over infinite models, an extra self-loop doing nothing is always added to make the traces to be infinite when the program is terminable. Then to check whether a path is accepted by an LTL specification is quite nontrivial algorithmically due to the required fair cycle test in LTL satisfaction. This makes a easier problem solved in a way with unnecessary overhead. Thus, we are inspired to use LTL confined in finite traces to specify temporal properties of terminable programs. For convenience, in the rest of this section, we write LTL over finite models as LTL for convenience unless noted otherwise.

3.1 Linear Temporal Logic

The syntax of LTL over finite models is the same as the original one over infinite models. The only difference is that the former is interpreted over finite models while the latter over infinite models [25]. Given a nonempty finite set of atomic propositions AP, the set of LTL formulas over AP is the set of formulas built from elements in AP using negation ($\neg$), conjunction ($\wedge$), next ($\bigcirc$), until (U), and release (R) operators. The syntax is presented as follows [7]:

$$P ::= p \mid \neg\phi \mid \varphi \wedge \psi \mid \bigcirc\phi \mid \varphi \ U \ \psi \mid \varphi \ R \ \psi$$

where $p \in$ AP, $\bigcirc$ (Next), U (Until), and R (Release) are temporal operations.

LTL formulas are interpreted over finite linear-time structures. A linear-time structure over AP is a finite sequence $x = x(0), x(1), \cdots$ where each $x(i)$ is a valuation AP $\rightarrow \{true, false\}$. Whether or not a formula ϕ holds on a finite linear-time structure x at a position i, denoted by $x, i \models \phi$ is defined by the following semantics:

$x, i \models p$ if $x(i)(p) = true$, for $p \in$ AP,
$x, i \models \neg\phi$ if $x, i \not\models \phi$,
$x, i \models \varphi \vee \psi$ if $x, i \models \varphi$ or $x, i \models \psi$,
$x, i \models \bigcirc\varphi$ if i is not the last state of the sequence, and $x, i + 1 \models \varphi$
$x, i \models \varphi \ U \ \psi$ if there exists $j \geq i$ such that $x, i' \models \varphi$ for all $i' \in \{i, i+1, \ldots, j-1\}$,
       and $x, j \models \psi$
$x, i \models \varphi \ R \ \psi$ if either $x, j \models \psi$ for all $j \geq i$, or there exists $j \geq i$ such that
       $x, i' \models \psi$ for $i' \in \{i, i+1, \ldots, j\}$ and $x, j \models \varphi$

The abbreviations $true$, $false$, $\wedge$, $\rightarrow$ and $\leftrightarrow$ are defined as usual. In particular, $true \stackrel{\text{def}}{=} \phi \vee \neg\phi$ and $false \stackrel{\text{def}}{=} \phi \wedge \neg\phi$ for any formula ϕ. In addition, eventually ($\Diamond\phi$) and always ($\Box\phi$) temporal constructs can be derived by $\Diamond\phi \stackrel{\text{def}}{=} true \ U \ \phi$ and $\Box\phi \stackrel{\text{def}}{=} \neg\Diamond\neg\phi$, respectively. Since the formulas are interpreted over finite models, a new abbreviation *empty* is defined by: $empty \stackrel{\text{def}}{=} \neg \bigcirc true$ for convenience. Intuitively, *empty* means that there exists no 'next' states [8].

In what follows, Deterministic Normal Form (DNF) is presented for LTL formulas.

Definition 2 (Deterministic Normal Form, DNF). *DNF of an LTL formula ϕ is defined by:* $\phi = \beta \wedge empty \vee \bigvee_i \beta_i \wedge \bigcirc \phi_i$ *where β and each β_i is a typical propositional logic formula (called state formula) without any temporal operators, and ϕ_i an arbitrary LTL formula. The restriction is that for any different i and j, $\beta_i \wedge \beta_j = false$.*

Each disjunct in a DNF explicitly expresses a deterministic transition relation as depicted in Fig. 1.

Intuitively, it shows that to satisfy ϕ, there must exist a unique i such that the state formula β_i is satisfied at the current state, and ϕ_i is required to hold at the next one; or β holds at the current state but there exist no next states. For convenience, we call $\beta \wedge empty$ the terminating part while $\bigvee_i \beta_i \wedge \bigcirc \phi_i$ the non-terminating part in the DNF. Also, we use $Dnf(\phi)$ to denote the DNF of formula ϕ and $Pre\_Dnf(\phi)$ a pre deterministic normal form of ϕ which is nearly the same as DNF except that $\beta_i \wedge \beta_j = false$ is not required for all different i and j.

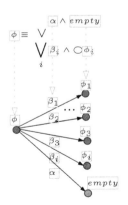

Fig. 1. Intuition of normal form

Theorem 1. *Any LTL formula can be transformed in deterministic normal form.*

Proof: The proof proceeds by induction on the structures of LTL formulas. We just consider $\wedge$, $\vee$, $\bigcirc$, U and R operations since $\neg$ can be put forward in the front of only atomic propositions [17].

- $Dnf(\phi) = \phi \wedge empty \vee \phi \wedge \bigcirc true$, if $\phi \in \mathsf{AP}$.
- $Dnf(\phi) = \neg\varphi \wedge empty \vee \neg\varphi \wedge \bigcirc true$ if $\phi = \neg\varphi$ and $\varphi \in \mathsf{AP}$.
- $Dnf(\phi) = Dnf(\varphi) \wedge Dnf(\psi)$ if $\phi = \varphi \wedge \psi$.
- $Dnf(\phi) = true \wedge \bigcirc\varphi$ if $\phi = \bigcirc\varphi$.
- $Pre\_Dnf(\phi) = Dnf(\varphi) \vee Dnf(\psi)$ if $\phi = \varphi \vee \psi$.
- $Pre\_Dnf(\phi) = Dnf(\psi) \vee Dnf(\varphi) \wedge \bigcirc(\varphi \mathsf{\ U\ } \psi)$ if $\phi = \varphi \mathsf{\ U\ } \psi$.
- $Pre\_Dnf(\phi) = Dnf(\varphi) \wedge Dnf(\psi) \vee Dnf(\psi) \wedge \bigcirc(\varphi \mathsf{\ R\ } \psi)$ if $\phi = \varphi \mathsf{\ R\ } \psi$.

For the first four cases above, we have already represented them in DNF. However, for the last three ones, further transformation is required such that the state formulas in the non-terminating part are pairwise exclusive. Actually, the results of the last three cases are all in the form of $\bigvee_i \alpha_i \wedge \bigcirc\phi_i \vee \bigvee_j \beta_j \wedge \bigcirc\varphi_j$, where $\beta_m \wedge \beta_n = false$ and $\alpha_m \wedge \alpha_n = false$ for any different m and n. For the formula in this form, it can be further equivalently transformed to DNF by

$$\bigvee_i \alpha_i \wedge \bigcirc\phi_i \vee \bigvee_j \beta_j \wedge \bigcirc\varphi_j = \bigvee_i \bigvee_j \alpha_i \wedge \beta_j \wedge \bigcirc(\phi_i \vee \varphi_j)$$
$$\vee \alpha_i \wedge \neg\beta_j \wedge \bigcirc\phi_i \vee \neg\alpha_i \wedge \beta_j \wedge \bigcirc\phi_i$$

As a result, any LTL formula can be transformed as DNF.   □

With DNFs of LTL formulas, an equivalent Deterministic Finite Automaton (DFA) can be constructed for any LTL formulas. The general idea for constructing DFA is simple. To construct DFA of ϕ, initially, a root node ϕ is created. Then we transform ϕ to its DNF: $\phi = \beta \wedge empty \vee \bigvee_i \beta_i \wedge \bigcirc\phi_i$. Based on it, for each i, a new node ϕ_i is created and a relative transition from ϕ to ϕ_i is created with the label being β_i. Meanwhile, the node $empty$ with no successors and the relative transition are also produced. To construct the whole graph structure of ϕ's DFA, the above procedure should then be applied similarly on the new created nodes repeatedly until no new nodes can be produced. The initial node in the DFA is the root node ϕ and the only accepting node is the $empty$ node. The equivalence of the obtained DFA and the original formula ϕ is ready to be proved since DNFs precisely rely on the semantics of LTL formulas. The detail of the proof is omitted here to save space. The algorithm for construction DFA of an LTL formula is presented in Algorithm 3.1 where a state S_Stack is utilized to record the states (formulas) whose successor states have not been produced via DNF. At the beginning, the initial state ϕ is created and pushed inside the stack. Next, the following three steps of operations are repeated until the stack is empty. First, the top element φ of the stack is popped and put into S. Second, φ is transformed into DNF. Third, if the terminating part exists, $empty$ state is put into S and the relative transition is put in T; for the non-terminating part, w.r.t to each disjunct $\beta_i \wedge \bigcirc\varphi_i$, φ_i is pushed into the stack and the relative transition is put into T. Eventually, when the stack is empty, the DFA is output with $empty$ being the only acceptable state.

3.2   Producing Counterexamples On-the-Fly

Even though most of the operations on DFAs are much easier than the ones on NBAs, to construct the whole DFA of a given LTL formula is still expensive.

Algorithm 3.1. LTL2DFA

Input: An LTL formula ϕ
Output: DFA: (S, s_0, T, a)
1 Stack S_Stack;
2 $s_0 = \phi$;
3 $push(s_0)$;
4 **while** $S\_Stack \neq \emptyset$ **do**
5 $\quad$ $\varphi = pop(S\_Stack)$;
6 $\quad$ Put φ in S;
7 $\quad$ **if** $\beta \wedge empty$ in $Dnf(\varphi)$ **then**
8 $\quad\quad$ Put $empty$ in S;
9 $\quad\quad$ Put $(\varphi, \beta, empty)$ in T;
10 $\quad$ **for** $each$ $\beta_i \wedge \bigcirc \varphi_i$ **do**
11 $\quad\quad$ $push(\varphi_i)$;
12 $\quad\quad$ Put $(\varphi, \beta_i, \varphi_i)$ in T
13 Return: (S, s_0, T, a);

Hence, in practice, we are not required to build the whole DFA in advance. Instead, we construct the DFA on-the-fly as long as the ART is constructed. As a result, only parts of the DFA which are necessary for the verification are constructed.

We still construct an eARG for producing a counterexample. Here, an eART can be seen as the product of an ART of the program and the DFA of the undesired property. Note that $n.f$ of a node here is an LTL formula since the states in DFA are named with LTL formulas as shown in Algorithm 3.1.

Given the CFA of a program and an undesired temporal property ϕ in LTL, a candidate counterexample can be produced by Algorithm 3.2 where global variables $node\_set$ in set and $node\_stack$ in stack are utilized to record all the visited nodes as well as the nodes whose descendants are still need to be checked, respectively. Initially, the root node n_0 of the eART is created with $n_0.q$ being the initial location in the CFA, $n_0.s$ an empty string, $n_0.p$ an empty set, and $n_0.f$ the undesired property ϕ. The root node is pushed into the stack as soon as it is created. Whenever the stack is not empty, the top node n is popped and put inside $node\_set$ immediately. Then, if $Suc(n.q) \neq \emptyset$, the set of n's successors $suc\_n = \{n' \mid n'.q \in Suc(n.q), n'.p = \beta$ $where$ $\beta \wedge \bigcirc \phi' \in Nf(\phi), I(n.q, n'.q) \wedge \beta \neq false$, and $n'.f = \phi'\}$ are created and pushed into the stack $Node\_Stack$; otherwise, if $Suc(n.q) = \emptyset$, n's successors $suc\_n = \{n' \mid n'.q = exit, n'.p = \beta$ $where$ $\beta \wedge empty \in Nf(\phi)$, and $n'.f = empty\}$ are created. Obviously, in this case suc_n is either a set with unique member or an empty set. If $suc\_n \neq \emptyset$, a candidate counterexample is created by back traversing from n' to the root. When the stack becomes empty, it is returned that the desired property is valid on the program.

Algorithm 3.2. Producing a candidate counterexample

Input: CFA of a program and the undesired property ϕ
Output: A candidate counterexample

1 Set $Node\_Set$;
2 Stack $Node\_Stack$;
3 Create the root node $n_0 : (q_0, s_0, p_0, f_0)$ with $n_0.q$ being the initial location in the CFA, $n_0.s$ empty, $n_0.p$ empty, and $n_0.f$ ϕ;
4 push($Node\_Stack, n_0$);
5 **while** $Node\_Stack \neq \emptyset$ **do**
6 $\quad$ $n = pop(Node\_Stack)$;
7 $\quad$ put n in $Node\_Set$;
8 $\quad$ **if** $Suc(n.q) \neq \emptyset$ **then**
9 $\quad$ $\quad$ $suc\_n = \{n' \mid n'.q \in Suc(n.q), n'.p = \beta \ where \ \beta \wedge \bigcirc \phi' \in Nf(\phi), I(n.q, n'.q) \wedge \beta \neq false, \ and \ n'.f = \phi'\}$;
10 $\quad$ $\quad$ push all the nodes in suc_n into $Node\_Stack$;
11 $\quad$ **else**
12 $\quad$ $\quad$ $suc\_n = \{n' \mid n'.q = exit, n'.p = \beta \ where \ \beta \wedge empty \in Nf(\phi), \ and \ n'.f = empty\}$;
13 $\quad$ $\quad$ **if** $suc\_n \neq \emptyset$ **then**
14 $\quad$ $\quad$ $\quad$ Return: a candidate counterexample

15 Return: no counterexamples are found;

3.3 Working Together with CEGAR

A candidate counterexample produced in an eARG presents a flaw that violates the desired property. However, it is possible a spurious path that is infeasible actually. To eliminates spurious counterexamples, the verification proceeds on the CEGAR loop. That is when a candidate counterexample is produced by Algorithm 3.2, its feasibility is checked by an SMT solver. If it is feasible, we return it as a real counterexample. Otherwise, new predicates are discovered by interpolant and added at a proper node n_a. Then the eARG is rebuilt from n_a in the same way in Algorithm 3.2.

To work in coopration with lazy abstraction supplemented CEGAR, Algorithm 3.2 is replenished as Algorithm 3.3 which is nearly the same as Algorithm 3.2 except for that when a candidate counterexample is found at line 14, whether or not it is spurious is checked. In the case the path is not spurious, it is returned as a real counterexample; otherwise, it is refined by lines 18–20.

4 Implementation

We have implemented the proposed approach in TPCHECKER to support the verification of temporal properties of C programs expressible in LTL formulas. It is developed upon the existing data structures, rules for forming path formulas, lazy abstraction based CEGAR, Craig interpolant, and graphical system in

Algorithm 3.3. Produce a counterexample

Input: CFA of a program and the undesired property ϕ
Output: A counterexample

1 Set $Node\_Set$;
2 Stack $Node\_Stack$;
3 Create the root node $n_0 : (q_0, s_0, p_0, f_0)$ with $n_0.q$ being the initial location in the CFA, $n_0.s$ being empty, $n_0.p$ being empty, and $n_0.f$ being ϕ;
4 push($Node\_Stack, n_0$);
5 **while** $Node\_Stack \neq \emptyset$ **do**
6    $n = pop(Node\_Stack)$;
7   put n in $Node\_Set$;
8   **if** $Suc(n.q) \neq \emptyset$ **then**
9      $suc\_n = \{n' \mid n'.q \in Suc(n.q), n'.p = \beta \text{ where } \beta \wedge \bigcirc \phi' \in Nf(\phi), I(n.q, n'.q) \wedge \beta \neq false, \text{ and } n'.f = \phi'\}$;
10   push all the nodes in suc_n to $Node\_Stack$;
11   **else**
12      $suc\_n = \{n' \mid n'.q = exit, n'.p = \beta \text{ where } \beta \wedge empty \in Nf(\phi), \text{ and } n'.f = empty\}$;
13   **if** $suc\_n \neq \emptyset$ **then**
14   check the feasibility of the path from the root to n' (a candidate counterexample);
15   **if** $the\ path\ is\ feasible$ **then**
16   Return: a counterexample
17   **else**
18          $n_a, Predicate = $ Interpolant();
19   add $Predicate$ in $n_a.p$;
20   deleting the descendant nodes of n_a in both $Node\_Stack$ and $Node\_Set$;

21 Return: no counterexamples are found;

CPAChecker. Figure 2 presents the outline of TPCHECKER. It takes the CFA created by the *C2CFA* module and the undesired property expressed with an LTL formula as the input to build eART. *LTL2DNF* and *LTL2BA* modules are developed to transform an LTL formula into its deterministic normal form or Büchi automaton, respectively. When a candidate counterexample is formed in *DFOTrav*, it calls *SpuriousCheck* to determine whether the path is feasible. In the case in which the path is feasible, it is output as a counterexample that violates the desired property. Otherwise, if the path is found to be spurious, the path formula is passed to *Craig Interpolant* for discovering new predicates and the proper node for further refinement. Getting the discovered predicates provided by *Craig Interpolant*, *Lazy* module refines the current path and then back to the *DFOTrav* module to build the eARG again. Whenever no new nodes can be created by *DFOTrav*, the program is proved to be free of the specified errors.

In TPCHECKER, modules *C2CFA*, *SpuriousChecking*, *Interpolant*, and *Lazy*, are directly adopted from CPACHcker.

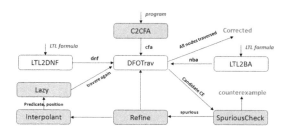

Fig. 2. Outline of TPCHECKER

5   Experiments

This section demonstrates the practical effectiveness of our approach for temporal property verification of C programs. We evaluate 2 aspects of TPCHECKER's effectiveness to answer the following questions:

(1) How does TPCHECKER's effectiveness compare to the existing approaches?
(2) How about TPCHECKER's ability on the verification of real-world programs with industrial scale?

All experiments in this paper were done on a PC with one processor Intel (R) Core (TM) i7 CPU 870 @2.93GHz, 8GB RAM and Microsoft Windows 7 ultimate version 2009 Service Pack 1 (64 bit) with Eclipse.

5.1   Comparison with Existing Approaches

Among the existing tools, Ultimate LTL automizer developed in [26] is the most recent one that outperforms DP in [13] and Termination in [12]. T2 improves on TERMINATPR project [30], which supports CTL, Fair-CTL, and CTL* specifications to verify user-provided liveness and safety properties for C programs. We compare our tool TPCHECKER with Ultimate LTL automizer and T2 on the benchmark programs drawn out from industrial code based utilized in [26] which are also once utilized in [12,13] for evaluating termination and DP.

In Table 1, the experimental results are compared with Ultimate LTL automizer and. The first column describes the code artifact. A symbol $\sqrt{}$ indicates that the tool proved the property, and $\times$ is used to denote cases where bugs were found. In the case where the tool exceeded the timeout threshold of 20 min, "T.O." is used to represent the time, and ??? the result. In the case in which the tool runs out of memory, "O.M." is used to represent the verification result. It is obvious that less time is consumed by TPCHECKER on most of the

Table 1. Experimental results

Program	Lines	Property	UL Automizer		T2		TPCHECKER	
			Time (ms)	Result	Time (ms)	Result	Time (ms)	Result
Ex. Sect. 2 of [13]	5	$\diamond\square p$	659	$\checkmark$	649	$\checkmark$	780	$\checkmark$
Ex. Fig. 8 of [12]	34	$\square(p \rightarrow \diamond q)$	1098	$\checkmark$	7117	$\times$	1218	$\checkmark$
Toy acquire/release	14	$\square(p \rightarrow \diamond q)$	1228	$\checkmark$	10203	$\checkmark$	874	$\checkmark$
Toy linear arith. 1	13	$p \rightarrow \diamond q$	1526	$\times$	3101	$\times$	1223	$\times$
Toy linear arith. 2	13	$p \rightarrow \diamond q$	1603	$\times$	1188	$\checkmark$	905	$\times$
PostgreSQL strmsrv	259	$\square(p \rightarrow \diamond\square q)$	1594	$\checkmark$	1521	$\checkmark$	1436	$\checkmark$
PostgreSQL strmsrv + bug	259	$\square(p \rightarrow \diamond\square q)$	1768	$\checkmark$	225783	$\times$	1795	$\checkmark$
PostgreSQL pgarch	61	$\diamond\square p$	1399	$\times$	2362	$\times$	1283	$\times$
PostgreSQL dropbuf	152	$\square p$	3429	$\times$	1444	$\times$	1374	$\times$
PostgreSQL dropbuf	152	$\square(p \rightarrow \diamond q)$	2003	$\checkmark$	4962	$\checkmark$	1355	$\checkmark$
Apache accept()	314	$\square p \rightarrow \square\diamond q$	480	O.M.	2621	$\times$	1124	$\checkmark$
Apache progress	314	$\square(p \rightarrow (\diamond q_1 \vee \diamond q_2))$	3153	$\checkmark$	6757	$\times$	920	$\checkmark$
Windows OS 1	180	$\square(p \rightarrow \diamond q)$	28783	$\checkmark$	1954	$\times$	1718	$\checkmark$
Windows OS 2	158	$\diamond\square p$	1027	$\checkmark$	1341	$\checkmark$	912	$\checkmark$
Windows OS 2 + bug	158	$\diamond\square p$	1696	$\times$	3408	$\times$	1171	$\times$
Windows OS 3	14	$\diamond\square p$	801	$\checkmark$	1165	$\checkmark$	919	$\checkmark$
Windows OS 4	327	$\square(p \rightarrow \diamond q)$	4119	$\checkmark$	218845	$\times$	4030	$\checkmark$
Windows OS 4	327	$(\diamond p) \vee (\diamond q)$	600	O.M.	19542	$\checkmark$	1749	$\times$
Windows OS 5	648	$\square(p \rightarrow \diamond q)$	34952	$\checkmark$	863	$\checkmark$	2799	$\checkmark$
Windows OS 6	13	$\diamond\square p$	T.O.	???	2803	$\checkmark$	1040	$\checkmark$
Windows OS 6 + bug	13	$\diamond\square p$	1033	$\times$	1217	$\times$	999	$\times$
Windows OS 7	13	$\square\diamond p$	3651	$\checkmark$	8438	$\checkmark$	931	$\checkmark$
Windows OS 8	181	$\diamond\square p$	778165	$\checkmark$	671	$\checkmark$	1046	$\checkmark$
23 programs in total			946767	20 (86.96%)	527955	17 (73.91%)	31611	23 (100%)

programs. Totally, only about 3.3% time consumed by Ultimate LTL automizer is required by TPCHECKER to accomplish the verification task. Compared with T2, the percentage is 5.99%. In addition, among the 23 programs in the benchmark, TPCHECKER successfully outputs the results on all the programs while only 86.96% are worked out by Ultimate LTL automizer and 73.91% by T2.

5.2   Scalability Evaluation on RERS

To evaluate the scalability of TPCHECKER on the verification of real world programs, we apply it on the on-site problems from the RERS Grey-Box challenge 2012 [29]. We directly download the benchmark including 6 problem classifications (P14–19) that are verified by Ultimate LTL automizer. The classification encodes the size and assumed difficulty of the problem class: P14 and P15 are small, P16 and P17 are medium, and P18 and P19 are large problems. The larger number means a higher difficulty. As known in [26], Ultimate LTL automizer fails on all the 50 programs in P19 where the average size of the programs is 8079 lines. As our target is to evaluate the scalability of TPCHECKER, we work only on P19 which contains the largest problems by both tools. While Ultimate LTL automizer still fails on all 50 programs, TPCHECKER successfully reports the verification results on 25 of 50 programs in the timeout threshold of 20 min as shown in Table 2.

Table 2. Scalability evaluation on RERS

Program set	Amount	Avg. lines	√	×	O.M	T.O
RERS P19	50	8079	24	1	0	25

6   Related Work

Lazy abstraction supplemented CEGAR has been implemented in software model checkers such as BLAST [5], CPAChecker [3], SLAM [4], and so forth. Thanks to these efforts, software model checkers are able to work on software systems in industrial circles. Among them, CPAChecker and BLAST are most related to ours. Both tools are typically used for the verification of safety properties expressed as assertions in the code. But they can only be utilized to verify limited liveness properties of programs. Our work strengthens lazy abstraction supplemented CEGAR-based software model checking with the ability of LTL specified temporal property verification. That is we can verify temporal properties of programs which can be expressed as LTL formulas. As a matter of fact, LTL specifications subsume safety properties. Hence, the original safety property verification with lazy abstraction supplemented CEGAR approach is still supported. The difference is that it is not checked by instrumenting the programs with assertions and then checks the reachability. Instead, all temporal properties, including safety properties, which can be specified with LTL formulas are all carried on in a unified approach.

LTL specified temporal property verification has been studied in several tools which can be classified mainly into two categories. The first one includes the explicit-state model checkers where the verification relies on the dynamic execution of the program under a given input. Thus, verification in this way is closely relative to the testing approach since it is hard to enumerate all the possible input. Verification of software in this way is inherited from the traditional model checking approach on finite state systems such as protocols and circuits. Tools in this category includes SPIN [15], Divine [9], Bandera [27], Cadence SMV [28] and so on. Among them, SPIN and Divine can support LTL model checking of C programs and Bandera for Java programs. To verify an LTL specification of C programs with SPIN [14,15], a front-end tool Modex is used to transform a C program as a Promela program. Then SPIN runs the Promela program with an interpreter to check whether the specification is valid on the Promela model [14].

The second category contains the tools which do not rely on dynamic execution of the program. Since the state space of programs is infinite even if we restrict programs to be terminable. The verification is indeed a proof of the program instead of testing as in the first category. In this category, an earlier approach is proposed in [12] which reduces the problem to fair termination checking. The mostly recent work in [26] improves it by checking fair termination only when it is necessary. Thus, a large number of termination checks are avoided. In [10,13], the authors reduce the LTL model checking problem to the problem of checking $\forall CTL$ by first approximating the LTL formula with a suitable CTL formula and then refining counterexamples that represent multiple paths by introducing non-deterministic prophecy variables, which is removed subsequently through a determinization procedure, in their program representation. With this approach, they reduce the problem to a termination proof task. Our work belongs to the second category. In contrast to the existing work, we rely on the mature lazy-abstraction supplemented CEGAR based program analysis approach to verify LTL specification. The things required are checked among the process for constructing eARTs. Considering the fact that most of the programs in real-world are terminable, we also use LTL confined in finite traces to specify temporal properties. As a result, the nontrivial algorithmically fair cycle test in LTL satisfaction checking can be avoided in case the program to be verified is terminable. Among the existing tools, Ultimate LTL automizer developed in [26] is the most recent one that outperforms DP in [13] and Termination in [12]. We evaluate our tool TPCHECKER on the benchmark utilized in [26]. Experiments show that our tool is competitive with Ultimate LTL automizer.

7   Conclusions

To verify temporal properties of C programs practically, this paper presents a lazy abstraction supplemented CEGAE based temporal property verification approach of C programs. To evaluate it, we have implemented the proposed approach in TPCHECKER. Experimental results show that TPCHECKER performs well in practice.

In the near future, different kinds of properties that are required to be verified in C programs will be studied and automatic temporal property formalizing methods will be investigated. Strategies for improving the efficiency will also be carried out.

References

1. Clarke, E.M., Emerson, E.A.: Design and synthesis of synchronization skeletons using branching time temporal logic. In: Kozen, D. (ed.) Logic of Programs 1981. LNCS, vol. 131, pp. 52–71. Springer, Heidelberg (1982). doi:10.1007/BFb0025774
2. Queille, J.P., Sifakis, J.: Specification and verification of concurrent systems in CESAR. In: Dezani-Ciancaglini, M., Montanari, U. (eds.) Programming 1982. LNCS, vol. 137, pp. 337–351. Springer, Heidelberg (1982). doi:10.1007/3-540-11494-7_22
3. Beyer, D., Keremoglu, M.E.: CPACHECKER: a tool for configurable software verification. In: Gopalakrishnan, G., Qadeer, S. (eds.) CAV 2011. LNCS, vol. 6806, pp. 184–190. Springer, Heidelberg (2011). doi:10.1007/978-3-642-22110-1_16
4. Ball, T., Bounimova, E., Kumar, R., Levin, V.: SLAM2: static driver verification with under 4% false alarms. In: FMCAD 2010, pp. 35–42 (2010)
5. Henzinger, T.A., Jhala, R., Majumdar, R., Sutre, G.: Software verification with BLAST. In: Ball, T., Rajamani, S.K. (eds.) SPIN 2003. LNCS, vol. 2648, pp. 235–239. Springer, Heidelberg (2003). doi:10.1007/3-540-44829-2_17
6. Pnueli, A.: The temporal logic of programs. In: Proceedings of 18th IEEE Symposium on Foundations of Computer Science, pp. 46–57 (1977)
7. Emerson, E.A.: Temporal and modal logic. In: van Leeuwen, J. (ed.) Handbook of Theoretical Computer Science, volume B: Formal Methods and Semantics, pp. 995–1072 (1990)
8. Duan, Z., Tian, C., Zhang, L.: A decision procedure for propositional projection temporal logic with infinite models. Acta Informatica **45**(1), 43–78 (2008)
9. http://divine.fi.muni.cz/
10. Koskinen, E.: Temporal verification of programs, Ph.D. thesis, University of Cambridge (2012)
11. Craig, W.: Linear reasoning. A new form of the Herbrand - Gentzen theorem. Symb. Log. **22**(3), 250–268 (1957)
12. Cook, B., Gotsman, A., Podelski, A., Rybalchenko, A., Vardi, M.Y.: Proving that programs eventually do something good. In: POPL 2007, pp. 265–276 (2007)
13. Cook, B., Koskinen, E.: Making prophecies with decision predicates. In: POPL 2011, pp. 399–410 (2011)
14. Holzmann, G.J.: The model checker spin. IEEE Trans. Softw. Eng. **23**(5), 279–295 (1997)
15. http://spinroot.com/spin/whatispin.html
16. Henzinger, T.A., Jhala, R., Majumdar, R., Sutre, G.: Lazy abstraction. In: Proceedings of Symposium on Principles of Programming Languages, pp. 58–70 (2002)
17. Gastin, P., Oddoux, D.: Fast LTL to Büchi automata translation. In: Berry, G., Comon, H., Finkel, A. (eds.) CAV 2001. LNCS, vol. 2102, pp. 53–65. Springer, Heidelberg (2001). doi:10.1007/3-540-44585-4_6

18. Kroening, D., Weissenbacher, G.: Verification and falsification of programs with loops using predicate abstraction. Formal Asp. Comput. **22**(2), 105–128 (2010)
19. Graf, S., Saidi, H.: Construction of abstract state graphs with PVS. In: Grumberg, O. (ed.) CAV 1997. LNCS, vol. 1254, pp. 72–83. Springer, Heidelberg (1997). doi:10. 1007/3-540-63166-6_10
20. Henzinger, T.A., Jhala, R., Majumdar, R., McMillan, K.L.: Abstractions from proofs. In: Principles of Programming Languages (POPL), pp 232–244. ACM Press, New York (2004)
21. Jhala, R., McMillan, K.L.: A practical and complete approach to predicate refinement. In: Hermanns, H., Palsberg, J. (eds.) TACAS 2006. LNCS, vol. 3920, pp. 459–473. Springer, Heidelberg (2006). doi:10.1007/11691372_33
22. Terauchi, T., Unno, H.: Relaxed stratification: a new approach to practical complete predicate refinement. In: Proceedings of the 24th European Symposium on Programming (ESOP 2015) (2015)
23. Cordeiro, L., Fischer, B., Verifying multi-threaded software using SMT-based context-bounded model checking. In Proceedings of the International Conference on Software Engineering (ICSE 2011), pp. 331–340. ACM (2011)
24. Sistla, A.P., Clarke, E.M.: The complexity of propositional linear temporal logic. J. ACM **32**, 733–749 (1985)
25. De Giacomo, G., Vardi, M.: Linear temporal logic and linear dynamic logic on finite traces. In: Proceedings of the Twenty-Fourth International Joint Conference on Artificial Intelligence, IJCAI 2013, pp. 2000–2007 (2013)
26. Dietsch, D., Heizmann, M., Langenfeld, V., Podelski, A.: Fairness modulo theory: a new approach to LTL software model checking. In: Kroening, D., Păsăreanu, C.S. (eds.) CAV 2015. LNCS, vol. 9206, pp. 49–66. Springer, Cham (2015). doi:10. 1007/978-3-319-21690-4_4
27. Corbett, J.C., Dwyer, M.B., Hatcliff, J., Laubach, S., Pasareanu, C.S.: Bandera: extracting finite-state models from Java source code. In: ICSE 2000, pp. 439–448 (2000)
28. Cadence SMV. http://www.kenmcmil.com/smv.html
29. Howar, F., Isberner, M., Merten, M., Steffen, B., Beyer, D.: The RERS greybox challenge 2012: analysis of event-condition-action systems. In: Margaria, T., Steffen, B. (eds.) ISoLA 2012. LNCS, vol. 7609, pp. 608–614. Springer, Heidelberg (2012). doi:10.1007/978-3-642-34026-0_45
30. Brockschmidt, M., Cook, B., Ishtiaq, S., Khlaaf, H., Piterman, N.: T2: temporal property verification. In: Chechik, M., Raskin, J.-F. (eds.) TACAS 2016. LNCS, vol. 9636, pp. 387–393. Springer, Heidelberg (2016). doi:10.1007/978-3-662-49674-9_22

Combining Event-B and CSP: An Institution Theoretic Approach to Interoperability

Marie Farrell$^{(\boxtimes)}$, Rosemary Monahan, and James F. Power

Department of Computer Science, Maynooth University, Maynooth, Ireland
`mfarrell@cs.nuim.ie`

Abstract. In this paper we present a formal framework designed to facilitate interoperability between the Event-B specification language and the process algebra CSP. Our previous work used the theory of institutions to provide a mathematically sound framework for Event-B, and this enables interoperability with CSP, which has already been incorporated into the institutional framework. This paper outlines a comorphism relationship between the institutions for Event-B and CSP, leveraging existing tool-chains to facilitate verification. We compare our work to the combined formalism Event-B‖CSP and use a supporting example to illustrate the benefits of our approach.

1   Introduction

Event-B is an industrial strength formal method that allows us to model a system's specification at various levels of abstraction using refinement and prove its safety properties [1]. The most primitive components of an Event-B specification are events, which are triggered non-deterministically once their guards evaluate to true. Much work has been done on imposing control on when events are triggered, as this models state changes in the system [7,18,21]. Our contributions seek to provide a mathematical grounding to this work using the theory of institutions and its underlying category theoretic framework [5]. As a result, we provide developers with the ability to add (CSP) control to Event-B specifications. This is achieved through our description of an institution comorphism between an institutional representation of Event-B ($\mathcal{EVTCASL}$) and an institutional representation of CSP-CASL ($\mathcal{CSPCASL}$) [16].

This document is structured as follows. In the remainder of Sect. 1 we outline the relevant background, motivate our work, and introduce our running example of a bounded retransmission protocol. Section 2 contains a brief overview of the institutions for $\mathcal{CASL}$ (the Common Algebraic Specification Language), $\mathcal{EVTCASL}$ and $\mathcal{CSPCASL}$. In Sect. 3 we outline the comorphism relating the institutions $\mathcal{EVTCASL}$ and $\mathcal{CSPCASL}$. We illustrate the use of the syntactic components of this comorphism with respect to our running example in Sect. 4 and discuss implications for refinement of specifications [1,19]. Finally, we conclude by outlining directions for future work.

M. Farrell–This work is funded by a Government of Ireland Postgraduate Grant from the Irish Research Council.

© Springer International Publishing AG 2017
Z. Duan and L. Ong (Eds.): ICFEM 2017, LNCS 10610, pp. 140–156, 2017.
https://doi.org/10.1007/978-3-319-68690-5_9

1 CONTEXT brp_c0
2 SETS STATUS
3 CONSTANTS *working*, *success*, *failure*
4 AXIOMS
5   axm1: $STATUS = \{working,\ success,$
            $failure\}$
6   axm2: $working\ \neq\ success$
7   axm3: $working\ \neq\ failure$
8   axm4: $success\ \neq\ failure$
9 END

10 MACHINE b_0 SEES brp_c0
11 VARIABLES $r\_st,\ s\_st$
12 INVARIANTS
13   inv1: $r\_st\ \in\ STATUS$
14   inv2: $s\_st\ \in\ STATUS$
15 EVENTS
16 Initialisation
17   then
18   act1: $r\_st\ :=\ working$
19   act2: $s\_st\ :=\ working$
20 Event brp $\widehat{=}$ ordinary
21   when
22   grd1: $r\_st\ \neq\ working$
23   grd2: $s\_st\ \neq\ working$
24   then
25   Skip
26 Event RCV_progress $\widehat{=}$ anticipated
27   then
28   act1: $r\_st\ :\in\ \{success,\ failure\}$
29 Event SND_progress $\widehat{=}$ anticipated
30   then
31   act1: $s\_st\ :\in\ \{success,\ failure\}$
32 END

Fig. 1. An Event-B model of the bounded retransmission protocol, consisting of a context (lines 1–9) that specifies a new data type called STATUS, and a specification for an abstract machine b_0 (lines 10–32) [1].

1.1   Event-B and a Running Example

Event-B is a state-based formalism for system-level modelling and analysis. It uses set theory as a modelling notation, refinement to represent systems at different levels of abstraction and mathematical proof to verify consistency between refinement levels [1]. In an Event-B model, static aspects of a system are specified in *contexts*, while dynamic aspects are modelled in *machines*. Each machine specifies states and events which update that state. Refinement between machines involves the addition of new variables and events, making the initial model more concrete. Refinement steps generate proof obligations so as to ensure that the refined machine does not invalidate the original model. Event-B is supported by its Eclipse-based IDE, the *Rodin Platform*, which provides support for refinement and automated proof [2].

Figure 1 contains an Event-B specification of a *bounded retransmission protocol* which we use as a running example throughout this paper [1,19]. The specification corresponds to the sequential file transfer from a sender site to a receiver site [1, Ch. 6]. The Event-B context specifies a data type called STATUS (line 2) that contains the three distinct values working, success and failure (lines 3–8). The corresponding abstract machine introduces two state variables of type STATUS: these are r_st for the receiver and s_st for the sender (lines 11–14). The Initialisation event (lines 16–19) sets both of these variables to the value working.

The events RCV_progress and SND_progress update the associated state variable to either success or failure (lines 26–28 and 29–31 respectively). Both events have the status anticipated which means that they must not increase the

```
1  P₀ = S₀ ∥ R₀
2  S₀ = SND_progress → brp → STOP
3  R₀ = RCV_progress → brp → STOP
```

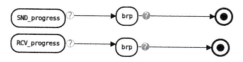

Fig. 2. An Event-B∥CSP process specification [19].

Fig. 3. Using the flows plugin to model the Event-B∥CSP process specification in Fig. 2.

variant expression in the machine. However, since there is no variant expression in this machine, this condition is not evaluated. While this labelling may seem redundant, it is a common development strategy used in Event-B and, in this case, reminds developers that these events should be refined to `convergent` events in future refinement steps. The event `brp` (lines 20–25) is triggered when both variables are no longer set to `working`, thus indicating that the protocol has completed [19].

1.2 Related Work on Adding Event Ordering to Event-B Machines

Developers often wish to model the *order* in which events are triggered, and specifically, how newly added events relate to previous events. Currently, control can only be implemented in Event-B in an ad hoc manner, typically by adding a machine variable to represent the current state. Each event must then check the value of this variable in its guard, and if this value indicates that the machine is ready to move into the next state then the appropriate event is triggered.

An alternative approach to introducing control is provided by the Event-B∥CSP formalism which combines Event-B with CSP, so that CSP controllers can be specified alongside Event-B machines facilitating an explicit approach to control flow [18]. CSP is a process algebra specifically designed to specify control oriented applications, using *processes* that can be composed in a variety of ways [6]. The subset of CSP made available by Event-B∥CSP is:

$$P ::= e \to P \mid P_1 \,\square\, P_2 \mid P_1 \,\sqcap\, P_2 \mid P_1 \| P_2 \mid S$$

where P, P_1 and P_2 are processes, e is a CSP event and S is a process variable. The semantics of CSP can be evaluated over a number of semantic domains. These include the traces (sequences of events that a process can engage in after the `Initialisation` event), failures (events the process might refuse after a trace) and divergences (traces after which the process might diverge).

The combination of Event-B and CSP in Event-B∥CSP results in a clear separation between the data-dependent and control-dependent aspects of a model, allowing proof obligations concerning control-flow to be discharged within the CSP framework. However, at the time of writing, no tool support has been explicitly provided for this approach, at either the Event-B or CSP level. The ProB animator and model checker can be used to explore Event-B models with CSP controllers for consistency [10]. Since it was not developed with Event-B∥CSP in mind there are some incompatibility issues: in particular, it is only feasible to check refinement for small examples.

Figure 2 contains an Event-B‖CSP process specification to be used alongside the Event-B model in Fig. 1. Here, three CSP processes are defined for use with the machine b_0, splitting the specification into sender and receiver controllers (S_0 and R_0 respectively) that are combined in parallel by P_0. This approach was taken by Schneider et al. to model the repeating behaviour of the sender and receiver using CSP, and to model the state using Event-B [19].

Another perspective is provided by the *Flows* plugin for Rodin, which extends Event-B models with event ordering(s) [7]. Flow diagrams represent the possible use cases of Event-B models. These *flows* resemble those used in process algebras such as CSP. A simple graphical notation is used, with a trace semantics provided over the sequence of events in the machine. No new Event-B specifications are generated by the *Flows* plugin. Instead new proof obligations are created to assist reasoning about whether or not a flow is feasible in a given Event-B model. The generated proof obligations characterise the relationship between the after-state of one event and the guard (before-state) of another.

Figure 3 illustrates a potential use case using the *flows* plugin, corresponding to the Event-B‖CSP specification in Fig. 2, introducing control to the Event-B machine b_0 (Fig. 1). Notice that it is not possible to indicate parallel composition here using the *flows* plugin. We can only specify S_0 and R_0 separately. Therefore, we conclude that the Event-B‖CSP specification outlined in Fig. 2 is much more expressive that the flow described in Fig. 3.

2   Background on Institutions

The theory of institutions was originally developed by Goguen and Burstall in a series of papers originating from their work on algebraic specification [5]. An institution is composed of signatures (vocabulary), sentences (syntax), models and a satisfaction condition (semantics). Figure 4 contains a summary of the definitions for these components. The key observation is that once the syntax and semantics of a formal system have been defined in a uniform way, using some basic constructs from category theory, then a set of *specification-building operators* can be defined that allow specifications to be written and modularised in a formalism-independent manner [17].

Institutions have been defined for many logics and formalisms, including formal languages such as Event-B, UML and CSP [3,9,12]. We can achieve interoperability between different logics by constructing a *comorphism* between their institutions. Figure 5 contains a summary of the definitions for the components of an institution comorphism, which broadly consist of mappings for each of the elements in an institution, as referred to in Fig. 4. Figures 4 and 5 are brief summaries of the relevant constructions; full details can be found in the literature [5,17]. Readers familiar with *Unifying Theories of Programming* may note that the notion of institutions, in this way, is similar to that of a "theory supermarket" where one can shop for theories with the confidence that they will work together [4].

An institution is composed of:

Vocabulary: A category **Sign** of *signatures*, with signature morphisms $\sigma : \Sigma \to \Sigma'$ for each signature $\Sigma, \Sigma' \in |\textbf{Sign}|$.

Syntax: A functor **Sen** : **Sign** $\to$ *Set* giving a set **Sen**(Σ) of Σ-*sentences* for each signature Σ and a function **Sen**(σ) : **Sen**$(\Sigma) \to$ **Sen**(Σ') which translates Σ-sentences to Σ'-sentences for each signature morphism $\sigma : \Sigma \to \Sigma'$.

Semantics: A functor **Mod** : **Sign**$^{op} \to$ **Cat** giving a category **Mod**(Σ) of Σ-*models* for each signature Σ and a functor **Mod**(σ) : **Mod**$(\Sigma') \to$ **Mod**(Σ) which translates Σ'-models to Σ-models (and Σ'-morphisms to Σ-morphisms) for each signature morphism $\sigma : \Sigma \to \Sigma'$.

A Satisfaction Relation $\models_{\mathcal{INS},\Sigma} \subseteq |\textbf{Mod}(\Sigma)| \times \textbf{Sen}(\Sigma)$, determining satisfaction of Σ-sentences by Σ-models for each signature Σ.

An institution must uphold the **satisfaction condition:** for any signature morphism $\sigma : \Sigma \to \Sigma'$ the translations **Mod**(σ) of models and **Sen**(σ) of sentences

$$M' \models_{\mathcal{INS},\Sigma'} \textbf{Sen}(\sigma)(\phi) \quad \Leftrightarrow \quad \textbf{Mod}(\sigma)(M') \models_{\mathcal{INS},\Sigma} \phi$$

for any $\phi \in \textbf{Sen}(\Sigma)$ and $M' \in |\textbf{Mod}(\Sigma')|$ [5].

Fig. 4. A brief summary of the definitions for the main components of an institution.

An institution comorphism $\rho : \textbf{INS} \to \textbf{INS}'$ is composed of:

A functor: $\rho^{Sign} : \textbf{Sign} \to \textbf{Sign}'$

A natural transformation: $\rho^{Sen} : \textbf{Sen} \to \rho^{Sign}$; **Sen**$'$, that is, for each $\Sigma \in |\textbf{Sign}|$, a function $\rho^{Sen}_{\Sigma} : \textbf{Sen}(\Sigma) \to \textbf{Sen}'(\rho^{Sign}(\Sigma))$.

A natural transformation: $\rho^{Mod} : (\rho^{Sign})^{op}$; **Mod**$' \to$ **Mod**, that is, for each $\Sigma \in |\textbf{Sign}|$, a functor $\rho^{Mod}_{\Sigma} : \textbf{Mod}'(\rho^{Sign}(\Sigma)) \to \textbf{Mod}(\Sigma)$.

An institution comorphism must ensure that for any signature $\Sigma \in |\textbf{Sign}|$, the translations ρ^{Sen}_{Σ} of sentences and ρ^{Mod}_{Σ} of models preserve the satisfaction relation, that is, for any $\psi \in \textbf{Sen}(\Sigma)$ and $M' \in |\textbf{Mod}(\rho^{Sign}(\Sigma))|$:

$$\rho^{Mod}_{\Sigma}(M') \models_{\Sigma} \psi \quad \Leftrightarrow \quad M' \models'_{\rho^{Sign}(\Sigma)} \rho^{Sen}_{\Sigma}(\psi)$$

and the relevant diagrams in **Sen** and **Mod** commute for each signature morphism in **Sign** [5].

Fig. 5. A brief summary of the main components of an institution comorphism, which is one way of combining specifications from different institutions.

The institutions relevant to this paper are the institutions for CASL, $\mathcal{CASL}$, CSP-CASL, $\mathcal{CSPCASL}$, and our definition of the institution for Event-B, $\mathcal{EVT}$-$\mathcal{CASL}$. Originally, we defined the institution $\mathcal{EVT}$ for Event-B to be built on top of the institution for first-order predicate logic with equality [3]. In this paper, we build our institution $\mathcal{EVTCASL}$ on top of the (more general) institution for $\mathcal{CASL}$, of which $\mathcal{FOPEQ}$ is a sublogic. The main components of these are summarised in Fig. 6. We do not delve deeply into their components here, but refer the reader to the literature and our website for further information[1].

The $\mathcal{CSPCASL}$ institution is built on the definition of the institutions $\mathcal{CSP}$ and $\mathcal{CASL}$ [12,13]. A specification over $\mathcal{CSPCASL}$ consists of a data part (written as a structured CASL specification), a channel part and a process part

---

[1] http://www.cs.nuim.ie/~mfarrell/extended.pdf.

$\mathcal{CASL}$: The institution for CASL [13]:
- **Signatures** are triples of the form $\langle S, \Omega, \Pi \rangle$, containing sort names, sort/arity indexed operation names (representing total and partial functions), sort-indexed predicate names and a subsort relation.
- **Sentences** are first order formulae and term equalities.
- **Models** contain a carrier set corresponding to each sort name, a function over sort carrier sets for each operation name and a relation over sort carrier sets for each predicate name.
- **The satisfaction relation** is the usual satisfaction of first-order structures in first-order sentences.

$\mathcal{CSPCASL}$: The institution for CSP-CASL [16]:
- **Signatures** are tuples $\langle \Sigma_{Data}, C, \Sigma_{Proc} \rangle$ where Σ_{Data} is a basic $\mathcal{CASL}$ signature, C is a set of sort-indexed channel names and $\Sigma_{Proc} = N_{w,comms}$ is a family of finite sets of process names. For every $n \in N_{w,comms}$, w is a sequence of sort names corresponding to the parameter type of n and $comms \subseteq S$ is the set of all types of events that n can engage in.
- **Sentences** are either $\mathcal{CASL}$ sentences or $\mathcal{CSP}$ process sentences.
- **Models** are pairs of the form $\langle A, I \rangle$ where A is a $\mathcal{CASL}$-model and I is a family of process interpretation functions. Each process interpretation function takes as arguments a process name and suitable parameters, and returns a $\mathcal{CSP}$ denotation for the appropriate CSP semantic domain (traces/failures/divergences).
- **The satisfaction relation** for process sentences is two-phase: (i) process terms are evaluated in process sentences using the $\mathcal{CASL}$ semantics, thus replacing each term by its valuation; (ii) the CSP semantics is than applied in the usual way for the specific semantic domain (traces/failures/divergences).

$\mathcal{EVTCASL}$: The institution for Event-B [3]:
- **Signatures** are tuples of the form $\langle S, \Omega, \Pi, E, V \rangle$, where $\langle S, \Omega, \Pi \rangle$ is a $\mathcal{CASL}$ signature, E is a set of (event name, status) pairs, and V is a set of sort-indexed variable names.
- **Sentences** are pairs of the form $\langle e, \phi(\overline{x}, \overline{x}') \rangle$ where e is an event name and $\phi(\overline{x}, \overline{x}')$ is a $\mathcal{CASL}$-formula. Here $\overline{x}$ is the set of free variable names from V and $\overline{x}'$ is the same set with each variable name primed.
- **Models** are triples $\langle A, L, R \rangle$ where A is a $\mathcal{CASL}$ model, L contains sets of variable-to-value mappings for each of the primed versions of the variable names in V. R is a set of relations over the before and after variable-to-value mappings for every (non-initial) event name in E.
- **The satisfaction relation** uses a comorphism between $\mathcal{CASL}$ and $\mathcal{EVT}$ to evaluate the satisfaction of $\mathcal{EVTCASL}$ sentences and models over $\mathcal{CASL}$.

Fig. 6. The principal components of the institutions for the common algebraic specification language ($\mathcal{CASL}$), CSP-CASL ($\mathcal{CSPCASL}$) and Event-B ($\mathcal{EVTCASL}$).

(written using CSP) [16]. The inclusion of channels is a form of syntactic sugaring as specifications with channels can easily be translated into those without but they provide a more convenient notation so we include them to aid in readability [14].

In Sect. 3, we outline the institution comorphism between $\mathcal{CSPCASL}$ and our institution for Event-B, $\mathcal{EVTCASL}$. This is the theoretical foundation and main contribution of our work and we use it to create a sound mechanism that has enabled us to achieve interoperability between CSP and Event-B.

2.1   Tool Support and Avenues to Interoperability

The Heterogeneous Toolset (HETS), written in Haskell, provides a general framework for parsing, static analysis and for proving the correctness of specifications in a formalism independent and thus heterogeneous manner [11]. In HETS, each formalism (expressed as an institution) is represented as a logic. In this setting, interoperability between formalisms is defined using institution comorphisms to relate the syntax of different logics and formalisms.

The institutions for $\mathcal{CASL}$ and $\mathcal{CSPCASL}$ have already been implemented in HETS. One notable feature available via HETS is the *CSPCASLProver*, a prover for $\mathcal{CSPCASL}$ based on the CSP-Prover [8]. It uses the Isabelle theorem prover to prove properties about specifications over the permitted CSP semantic domains [15]. We have added an implementation for our institution for Event-B, $\mathcal{EVTCASL}$, to HETS.

In previous work, we have defined a translational semantics for Event-B specifications using the institutional language of $\mathcal{EVTCASL}$. We have implemented this via a parser for the Event-B files that are generated by Rodin. In this way we bridge the gap between the Rodin and HETS software ecosystems, enabling the analysis and manipulation of Event-B specifications in the interoperability-friendly environment made available by HETS. Using our translational semantics for Event-B [3] we generate the $\mathcal{EVTCASL}$ signatures and sentences (as shown in Fig. 7) that correspond to the Event-B model defined in Fig. 1.

```
1   Σ_brp_c0 = ⟨ S, Ω, Π, E, V ⟩ where
2     S = {STATUS},
3     Ω = {working:STATUS, success:STATUS,
4           failure:STATUS},
5     Π = {}, E = {}, V = {}

6   Σ_b_0 = ⟨ S, Ω, Π, E, V ⟩ where
7     S = {STATUS,BOOL},
8     Ω = {working:STATUS, success:STATUS,
9           failure:STATUS},
10    Π = {},
11    E =
12      {(brp, Ordinary),
13       (RCV_progress, Anticipated),
14       (SND_progress, Anticipated),
15       (e_init, Ordinary)},
16    V = {(r_st:STATUS), (s_st:STATUS)}
```

The sentences in $\mathbf{Sen}(\Sigma_{brp\_c0})$ that correspond to the Event-B context in Figure 1 are:

```
17    {⟨e_init, STATUS = {working, success,failure}⟩
18     ⟨e_init, working ≠ success⟩
19     ⟨e_init, working ≠ failure⟩
20     ⟨e_init, success ≠ failure⟩}
```

The sentences in $\mathbf{Sen}(\Sigma_{b\_c0})$ that correspond to the Event-B machine in Figure 1 are:

```
21    {⟨e_init, STATUS = {working, success, failure}⟩
22     ⟨e_init, working ≠ success⟩
23     ⟨e_init, working ≠ failure⟩
24     ⟨e_init, success ≠ failure⟩
25     ⟨e_init, (r_st' = working ∧ s_st' = working)⟩
26     ⟨brp, (r_st ≠ working ∧ s_st ≠ working)⟩
27     ⟨RCV_progress, (r_st :∈ {success, failure})⟩
28     ⟨SND_progress, (s_st :∈ {success, failure})⟩}
```

Fig. 7. The $\mathcal{EVTCASL}$ signatures and sentences generated, using our translational semantics parser, from the Event-B model in Fig. 1. We use subscript notation to indicate the origin of each of these signatures and sentences.

3   Translating $\mathcal{EVTCASL}$ specifications to $\mathcal{CSPCASL}$ specifications

We outline a comorphism-based translation between $\mathcal{EVTCASL}$ and $\mathcal{CSPCASL}$. Both of these institutions rely on $\mathcal{CASL}$ to model the static components of a specification, with Event-B events and CSP processes used to model dynamic behaviour. There are a number of potential approaches to the construction of a comorphism. We could have opted to translate specifications written over both institutions into specifications written over $\mathcal{CASL}$, as $\mathcal{CASL}$ is the base layer of both $\mathcal{EVTCASL}$ and $\mathcal{CSPCASL}$. However, this would lead to the loss of event, channel and process names, unless we used additional annotations alongside the translation. Instead, our approach translates directly from $\mathcal{EVTCASL}$ to $\mathcal{CSPCASL}$, thus ensuring that the event, channel and process names are not lost. We use the event names in $\mathcal{CSPCASL}$ process definitions in order to introduce control over $\mathcal{EVTCASL}$ specifications.

3.1   An Institution Theoretic Translation

Here we outline the process that we used to define our institution theoretic translation $\rho : \mathcal{EVTCASL} \to \mathcal{CSPCASL}$ and the difficulties that we encountered. There are three components to an institution comorphism but only the first two are required in order to implement a comorphism translation in HETS. These are the signature and sentences translations described below.

Signature Translation:

$$\rho^{Sign} : \mathbf{Sign}_{\mathcal{EVTCASL}} \to \mathbf{Sign}_{\mathcal{CSPCASL}}$$

Given the $\mathcal{EVTCASL}$ signature $\langle S, \Omega, \Pi, E, V \rangle$, we form the $\mathcal{CSPCASL}$ signature $\langle \Sigma_{Data}, C, \Sigma_{Proc} \rangle$. Since both institutions are based on $\mathcal{CASL}$, we map $\langle S, \Omega, \Pi \rangle$ to Σ_{Data}. We enrich S, the set of sort names, with the new sort $\mathtt{Event}$ whose carrier set consists of $dom(E)$. For each event name $e \in dom(E)$, we construct the 0-ary operation $\mathtt{e}$, of sort $\mathtt{Event}$, and add it to Ω. Finally, we equip Σ_{Proc} with the new process names $\mathtt{E\_e}$, one for each $e \in dom(E)$. Each variable in V is represented by two channels in C of the variable's sort, one for its before value and one for its after value, in order to facilitate variable input for processes.

Sentence Translation:

$$\rho^{Sen} : \mathbf{Sen}_{\mathcal{EVTCASL}} \to \rho^{Sign}; \mathbf{Sen}_{\mathcal{CSPCASL}}$$

Each $\mathcal{EVTCASL}$ sentence is of the form $\langle e, \phi(\overline{x}, \overline{x}\prime) \rangle$ where e is the event name and $\phi(\overline{x}, \overline{x}\prime)$ is a formula over the before and after values of the variables in the signature Σ. As $\mathcal{CSPCASL}$ specifications are over some base logic we assume that this logic corresponds to the base logic of the mathematical predicate language of Event-B for the processes that we construct [12]. Then for each $\mathcal{EVTCASL}$ sentence ρ^{Sen} yields the following $\mathcal{CSPCASL}$ process sentence:

$$\mathtt{E\_e} \quad = \quad ?c_1.\overline{x}_1 \ldots c_{2n}.\overline{x}'_{2n} \to (\mathtt{if}\ \phi(\overline{x}, \overline{x}\prime)\ \mathtt{then}\ \mathtt{e} \to \mathtt{STOP}\ \mathtt{else}\ \mathtt{STOP})$$

The notation $?c_1.\overline{x}_1 \ldots c_{2n}.\overline{x}'_{2n}$ takes a sort appropriate value for each the variables $\overline{x}_1, \ldots, \overline{x}'_{2n}$ as input on the designated channel for that variable. This indicates that if the formula $\phi(\overline{x}, \overline{x}')$ evaluates to true then the corresponding event e has been triggered. Using the process STOP is safe as it does nothing.

Model Translation: The signature and sentence translations described above are sufficient for the implementation of an institution comorphism in HETS. However, in order to provide a theoretic underpinning to this translation by correctly defining an institution comorphism we must also provide a translation for the models:

$$\rho^{Mod} : (\rho^{Sign})^{op}; \; \mathbf{Mod}_{\mathcal{CSPCASL}} \to \mathbf{Mod}_{\mathcal{EVTCASL}}$$

Here $\rho^{Mod}(\langle A, I \rangle) = \langle A, L, R \rangle$ and consists of two maps, the identity map on the $\mathcal{CASL}$ model components and a map from I to $\langle L, R \rangle$. Given a $\mathcal{CSPCASL}$-sentence of the form described above, $I(\text{E\_e})$ returns a CSP denotation for the process E_e in a specified semantic domain $\mathcal{D} \in \{\mathcal{T}, \mathcal{N}, \mathcal{F}\}$. As the primary concern of Event-B is safety we examine the traces model which gives the following set of traces:

$$\{\ldots, \langle\rangle, \langle c_1.a_1, \ldots, c_{2n}.a_{2n}, \mathsf{e}\rangle, \ldots, \langle c_1.b_1, \ldots, c_{2n}.b_{2n}\rangle, \ldots\}$$

where traces of the form $\langle c_1.a_1, \ldots, c_{2n}.a_{2n}, \mathsf{e}\rangle$ indicate that the predicate $\phi(\overline{x}, \overline{x}')$ evaluated to true when the values listed in $c_1.a_1, \ldots, c_{2n}.a_{2n}$ were given to the variables $\overline{x}_1, \ldots, \overline{x}'_{2n}$. Then, traces of the form $\langle c_1.b_1, \ldots, c_{2n}.b_{2n}\rangle$ indicate that the predicate $\phi(\overline{x}, \overline{x}')$ evaluated to false on these variable values. We use this traces model to generate the R component (which is made up of the relations $R.e$ for $e \in dom(E) \neq \mathtt{Init}$) of the $\mathcal{EVTCASL}$-model such that:

$$R.e = \{\{\overline{x}_1 \mapsto a_1, \ldots \overline{x}'_{2n} \mapsto a_{2n}\} \mid \langle c_1.a_1, \ldots, c_{2n}.a_{2n}, \mathsf{e}\rangle \in I(\text{E\_e})_{\mathcal{T}}\}$$

Note that in what follows, we abbreviate the Initialisation event to Init. We only include the values from the traces model that caused the predicate $\phi(\overline{x}, \overline{x}')$ to evaluate to true, since these variable values will also satisfy the $\mathcal{EVTCASL}$-sentence $\langle e, \phi(\overline{x}, \overline{x}')\rangle$ in the $\mathcal{EVTCASL}$ institution. These are easily identified as the traces that ended with the event name e thus indicating that the event e was triggered. In the case where $\mathsf{e} = \mathtt{Init}$ we construct L in a similar fashion, otherwise, $L = \{\varnothing\}$.

Comorphisms are defined such that for any signature $\Sigma \in |\mathbf{Sign}_{\mathcal{EVTCASL}}|$, the translations $\rho^{Sen}_\Sigma : \mathbf{Sen}_{\mathcal{EVTCASL}}(\Sigma) \to \mathbf{Sen}_{\mathcal{CSPCASL}}(\rho^{Sign}(\Sigma))$ of sentences and $\rho^{Mod}_\Sigma : \mathbf{Mod}_{\mathcal{CSPCASL}}(\rho^{Sign}(\Sigma)) \to \mathbf{Mod}_{\mathcal{EVTCASL}}(\Sigma)$ of models preserve the satisfaction relation. That is, for any $\psi \in \mathbf{Sen}_{\mathcal{EVTCASL}}(\Sigma)$ and $M' \in |\mathbf{Mod}_{\mathcal{CSPCASL}}(\rho^{Sign}(\Sigma))|$

$$\rho^{Mod}_\Sigma(M') \models^{\mathcal{EVTCASL}}_\Sigma \psi \quad \Leftrightarrow \quad M' \models^{\mathcal{CSPCASL}}_{\rho^{Sign}(\Sigma)} \rho^{Sen}_\Sigma(\psi)$$

Note that in the special case where the formula $\phi(\overline{x}, \overline{x}')$ denotes a contradiction (there are no variable values that cause it to evaluate to true), then the comorphism satisfaction condition fails to hold. In this case, the corresponding $R.e$ will be empty but as there are variables in the $\mathcal{EVTCASL}$ signature, the generated $\mathcal{EVTCASL}$-model is not a valid one. We are currently investigating alternative constructions of ρ^{Mod} and alternative institution-based translations in order to resolve this issue. The case study that we present in this paper utilises HETS which has no notion of the model translation component of a comorphism so we illustrate how the syntactic components (ρ^{Sign} and ρ^{Sen}) can, in general, be applied to translate $\mathcal{EVTCASL}$ specifications into $\mathcal{CSPCASL}$ specifications that can be processed by HETS.

3.2   Translation via ρ^{Sign} and ρ^{Sen}

Figure 8 contains the $\mathcal{CSPCASL}$ specification corresponding to the Event-B specification in Fig. 1. Our translation from Event-B to $\mathcal{CSPCASL}$ involves two distinct steps. First, an Event-B specification (Fig. 1) is translated into a specification in the language of $\mathcal{EVTCASL}$ using our translational semantics parser (Fig. 7). Next, we apply ρ^{Sign} and ρ^{Sen}, the signature and sentence translations described earlier, to the $\mathcal{EVTCASL}$ specification to generate the corresponding $\mathcal{CSPCASL}$ specification (Fig. 8). This translation is represented by the dashed arrows in the refinement cube in Fig. 10 and the resultant $\mathcal{CSPCASL}$ specification corresponds to the vertex labelled B_0.

Applying ρ^{Sign} to the $\mathcal{EVTCASL}$ signatures in Fig. 7 (lines 1–16) generates the $\mathcal{CSPCASL}$ signature $\langle \Sigma_{Data}, C, \Sigma_{Proc} \rangle$ where the sort component of the data signature Σ_{Data} is augmented with new sorts Event and STATUS. The operation component of Σ_{Data} is augmented with one 0-ary operator per event name in $dom(E)$ of the $\mathcal{EVTCASL}$ signature Σ, yielding the set:

$$\{\text{Init}, \text{brp}, \text{RCV\_progress}, \text{SND\_progress} : \text{Event}\}$$

C contains two sort-appropriate channels for each variable in V (before and after values). In this $\mathcal{EVTCASL}$ example, there are two variables of sort STATUS, yielding four channels of sort STATUS in the corresponding $\mathcal{CSPCASL}$ specification. The Σ_{Proc} component of the $\mathcal{CSPCASL}$ signature is augmented a new process E_e for every $e \in dom(E)$.

Applying ρ^{Sen} to the sentences in $\mathbf{Sen}(\Sigma)$ (Fig. 7, lines 17–28) gives the (syntactically sugared) $\mathcal{CSPCASL}$ specification in Fig. 8. Note that we have manually added the process M to describe the behaviour of the Event-B machine in its entirety. We use parallel composition to indicate that events are triggered in any order. This specification has been proven consistent, using the Darwin and FACT consistency checkers available in HETS [11]. For readability, we have not included the invariant sentences given in Fig. 7 (lines 17–24). The formulae corresponding to each of these sentences is appended by logical conjunction to each of the formulae in the event process definitions in Fig. 8 (lines 14–29). We have included the context axiom sentences as predicates (lines 4–8) of the $\mathcal{CSPCASL}$ specification, corresponding to the context in Fig. 1.

A $\mathcal{CSPCASL}$ representation of the Event-B‖CSP specification in Fig. 2 is illustrated in Fig. 9 (lines 1–7). This shows that once the Event-B component of the Event-B‖CSP specification has been translated into $\mathcal{CSPCASL}$, then the CSP component can be easily written using $\mathcal{CSPCASL}$. These specifications

```
 1  spec BRP_C0 over CASL
 2    sort STATUS
 3    ops
 4    preds STATUS = {working, success,
 5      failure}
 6      working ≠ success
 7      working ≠ failure
 8      success ≠ failure
 9  end
```

```
10  spec B_0 over CSPCASL
11    data BRP_C0
12    channel c₁, c₂, c₃, c₄: STATUS
13    process
14      E_Init =
15        ?c₁.r_st.c₂.s_st.c₃.r_st'.c₄.s_st' →
16          if r_st' = working ∧ s_st' = working
17          then (Init → M) else STOP
18      E_brp =
19        ?c₁.r_st.c₂.s_st.c₃.r_st'.c₄.s_st' →
20          if r_st ≠ working ∧ s_st ≠ working
21          then (brp → M) else STOP
22      E_RCV_progress =
23        ?c₁.r_st.c₂.s_st.c₃.r_st'.c₄.s_st' →
24          if r_st :∈ {success, failure}
25          then (RCV_progress → M) else STOP
26      E_SND_progress =
27        ?c₁.r_st.c₂.s_st.c₃.r_st'.c₄.s_st' →
28          if s_st :∈ {success, failure}
29          then (SND_progress → M) else STOP
30      M = E_Init ∥ E_brp∥E_RCV_progress
31           ∥E_SND_progress
32  end
```

Fig. 8. $CSPCASL$ specification that is generated using ρ^{Sign} and ρ^{Sen} as described in Sect. 3. This specification has been syntactically sugared for presentation. We provide the full specification that can be input to HETS on our website.

```
1  spec EB∥CSP_B_0 over CSPCASL
2    B_0 then
3    process
4      P₀ = S₀ ∥ R₀
5      S₀ = SND_progress → brp → STOP
6      R₀ = RCV_progress → brp → STOP
7  end
```

```
8  refinement ref0 =
9    B_0 refined to EB∥CSP_B_0
```

Fig. 9. A $CSPCASL$ specification corresponding to the Event-B∥CSP specification in Fig. 2 and a statement of refinement in the notation of HETS between the $CSPCASL$ specifications B_0 and EB∥CSP_B_0.

are thus provided with tool support in HETS [11], an environment designed to facilitate interoperability.

4   The Refinement Cube

The refinement cube in Fig. 10 depicts the specifications and translations that will be presented throughout this section. In this cube, the labelled vertices represent specifications and the arrows between them describe how they are related. The front face of the cube corresponds to specifications that were developed in Rodin and the combined formalism Event-B∥CSP, the rear face corresponds to those completed in HETS using $CSPCASL$. The vertex labelled b_0 corresponds to the Event-B specification in Fig. 1 and the vertex labelled EB∥CSP_b_0 corresponds to the Event-B∥CSP specification in Fig. 2. The vertical arrow between them indicates that b_0 is used alongside EB∥CSP_b_0.

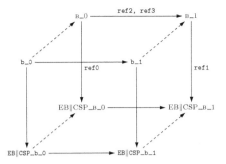

Fig. 10. Refinement cube: solid lines represent refinement relations and the dashed lines represent our translation into $\mathcal{CSPCASL}$.

4.1 Event and Process Refinement

In this subsection, we describe the refinement steps that correspond to the solid horizontal arrows in the refinement cube of Fig. 10. The theory of institutions equips us with a basic notion of refinement as *model-class inclusion* where the class of models of the concrete specification are a subset of the class of models of the abstract specification [17]. When the signatures are the same we simply denote this refinement as:

$$SP_A \sqsubseteq SP_C \quad \Leftrightarrow \quad Mod(SP_C) \subseteq Mod(SP_A)$$

where SP_A is an abstract specification that refines ($\sqsubseteq$) to a concrete specification SP_C.

If the signatures are different then we must define a signature morphism $\sigma : Sig[SP_A] \rightarrow Sig[SP_C]$, and can then use the corresponding model morphism to interpret the concrete specification as containing only the signature items from the abstract specification. This refinement is the model-class inclusion of the models of the concrete specification, restricted using the model morphism, into the class of models of the abstract specification. In this case write:

$$SP_A \sqsubseteq SP_C \quad \Leftrightarrow \quad Mod(\sigma)(SP_C) \subseteq Mod(SP_A)$$

where $Mod(\sigma)(SP_C)$ is the model morphism applied to the model-class of the concrete specification SP_C. This interprets each of the models of SP_C as models of SP_A before a refinement relationship is determined. In our running example, all refinement steps involve a change of signature. A similar approach taken by Schneider et al. involves using a renaming function, f, to relate concrete events to their abstract counterparts before a refinement relation is evaluated [20]. This was used to prove the refinement indicated by the horizontal arrow from EB‖CSP_b_0 to EB‖CSP_b_1 in Fig. 10.

Figure 11 contains a refined version of the abstract Event-B machine from Fig. 1. Here, each of the events RCV_progress and SND_progress are refined and split into two events (RCV_success, RCV_failure, SND_success and

```
 1  MACHINE b_1 refines b_0 SEES brp_c0        24  Event RCV_failure ≙convergent
 2  VARIABLES r_st, s_st                       25    refines RCV_progress
 3  INVARIANTS                                 26    when
 4    inv1 s_st = success ⇒ r_st = success     27      grd1  r_st  =   working
 5  VARIANT                                    28      grd2  s_st  =   failure
 6    {success, failure, s_st, r_st}           29    then
 7  Initialisation ordinary                    30      act1  r_st  :=  failure
 8    then                                     31  Event SND_success ≙convergent
 9      act1  r_st  :=  working                32    refines SND_progress
10      act2  s_st  :=  working                33    when
11  Event brp ≙ ordinary                       34      grd1  s_st  =   working
12    refines brp                              35      grd2  r_st  =   success
13    when                                     36    then
14      grd1  r_st  ≠  working                 37      act1  s_st  :=  success
15      grd2  s_st  ≠  working                 38  Event SND_failure ≙convergent
16    then                                     39    refines SND_progress
17      Skip                                   40    when
18  Event RCV_success ≙convergent              41      grd1  s_st  =   working
19    refines RCV_progress                     42    then
20    when                                     43      act1  s_st  :=  failure
21      grd1  r_st  =  working                 44  END
22    then
23      act1  r_st  :=  success
```

Fig. 11. A refined version of the Event-B machine that was described in Fig. 1.

```
 1  spec B_1 over CSPCASL
 2    data BRP_C0
 3    channelc_1,c_2,c_3,c_4: STATUS
 4    process
 5      E_Init =                                    34  spec EB‖CSP_B_1 over CSPCASL
 6        ?c_1.r_st.c_2.s_st.c_3.r_st'.c_4.s_st' →   35    B_1 then
 7          if r_st' = workings ∧ st' = working     36    process
 8          then (Init → M) else STOP               37      P_1 = S_1 ‖ R_1
 9      E_brp =                                      38      S_1 = (SND_success → brp → STOP)
10        ?c_1.r_st.c_2.s_st.c_3.r_st'.c_4.s_st' →   39          □ (SND_failure → brp → STOP)
11          if r_st ≠ working ∧ s_st ≠ working      40      R_1 = (RCV_success → brp → STOP)
12          then (brp → M) else STOP                41          □ (RCV_failure → brp → STOP)
13      E_RCV_success =                              42    end
14        ?c_1.r_st.c_2.s_st.c_3.r_st'.c_4.s_st' →
15          if r_st = working ∧ r_st' = success ∧ var   43  refinement ref1 = B_1 to EB‖CSP_B_1
16          then (RCV_success → M) else STOP
17      E_RCV_failure =                              44  refinement ref2 = B_0 refined via
18        ?c_1.r_st.c_2.s_st.c_3.r_st'.c_4.s_st' →   45    RCV_progress |-> RCV_success
19          if r_st = working ∧ s_st = failure ∧ var 46    SND_progress |-> SND_success
20            ∧ r_st' = failure                      47    E_RCV_progress |-> E_RCV_success
21          then RCV_failure → M) else STOP          48    E_SND_progress |-> E_SND_success
22      E_SND_success =                              49  to B_1
23        ?c_1.r_st.c_2.s_st.c_3.r_st'.c_4.s_st' →
24          if s_st = working ∧ r_st = success ∧ var 50  refinement ref3 = B_0 refined via
25            ∧ s_st' = success                      51    RCV_progress |-> RCV_failure
26          then (SND_success → M) else STOP         52    SND_progress |-> SND_failure
27      E_SND_failure =                              53    E_RCV_progress |-> E_RCV_failure
28        ?c_1.r_st.c_2.s_st.c_3.r_st'.c_4.s_st' →   54    E_SND_progress |-> E_SND_failure
29          if s_st = working ∧ s_st' = failure ∧ var 55 to B_1
30          then (SND_failure → M) else STOP
31      M = E_Init‖E_brp‖E_RCV_success‖E_SND_success
32          ‖E_RCV_failure‖E_SND_failure
33  end
```

Fig. 12. $\mathcal{CSPCASL}$ specification corresponding to the concrete machine from Fig. 11 as well as the refinement relations. We have also included the corresponding $\mathcal{CSPCASL}$ for the Event-B‖CSP specification used by Schneider et al. on lines (34–42) [19] .

SND_failure). The status of these events has been changed from anticipated to convergent during the refinement. Thus, the variant expression on line 6 must now be decreased by these events. This amounts to ensuring that in these events the following condition, that we refer to as var in Fig. 12, holds:

$$|\{\text{success, failure, s\_st', r\_st'}\}| < |\{\text{success, failure, s\_st, r\_st}\}|$$

When one of the variables moves from working to success or failure then the cardinality of the first set decreases, and this condition will evaluate to true. We apply the same process to this Event-B specification, using our translational semantics and the comorphism that we have described in Sect. 3. The resulting $\mathcal{CSPCASL}$ specification is shown in Fig. 12.

Specifying refinement between Event-B and Event-B‖CSP: We have successfully proven that the Event-B‖CSP specification (given in Fig. 2 and written as a $\mathcal{CSPCASL}$ specification in Fig. 9 (lines 1–7)) is a refinement of the translation of the Event-B model (given in Fig. 1 and written as a $\mathcal{CSPCASL}$ specification in Fig. 8) using the Auto-DG-Prover available in HETS.

This refinement is specified in HETS as shown on lines 8–9 of Fig. 9, and essentially adds the processes P_0, S_0 and R_0 to the $\mathcal{CSPCASL}$ specification of B_0 from lines 10–32 of Fig. 8. This inclusion is indicated by the use of the "then" specification-building operator (line 2 of Fig. 9), which corresponds to proving that the Event-B‖CSP specification (Fig. 2) is a refinement of the Event-B model (Fig. 1). This is a logical conclusion to draw since Event-B‖CSP is intended to be used alongside the Event-B machine specification and thus adds a level of deterministic behaviour to the Event-B model.

Similarly, we proved that the Event-B‖CSP specification on lines 34–42 of Fig. 12 is a refinement of the refined Event-B machine in Fig. 11 by translating the Event-B specification into $\mathcal{CSPCASL}$ via our translational semantics and the comorphism that we outlined earlier. These refinement steps are indicated by the downwards arrows in the back face of the refinement cube in Fig. 10 and by the refinement statements ref0 on lines 8–9 of Fig. 9 and ref1 on line 43 of Fig. 12.

Using CSPCASLProver to preserve Event-B Refinement: Using HETS and the CSPCASLProver we proved a refinement relation between the two $\mathcal{CSPCASL}$ specifications (Fig. 8 and lines 1–33 of Fig. 12) that we generated using our comorphism. This is indicated by the top horizontal arrow in the back face of the refinement cube (Fig. 10).

Since the corresponding refinement step in Event-B split a single event into two events, we had to define two separate refinements in HETS, ref2 and ref3 on lines 44–55 in Fig. 12. The syntax of these refinement specifications differs to the previous ones that we have discussed, because this refinement is not the simple addition of processes. Here, the refinement relation specifies the relationship between the signatures of the abstract and refined specifications.

For example, for ref2 we prove that the following are derivable from the specification in Fig. 12:

```
E_RCV_success  =  if r_st' = success ∨ r_st' = failure
                  then RCV_success → M else STOP
E_SND_success  =  if s_st' = success ∨ s_st' = failure
                  then SND_success → M else STOP
           M   =  E_Init||E_brp || E_RCV_success || E_SND_success
```

This corresponds to changing the names of the abstract processes E_RCV_progress and E_SND_progress to E_RCV_success and E_SND_success respectively. Thus the concrete processes still preserve the truth of the abstract ones that they refine. A similar construction follows for ref3.

Schneider et al. provide a CSP account of Event-B refinement by adding a new event status devolved, which indicates events where the CSP controller must ensure convergence [20]. In this paper, we have translated the Event-B specification into $\mathcal{CSPCASL}$ so all convergence checks occur within the same formalism. Therefore we do not need this new status.

These proofs were mostly automatic. Some path issues, caused by the translation from HETS to CSPCASLProver (which uses Isabelle), resulted in a small manual effort to discharge these proofs in Isabelle. Our findings illustrate that the notions of refinement, although expressed differently, in Rodin and HETS are preserved using this comorphism. Thus highlighting the benefits of our institution theoretic approach to interoperability by maintaining that *"truth is invariant under change of notation"* [5].

5   Conclusions and Future Work

Until now, interoperability between Event-B and CSP has been mostly theoretical, offering little in terms of tool support. By devising a means of forming HETS-readable $\mathcal{CSPCASL}$ specifications from those in Event-B we have created tool support for the combination of Event-B and CSP using the theory of institutions. The institutional approach supplies a general framework within which we can achieve interoperability, offering more freedom and a more formal foundation than the approach taken by both the *flows* plugin and the combined formalism Event-B∥CSP, with the advantage of tool support via HETS.

It has been shown that the institutions for both $\mathcal{EVTCASL}$ and $\mathcal{CSPCASL}$ have good behaviour with respect to the institution-theoretic amalgamation property [12,13]. As a result, we are now able to write *modular* Event-B specifications and interoperate with $\mathcal{CSPCASL}$ using specification-building operators that are made available in the theory of institutions and supported by HETS. In future work, we will investigate the relationships between these specification-building operators and the modularisation constructs in Event-B and CSP. We will define and prove that ρ^{Mod} obeys the required properties. We will also examine whether other kinds of institution morphisms could exist between these two formalisms with particular focus on providing a more heterogeneous specification similar to that of the Event-B∥CSP formalism.

References

1. Abrial, J.-R.: Modeling in Event-B: System and Software Engineering, 1st edn. Cambridge University Press, New York (2010)
2. Abrial, J.-R., Butler, M., Hallerstede, S., Hoang, T.S., Mehta, F., Voisin, L.: Rodin: an open toolset for modelling and reasoning in Event-B. Int. J. Softw. Tools Technol. Transf. **12**(6), 447–466 (2010)
3. Farrell, M., Monahan, R., Power, J.F.: Providing a semantics and modularisation constructs for Event-B using institutions. In: International Workshop on Algebraic Development Techniques (2016)
4. Fitzgerald, J., Larsen, P.G., Woodcock, J.: Foundations for model-based engineering of systems of systems. In: Aiguier, M., Boulanger, F., Krob, D., Marchal, C. (eds.) Complex Systems Design & Management, pp. 1–19. Springer, Cham (2014)
5. Goguen, J.A., Burstall, R.M.: Institutions: abstract model theory for specification and programming. J. ACM **39**(1), 95–146 (1992)
6. Hoare, C.A.R.: Communicating sequential processes. In: Hansen, P.B. (ed.) The Origin of Concurrent Programming, pp. 413–443. Springer, New York (1978)
7. Iliasov, A.: On Event-B and control flow. Technical report, Newcastle University, Newcastle Upon Tyne, U.K (2009)
8. Isobe, Y., Roggenbach, M.: CSP-Prover - a proof tool for the verification of scalable concurrent systems. Inf. Media Technol. **5**(1), 32–39 (2010)
9. Knapp, A., Mossakowski, T., Roggenbach, M., Glauer, M.: An institution for simple UML state machines. In: Egyed, A., Schaefer, I. (eds.) FASE 2015. LNCS, vol. 9033, pp. 3–18. Springer, Heidelberg (2015). doi:10.1007/978-3-662-46675-9_1
10. Leuschel, M., Butler, M.: ProB: an automated analysis toolset for the B method. Int. J. Softw. Tools Technol. Transf. **10**(2), 185–203 (2008)
11. Mossakowski, T., Maeder, C., Lüttich, K.: The heterogeneous tool set, HETS. In: Grumberg, O., Huth, M. (eds.) TACAS 2007. LNCS, vol. 4424, pp. 519–522. Springer, Heidelberg (2007). doi:10.1007/978-3-540-71209-1_40
12. Mossakowski, T., Roggenbach, M.: Structured CSP – a process algebra as an institution. In: Fiadeiro, J.L., Schobbens, P.-Y. (eds.) WADT 2006. LNCS, vol. 4409, pp. 92–110. Springer, Heidelberg (2007). doi:10.1007/978-3-540-71998-4_6
13. Mosses, P.D. (ed.): CASL Reference Manual. The Complete Documentation of the Common Algebraic Specification Language. LNCS, vol. 2960. Springer, Heidelberg (2004)
14. O'Reilly, L.: Structured Specification with Processes and Data. Ph.D. thesis, Swansea University, Swansea, U.K (2012)
15. O'Reilly, L., Roggenbach, M., Isobe, Y.: CSP-CASL-Prover: a generic tool for process and data refinement. Electron. Notes Theor. Comput. Sci. **250**(2), 69–84 (2009)
16. Roggenbach, M.: CSP-CASL - a new integration of process algebra and algebraic specification. Theor. Comput. Sci. **354**(1), 42–71 (2006)
17. Sanella, D., Tarlecki, A.: Foundations of Algebraic Specification and Formal Software Development. Springer, Heidelberg (2012)
18. Schneider, S., Treharne, H., Wehrheim, H.: A CSP approach to control in Event-B. In: Méry, D., Merz, S. (eds.) IFM 2010. LNCS, vol. 6396, pp. 260–274. Springer, Heidelberg (2010). doi:10.1007/978-3-642-16265-7_19
19. Schneider, S., Treharne, H., Wehrheim, H.: Bounded retransmission in Event-B‖CSP: a case study. Electron. Notes Theor. Comput. Sci. **280**, 69–80 (2011)

20. Schneider, S., Treharne, H., Wehrheim, H.: The behavioural semantics of Event-B refinement. Formal Aspects Comput. **26**, 251–280 (2014)
21. Snook, C., Butler, M.: UML-B and Event-B: an integration of languages and tools. In: IASTED International Conference on Software Engineering, pp. 336–341, Innsbruck, Austria (2008)

Refinement-Based Modelling and Verification of Design Patterns for Self-adaptive Systems

Thomas Göthel$^{(\boxtimes)}$, Nils Jähnig, and Simon Seif

Technische Universität Berlin, Berlin, Germany
thomas.goethel@tu-berlin.de

Abstract. Design patterns are essential for designing complex systems by reusing recurring design principles. Various design patterns were proposed for self-adaptive systems, but their integration into a model-driven design process that, at the same time, provides formal guarantees is still a challenge. This is especially true for self-adaptive design patterns that are generic and abstract enough to provide general solutions that need to be refined prior to their concrete instantiations. In this paper, we present a structured and comprehensible modelling approach for design patterns in the refinement-based process calculus CSP. We formally show crucial properties of them and analyse the refinement-based relationship between their components, which generalises to entire patterns. Based on these analysis results, we are able to provide a first step towards a general, formally well-founded framework providing generic solutions for recurring problems in the management of self-adaptive systems.

Keywords: Design patterns · Self-adaptive systems · Refinement · Formal verification · Process calculus · CSP

1 Introduction

Design patterns offer an efficient way to develop complex software systems by reusing established structures that occur in various systems. Examples are the well-known server-client or the publisher-subscriber pattern. In this paper, we are interested in design patterns for the design of self-adaptive systems. Such systems interact with environments whose behaviours may unpredictably change at run-time. To cope with that, feedback loops can be employed. The MAPE-K loop [1] is one of the standard architectures for self-adaptive systems. It consists of a **M**onitoring, an **A**nalysis, a **P**lanning, and an **E**xecution phase. Firstly, the environment behaviour is monitored and analysed. Then, an adaptation plan is generated if necessary and finally executed in the managed system. All these phases share a common **K**nowledge base to transfer data between them.

In [12,13] more than thirty adaptive system implementations are studied. The authors extract twelve design patterns describing recurring elements in the management of self-adaptive systems. They are presented in a similar fashion like in [4] and are modelled informally. The extracted patterns are categorised

© Springer International Publishing AG 2017
Z. Duan and L. Ong (Eds.): ICFEM 2017, LNCS 10610, pp. 157–173, 2017.
https://doi.org/10.1007/978-3-319-68690-5_10

according to their general purpose (creational, behavioural, structural) and their relationship to the MAPE phases (monitoring, decision-making, reconfiguration). The presentation of [12] comprises a context under which the pattern can be applied, a description of the pattern elements, their relations and responsibilities, and consequences of the pattern (i.e. the results and tradeoffs). The patterns are presented in the context of a model-based development process [17]. Furthermore, linear temporal logic (LTL) is used to formally capture invariants of the patterns. Although the authors incorporate automated tools such as the SPIN model checker [8] to check for violations of the constraints, this can only be done with completely instantiated and concretely defined versions of a pattern. This precludes incremental design in which previously verified properties are preserved to lower levels.

To overcome this problem, we provide a structured and comprehensible modelling approach with which we have formally modelled five representative design patterns from [13] in the CSP *(Communicating Sequential Processes)* process calculus [14]. They are representative because they cover all categories as mentioned above. In this paper, due to space restrictions, we present two of them as examples to illustrate that they share many similarities that are furthermore present in all these design patterns. As part of our first main contribution, we formally model the pattern components as single abstract CSP processes. The advantage is that the behaviour of each component can be refined separately due to the compositional semantics of CSP. We discuss common design principles that facilitate their uniform modelling in CSP. We furthermore verify important properties of the patterns using the powerful notion of CSP refinement and its automatic verification support in the FDR refinement checker [6]. As our second main contribution, we analyse the relationship between pattern components and entire patterns based on our definition of behavioural extension. By this, a pattern component or an entire pattern inherits proved properties from other components or patterns even though new behaviour is introduced which stands in contrast to standard CSP refinement. As a result, we lay the foundation for a formally well-founded framework for design patterns for self-adaptive systems that are extensible, refinable, verifiable, and combinable w.r.t. interoperability.

In Sect. 2, we discuss related work of this paper. Then, we present background on the design patterns of [12] and on CSP in Sect. 3. The first part of our contribution is presented in Sect. 4 where we focus on the structured modelling of design patterns and the verification of their properties. Then, in Sect. 5, we present the second part of our contribution consisting of a formal relationship between pattern components and the patterns themselves based on our definition of behavioural extensions. Finally, in Sect. 6, we summarise and discuss our approach and point out possible directions for future work.

2   Related Work

In the following, we sketch some approaches on formal verification of self-adaptive systems and on formal modelling/verification of self-adaptive design patterns.

In [18], a modular approach for model-checking adaptive systems is presented. Invariant properties are stated in the temporal logic A-LTL. Modular verification is performed by decomposing the system and by applying assume-guarantee reasoning. In contrast to our work, refinement aspects and general design patterns are not considered. In [10], a formal model for policy-based adaptive systems is presented. According to environment changes, a managing component switches between configurations enforcing a certain adaptive policy. A formalism called PobSAM is presented with a formal semantics. Several equivalence relations and abstract results are provided. The results of the paper are rather abstract and it is not shown how to model concrete adaptive systems or parts of them. In [11], a UML-based modelling language for adaptive systems is presented. Based on its formal semantics, deadlock freedom and stability can be verified. In contrast, our work enables the stepwise development and furthermore the verification of general functional and adaptation properties. In [9], various formal design patterns are presented using timed automata that form components of a MAPE-K loop. In addition, specification templates for verification of properties are given. In contrast, our work formalises more detailed patterns that can themselves be used to design MAPE-K components. Furthermore, we enable the refinement-based design of patterns and examine the relationship between them. In [7], we have modelled and analysed a possible general structure of distributed adaptive real-time systems in CSP. This structure was rather abstract and independent of concrete feedback loops. In this paper, we provide more detailed design patterns that are relevant for the design of different MAPE-K components.

A conceptual framework for adaptation is presented in [2]. The work attempts to answer the general question under which conditions a software system can be considered adaptive. A formal model is presented that is based on labelled transition systems. To validate the framework, the authors discuss how several well-accepted adaptive architectures and computational paradigms fit into the framework, such as MAPE-K. However, due to the abstract nature of this paper, it is not clear how the presented framework can be used to build a concrete self-adaptive system. In [16], design patterns for decentralised control in self-adaptive systems are described. The patterns focus on the arrangement and interaction of multiple MAPE-K loops and are derived from their use in practice. In contrast to our work, this work is more abstract, as it takes an architecture-centric perspective. The presented patterns only focus on the structural arrangement of different components. They do not cover how communication between components is organised or how a common knowledge base for all the components is realised. In [3], the formal language SCEL is used to model general adaptation patterns consisting of service components that interact with each other according to the underlying pattern. The authors do not perform analysis of their patterns. Furthermore, the authors do not focus on refinement of patterns.

3   Background

In this section, we give an overview of the design patterns presented in [12], which is the basis for our work. We then briefly introduce CSP, which we use for modelling and verification of self-adaptive design patterns.

3.1   Design Patterns for Self-adaptive Systems

The work of [12] classifies design patterns for self-adaptive systems in three main categories based on their overall objective. *Monitoring* (M): Probing and distribution of information. *Decision-Making* (DM): Detect the necessity of adaptation and create a plan to perform a corresponding adaptation. *Reconfiguration* (R): Safely reconfigure the system according to an adaptation plan. Monitoring patterns can further be classified as *creational* (C) or *structural* (S), while reconfiguration design patterns can be further classified as *structural* (S) or *behavioural* (B). All considered decision-making patterns are classified as *structural* (S). *Creational* patterns are concerned with the creation and introduction of new elements into an existing system. *Behavioural* patterns describe how different components must interact in order to fulfil a common objective. Patterns that focus on how different components are arranged, are called *structural*.

In Table 1, we list the design patterns of [12] with their classifications and descriptions. All of them were modelled in the semi-formal modelling language UML. We formally modelled and analysed the patterns highlighted in italics in a Master's thesis [15] using CSP. In Sect. 4, we present the formalisations and analysis results of the *sensor factory* and the *adaptation detector*.

3.2   Communicating Sequential Processes

Process calculi are well suited to formally model and verify self-adaptive systems for several reasons. Firstly, they are inherently able to express characteristics of self-adaptive systems such as multiple concurrent and non-terminating processes. Secondly, process calculi offer compositionality features that allow for proofs to decompose a complex system into smaller subsystems. Lastly, refinement or equivalence can be used to relate an implementation to a specification. We decide in favour of CSP [14] because of its mature tool support, namely FDR [6].

The basic processes of CSP are $STOP$ (deadlock) and $SKIP$ (successful termination). The occurrence of an event is modelled using the *Prefix* operator $c.v \rightarrow P$, where the *value* v is communicated via *channel* c and then the process behaves as P. Receiving data on a channel is denoted by $c?x$. Choices between processes can be resolved by *External Choice* ($P \,\square\, Q$) or internally (non-deterministically) by *Internal Choice* ($P \,\sqcap\, Q$). To synchronise processes, *Parallel Composition* ($P \parallel_A Q$) is used describing that P and Q run independently, synchronising on events in A. Pure interleaving is denoted $P \,|||\, Q$. The *Hiding* operator ($P \setminus A$) is used to describe a process where all events in A are internalised within P, thus not visible to other processes and the environment.

Table 1. List of design patterns for self-adaptive systems.

Design pattern	Classification	Description
Sensor factory	M (C)	Systematically deploy sensors across a network
Reflective monitoring	M (S)	Perform introspection on a component and alter its behaviour
Content-based routing	M (S)	Route monitoring information based on the content of the readings
Case-based reasoning	DM (S)	Select an adaption plan based on rules
Divide & Conquer	DM (S)	Decompose a complex adaption plan into simpler adaption plans
Adaptation detector	DM (S)	Analyse monitoring data and determine whether adaption is necessary
Architectural-based	DM (S)	Architecture-based approach for selecting adaption plans
Tradeoff-based	DM (S)	Decide which adaption plan offers the best balance between competing objectives
Component insertion	R (S)	Insert components into a system during run time in a safe fashion
Component removal	R (S)	Remove components from a system during run time in a safe fashion
Server reconfiguration	R (B)	Reconfigure a server-client system during runtime without creating down times
Decentralized	R (B)	Insert and remove components from a system during run time in a safe fashion

FDR [6] enables the simulation and formal refinement-based verification of processes described in CSPm. This language extends CSP by a functional language for the formal description of datatypes, channels, sets, functions, and more. Expansion of channels is denoted by $\{|\ c\ |\}$ and describes the set of all possible communicated events on that channel.

The idea of refinement is that an implementation process has fewer possible behaviours than a specification process, thus describing a specification/implementation relationship. Properties like deadlock-freedom can also be defined as processes. The refinement $Prop \sqsubseteq Sys$ is used to show properties $Prop$ to be satisfied by Sys. Refinement is usually considered in the semantical traces or (stable) failures model [14]. The traces of a process describe its possible finite sequences of events and trace refinement $P \sqsubseteq_T Q$ (denoting $traces(Q) \subseteq traces(P)$) can be used to verify safety properties. In contrast, stable failures additionally record a set of refused events after a trace and thereby allow for the verification of liveness properties ($P \sqsubseteq_F Q$). The most important property concerning all the semantical models of CSP is their compositionality. From the refinements $P \sqsubseteq P'$ and $Q \sqsubseteq Q'$ it follows that in any arbitrary composition $\otimes$ also $P \otimes Q \sqsubseteq P' \otimes Q'$ holds, i.e., refinement can be shown component-wise. This enables modular verification in CSP, which we exploit in the context of our adaptive system patterns.

4   Formalisation of Adaptive Design Patterns

To facilitate the abstract design and verification of self-adaptive systems, we have formalised a representative subset of the adaptive design patterns presented in [12] in CSP. As described in Sect. 3, [12] classifies adaptive design patterns in several categories. In a Master's thesis [15], we have formally modelled and analysed one pattern for each category. The main challenge was to capture their similarities explicitly to establish formal relationships between components and patterns. This enables systematic reuse and reduces verification effort.

The formal model of each pattern consists of the pattern components (processes) and their interactions (composition). Here, we provide our pattern models on an abstract and generic level, which enables us to focus on their essential ideas. Note that implementation details can be introduced using formal refinement and behavioural extensions, as introduced in Sect. 5. Thus, design options can be chosen and detailed data-oriented behaviour can be introduced. The modelling of the essential nature of pattern components and patterns allows us, furthermore, to focus on similarities of different patterns that facilitates reuse of modelling principles and can be used for interoperability. The abstract models enable us to automatically show general safety and liveness properties using the FDR refinement checker. We exploit the compositional properties of CSP refinement such that only the relevant components of an abstract pattern need to be considered. We base our considered properties on the ones listed in [12].

Due to space limitations, we focus on two patterns, the *sensor factory* and the *adaptation detector*, in this paper. These allow us to illustrate our structured modelling approach, which exploits similarities between these models. As part of these similarities, we make use of a common subcomponent, the generic *adaptable component*, which originally stems from the *component insertion/removal* pattern. For the remaining design patterns, similar observations concerning reusability of modelling principles and common subcomponents can be made [15].

4.1   Adaptable Component

In the following, we first present our CSP model of the *adaptable component* together with a graphical notation for the ease of presentation that we use throughout the paper. Then, we present our formalisations and analysis results of the *sensor factory* and *adaptation detector*.

Definitions. ID is a set of unique identifiers for *adaptable components* that can interact. $\mathcal{L} = ID \times ID$ is a set of links between *adaptable components*. $\mathcal{L}_{id}^{CC} = \{id.c,\ c.id \mid c \in CC\}$ is the set of possible links for a component $id \in ID$ to other cooperating components $CC \subseteq ID$.

```
AdaptableComponentPassive(id, coopDom, links) =
   if card(links)==0
      then  (stopComponent.id -> AdaptableComponent(id, coopDom)
             [] AdaptableComponentPassive'(id, coopDom, links))
      else  AdaptableComponentPassive'(id, coopDom, links)

AdaptableComponentPassive'(id, coopDom, links) =
      destroyLink? link : links ->
         AdaptableComponentPassive(id,coopDom,diff(links,{link}))
   [] spawnLink?link : diff(possibleLinks(id, coopDom), links) ->
         AdaptableComponentPassive(id,coopDom,union(links,{link}))
   [] activateComponent.id ->
         AdaptableComponentActive(id, coopDom, links)
```

Fig. 1. Behaviour of an *Adaptable component*

$P = (a \in \{load, unload\}, c \in ID, L \subseteq \mathcal{L})$ is an adaptation plan to *load* or *unload* an *adaptable component* c along with a set of links L that need to be removed or created. Within the component-insertion-removal pattern, an adaptation driver creates adaptation plans.

CSP Model. The behaviour of an *adaptable component* is depicted in Fig. 1. In the upper part, we give an excerpt of the exact definition in CSPm syntax. Below, we give a simplified graphical representation of the entire process.

An *adaptable component* is uniquely identified by an $id \in ID$. Initially, it is in a stopped state. It will remain there until it is explicitly initialised via an *initComponent.id* event. Immediately after initialisation, the component resides in a passive state. Only in this passive state, links to other components can be created or destroyed. The component can be activated with an *activateComponent.id* event. While the component is active, it may process arbitrary transactions with linked components. Although this version of an *adaptable component* is rather abstract, it demands a specific availability of the *processTransaction* events. To this end, we use external choice on the *processTransaction* channel. An *adaptable component* is restricted to cooperate only with other components from a set $CC \subseteq ID$. This cooperation domain CC (denoted coopDom in the CSP script) enables us to partition the set of all components into distinct groups. This feature will be rather useful if multiple types of *adaptable components* are composed into a larger system. Note that this does not necessarily restrict our expressiveness. We can simply instantiate an *adaptable component* with $CC = ID$, lifting any restriction in communication. For two *adaptable components* we can show that $AC(id, ID) \sqsubseteq_T AC(id, CC \subseteq ID)$.

4.2 Sensor Factory

The *sensor factory* pattern is suited to (a) manage *sensors* in a loosely coupled system, to (b) provide a central instance to retrieve *sensors* in a uniform fashion, and to (c) enforce resource constraints across the system. The overall system is given by the parallel composition of the involved processes as follows.

$$Sensors = \left|\right|\right|_{i \in ID_S} Sensor(i, ID_C)$$

$$Clients = \left|\right|\right|_{i \in ID_C} Client(i, ID_S)$$

$$SensorInfrastructure = SensorFactory \underset{A_1}{\|} ResourceManager$$

$$System = (Clients \underset{A_2}{\|} Sensors) \underset{A_3}{\|} SensorInfrastructure$$

$A_1 = \{\!|allocateResources, freeResources, resourcesDenied, resourcesGranted|\!\}$

$A_2 = \{\!|spawnLink, destroyLink, read|\!\}$

$A_3 = \{\!|initComponent, stopComponent, activateComponent,$

   $passivateComponent, getSensor, releaseSensor, sensorGranted,$

   $sensorDenied, spawnLink, destroyLink|\!\}$

It deviates in several points from the original version described in [12]:

- We have abstracted away various methods and variables. We only cover the structural and behavioural essence of the pattern.
- Both simple sensor and complex sensor classes are covered by our single *sensor* process. The explicit transmission of values (and their types) is omitted.
- Our model of the resource manager is highly abstract. It decides whether resources can be allocated or not non-deterministically, which is the usual way to represent abstract behaviour in CSP.

In the following, we use a set of unique component identifiers *ID*, partitioned into identifiers for *sensors* (ID_S) and *clients* (ID_C), respectively. The set of all links is described by $\mathcal{L} = ID \times ID$. The set of possible links from a component with $id \in ID$ to other cooperating components $CC \subseteq ID$ is described by $\mathcal{L}_{id}^{CC} = \{id.c, c.id \mid c \in CC\}$.

The *sensors* and the *clients* are the managed components within this pattern. The purpose of a *sensor* is to provide data from the environment to the *client* components. A *sensor* is uniquely identified by an $id \in ID_S$. It keeps track of its active links to *clients* via a set of links $L \subseteq \mathcal{L}_{id}^{CC}$. CC is usually initialised with the set of *clients* ID_C. The behaviour of a *sensor* is very similar to that of the abstract *adaptable component* as given in Fig. 1. The main difference is that the cooperation components are clients and that the abstract *processTransation* channel is concretised to the *read* channel. Initially, a *sensor* is in an idle state until it is explicitly started via the *initComponent.id* event. Once started, the *sensor* can be linked with a *client* via the *spawnLink.l* event. After being activated via the *activateComponent.id* event, the *sensor* can communicate with a linked *client*. Communication is abstractly modelled by the *read.l* event. A *sensor* may also be passivated (*passivateComponent.id*) again, so that existing links can be destroyed (*destroyLink.l*) or new links can be spawned (*spawnLink.l*). If a *sensor* has no more linked *clients*, it can again return to the idle state.

The role of a *client* is to read data provided by *sensors*. Rather than accessing or creating *sensor* instances at will, it requests access to a *sensor* at a central manager, the *sensor factory*. A *client* is uniquely identified by an $id \in ID_C$ and keeps track of its active links to *sensors* via a set $L \subseteq \mathcal{L}_{id}^{CC}$ with CC usually being the set of *sensors* ID_S. S, the set of *sensors* that are connected to a *client*, can be computed from the link set L. Its behaviour is depicted in Fig. 2. Initially, a *client* is in an idle state until it is explicitly started via an *initComponent.id* event. To perform an active role within the system, it needs further to be activated (*activateComponent.id*). A *client* may then request a *sensor* s via the *getSensor.id.s* event if it is not yet linked to this *sensor*. If the request is denied (*sensorDenied.id.s*), the *client* simply returns to its previous state and is free to retry its attempt later or with a different *sensor*. If the request is granted (*sensorGranted.id.s*), the *client* waits for the *sensor factory* to perform a *passivateComponent.id* event. Only in the passive state, links may either be created or destroyed. Once linked to a *sensor*, the *client* can read data provided by the *sensor* via the corresponding *read.l* events. The *client* can release a *sensor* after it has been deployed via the *releaseSensor.id.s* event.

The *sensor factory* provides an interface to *clients* for retrieving *sensors*. Thus, it introduces a level of indirection between *clients* and *sensors*. This not only allows *clients* to access *sensors* in a uniform fashion, but also enables the

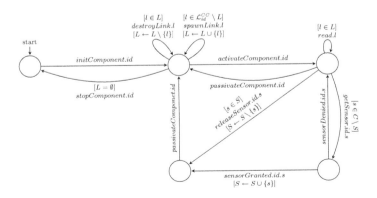

Fig. 2. Behaviour of a *Client Component*

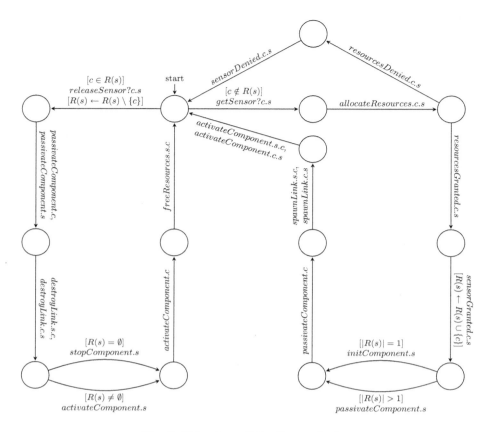

Fig. 3. Behaviour of the *Sensor factory*

factory to enforce resource constraints. The behaviour of the *sensor factory* is depicted in Fig. 3. The factory keeps track of all active links between *clients* and *sensors* with a registry map $R : ID_S \rightarrow \mathcal{P}(ID_C)$. A *client* c may request a *sensor* s via a *getSensor.c.s* event if it is not yet linked to this *sensor*. It is the responsibility of the *sensor factory* to allocate resources for the requested link via an *allocateResources.c.s* event. If the resource manager cannot allocate the requested resources, a *resourcesDenied.c.s* event is fired. Subsequently, the *sensor factory* informs the *client* about the denial via the *sensorDenied* channel. If, however, the resources could be allocated (*resourcesGranted.c.s*), the decision is forwarded via a *sensorGranted.c.s* event. Creating or destroying a link between a *client* and a *sensor* constitutes an adaptation of the system. The adaptation will be performed in an atomic fashion. To this end, the *sensor factory* will first passivate both involved components. Once the *sensor* and the *client* are passivated, their links will be created or destroyed via *spawnLink* or *destroyLink* events, respectively. Normal operation can resume as soon as both components have been reactivated. A *client* may unlink itself from the *sensor* at any time via the *releaseSensor* channel. Releasing a *sensor* constitutes another adaptation of the system. The procedure is analogous to the adaptation performed when a *sensor* is linked to a *client*. In addition, the *sensor factory* will notify the resource manager about the freed resources via a *freeResources* event. If a *sensor* becomes unused afterwards, i.e. there are no more linked active *clients*, it will be stopped.

The resource manager tracks the current resources of the system. It communicates only with the *sensor factory*. If the *sensor factory* tries to allocate resources for a new link between a *client* and a *sensor* via the *allocateResources* channel, the resource manager evaluates whether the system can spare the requested resources. If the request can be fulfilled, a *resourcesGranted* event is fired, *resourcesDenied* otherwise. Resources are freed via the *freeResources* channel.

For the *sensor factory*, we have proved four important safety properties automatically using the FDR refinement checker: (SF1) *clients* and *sensors* are only linked if the resource manager agrees, (SF2) *sensors* are not started without permission of the resource manager, (SF3) *clients* cannot access *sensors* without being linked by the *sensor factory* first, and (SF4) links are only destroyed after the *client* explicitly releases the *sensor*. To formally capture safety properties, we have defined generic safety property processes in CSP as follows.

$$P(A, B) = \left(\prod_{x \in \text{Events} \setminus A \cup B} x \rightarrow P(A, B) \right) \sqcap \left(\prod_{a \in A} a \rightarrow Q(A, B) \right)$$

$$Q(A, B) = \left(\prod_{x \in \text{Events} \setminus A \cup B} x \rightarrow Q(A, B) \right) \sqcap \left(\prod_{b \in B} b \rightarrow P(A, B) \right)$$

The basic idea is to first accept all events of the alphabet except for the events $b \in B$ that must not occur without the previous occurrence of another event $a \in A$. If some a occurs, the generic process goes to another state where b events are allowed, but no a events. When a b event occurs there, the process goes back to the initial state. Thereby, the property process has only those traces where each occurrence of a b event is preceded by exactly one corresponding a event.

4.3   Adaptation Detector

The adaptation detector pattern monitors the overall health of a system using *health indicators* and possibly triggers an adaptation if necessary. The overall pattern is given by the parallel composition of the involved processes as follows.

$$HM(id, s, t) = HI(id, s) \underset{A_1}{\parallel} Analyser(id, s, t)$$

$$HM = \underset{id \in ID_C, (s,t) \in P}{\big\vert\big\vert\big\vert} HM(id, s, t)$$

$$System = SensorInfrastructure \underset{A_3}{\parallel} (Sensors \underset{A_2}{\parallel} HM)$$

$$A_1 = \{analyse, analysis\}$$
$$A_2 = \{spawnLink, destroyLink, read\}$$
$$A_3 = \{initComponent, stopComponent, activateComponent,$$
$$passivateComponent, getSensor, releaseSensor,$$
$$sensorGranted, sensorDenied, spawnLink, destroyLink\}$$

It deviates in several points from the original version described in [12]:

– Various methods and variables have been omitted. Our model only covers the structural and behavioural essence of the pattern.
– The observer is omitted – a *health indicator* is directly linked with a *sensor*.
– The model reuses the *sensor factory* pattern as described above for the management of *sensors* and *health indicators*.

In the following, we use a set of unique component identifiers ID, partitioned into identifiers for *sensors* (ID_S) and *health indicator* components (ID_C), respectively. $\mathcal{L} = ID \times ID$ describes a set of links, $\mathcal{L}_{id}^{CC} = \{id.c, c.id \mid c \in CC\}$, the set of possible links from a component with $id \in ID$ to other cooperating components $CC \subseteq ID$. $P = ID_S \times T$ describes the set of possible health parameters, where T is a non-empty finite set of possible thresholds. $E = \{Normal, Abnormal\}$ is the set of possible evaluations.

A *health indicator* monitors an environment parameter. To this end, the indicator retrieves information about the system from a *sensor*, which is analysed by an *analyser*. If corresponding thresholds are violated, a system adaptation is initiated. The behaviour of a *health indicator* is depicted in Fig. 4. It is uniquely identified by an $id \in ID_C$ and is bound to a specific *sensor* $s \in ID_S$. To monitor an environment parameter, the *health indicator* regularly reads its assigned *sensor* via the *read* channel. The *health indicator* sends the acquired sensor data to its *analyser* process via the *analyse* channel and awaits the analysis result on the *analysis* channel. Note that we abstract from the actual *sensor* value. If the *analyser* detects abnormal behaviour, the *health indicator* is responsible to trigger an adaptation via the *trigger* channel. In our abstract model, the trigger event only contains the *sensor* s that reported the abnormal value.

An *analyser* decides whether a reported *sensor* value deviates from a defined threshold. It may implement arbitrarily complex analysis functions. An *analyser* is directly linked to a *health indicator* and its implementation is specific to a *sensor* and threshold. The *health indicator* may ask the *analyser* to perform analysis on a *sensor* value via the *analyse* channel. The *analyser* will then respond with an analysis result of the presented value containing an evaluation via the *analysis* channel. In practice, there would be different implementations of *analysers* that incorporate different logic to judge whether a presented value exceeds a threshold or not. In our model, the actual *sensor* value again has been omitted. The *analyser* in our model is highly abstract and decides non-deterministically whether a threshold is exceeded or not.

Sensors describe a class of managed components within this pattern. A system using this pattern may consists of one or more *sensors*. The purpose of a *sensor* component is to provide data about the environment to a *health indicator*. The *sensor factory* enables *health indicators* to retrieve *sensors*.

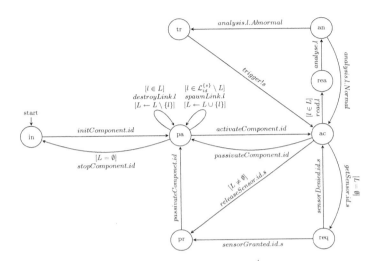

Fig. 4. Behaviour of a *Health indicator*

For the adaptation detector, we have proved four important properties automatically using the FDR refinement checker: (HM1) An adaptation trigger event must only be fired if the analysis indicated abnormal behaviour, (HM2) any *sensor* data obtained by a *health indicator* must eventually be presented to an *analyser* for analysis, and (HM3) any report of a threshold exceeded will eventually cause an adaptation trigger. HM1 is a safety property, whereas HM2 and HM3 are liveness properties. To capture liveness properties, we have defined a generic liveness property process in CSP as follows.

$$P(A, B) = \left(\sqcap_{x \in \Sigma \setminus A} x \to P(A, B) \right) \qquad \sqcap \left(\sqcap_{a \in A} a \to Q(A, B, n_{max}) \right)$$

$$Q(A, B, 0) = \left(\sqcap_{x \in \Sigma \setminus B} x \to Q(A, B, 0) \right) \qquad \square \left(\sqcap_{b \in B} b \to P(A, B) \right)$$

$$Q(A, B, n) = \left(\sqcap_{x \in \Sigma \setminus B} x \to Q(A, B, n - 1) \right) \quad \sqcap \left(\sqcap_{b \in B} b \to P(A, B) \right)$$

First, this process can non-deterministically choose an event from the alphabet including some events $a \in A$ that should enable some events $b \in B$, subsequently. If some a occurs, the generic property process goes into a state where alphabet events and b are non-deterministically chosen. However, after at most n steps without performing b, b is enabled using external choice. This means that the liveness property process models the most non-deterministic process that stably enables b eventually after a occurred. Note that eventuality cannot be expressed unboundedly in CSP, but only w.r.t. a fixed maximal number n of steps.

Note that the conjunction of HM1 and HM3 imposes a restriction on the design: A *health indicator* cannot implement an analysis of *sensor* values that deviates from the behaviour of its *analyser*. Thus, a *health indicator* is unable to directly implement a higher-level analysis, e.g. a compound analysis involving multiple *sensors*. This enables us to reduce the complexity of *health indicators* and *health monitors* as they are now bound to a single *sensor*. Note that our models can easily be used to define less restrictive variations of this pattern.

In this section, we have formally modelled two design patterns in a structured way exploiting similarities between them. Furthermore, we have automatically proved general important properties of them. In the next section, we present our notion of behavioural extension to formally relate components of different patterns that enables formal interoperability between patterns.

5   Formal Relations Between Adaptive Design Patterns

To enable the transfer of proved properties of pattern components, we show that they extend each other. To this end, we define an appropriate *extension* relation.

5.1   Behavioural Extension

As an example for behavioural extension, the *adaptable component* (AC, from the *component insertion/removal* patterns) defines just the behaviour of the adaptation logic, and the *client* (C, from the *sensor factory* pattern) additionally specifies its interaction with the *sensor factory*. To relate these processes, both traces refinement and failures refinement are insufficient. These kinds of refinements require all possible behaviour to be present in the abstract specification already. Instead, we need an adapted notion of refinement that preserves behaviour (in the sense of traces or failures refinement) on process parts that are not extended and ignores the extended behaviour itself to a certain degree. We propose a relation $\sqsubseteq^{(\cdot)}$ with EX as parameter for the extension alphabet, hidden within Q so that only events of P's alphabet remain visible.

$$P \sqsubseteq^{(EX)} Q := P \sqsubseteq (Q \setminus EX)$$

Using only original CSP theory enables us to inherit CSP compositionality and to directly use verification tools such as FDR [6]. The $\sqsubseteq^{(\cdot)}$ relation is transitive [1] and works with all three refinement models (traces, failures, failures-divergence). As usual, it is possible to rename events. For example, in the *adaptable component* a generic *processTransaction* is used, which is called *read* in the *client*.

---

[1] $P \sqsubseteq^{(A)} Q \wedge Q \sqsubseteq^{(B)} R \Longrightarrow P \sqsubseteq^{(A \cup B)} R.$

5.2   Relations Between Pattern Components

The *health indicator* component can be described as an extension of the *client*. Basically, the *health indicator* is a *client* that is bound to a single *sensor* and cooperates with an *analyser* component. Formally, we can show a refinement relation between the *client* and the *health indicator*. Let $id \in ID_C$ and $s \in ID_S$ be identifiers. We instantiate the two processes as follows.

$$C = Client(id, \{s\})$$
$$HI = HealthIndicator(id, s)$$

The instantiation of the *client* restricts the component to only cooperate with a single *sensor*, namely s. This is somewhat different from the usual instantiation of the component, where we usually pass ID_S, i.e. the set of all *sensors*.

The communication of the *health indicator* with its *analyser* component is limited to the event set $\{\!|analyse, analysis|\!\}$, while its interface to the environment is just the event *trigger*. Let EX be the set of these events, formally $\{\!|analyser, analysis, trigger|\!\}$. In our formalisation, it holds that

$$C \sqsubseteq_F^{(EX)} HI$$

The *health indicator* extends the *client* by an interface to an *analyser*. Thus, the *health indicator* inherits all safety and liveness properties of the *client*.

With this and $AC \sqsubseteq_T^{(SF)} C$ (SF being the interface of the *client* to the *sensor factory*), we can show that the *health indicator* satisfies by transitivity of $\sqsubseteq_T$ all safety properties of the *adaptable component*. However, $AC \sqsubseteq_F^{(SF)} C$ does not hold, because hiding SF in C creates invisible loops which lead to divergences. This is a common problem with hiding. The situation above is different when extending the *client* to the *health indicator*. The *client* already uses the event *read*, which is "action refined" in the *health indicator*, i.e., the loop consisting of the event *read* is replaced by a loop consisting of a sequence starting with *read*. Thus, when hiding the extension events, there is still one visible event in the loop, namely *read*, so the loop does not get divergent after hiding. The *adaptable component* is also extended w.r.t. traces by the *server* and the *sensor*, respectively. An overview of the extensions is depicted in Fig. 5.

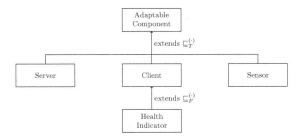

Fig. 5. Overview of extension relations between components across design patterns.

Within a pattern, we can replace a component with a behavioural extension, thus generalising extension to entire patterns. The extension relation allows us not only to reuse patterns but also to inherit their properties. This complements the ordinary refinement of CSP where behaviour is removed with an extension mechanism where new behaviour is introduced that preserves shown properties.

6   Conclusion and Future Work

In this paper, we have presented an approach for the structured modelling and verification of self-adaptive design patterns within CSP. The advantage of CSP is that refinement can be carried out compositionally and that it enables the transfer of verified properties from abstract levels to concrete ones. This allows us not only to verify these design patterns and their components but also to establish formally well-founded relations between components of different patterns. To this end, we have defined the notion of behavioural extension, which also allows to introduce new behaviour. Furthermore, this enables a formally sound embedding of entire design patterns within other patterns.

In future work, we plan to formalise further adaptive design patterns in CSP. Our goal is a comprehensive set of verified basic components that can be used to combine different patterns. To build actual running adaptive systems, we currently study adaptive design patterns together with the implementation framework of CSP++ [5], which enables us to define a model-driven design approach for self-adaptive systems from high-level specification down to executable code. In CSP++, events are bound to C++ functions to realise complex computations that are irrelevant within the abstract CSP models. This approach allows us to reduce the semantic gap between models that are formally refined and their final implementation as the important implementation infrastructure code is automatically generated. The generated infrastructure code ensures that formal guarantees are preserved to the implementation level. Our case study is given by an adaptive cruise control where several lorries can autonomously create and dissolve convoys to save fuel. Finally, we have started to analyse the applicability of adaptive design patterns in distributed systems. In our current models, communication works perfectly and components cannot fail. The consideration of such effects would lead to more robust adaptive design patterns.

References

1. An architectural blueprint for autonomic computing. Technical report, IBM, June 2005
2. Bruni, R., Corradini, A., Gadducci, F., Lluch Lafuente, A., Vandin, A.: A conceptual framework for adaptation. In: de Lara, J., Zisman, A. (eds.) FASE 2012. LNCS, vol. 7212, pp. 240–254. Springer, Heidelberg (2012). doi:10.1007/978-3-642-28872-2_17
3. Cesari, L., De Nicola, R., Pugliese, R., Puviani, M., Tiezzi, F., Zambonelli, F.: Formalising adaptation patterns for autonomic ensembles. In: Fiadeiro, J.L., Liu, Z., Xue, J. (eds.) FACS 2013. LNCS, vol. 8348, pp. 100–118. Springer, Cham (2014). doi:10.1007/978-3-319-07602-7_8

4. Gamma, E., Helm, R., Johnson, R., Vlissides, J.: Design Patterns: Elements of Reusable Object-Oriented Software. Addison-Wesley, Reading (1995)
5. Gardner, W.B., Gumtie, A., Carter, J.D.: Supporting selective formalism in CSP++ with process-specific storage. In: 12th International Conference on Embedded Software and Systems, ICESS 2015, pp. 1057–1065. IEEE (2015)
6. Gibson-Robinson, T., Armstrong, P., Boulgakov, A., Roscoe, A.W.: FDR3 — a modern refinement checker for CSP. In: Ábrahám, E., Havelund, K. (eds.) TACAS 2014. LNCS, vol. 8413, pp. 187–201. Springer, Heidelberg (2014). doi:10.1007/978-3-642-54862-8_13
7. Göthel, T., Klös, V., Bartels, B.: Modular design and verification of distributed adaptive real-time systems based on refinements and abstractions. EAI Endorsed Trans. Self-Adapt. Syst. **15**(1), 5:1–5:12 (2015)
8. Holzmann, G.: The Spin Model Checker: Primer and Reference Manual. Addison-Wesley, Reading (2003)
9. de la Iglesia, D.G., Weyns, D.: MAPE-K formal templates to rigorously design behaviors for self-adaptive systems. ACM Trans. Auton. Adapt. Syst. **10**(3), 15:1–15:31 (2015)
10. Khakpour, N., Jalili, S., Talcott, C., Sirjani, M., Mousavi, M.: Formal modeling of evolving self-adaptive systems. Sci. Comput. Program. **78**(1), 3–26 (2012)
11. Luckey, M., Engels, G.: High-quality specification of self-adaptive software systems. In: Proceedings of the 8th International Symposium on Software Engineering for Adaptive and Self-Managing Systems, SEAMS 2013, pp. 143–152. IEEE (2013)
12. Ramirez, A.J.: Design patterns for developing dynamically adaptive systems. Master's thesis, Michigan State University (2008)
13. Ramirez, A.J., Cheng, B.H.C.: Design patterns for developing dynamically adaptive systems. In: Proceedings of the 2010 ICSE Workshop on Software Engineering for Adaptive and Self-Managing Systems, pp. 49–58. ACM (2010)
14. Roscoe, A.: Understanding Concurrent Systems. Springer, London (2010)
15. Seif, S.: Formalisation and analysis of design patterns for self-adaptive systems and their formal relationship. Master's thesis, Techn. Universität Berlin (2015)
16. Weyns, D., et al.: On patterns for decentralized control in self-adaptive systems. In: de Lemos, R., Giese, H., Müller, H.A., Shaw, M. (eds.) Software Engineering for Self-Adaptive Systems II. LNCS, vol. 7475, pp. 76–107. Springer, Heidelberg (2013). doi:10.1007/978-3-642-35813-5_4
17. Zhang, J., Cheng, B.H.C.: Model-based development of dynamically adaptive software. In: Proceedings of the 28th International Conference on Software Engineering, pp. 371–380. ACM (2006)
18. Zhang, J., Goldsby, H.J., Cheng, B.H.: Modular verification of dynamically adaptive systems. In: Proceedings of the 8th ACM International Conference on Aspect-Oriented Software Development, AOSD 2009, pp. 161–172. ACM (2009)

Assertion Generation Through Active Learning

Long H. Pham$^{(\boxtimes)}$, Ly Ly Tran Thi, and Jun Sun

ISTD, Singapore University of Technology and Design, Singapore, Singapore
honglong_pham@mymail.stud.edu.sg

Abstract. Program assertions are useful for many program analysis tasks. They are however often missing in practice. Many approaches have been developed to generate assertions automatically. Existing methods are either based on generalizing from a set of test cases (e.g., DAIKON), or based on some forms of symbolic execution. In this work, we develop a novel approach for generating likely assertions automatically based on active learning. Our targets are complex Java programs which are challenging for symbolic execution. Our key idea is to generate candidate assertions based on test cases and then apply active learning techniques to iteratively improve them. We evaluate our approach using two sets of programs, i.e., 425 methods from three popular Java projects from GitHub and 10 programs from the SVComp repository. We evaluate the 'correctness' of the assertions either by comparing them with existing assertion-like checking conditions, or by comparing them with the documentation, or by verifying them.

1 Introduction

Assertions in programs are useful for many program analysis tasks [15]. For instance, they can be used as oracles for program testing, or correctness specification for static program verification. They are however often insufficiently written in practice [15]. It is thus desirable to generate them automatically.

A variety of approaches have been developed for assertion generation. We broadly divide them into three categories. The approaches in the first category rely on summarizing and generalizing a set of test cases. One well-known example is DAIKON [11]. DAIKON takes a set of test cases as inputs and summarizes the program states at a given program location based on a set of predefined templates. Typically, these approaches are scalable and thus can be applied to complex programs. However, it is also known if only a limited number of test cases are available, the generated assertions are often not 'correct' [32]. Unfortunately, as reported in [4,5], the number of test cases available in practice is often limited.

The second category contains approaches which rely on some forms of symbolic execution or constraint solving, e.g., [3,6,10]. These approaches often provide some guarantee on the quality of the generated assertions. However, since programs must be encoded as symbolic constraints and be solved, these approaches are often limited to relatively simple programs.

© Springer International Publishing AG 2017
Z. Duan and L. Ong (Eds.): ICFEM 2017, LNCS 10610, pp. 174–191, 2017.
https://doi.org/10.1007/978-3-319-68690-5_11

The third category combines the techniques of the two categories, e.g., the guess-and-check approaches [13,24,25]. The idea is to *guess* candidate assertions and then *check* their correctness based on symbolic execution or similar techniques. If the candidate assertion is found to be incorrect, a counterexample is identified as a new test case and used to refine the candidate assertion. Similarly, the work in [35] generates candidate invariants and then instruments the candidate invariants into the programs. Afterwards, symbolic execution is applied to generate new test cases, which are used to improve the candidates. Similar to those approaches in the second category, these approaches are often limited to relatively simple programs as symbolic execution is applied.

In this work, we propose a new approach for assertion generation. Our targets are complex Java programs and thus we would like to avoid heavy-weight techniques like symbolic execution. We also would like to overcome the issue of not having sufficiently many test cases in practice and be able to generate 'correct' assertions. Briefly, our approach works as follows. We first learn some initial candidate assertions using a set of templates and machine learning algorithms (e.g., [7] and Support Vector Machine [23]). Next, we apply active learning techniques to improve the candidate assertions. That is, we automatically generate new program states based on the candidate assertions. Then, we re-learn the assertion using the testing results from new states and iteratively improve the assertions until they converge. Compared to existing approaches, our main idea is to automatically mutate program states based on active learning to refine the candidate assertions. This is motivated by recent studies in [30,31] which show that active learning can help to learn 'correct' predicates (i.e., with bounded error) with a small number of labeled data.

Our approach has been implemented in a tool named ALEARNER. To evaluate the effectiveness and efficiency of ALEARNER, we conduct two sets of experiments. Firstly, we apply ALEARNER to 425 methods from three popular Java projects from GitHub. ALEARNER successfully generates 243 assertions. We manually inspect the generated assertions and confirm that 168 of them (69%) are correct, i.e., necessary and sufficient to avoid failure. Furthermore, we notice that 186 out of the 425 methods contain some assertion-like checking condition at the beginning of the method. For 116 of those methods (62%), ALEARNER successfully generates an assertion identical to the condition. Secondly, we apply ALEARNER to a set of 10 programs from the software verification competition (SVComp [2]). Given the postcondition in the program, we use ALEARNER to automatically learn a precondition, without any user-provided test cases. We show that for 90% of the cases, ALEARNER learns a precondition which is weaker than the user-provided precondition yet strong enough to prove the postcondition. Lastly, we evaluate the efficiency of ALEARNER and show that the computational overhead is mild.

The remainder of the paper is organized as follows. Section 2 illustrates how our approach works with examples. Section 3 presents details of each step in our approach. Section 4 presents the implementation of ALEARNER and evaluation results. Section 5 discusses the related work. Section 6 concludes.

2   Overview with Examples

In the following, we briefly describe how our approach works. Without loss of generality, we assume the input to our method is a Java method with multiple parameters (which may call other methods) as well as a set of user-provided test cases. For instance, assume that the input is the method $withMonthOfYear$ shown in Fig. 1, which is a method from the $joda$-$time$ project on GitHub. This method returns a new $MonthDay$ object based on the current object and sets its month value as the input $monthOfYear$. A series of methods are invoked through inheritance and polymorphism to create a new $MonthDay$ object, including method $verifyValueBounds$ in class $FieldUtils$ (shown in Fig. 1). Method $verifyValueBounds$ checks if the value of $monthOfYear$ is within the range defined by the parameters $lowerBound$ (i.e., 1) and $upperBound$ (i.e., 12).

```
public MonthDay withMonthOfYear(int monthOfYear) {
    int[] newValues = getValues();
    newValues = getChronology().monthOfYear().
    set(this,MONTH_OF_YEAR,newValues,monthOfYear);
    return new MonthDay(this, newValues);
}
...
public static void verifyValueBounds(DateTimeField field, int value,
        int lowerBound, int upperBound) {
    if ((value<lowerBound)||(value>upperBound)) {
        throw new IllegalFieldValueException(
            field.getType(), Integer.valueOf(value),
            Integer.valueOf(lowerBound), Integer.valueOf(upperBound));
    }
}
```

Fig. 1. Example from class $MonthDay$ in project $JodaOrg/joda$-$time$

Our first step is *data collection*. Given a program location in the given program, we instruct the program to output the program states during the execution of the test cases. We collect two sets of program states, one containing program states which lead to failure and the other containing the rest. In the above example, assume that we are interested in generating a precondition of method $monthOfYear$, i.e., an assertion at the beginning of the method. In the project, there are three user-provided test cases for this method, with the input $monthOfYear$ being 5, 0, and 13 respectively. The latter two test cases result in failure, whereas the first runs successfully. Thus, we have two sets of program states, one containing the state of $monthOfYear$ being 0 or 13 and the other containing the state of $monthOfYear$ being 5.

The second step is *classification*. Given the two sets of program states, we apply learning techniques to identify predicates which could perfectly classify the two sets. In ALEARNER, we support two learning algorithms to identify such predicates. The first algorithm uses the predefined templates and applies the learning algorithm in [7] to learn boolean combination of the templates. The second one is inspired by [27], which applies Support Vector Machine (SVM) to learn conjunction of linear inequalities as classifiers. In our example, given the two sets of program states, applying the first algorithm, ALEARNER tries the templates one by one and identifies a candidate assertion $monthOfYear = 5$ (i.e., when $monthOfYear$ is 5, there is no failure). While this assertion is consistent with the three test cases, it is 'incorrect' and the reason is the lack of test cases. For instance, if we are provided with a test case with $monthOfYear$ being 4, assertion $monthOfYear = 5$ would not be generated. This shows that assertion generation based only on a limited set of test cases may not be effective. Using SVM, we learn the assertion: $3 \leq monthOfYear \leq 9$.

The third step is *active learning*. To solve the above problem, we apply active learning techniques to iteratively improve the assertion until it converges. This is necessary because the assertion should define the boundary between failing program states from the rest, whereas it is unlikely that the provided (or generated) test cases are right on the boundary. Active learning works by generating new states based on the current boundary. Then, we execute the program with new states to check whether they lead to failure or not (a.k.a. labeling). Step 2 and subsequently step 3 are then repeated until the assertion converges.

For simplicity, we show only how the candidate assertion $3 \leq monthOfYear \leq 9$ is refined in the following. Applying active learning, we generate two new states where $monthOfYear$ is 3 and 9 respectively. After testing, since both states run successfully, the two sets of program states are updated so that the passing set contains the states of $monthOfYear$ being 3, 5 and 9; and the failing set contains 0 and 13. Afterwards, the following assertion is identified using SVM: $2 \leq monthOfYear \leq 11$. Repeating the same process, we generate new states where $monthOfYear$ is 2 and 11 and get the assertion: $1 \leq monthOfYear \leq 12$. We then generate states where $monthOfYear$ is 1 and 12 and learn the same assertion again. This implies that we have converged and thus the assertion is output *for user inspection*.

The above example shows a simple assertion which is generated using ALEARNER. In comparison, because $withMonthOfYear$ calls many methods as well as inheritance and polymorphism in the relevant classes, applying assertion-generation methods based on symbolic execution is non-trivial[1]. ALEARNER can also learn complex assertions with disjunction and variables from different domains. An example is the precondition generated for method $minus$ in class $Days$ shown in Fig. 2. Each $Days$ object has a field $iPeriod$ to represent the number of days. The method receives a $Days$ object $days$ as input. If $days$ is $null$, the method returns the *this* object. Otherwise, it negates the number of days in $days$. Then, it returns a new $Days$ object whose number of days is the sum of the negation and the number of day in the *this* object. An arithmetic exception is thrown when the number of days of $days$ equals $Integer.MIN\_VALUE$ or when the result of the sum is overflow. ALEARNER generates the assertion: $days = null \; || \; (this.iPeriod - days.iPeriod \; is \; not \; overflow \; \&\& \; days.iPeriod \neq Integer.MIN\_VALUE)$ for the method.

---

[1] Refer to recent development on supporting polymorphism in symbolic execution in [17].

```
public Days minus(Days days) {
    if (days == null) return this;
    return minus(days.getValue());
}
public Days minus(int days) {
    return plus(FieldUtils.safeNegate(days));
}
```

Fig. 2. Example from class *Days* in project *JodaOrg/joda-time*

3 Detailed Approach

In this section, we present the details of each step in our approach. Recall that the inputs include a Java program in the form of a method with multiple parameters and a set of test cases. The output is the assertions at different program locations. We assume the program is deterministic with respect to the testing results. This is necessary because our approach learns based on the testing results, which become unreliable in the presence of non-determinism.

Step 1: Data Collection. Our goal is to dynamically learn likely assertions at different program locations. To choose program locations to learn, we build a control flow graph of the program and choose the locations heuristically based on the graph. For instance, we generate assertions at the beginning of a method or the end of a loop inside a method. Another candidate program location is the beginning of a loop. However, an assertion in a loop or a recursion must be inductive. Learning inductive assertions is itself a research topic (e.g., [24,28]) and we leave it to future work.

We instruct at the program location with statements to output the program states during the execution of the test cases. In ALEARNER, there can be two sources of test cases. The first group contains the user-provided test cases. However, our experience is that often user-provided test cases are rather limited and they may or may not contain the ones which result in failure. The second group contains random test cases we generate using the Randoop approach [20]. We remark that Randoop is adopted because it is relatively easy to implement.

To collect only relevant features of the program states, we identify the relevant variables. Given a failed test case, we identify the statement where the failure occurs and find all the variables which it has a data/control dependence on through dynamic program slicing. Among these variables, the ones accessible at the program location are considered relevant. Next, we extract features from the relevant variables. For variables of primitive types (e.g., int, $float$), we use their values. For reference type variables, we can obtain values from the fields of the referenced objects, the fields of those fields, or the returned value of the inspector methods in the class. As a result, we can obtain many values from a single variable. In ALEARNER, we set the bound on the number of de-referencing to be 2 by default, i.e., we focus on the values which can be accessed through two or less de-referencing. This avoids the problem of infinite de-referencing in dealing with recursive data types.

After executing the test cases with the instrumented program, we obtain a set of program states, in the form of an ordered sequence of features (a.k.a. feature vectors). We then categorize the feature vectors into two sets according to the testing results, one denoted as S^+ containing those which do not lead to failure and the other denoted by S^- containing the rest. Note that the feature vectors obtained from different test cases may not always have the same dimension. For instance, in one test case, a reference type object might have the value $null$, whereas it may not be $null$ in another test case so that we can obtain more features. We then apply standard techniques to normalize feature vectors in S^+ and S^-, i.e., we mark missing features as $null$. With this normalization, all vectors have the same number of features.

Step 2: Classification. The feature vectors in S^+ are samples of 'correct' program behaviors, whereas the ones in S^- are samples of 'incorrect' program behaviors. Intuitively, an assertion should perfectly classify S^+ from S^-. We thus borrow ideas from the machine learning community to learn the assertions through classification. We support two classification algorithms in this work. One applies the learning algorithm in [7] to learn boolean combination of propositions generated by a set of predefined templates inspired by DAIKON. The other applies SVM to learn assertions in the form of conjunctions of linear inequalities. Both algorithms are coupled with an active learning strategy as we discuss later.

Table 1. Sample templates for assertions

Sample template	Sample selective sampling
x * y = z	Predefined values for x, y, and z
x = c	$(x = c \pm 1)$
x != c	$(x = c \pm 1)$
x = true	$(x = true)$; $(x = false)$
ax + by = c	Solve for x based on y and vice versa

Template based Learning. We first introduce our template based assertion generation approach. We adopt most of the templates from DAIKON. In the following, we first introduce the primitive templates (i.e., propositions without logical connectors) supported by ALEARNER and then explain how to learn boolean combinations of certain primitive templates.

A few sample primitive templates are shown in Table 1. In total, we have 120 primitive templates and we refer the readers to [1] for the complete list. A template may contain zero or more unknown coefficients which can be precisely determined with a finite set of program states. For instance, the template which checks whether two variables have the same value has zero coefficient and we can determine whether it is valid straightforwardly; the template which checks whether a variable has a constant value has one unknown coefficient (i.e., the constant value) which can be determined with one program state in S^+. Some templates have multiple coefficients, e.g., the template $ax + by = c$ where x and y are variables and a, b, c are constant coefficients. We need at least three pairs of x, y values in S^+ to identify the values of a, b, and c.

In order to generate candidate assertions in the form of a primitive template, we randomly select a sufficient number of feature vectors from S^+ and/or S^- and compute the coefficients. Once we compute the values for the coefficients, we check whether the resultant predicate is valid. A template with concrete values for its coefficients is called valid if it evaluates to true for all feature vectors in S^+ and evaluates to false for all feature vectors in S^-. If feature vectors are not enough to identify the coefficients, or the template requires more features than those in the feature vectors, or the template is not applicable to the input values, the template is skipped. If a template requires only a subset of the features in the feature vectors, we try all subsets of the features.

Like DAIKON, we limit the number of variables in the primitive templates to be no more than 3 and hence the number of combinations of features is cubic in the total number of features. We remark that because we learn from S^- as well, we are able to support templates which are not supported by DAIKON. One example is the template $x \neq a$ (where a is an unknown coefficient). With only program states in S^+, it is impossible to identify the value of a (since there are infinitely many possibilities). However, since the negation of $x \neq a$ must be satisfied by program states in S^-. With one feature vector from S^-, we can precisely determine the value of a.

We sometimes need assertions in the form of boolean combinations of primitive templates. In the following, we describe how to learn boolean combination of primitive templates. We start with identifying a set of predicates (in a form defined by a primitive template) which correctly classify some feature vectors in S^+ or S^-. For instance, we have the predicate $x = y$ if there is a feature vector such that $x = y$ in S^+ or $x \neq y$ in S^-. In general, it might be expensive to identify all of such predicates if the primitive template has multiple coefficients. For instance, in order to identify all such predicates in the form of $ax + by = c$, we must try all combinations of three feature vectors in S^+ to identify the value of a, b and c, which has a complexity cubic in the size of S^+. We thus limit ourselves to predicates defined by primitive templates with zero coefficient for learning boolean combination of the templates.

Once we have identified the set of predicates, we apply the algorithm in [7] to identify a boolean combination of them which perfectly classifies all feature vectors in S^+ and S^-. Informally, we consider each feature vector in S^+ and S^- as data points in certain space. Each data point in S^+ is connected to every one in S^- by an edge. The problem then becomes finding a subset of the predicates (which represent lines in this space) such that every edge is cut by some predicates. The algorithm in [7] works by greedily finding the predicate which can cut the most number of uncut edges until all edges are cut. The set of predicates identified this way partition the space into regions which only contains data points in S^+ or S^- but not both. Each region is a conjunction of the predicates. The disjunction of all regions containing S^+ is a perfect classifier. We remark that DAIKON generates multiple assertions at a program location, which are logically in conjunction, and has limited support for disjunctive assertions.

SVM-based Learning. In addition to template-based learning, we support learning of assertions in the general form of $c_1x_1 + c_2x_2 + \cdots \geq k$ (a.k.a. a half space) where there might be 1, 2, 3, or more variables in the expression. To generate such an assertion, we need to find coefficients $c_1, c_2, \cdots, k$ such that $c_1x_1 + c_2x_2 + \cdots \geq k$ for all feature vectors in S^+ and $c_1x_1 + c_2x_2 + \cdots < k$ for all feature vectors in S^-. With a finite set of feature vectors, we may have infinitely many coefficients $c_1, c_2, \cdots, k$ satisfying the above condition. In this work, we apply SVM classification [23] to identify the coefficients for this template.

SVM is a supervised machine learning algorithm for classification and regression analysis. We use its binary classification functionality, which works as follows. Given S^+ and S^-, it tries to find a half space $\Sigma_{i=1}^d c_i x_i \geq k$ such that (1) for every feature vector $[x_1, x_2, \cdots, x_d] \in S^+$ such that $\Sigma_{i=1}^d c_i x_i \geq k$ and (2) for every feature vector $[x_1, x_2, \cdots, x_d] \in S^-$ such that $\Sigma_{i=1}^d c_i x_i < k$. If S^+ and S^- are linearly separable, SVM is guaranteed to find a half space. The complexity of SVM is $O(max(n, d) * min(n, d)^2)$, where n is the number of feature vectors and d is the number of dimensions [8], i.e., the number of values in a feature vector in S^+ or S^-.

It has been shown that SVM can be extended to learn more expressive classifiers, e.g., polynomial inequalities using the polynomial kernel and conjunctions of half spaces. In the following, we briefly describe how ALEARNER learns conjunction of multiple half spaces as the assertions (in the form of $c_1^1 x_1 + c_2^1 x_2 + \cdots \geq k^1 \wedge c_1^2 x_1 + c_2^2 x_2 + \cdots \geq k^2 \wedge \cdots$) adopting the algorithm proposed in [27]. Given the feature vectors in S^+ and S^-, we first randomly select a vector s from S^- and learn a half space ϕ_1 to separate s from all vectors in S^+. We then remove all vectors s' in S^- such that ϕ_1 evaluates to false given s'. Next, we select another vector from S^- and find another half space ϕ_2. We repeat this process until S^- becomes empty. The conjunction of all the half spaces $\phi_1 \wedge \phi_2 \wedge \cdots$ perfectly classifies S^+ from S^- and is reported as a candidate assertion.

We remark that we prefer simple assertions rather than complex ones. Thus, we first apply the primitive templates. We then apply SVM-based learning if no valid assertion is generated based on the primitive templates. Boolean combinations of primitive templates are tried last. The order in which the templates are tried has little effect on the outcome because invalid assertions are often filtered through active learning, which we explain next.

Step 3: Active Learning. The assertions generated as discussed above are often not correct due to the limited number of test cases we learn from, as we have illustrated in Sect. 2. This is a known problem in the machine learning community and one remedy for solving the problem is active learning [9].

Active learning is proposed in contrast to passive learning. A passive learner learns from a given set of data over which it has no control, whereas an active learner actively selects what data to learn from. For instance, DAIKON could be regarded as a passive learner for assertions. It has been shown that an active learner can sometimes achieve good performance using far less data than would otherwise be required by a passive learner [30, 31]. Active learning can be applied for classification or regression. In this work, we apply it for improving the candidate assertions generated by the above-discussed classification algorithms.

In the following, we explain how active learning is adopted in our work. Once a candidate assertion is generated, we selectively generate new feature vectors, which are then turned into new program states so as to improve the assertion. For template-based learning, we design heuristics to select the data on and near by the classification boundary for each template. A few examples are shown in the second column of Table 1. For example, if the assertion is $x = c$ and x is of type integer, the generated feature vectors would be $x = c + 1$ or $x = c - 1$. For templates with zero coefficients such as $x * y = z$, we choose some predefined values on and near by the boundary of $x * y = z$ as the selected feature vectors.

For SVM-based learning, we adopt the active learning strategy in [23]. The idea is to select a fixed number (e.g., 5 as in [23]) of data points on the classification boundary as the selected feature vectors. For instance, if the candidate assertion is $3x + 2y \geq 5$, we solve the equation $3x + 2y = 5$ to get a few pairs of x, y values. Note that if the candidate assertion contains multiple clauses (e.g., it is the conjunction of multiple inequalities), we apply the above strategy to each of its clauses (e.g., if it is from a template, we apply the corresponding heuristics).

After selecting the feature vectors, we automatically mutate the program so as to set the program state at the program location according to the selected feature vectors. For instance, if the selected feature vectors are $x = 4$ and $x = 6$, we generate two versions of the program. The first version inserts an additional statement $x = 4$ right before the program location in the original program, and the second version inserts the additional statement $x = 6$. Next, we run the test cases with the modified programs so as to check whether the test cases lead to failure or not. If executing a test case with the first version of the program leads to failure, the program state $x = 4$ is added to S^- or otherwise it is added to S^+. Similarly, if executing a test case with the second version leads to failure, the program state $x = 6$ is added to S^- or otherwise it is added to S^+. Afterwards, we repeat the classification step to identify new candidate assertions and then apply active learning again. The process repeats until the assertion converges.

Note that selective sampling may create unreachable states in the program. If the unreachable states are labeled negative, they do not affect the learning result because we try to exclude them. If they are labeled positive, we learn an invariant which is weaker than the 'actual' one. It is not a problem as our goal is to learn invariants which are sufficiently strong to avoid program failure.

4   Implementation and Evaluation

We have implemented the proposed method in a self-contained tool named ALEARNER, which is available at [1]. ALEARNER is written in Java with 91600 lines of code. In the following, we evaluate ALEARNER in order to answer the following research questions.

- RQ1: Can ALEARNER generate correct assertions?
- RQ2: Is active learning helpful?
- RQ3: Is ALEARNER sufficiently efficient?

As a baseline, we compare ALEARNER with DAIKON. To have a fair comparison, the experiments are set up such that ALEARNER and DAIKON always have the same set of test cases except that the test cases which result in failure are omitted for DAIKON since DAIKON learns only from the correct program executions.

Our experimental subjects include two sets of programs. The first set contains 425 methods selected from three Java projects on GitHub. Project *pedrovgs/Algorithms* is a library of commonly used algorithms on data structures and some math operations; project *JodaOrg/joda-time* is a library for working with date and time; and project *JodaOrg/joda-money* is a library for working with currency. We apply ALEARNER to all classes in the first project. For the other two projects, we focus on classes in the main packages (*org.joda.time* and *org.joda.money*) as those classes contain relatively more unit test cases. We select all methods which have at least one passed test case and one failed test case, except the constructors or the methods that are inherited without overriding (due to limitation of our current implementation). We systematically apply ALEARNER to each method, using existing test cases in the projects only. As shown in Table 5, there are a total of 2137 test cases for all the methods, i.e., on average 5 per method. *We do not generate random test cases for this set of programs*, so as to reduce randomness as well as to evaluate whether ALEARNER works with limited user-provided test cases only.

The second set contains 10 programs from the software verification competition (SVComp) repository. These programs are chosen because we can verify the correctness of the learned assertions. The programs are selected based on the following criteria. First, because ALEARNER is designed for Java programs and the programs in the repository are in C, we have to manually translate the selected programs into Java. We thus avoid programs which rely on C specific language constructs. For the same reason, we are limited to a small set of programs due to manual effort required in translating the programs. Furthermore, we skip programs with no precondition (i.e., the precondition is *true*) and non-deterministic programs. These programs are relatively small, contain relatively strong user-provided assertions (i.e., a pair of precondition and postcondition for each program) and no test cases. These 10 programs are not easy to analyze. Most of them rely on *float* or *double* variables and are hard to verify.

We randomly generate 20 test cases for each program. Since these programs take *float* or *double* type numbers as inputs which have a huge domain, we perform a simple static analysis of the postcondition, to heuristically set the range of random number generation for generating test cases. For instance, if we are to verify that some variable is always within the range of $[-10, 10]$, we use an enlarged range (e.g., $[-100, 100]$) to generate input values (often for different variables). Furthermore, we manually examine the results and round the coefficients in the learned assertions to the number of decimal places that are enough to prove the postcondition based on programs specification.

All experiments are conducted in macOS on a machine with an Intel(R) Core(TM) i7, running with one 2.20 GHz CPU, 6M cache and 16 GB RAM. All details of the experiments are at [1]. For all the programs, we configure ALEARNER to learn an assertion at the beginning of the method, i.e., a precondition. For each program, if random test case generation is applied, we repeat the experiment 20 times and report the average results. We set a time out of 3 min so that we terminate if we do not learn anything (e.g., if SVM could not find a classifier, it usually takes a long time to terminate) or active learning takes too long to converge.

RQ1: Can ALEARNER *generate correct assertions?* In this work, we define the correctness of an assertion in terms of whether there is a correlation between the learned assertion and whether failure occurs or not. Depending on what the correlation is, the assertions are categorized into four categories. An assertion is called *necessary* if it is (only) a necessary condition for avoiding failure; it is *sufficient* if it is (only) a sufficient condition; and *correct* if it is both necessary and sufficient (i.e., there is no failure if and only if the assertion is satisfied). Ideally, we should learn correct assertions. Lastly, an assertion is called *irrelevant* if it is neither necessary nor sufficient. For instance, given a program which contains an expression 5/x, assertion *true* is necessary; $x \geq 2$ is sufficient; $x \neq 0$ is correct; and $x > -13$ is irrelevant.

We start with the experiment results on the GitHub projects, which are shown in Table 2. As shown in column *#asse*, a total of 243 assertions are learned by ALEARNER, i.e., ALEARNER is able to learn an assertion at the beginning of 57% of the methods. For comparison, the second last column shows the corresponding number using DAIKON. It can be observed that ALEARNER learned fewer assertions than DAIKON for all three projects. This is expected because DAIKON generates one assertion for each of its templates which is consistent with the test cases (after certain filtering [11]), whereas an assertion learned by ALEARNER must be consistent with not only the passed test cases but also the ones which trigger failure.

We first evaluate the correctness of these assertions by manually categorizing them. Table 2 shows the number of assertions in each category. Note that DAIKON often generates multiple assertions and it is often meaningless if we take the conjunction of all of them as one assertion. We thus manually check whether some assertions generated by DAIKON can be conjuncted to form correct assertions and count them as correct assertions. Necessary and sufficient assertions for DAIKON are counted similarly. Then we count the rest of DAIKON's assertions as irrelevant. In comparison, ALEARNER generates only one assertion at one program location. We can see that ALEARNER successfully generates many correct assertions, i.e., 168 out of all 243 (about 69%) are correct. In comparison, only 18 out of 516 (about 3.5%) assertions learned by DAIKON are correct, whereas majority of those learned by DAIKON are sufficient only (35%) or irrelevant (60%). This is expected as DAIKON learns based on the program states in the passed test cases only. Given that the number of test cases is limited, often the learned assertions have limited correctness.

In all three projects, ALEARNER learned more correct or necessary (i.e., over-approximation) assertions than DAIKON and much fewer sufficient or irrelevant ones. There are two main reasons why ALEARNER may not always learn the correct assertion. Firstly, ALEARNER may not always be able to perform active learning. For instance, a field of an object may be declared as *final* and thus altering its value at runtime is infeasible. Secondly, the test cases are biased for some methods. For example, in one method in project *Algorithm*, the correct assertion should be $tree1 \neq null \,||\, tree2 \neq null$. But in the test cases, only the value of variable *tree1* varies (e.g., being *null* in one test and being not *null* in another) and variable *tree2* remains the same. As a result, ALEARNER learns the assertion $tree1 \neq null$, which is sufficient but not necessary.

Table 2. Experiment results on GitHub projects and Java standard library

Project	#meth	ALEARNER					DAIKON					ALEARNER wo AL				
		#asse	corr	necc	suff	irre	#asse	corr	necc	suff	irre	#asse	corr	necc	suff	irre
Algorithms	96	85	69	10	2	4	135	5	0	93	37	88	64	15	3	6
Joda-time	236	133	83	43	0	7	307	8	7	84	208	153	25	31	37	60
Joda-money	93	25	16	9	0	0	74	5	2	3	64	30	16	9	0	5

There are cases where ALEARNER cannot learn any assertion. The reason is the correct assertions require templates which are currently not supported by ALEARNER. For example, there are multiple methods which take *String* objects as inputs and throws *RuntimeException* if the input *String* objects do not follow certain patterns, such as patterns for scientific numbers in *Algorithm* and patterns for day and time format in *joda-time*. In another example, multiple methods throw *RuntimeException* if and only if an input object is not of a type which is a subclass of certain class. ALEARNER does not support templates related to typing and cannot learn those assertions.

We observe that, for 186 out of these 425 methods, the authors have explicitly put in code which is used to check the validity of the inputs (which is used to prevent the inputs from crashing the program by causing *RuntimeException*). This provides an alternative way of evaluating the quality of the learned assertion. That is, we assume the conditions used in these checking code are correct assertions and compare them with the learned assertions. For 116 out of the 186 (62%) methods, the assertion learned by ALEARNER is the same as the checking condition. In comparison, for only 8 out of the 186 (4.3%) methods, the condition is one of those assertions generated by DAIKON for the respective method.

Next, we evaluate the assertions generated for the SVComp programs. We formally verify the correctness of the learned precondition (by either existing program verifier or referring to the original proof of the program). Table 3 shows the experiment results. Column *correct* shows how many times (out of 20) we learn the correct assertion. The reason that ALEARNER may not always learn the same assertion is the random test cases could be different every time. Column

Table 3. Experiment results on SVComp programs

Subject	ALEARNER		DAIKON		ALEARNER wo AL	
	Useful	Correct	Useful	Correct	Useful	Correct
exp_loop	0	0	0	0	0	0
inv_sqrt	20	20	0	0	0	0
sqrt_biN	12	11	0	0	1	0
sqrt_H_con	15	15	0	0	0	0
sqrt_H_int	13	12	0	0	0	0
sqrt_H_pse	15	13	0	0	0	0
sqrt_N_pse	13	10	0	0	0	0
square_8	15	0	0	0	0	0
zono_loose	16	16	0	0	9	1
zono_tight	14	14	0	0	11	2

useful shows the number of times we learn a useful assertion, i.e., a sufficient condition for proving the postcondition which is implied by the given precondition. It is useful as it can be used to verify the program indirectly.

We first observe that DAIKON failed to learn any correct or useful assertion for these programs with the same passing test cases. One reason is because these programs require some precise numerical values in the assertions which are often missing from the randomly generated test cases. For 9 programs, ALEARNER learns useful assertions most of the time; and for 8 programs, ALEARNER learns the correct assertions. Further, for all these 8 cases, ALEARNER learns correct assertions which are strictly weaker than the corresponding precondition, which implies that with ALEARNER's result, we prove a stronger specification of the program. For program *exp_loop*, ALEARNER learned the assertion $a \neq 0$, which is implied by the given precondition $a \geq 1e-10$ && $a \leq 1e10$. However, it is necessary but not sufficient to prove the postcondition $c \geq 0$ && $c \leq 1e6$. A closer look reveals that the postcondition is violated if a is greater than 2.1e12 or less than $-2.1e12$. Because we never generated a random test case with such huge number, ALEARNER failed to learn the correct assertion. For program *square_8*, we discover that the correct assertion contains two irrational number coefficients, which is beyond the capability of ALEARNER.

Based on the experiment results discussed above, we conclude that the answer to RQ1 is that ALEARNER can learn correct assertions and does so often.

RQ2: Is active learning helpful? To answer this question, we compare the performance of ALEARNER with and without active learning. The results are shown in the last columns of Tables 2 and 3. Without active learning, the number of learned assertions and irrelevant ones increases. For instance, for methods in *joda-time*, the number of irrelevant assertions increases from 7 (i.e., 5%) to 60

Table 4. DAIKON results with selective sampling

	corr	necc	suff	irre
Without AL test cases	0	0	28	13
With AL test cases	0	0	2	8

(i.e., 39%). Furthermore, without active learning, we almost never learn correct assertions for the SVComp programs. This is expected as without active learning, we are limited to the provided test cases and many templates cannot be filtered. As the correct assertions for these programs contain specific numerical values, active learning works by iteratively improving the candidate assertions until the correct numerical values are identified.

Next, we conduct experiments to see whether the additional programs states generated by ALEARNER during active learning could be used to improve DAIKON. The rationale is that if it does, active learning could be helpful not only for ALEARNER but also DAIKON. We randomly selected about 10% of the methods (43 of them), created additional test cases based on the new program states, then feed those test cases (together with the provided ones) to DAIKON. The results are shown in Table 4. We can see that with additional test cases, DAIKON can filter a lot of sufficient and irrelevant assertions. We conclude that active learning is helpful for ALEARNER and may potentially be helpful for DAIKON.

RQ3: Is ALEARNER sufficiently efficient? To answer this question, we would like to evaluate whether the overhead of active learning is acceptable. Table 5 shows the execution time of ALEARNER (with and without active learning) as well as DAIKON's. In addition, we show the lines of the code in the projects and the number of test cases we use to analyze methods since they are relevant to the efficiency. It can be observed that ALEARNER is slower than DAIKON (about one order of magnitude), which is expected as ALEARNER relies on learning algorithms which are more time consuming than template matching in DAIKON. On average ALEARNER takes about 40 seconds to learn an assertion, which we consider as reasonably efficient for practical usage. Without active learning, ALEARNER runs faster but only by a factor of 2, which means active learning converges relatively quickly. Given that the quality of the generated assertions improve with active learning, we consider the overhead is acceptable.

Threat to Validity. Firstly, we acknowledge that the subjects used for evaluation might be biased. Though the three GitHub projects are selected randomly, they may not be representative of other projects. So are the programs from the SVComp repository. Secondly, although we did our best to configure DAIKON to achieve its best performance, it is not impossible that experts on DAIKON may be able to tune it for better performance. The issue of lacking test cases is a fundamental limitation for DAIKON.

Table 5. Experiment results on efficiency

Project	LOC	#tests	ALEARNER(w/wo AL)(s)	DAIKON(s)
Algorithms	6512	414	2496/1682	223
Joda-time	85785	1163	5970/4701	665
Joda-money	8464	560	1947/1739	236
SVComp	276	200	471/193	22

5 Related Work

This work is closely related to the line of work on dynamic invariant generation, a technique pioneered by Ernst *et al.* to infer likely invariants. In particular, ALEARNER is inspired by DAIKON [11,12]. DAIKON executes a program with a set of test cases. Then it infers precondition, postcondition, and loop invariant by checking the program states against a set of predefined templates. The templates that satisfy all these program states are likely invariants. Nguyen *et al.* extends DAIKON's approach by proposing some templates that can describe inequality, nested array [18], and disjunction [19]. They also propose to validate the inferred invariants through k-induction.

ALEARNER is different from the above-mentioned approaches. Firstly, above approaches learn invariants through summarising the program states of the passed test cases using some templates. ALEARNER learns not only from the passed test cases but also the failed ones. Therefore, it is able to learn assertions with a number of templates which cannot be supported otherwise. Secondly, ALEARNER relies on active learning to overcome the lack of user-provided test cases, which we believe is a threat to the usefulness of the above-mentioned test cases based learning tools.

Our approach is related to iDiscovery [35], which improves invariants in DAIKON by generating more test cases based on current candidate invariants and symbolic execution. In comparison, ALEARNER avoids symbolic execution. Moreover, because iDiscovery uses DAIKON to generate invariants, it only learns from passed test cases. Xie and Notkin also propose an approach similar to ours, in which test cases generation and specification inference are enhanced mutually [34]. Their work, however, does not provide any experiment results.

Sharma *et al.* proposed a number of guess-and-check approaches to infer loop invariants. They categorize program states into two sets of good and bad states. Several learning algorithms are used to learn a predicate that can separate these two sets, such as PAC learner [26], null space [25], or randomised search [24]. The predicate is then checked by a verifier to see if it is valid loop invariant. If it is not, verifier returns a counterexample and the counterexample is used to improve the learned predicate. Garg *et al.* extend above idea by introducing ICE framework [13] and a method to learn invariants by solving a SMT formula. A new method using decision tree to learn invariants in ICE framework is presented in [14]. Krishna *et al.* also use decision tree to learn invariant in their approach [16].

These guess-and-check methods can infer correct invariants. However, they rely on the program verification and thus are limited to relatively simple programs. In comparison, our approach relies on machine learning techniques.

Padhi *et al.* present the idea of learning precondition to avoid exception with a method that can add more features in the learning process automatically [21]. In [22], the authors use decision tree to learn likely precondition from a partial truth table of a set of predicates. Lastly, our idea of using SVM to learn assertions is inspired by [27,29,33]. However, those works have very different goals from this one.

6   Conclusion

In this work, we present an approach that can infer likely assertions from complex Java programs. The novelty in our approach is to apply active learning techniques to learn and refine assertions. While active learning helps to overcome the issue of lacking test cases in many cases, the effectiveness of ALEARNER is still dependent on the availability of certain test cases. For instance, if a failure occurs only if some complex path conditions are satisfied and there are no test cases for triggering that exception, the condition to avoid that failure will not be learned. To solve the problem, we would like to use more systematic test case generation techniques to get better initial test cases.

Acknowledgments. This research was funded by the project T2MOE1704.

References

1. http://sav.sutd.edu.sg/alearner
2. http://sv-comp.sosy-lab.org/2016/
3. Alur, R., Černỳ, P., Madhusudan, P., Nam, W.: Synthesis of interface specifications for java classes. In: POPL, pp. 98–109. ACM (2005)
4. Beller, M., Gousios, G., Panichella, A., Zaidman, A.: When, how, and why developers (do not) test in their IDEs. In: ESEC/FSE, pp. 179–190. ACM (2015)
5. Beller, M., Gousios, G., Zaidman, A.: How (much) do developers test? In: ICSE, pp. 559–562. IEEE (2015)
6. Boshernitsan, M., Doong, R., Savoia, A.: From daikon to agitator: lessons and challenges in building a commercial tool for developer testing. In: ISSTA, pp. 169–180. ACM (2006)
7. Bshouty, N.H., Goldman, S.A., Mathias, H.D., Suri, S., Tamaki, H.: Noise-tolerant distribution-free learning of general geometric concepts. JACM **45**(5), 863–890 (1998)
8. Chapelle, O.: Training a support vector machine in the primal. Neural Comput. **19**(5), 1155–1178 (2007)
9. Cohn, D.: Active learning. In: Sammut, C., Webb, G.I. (eds.) Encyclopedia of Machine Learning, pp. 10–14. Springer, New York (2010)
10. Csallner, C., Tillmann, N., Smaragdakis, Y.: DySy: Dynamic symbolic execution for invariant inference. In: ICSE, pp. 281–290. ACM (2008)

11. Ernst, M.D., Cockrell, J., Griswold, W.G., Notkin, D.: Dynamically discovering likely program invariants to support program evolution. IEEE Trans. Software Eng. **27**(2), 99–123 (2001)

12. Ernst, M.D., Perkins, J.H., Guo, P.J., McCamant, S., Pacheco, C., Tschantz, M.S., Xiao, C.: The daikon system for dynamic detection of likely invariants. Sci. Comput. Program. **69**(1), 35–45 (2007)

13. Garg, P., Löding, C., Madhusudan, P., Neider, D.: ICE: a robust framework for learning invariants. In: Biere, A., Bloem, R. (eds.) CAV 2014. LNCS, vol. 8559, pp. 69–87. Springer, Cham (2014). doi:10.1007/978-3-319-08867-9_5

14. Garg, P., Neider, D., Madhusudan, P., Roth, D.: Learning invariants using decision trees and implication counterexamples. In: POPL, pp. 499–512. ACM (2016)

15. Hoare, C.A.R.: Assertions: a personal perspective. IEEE Ann. Hist. Comput. **25**(2), 14–25 (2003)

16. Krishna, S., Puhrsch, C., Wies, T.: Learning invariants using decision trees. arXiv preprint arXiv:1501.04725 (2015)

17. Li, L., Lu, Y., Xue, J.: Dynamic symbolic execution for polymorphism. In: CC, pp. 120–130. ACM (2017)

18. Nguyen, T., Kapur, D., Weimer, W., Forrest, S.: DIG: a dynamic invariant generator for polynomial and array invariants. ACM Trans. Softw. Eng. Methodol. **23**(4), 30 (2014)

19. Nguyen, T., Kapur, D., Weimer, W., Forrest, S.: Using dynamic analysis to generate disjunctive invariants. In: ICSE, pp. 608–619. ACM (2014)

20. Pacheco, C., Lahiri, S.K., Ernst, M.D., Ball, T.: Feedback-directed random test generation. In: ICSE, pp. 75–84. IEEE (2007)

21. Padhi, S., Sharma, R., Millstein, T.: Data-driven precondition inference with learned features. In: PLDI, pp. 42–56. ACM (2016)

22. Sankaranarayanan, S., Chaudhuri, S., Ivančić, F., Gupta, A.: Dynamic inference of likely data preconditions over predicates by tree learning. In: ISSTA, pp. 295–306. ACM (2008)

23. Schohn, G., Cohn, D.: Less is more: active learning with support vector machines. In: ICML, pp. 839–846 (2000)

24. Sharma, R., Aiken, A.: From invariant checking to invariant inference using randomized search. In: Biere, A., Bloem, R. (eds.) CAV 2014. LNCS, vol. 8559, pp. 88–105. Springer, Cham (2014). doi:10.1007/978-3-319-08867-9_6

25. Sharma, R., Gupta, S., Hariharan, B., Aiken, A., Liang, P., Nori, A.V.: A data driven approach for algebraic loop invariants. In: Felleisen, M., Gardner, P. (eds.) ESOP 2013. LNCS, vol. 7792, pp. 574–592. Springer, Heidelberg (2013). doi:10.1007/978-3-642-37036-6_31

26. Sharma, R., Gupta, S., Hariharan, B., Aiken, A., Nori, A.V.: Verification as learning geometric concepts. In: Logozzo, F., Fähndrich, M. (eds.) SAS 2013. LNCS, vol. 7935, pp. 388–411. Springer, Heidelberg (2013). doi:10.1007/978-3-642-38856-9_21

27. Sharma, R., Nori, A.V., Aiken, A.: Interpolants as classifiers. In: Madhusudan, P., Seshia, S.A. (eds.) CAV 2012. LNCS, vol. 7358, pp. 71–87. Springer, Heidelberg (2012). doi:10.1007/978-3-642-31424-7_11

28. Somenzi, F., Bradley, A.R.: IC3: where monolithic and incremental meet. In: FMCAD, pp. 3–8 (2011)

29. Sun, J., Xiao, H., Liu, Y., Lin, S., Qin, S.: TLV: abstraction through testing, learning, and validation. In: ESEC/FSE, pp. 698–709. ACM (2015)

30. Tong, S., Chang, E.Y.: Support vector machine active learning for image retrieval. In: MULTIMEDIA, pp. 107–118. ACM(2001)

31. Tong, S., Koller, D.: Support vector machine active learning with applications to text classification. J. Mach. Learn. Res. **2**, 45–66 (2001)
32. Wei, Y., Furia, C.A., Kazmin, N., Meyer, B.: Inferring better contracts. In: ICSE, pp. 191–200. ACM (2011)
33. Xiao, H., Sun, J., Liu, Y., Lin, S., Sun, C.: TzuYu: Learning stateful typestates. In: ASE, pp. 432–442. IEEE (2013)
34. Xie, T., Notkin, D.: Mutually enhancing test generation and specification inference. In: Petrenko, A., Ulrich, A. (eds.) FATES 2003. LNCS, vol. 2931, pp. 60–69. Springer, Heidelberg (2004). doi:10.1007/978-3-540-24617-6_5
35. Zhang, L., Yang, G., Rungta, N., Person, S., Khurshid, S.: Feedback-driven dynamic invariant discovery. In: ISSTA, pp. 362–372. ACM (2014)

Detecting Energy Bugs in Android Apps Using Static Analysis

Hao Jiang[1], Hongli Yang[1(✉)], Shengchao Qin[2], Zhendong Su[3], Jian Zhang[4], and Jun Yan[4]

[1] Beijing University of Technology, Beijing, China
yhl.yang@gmail.com
[2] Teesside University, Middlesbrough, UK
[3] University of California, Davis, USA
[4] State Key Laboratory of Computer Science, Institute of Software,
Chinese Academy of Sciences, Beijing, China

Abstract. Energy bugs in Android apps are defects that can make Android systems waste much energy as a whole. Energy bugs detection in Android apps has become an important issue since smartphones usually operate on a limited amount of battery capacity and the existence of energy bugs may lead to serious drain in the battery power. This paper focuses on detecting two types of energy bugs, namely resource leak and layout defect, in Android apps. A resource leak is a particular type of energy wasting phenomena where an app does not release its acquired resources such as a sensor and GPS. A layout defect refers to a poor layout structure causing more energy consumption for measuring and drawing the layout. In this paper, we present a static analysis technique called SAAD, that can automatically detect energy bugs in a context-sensitive way. SAAD detects the energy bugs by taking an inter-procedural analysis of an app. For resource leak analysis, SAAD decompiles APK file into Dalvik bytecodes files and then performs resource leak analysis by taking components call relationship analysis, inter-procedure and intra-procedure analysis. For detecting layout defect, SAAD firstly employs *Lint* to perform some traditional app analysis, then filters energy defects from reported issues. Our experimental result on 64 publicly-available Android apps shows that SAAD can detect energy bugs effectively. The accuracies of detecting resource leak and layout energy defect are 87.5% and 78.1% respectively.

1 Introduction

With the rapid development of mobile technology, smartphones, especially Android phones, provide people with convenient services. Android application markets like Google Play provide abundant apps for users. In order to enrich the user experience, Android systems are equipped with a wide range of hardware

Supported by National Natural Science Foundation of China (No. 61672505) and the CAS/SAFEA International Partnership Program for Creative Research Teams.

Z. Duan and L. Ong (Eds.): ICFEM 2017, LNCS 10610, pp. 192–208, 2017.
https://doi.org/10.1007/978-3-319-68690-5_12

components, such as Sensors, WIFI, GPS, Camera and so on. Because of rich functionalities and convenient services, a majority of developers are attracted to develop apps on Android platforms.

Meanwhile, the usage time of a smartphone is constrained by its battery capacity. Since the existing techniques have not yet allowed the smartphones to be charged anywhere, and at anytime, services and functions will be constrained, and even forced to close. And as a consequence, the battery energy has great impacts on user experiences. The battery energy is mostly consumed by apps installed in smartphones, as the service and some resource intensive hardware components (such as screen, GPS, WIFI, and CPU) are usually invoked when apps are running [2].

Typical energy bugs [1,3] that may be hidden in smartphone apps can be classified into either resource leak or layout defect. A resource leak refers to a case that an app does not release acquired resources such as sensor, GPS, wakelock, memory etc., and thus may hinder system from entering an idle state, making hardware reside at a continuous energy consumption situation. A layout defect can be caused by a poor layout structure (layout is too deep, too many or ineffective widgets, etc.) which leads to high energy consumption for measuring and drawing of this layout. Both types of bugs can result in unnecessary energy consumption.

There are some work related with energy bugs detection. However, they focus on detecting either background programs or foreground ones such as user interfaces. Comparatively, we focus on detecting both resource leaks and layout defects, which are more latent to the users.

This paper makes the following contributions:

- We propose a novel approach, called *SAAD* (Static Application Analysis Detector). It analyzes not only resource leak at background programs, but also layout defects at foreground. The generated reports of energy bugs help analyzers and developers improve their apps.
- *SAAD* detects resource leak by context sensitive analysis, which combines component call analysis, inter-procedural analysis and intra-procedural analysis. It considers the calling context when analyzing the target of a function call. In order to improve efficiency, It focuses on analyzing effective paths that are involved in resource applying/releasing operations. In particular, *SAAD* can detect more than eighty resources leak by automatically getting those resources API information from Android official website by Web crawler.
- We have implemented a tool to support *SAAD* and evaluated it on 64 free-available Android applications. Our results show that *SAAD* can detect energy bugs effectively. The accuracies of detecting resource leak and layout energy defect are 87.5% and 78.1%, respectively.

The rest of the paper is organised as follows. Section 2 introduces background about the classifications of resource leak and layout defect. Section 3 gives an overview of our energy bugs detection framework. Section 4 presents analysis approach of resource leak and layout defect. Section 5 demonstrates experimental results of 64 real practical Android apps for evaluating our approach *SAAD*. Section 6 presents related work, while Sect. 7 concludes.

2   Background

2.1   Resource Leak Classification

Some typical energy bugs due to resource leak are listed as follows:

- Non sleep bug: An app applies a wakelock object to keep CPU and Screen to reside in an active state, and does not release the object in time. It results in that the CPU and the LCD component cannot enter a dormant state with sustainable energy consumption. An example of non sleep bug is illustrated in Fig. 1. A *Wakelock* resource is applied in the *try* block, then after running a task, this resource is released using *release()* method. However, if an exception takes place when the task runs, the execution of the method *runInWakeLock()* will throw exceptions and enter the *catch* block. It means the release operation cannot be completed at the end, causing a resource leak.
- Sensor leak: Sensors (e.g., pressure sensors, direction sensors) are acquired, while the sensor object may not be released when the Android system enters its background state, making sensors stay active.
- Camera leak: The camera resource is occupied during an app's execution process, but fails to be released when the app switches into the background, leaving the camera driver stay in active state. In particular, since a camera resource in a smartphone is usually exclusive, if it is not released, other apps may not be able to access.
- Multimedia leak: A media player object or an audio manager object may be acquired by apps to play video or audio files. However, the corresponding object resource may not be released when an app enters its background state, and the leak makes the devices work continuously.
- Memory leak: The running system continues to allocate memory space for apps. Because of negligence or errors, it fails in releasing the corresponding memory space when apps are closed.

```
public void runInWakeLock(PowerManager pm,Runnable task, int flags){
    PowerManager.WakeLock wl = pm.newWakeLock(flags,"My WakeLock");
    try{
        wl.acquire();  //wake lock acquire
        task.run();    //execute task
        wl.release();  //wake lock release
    }catch(Exception e){
        System.out.print(e);
    }
}
```

Fig. 1. An example of non sleep energy bug

Resource leaks are not limited to the above cases only. We use Web crawler to explore as many resources as possible according to characteristics (such as their operation names containing key words *open/release*, *start/stop* and *register/unregister*). We get more than eighty resources API information, and store them in a configuration file to support energy bugs detection.

2.2 Layout Defect Classification

Unlike resource leaks, layout defects are mainly about bad designs of the layout structure, which may cause more unnecessary CPU time or memory spaces. Traditionally, each layout file uses an XML format to define and manage widgets. It is composed of several *View* objects and *ViewGroup* objects, organized in a tree hierarchy. A layout can be nested and referenced to other sub layout files. Under normal circumstances, each activity component is associated with a specific layout file. When an activity starts, it will load its layout file by invoking the *setContentView*() method. After finishing the steps of reading, parsing and measuring, the corresponding widgets in a layout are arranged to a coordinate position and the system begins to render and show them on the screen. As the number of widgets becomes bigger, or nesting level becomes deeper, the complexity of the layout file can be high, requiring much resources like CPU and memory space to be consumed. Compared with resource leak, layout defect may not increase energy consumption very obviously, and thus are often less concerned by developers, but it is surely a problem to energy inefficiency. The typical classification of layout defects are:

- Too many views: in a layout file, the default maximum widget number is 80 by default. When the number is greater than the default value, the system's running fluency can be decreased.
- Too deep layout: the default maximum nesting depth is 10. Similarly, the system may not run fluently when the depth is more than the default value.
- Compound drawables: it implies that a pair of widgets defined in a layout file can be replaced by one compound widget, such as a combination of an *ImageView* and a *TextView* can always be replaced by a *TextView* using a compound drawable.
- Useless leaf: if a widget does not have a child node or does not have a set of background properties, it is treated as a useless leaf node. A useless leaf node can be removed in order to reduce the complexity of the layout structure.
- Useless parent: if a widget has only one child node, and it is not a *scrollview* or a root node. Without the background properties, a useless parent can be removed so that the child node moves to its position.

The layout defects are common, and can also raise the complexity of layout structures, while they are less researched.

3   Framework Overview

An overview of our bug-detection framework is shown in Fig. 2. The input of the framework is an *APK* file, the outputs comprise a resource leak report and a layout defect report, and the modules of the dashed box perform energy bugs analysis and detection, using *Apktool* [4], *SAAF* [6], *Lint* [5], resource leak analysis and layout defect analysis, and a report generator.

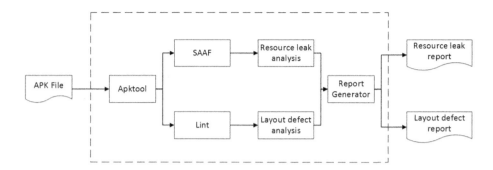

Fig. 2. The framework of energy bug detection

The *Apktool* is a reverse-engineering tool that decompiles an *Apk* file to generate a manifest configuration file, several bytecode files named *Dalvik* [7] bytecode and layout files of an app. Generally, the components of an app are defined in its manifest file.

The *SAAF* is an open source static Android analysis framework which makes use of program slicing and static analysis techniques to uncover any suspicious behaviors. In the analysis, *SAAF* parses *Dalvik* bytecodes generated by *Apktool* and encapsulates them into data models provided by itself. There are different models such as the *Instruction* model, the *BasicBlock* model, the *Method* model, the *SmaliClass* model and so on. For example, a *SmaliClass* model encapsulates the current class's information including its name and method list, path and the type of its super class. *SAAF* also provides available APIs to retrieve such information.

Lint is a static analysis tool for Android project source code, which detects potential bugs in the project and performs corresponding optimizations. The input of *Lint* contains two parts, the Android project source files (including java source files, configuration files, layout files and others), and an XML file named *lint.xml*, that defines severity levels of problems. *Lint* will detect performance problems of the code structure. For any problems detected, *Lint* gives an analysis report, and developers can fix these problems before releasing the apps.

The resource leak analysis module and the layout defect analysis module are the core parts in the framework. The resource leak analysis module judges whether the resource leak problems exist, and the layout defect analysis module further analyzes defects related to energy consumption based on the output of the *Lint* tool. We will present the two modules in Sect. 4 in detail.

4   Analysis

4.1   Resource Leak Analysis

This section introduces resource leak analysis module in Fig. 2. It performs component call analysis, inter-procedural analysis, intra-procedural analysis and resource leak detection.

Components Call Analysis. Usually, each app is composed of multiple components declared in its Manifest file. Each component can invoke methods such as *startActivity()* and *startService()* to call another component. The components relationship can be abstracted into a component call graph. In order to build the component call relationship, we find out an app's entry point, which is usually an activity targeted with *Android.intent.action.MAIN*. Then we search for *intent* objects, which are data objects for recording data that needs to be transmitted. A target component is defined as a parameter in an *intent* object.

After building the component call graph, we can extract a set of component call paths from the graph. Our framework can analyze each path whether there exists a resource leak or not.

Figure 3 shows component call graph of a smart home app. Here each node represents a component, and each arrow stands for the call relationship between the corresponding components.

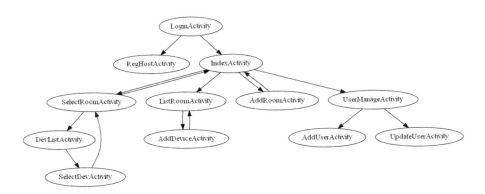

Fig. 3. Component call graph of smart home app

Figure 4 shows algorithm *generateCCGPaths* for extracting component call paths. The input is a list of components *cp_list*. The result *result_set* stores a set of component call paths. Lines 3–6 traverse list of components and find out entry component, which is the first node of each path. Then sub-function *ccgTraverse* is called to traverse the component call graph.

The algorithm *ccgTraverse* in Fig. 5 takes component *cp*, *path_list* and *result_set* as parameters. Lines 1–2 extract one path and add it to the result

generateCCPaths(*cp_list*)

1   *create a list as path_list*
2   *create a set as result_set*
3   **foreach** *cp in cp_list* **do**
4   **if** *cp is EntryComponent* **then**
5   *path_list.add(cp)*
6   *ccgTraverse(cp, path_list, result_set)*
7   **return** *result_set*

Fig. 4. Generating component call paths algorithm

set if *cp* has been visited and its calling target component list *cp.targetList* is empty. Lines 3–7 traverse *cp.targetList*. Each target component is added into path list if it is not visited, and recursively traversed by calling *ccgTraverse*. Lines 8–9 process pop stack operations, which delete the last node of current path in order to traverse other target components of its source component.

ccgTraverse (*cp, path_list, result_set*)

1   **if** *cp is visited ∧ cp.targetList is Empty* **then**
2   *result_set.add(path_list)*
3   **foreach** *target in cp.targetList* **do**
4   **if** *target is not visited* **then**
5   *target.visited ← true*
6   *path_list.add(target)*
7   *ccgTraverse(target, path_list, result_set)*
8   *path_list.remove(path_list.size − 1)*
9   *target.visited ← false*
10   **return** *result_set*

Fig. 5. Traversing component call graph algorithm

Inter-procedural Analysis. Based on each component call path, we analyze each component in its own life cycle, taking into account its inter-procedural information such as the function call relations, in order to understand the comprehensive behavior and status of an app. Particularly, we explore the function call path related with resource applying and releasing.

(a) Resource APIs

Resource APIs are used for deciding whether a function call path is involved in applying or releasing system resource. Android resource APIs have been published as webpages at its official website. We use the Web crawler technique to automatically extract more than eighty resource APIs including bluetooth, wifi, camera, multimedia, GPS, sensor, memory etc. Each resource API is defined with both apply and release methods information such as class path, method name, parameter list and return type.

(b) Function Abstraction

In order to build function call relationships, we perform function abstraction for simplifying function analysis. A function abstraction is a semantic abstraction of a function, which includes the name of a function, the class it belongs to, the parameter list, the type of its return value and an invoked functions list. It saves an XML format for further processing. We use function abstractions to construct function call relationship.

(c) Effective Path

Before detecting resource leak, our framework filters function call paths obtained from step (b), and only analyzes effective paths where resources are acquired or released. This preprocessing decreases the number of paths to be analyzed, making the analysis more efficient. Figure 6 is an example of a function call graph, in which three paths can be extracted.

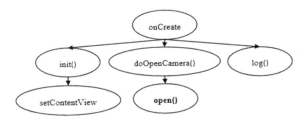

Fig. 6. An example of a function call graph

1. $onCreate() \rightarrow init() \rightarrow setContentView()$
2. $onCreate() \rightarrow doCameraOpen() \rightarrow open()$
3. $onCreate() \rightarrow log()$

However, only path 2 contains an instruction for opening a camera. Here the function $open()$ is an API for opening camera resource. It is invoked to use the camera device. So this path is an effective path while the others are omitted in analysis. The following is the definition of effective path.

Definition 1. *An effective path is a 4-tuple $\langle com, path, res, op \rangle$. Here com is the current component, path is a list of methods. res represents used system resource on this path and op denotes the operation on corresponding resources. There are two kinds of resource operations, which is either apply or release.*

Figure 7 shows the algorithm $extractEftPath$, which takes three parameters: the current method m, a list of methods $path\_list$ and a set of effective paths

extractEftPath $(cp, m, path\_list, result\_set)$

```
1    path_list.add(m)
2    if m.hasResource() is not null  then
3      create a path as eftPath
4      eftPath.com  ←  cp
5      eftPath.path  ←  path_list
6      eftPath.res  ←  m.hasResource()
7      result_set.add(eftPath)
8    if m.abList is empty  then
9      path_list.remove(size − 1)
10   else foreach ab in ablist do
11     nextMethod  ←  getMethod(ab)
12     extractEftPath(nextMethod, path_list, result_set)
13     path_list.remove(size − 1)
14   return result_set
```

Fig. 7. Extracting effective paths algorithm

$result\_set$. Line 1 adds the current method m into list $path\_list$, and line 2 checks if current method has resource operation. If it has, lines 3–7 create an effective path $eftPath$, and sets its corresponding component, path and used resource, and add it to the result set. Otherwise lines 8–13 recursively traverse the next invoked method of m. Here the function $m.hasResource$ will check whether method m invokes resource APIs and returns resource type and operation in case of invoking. The function $getMethod(ab)$ takes the function ab as a parameter and returns the corresponding method.

(d) Event Response and Callback Functions

Android apps are usually event driven. When an event response function calls a resource related API, it will be included in the corresponding effective path. Considering button events, our framework builds a hash table for mapping button objects into their monitoring objects. Thus it is easy to find out the event response functions defined in the monitoring class.

The callback mechanism is popular in Android system. For instance, the *Activity* component's life cycle functions *onCreate*, *onStart* etc. are system callback functions, which are automatically invoked by the system. A common example is the *Thread* class. When a thread object executes the *start* function, it actually executes the *run* function. However, the relation between *start* and *run* functions are implicit. This situation causes some function call paths break in analysis. Our framework firstly tries to build a map between callback functions and real executed functions, and adds a callback function to the corresponding function call path.

Intra-procedural Analysis. The aim of the intra-procedural analysis is to analyze a single function. Based on basic blocks of a function, we build the control flow graph of the function. Our framework employs *SAAF* to generate a control flow graph of a function, and further extract a set of execution paths. The details are omitted here due to the page limitation.

Resource Leak Detection. By combining the above analyses, Fig. 8 provides our algorithm for resource leak checking. The input *cpPath_set* is a set of component call paths obtained by component analysis. For each effective path *eftPath* of the component *cp*, lines 4–6 add the resource into *apply_list* if the operation of the current path is an *apply* operation. For *release* operation, lines 7–16 traverse each method *method* on effective path and make sure that: (1) its control flow paths *method.cfg* must call the next method on the same path before getting to the last method; (2) when traversing the last method on the path, each of its control flow path must release the corresponding resource. If both conditions are satisfied, the resource *res* of current effective path is added into *release_list*. Lines 17–19 compare *apply_list* and *release_list*, and if they are matched, return *false* for no release leak. Otherwise the algorithm returns *true* for exiting release leak.

---

checkResourceLeak (*cpPath_set*)

```
1    create an apply_list and a release_list
2    foreach cpPath in cpPath_set do
3      foreach cp in cpPath do
4        foreach eftPath in cp.getEftPath() do
5          if eftPath.op is apply then
6            apply_list.add(eftPath.res)
7          else if eftPath.op is release then
8            for i = 0; i ≤ eftPath.size − 1; i + + do
9              method ← eftPath.getMethod(i)
10             if i ≤ eftPath.size − 2 then
11               next_method ← eftPath.getMethod(i + 1)
12               if method.cfg do not invoke next_method then
13                 break
14             else
15               if method.cfg do release then
16                 release_list.add(eftPath.res)
17   if apply_list equals with release_list then
18       return false
19   else return true
```

Fig. 8. Checking resource leak algorithm

4.2 Layout Defect Detection

Figure 9 shows the process of our layout defect analysis. The input is an *APK* file that needs to be decompiled by *Apktool*, and the output is a defect report. The analysis module and the filter module are explained as follows.

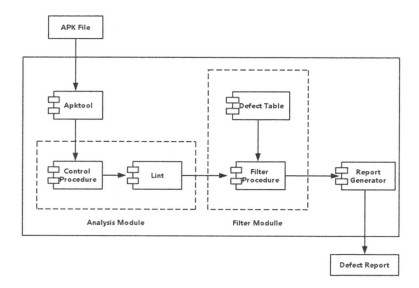

Fig. 9. Layout defect analysis process

Analysis Module. The analysis module mainly conducts an overall analysis of the layout files, including correctness, security, performance, usability and accessibility analysis. After receiving the paths of the layout files, that come from the result of decompiling of the *APK* file, the *Control Procedure* starts *Lint* to execute the layout file analysis. Finally, *Lint* will output an *XML* report about the issues for each layout file.

Filter Module. Since the output of the analysis module includes different types of layout issues, which may or may not be energy consumption related layout defects. The Filter module extracts energy defects from the issues report of *Lint*. It is composed of a *Defect Table* and a *Filter Procedure*: the former acts as a set of filter rules, which are identified from layout defect classification in Sect. 2.2, and the latter uses filter rules to find out layout energy defects.

5 Evaluation

We have implemented the proposed analysis as a prototype tool called *SAAD*. In order to evaluate our tool, we have conducted experiments on 64 real *APK* files, with 28 of them from well-known markets, and the other 36 are open source apps. In order to complete a more comprehensive experiment, we select these apps belonging to different classifications. In the process of the experiment, we collect the statistics of apps based on characteristics and scale, some of them are shown in Table 1.

Table 1. Scale statistics of apps (part)

APP	File size	Component number	Layout number
Agenda Plus	1.91 M	3	9
Heart Rate Runtastic	6.75 M	24	101
Duomi Radio Station	8.79 M	14	25
Drifting Bottle	7.29 M	23	49
Constellation Camera	9.04 M	42	93

5.1 Result of Resource Leak Detection

With code confirmation by manual inspection, we have detected 8 false positives, 4 leak free and 52 resource leaks. The accuracy rate is 87.5%. Among the 52 apps that have resource leaks, three kinds of leaks can be detected after we review their source codes.

- no release operation. The current component in an app does not take initiatives to release resources. For example, the *Drifting Bottle* application in Table 1, uses the *SoundPool* class without releasing the obtained resources. Table 2 shows the details of the invoking path. It appears in an activity named *HrLoginSelectionActivity*, which is invoked by *SplashScreenActivity*.
- The path of existing release operation may be blocked, e.g., by exception handlings.
- The release operation has not been activated by an event. In this situation, an app has a release operation, while it releases only when a specific event such as *onClick*, *onKeyDown* and so on occurs. If the user cannot trigger any of these events, the related resources cannot be released.

5.2 Result of Layout Defect Detection

We have detected that 5 apps are defect free, 14 apps are false positives and 45 apps have layout defects. The accuracy rate is 78.1%. To validate the experimental results, we re-design layouts reported with defects, confirm the new layouts are equivalent to the old ones, and analyze the new layouts again. Moreover, we employ a view hierarchy tool called *HierarchyViewer* [8] to visualize the nested structure of layout files when running applications.

Table 2. Report fragment of resource leak

<class name=" HrLoginSelectionActivity">
  <path>
    SplashScreenActivity,HrLoginSelectionActivity
  </path>
  <leak>[Landroid/media/SoundPool;]</leak>
</class>

There are two types of false positives: *UselessParent* or *UselessLeaf*, which are raised by the static analysis of *Lint*. Since the widgets of a layout can be loaded only during an app's execution, we monitor the behavior of the layout by *HierarchyViewer*, and identify all of the 14 false positives. In addition, *HierarchyViewer* can report the start time of each widget and its drawing time, which helps to confirm that layout defects consume system resources and time.

Figure 10 summarizes 45 apps that have layout defects. The x-axis denotes the number of layout defects. Through the experimental results, we can see some defects appear more frequently, including *Useless Parent, Inefficient Weight, Compound Drawables* etc. It indicates that some developers may not design the layout structure rigorously, and thus create some useless widget and useless properties, resulting in a more complex layout structure and causing unnecessary consumption of CPU resources and memory.

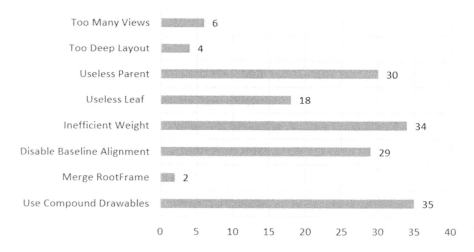

Fig. 10. Summary of layout defect

6   Related Work

We present related work in the following three aspects: (1) detecting and testing energy bugs; (2) estimating energy consumption; (3) optimizing energy.

6.1   Detecting and Testing Energy Bugs

The researches in [21,23,26] are strongly relevant with our work. Guo et al. [26] aim to detect resource leak of Android apps. However, the provided approaches are not context sensitive. For instance, considering resource leak, if there exists one releasing resource path, no resource leak report is given, causing false negatives. Wu et al. [21,23] present Relda2, a light-weight static resource leak detection tool, which takes model checking technology to detect resource leak. Comparatively, our approach combines function call analysis with control flow analysis to locate the real paths related to energy bugs.

There are some other work related with detecting and testing energy bugs. Wu et al. [12] focus on detecting energy-related defects in the UI logic of an Android application. The authors identify two patterns of behavior in which location listeners are leaking. Liu et al. [11,18] implement a static code analyzer, *PerfChecker*, to detect identified performance bug patterns. Moreover, they build a tool called *GreenDroid* for automatically analyzing an app's sensory data utilization at different states and reporting actionable information to help developers locate energy inefficiency problems and identify their root causes [10]. Wan et al. [19] present a technique for detecting display energy hotspots and prioritizing them for developers. Abhik et al. [24] present an automated test generation framework, which systematically generates test inputs that are likely to capture energy hotspots/bugs.

6.2   Estimating Energy Consumption

Energy is a critical resource for smartphones. However, developers usually lack quantitative information about the behavior of apps with respect to energy consumption. Lu et al. [22] propose a lightweight and automatic approach to estimating the method-level energy consumption for Android apps. Li et al. [14] provide code-level estimates of energy consumption using program analysis and per-instruction energy modeling. [15] presents an approach to calculating source line level energy consumption information by combining hardware-based power measurements with program analysis and statistical modeling. Mario et al. [20] present a quantitative and qualitative empirical investigation by measuring energy consumption of method calls when executing typical usage scenarios in 55 mobile apps from different domains. Ferrari et al. [9] present the design and implementation of a Portable Open Source Energy Monitor (POEM) to enable developers to test and measure the energy consumption of the basic blocks, the call graph, and the Android API calls, allowing developers to locate energy leaks with high accuracy. [25] presents the design, implementation and evaluation of eprof, the first fine-grained energy profiler for smartphone apps. Eprof also reveals several "wakelock bugs", a family of "energy bugs" in smartphone apps.

6.3 Optimizing Energy

A smartphone's display is usually one of its most energy consuming components. There are several researches focusing on optimization issues. Li et al. [16] develop an approach for automatically rewriting web applications so that they can generate more energy efficient web pages. Kim et al. [13] propose a novel static optimization technique for eliminating drawing commands to produce energy-efficient apps.

Making HTTP requests is one of the most energy consuming activities in Android apps, Li et al. [17] propose an approach to reducing the energy consumption of HTTP requests by automatically detecting and then bundling multiple HTTP requests.

7   Conclusion and Future Work

Due to the limited capacity of the battery power in (Android) smartphones, energy bugs in Android apps may cause serious battery drain. In this paper, we have proposed a static analysis approach to detect both resource leak and layout defect in Android applications. Compared with dynamic methods such as Google run-time monitoring, the static analysis will check all possible execution paths. We have implemented our analysis in the $SAAD$ tool and have used it to analyze 64 real applications. In our experiment, we have found that 52 apps have resource leakage, and 45 apps have layout defects. The corresponding accuracies are 87.5% and 78.1%. The results show that our $SAAD$ tool can effectively analyze energy bugs of Android apps.

For the future work, due to the limitations of static analysis, we will combine static analysis with dynamic monitoring together for checking energy bugs. Moreover, although a number of callback functions and event response functions are available in Android system, our framework only analyzes some common functions. As future work, we will include more functions analysis into the framework.

Acknowledgment. We thank the ICFEM reviewers for their valuable feedback, and also thank Dr. Yuting Chen and Dr. Zhoulai Fu for many useful comments on the presentation.

References

1. Pathak, A., Hu, Y.C., Zhang, M.: Bootstrapping energy debugging on smartphones: a first look at energy bugs in mobile devices. In: Proceeding of The 10th ACM Workshop on Hot Topics in Networks, HotNets-X (2011)
2. Banerjee, A., Chong, L.K., Chattopadhyay, S., et al.: Detecting energy bugs and hotspots in mobile apps. In: Proceedings of the 22nd ACM SIGSOFT International Symposium on Foundations of Software Engineering, pp. 588–598. ACM (2014)
3. Zhang, J., Musa, A., Le, W.: A comparison of energy bugs for smartphone platforms. In: Engineering of Mobile-Enabled Systems (MOBS), pp. 25–30. IEEE (2013)

4. APKTool. https://code.google.com/p/android-apktool/
5. Lint. http://tools.android.com/tips/lint
6. Hoffmann, J., Ussath, M., Holz, T., et al.: Slicing droids: program slicing for smali code. Automated Software Engineering (ASE), Coimbra, Portugal, 18–22 March 2013, pp. 1844–1851. IEEE (2013)
7. Dalvik. https://en.wikipedia.org/wiki/Dalvik
8. Hierarchy Viewer. http://developer.android.com/tools/help/hierarchy-viewer. html
9. Ferrari, A., Gallucci, D., Puccinelli, D., et al.: Detecting energy leaks in Android app with POEM. In: Pervasive Computing and Communication Workshops (PerCom Workshops). IEEE (2015)
10. Liu, Y., Xu, C., Cheung, S.C.: Where has my battery gone? Finding sensor related energy black holes in smartphone applications. In: Pervasive Computing and Communications (PerCom), pp. 2–10. IEEE (2013)
11. Liu, Y., Xu, C., Cheung, S.C.: Characterizing and detecting performance bugs for smartphone applications. In: Proceedings of the 36th International Conference on Software Engineering, pp. 1013–1024 (2014)
12. Wu, H., Yang, S., Rountev, A.: Static detection of energy defect patterns in Android applications. In: Proceedings of the 25th International Conference on Compiler Construction, pp. 185–195. ACM (2016)
13. Kim, P., Kroening, D., Kwiatkowska, M.: Static program analysis for identifying energy bugs in graphics-intensive mobile apps. In: Proceedings of the 24th IEEE International Conference on Modelling, Analysis and Simulation of Computer and Telecommunication Systems, MASCOTS 2016. IEEE CS Press (2016)
14. Hao, S., Li, D., Halfond, W.G.J., Govindan, R.: Estimating mobile application energy consumption using program analysis. In: Proceedings of the 35th International Conference on Software Engineering (ICSE), May 2013
15. Li, D., Hao, S., Halfond, W.G.J., Govindan, R.: Calculating source line level energy information for Android applications. In: ISSTA (2013)
16. Li, D., Tran, A.H., Halfond, W.G.J.: Making web applications more energy efficient for OLED smartphones. In: Proceedings of the International Conference on Software Engineering (ICSE), June 2014
17. Li, D., Lyu, Y., Gui, J., Halfond, W.G.J.: Automated energy optimization of HTTP requests for mobile applications. In: Proceedings of the 38th International Conference on Software Engineering (ICSE), May 2016
18. Liu, Y., Chang, X., Cheung, S.C., Lu, J.: GreenDroid: automated diagnosis of energy inefficiency for smartphone applications. IEEE Trans. Software Eng. **40**(9), 911–940 (2014)
19. Wan, M., Jin, Y., Li, D., Halfond, W.G.J.: Detecting display energy hotspots in Android apps. In: Proceedings of the 8th IEEE International Conference on Software Testing, Verification and Validation (ICST), April 2015
20. Vsquez, M.L., Bavota, G., Bernal-Crdenas, C., et al.: Mining energy-greedy API usage patterns in Android apps: an empirical study. In: 11th Working Conference on Mining Software Repositories, MSR 2014, pp. 2–11 (2014)
21. Tianyong, W., Liu, J., Zhenbo, X., Guo, C., Zhang, Y., Yan, J., Zhang, J.: Lightweight, inter-procedural and callback-aware resource leak detection for Android apps. IEEE Trans. Software Eng. **42**(11), 1054–1076 (2016)
22. Lu, Q., Wu, T., Yan, J., Yan, J., Ma, F., Zhang, F.: Lightweight method-level energy consumption estimation for Android applications. In: TASE 2016, pp. 144–151 (2016)

23. Wu, T., Liu, J., Deng, X., Yan, J., Zhang, J.: Relda2: an effective static analysis tool for resource leak detection in Android apps. In: ASE 2016, pp. 762–767 (2016)
24. Banerjee, A., Chong, L.K., Chattopadhyay, S., Roychoudhury, A.: Detecting energy bugs and hotspots in mobile apps. In: SIGSOFT FSE 2014, pp. 588–598 (2014)
25. Pathak, A., Hu, Y.C., Zhang, M.: Where is the energy spent inside my app?: Fine grained energy accounting on smartphones with Eprof. In: Proceedings of the 7th ACM European Conference on Computer Systems, EuroSys 2012, pp. 29–42 (2012)
26. Guo, C., Zhang, J., Yan, J., Zhang, Z., Zhang, Y.: Characterizing and detecting resource leaks in Android applications. In: IEEE/ACM 28th International Conference on Automated Software Engineering, ASE 2013, pp. 389–398 (2013)

A Flexible Approach for Finding Optimal Paths with Minimal Conflicts

Juliana K.F. Bowles[(✉)] and Marco B. Caminati

School of Computer Science,
University of St Andrews, St Andrews KY16 9SX, UK
{jkfb,mbc8}@st-andrews.ac.uk

Abstract. Complex systems are usually modelled through a combination of structural and behavioural models, where separate behavioural models make it easier to design and understand partial behaviour. When partial models are combined, we need to guarantee that they are consistent, and several automated techniques have been developed to check this. We argue that in some cases it is impossible to guarantee total consistency, and instead we want to find execution paths across such models with minimal conflicts with respect to a certain metric of interest. We present an efficient and scalable solution to find optimal paths through a combination of the theorem prover Isabelle with the constraint solver Z3. Our approach has been inspired by a healthcare problem, namely how to detect conflicts between medications taken by patients with multiple chronic conditions, and how to find preferable alternatives automatically.

1 Introduction

In complex systems design, it is common to model components separately in order to facilitate the understanding and analysis of their behaviour. Nonetheless, modelling the complete behaviour of a component is hard [25], and often sets of possible scenarios of execution are captured instead. A scenario describes a particular situation that may involve a component and how it behaves and interacts with other components. In practice, UML's sequence diagrams are commonly used to model scenarios [20]. From such individual scenarios, we then need to be able to derive the complete behaviour of a component. The same ideas apply if we model (partial) business processes within an organisation, for instance using BPMN [19]. In either case, we need a means to compose models (scenarios or processes), and when this cannot be done, detect and resolve inconsistencies.

Composing systems manually can only be done for small systems. As a result, in recent years, various methods for automated model composition have been introduced [1,4–6,11,13,22,23,26–28]. Most of these methods introduce algorithms to produce a composite model from partial specifications and assume a formal underlying semantics [11]. In our recent work [4,6], we have used constraint solvers (Alloy [9] and Z3 [17] respectively) for automatically constructing

---

This research is supported by EPSRC grant EP/M014290/1.

Z. Duan and L. Ong (Eds.): ICFEM 2017, LNCS 10610, pp. 209–225, 2017.
https://doi.org/10.1007/978-3-319-68690-5_13

the composed model. This involves generating all constraints associated to the models, and using an automated solver to find a solution (the composed model) for the conjunction of all constraints. Using Alloy for model composition (usually only for structural models), is an active area of research [23, 28], but the use of Z3 is a novelty of [6]. In [6] we did not exploit Z3's arithmetic capabilities which we have done more recently in [7]. Most existing approaches can detect inconsistencies, but fail to provide a means to resolve them.

We argue that in some cases it is impossible to guarantee total consistency between scenarios of execution. Instead we want to find execution paths across such models with minimal conflicts with respect to a certain metric of interest. We present an efficient and scalable solution to find optimal paths through a combination of the theorem prover Isabelle [18] with the constraint solver Z3. Our approach has been inspired by a healthcare problem, namely how to detect conflicts between medications taken by patients with multiple chronic conditions, and how to find preferable alternatives automatically. In this paper, we focus on the theoretical foundations required to address the problem and our medical domain, but remind the reader of the more general applicability of our work and considerable practical benefits.

This paper provides a formal statement of the problem, a measure of inconsistency, and shows how the obtained problem can be turned into an optimisation problem. In addition, it illustrates how a SMT solver can be used to find a scalable solution to the proposed problem. As a final contribution, the paper introduces a general technique to combine Z3 with Isabelle in order to ensure that the SMT translation of the problem is formally correct.

Paper structure: Sect. 2 introduces the formalisation of the problem and our solution. Section 3 translates this formulation into an SMT context. In Sect. 4, a concrete application in the healthcare domain is introduced to motivate the approach introduced in this paper, and is used to evaluate our design through a basic implementation featuring simple input and output interfaces. Section 5 exposes the general technique we used to combine the theorem prover Isabelle and the SMT solver to guarantee the correctness of the SMT code illustrated in Sect. 3. Section 6 discusses related work, and Sect. 7 concludes.

2 Description of the Problem and Approach

Our problem is formulated formally as follows: we are given a list of simple directed acyclic graphs $G_i, i = 1, \ldots, n$, each with exactly one source node. Since each of the graphs is simple, each G_i can be thought of as a finite set of ordered pairs of nodes (j, k), each representing a directed edge from node j to node k. Therefore, we can define $G := \bigcup_{i=1}^n G_i$, and denote by $V(G')$ the set of nodes touched by any edge in $G' \subseteq G$. Further, we assume that $V(G_{i_1}) \cap V(G_{i_2}) = \emptyset$ for any $i_1 \neq i_2 \in \{i_1, \ldots, i_n\}$: i.e., distinct graphs have no nodes in common.

We want to obtain a list of paths, one for each given graph, each leading from the source of the corresponding graph to one of it sinks (we recall that a source is a node with no incoming edges and a sink one with no exiting edges). Such a list of paths must be determined so as to maximise a given *score*, which can be thought of as a metric of the compatibility of the resulting execution paths. Before defining how this score is computed, we need to describe how the needed input data and the output are encoded. Examples later clarify the need for these notions.

2.1   Score Model

To compute the score, we assume to be given further input, besides the list of graphs $G_1, \ldots, G_n$, as follows.

1. A map $t : G \to \mathbb{N} \times \mathbb{N}$ associating to each edge e a pair $(t^- (e), t^+ (e))$, where $t^- (e)$ is the minimal time and $t^+ (e)$ is the maximal time e has to wait before e can occur. We require $t^- (e) \leq t^+ (e)$ for any $e \in G$. It can be used to bound the occurrence of tasks associated to nodes in a graph. For example, t^- expresses that the next task cannot start before t^- time units, and t^+ expresses that it must occur before t^+ time units.
2. A list $\tau := \{\tau_1, \ldots, \tau_n\}$ of integers, where τ_i specifies the instant at which the source node of the graph G_i is executed. This list can be used to express the requirement that different models start their execution at different times.
3. A finite set R of *resources*.
4. A map $M : V (G) \to 2^R$. $M(j)$ specifies a subset of resources among which one can be chosen in order to perform the task corresponding to node j.
5. A map $g : R \to \mathbb{Z} \times \mathbb{N}$ associating to each resource r an *effectiveness score* $g_1(r)$ and an *amount* $g_2(r)$. The effectiveness is a measure of how well a given resource performs a task, and the amount is how much of the resource is consumed for performing the task. For example, a hardware resource is needed for a given time, a medication must be taken at a given dosage, etc.
6. A map $I : R \times R \to \mathbb{Z}$ yielding an *interaction*. The interaction is an integer expressing how much two resources mutually boost or interfere, where a negative interaction means a counter-productive effect (i.e., diminishing the overall effectiveness of the two interacting resources).
7. A map $f : \mathbb{Z} \times \mathbb{N} \times \mathbb{N} \times \mathbb{N} \to \mathbb{Z}$ combining an interaction between two resources, a time distance, and the amounts of the two resources to yield the component of the overall score for a given pair of resources. f takes into account the fact that the actual interaction between resources occurring at distinct nodes depends not only on the interaction between the resources (as defined at the previous point), but on their amount and on how much time passes between their occurrences. We will refer to the integer values returned by f as *interaction scores*.

2.2   Output

Given a list $G_1, \ldots G_n$ of directed acyclic graphs, a set of resources R and maps f, g, I, M, t as introduced in the previous section, the output is a triple of functions (F, c, m), each defined on the set of all nodes, $V (G)$.

F is a boolean function telling us which nodes are executed, $c(j)$ returns the instant at which node j is executed, while $m(j)$ is the resource picked to perform the task associated to the node j. We will use the notation $P[X]$ to indicate the image of the set X through the relation P; for example, $F[\{true\}]$ is the set of executed nodes. With this notation in place, we require that F, c and m satisfy all the following conditions:

1. the set on which F is true determines one path for each G_i, starting from the source of G_i and ending at one of its sinks; this is a way to represent the paths that we anticipated as our main goal at the beginning of this section. More formally, F satisfies the following requirement: for any $i \in \{1, \ldots, n\}$ there is a finite sequence w^i of nodes of G_i such that (a) w_0^i is the source of G_i, (b) $w_{|w^i|-1}^i$ is a sink of G_i, (c) $\forall j \in \{1, \ldots, |w^i| - 1\}$ $(w_{j-1}^i, w_j^i) \in G_i$, and (d) $\left\{ w_0^i, \ldots, w_{|w^i|-1}^i \right\} = F^{-1}[\{true\}] \cap G_i$.
2. $\forall j \in V(G)$, $F(j) \rightarrow m(j) \in M(j)$;
3. for any $i \in \{1, \ldots, n\}$, if j is the source node of G_i, then $c(j) = \tau_i$;
4. if there is an edge going from the node j to the node k, and j and k are executed, then

$$t^-(j,k) \leq c(k) - c(j) \leq t^+(j,k);$$

5. the global score:

$$\sum_{j \in F^{-1}[\{true\}]} g_1(m(j)) +$$

$$\sum_{\substack{i_1, i_2 \in \{1, \ldots, n\}, i_1 < i_2 \\ j \in F^{-1}[\{true\}] \cap V(G_{i_1}) \\ k \in F^{-1}[\{true\}] \cap V(G_{i_2})}} f(I(m(j), m(k)), |c(k) - c(j)|, g_2(m(j)), g_2(m(k)))$$

$$(1)$$

is maximal.

The first term in (1) sums the effectiveness of each picked resource for each executed node, irrespectively of whether distinct picked resources interact. The second term sums together the interaction scores of each pair of resources picked in distinct graphs. The interaction score for each of such pairs depends on the absolute interaction of the two resources (specified by I), the time distance separating the occurrence of the two resources, and the amount.

2.3   An Illustrative Example

We use a simplified example to motivate our formal problem. A more realistic example and our solution is given in Sect. 4.

Assume that a patient with an acute condition is hospitalised on day 0. There are two possible treatments for the condition: a non-surgical treatment and surgery. The two alternatives are represented by the two branches in the directed graph of Fig. 1 (left), where the source node represents the hospitalisation. The right branch represents the choice of surgery with nodes n_3 and n_4 denoting the steps implied by this choice (n_3: pre-surgical testing and n_4: the surgery itself). Each node in a treatment graph may have one or more ways of performing it. For example, in the case of pre-surgical testing it involves administering one of two drugs (d_1 or d_2), while in the case of the surgery, only one resource is present (we assume here that there is only one way to perform it). The left branch (with n_2) models the non-surgical choice, here associated to the prescription of drug d_0 (with no other choice available). The weights on the edges are the time constraints for the subsequent step: for example, after pre-surgical testing was performed (n_3), surgery cannot happen before 2 days have passed, but should happen within 4 days (for illustration purposes only).

Additionally, this particular patient suffers from a chronic condition, which requires him to take drug d_3 on even days and d_4 on odd days. This can be represented by a path graph, unfolding the alternation of d_3 and d_4 for a given finite number of days (Fig. 1 right).

It is known that surgery is preferred, but d_1 interacts negatively with d_3 and d_2 with d_4. We ignore drug dosages here, which our formalisation can handle as well. The problem we want to solve is to find how to best schedule steps in the hospitalisation, and how to choose between the non-surgical and the surgical treatment, taking into account the

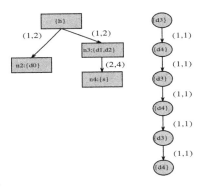

Fig. 1. A simple example problem.

respective effectiveness and the interaction with the treatments for the chronic condition.

3   SMT Translation

We now need to represent the notions presented in Sect. 2 in a way amenable to SMT computations. In doing so, we will write formulas close to the first-order logic language used by SMT solvers; for the sake of readability, however, we will employ some notational simplifications. In particular, we adopt infix notation instead of prefix notation, we omit type specifications, and we use subscripts and other typographic features not available in plain-text syntax of SMT-LIB.

To represent the output F, we introduce one boolean variable node$_i$ for each node i (i.e., the truth value of node$_i$ will yield $F(i)$). First, we must pick all the sources of the G_i's, so that the corresponding node variables will be asserted to be true. Afterwards, for each source, we must assert that exactly one of its children must be true. Then, for every child set to true, we must ask that exactly one of its children must be true, and so on, until no node has children (we reached a sink). Besides doing that, we want to make sure that no other node is selected.

Correspondingly, we generate, for the node i, the assertions

$$\text{node}_i \rightarrow \bigvee_{j|(i,j)\in G} \left(\left(\bigwedge_{\substack{k\neq j, \\ k|(i,k)\in G}} (\neg \text{node}_k)\right) \wedge \text{node}_j\right) \tag{2}$$

$$\left(\bigwedge_{(j,i)\in G} (\neg \text{node}_j)\right) \rightarrow \neg \text{node}_i, \tag{3}$$

where we adopted an informal intentional implosion of the arguments of connectives for reader's convenience, rather than writing the extensional form actually needed for SMT-LIB. For example, the expression $\bigwedge_{(j,i)\in G} (\neg \text{node}_j)$ appearing in (3) is a shortcut for scanning the input G to take all the first components of pairs having i as a second component (let us assume they are $\text{node}_{i_1}, \dots, \text{node}_{i_p}$), and then writing the SMT expression and $\text{node}_{i_1} \dots \text{node}_{i_p}$.

3.1 Scores in SMT

To represent the output c, we introduce one numerical variable clock_j for each node j. For each j, k such that $(j,k) \in G$, we create the following assertion:

$$\text{node}_j \wedge \text{node}_k \rightarrow \text{clock}_k - \text{clock}_j \geq t^- (j,k) \wedge \text{clock}_k - \text{clock}_j \leq t^+ (j,k).$$

Additionally, we impose that each source node happens at the time specified by τ; therefore, if j is the source node of G_i, we assert:

$$\text{clock}_j = \tau_i. \tag{4}$$

To represent the output m, we introduce one variable label_j for each node j, whose value is the name of the drug picked for the node j. Now we can introduce two kinds of scores, represented by integer SMT variables score_j and $\text{score}_{j,k}$, respectively: the first represents the effectiveness of the prescription associated to node j, while the second is the score generated by possible conflicts between the prescriptions picked for node j and for node k. We first zero out the scores for the non-executed nodes:

$$\neg \text{node}_i \rightarrow \text{score}_{i,j} = 0 \wedge \text{score}_i = 0 \wedge \text{score}_{j,i} = 0.$$

Since the variables node_j describe whether a node is executed the final optimisation, we generate the following assertions for each possible j, k:

$$\text{node}_j \wedge \text{node}_k \rightarrow \text{score}_{j,k} =$$
$$f \left(I \left(\text{label}_j, \text{label}_k\right), |\text{clock}_k - \text{clock}_j|, g_2 \left(\text{label}_j\right), g_2 \left(\text{label}_k\right)\right).$$

We finally assign the sum of all $\text{score}_{i,j}$'s and score_i's to a variable, and ask for an SMT solution to all the assertions which maximises that variable; this requires the optimizing version of the SMT solver Z3, νZ (also known as μZ or Z3Opt) [2].

The map I assigns a degree to the possible conflicts; this assignment, together with f, determines how the interactions influence the resulting choice of resources, timing, and the execution paths in the different models. These choices add flexibility to the whole approach but, on the other hand, need to be done by a domain expert.

4   Evaluation and Use Cases

In healthcare management and practice, as in other domains, clinical and medical procedures are streamlined by adopting standardised guidelines. In particular, treatments for common chronic conditions have been subject to various clinical trials, and the outcomes documented in *clinical pathways* specifying accepted treatment steps, possible alternatives, and recommendations to follow. Clinical pathways are informal flowcharts, with natural language annotations, and as such they can be formalised as directed acyclic graph structures, usually with one initial node (the source), and each node representing a medication prescription. Applying a single clinical pathway to a given patient is subject to a number of variable aspects and requirements, for example:

1. pathways typically present alternatives from which one is chosen;
2. there is often a choice to be taken among equivalent drugs in a group;
3. the time separating subsequent steps in a pathway is typically not fixed, being liable to be adapted to the context and the patient situation;
4. the dosage of the chosen drugs influences how drugs mutually interact;
5. the set of chronic conditions typically changes over the patient's life span: when this happens, even the treatment of the pre-existing conditions must be reconsidered.

On patients suffering from multiple chronic conditions, several pathways have to be applied concurrently, so that the number of possible combinations of these parameters increases dramatically. Our goal is to present the clinician suggestions about which choice of the parameters above is the best. The model presented in the previous sections allows us to capture all these aspects: the resources correspond to the single treatments (e.g., drugs, or surgical procedures), the effectiveness score expresses how well a single treatment performs, the amount can be used to express the dosage of a drug, and I can model, for example, drug-drug interaction. For consistency and comparison, we evaluate our design on a well-known case [8] of a hypothetical 79-year-old woman with five diseases: chronic obstructive pulmonary disease (COPD), diabetes mellitus (type 2), hypertension, osteoarthritis, and osteoporosis. To this end, we extracted data to represent pathways and scores from two sources, respectively: NICE pathways[1], publicly available as informal flowcharts with accompanying text, and the website drugs.com to derive the scores.

Given the form in which pathways from NICE are presented, we extracted the data needed as input to our design manually, for each of the five conditions we are considering (see [12]). We pruned the nodes not liable to cause conflicts (e.g., "ongoing monitoring of HbA_{1c}"), generated an adjacency relation describing the underlying graph, and attached a list of possible medications for each node (for example, when a medication group such as *Sulfonylurea* was associated to a node, we inserted the list of all the medications in the group in the corresponding node of the graph we generated). The resulting graphs are visible in Figs. 2 and 3,

---

[1] http://pathways.nice.org.uk/.

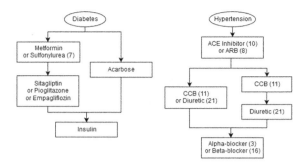

Fig. 2. Pharmaceutical graphs for Diabetes and Hypertension based on NICE pathways. ACE – angiotensin-converting-enzyme, ARB – angiotensin receptor blocker, CCB – calcium channel blocker.

where numbers in brackets represent the number of individual medications in a group. They contain a total of 127 distinct medications. Some of the graph parameters, such as the duration limits (described by the functions t^- and t^+ introduced in Sect. 2) can depend on the single patient and on the context, and are therefore not present in the data provided by NICE. For evaluation purposes, we generated suitable data reasonable for our purposes to fill the gaps (this will be done by clinicians in the future). To retrieve all the possible drug conflicts, we used the interaction engine on the mentioned site drugs.com[2], and obtained a classification (minor, moderate and major): 178 minor conflicts, 3033 moderate conflicts, 270 major conflicts, for a total of 3481 conflicts, an amount too large to analyse manually.

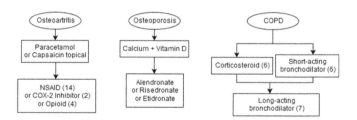

Fig. 3. Pharmaceutical graphs for three additional conditions. NSAID – nonsteroidal anti-inflammatory drug, COX-2 – Cyclooxygenase-2.

4.1 Results

The data extracted as explained above was represented in a textual, comma-separated value (CSV) format, and we built a simple implementation of our

---

[2] http://www.drugs.com/drug_interactions.html.

design, parsing these files, generating SMT code, producing text representations of (F, c, m), together with a graphical representation of the output using Cytoscape[3] [24]. For computations, we assigned the values of -100, -1000 and -5000 to minor, moderate and major conflicts, respectively. Another important parameter we had to set is f, which weights the conflicts according to time separation and dosage. We chose a simple form, which takes the conflict and zeroes it as soon as the time distance is greater than 8 time units or one of the dosages is less than 10 dosage units.

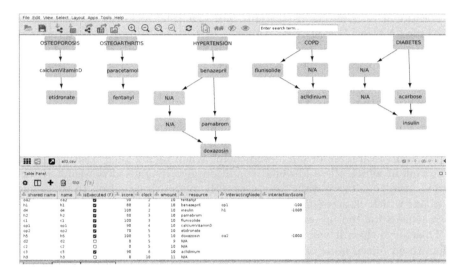

Fig. 4. Time- and dosage- aware optimal solution generated by Z3 for a hypothetical five-comorbid patient, as represented in the graphical front-end.

The output is shown in Fig. 4: the text in the nodes of Figs. 2 and 3 have been substituted by the drug ultimately picked in the maximised solution, except for the non-executed nodes, which are marked with "N/A". In the lower part of the interface, the user can see the node list with all the relevant information: the picked drug, the clock (i.e., the value returned by c introduced in Sect. 2.2) for the corresponding event, the score, the conflicting nodes (if any) and the conflict score (if any). The user can also click on single node to highlight only the relevant data. For this example, the total score is -1220, while the total conflict is -2100, composed as follows:

---

[3] Cytoscape is a software platform for the visualisation of complex network integrated with any type of attribute data, with a focus on molecular interaction networks. It was chosen among several other visualisation platforms because of the variety of layout algorithms available, the simple data import/export format available, and the relatively moderate adoption effort it required from us.

- the insulin-benazepril interaction contributes -1000,
- the doxazosin-fentanyl interaction contributes -1000,
- the benazepril-calciumVitaminD interaction contributes -100.

To assess the performance of the proposed approach, we timed the presented implementation. The average running time is $28.1\,s$, including the SMT code generation from the input data (which, however, takes a negligible amount of time); these results were obtained on an off-the-shelf laptop with 4GB RAM and a dual-core 2GHz CPU, running a 32-bit Linux OS. The actual run-times would likely be less, since in real situations a number of possibilities are excluded and additional restrictions often apply. For example, a portion of drugs could be excluded a priori because not available, or because known to have too many interactions; what is more, the doctor might impose manually a choice in a graph branch, thereby reducing the combinations.

4.2 Introducing Time Offsets

Suppose a patient is being treated for a number of conditions, when she gets diagnosed an additional condition (requirement (5) of Sect. 4). We want to show how the time-awareness of our design helps when facing such a situation. Let the instant in which the additional condition gets diagnosed be denoted by 0. Starting from time 0, we want to re-assess the patient's situation to get suggestion about which changes in the therapy should be implemented, assuming that the treatment for the pre-existing conditions started at some time in the past $-x$. To achieve that, it will suffice to change condition (4) (Sect. 3.1) whenever j refers to an initial node of the pre-existing conditions:

$$\text{clock}_j = -x,$$

while we assert $\text{clock}_j = 0$ when the index j refers to the new condition.

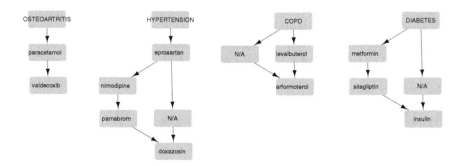

Fig. 5. Time- and dosage- aware optimal solution generated by Z3 with four concurrent morbidities.

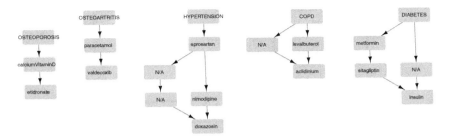

Fig. 6. The optimal solution after a fifth condition was added with a time offset.

We evaluated how this can change the recommendation given by our system in a very simple case. First, we ran the simulation as in the preceding section, except that we did not include osteoporosis, and obtained the solution shown in Fig. 5. Then we added back osteoporosis with a starting time 0, while changing the starting time of the remaining four conditions to −6. The result is shown in Fig. 6. As it can be seen by comparing the results, the addition of the new condition (osteoporosis) modified the suggested pathway for one of the existing conditions (hypertension). This means that the clinician could consider backtracking and changing the previously established therapy in view of the modified clinical situation. It should be noted that the running time for these examples is substantially the same as that for the example in the previous section (≤30 s).

5 Formal Verification

Formulas (2) and (3) correspond to SMT assertions whose number quickly grows even for small graphs. There are more immediate ways of expressing the same problem as an SMT problem, but they turn out to be significantly less efficient. Our idea (extending the approach taken in [7]) is to exploit Isabelle's SMT-LIB generator to automatically produce SMT code from Isabelle definitions that we can formally prove to be correct via formal Isabelle theorems. This SMT code will typically be not as efficient as the SMT code that we will effectively run; however, we can use an SMT solver to prove that the two are equivalent. This allows us to infer (if we trust the SMT solver) that the formal correctness theorems proved in Isabelle apply to the SMT code that we will effectively run.

This approach is illustrated in Fig. 7. While this scheme can be applied generally, we use formulas (2) and (3) (Sect. 3) to illustrate it. We rewrite them as the following equivalent Isabelle/HOL definitions:

```
abbreviation "conditionTwo' G F ==
(∀ p. (F p & ¬ isSink' G p) → (∃! c. (G p c & F c)))"
```

```
abbreviation "conditionThree' G F ==
∀ c. (¬ isSource' G c & (∀ p. G p c → ¬ F p)) → (¬ F c)"
```

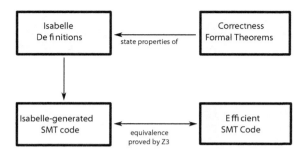

Fig. 7. Overview of the formal verification of the SMT code.

Here, G is a graph and F is a set of nodes expressed as predicates (i.e., there is an edge from m to n if and only if $G\ m\ n$ is true, and the node m is selected if and only if Fm is true), and isSink' G s is a predicate telling whether s is a sink for the graph G; similarly for isSource'. To these definitions, we add another, corresponding to the requirement that all the sources must be selected:

```
abbreviation "conditionOne' G F =
              (∀ s. isSource' G s → F s)"
```

Now, we put together these conditions:

```
abbreviation "formalConditions' G F = conditionOne' G F &
              conditionTwo' G F & conditionThree' G F"
```

and use Isabelle's SMT generator to produce corresponding SMT code:

```
lemma assumes "formalConditions' G F" shows False
sledgehammer[provers=z3, minimize=false,
              timeout=1, overlord=true] (assms).
```

sledgehammer is an Isabelle tool for theorem proving, and it works by negating the thesis of the considered theorem, and to challenge an SMT solver (or other tools) to consider whether the obtained problem is satisfiable. If it is not, it can use the information to find a proof. In this case, we are not interested in theorem proving, but only in the generated SMT code. More details can be found in [7], where we directly use the generated code to compute. Here, we make an indirect use of it: the generated code is used to define a boolean SMT variable formal, containing all the corresponding assertions. That is, formal will be true if and only if the automatically generated formalConditions' G F is true. We do the same for the assertions illustrated at the beginning of Sect. 3, to obtain an SMT variable that we call efficient. In other words, efficient will be true if and only if each node$_j$ obeys the group of assertions in Sect. 3. We add the requirement that $Fj = \text{node}_j$ for any node j. If this group assertions and the group of assertions enclosed in formalConditions' introduced above were not equivalent, there should be a choice of F satisfying one but not the other group. Therefore, we express the following SMT assertion:

```
(assert (or (and formal (not efficient))
            (and (not formal) efficient))).
```

If the SMT solver returns (unsat), this means that the two conditions are indeed equivalent. It should be noted that this check is only needed once; for the example of Sect. 4, we obtained an (unsat) answer in about 5 s.

Once we have the guarantee of the equivalence between the SMT code that we run and the SMT code generated from Isabelle definitions, we can start proving formal theorems in Isabelle about these definitions, in order to make sure they present the intended properties.

As an example, we discuss how to prove that the nodes selected by the SMT assertions labelled as formal is indeed a path leading from a source to a sink for the corresponding graph. To do so, we start from defining in Isabelle/HOL the canonical notion of walk in a simple directed graph:

```
definition "isWalk G w == w≠[] →
                  (∀i∈{1..<size w}. (w!(i−1),w!i)∈G)",
```

which amounts to asking that any consecutive entries of the node list w are joined by an edge (note that w!0, w!1, ... are the entries of the list w). We want to prove that any selection of nodes of a given graph G obtained from the assertions formal are the entries of a walk which starts from the source of G, ends in a sink of G and has no repetitions. To this end, we formally proved the following theorem:

```
theorem assumes "finite G" "card (sources G)=1"
"irrefl (trancl G)" "conditionOne (set2pred G) (unset F)"
"conditionTwo (set2pred G) (unset F)"
"conditionThree (set2pred G) (unset F)" shows
"∃ w. distinct w & isWalk G w & last w∈sinks G &
                {hd w}=F∩sources G & set w=F∩nodes G"
```

The converter set2pred serves to pass from G represented as a set of pairs to its representation as a binary boolean predicate. In Isabelle, they have different types, and using sets is more expressive than using predicates, leading to more readable statements; on the other hand, sets are not present natively in the SMT-LIB language, and using predicates is therefore preferable. Similarly, unset passes from the set F to its representation as a unary boolean predicate.

The theorem assumes that the graph is finite, and that there is only one source. Given that it is represented as a set of ordered pairs, it is inherently directed, while irrefl (trancl G) states that its transitive closure is not reflexive. This is the set-theoretical way of requiring that G is acyclic. Under these assumptions, plus the requirements that the SMT solver proved to be equivalent to the SMT assertions that we execute, the theorem states that the set F∩nodes G is the entries set of some walk w for G which starts at the source (hd w is the first entry of w), ends at a sink, and has no repetitions (keyword distinct). The conditions about w in the thesis of the theorem above correspond to requirements at the point (1) of the list of conditions at the beginning of Sect. 2.2.

6   Related Work

The problem of model composition has been treated by using SMT solvers or constraint solvers in previous works [4,6,23,27,28]. To the best of our knowledge, no other existing approach to the problem adopts a metric to be maximised, as we did here. From an abstract viewpoint, there are some similarities between the model we proposed in Sect. 2 and that presented in [14] where, however, there is only one graph involved, and the semantics associated to it and the problem to be solved are entirely different. In [12], the specific problem of the composition of pharmaceutical graphs is solved by the usage of SMT solvers in a way which inspired the present paper. Here, we addressed two of the main limitations conceded in [12], namely the lack of dosage and timing information, presenting an SMT-based design which adds those information coordinates to obtain a more flexible and realistic solution to the problem of minimising conflict in multiple pathway applications on multimorbid patients.

The issue of verifying SMT code, a solution to which we discussed in Sect. 5, is underexplored: indeed, SMT solvers are typically used the other way around, i.e., to aid in the verification of software or in formal proofs [3].

The problem of automated detection and resolution of pathway conflicts in patients with multimorbidity is gaining considerable attention. In [10], ontologies are used to represent pathways, with one additional ontology (Merge Representation Ontology, MRO) created by interviewing clinicians to identify merging criteria, and instantiated to find merge points of two given pathways. No information is given, however, on how adaptable the approach is and whether the instantiation process is automatic. Similarly, recent work proposing extensions to the existing GLARE project [21] also uses ontologies, but focuses on soliciting clinicians' input for conflicts solution, rather than automating it. Constraint logic programming (CLP) to express and deal with conflicts is proposed in [16]. While CLP solvers and SMT solvers have fundamental similarities, their expressiveness, background technologies and domains of application differ. With the efficiency of the current, mutually competitive, SMT solvers growing at a steadfast pace, their lower expressiveness is getting more and more effectively compensated. Another route has been brought forward in [15], where an ad-hoc algorithm is proposed based on formal rules expressing the actions to be taken upon the happening of given premises expressing conflicts. Whereas this solution has the advantage of accurately solving conflicts, based on the actual medical meaning of the rules themselves, it relies on specific software, which looks problematic in view of extensions and further development.

7   Conclusions

We introduced a general way of expressing the problem of execution paths across combined behavioural models of complex systems as an optimisation problem on a suitably defined score metric, expressed the latter problem in SMT language and evaluated the whole approach on a concrete, well-known healthcare problem.

Additionally, we formally proved the correctness of our SMT code through a novel application of theorem prover Isabelle, exploiting the latter's ability of generating SMT code. This is important because writing SMT code directly is time-consuming and error-prone while, and the existing interfaces of SMT solvers with higher-level languages (e.g., APIs) are currently (as far as we know) not formally verified.

Our approach can be adapted to a wide range of conditions: for example, by imposing manual restrictions on the number of resources, by manually imposing a chosen path in some of the graphs, by changing how f operates, or by offsetting the application of distinct models time-wise; in the latter case, we showed how this can be exploited in a simple way to manage the changes to a patient's therapy following the diagnose of a new condition.

While the current execution time is tolerable for interactive use, we believe that in real situations it can be dramatically lower, on average. Nonetheless, we are experimenting with *scopes*, a feature of Z3 which allows incremental solving by specifying a block of assumptions which are always held, together with a stack of additional assumptions which can be pushed and popped repeatedly. When suitably handled, this feature is likely to allow to reduce the SMT computation time upon modifications of the inputs, since a relevant part of it will remain unchanged throughout the modifications (e.g., the topology of the graphs). As a further, orthogonal code improvement strategy, we are investigating restrictions of the theory known to the solver (using the (set−logic) command); this requires expressing our SMT-LIB code into a form allowed by the selected restriction. The code presented here can be run under the UFLIA theory, but we are positive about it being adaptable to a fragment of UFLIA (e.g., QF_UFLIA), which would likely result in better performance.

The presented design has some limitations. First, while it can find an execution minimising the conflict, it cannot suggest additional remedies to neutralise or mitigate the arising conflicts. Secondly, it does not handle, currently, directed graph presenting cycles (we are not aware of any existing approach supporting the presence of cycles in our main application domain, e.g., clinical pathways composition). Third, the score calculation could be made context-aware by considering previously occurred resources in the same graphs. A possible attack to the last issue could consist in generalising the maps f and g by adding arguments to them expressing the context: we are experimenting in this sense.

References

1. Araújo, J., Whittle, J., Kim, D.: Modeling and composing scenario-based requirements with aspects. In: Proceedings of the 12th IEEE International Requirements Engineering Conference, pp. 58–67. IEEE Computer Society Press (2004)
2. Bjørner, N., Phan, A.-D., Fleckenstein, L.: vZ - an optimizing SMT solver. In: Baier, C., Tinelli, C. (eds.) TACAS 2015. LNCS, vol. 9035, pp. 194–199. Springer, Heidelberg (2015). doi:10.1007/978-3-662-46681-0_14
3. Bobot, F., Filliâtre, J.C., Marché, C., Paskevich, A.: Why3: shepherd your herd of provers. In: Boogie 2011: First International Workshop on Intermediate Verification Languages, pp. 53–64 (2011)

4. Bowles, J.K.F., Bordbar, B., Alwanain, M.: A logical approach for behavioural composition of scenario-based models. In: Butler, M., Conchon, S., Zaïdi, F. (eds.) ICFEM 2015. LNCS, vol. 9407, pp. 252–269. Springer, Cham (2015). doi:10.1007/978-3-319-25423-4_16

5. Bowles, J., Bordbar, B.: A formal model for integrating multiple views. In: Seventh International Conference on Application of Concurrency to System Design, 2007, ACSD 2007, pp. 71–79. IEEE Computer Society Press (2007)

6. Bowles, J., Bordbar, B., Alwanain, M.: Weaving true-concurrent aspects using constraint solvers. In: Application of Concurrency to System Design (ACSD 2016). IEEE Computer Society Press, June 2016

7. Bowles, J.K.F., Caminati, M.B.: Mind the gap: addressing behavioural inconsistencies with formal methods. In: 2016 23rd Asia-Pacific Software Engineering Conference (APSEC). IEEE Computer Society (2016)

8. Boyd, C.M., Darer, J., Boult, C., Fried, L.P., Boult, L., Wu, A.W.: Clinical practice guidelines and quality of care for older patients with multiple comorbid diseases: implications for pay for performance. JAMA **294**(6), 716–724 (2005)

9. Jackson, D.: Software Abstractions: Logic, Language and Analysis. MIT Press, Cambridge (2006)

10. Jafarpour, B., Abidi, S.S.R.: Merging disease-specific clinical guidelines to handle comorbidities in a clinical decision support setting. In: Peek, N., Marín Morales, R., Peleg, M. (eds.) AIME 2013. LNCS, vol. 7885, pp. 28–32. Springer, Heidelberg (2013). doi:10.1007/978-3-642-38326-7_5

11. Klein, J., Hélouët, L., Jézéquel, J.: Semantic-based weaving of scenarios. In: Proceedings of the 5th International Conference on Aspect-Oriented Software Development, pp. 27–38. ACM (2006)

12. Kovalov, A., Bowles, J.K.F.: Avoiding medication conflicts for patients with multimorbidities. In: Ábrahám, E., Huisman, M. (eds.) IFM 2016. LNCS, vol. 9681, pp. 376–390. Springer, Cham (2016). doi:10.1007/978-3-319-33693-0_24

13. Liang, H., Diskin, Z., Dingel, J., Posse, E.: A general approach for scenario integration. In: Czarnecki, K., Ober, I., Bruel, J.-M., Uhl, A., Völter, M. (eds.) MODELS 2008. LNCS, vol. 5301, pp. 204–218. Springer, Heidelberg (2008). doi:10.1007/978-3-540-87875-9_15

14. Lombardi, M., Milano, M., Benini, L.: Robust scheduling of task graphs under execution time uncertainty. IEEE Trans. Comput. **62**(1), 98–111 (2013)

15. López-Vallverdú, J.A., Riaño, D., Collado, A.: Rule-based combination of comorbid treatments for chronic diseases applied to hypertension, diabetes mellitus and heart failure. In: Lenz, R., Miksch, S., Peleg, M., Reichert, M., Riaño, D., ten Teije, A. (eds.) KR4HC/ProHealth -2012. LNCS, vol. 7738, pp. 30–41. Springer, Heidelberg (2013). doi:10.1007/978-3-642-36438-9_2

16. Michalowski, M., Wilk, S., Michalowski, W., Lin, D., Farion, K., Mohapatra, S.: Using constraint logic programming to implement iterative actions and numerical measures during mitigation of concurrently applied clinical practice guidelines. In: Peek, N., Marín Morales, R., Peleg, M. (eds.) AIME 2013. LNCS, vol. 7885, pp. 17–22. Springer, Heidelberg (2013). doi:10.1007/978-3-642-38326-7_3

17. de Moura, L., Bjørner, N.: Z3: an efficient SMT solver. In: Ramakrishnan, C.R., Rehof, J. (eds.) TACAS 2008. LNCS, vol. 4963, pp. 337–340. Springer, Heidelberg (2008). doi:10.1007/978-3-540-78800-3_24

18. Nipkow, T., Wenzel, M., Paulson, L.C. (eds.): Isabelle/HOL: A Proof Assistant for Higher-Order Logic. LNCS, vol. 2283. Springer, Heidelberg (2002). doi:10.1007/3-540-45949-9

19. OMG: Business Process Model and Notation. Version 2.0. OMG (2011). http://www.omg.org, document id: formal/2011-01-03
20. OMG: UML: Superstructure. Version 2.4.1. OMG (2011). http://www.omg.org, document id: formal/2011-08-06
21. Piovesan, L., Molino, G., Terenziani, P.: An ontological knowledge and multiple abstraction level decision support system in healthcare. Decision Anal. **1**(1), 1 (2014)
22. Reddy, R., Solberg, A., France, R., Ghosh, S.: Composing sequence models using tags. In: Proceedings of MoDELS Workshop on Aspect Oriented Modeling (2006)
23. Rubin, J., Chechik, M., Easterbrook, S.: Declarative approach for model composition. In: MiSE 2008, pp. 7–14. ACM (2008)
24. Shannon, P., Markiel, A., Ozier, O., Baliga, N.S., Wang, J.T., Ramage, D., Amin, N., Schwikowski, B., Ideker, T.: Cytoscape: a software environment for integrated models of biomolecular interaction networks. Genome Res. **13**(11), 2498–2504 (2003)
25. Uchitel, S., Brunet, G., Chechik, M.: Synthesis of partial behavior models from properties and scenarios. IEEE Trans. Softw. Eng. **35**(3), 384–406 (2009)
26. Whittle, J., Araújo, J., Moreira, A.: Composing aspect models with graph transformations. In: Proceedings of the 2006 International Workshop on Early Aspects at ICSE, pp. 59–65. ACM (2006)
27. Widl, M., Biere, A., Brosch, P., Egly, U., Heule, M., Kappel, G., Seidl, M., Tompits, H.: Guided merging of sequence diagrams. In: Czarnecki, K., Hedin, G. (eds.) SLE 2012. LNCS, vol. 7745, pp. 164–183. Springer, Heidelberg (2013). doi:10.1007/978-3-642-36089-3_10
28. Zhang, D., Li, S., Liu, X.: An approach for model composition and verification. In: NCM 2009, pp. 1102–1107. IEEE Computer Society Press (2009)

A Certified Decision Procedure for Tree Shares

Xuan-Bach Le[1][(✉)], Thanh-Toan Nguyen[1], Wei-Ngan Chin[1],
and Aquinas Hobor[1,2]

[1] School of Computing, National University of Singapore, Singapore, Singapore
bachdylan@gmail.com
[2] Yale-NUS College, National University of Singapore, Singapore, Singapore

Abstract. We develop a certified decision procedure for reasoning about systems of equations over the "tree share" fractional permission model of Dockins *et al.* Fractional permissions can reason about shared ownership of resources, *e.g.* in a concurrent program. We imported our certified procedure into the HIP/SLEEK verification system and found bugs in both the previous, uncertified, decision procedure and HIP/SLEEK itself. In addition to being certified, our new procedure improves previous work by correctly handling negative clauses and enjoys better performance.

1 Introduction

The last decade has enjoyed much progress in formal methods for concurrency in both theoretical understanding [12,20,22,34,35] and tool support [11,14, 19,23,24,28,33]. Fractional shares enable reasoning about shared ownership of resources between multiple parties, *e.g.* in a concurrent program [5]. The original model for fractional shares was rational numbers in $[0, 1]$, with 0 representing no ownership, 1 representing full ownership, and $0 < x < 1$ representing partial ownership. A *policy* maps permission quanta to allowed actions. One simple policy maps 1 to the ability to both read and write a memory cell, $0 < x < 1$ to the ability to read—but not write—the cell, and 0 denying both reading and writing. We can prevent dangerous read/write and write/write data races by enforcing that the combined total ownership of each address is no more than 1.

Unfortunately, rational numbers are not an ideal model for shares. Consider the following recursive predicate definition for fractionally-owned binary trees:

$$\mathsf{tree}(\ell, \pi) \overset{\mathrm{def}}{=} (\ell = \mathsf{null} \ \wedge \mathsf{emp}) \ \vee$$
$$\exists \ell_l, \ell_r. \ (\ell \overset{\pi}{\mapsto} (\ell_l, \ell_r) \star \mathsf{tree}(\ell_l, \pi) \star \mathsf{tree}(\ell_r, \pi)) \tag{1}$$

Here we write $a \overset{\pi}{\mapsto} b$ to indicate that memory location a contains value b and is owned with (positive/nonempty) share π. We can split and join ownership of a cell with addition: $a \overset{\pi_1}{\mapsto} b \star a \overset{\pi_2}{\mapsto} b \dashv\vdash a \overset{\pi_1 \oplus \pi_2}{\longmapsto} b$; note we use $\oplus$ instead of $+$ to indicate that the addition is bounded in $[0,1]$ and thus partial (*e.g.* $0.6 \oplus 0.6$ is undefined). This tree predicate is obtained directly from the standard recursive predicate for binary trees in separation logic by asserting only π ownership of the

© Springer International Publishing AG 2017
Z. Duan and L. Ong (Eds.): ICFEM 2017, LNCS 10610, pp. 226–242, 2017.
https://doi.org/10.1007/978-3-319-68690-5_14

root and recursively doing the same for the left and right substructures, and so at first glance looks obviously correct. The problem is that when $\pi \in (0, 0.5]$, then tree can describe some non-tree directed acyclic graphs such as the following:

$$\texttt{root} \xmapsto{0.3} (\texttt{left}, \texttt{right}) \; *$$
$$\texttt{left} \xmapsto{0.3} (\texttt{null}, \texttt{grand}) \; *$$
$$\texttt{right} \xmapsto{0.3} (\texttt{grand}, \texttt{null}) \; *$$
$$\texttt{grand} \xmapsto{0.6} (\texttt{null}, \texttt{null})$$

This heap satisfies $\texttt{tree}(\texttt{root}, 0.3)$ despite actually being a DAG ($\texttt{grand}$ is owned with share $0.3 \oplus 0.3 = 0.6$).

Parkinson proposed a model based on sets of natural numbers that solved this issue but introduced others [31], and then Dockins *et al.* [13] proposed the following "tree share" model, which fixes all of the aforementioned issues. A tree share $\tau \in \mathbb{T}$ is inductively defined as a binary tree with boolean leaves:

$$\tau \triangleq \circ \mid \bullet \mid \widehat{\tau \; \tau}$$

Here $\circ$ denotes an "empty" leaf while $\bullet$ a "full" leaf. The tree $\circ$ is thus the empty share, and $\bullet$ the full share. There are two "half" shares: $\widehat{\circ \bullet}$ and $\widehat{\bullet \circ}$, and four "quarter" shares, beginning with $\widehat{\underset{\bullet \; \circ}{\frown} \circ}$. It is a feature, rather than a bug, that the two half shares are distinct from each other.

Notice that we presented the first quarter share as $\widehat{\underset{\bullet \; \circ}{\frown} \circ}$ instead of *e.g.*
$\underset{\bullet \; \circ \; \circ \; \circ}{\frown}$. This is deliberate: the second choice is not a valid share because the tree is not in *canonical form*. A tree is in canonical form when it is in its most compact representation under the relation $\cong$:

$$\overline{\circ \cong \circ} \qquad \overline{\bullet \cong \bullet} \qquad \overline{\circ \cong \widehat{\circ \; \circ}} \qquad \overline{\bullet \cong \widehat{\bullet \; \bullet}} \qquad \frac{\tau_1 \cong \tau_1' \quad \tau_2 \cong \tau_2'}{\widehat{\tau_1 \; \tau_2} \cong \widehat{\tau_1' \; \tau_2'}}$$

Maintaining canonical form is a headache in Coq but does not introduce any fundamental difficulty. Accordingly, for this presentation we will simply fold and unfold trees to/from canonical form when required by the narrative.

Defining the "join" operation $\oplus$ on tree shares formally is somewhat technical due to the necessity of managing the canonical forms [27, Sect. A] but the core idea is quite straightforward. Simply unfold both trees under $\cong$ into the same shape and join them leafwise using the rules $\circ \oplus \circ = \circ$, $\circ \oplus \bullet = \bullet$, and $\bullet \oplus \circ = \bullet$; afterwards refold under $\cong$ back into canonical form. Here is an example:

$$\widehat{\underset{\bullet \; \circ}{\frown} \circ} \oplus \underset{\circ \; \bullet \; \bullet}{\frown} \cong \underset{\bullet \; \circ \; \circ}{\frown} \oplus \underset{\circ \; \bullet \; \bullet}{\frown} = \underset{\bullet \; \bullet \; \bullet}{\frown} \cong \widehat{\underset{\bullet \; \bullet}{\frown} \circ}$$

Because $\bullet \oplus \bullet$ is undefined, the join relation on trees is a partial operation. Dockins *et al.* [13] prove that the join relation satisfies a number of useful axioms *e.g.* associativity and commutativity (Sect. 2.1 has the full list). One key axiom, not satisfied by $(\mathbb{Q}, \oplus)$, is "disjointness": $x \oplus x = y \Rightarrow x = \circ$. Disjointness is the axiom that forces the **tree** predicate—Eq. 1—to behave properly: we saw above that we get a DAG in $\mathbb{Q}$ since $x \oplus x$ need not be 0.

Due to their good metatheorical properties, various program logics [16,17] and tools [1,19,36] incorporate tree shares. Gherghina detailed a number of programs whose verifications used tree shares heavily [15, Chap. 4]; these form the core of our benchmark in Sect. 4.2. However, most tools have avoided using tree shares in part because they lacked algorithms that could decide entailments involving fractionals. Hobor and Gherghina [19] showed how to divide an entailment between separation logic formulae incorporating fractional ownership into (1) a fraction-free separation logic entailment, and (2) an entailment between systems of share equations; this encouraged shares to be studied as a standalone domain.

Le *et al.* developed a tool to decide tree share entailments [25]. The present paper improves on their work in several ways. From a practical point of view, our new tool is fully machine-checked in Coq, giving the highest level of assurance that both its implementation and underlying theory are rock solid. By comparing our new tool with Le *et al.*'s, we discovered weaknesses in both the latter's implementation and its theory. Moreover, a trend in recent years has been to develop verification toolsets within Coq [1,2,8]; since certified tools generally only depend on other certified tools, such tools have not been able to use Le *et al.*'s implementation, but they can use our new tool. Happily, despite the challenges involved in developing an implementation in Coq, our new tool exhibits improved performance over Le *et al.*'s due to a number of heuristics that meaningfully improve performance without sacrificing soundness or completeness; some of these heuristics should be applicable to future certified procedures.

From a theoretical point of view, our major improvement over Le *et al.* is a sound treatment of negations. Negative clauses in logic are often more difficult to handle than positive ones are. Le *et al.*'s theory purported to support a very limited form of negation, which allowed them to force variables to be nonempty, *i.e.* $\pi \neq \circ$. We believe the previous theory is unsound when there are a sufficiently high number of nonempty variables on both sides of an implication. Our new theory handles arbitrary negative clauses, *i.e.* $\neg(\pi_1 \oplus \pi_2 = \pi_3)$ and is fully mechanized in Coq. A second theoretical improvement is a more careful treatment of existential variables.

The rest of this paper is organized as follows. In Sect. 2 we define the central decision problem and give an overview of our procedure. In Sect. 3 we show the key algorithms and outline why they are correct. All our proofs are mechanized in Coq; additional pen-and-paper details are also available in our appendix [27]. In Sect. 4 we discuss our 38.6k LOC certified implementation, describe how we have incorporated it into the HIP/SLEEK verification toolset [30], and benchmark its performance. Finally, in Sect. 5 we discuss related and future work and conclude.

2   Share Constraints and Their Decision Procedures

In Sect. 2.1, we introduce the decision problems over tree shares, satisfiability and entailment over *share equation systems*. Next we overview our decision procedure in Sect. 2.2 together with a brief description of their components' functionality. For **convenience**, we will use the symbol $\mathcal{L}$ to represent $\widehat{\bullet \circ}$ and $\mathcal{R}$ for $\widehat{\circ \bullet}$.

2.1 Share Constraints

Given a SL entailment $P \vdash Q$ with fractional permissions, there are standard procedures to separately extract a heap constraint and a share constraint [15, 19, 25]. For example, the entailment $x \xmapsto{v_1} 1 * y \xmapsto{\mathcal{R}} 2 \vdash x \xmapsto{\mathcal{L}} 1$ yields constraints $v_1 \neq \circ \wedge v_2 = \mathcal{R} \vdash \exists v_3. \mathcal{L} \oplus v_3 = v_1$. Tree constraints pose a technical difficulty due to the infinite tree domain, e.g., $v_1 \oplus v_2 = \bullet$ has infinitely many solutions $\{(\bullet, \circ), (\mathcal{L}, \mathcal{R}), \ldots\}$. The type of tree constraints we need to deal with can be represent as $\Sigma_1 \vdash \Sigma_2$ where Σ_i is *share equation system*:

Definition 1. *A share equation system Σ is a quadruple $(l^\exists, l^=, l^+, l^-)$ in which:*

1. *$l^\exists$ is the list of existential variables.*
2. *$l^=$ is the list of equalities $\pi_1 = \pi_2$.*
3. *l^+ is the list of equations $\pi_1 \oplus \pi_2 = \pi_3$.*
4. *l^- is the list of disequations $\neg(\pi_1 \oplus \pi_2 = \pi_3)$.*

The entailment $\Sigma_1 \vdash \Sigma_2$ can be informally understood as "all solutions of Σ_1 are also solutions of Σ_2". In theory, it is conventional to treat equalities $\pi_1 = \pi_2$ as macros for $\pi_1 \oplus \circ = \pi_2$, although our certified tool tracks equalities separately for optimization purposes. For **convenience**, we will usually illustrate equation system as $\Sigma = \{x_1, \ldots, x_n, g_1, \ldots, g_m\}$ in which x_i is existential variable and g_i is either equality, equation or disequation.

To define the semantics of Σ, let *context* ρ be a mapping from variable names to tree shares. We then override ρ over tree constants as identity, i.e., $\rho(\tau) = \tau$. To handle existential variable lists, we define the notion of a *context override*:

$$\rho[\rho' \Leftarrow l] \overset{\text{def}}{=} \lambda x. \ \rho'(v) \text{ if } x \in l \text{ else } \rho(v)$$

The semantics of forcing, written $\rho \models \Phi$, follows natural, e.g., $\rho \models \pi_1 \oplus \pi_2 = \pi_3$ iff $\rho(\pi_1) \oplus \rho(\pi_2) = \rho(\pi_3)$ and $\rho \models P \wedge Q$ iff $\rho \models P$ and $\rho \models Q$. We say ρ is a solution of Σ, denoted by $\rho \models \Sigma$, if there exists a context ρ' such that $\rho[\rho' \Leftarrow l^\exists] \models l^= \wedge l^+ \wedge l^-$. Consequently, we say Σ_1 entails Σ_2 if all solutions of Σ_1 are also solutions of Σ_2. In this paper, we propose *certified algorithms* to solve the satisfiability and entailment over tree shares:

Problem. Let Σ_1, Σ_2 be share equation systems. Construct a sound and complete procedure to handle the following queries:

1. **SAT(Σ_1)**: Is Σ_1 satisfiable, i.e., $\exists \rho. \ \rho \models \Sigma_1$?
2. **IMP(Σ_1, Σ_2)**: Does Σ_1 entail Σ_2, i.e., $\forall \rho. \ \rho \models \Sigma_1 \Rightarrow \rho \models \Sigma_2$?

Despite allowing negative clauses, entailment is not subsumed by satisfiability due to the quantifier alternation in the consequent. One interesting exercise is to examine the metatheoretical properties of tree shares described by Dockins

Functional: $x \oplus y = z_1 \;\; \Rightarrow \;\; x \oplus y = z_2 \;\; \Rightarrow \;\; z_1 = z_2$
Commutative: $x \oplus y \;=\; y \oplus x$
Associative: $x \oplus (y \oplus z) \;=\; (x \oplus y) \oplus z$
Cancellative: $x_1 \oplus y = z \;\; \Rightarrow \;\; x_2 \oplus y = z \;\; \Rightarrow \;\; x_1 = x_2$
Unit: $\exists u. \; \forall x. \; x \oplus u = x$
Disjointness: $x \oplus x = y \;\; \Rightarrow \;\; x = y$
Cross split: $a \oplus b = z \wedge c \oplus d = z \Rightarrow \exists ac, ad, bc, bd.$
  $ac \oplus ad = a \wedge bc \oplus bd = b \wedge ac \oplus bc = c \wedge ad \oplus bd = d$

$$\forall \; \boxed{a \mid b} \;\; \boxed{\genfrac{}{}{0pt}{}{c}{d}} \;\; \exists \; \boxed{\genfrac{}{}{0pt}{}{ac \mid bc}{ad \mid bd}}$$

Infinite splitability: $x \neq \circ \;\; \Rightarrow \;\; \exists x_1, x_2. \; x_1 \neq \circ \;\wedge\; x_2 \neq \circ \;\wedge\; x_1 \oplus x_2 = x$

Fig. 1. Properties of tree shares

et al. [13]; these are given in Fig. 1. Several of these are the standard properties of separation algebras [6], but others are part of what make the tree share model special. In particular, tree shares are one of the fractional permission models that simultaneously satisfy Disjointness (forces the **tree** predicate—Eq. 1—to behave properly), Cross-split (used *e.g.* in settings involving overlapping data structures), and Infinite splitability (to verify divide-and-conquer algorithms). Encouragingly, all of the properties except for "Unit" are expressible as entailments in our format; *e.g.* associativity is expressed as:

$$\{x \oplus a = b, y \oplus z = a\} \;\; \vdash \;\; \{c, x \oplus y = c, c \oplus z = b\}$$

Unit requires the order of quantifiers to swap; our format can express the weaker "Multiunit axiom" $\forall x. \; \exists u. \; x \oplus u = x$ as well as $\forall x. \; x \oplus \circ = x$.

2.2 Overview of Our Decision Procedure

We use **SAT** and **IMP** for the problems and SAT and IMP for the decision procedures themselves. Although the entailment checker IMP is our main concern, the satisfiability checker SAT is helpful for at least two reasons. First, SAT helps to prune the search space; *e.g.*, if the antecedent Σ_1 for IMP is unsatisfiable, we can immediately conclude $\Sigma_1 \vdash \Sigma_2$. Second, the correctness of some of the transformations in IMP require that Σ_1 be satisfiable.

The architecture of our system is given in Fig. 2. We have two procedures to solve problems over share formulas, one for satisfiability and the other for entailment, both written in Gallina and certified in Coq. Identically-named components in the two procedures are similar in spirit but not identical in operation; thus *e.g.* there are two different SIMPLIFIER components, one for SAT and another for IMP. The PARTITIONER, BOUNDER, and SIMPLIFIER components substantially improve the performance of our procedures in practice but are not complete solvers: in the worst case they do nothing. Since they are included for performance we will discuss them in more detail in Sect. 4.

The DECOMPOSER and TRANSFORMER components form the heart of our procedure. While the $\oplus$ operation has many useful properties that enable sophisticated reasoning about shared ownership in program verifications (*e.g.* Fig. 1), they are not strong enough for techniques like Gaussian elimination (which even in $\mathbb{Q}$ cannot handle negative clauses). In Sect. 3 we will describe DECOMPOSER in detail after developing the necessary theory. Briefly, DECOMPOSER takes a system of equations with constants of arbitrary complexity and eventually produces a much larger equivalent system in which each constant is either $\circ$ or $\bullet$ (*i.e.*, the final system has *height* zero).

TRANSFORMER is a very sophisticated component mathematically, yet also the simplest computationally: it just changes the **type** of the system. That is, it inputs a **tree** system of height zero and outputs an equivalent, essentially identical **Boolean** system. The only actual computational content is by swapping $\circ$ for $\bot$ and $\bullet$ for $\top$. The join relation on Booleans is simply disjoint disjunction:

$$\top \oplus \bot = \top \qquad \bot \oplus \top = \top \qquad \bot \oplus \bot = \bot$$

The last option, $\top \oplus \top$, is undefined.

INTERPRETER translates Boolean systems of equations into Boolean sentences by rewriting positive and negative equations using the rules

$$\pi_1 \oplus \pi_2 = \pi_3 \rightsquigarrow (\pi_1 \wedge \neg\pi_2 \wedge \pi_3) \vee (\neg\pi_1 \wedge \pi_2 \wedge \pi_3) \vee (\neg\pi_1 \wedge \neg\pi_2 \wedge \neg\pi_3)$$

$$\neg(\pi_1 \oplus \pi_2 = \pi_3) \rightsquigarrow (\neg\pi_1 \vee \pi_2 \vee \neg\pi_3) \wedge (\pi_1 \vee \neg\pi_2 \vee \neg\pi_3) \wedge (\pi_1 \vee \pi_2 \vee \pi_3)$$

Next, it adds the appropriate quantifiers depending on the query type to reach a closed sentence. INTERPRETER's code and correctness proof are straightforward.

SMT_SOLVER uses simple quantifier elimination to check the validity of boolean sentences. Our SMT solver is rather naïve, and thus is the performance bottleneck of our tool, but we could not find a suitable Gallina alternative. As discussed in Sect. 4, despite its naïveté our overall performance seems acceptable in practice due to the heuristics in PARTITION, BOUNDER, and SIMPLIFIER.

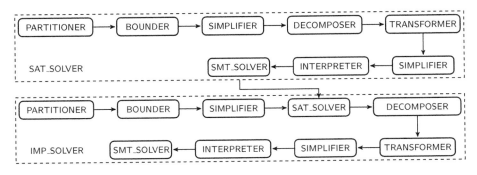

Fig. 2. SATsolver and IMP solver

Algorithm 1. Solver SAT for systems with disequations

1: **function** SAT(Σ)
2:     **if** SAT$^+$(Σ^+) $= \bot$ **then return** $\bot$
3:     **else if** $l^- = $ nil **then**   ▷ l^- is the disequation list in Σ
4:         **return** $\top$
5:     **else**   **let** $l^- = [\eta_1, \ldots, \eta_n]$
6:         **return** $\bigwedge_{i=1}^n$ SSAT(Σ^{η_i})

3   Core Algorithms for the Decision Procedures

We begin with some basic definitions and notions in Sect. 3.1 that are essential for the algorithms and their correctness proofs. In Sects. 3.2 and 3.3, we propose our decision procedures to solve **SAT** and **IMP** together with illustrated examples.

3.1   Definitions and Notations

We adopt the following definitions and notations. We use nil to denote empty list, $[e_1, \ldots, e_n]$ to represent list's content, and $l + l'$ for list concatenation. We use the metavariable η to represent a single disequation. The symbols Σ and Π are reserved for systems and pairs of systems respectively; if the exact form of our systems is not important or is clear from the context, we may refer it as Γ. The symbol ρ and S are for contexts and solutions respectively. We use $|\tau|$ to indicate the height of τ. Also, we will override the height function $|\cdot|$ for equation systems and contexts to indicate the height of the highest tree constant. For a tree τ, we let τ_l and τ_r to be the left and right sub-trees of τ, i.e., $\tau = \tau_l = \tau_r$ if $\tau \in \{\circ, \bullet\}$ and $\tau = \widehat{\tau_l \ \tau_r}$ otherwise. We define several basic systems for SAT and IMP as the building blocks of the decision procedures:

Definition 2. Let $\Sigma, \Sigma_1, \Sigma_2$ be share equation systems and η, η_1, η_2 disequations. Let l be a list of disequations, we define Σ^l to be the new equation system in which the disequation list in Σ is replaced with l. For convenience, we write Σ^η as shortcut for $\Sigma^{[\eta]}$, and Σ^+ as shortcut for Σ^{nil}. Then:

1. If the disequation list in Σ is empty then Σ is called a positive system.
2. If there is exactly one disequation in Σ then Σ is called a singleton system.
3. If Σ_1 is positive and Σ_2 is singleton then (Σ_1, Σ_2) is called a Z-system.
4. If both Σ_1 and Σ_2 are singleton then (Σ_1, Σ_2) is called a S-system.

   In particular, Σ^+ is always a positive system, Σ^η is always a singleton system, $(\Sigma_1^+, \Sigma_2^\eta)$ is always a Z-system, and $(\Sigma_1^{\eta_1}, \Sigma_2^{\eta_2})$ is always an S-system.

3.2   Decision Procedure for SAT

We propose the procedure SAT (Algorithm 1) to solve **SAT** of systems with disequations. For **SAT**(Σ), the existential list is redundant and thus will be ignored. Our new decision procedure SAT also makes use of the old decision procedure

---

Algorithm 2. Solver SSAT for singleton systems

1: **function** SSAT(Σ^η)
Require: Σ^η is singleton and Σ^+ is satisfiable
  2:    $[\Sigma_1, \ldots, \Sigma_n] \leftarrow$ DECOMPOSE(Σ^η)
  3:    transform each Σ_i into Boolean formula Φ_i
  4:    $\Phi \leftarrow \bigvee_{i=1}^{n} \Phi_i$
  5:    **return** SMT_SOLVER(Φ)

SAT^+ from previous work [25] for systems without disequations, *e.g.*, positive systems. To help the readers gain intuition, we will abstract away all the tedious low-level implementations and only discuss about the high-level structure. The execution of SAT consists of two major steps which are described in Algorithm 1. First, the system Σ is separated into a list of singleton systems; each contains a single disequation taken from the disequation list of Σ. In the second step, each singleton system is solved individually using the subroutine SSAT, then their results are conjoined to determine the result of SAT(Σ).

The solver SSAT for singleton system (Algorithm 2) calls subroutine DECOMPOSE (Algorithm 3) that helps decompose a share system into sub-systems of height zero. These subs-systems subsequently go though a 2-phase process to be transformed into Boolean formulas. In the first phase, the sub-routine TRANSFORM trivially converts tree type into Boolean type using the conversions $\bullet \rightsquigarrow \top$ and $\circ \rightsquigarrow \bot$. Correspondingly, the share system is converted into the Boolean system. In the second phase, the subroutine INTERPRET helps to interpret the Boolean system into an equivalent Boolean formula by adding necessary quantifiers ($\exists$ for **SAT**, $\forall$ for **IMP**) and conjunctives among equations and disequations. Finally, Theorem 1 states the correctness of SAT whose proof is verified in Coq.

Theorem 1. *Let Σ be a share system then Σ is satisfiable iff* SAT(Σ) = $\top$.

Example 1. Let $\Sigma = \{v_1 \oplus v_2 = \bullet, \neg(v_1 = \mathcal{L}), \neg(v_2 = \circ)\}$ then **SAT**(Σ) is the valid formula ($v_1 = \mathcal{R}$, $v_2 = \mathcal{L}$ is a solution):

$$\exists v_1 \exists v_2.\ v_1 \oplus v_2 = \bullet \ \wedge \ \neg(v_1 = \mathcal{L}) \ \wedge \ \neg(v_2 = \circ)$$

First, $SAT^+(\Sigma^+)$ is called to check $\exists v_1 \exists v_2.\ v_1 \oplus v_2 = \bullet$ (which returns $\top$ as $v_1 = \circ$, $v_2 = \bullet$ is a solution). After that, Σ is split into two singleton systems:

$$\Sigma^1 = \{v_1 \oplus v_2 = \bullet, \neg(v_1 = \mathcal{L})\} \text{ and } \Sigma^2 = \{v_1 \oplus v_2 = \bullet, \neg(v_2 = \circ)\}$$

When NSAT(Σ^1) is called, Σ^1 is split into Σ^1_1 and Σ^1_2 by DECOMPOSER:

$$\Sigma^1_1 = \{v_1 \oplus v_2 = \bullet, \neg(v_1 = \bullet)\} \text{ and } \Sigma^1_2 = \{v_1 \oplus v_2 = \bullet, \neg(v_1 = \circ)\}$$

The two systems Σ^1_1, Σ^1_2 are transformed into boolean formulas Φ^1_1 and Φ^1_2:

$$\begin{aligned}
\Phi^1_1 &= \exists v_1 \exists v_2.\ ((v_1 \wedge \neg v_2) \ \vee \ (\neg v_1 \wedge v_2)) \ \wedge \ \neg v_1 \\
\Phi^1_2 &= \exists v_1 \exists v_2.\ ((v_1 \wedge \neg v_2) \ \vee \ (\neg v_1 \wedge v_2)) \ \wedge \ v_1
\end{aligned}$$

Algorithm 3. Decompose system into sub-systems of height zero

---

1: **function** DECOMPOSE(Γ)
Require: Γ is either one system (**SAT**) or pair of systems (**IMP**)
Ensure: A list of sub-systems of height zero
2:     **if** $|\Gamma| = 0$ **then return** $[\Gamma]$
3:     **else**
4:         $(\Gamma_1, \Gamma_2) \leftarrow$ SINGLE_DECOMPOSE(Γ)
5:         **return** DECOMPOSE(Γ_1) $+\!\!+$ DECOMPOSE(Γ_2)

6:

7: **function** SINGLE_DECOMPOSE(Γ)
Require: Γ is either one system (**SAT**) or pair of systems (**IMP**)
Ensure: A pair of left and right sub-system
8:     **if** $|\Gamma| = 0$ **then return** (Γ, Γ)
9:     **else**
10:         $\Gamma_l \leftarrow$ replace each tree constant τ in Γ with its left sub-tree τ_l
11:         $\Gamma_r \leftarrow$ replace each tree constant τ in Γ with its right sub-tree τ_r
12:         **return** (Γ_l, Γ_r)

As both Φ_1^1 and Φ_2^1 are valid, NSAT(Σ^1) returns $\top$. Similarly, one can verify that NSAT(Σ^2) also returns $\top$ and thus SAT(Σ) returns $\top$ as the result.   □

Additional details of the soundness proof for SAT can be found in [27, Sect. B.1], which uses a technique we call "domain reduction", explained in [27, Sect. A.1]. We finish Sect. 3.2 by pointing out a decidability result of $\oplus$:

Corollary 1. *The $\exists$-theory of* $\mathcal{M} = \langle \mathbb{T}, \oplus, = \rangle$ *is decidable.*

Proof. Let Ψ be a quantifier-free formula in $\mathcal{M}$, we convert Ψ into Disjunctive Normal Form $\bigvee_{i=1}^{n} \Psi_i$ then each Ψ_i can be represented as a constraint system Σ_i. As a result, Ψ is satisfiable iff some Σ_i is satisfiable which can be solved using Algorithm 1. Thus the result follows.

3.3   Decision Procedure for IMP

Our IMP procedure (Algorithm 4) deploys a similar strategy as for SAT by reducing the entailment into several entailments of the basic systems (*e.g.* Z-system and S-system). In detail, IMP verifies the entailment $\Sigma_1 \vdash \Sigma_2$ by first calling two solvers SAT(Σ_1) and IMP$^+$(Σ_1^+, Σ_2^+)[1] (line 2 and 3). Then the lengths of the two disequation lists (l_1^- in Σ_1 and l_2^- in Σ_2) critically determine the subsequent flow of IMP. To be precise, there are three different cases of l_1^- and l_2^- that fully cover all the possibilities:

1. If $l_2^- =$ nil (line 5) then the answer is equivalent to IMP$^+$(Σ_1^+, Σ_2^+), *i.e.*, $\top$.

---

[1] This is the entailment checker for positive constraints from previous work [25].

Algorithm 4. Solver IMP for entailment of share systems with disequations

```
1: function IMP(Σ₁, Σ₂)
2:     if SAT(Σ₁) = ⊥ then return ⊥
3:     else if IMP⁺(Σ₁⁺, Σ₂⁺) = ⊥ then return ⊥
4:     else  let l₁⁻, l₂⁻ be disequation lists of Σ₁, Σ₂
5:         if l₂⁻ = nil then return ⊤
6:         else  let l₂⁻ = [η₂¹, ..., η₂ⁿ]
7:             if l₁⁻ = nil then return ⋀ᵢ₌₁ⁿ ZIMP(Σ₁⁺, Σ₂^{η₂ⁱ})
8:             else  let l₁⁻ = [η₁¹, ..., η₁ᵐ]
9:                 for i = 1 ... n and j = 1 ... m do
10:                    let Zᵢ ← ZIMP(Σ₁⁺, Σ₂^{η₂ⁱ}) and Sᵢʲ ← SIMP(Σ₁^{η₁ʲ}, Σ₂^{η₂ⁱ})
11:                return ⋀ᵢ₌₁ⁿ(Zᵢ ∨ (⋁ⱼ₌₁ᵐ Sᵢʲ))
```

Algorithm 5. Solvers for entailment of Z-systems and S-systems

```
1: function ZIMP(Σ₁, Σ₂)
Require: (Σ₁, Σ₂) is Z-system, Σ₁ is satisfiable and Σ₁ ⊢ Σ₂⁺
2:     [Γ₁, ..., Γₙ] ← DECOMPOSE(Σ₁, Σ₂)
3:     transform each Γᵢ into Boolean formula Φᵢ
4:     Φ ← ⋁ᵢ₌₁ⁿ Φᵢ
5:     return SMT_SOLVER(Φ)
6:
7: function SIMP(Σ₁, Σ₂)
Require: (Σ₁, Σ₂) is S-system, Σ₁⁺ is satisfiable, Σ₁⁺ ⊢ Σ₂⁺ and Σ₁⁺ ⊬ Σ₂
8:     [Γ₁, ..., Γₙ] ← DECOMPOSE(Σ₁, Σ₂)
9:     transform each Γᵢ into Boolean formula Φᵢ
10:    Φ ← ⋀ᵢ₌₁ⁿ Φᵢ
11:    return SMT_SOLVER(Φ)
```

2. Otherwise, we check whether $l_1^- =$ nil (line 7) from which the answer is conjoined from several entailments of Z-systems $(\Sigma_1, \Sigma_2^{\eta_2^i})$; each is constructed from (Σ_1, Σ_2) by removing all disequations in Σ_2 except for one. Here we call the subroutine ZIMP which is a specialized for entailment of Z-systems.
3. The third case is neither l_1^- nor l_2^- is empty (line 8). Then $\Sigma_1 \vdash \Sigma_2$ is derived by taking the conjunction of several entailments of Z-systems and S-systems altogether. Here we use SIMP to solve S-system entailments.

Two specialized solvers ZIMP and SIMP are described in Algorithm 5. For ZIMP, we first call the subroutine DECOMPOSE to split the Z-system into sub-systems of height zero. Next, each sub-system is transformed in to Boolean formula by adding necessary quantifiers and logical connectives. These Boolean formulas are then combined using disjunctions to form a single Boolean formula; and this formula is solved using standard SMT solvers to determine the result of the entailment. The procedure for SIMP has a similar structure, except that the final Boolean formula is formed using conjunctions. Also, it is worth noticing that there are certain preconditions for both solvers; and all of them are important to shape the correctness of the solvers. Last but not least, the correctness of IMP is mentioned in Theorem 2; and its proof is verified entirely in Coq.

Theorem 2. *Let Σ_1, Σ_2 be share systems then $\Sigma_1 \vdash \Sigma_2$ iff* $\mathsf{IMP}(\Sigma_1, \Sigma_2) = \top$.

Example 2. The infinite splitability of tree share (Fig. 1):

$$\forall v. \ (v \neq \circ \Rightarrow \exists v_1 \exists v_2. \ v_1 \oplus v_2 = v \wedge v_1 \neq \circ \wedge v_2 \neq \circ)$$

can be represented as the entailment $\Sigma_1 \vdash \Sigma_2$ s.t.:

$$\Sigma_1 = \{\neg(v = \circ)\} \text{ and } \Sigma_2 = \{v_1, v_2, v_1 \oplus v_2 = v, \neg(v_1 = \circ), \neg(v_2 = \circ)\}$$

This entailment will go though Algorithm 4 until line 8 because both disequation lists are nonempty. As there are two disequations in Σ_2, namely $\eta_1 : v_1 \neq \circ$ and $\eta_2 : v_2 \neq \circ$, we need to verify the conjunction $P_1 \wedge P_2$ s.t.:

$$P_1 = \mathsf{ZIMP}(\Sigma_1^+, \Sigma_2^{\eta_1}) \vee \mathsf{SIMP}(\Sigma_1, \Sigma_2^{\eta_1}) \text{ and } P_2 = \mathsf{ZIMP}(\Sigma_1^+, \Sigma_2^{\eta_2}) \vee \mathsf{SIMP}(\Sigma_1, \Sigma_2^{\eta_2})$$

For P_1, $\mathsf{ZIMP}(\Sigma_1^+, \Sigma_2^{\eta_1})$ is equivalent to $\forall v. \ (\top \Rightarrow \exists v_1, v_2. \ v_1 \oplus v_2 = v \wedge v_1 \neq \circ)$ which is false by choosing $v = \circ$ so that both v_1 and v_2 must also be $\circ$. Likewise, $\mathsf{SIMP}(\Sigma_1, \Sigma_2^{\eta_1})$ is equivalent to $\forall v. \ (v \neq \circ \Rightarrow \exists v_1, v_2. \ v_1 \oplus v_2 = v \wedge v_1 \neq \circ)$ which is transformed into the boolean formula:

$$\Phi_1 = \forall v. \ (v \Rightarrow \exists v_1, v_2. \ ((\neg v_1 \wedge \neg v_2 \wedge \neg v) \vee (v_1 \wedge \neg v_2 \wedge v) \vee (\neg v_1 \wedge v_2 \wedge v)) \wedge v_1)$$

As Φ_1 is valid, P_1 is true. Same result holds for P_2 and thus $\Sigma_1 \vdash \Sigma_2$.   □

Additional details of the soundness proof for IMP can be found in [27, Sect. B.2], again using domain reduction [27, Sect. A.1].

4   Performance, Evaluation, and Implementation

Having described the heart of our decision procedures, what remains is to describe the practical aspects of their development and evaluation. In Sect. 4.1 we describe various techniques that enable good performance in practice. In Sect. 4.2 we describe how we benchmarked our tool running inside Coq, running as a standalone compiled program, and after incorporating it into the HIP/SLEEK verification toolset. In [27, Sect. C] we document the files in the development itself; we have approximately 38.6k lines of code in 31 files.

4.1   Performance-Enhancing Components

The architecture of our tool was given in Sect. 2.2 (Fig. 2). The key DECOMPOSER, TRANSFORMER and INTERPRETER components were discussed in Sects. 2.2, 3.2, and 3.3. Here we give details on the PARTITIONER, BOUNDER, and SIMPLIFIER modules. Their principal goal is to shrink the search space and uncover contradictions, although they each do so in a very different way. Although in practice they can substantially improve performance, none of these components is a complete solver. The key ideas in these components were developed previously [19,25], although not all together. We have made a number of incremental enhancements, but our major contribution for these is components is the development of high-performing general-purpose certified implementations.

PARTITIONER. The goal of this module is to separate a constraint system into *independent subsystems*. Two systems are independent of each other if they do not share any common variable (with existential variables bound locally).

The partition function is implemented *generically*: in other words it does not assume very much about the underlying domain. To build the module, we must specify types of *variables* V, *equations* E, and contexts C. We also provide a function $\sigma : E \Rightarrow L(V)$ that extracts a list of variables from an equation, an overriding function written $\rho'[\rho \Leftarrow l]$, and an evaluation relation written $c \models e$. The soundness proof requires two properties that relate these inputs as follows:

$$\frac{\rho \models e \qquad \sigma(e) \cap l = \varnothing}{\rho[\rho' \Leftarrow l] \models e} \; disjointness \qquad\qquad \frac{\rho \models e \qquad \sigma(e) \subset l}{\rho'[\rho \Leftarrow l] \models e} \; inclusion$$

Disjointness and inclusion jointly specify that satisfaction of an equation only depends on the variables it contains: overriding variables not in the equation does not matter; and from any context, if we override all of the variables that are in an equation then we can ignore the original context.

It is simple to use PARTITIONER for **SAT**, but to handle **IMP** is harder. We can "tag" equations and variables as coming from the antecedent or consequent before partitioning and then use these tags to separate the resulting partitioned systems into antecedents and consequents afterwards.

The implementation of PARTITIONER is nontrivial in purely functional languages like Coq. One reason is that we need a purely functional union-find data structure, which we obtain via the impure-to-pure transformation of Pippenger [32] applied to the canonical imperative algorithm [9]. In other words, we substitute red-black trees for memory (mapping "addresses" to "cell contents") and pay a logarithmic access penalty, yielding an $O(n \cdot \log(n) \cdot \alpha(n))$ algorithm.

The termination of "find" turns out to be subtle. Parent pointers are represented as cells that "point to" other cells; however, those parent cells can be anywhere in the red-black tree (*e.g.* item 5 can be the parent of item 10, or the other way around.) Accordingly an important invariant of the structure is that "nonlocal links" form acyclic chains, which is the key termination argument.

Given union-find, the algorithm is straightforward: each variable is put into a singleton set, and then while processing each equation we union the corresponding sets. Lastly, we extract the sets and filter the equations into components.

BOUNDER. The bounder uses order theory to prune the space. Each variable v is given an initial bound $\circ \subseteq v \subseteq \bullet$. The bounder then tries to narrow these bounds by forward and backward propagation. For example, if $\tau_1 \subseteq v_1 \subseteq \bullet$, $\tau_2 \subseteq v_2 \subseteq \bullet$, and $\circ \subseteq v_3 \subseteq \bullet$, then if $v_1 \oplus v_2 = v_3$ is an clause we can conclude that v_3's lower bound can be increased from $\circ$ to $\tau_1 \sqcup \tau_2$ (where $\sqcup$ computes the union in an underlying lattice on trees). In some cases, the bounds for a variable can be narrowed all the way to a point, in which case we can substitute the variable away. In other cases we can find a contradiction (when the upper bound goes below the lower bound), allowing us to terminate the procedure.

The bounder is an updated version of the incomplete solver developed by Hobor *et al.* [19]. Although our main contribution here is the certified implementation, we managed to tighten the bounds in certain cases.

SIMPLIFIER. The simplifier is a combination of a substitution engine and several effective heuristics for reducing the overall difficulty via calculation. For example, from $v \oplus \tau_1 = \tau_2$, where τ_i are constants, we can compute an exact value for v using an inverse of $\oplus$: $v = \tau_2 \ominus \tau_1$. SIMPLIFIER also hunts for contradictions: for example, from $v \oplus v = \bullet$ we can reach a contradiction due to the "disjointness" axiom from Fig. 1. The core idea of simplifier was contained in the work of Le *et al.* [25], so our main contribution here is our certified implementation.

4.2   Experimental Evaluation

Our procedures are implemented and certified in Coq. Users who wish to use our code outside of Coq can use Coq's extraction feature to generate code in OCaml and Haskell, although at present a small bug in Coq 8.4pl5's extraction mechanism requires a small human edit to the generated code.

We benchmarked our code in three ways using an Intel i7 with 8GB RAM. First, we used a suite of 102 standalone test cases developed by Le *et al.* (53 **SAT** and 49 **IMP**) [25] and the 9 metatheoretic properties described in Sect. 2. These tests cover a variety tricky cases such as large number of variables, deep tree constants, etc. Even running as interpreted Gallina code within Coq, the time is extremely encouraging at **17 s** to check all 111 tests. After we port to Coq 8.5 we can use the native_compute tactic to increase performance.

Second, we compiled the extracted OCaml code with ocamlopt. The total running time to test all 111 previous tests is **0.02 s**, despite our naïve SMT solver; our previous tool took 1.4 s. Since our SMT solver is a separate module, it can be replaced with a more robust external solver such as Z3 [10] if performance is bottleneck in that spot in the future.

Finally, we incorporated our solver into the HIP/SLEEK verification toolset, which was previously using the uncertified solver by Le *et al.* We did so by writing a short (approximately 150 line) "shim" that translated the format used by the previous tool into the format expected by the new tool.

We then benchmarked our tool against a suite of 23 benchmark programs as shown in Fig. 3. 15 of those programs were developed by Gherghina [15] and utilize a concurrent separation logic for pthreads-style barriers that exercise share provers extensively. Another 7 tests were developed for the HipCAP project [7], which extended HIP/SLEEK to reason in a Concurrent Abstract Predicate [12] style. Finally, we wrote a simple fork/join program for our initial testing.

The results are rather interesting! The left column gives the input file name to HIP/SLEEK and the second the number of lines in that file. The third column is the total number of calls into the solver (both **SAT** and **IMP**). **The fourth column is the number of times the previous solver by Le *et al.* answered**

File	LOC	# calls	# wrong	Le *et al.* [25]	Our tool
MISD_ex1_th1.ss	36	294	48	2.21	2.37
MISD_ex1_th2.ss	36	495	67	4.36	4.48
MISD_ex1_th3.ss	36	726	94	6.95	6.58
MISD_ex1_th4.ss	36	1,003	123	9.09	8.36
MISD_ex1_th5.ss	36	1,320	134	15.74	12.38
MISD_ex2_th1.ss	47	837	107	16.77	18.97
MISD_ex2_th2.ss	52	1,044	157	29.34	26.02
MISD_ex2_th3.ss	87	1,841	260	69.09	64.21
MISD_ex2_th4.ss	105	3,023	374	194.17	194.64
PIPE_ex1_th2.ss	35	283	7	2.49	2.78
PIPE_ex1_th3.ss	44	467	12	4.92	4.65
PIPE_ex1_th4.ss	56	678	15	7.00	7.53
PIPE_ex1_th5.ss	66	931	18	9.67	9.37
SIMD_ex1_v2_th1.ss	74	1,167	281	18.46	17.64
SIMD_ex1_v2_th2.ss	95	2,029	392	63.83	53.50
cdl-ex1a-fm.ss	49	7	0	0.10	0.08
cdl-ex2-fm.ss	50	9	0	0.12	0.09
cdl-ex3-fm.ss	51	10	0	0.11	0.12
cdl-ex4-race.ss	50	5	0	0.09	0.09
cdl-ex4a-race.ss	50	9	0	0.10	0.08
cdl-ex5-deadlock.ss	42	5	0	0.10	0.10
cdl-ex5a-deadlock.ss	42	9	0	0.08	0.08
ex-fork-join.ss	25	47	22	0.19	0.16
total		**10,252**	**534**	**455.01**	**434.30**

Fig. 3. Evaluation of our procedures using HIP/SLEEK

the query incorrectly. The fifth column gives the time (in seconds) spent by Le *et al.*'s uncertified solver and the sixth column gives the time spent by our new certified solver. HIP/SLEEK was benchmarked on a more powerful machine with 16 cores and 64 GB RAM.

The uncertified solver got approximately 5.2% of the queries wrong! In our subsequent investigation, we discovered a number of bugs in the original solver: code rot (due to a change in the correct mechanism to call the SMT backend), improper error handling and signaling, general coding errors, and the incorrect treatment of nonzero variables. We also discovered bugs in HIP/SLEEK itself, which did not always use the result of the solver in the correct way; this is why the regression tests were passing even though the solver was reporting the incorrect answer. Our discovery of bugs on this scale, despite the large benchmarks developed by Le *et al.* [25] and Gherghina [15], illustrates the value of developing certified decision procedures.

Our timing results are reasonable: despite our naïve SMT solver backend and the difficulties in writing the algorithms in a purely functional style, our tool is approximately 4.6% faster than Le *et al.*'s uncertified solver.

5   Related Work, Future Work, and Conclusion

Boyland first proposed fractional shares over $\mathbb{Q}$ [5]. Subsequently, Bornat *et al.* [3] improved the rational model by adding natural counting permissions to reason about critical sections. Other notable refinements of the rationals are achieved by Boyland *et al.* [4], Huisman *et al.* [21] and Müller *et al.* [29] that work well on programs with fork, join and lock. Parkinson showed that $\mathbb{Q}$'s lack of disjointness caused trouble and proposed modelling shares as subsets of $\mathbb{N}$ [31]. Dockins *et al.* proposed the tree share model used in the present paper to fix issues with Parkinson's model [13]. Hobor *et al.* were the first to use tree shares in a program logic [18], followed by Hobor and Gherghina [16] and Villard [36]. Hobor and Gherghina [19], Villiard [36], and Appel *et al.* [1] subsequently integrated shares into program verification tools with various incomplete solvers. Le *et al.* [25] developed sound and complete procedures to handle tree share constraints but their correctness proof only justifies the case when there is no disequation.

Future work. We have plans to examine the theory further to support general logical formulae (including arbitrary quantifier use) and perhaps monadic second-order logic. Dockins *et al.* also define a kind of multiplicative operation $\bowtie$ between shares whose computability and complexity was first analyzed by Le *et al.* [26]. Interestingly, this operator can be used to scale permissions over arbitrary predicates and thus our decision procedures need to be generalized to handle constraints that contain both $\oplus$ and $\bowtie$.

Conclusion. We have used tree shares to model permissions for integration into program logics. We proposed two decision procedures for tree shares and proved their correctness in Coq. The two algorithms perform well in practice and have been integrated into a sizable verification toolset.

References

1. Appel, A.W., Dockins, R., Hobor, A., Beringer, L., Dodds, J., Stewart, G., Blazy, S., Leroy, X.: Program Logics for Certified Compilers. Cambridge University Press, New York (2014)
2. Bengtson, J., Jensen, J.B., Birkedal, L.: Charge! - a framework for higher-order separation logic in Coq. In: ITP, pp. 315–331 (2012)
3. Bornat, R., Calcagno, C., O'Hearn, P., Parkinson, M.: Permission accounting in separation logic. In: POPL, pp. 259–270 (2005)
4. Boyland, J.T., Müller, P., Schwerhoff, M., Summers, A.J.: Constraint semantics for abstract read permissions. In: FTfJP, pp. 2:1–2:6 (2014)
5. Boyland, J.: Checking interference with fractional permissions. In: Cousot, R. (ed.) SAS 2003. LNCS, vol. 2694, pp. 55–72. Springer, Heidelberg (2003). doi:10.1007/3-540-44898-5_4
6. Calcagno, C., O'Hearn, P.W., Yang, H.: Local action and abstract separation logic. In: LICS, pp. 366–378 (2007)
7. Chin, W.N., Le, T.C., Qin, S.: Automated verification of countdownlatch (2017)

8. Chlipala, A.: The bedrock structured programming system: combining generative metaprogramming and hoare logic in an extensible program verifier. In: ICFP, pp. 391–402 (2013)
9. Cormen, T.H., Stein, C., Rivest, R.L., Leiserson, C.E.: Introduction to Algorithms, 3 edn. MIT Press (2009)
10. de Moura, L., Bjørner, N.: Z3: an efficient SMT solver. In: Ramakrishnan, C.R., Rehof, J. (eds.) TACAS 2008. LNCS, vol. 4963, pp. 337–340. Springer, Heidelberg (2008). doi:10.1007/978-3-540-78800-3_24
11. Dinsdale-Young, T., da Rocha Pinto, P., Andersen, K.J., Birkedal, L.: CAPER: Automatic verification for fine-grained concurrency. In: Yang, H. (ed.) ESOP 2017. LNCS, vol. 10201, pp. 420–447. Springer, Heidelberg (2017). doi:10.1007/978-3-662-54434-1_16
12. Dinsdale-Young, T., Dodds, M., Gardner, P., Parkinson, M.J., Vafeiadis, V.: Concurrent abstract predicates. In: D'Hondt, T. (ed.) ECOOP 2010. LNCS, vol. 6183, pp. 504–528. Springer, Heidelberg (2010). doi:10.1007/978-3-642-14107-2_24
13. Dockins, R., Hobor, A., Appel, A.W.: A Fresh Look at Separation Algebras and Share Accounting. In: Hu, Z. (ed.) APLAS 2009. LNCS, vol. 5904, pp. 161–177. Springer, Heidelberg (2009). doi:10.1007/978-3-642-10672-9_13
14. Fiedor, J., Letko, Z., Lourenço, J., Vojnar, T.: Dynamic validation of contracts in concurrent code. In: Moreno-Díaz, R., Pichler, F., Quesada-Arencibia, A. (eds.) EUROCAST 2015. LNCS, vol. 9520, pp. 555–564. Springer, Cham (2015). doi:10.1007/978-3-319-27340-2_69
15. Gherghina, C.A.: Efficiently verifying programs with rich control flows. Ph.D. thesis, National University of Singapore (2012)
16. Hobor, A., Gherghina, C.: Barriers in concurrent separation logic. In: Barthe, G. (ed.) ESOP 2011. LNCS, vol. 6602, pp. 276–296. Springer, Heidelberg (2011). doi:10.1007/978-3-642-19718-5_15
17. Hobor, A.: Oracle semantics. Ph.D. thesis, Princeton University, Department of Computer Science, Princeton, NJ, October 2008
18. Hobor, A., Appel, A.W., Nardelli, F.Z.: Oracle semantics for concurrent separation logic. In: Drossopoulou, S. (ed.) ESOP 2008. LNCS, vol. 4960, pp. 353–367. Springer, Heidelberg (2008). doi:10.1007/978-3-540-78739-6_27
19. Hobor, A., Gherghina, C.: Barriers in concurrent separation logic: now with tool support!. Logical Methods Comput. Sci. 8(2), 1–36 (2012)
20. Hoenicke, J., Majumdar, R., Podelski, A.: Thread modularity at many levels: a pearl in compositional verification. In: POPL, pp. 473–485 (2017)
21. Huisman, M., Mostowski, W.: A symbolic approach to permission accounting for concurrent reasoning. In: ISPDC, pp. 165–174 (2015)
22. Jung, R., Swasey, D., Sieczkowski, F., Svendsen, K., Turon, A., Birkedal, L., Dreyer, D.: Iris: monoids and invariants as an orthogonal basis for concurrent reasoning. In: POPL, pp. 637–650 (2015)
23. Křena, B., Letko, Z., Vojnar, T., Ur, S.: A platform for search-based testing of concurrent software. In: PADTAD, pp. 48–58 (2010)
24. Le, D.-K., Chin, W.-N., Teo, Y.M.: Threads as resource for concurrency verification. In: PEPM, pp. 73–84 (2015)
25. Le, X.B., Gherghina, C., Hobor, A.: Decision procedures over sophisticated fractional permissions. In: Jhala, R., Igarashi, A. (eds.) APLAS 2012. LNCS, vol. 7705, pp. 368–385. Springer, Heidelberg (2012). doi:10.1007/978-3-642-35182-2_26
26. Le, X.-B., Hobor, A., Lin, A.W.: Decidability and complexity of tree shares formulas. In: FSTTCS (2016)

27. Le, X.-B., Nguyen, T.-T., Chin, W.-N., Hobor, A.: A certified decision procedure for tree shares (extended) (2017). http://www.comp.nus.edu.sg/~lxbach/certtool/
28. Meng, W., He, F., Wang, B.-Y., Liu, Q.: Thread-modular model checking with iterative refinement. In: Goodloe, A.E., Person, S. (eds.) NFM 2012. LNCS, vol. 7226, pp. 237–251. Springer, Heidelberg (2012). doi:10.1007/978-3-642-28891-3_24
29. Müller, P., Schwerhoff, M., Summers, A.J.: Viper: a verification infrastructure for permission-based reasoning. In: Jobstmann, B., Leino, K.R.M. (eds.) VMCAI 2016. LNCS, vol. 9583, pp. 41–62. Springer, Heidelberg (2016). doi:10.1007/978-3-662-49122-5_2
30. Nguyen, H.H., David, C., Qin, S., Chin, W.-N.: Automated verification of shape and size properties via separation logic. In: Cook, B., Podelski, A. (eds.) VMCAI 2007. LNCS, vol. 4349, pp. 251–266. Springer, Heidelberg (2007). doi:10.1007/978-3-540-69738-1_18
31. Parkinson, M.: Local reasoning for Java. Ph.D. thesis, University of Cambridge (2005)
32. Pippenger, N.: Pure versus impure LISP. In: POPL, pp. 104–109 (1996)
33. Sergey, I., Nanevski, A., Banerjee, A.: Mechanized verification of fine-grained concurrent programs. In: PLDI, pp. 77–87 (2015)
34. Svendsen, K., Birkedal, L.: Impredicative concurrent abstract predicates. In: Shao, Z. (ed.) ESOP 2014. LNCS, vol. 8410, pp. 149–168. Springer, Heidelberg (2014). doi:10.1007/978-3-642-54833-8_9
35. Turon, A., Dreyer, D., Birkedal, L.: Unifying refinement and hoare-style reasoning in a logic for higher-order concurrency. In: ICFP, pp. 377–390 (2013)
36. Villard, J.: Heaps and Hops. Ph.D. thesis, Laboratoire Spécification et Vérification, École Normale Supérieure de Cachan, France, February 2011

Classification-Based Parameter Synthesis for Parametric Timed Automata

Jiaying Li[1(✉)], Jun Sun[1], Bo Gao[1], and Étienne André[2]

[1] Singapore University of Technology and Design, Singapore, Singapore
jiaying_li@mymail.sutd.edu.sg, {sunjun,bo_gao}@sutd.edu.sg
[2] LIPN, University Paris 13, Villetaneuse, France
Etienne.Andre@univ-paris13.fr

Abstract. Parametric timed automata are designed to model timed systems with unknown parameters, often representing design uncertainties of external environments. In order to design a robust system, it is crucial to synthesize constraints on the parameters, which guarantee the system behaves according to certain properties. Existing approaches suffer from scalability issues. In this work, we propose to enhance existing approaches through classification-based learning. We sample multiple concrete values for parameters and model check the corresponding non-parametric models. Based on the checking results, we form conjectures on the constraint through classification techniques, which can be subsequently confirmed by existing model checkers for parametric timed automata. In order to limit the number of model checker invocations, we actively identify informative parameter values so as to help the classification converge quickly. We have implemented a prototype and evaluated our idea on 24 benchmark systems. The result shows our approach can synthesize parameter constraints effectively and thus improve parametric verification.

1 Introduction

Timed-automata [2] are finite-state automata extended with real-valued clock variables which capture the passage of time. As a modeling language, timed-automata are used to model embedded software, timed protocols, cyber-physical systems, etc. To verify such systems, a number of verifiers on timed automata have been developed [11,20,37,39], including the well-known UPPAAL [11] model checker, which has been applied to several industrial applications [38].

In timed automata, clock variables are compared with concrete constants within clocks guards. However, these constants may be unknown at the design time. If an embedded software interacts with an external environment, the constants may depend on the environment. Furthermore, the use of parameters is fundamental in the early phases of the development, giving the possibility to explore different design choices [13]. For example, "given a real-time system M with unknown constants d and r, representing the deadline and the delay in receiving an acknowledgment, one may wish to verify a property F of the system." [23]. To design such a system robustly, it may be useful to have a

© Springer International Publishing AG 2017
Z. Duan and L. Ong (Eds.): ICFEM 2017, LNCS 10610, pp. 243–261, 2017.
https://doi.org/10.1007/978-3-319-68690-5_15

timed automaton model where r and d are kept as unknown parameters, since concrete values for them make sense only in a given concrete environment.

Therefore, parametric timed automata (PTA [3]) which extend timed automata with parametric clock guards have been proposed. The concrete behavior of a PTA depends on the valuation of its parameters, and therefore a given property can be verified for some valuations only in general. A main goal of system verification will be to synthesize a set of valuations (often in the form of a convex or non-convex constraint) for which a PTA satisfies a property; this is also a way to explore various design choices at once. However, manual estimation is time-consuming and does not always generate optimal solutions for specific design problems. In contrast, parametric model checking (i.e., model checking of parametric models [8,22,24,25]) aims to automatically synthesize the region of property-satisfying parameter values, in the form of a constraint.

Existing work on the PTA verification problem relies on exploring PTA models and synthesizing constraints based on "bad states" or "good states". Given a set of property-violating states (hence "bad") or property-satisfying states (hence "good"), we can synthesize a sound constraint by either covering all the "good states" or avoiding all the "bad states". For instance, [16] proposes a method based on the counterexample-guided abstraction refinement (CEGAR). Firstly, the PTA is explored through model checking where parameters are kept as a part of the symbolic state space. After finding a counterexample, a constraint which makes the counterexample infeasible is identified. Afterwards, a different counterexample is identified and subsequently a different constraint. Once all the counterexamples are eliminated, the disjunction of these identified constraints captures all the property-satisfying parameter values.

Note that these approaches often suffer from scalability problem, which limits their power in practice. For example, IMITATOR [5] times out when applied to check a parametric Fischer protocol with 5 processes. In comparison, UPPAAL can verify the non-parametric Fischer protocol with dozens of processes [10]. Furthermore, existing approaches provide no information if they fail to handle a given model.

In this work, we propose an approach to enhance the scalability of existing model checkers for PTA by adopting machine learning techniques. The idea is to form conjectures on the constraint based on sampling and classification techniques. Our approach takes a PTA as input and works as follows. Firstly, we generate random parameter values and construct the corresponding non-parametric timed automata. Next, we verify the timed automata using existing model checker (i.e., UPPAAL). Based on the checking results, we form conjectures on the constraint through machine learning, which can be subsequently checked using existing model checkers for PTA (i.e., IMITATOR). Moreover, we actively seek out informative parameter values and check the corresponding timed automata so that we converge to an accurate conjecture quickly. We implement our approach as a tool called PTA-LEARN and evaluate it on benchmark systems. We also compare it with state-of-the-art tools such as IMITA-TOR [5]. The results show our approach can synthesize parameter constraints effectively and thus improve parametric verification. Since machine learning algorithms used in our approach are agnostic with the underlying system and learn only based on the verification results of the non-parametric timed automata, our approach is more scalable than the existing approaches.

The remainders of the paper are organized as follows. Section 2 introduces a simple protocol and then illustrates how our approach works step-by-step. Then, Sect. 3 shows how candidate constraints are generated through classification and refined through active learning. Next, Sect. 4 evaluates our approach using a set of benchmark models. Section 5 reviews related work and Sect. 6 concludes in the end.

2   The Overall Approach

In this section, we first define the parametric model checking problem of timed automata and then illustrate how our approach works on an example system. We start with defining our model, i.e., timed automata and parametric timed automata.

2.1   Problem Definition

Let $\mathbb{R}^{\geq 0}$ be the set of non-negative real numbers. Given a set of clocks X, we define $\Phi(C)$ as the set of clock constraints. Each clock constraint is inductively defined by: $\delta := true \mid x \sim n \mid \delta_1 \wedge \delta_2 \mid \neg \delta_1$ where $\sim \in \{=, \leq, \geq, <, >\}$; x is a clock in X and $n \in \mathbb{N}^{\geq 0}$ is a constant. The set of downward constraints obtained with $\sim \in \{\leq, <\}$ is denoted as $\Phi_{\leq,<}(X)$. A clock valuation v for a set of clocks X is a function which assigns a real value to each clock. A clock constraint can be viewed as the set of clock valuations which satisfy the constraint. A clock valuation v satisfies a clock constraint δ, written as $v \in \delta$, iff δ evaluates to be true using the clock values given by v.

Definition 1. *A timed automaton is a tuple $\mathcal{A} = (S, Init, \Sigma, X, L, T)$ where S is a finite set of locations; $Init \subseteq S$ is a set of initial locations; Σ is an alphabet; X is a finite set of clocks; $L : S \to \Phi_{\leq,<}(X)$ labels each state with an invariant; $T \subseteq S \times \Sigma \times \Phi(X) \times 2^{|X|} \times S$ is a labelled transition relation.*

Intuitively, a transition $(s, e, \delta, \chi, s') \in T$ can be fired if δ is satisfied. After event e occurs, clocks in χ are set to zero. The concrete semantics of $\mathcal{A}$ is an infinite-state labelled transition system (LTS), denoted as $\mathcal{C}(\mathcal{A}) = (S_x, Init_x, \mathbb{R}^{\geq 0} \times \Sigma, T_x)$ such that S_x is a set of concrete states of $\mathcal{A}$, each of which is a pair (s, v) where $s \in S$ is a state and v is a clock valuation; $Init_x = \{(s, X = 0) \mid s \in Init\}$ is a set of initial concrete states; and T_x is a set of concrete transitions of the form $((s, v), (d, e), (s', v'))$ such that there exists a transition $(s, e, \delta, \chi, s') \in T$; $v + d \in \delta$; $v + d \in L(s)$; $[\chi \mapsto 0](v + d) = v'$; and $v' \in L(s')$. Intuitively, the system idles for d time units at state s and then take the transition (generating event e) to reach state s'.

Given a property, the model checking problem of timed automata is to model check whether the given timed automaton satisfies the property. We skip the details on how to model check timed automata and refer the readers to [42] for details.

By generalizing the timed automata theory [2], Alur et al. first defined parametric timed automata in [3], where guards and state invariants are allowed to be parametric. Let $P = \{p_1, \cdots, p_M\}$ be a set of parameters. Throughout this paper, we assume parameters are integer-valued. Let $\Phi(X, P)$ be the set of parametric clock constraints which are inductively defined by: $\gamma := \delta \mid x \sim \alpha \mid \gamma_1 \wedge \gamma_2 \mid \neg\gamma_1$ where $\delta \in \Phi(C)$ is a non-parametric constraint; $\sim \in \{=, \leq, \geq, <, >\}$; and α is a parametric linear term in the form of $\Sigma_i a_i * p_i + d$ where both a_i and d are integer constants. The set of downward parametric constraints obtained with $\sim \in \{\leq, <\}$ is denoted as $\Phi_{\leq,<}(X, P)$.

Definition 2. *A PTA $\mathcal{A}(P)$ with parameters P is a 7-tuple $(S, Init, \Sigma, X, \phi, L, T)$ where S, Init, Σ, and X are the same in the timed automata definition; and*

- *$\phi \in \Phi(X, P)$ is a constraint on the parameters P;*
- *L is the invariant assigning to every $q \in S$ a constraint $L(q) \in \Phi_{\leq,<}(X, P)$ on the clocks and the parameters;*
- *and $T \subseteq S \times \Sigma \times \Phi(X, P) \times 2^{|X|} \times S$ is a labelled transition relation.*

Both timed automata and PTA can be composed in parallel. The parallel composition of two timed automata or PTA is defined in the standard way (refer to [2]). Figure 1 shows two example PTA, and the overall system is defined as their parallel composition. In this example, we use discrete integer-valued shared variables (e.g., nb), supported by most model checkers (such as UPPAAL and IMITATOR). When bounded, these variables do not add expressiveness, but act as syntactic sugar for extra locations.

Given a PTA $\mathcal{A}(P)$ and a parameter valuation v, we can construct the corresponding timed automata, written as $\mathcal{A}(v)$, by substituting the parameter values in the parameter constraints with v. Given a PTA $\mathcal{A}(P)$ and a property ρ, the parametric model checking problem is to synthesize a constraint π such that for any parameter valuation v, $\mathcal{A}(v)$ satisfies ρ if and only if v satisfies π. In particular, we say that π is sound with respect to ρ if $\mathcal{A}(v)$ satisfies ρ for all $v \in \pi$; we say that π is complete with respect to ρ if $v \in \pi$ as long as $\mathcal{A}(v)$ satisfies ρ; and we say π is perfect if it is both sound and complete. We remark existing approaches often focus on identifying sound constraints, since identifying perfect constraints are often infeasible.

2.2   Overall Approach with an Illustrative Example

In the following, we illustrate how our approach works through a simple example. We fix a PTA $\mathcal{A}(P) = (S, Init, \Sigma, X, \phi, L, T)$ in the following.

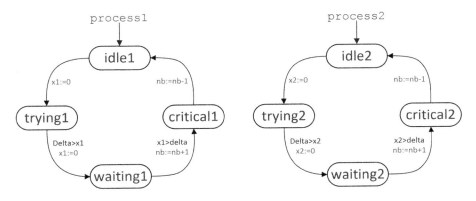

Fig. 1. Fischer protocol with 2 processes

Example 1. The Fischer's protocol is a mutual exclusion protocol proposed by Fischer [7]. Instead of using atomic test-and-set instructions or semaphores, it only assumes atomic reads and writes to a shared variable and achieves mutual exclusion between multiple processes by carefully placing bounds on the execution times of the instructions. For simplicity, we focus on the Fischer protocol with only two processes, which are modeled as the PTA in Fig. 1. Each child PTA models a process with a set of four locations, with one initial location at the top and contains one clock (i.e., $x1$ for process 1 and $x2$ for process 2). The parallel composition of the two processes forms the system model. Variable nb is a shared global variable which intuitively records the number of processes in the critical session. The protocol is designed for mutual exclusion, i.e., $\Box(nb \leq 1)$ which means no more than one process should be in the critical session at any time. There are two parameters: *delta* and *Delta*, which are used as bounds for the clocks. We remark in the original protocol [7], the property has been proved under the occasion that *delta* is set to be 4 and*Delta* is set to be 3. The goal of parametric model checking for this example is to find out a constraint which contains all the property-satisfying properties. For instance, one possible constraint is *delta* > *Delta*. In the following, we show how we can synthesize such a constraint automatically.

The overall work flow of our approach is shown in Fig. 2. Given a PTA $\mathcal{A}(P)$, we start with generating a set of random valuations for P, denoted as S, which satisfy ϕ. Hereafter, we refer to the valuations in S random samples and the process of generating them "random sampling". Random sampling provides us an initial set of samples to learn the very first candidate constraint. In this work, we generate random values for each parameter in P based on its domain, assuming a uniform probabilistic distribution over all values in its domain. With each parameter valuation $v \in S$, we can generate a timed automaton model $\mathcal{A}(v)$. Next, we employ the UPPAAL to check whether $\mathcal{A}(v)$ satisfies the property. Depending on the verification results, we partition S into two sets P_S and N_S,

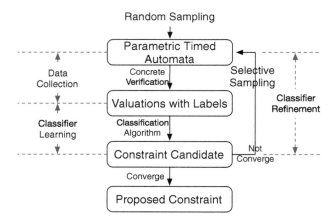

Fig. 2. Approach overview

where P_S contains all those valuations $v \in S$ such that $\mathcal{A}(v)$ satisfies the property and N_S contains all those valuations $v \in S$ such that $\mathcal{A}(v)$ fails the property.

Example 2. Continuing Example 1, assume that we generate four parameter valuations: $(6,7)$, $(8,2)$, $(5,3)$ and $(0,4)$ where each pair (d_1, d_2) denotes a valuation $\{delta \mapsto d_1, Delta \mapsto d_2\}$. Based on UPPAAL's verification results, these valuations are divided into two sets: P_S containing $\{(8,2),(5,3)\}$ and N_S containing $\{(6,7),(0,4)\}$.

Recall that the goal of parametric model checking is to synthesize a constraint which all parameter valuations in P_S should satisfy and all parameter valuations in N_S should not satisfy. We thus employ classification techniques, which have been extensively studied in machine learning community, to generate classifiers which can be treated as constraint candidates. Among the classification algorithms, e.g., [12,28,30]. we focus on two particular classification algorithms: Support Vector Machine (SVM [12]) and Kernel Query By Committee (KQBC [18]), which are introduced in Sect. 3.

Example 3. Continuing Example 2, assume that we apply SVM to generate a classifier to divide sets P_S and N_S. By tuning parameters in SVM, we can obtain a model as the classifier which make zero prediction error on the training set P_S and N_S. Converting the model into an explicit hyperplane, we learn the classifier as $delta - 2 * Delta \geq -4$.

Compared with the desired constraint mentioned in Example 1, this classifier is quite different. Although this desired constraint remains unknown in practice, the problem of classification on limited random samples is real. One way to solve this problem is to generate more random samples. In general, it is likely that a better constraint can be learned if more samples are provided. In our setting, it is expensive since we need to model check $\mathcal{A}(c)$ for each valuation c in order to categorize it. So it would be good if we are able to learn accurate constraints with a small number of samples.

Our remedy is to apply active learning techniques to select the most informative parameter valuations so that we converge fast. Which samples are considered most informative can be defined in different ways, depending the classification algorithms, which are detailed in Sect. 3. With these new samples and their corresponding labels, a new classifier can be learned. We iteratively adopt this learning and refining procedures until the generated constraint stays the same, in other words, converges. Then we can stop and report this constraint as a candidate for the constraint.

Example 4. Continuing with Example 3, given the classifier $delta - 2*$ *Delta* ≥ -4, we pick four more valuations $(3, 3)$, $(1, 2)$, $(4, 4)$, $(6, 5)$ which locate right by the classification boundary geometrically. After verifying the corresponding timed automata using UPPAAL, the valuations $(3, 3),(4, 4),(6, 5)$ are added into set P_S and $(1, 2)$ is added into set N_S. Then a new classifier: $delta - Delta \geq 0$ can be obtained by classification algorithms. With the observation that the constraint converges after multiple iterations of learn-and-refine, we report this classifier as the candidate constraint.

Once having a candidate constraint $\mathcal{C}$, we employ a parametric model checker (i.e., the state-of-the-art IMITATOR [5]) for checking the correctness of ρ. That is, we construct a new PTA $\mathcal{A}'(P) = (S, Init, \Sigma, X, \mathcal{C}, L, T)$ where ϕ is replaced by $\mathcal{C}$ and solve the parametric checking problem of $\mathcal{A}'(P)$. We remark that parametric checking $\mathcal{A}'(P)$ is often easier than $\mathcal{A}(P)$, as we show empirically in Sect. 4. Intuitively, this is because $\mathcal{C}$ is more restrictive than ϕ and thus IMITATOR needs to explore, symbolically, a smaller state space. However, even with the learned constraint $\mathcal{C}$, soundness and completeness may not be checked from time to time still due to the complexity in parametric model checking of timed automata. Compared to directly applying a parametric model checker to $\mathcal{A}(P)$, which provides no information at all if the model checker times out, our approach provides a conjecture $\mathcal{C}$, which could be useful for system design.

Example 5. Continuing Example 4, we apply IMITATOR to check the soundness and completeness of the learned constraint. For this example, IMITATOR confirms that it is both sound and complete. In fact, IMITATOR can generate the same constraint for this example if no constraint provided. However, if we increase the number of processes to 5, IMITATOR is unable to synthesize any sound constraint. On the contrary, with the learned constraint $delta - Delta \geq 0$, IMITATOR can prove the soundness and completeness of such a system, as shown in Sect. 4.

3   Classification

We have discussed the overall approach in Sect. 2. While most of the steps are self-explanatory, details on how candidate constraints are generated and refined

---

Algorithm 1. Algorithm $generate(P_S, N_S)$

---

1 **while** *not time out* **do**
2 | let C be a constraint generated by $classify(P_S, N_S)$;
3 | **if** C *is the same as the one obtained in the last iteration* **then**
4 | | return C;
5 | $V = select(C)$;
6 | **for** $v \in V$ **do**
7 | | add v into P_S if $\mathcal{A}(v)$ satisfies the property;
8 | | add v into N_S if $\mathcal{A}(v)$ fails the property;

---

are centric in our approach and thus will be explained in this section. The overall algorithm for generating candidate constraints is shown in Algorithm 1. Given two sets of labelled samples P_S and N_S, we first learn a candidate constraint using function $classify(P_S, N_S)$ at line 2. If the constraint is the same as the one obtained in the last iteration, we consider that the constraint has converged and return it. Otherwise, we selectively generate a set of new parameter valuations using function $select(C)$ at line 5. The loop from line 6 to 8 then checks whether each parameter valuation is property-satisfying or not and adds it into either P_S or N_S depending on the verification result. The outer loop from line 1 to 8 iterates until a constraint is returned at line 4 or a timeout has occurred. In the following, we present details of function $classify(P_S, N_S)$ and $select(C)$.

3.1 Classification

Function $classify(P_S, N_S)$ generates a candidate constraint based on classification techniques. Assume that π is the perfect constraint for which the PTA satisfies the property. Intuitively, since parameter valuations in P_S must satisfy π (since P_S contains valuations that have been checked to satisfy π) and valuations in N_S must not satisfy π, a constraint C separating the two sets (a.k.a. a classifier) thus can be regarded as a candidate for π. In the extreme case, if we can enumerate all the possible parameter valuations, a classifier which perfectly separates the sets is equivalent to π.

To automatically generate classifiers separating P_S and N_S, we apply existing classification techniques. In the machine learning setting, the assumption is that there is a training set containing samples X and the associated labels Y, and the goal of classification is to learn a function $f : X \to Y$ which accurately predicts the labels of samples arising in the future. There are many existing classification algorithms. For instance, k-nearest neighbors algorithm [14] clusters samples into groups based on their distances to others, while decision tree algorithm [30] splits set of samples step by step according to the maximal information gain of the unused features. Moreover, perceptron [28], Supported Vector Machine (SVM [12]) and Kernel Query By Committee (KQBC [18]) have been proposed to construct classifiers which can separate the samples with different labels apart.

In general, due to the noises in the training set, these classification algorithms prefer a function with small prediction error (rather than zero) on the training set to avoid the overfitting problem. However, in our setting, any prediction error is intolerable and thus the classification algorithms must be tuned to generate perfect classifiers. Formally, a perfect classifier π for P_S and N_S is a predicate such that $s \in \pi$ for all $s \in P_S$ and $s \notin \pi$ for all $s \in N_S$. Furthermore, in order to help system designer utilize the learned constraint, it is preferred to be human-interpretable. Considering all these mentioned above, we briefly introduce one of the classification algorithms, SVM, which we adopt in our work.

SVM is a commonly applied supervised machine learning algorithm for classification and regression analysis [12]. In the binary classification case, the functionality of SVM works as follows. Given P_S and N_S, SVM can generate a perfect classifier to separate them if there is any. We refer the readers to [29] for details on how the classifier is computed. In this work, we always choose the *optimal margin classifier* if possible. Intuitively, the optimal margin classifier could be seen as the strongest witness why P_S and N_S are different. SVM by default learns classifiers in the form of a linear inequality, i.e., a half space in the form of $c_1 x_1 + c_2 x_2 + \cdots \geq k$ where x_i are variables while c_i and k are constant coefficients.

As linear inequalities may not be sufficiently expressive for some parametric models, we discuss how SVM can be extended to learn more expressive constraints. A polynomial classifier can be obtained by systematically mapping the samples to a high dimensional space and then applying SVM in the high dimensional space. For instance, assume that the maximum degree of the polynomial is set to be 2, the sample valuation $\{x \mapsto 2, y \mapsto 1\}$ in P_S is mapped to $\{x \mapsto 2, y \mapsto 1, x^2 \mapsto 4, xy \mapsto 2, y^2 \mapsto 1\}$. Let P'_S and N'_S be the set of samples in the high dimensional space. SVM is then applied to learn a perfect linear classifier for P'_S and N'_S. Mathematically, a linear classifier in the high dimensional space is the same as a polynomial classifier in the original space [21].

To generate conjunctive classifiers, we adopt the algorithm proposed in [36]. The idea is to pick one sample s from N_S each time and identify a classifier $\mathcal{C}_i$ to separate P_S and $\{s\}$, remove all samples from N_S which can be correctly classified by $\mathcal{C}_i$, and then repeat the process until N_S becomes empty. The conjunction of all the classifiers $\mathcal{C}_i$ is then a perfect classifier separating P_S and N_S. We refer the readers to [36] for details of the algorithm. We remark that if we switch P_S and N_S, the negation of the learned classifier using this algorithm is a classifier which is in the form of a disjunction.

3.2 Candidate Refinement

Stone's celebrated theorem proves that even naive algorithms can get the optimal solution if given a large enough training sequence [18]. However, we always have obstacles in collecting such a large data set. In particular, labeling more samples is expensive in our setting because we are required to model check the system for each parameter valuation. One fundamental problem in applying classification techniques to learn the constraint is that with the limited samples in P_S and N_S, it is unlikely that we can obtain an "accurate" classifier. In the machine learning community, researchers have studied extensively on the problem "how can we learn an accurate classifier from a small number of labelled samples?". One of the remedies is active learning [33].

Active learning is proposed in contrast to passive learning. A passive learner learns from a given set of samples that it has no control over, whereas an active learner is able to adaptively select its samples. Intuitively, by selecting the right samples, active learning is able to learn much faster. In general, an active learner could choose the most informative samples to label based on the intermediate learning results. Specifically, a number of different active learning strategies on how to select the samples have been proposed. For instance, version space partitioning [31] tries to select samples on which there is maximal disagreement between classifiers in the current version space (e.g., the space of all classifiers which are consistent with the given samples); uncertainty sampling [26] maintains an explicit model of uncertainty and selects the sample that it is least confident about. The effectiveness of these strategies can be measured in terms of the labeling cost, i.e., the number of labelled samples needed in order to learn a classifier which has a classification error bounded by some threshold ϵ. An active learner can sometimes achieve good performance using far fewer samples than would otherwise be required by a passive learner [40,41]. Thus, in this work, we adopt two active learning strategies designed for different classification algorithms so that we can generate the constraint by invoking a model checker only a small number of times.

Selective Sampling for SVM We adopt the active learning strategy proposed in [32], called selective sampling, to improve the constraints generated by SVM. This strategy has been shown to be effective in different applications [40,41]. The idea is to generate multiple samples on the current classification boundary $\mathcal{C}$.

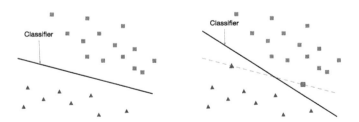

Fig. 3. Selective sampling for SVM

The exact details of function $select(\mathcal{C})$ in Algorithm 1 depends on the type of classifiers. For classifiers in the form of linear inequalities or polynomial inequalities, identifying samples on the classification boundary is straightforward, i.e., we turn the inequality into an equation and solve the equation. For the classifier $delta - 2 * Delta \geq -4$ in the above example, we solve the equation

---

Algorithm 2. Algorithm $kqbc\_classify(\mathcal{C}, P_S, N_S)$

---

1 $i \leftarrow 0$;
2 **while** $i <$ ITERATION **do**
3   let $\mathcal{C}_a, \mathcal{C}_b$ be two random hypotheses selected over $\mathcal{C}$;
4   get a parameter valuation v by solving $\mathcal{C}_a(v) * \mathcal{C}_b(v) < 0$;
5   model check $\mathcal{C}(v)$;
6   add v into P_S or N_S based on whether $\mathcal{C}(v)$ satisfies the property;
7   update $\mathcal{C}$;
8 $i \leftarrow i + 1$;

$delta - 2 * Delta = -4$ in the integer domain and obtain new valuations like $(4, 4)$, $(6, 5)$. Note that if there is no integer solution, we solve the equation in the real-number domain and select the nearest integer samples with unknown labels. In the case that the constraint is conjunctive or disjunctive, we apply the above selective sampling approach to each clause in the constraint to obtain new samples. For instance, if $\mathcal{C}$ is in the form of $\mathcal{C}_1 \wedge \mathcal{C}_2$ where $\mathcal{C}_i$ is a linear or polynomial inequality, we turn each $\mathcal{C}_i$ into an equation and solve it to obtain new samples.

Figure 3 visualizes how selective sampling works in a 2-D plane. In the left figure, the squares represent the samples in P_S, while the triangles represent the samples in N_S. Based on these samples, a classifier is learned to separate these samples, as shown in the left figure. Selective sampling allows us to identify those samples (i.e., those triangles and squares on the line) on the classification boundary based on the learned classifier. The classifier is then improved using the new samples generated by selective sampling, as shown in the right figure.

KQBC Although SVM is a widely used classification technique and its selective sampling strategy works often in practice [40, 41], it has been shown that SVM-based active learning in the worse case has the same labeling cost as random sampling, i.e., $\Omega(\frac{1}{\epsilon})$ where ϵ is the target classification error rate. A number of active learning algorithms with better worse case labeling cost have been proposed. One example is the Kernel Query By Committee (KQBC) algorithm [18]. It has been shown that KQBC has the optimal labeling cost: $O(d \lg \frac{1}{\epsilon})$ where d is the dimension of the samples [15, 19]. That is, if passive learning requires a million samples, KQBC may require just $\lg 1000000$ (≈ 20) to achieve the same accuracy. Thus, in this work, we additionally adopt KQBC and develop a particular sampling strategy for KQBC to solve our problem.

Compared to SVM, instead of learning one hyperplane for separating P_S and N_S, KQBC maintains a "committee", i.e., a cluster of models $\mathcal{C} = \langle \mathcal{C}^1, \mathcal{C}^2, \mathcal{C}^3, \cdots, \mathcal{C}^m \rangle$, based on the currently labelled samples. These models compose a version space, where each member is allowed to vote on the labels of a new sample (i.e., whether a parameter valuation would make the PTA satisfy the property). KQBC shrinks the version space whenever a newly labelled sample is provided. The essence of KQBC is to constrain the size of version space as much as possible with as few labelled samples and the classification task is to search for the best model within the version space.

In the original algorithm [18], KQBC takes a stream of unclassified samples and decides whether to ask for the label of a newly arrived sample. In our setting, we modify the algorithm in order to actively seek out samples which are effective in reducing the version space, and as a result we can potentially converge to the actual classifier. Algorithm 2 shows how KQBC is adopted in our setting, where the input parameter $\mathcal{C}$ represents the version space, P_S and N_S are the positive and negative samples. At line 3, we randomly pick two hypotheses (i.e., hyperplanes) $\mathcal{C}_a$ and $\mathcal{C}_b$ in the current version space $\mathcal{C}$. At line 4, we employ a constraint solver to solve the constraint $\mathcal{C}_a(v) * \mathcal{C}_b(v) < 0$ where $\mathcal{C}_a(v)$ is the label prediction of sample v, which is either 1 or -1. That is, by solving the constraint, we identify a controversial sample, i.e., one which is disagreed upon by two members of the committee. At line 5, we model check the timed automaton $\mathcal{C}(v)$ and we add v into P_S or N_S accordingly at line 6. At line 7, we update the version space. We skip the details on how the version space is updated and maintained and refer the readers to [18] for the technical details. The loop from line 2 from line 8 iterates until a pre-defined number of iterations has been reached.

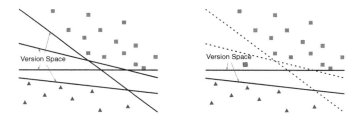

Fig. 4. Sampling in KQBC

Figure 4 illustrates how classfiers are obtained by KQBC in a binary classification task. In the left figure, the squares represent samples in P_S while the triangles represent samples in N_S. All the lines compose the committee for the current samples. Note that any member of the committee classifies the current samples perfectly. In order to reduce the committee, we select two lines by hit-and-run algorithm [27] and identify a sample which they disagree upon, represented as the bigger square in between the lines. After obtaining the label of this sample, two members of the committee represented by the dotted lines are ruled out. As a result, the version space is reduced.

4   Evaluation

We have implemented our approach for model checking of PTA in a tool named PTA-LEARN (available at [1]). PTA-LEARN is written using a combination of C++

and shell codes. It makes use of GSL to solve equation systems; and uses LibSVM for SVM-based classification. It relies on UPPAAL [11] for model checking timed automata and IMITATOR for model checking PTA with learned constraints. Note that both UPPAAL and IMITATOR are regarded as the state-of-the-art in their respective fields. In the following, we evaluate PTA-LEARN, to address the following three research questions.

- RQ1: Can PTA-LEARN improve scalability of IMITATOR?
- RQ2: Are the constraints generated by PTA-LEARN sound, or complete compared to those generated by IMITATOR?
- RQ3: Is our candidate refinement strategy helpful?

To answer the aforementioned research questions, we identify 24 parametric timed automata models from the IMITATOR benchmarks library, which in terms are collected from multiple sources. Since the models in [5] are written in a language different from the language supported by UPPAAL, we develop a translator to convert those models. The correctness of the translator is checked manually as well as through comparing verification results of UPPAAL and IMITATOR. All evaluated models are available at [1].

The parameters in our experiments are configured as follows. During the random sampling stage, given a parametric model $\mathcal{A}(P)$ and a property ρ, we try to generate random parameter valuations until there are at least one valuation v such that $\mathcal{A}(v)$ satisfies ρ and one valuation v' such that $\mathcal{A}(v')$ fails ρ. If all random valuations satisfy ρ after a threshold $64 * |P|$ of random values (where $|P|$ is the number of parameters), we stop the process and conjecture that the constraint is *true* (i.e., any parameter valuation is valid). Similarly, if all random valuations fail ρ, we conjecture that the constraint is *false* (i.e., no parameter valuation is valid).

During the learning stage, both SVM and KQBC are applied and we take the first converged constraint as the learning result. In the case of SVM, the parameter C (which controls the trade-off between avoiding misclassifying training samples and enlarging the decision boundary) in LibSVM and the inner iteration are set to their maximum values so that it generates only the perfect classifier, if there is. Selective sampling is applied repeatedly until the learned constraint remained unchanged after 2 consecutive iterations. We remark it is an open question on how to know that a classifier has converged. In the case of KQBC, we conduct a set of preliminary experiments with randomly generated predicate to test how many samples are necessary to learn the predicate. The details of the preliminary results are available at [1]. During the verification stage, if IMITATOR is applied, the timeout is set to be 300 seconds. If PTA-LEARN learns a constraint *true* or does not learn (i.e., timeout), we apply IMITATOR on the original model. Each experiment is repeated for 5 times and we report the median as the experiment results. All of the experiments are conducted using x64 Ubuntu 16.04.2 (kernel 4.8.0-49-generic) with 3.60 GHz Intel Core i7 and 32G DDR3.

The experiment results are shown in Table 1. To answer RQ1, we apply PTA-LEARN to each model and compare the performance with IMITATOR. The result verification time of IMITATOR is shown in the second column of Table 1.

The following two columns show the time spent on learning and verifying the constraint by PTA-LEARN. PTA-LEARN's *total time is the sum of numbers in these two columns.*

It can be observed that IMITATOR times out in 9 cases. In comparison, PTA-LEARN succeeds in learning constraints for 21 out of 24 benchmarks and fails to learn any constraint for the 3 remaining case studies. A close look reveals that in the 3 cases, 2 models involve many parameters (i.e., > 6) and thus our learning algorithms time out before converge. Note that IMITATOR times out on these two cases as well. We fail to learn on the other case because the actual constraint is a complicated constraint consisting of a mixture of conjunctions and disjunctions. Recall that if we do not learn any constraint, the original model is submitted to IMITATOR for parametric model checking. It can be observed that (as shown in the column "verify" under PTA-LEARN) that with the learned constraint, PTA-LEARN is able to verify 23 models and only times out on one model named LALSD14-FMS2p. In terms of efficiency, we highlight the approach between PTA-LEARN and IMITATOR which takes less time in parametric verification for each model. PTA-LEARN takes seconds on learning and verifies the models more efficiently with the learned constraint, than applying IMITATOR directly. Thus, we conclude that PTA-LEARN can be used to improve IMITATOR.

To answer RQ2, we measure the soundness and completeness of the learned constraint. Soundness of a learned constraint is checked by IMITATOR, i.e., we apply IMITATOR to check whether the PTA updated with the learned constraint always satisfies the property. We recall that a sound constraint is useful as it provides a guideline for choosing safe parameter values. Column *sound* under PTA-LEARN shows whether the learned constraint can satisfy the properties. The results show that, among the 21 constraints learned by PTA-LEARN, 19 are proved sound; 1 is not sound; and 1 is unknown as PTA-LEARN times out trying to prove its soundness.

A sound constraint may be too restrictive. In the extreme case, the constraint *false* is trivially sound and obviously not useful. Out of the 24 cases, in three cases, we learn the trivial constraint *false*, marked as "*" in Table 1. To checking the completeness of the learned constraint, we compare the learned constraint with the constrained obtained by applying IMITATOR directly. We consider the learned constraint is complete if and only if it is weaker than or equivalent to that obtained by IMITATOR. The results are shown in column *complete*. It is observed that out of the 12 constraints for which we can evaluate the completeness, 10 of them are complete. For the remaining two cases, IMITATOR finds constraints which are weaker than those found by PTA-LEARN. This is possible as PTA-LEARN is based on black-box learning, whereas as a white-box technique, IMITATOR explores the system paths systematically if it is able to finish.

To answer RQ3, we compare the performance of PTA-LEARN with and without active learning. In our evaluation, when active learning is not applied, we simply learn from randomly generated parameter valuations. That is, we keep generating random valuations until the constraints get converged. The columns

Table 1. Evaluation results, where "-" means "not applicable"

Model	IMITATOR	PTA-LEARN				PTA-LEARN-Active		
		learn	verify	sound	complete	learn	verify	sound
coffee	0.007	1.482	0.017	T	T	1.851	0.017	T
coffeeDrinker	0.019	timeout	0.019	-	-	timeout	0.019	-
counterexACSD15	timeout	1.49	0.018	T	T	1.128	timeout	-
ex1pPTA	timeout	3.134	0.030	T	-	20.34	0.018	T
exUPTA-allp	timeout	1.148	0.018	T	-	0.375	timeout	-
F3	0.184	0.171	0.014	T	T	0.175	0.014	T
F4	28.777	0.763	4.151	T	T	1.052	4.095	T
F5	timeout	0.851	227	T	-	1.073	243	T
FischerAHV93	0.040	7.835	0.039	T	T	12.56	0.405	F
fischerHRSV02-2	timeout	14.686	0*	T	-	10.88	timeout	-
fischerHRSV02-3	timeout	7.670	0*	T	-	7.22	timeout	-
fisherPAT.nocomment	0.05	2.886	0.036	T	T	2.917	0.0367	T
IMPO	0.013	timeout	0.013	-	-	timeout	0.013	-
JLR13-3tasks-npfp	36.84	1.91	0*	T	F	0.8	timeout	-
JLR-TACAS13	timeout	0.694	0.016	T	-	0.688	0.015	T
LALSD14-FMS2p	timeout	6.142	timeout	-	-	8.65	timeout	-
NuclearPlant	0.023	4.47	0.017	T	T	3.196	0.022	F
Pipeline-KP12-2-5	13.323	timeout	13.323	-	-	timeout	13.323	-
Sched2.100.0	1.11	3.84	0.318	T	F	1.654	1.347	F
Sched2.50.0	0.933	2.782	0.302	T	T	1.278	1.177	F
testBadWithoutDiscrete	0.019	1.212	0.018	T	T	0.347	0.018	T
testIM-IMK-IMunion	0.008	0.305	0.016	T	T	0.4	0.016	T
TestPattern1	0.018	2.95	0.031	F	-	2.28	0.035	F
WFAS-BBLS15-det	timeout	1.925	0.027	T	-	1.216	0.221	F

under **pta-Learn**-active show the results obtained by applying PTA-LEARN without active learning. Note that the number of sound constraints reduces from 19 to 9 when active learning is disabled. One reason is that without active learning, often different runs of the same experiment result in different constraints, which makes it hard for the constraints to converge. Comparing PTA-LEARN with and without active learning, we can see that the overhead of active learning is negligible. We thus conclude that active learning is helpful.

5   Related Work

Besides our method, several white-box tools have been developed to verify parametric systems by exploring system states with different strategies. For instance, LPMC [37] employs a partition refinement technique to generate an unstructured set of constraints; HyTech [20] verifies linear hybrid automata by exploring the state space through either forward reachability or partition refinement; [22] adopts a symbolic representation of the state space to synthesize linear parameter constraints. IMITATOR [5] implements the inverse method (or trace preservation synthesis), the behavioral cartography [4], bad state reachability synthesis (used in this work), parametric deadlock-freeness checking and non-Zeno parametric model checking. The behavioral cartography is close to our sampling that iterates on integer-valuations to generalize their discrete behavior; however, a main difference (and advantage) of our work is that we use non-parametric model checking on the sampled points, which is more efficient by an order magnitude, and we only use parametric model checking to assess the validity of the constraint. [6] uses an orthogonal approach based on learning for a subclass of PTA: in order to perform compositional parameter synthesis, they attempt to compute an abstraction of a non-parametric part of the system using an extension of Angluin's learning algorithm L^*.

To the best of our knowledge, we are the first to introduce learning techniques in verifying parametric systems. (Although the notion of learning we use in [6] is in fact different.) But this is not a genius creation, as learning has been already applied in many other areas successfully. For instance, there are many learning-based approaches in program verification field.

In particular, several papers [17,34–36] have deployed learning techniques to help software verification, and compiler optimization. In these works, program states are regarded as labelled samples and a variety of classification algorithms are applied to learn the relationship between a correct program with the program states. We remark that although we focus on PTA throughout this paper, our technique can be adapted to other models like parametric probabilistic models [9].

6   Conclusion

In this work, we propose an approach to automatically synthesize parameter constraints through learning. In particular, we apply active learning techniques so as to learn accurate candidate constraints prior to the checking phase. Furthermore, we adopt SVM and KQBC as the classification algorithms to learn constraints in different forms. In principle, our approach can be extended to learn arbitrary mathematical classifiers with kernel methods. Nonetheless, we focus on constraints in form of polynomial inequalities or conjunctions/disjunctions of polynomial inequalities in our evaluation. The results show that our approach effectively learns parameter constraints to guarantee the correctness of a set of benchmarks and hence helps the system verification and design.

Acknowledgement. This work is supported by NRF project "RG101NR0114A" and partially supported by the ANR national research program "PACS"(ANR-14-CE28-0002).

References

1. PTA-Learn repo (2017). https://github.com/lijiaying/pta-Learn
2. Alur, R., Dill, D.L.: A theory of timed automata. Theoret. Comput. Sci. **126**(2), 183–235 (1994)
3. Alur, R., Henzinger, T.A., Vardi, M.Y.: Parametric real-time reasoning. In: Proceedings of the 25th annual ACM symposium on Theory of Computing, pp. 592–601. ACM (1993)
4. André, É., Fribourg, L.: Behavioral Cartography of Timed Automata. In: Kučera, A., Potapov, I. (eds.) RP 2010. LNCS, vol. 6227, pp. 76–90. Springer, Heidelberg (2010). doi:10.1007/978-3-642-15349-5_5
5. André, É., Fribourg, L., Kühne, U., Soulat, R.: IMITATOR 2.5: a tool for analyzing robustness in scheduling problems. In: Giannakopoulou, D., Méry, D. (eds.) FM 2012. LNCS, vol. 7436, pp. 33–36. Springer, Heidelberg (2012). doi:10.1007/978-3-642-32759-9_6
6. André, É., Lin, S.-W.: Learning-based compositional parameter synthesis for event-recording automata. In: Bouajjani, A., Silva, A. (eds.) FORTE 2017. LNCS, vol. 10321, pp. 17–32. Springer, Cham (2017). doi:10.1007/978-3-319-60225-7_2
7. Angluin, D., Aspnes, J., Fischer, M.J., Jiang, H.: Self-stabilizing population protocols. In: International Conference On Principles Of Distributed Systems, pp. 103–117 (2005)
8. Aştefănoaei, L., Bensalem, S., Bozga, M., Cheng, C.-H., Ruess, H.: Compositional parameter synthesis. In: Fitzgerald, J., Heitmeyer, C., Gnesi, S., Philippou, A. (eds.) FM 2016. LNCS, vol. 9995, pp. 60–68. Springer, Cham (2016). doi:10.1007/978-3-319-48989-6_4
9. Baudrit, C., Dubois, D., Perrot, N.: Representing parametric probabilistic models tainted with imprecision. Fuzzy Sets Syst. **159**(15), 1913–1928 (2008)
10. Behrmann, G., David, A., Larsen, K.G., Pettersson, P., Yi, W.: Developing UPPAAL over 15 years. Softw. Pract. Exper. **41**(2), 133–142 (2011)
11. Bengtsson, J., Larsen, K., Larsson, F., Pettersson, P., Yi, W.: Uppaala tool suite for automatic verification of real-time systems. Hybrid Syst. **3**, 232–243 (1996)
12. Boser, B.E., Guyon, I.M., Vapnik, V.N.: A training algorithm for optimal margin classifiers. In: Workshop on Computational Learning Theory, pp. 144–152. ACM (1992)
13. Cimatti, A., Griggio, A., Mover, S., Tonetta, S.: Parameter synthesis with ic3. In: Formal Methods in Computer-Aided Design (FMCAD), pp. 165–168. IEEE (2013)
14. Cover, T., Hart, P.: Nearest neighbor pattern classification. IEEE Trans. Inf. Theory **13**(1), 21–27 (1967)
15. Dasgupta, S.: Coarse sample complexity bounds for active learning. In: NIPS, pp. 235–242 (2005)
16. Frehse, G., Jha, S.K., Krogh, B.H.: A counterexample-guided approach to parameter synthesis for linear hybrid automata. In: Egerstedt, M., Mishra, B. (eds.) HSCC 2008. LNCS, vol. 4981, pp. 187–200. Springer, Heidelberg (2008). doi:10.1007/978-3-540-78929-1_14
17. Garg, P., Löding, C., Madhusudan, P., Neider, D.: ICE: a robust framework for learning invariants. In: Biere, A., Bloem, R. (eds.) CAV 2014. LNCS, vol. 8559, pp. 69–87. Springer, Cham (2014). doi:10.1007/978-3-319-08867-9_5
18. Gilad-Bachrach, R., Navot, A., Tishby, N.: Kernel query by committee (KQBC). Technical report, Technical Report 2003–88, Leibniz Center, The Hebrew University (2003)

19. Gilad-Bachrach, R., Navot, A., Tishby, N.: Query by committee made real. In: NIPS, pp. 443–450 (2005)

20. Henzinger, T.A., Ho, P.-H., Wong-Toi, H.: HyTech: A model checker for hybrid systems. In: Grumberg, O. (ed.) CAV 1997. LNCS, vol. 1254, pp. 460–463. Springer, Heidelberg (1997). doi:10.1007/3-540-63166-6_48

21. Huang, T.-M., Kecman, V., Kopriva, I.: Kernel Based Algorithms for Mining Huge Data Sets, vol. 1. Springer, Heidelberg (2006)

22. Hune, T., Romijn, J., Stoelinga, M., Vaandrager, F.W.: Linear parametric model checking of timed automata. J. Logic Algebraic Program. **52–53**, 183–220 (2002)

23. Jahanian, F.: Verifying properties of systems with variable timing constraints. In: Proceedings Real Time Systems Symposium, pp. 319–328. IEEE (1989)

24. Jovanović, A., Lime, D., Roux, O.H.: Integer parameter synthesis for timed automata. IEEE Trans. Software Eng. **41**(5), 445–461 (2015)

25. Knapik, M., Penczek, W.: Bounded model checking for parametric timed automata. Trans. Petri Nets Other Models Concurrency **5**, 141–159 (2012)

26. Lewis, D.D., Gale, W.A.: A sequential algorithm for training text classifiers. In: Croft, B.W., van Rijsbergen, C.J. (eds.) SIGIR 1994. Springer, London (1994)

27. Lovász, L., Vempala, S.: Hit-and-run is fast and fun. Microsoft Research (2003, preprint)

28. Minsky, M., Papert, S.: Perceptrons: An Introduction to Computational Geometry, 2nd edn. The MIT Press, Cambridge (1972)

29. Platt, J., et al.: Sequential minimal optimization: a fast algorithm for training support vector machines (1998)

30. Quinlan, J.R.: Induction of decision trees. Mach. Learn. **1**(1), 81–106 (1986)

31. Ruff, R.A., Dietterich, T.G.: What good are experiments? In: Proceedings of the Sixth International Workshop on Machine Learning (ML 1989), pp. 109–112 (1989)

32. Schohn, G., Cohn, D.: Less is more: active learning with support vector machines. In: ICML, pp. 839–846 (2000)

33. Settles, B.: Active learning. In: Synthesis Lectures on Artificial Intelligence and Machine Learning. Morgan & Claypool Publishers (2012)

34. Sharma, R., Aiken, A.: From invariant checking to invariant inference using randomized search. In: Biere, A., Bloem, R. (eds.) CAV 2014. LNCS, vol. 8559, pp. 88–105. Springer, Cham (2014). doi:10.1007/978-3-319-08867-9_6

35. Sharma, R., Gupta, S., Hariharan, B., Aiken, A., Nori, A.V.: Verification as learning geometric concepts. In: Static Analysis Symposium, pp. 388–411 (2013)

36. Sharma, R., Nori, A.V., Aiken, A.: Interpolants as classifiers. In: Madhusudan, P., Seshia, S.A. (eds.) CAV 2012. LNCS, vol. 7358, pp. 71–87. Springer, Heidelberg (2012). doi:10.1007/978-3-642-31424-7_11

37. Spelberg, R.L., Toetenel, H., Ammerlaan, M.: Partition refinement in real-time model checking. In: Ravn, A.P., Rischel, H. (eds.) FTRTFT 1998. LNCS, vol. 1486, pp. 143–157. Springer, Heidelberg (1998). doi:10.1007/BFb0055344

38. Stoelinga, M.: Fun with firewire: A comparative study of formal verification methods applied to the ieee 1394 root contention protocol. Formal Aspects Comp. **14**(3), 328–337 (2003)

39. Sun, J., Liu, Y., Dong, J.S., Pang, J.: PAT: towards flexible verification under fairness. In: Bouajjani, A., Maler, O. (eds.) CAV 2009. LNCS, vol. 5643, pp. 709–714. Springer, Heidelberg (2009). doi:10.1007/978-3-642-02658-4_59

40. Tong, S., Chang, E.Y.: Support vector machine active learning for image retrieval. In: Proceedings of the 9th ACM International Conference on Multimedia, pp. 107–118 (2001)

41. Tong, S., Koller, D.: Support vector machine active learning with applications to text classification. J. Mach. Learn. Res. **2**, 45–66 (2001)

42. Yovine, S.: Model checking timed automata. In: Rozenberg, G., Vaandrager, F.W. (eds.) EEF School 1996. LNCS, vol. 1494, pp. 114–152. Springer, Heidelberg (1998). doi:10.1007/3-540-65193-4_20

A Verification Framework for Stateful Security Protocols

Li Li[1], Naipeng Dong[2(✉)], Jun Pang[3], Jun Sun[1], Guangdong Bai[2], Yang Liu[4], and Jin Song Dong[2,5]

[1] Singapore University of Technology and Design, Singapore, Singapore
[2] National University of Singapore, Singapore, Singapore
dcsdn@nus.edu.sg
[3] University of Luxembourg, Luxembourg, Luxembourg
[4] Nanyang Technological University, Singapore, Singapore
[5] Griffith University, Brisbane, Australia

Abstract. A long-standing research problem is how to efficiently verify security protocols with tamper-resistant global states, especially when the global states evolve unboundedly. We propose a protocol specification framework, which facilitates explicit modeling of states and state transformations. On the basis of that, we develop an algorithm for verifying security properties of protocols with unbounded state-evolving, by tracking state transformation and checking the validity of the state-evolving traces. We prove the correctness of the verification algorithm, implement both of the specification framework and the algorithm, and evaluate our implementation using a number of stateful security protocols. The experimental results show that our approach is both feasible and practically efficient. Particularly, we have found a security flaw on the digital envelope protocol, which cannot be detected with existing security protocol verifiers.

1 Introduction

Automatic formal verification is shown to be extremely useful in analyzing security protocols. Many security protocol verifiers have been developed, for instance, ProVerif [1], AVISPA [2] and Maude-NPA [3]. However, such verifiers fail in analyzing security protocols with shared objects such as databases, registers and memory locations [4]. Real-world examples include protocols involving security devices like IBM's 4758 CCA secure coprocessor platform and trusted platform module (TPM) [5] and protocols involving databases for websites and key servers [6].

As these shared objects must be maintained externally w.r.t. sessions, the objects are abstracted as global states; and protocols with these shared objects are refereed to as stateful protocols. The global states have three properties: (1) *mutable*: the value of a state can be updated, (2) *unbounded evolving*: the value updating of a state can be unbounded, and (3) *tamper-resistant*: the value of a state can only be updated by legitimate users. For instance, the following example is a simple stateful protocol, where the security device is a shared object, i.e., a global state.

Z. Duan and L. Ong (Eds.): ICFEM 2017, LNCS 10610, pp. 262–280, 2017.
https://doi.org/10.1007/978-3-319-68690-5_16

Example 1. Consider a security device SD (a variation of [6]), with a tamper-resistant memory initialized to a constant '*init*'. SD supports three public operations: (1) reading: the current value stored in the memory can be read; (2) updating: the memory with current value m, can be updated to $\mathsf{h}(m, x)$, where h is a hash function and x is an arbitrary value; (3) decrypting: when receiving a ciphertext of the form $\mathsf{enc_a}(\langle m_f, s_l, s_r \rangle, pub)$, i.e., a sequence of three values $\langle m_f, s_l, s_r \rangle$ asymmetrically encrypted by SD's public key pub, SD decrypts it. According to SD's current memory value m, it continues as follows: if $m = \mathsf{h}(m_f, left)$, SD sends out s_l; if $m = \mathsf{h}(m_f, right)$, SD sends out s_r, where *left* and *right* are two publicly known constants. Suppose *Bob*, a legitimate user, generates two secrets s_l and s_r, reads the memory of SD as m_f and sends a ciphertext $\mathsf{enc_a}(\langle m_f, s_l, s_r \rangle, pub)$ to SD. The SD ensures that a malicious *Bob* or any other attackers can never know both 's_l' and 's_r' at the same time, since SD cannot be configured as both '$\mathsf{h}(m_f, left)$' and '$\mathsf{h}(m_f, right)$' in one execution.

Verification of stateful protocols has been noticed as important and necessary but challenging [5] even for a simple protocol as Example 1. In particular, ProVerif – one of the popular and widely used verifier (e.g., used in [7–10]), reports false attacks for some stateful protocols such as Example 1. Recently, an extension StatVerif is proposed, which is specialized in verifying stateful protocols [6]. However, StatVerif can produce false attacks when the state-value mutates (e.g., when the security device in Example 1 reboots) and cannot terminate when the state-value mutates unboundedly (e.g., when the protocol in Example 1 keeps running).

We improve the Horn clause based verification (used in ProVerif and StatVerif) for analyzing stateful protocols with unbounded global state evolving (i.e., unbounded evolving steps with potentially unbounded values of a state). Horn clause reasoning is inherently monotonic – once an event (the basic element in Horn clause) is true, it cannot be set to false anymore, and thus does not work well for state-value mutation in ProVerif and StatVerif [4]. Therefore, we propose to distinguish global states from events. In particular, we explicitly model global states and their evolving transformations in specification. More importantly, on each step of reasoning in verification, we record the state-evolving constraints; and when a target event is derived, we instantiate a state-evolving trace satisfying the constraints in the derivation, i.e., the global states can evolve following the trace such that the derivation could happen. In such a way, we reduce the false attacks caused by global states' unbounded evolving.

For example, we model the security device as a global state $SD(\_)$, which consists of two parts: the name of the object (SD) used to distinguish different objects and its pre-defined fields ('$\_$') used to distinguish attributes of the same object (the field '$\_$' indicates the memory of the security device). Each field is filled with a concrete value of the attribute at any time, e.g., the memory field can be filled with '*init*', $\mathsf{h}(m_f, left)$, or $\mathsf{h}(m_f, right)$. Hence, $SD(init)$, $SD(\mathsf{h}(m_f, left))$, and $SD(\mathsf{h}(m_f, right))$ are the possible *instantiations* of the global state $SD(\_)$. A particular instantiation of a global state may be visited multiple times in one trace of the global state's evolving. To distinguish each appearance of an instantiation, we additionally add a distinct index a_i to the instantiation, and require all indexes in a trace to have chronological orders. We name an instantiation of a global state and its index a *snapshot*. The snapshots of a global state must form an evolving trace starting from an initial instantiation, based on the index's chronological order. We allow variables to appear in the snapshot to represent a set of snapshots, and name the snapshot with variables a snapshot *pattern*.

In verification, we explicitly validate the evolving traces of the snapshots. Suppose the adversary obtains message m_1 and m_2 at the following snapshot pattern respectively

$$\big(SD(\mathsf{h}(\mathsf{h}(x_1, x_2), \mathit{left})), a_1\big), \big(SD(\mathsf{h}(\mathsf{h}(\mathsf{h}(\mathit{init}, \mathit{right}), x_1')), \mathit{left})), a_2\big),$$

where variables x_1, x_2 and x_1' can be arbitrary values, a_1 and a_2 are indexes of the two snapshots (any ordering is possible). In order to conduct the attack that the adversary obtains both m_1 and m_2, the adversary tries to find an instantiation of the variables x_1, x_2 and x_1' such that a valid trace exists for the security device to evolve from its initial snapshot $(SD(\mathit{init}), a_0)$ to the above snapshots. We can see that the following evolving trace exists, when $x_1 = \mathsf{h}(\mathit{init}, \mathit{right})$, and $x_2 = x_1'$ can be an arbitrary value,

$$SD(\mathit{init}) \rightarrow SD(\mathsf{h}(\mathit{init}, \mathit{right})) \rightarrow SD(\mathsf{h}(\mathsf{h}(\mathit{init}, \mathit{right}), x_2))$$
$$\rightarrow SD(\mathsf{h}(\mathsf{h}(\mathsf{h}(\mathit{init}, \mathit{right}), x_2), \mathit{left})).$$

That is, the adversary tries to guide the protocol to perform the above global state transformation, and then obtains both m_1 and m_2 at the last snapshot. However, if an additional snapshot $\big(SD(\mathsf{h}(\mathit{init}, \mathit{left})), a_3\big)$ exists e.g., for the adversary to obtain m_3, then no valid evolving trace exists for the adversary to obtain m_1, m_2 and m_3, since the device memory cannot be set to $SD(\mathsf{h}(\mathit{init}, \mathit{left}))$ and $SD(\mathsf{h}(\mathit{init}, \mathit{right}))$ (contained in the snapshot with index a_2) no matter in which order in a single trace. Hence, the attack is infeasible for obtaining all three pieces of information.

We introduce the formal modeling of global states and their transformations in the subsequent section, then propose our verification algorithm in Sect. 3, and finally present our experimental results in Sect. 4 and discuss related works in Sect. 5.

2   Protocol Specification

To verify whether a protocol satisfies a security property, an analyzer needs to formally specify the protocol (without states in Sect. 2.1) and the property (Sect. 2.3). The key part is how the global states and state transformations are formalized (Sect. 2.2).

Table 1. Syntax hierarchy

Type	Expression			
Message(m)	$a[], b[], A[], B[], \bot$ (name)		$[n], [k], [N], [K]$	(nonce)
	x, y, z, X, Y, Z (variable)		$f(m_1, m_2, ..., m_n)$	(function)
Guard(g)	$m_1 \not\leadsto m_2$	$(\nexists \sigma, m_1 \cdot \sigma = m_2)$	$m_1 \neq m_2$	(inequivalence)
Event(e)	$know(m)$	(knowledge)	$new([n], l[])$	(generation)
	$init(m_1, \cdots, m_n)$	(initialization)	$accept(m_1, \cdots, m_n)$	(acceptance)
	$leak(m)$	(leakage)		
State(s)	$name(id_1, \cdots, id_s, m_1, \cdots, m_n)$ (state)			

2.1 Preliminary – Specification Syntax Without States

As in most verifiers, messages – the basic elements in protocols, are modeled by names, nonces, variables and functions (first row in Table 1). Names model constants; nonces are freshly generated random numbers; variables represent memory locations for holding messages, and functions can be applied to a sequence of messages. All messages are assumed to be well-typed and variables can be instantiated only once.

The relations between messages are as follows. A message containing variables can be instantiated by a *substitution*, e.g., $\sigma = \{x_1 \mapsto m_1, \cdots, x_n \mapsto m_n\}$ instantiates the variables $x_1, \cdots, x_n$ with the messages $m_1, \cdots, m_n$ respectively. Given two messages m_1 and m_2, when there exists a substitution σ such that $m_1 \cdot \sigma = m_2$, we say that m_1 *is unified to* m_2, denoted as $m_1 \leadsto_\sigma m_2$. When m_1 should not be unified to m_2, we write $m_1 \not\leadsto m_2$. For instance, when a message m should not be a tuple, we write $m \not\leadsto \langle m_1, m_2 \rangle$. Given two messages m_1 and m_2, if there exists a substitution σ such that $m_1 \cdot \sigma = m_2 \cdot \sigma$, we say m_1 *and m_2 are unifiable* and σ is a unifier of m_1 and m_2, denoted as $m_1 =_\sigma m_2$. If m_1 and m_2 are unifiable, the most general unifier of m_1 and m_2 is a unifier σ such that for any unifier σ' of m_1 and m_2 there exists a substitution σ'' such that $\sigma' = \sigma \cdot \sigma''$. When m_1 and m_2 should not be unifiable (a.k.a., inequivalence), we write $m_1 \neq m_2$. For instance, if the current branch condition is that the protocol responder r is not *Bob*, we write $r \neq Bob$. $m_1 \not\leadsto m_2$ and $m_1 \neq m_2$ form the guarding conditions (second row in Table 1) i.e., whether an rule (defined later) can be applied.

Based on the above definitions, a protocol is modeled as a set of logical rules, similar as in ProVerif [1] and Tamarin [11]. The basic elements of a rule are events. An event is applying a predicate to a message sequence. The following two events are used in the protocol specification:

- event $know(m)$ means that the adversary knows the message m; and the
- event $new([n], l[])$ models that a nonce $[n]$ (the concrete value of the nonce) is freshly generated at the location $l[]$ (symbolic value used to distinguish the nonce from other nonces in a specification) by a legitimate protocol participant. Note that nonce $[n_1] \ldots [n_k]$ with the same location $l[]$ are k concrete generation of the same nonce specification in k different sessions.

The intuition is that a protocol and its involved cryptographic primitives can be treated as oracles accessible to the adversary. The adversary having the required messages obtains the corresponding outputs. Once receiving an input, the oracle generates nonces, processes messages and outputs messages according to its specification. Each oracle is modeled as a rule $[\ G\ ]\ H \dashv\{\ \}\mapsto e$, where G is a set of guard conditions, H is a set of premise events, and e is a conclusion event, meaning that if the guard conditions in G and the premise events in H are satisfied, then the conclusion event in e is satisfiable.

Cryptographic primitives. The premises of a cryptographic primitive are a set of *know* events specifying the input parameters, and the conclusion is one *know* event representing the generated result, e.g., the asymmetric encryption and decryption used in Example 1 is modeled as follows, where m, pub and sk are variables.

$$know(m), know(pub) \dashv\{\ \}\mapsto know(\mathsf{enc_a}(m, pub)) \tag{1}$$

$$know(\mathsf{enc_a}(m, \mathsf{pk}(sk))), know(sk) \dashv\{\ \}\mapsto know(m) \tag{2}$$

Protocol. A pair of the message input and the subsequent output of a participant are specified as an oracle as well. The difference is that we need to additionally consider the nonce generation and potential guard conditions. Whenever a nonce at position $l[]$ is generated in a protocol, we model the nonce generation by adding a $new([d], l[])$ event to H of the oracle. Whenever $m_1 \neq m_2$ or $m_1 \not\mapsto m_2$ conditions are required (which rarely happen in protocol specification) in the current execution branch, we add the conditions into G. For example, *bob*'s behavior in Example 1 can be modeled as

$$new([bob_l], l_{s_l}[]), new([bob_r], l_{s_r}[]), know(m_f) \dashv\{\ \}\mapsto$$
$$know(\mathsf{enc_a}(\langle m_f, [bob_l], [bob_r]\rangle, \mathsf{pk}(sksd[]))) \tag{3}$$

2.2   Protocol Specification with States

As addressed in the introduction, we explicitly model the global states of a protocol as well as their transformations. There are two ways that the states are involved. First, we use snapshots to represent at which state a rule can be applied. Second, we use a rule to model how the state transforms.

For the first case, we introduce a set of snapshots S into the rule to denote the involved states, use M to record at which snapshot each event happens (each element in M is of the form $e_i :: a_j$ with $e_i \in H$ and a_j being the index of a snapshot in S), and use O to denote the constraints on chronically orders between snapshots (each element in O is of the form $a_i \mathcal{R} a_j$ with a_i and a_j being indexes of snapshots in S). We define three types of ordering relations between two snapshots a_i and a_j in $\mathcal{R}$: (1) $a_i \leq a_j$ means that a_i appears earlier than a_j; (2) $a_i \lessdot a_j$ means that the shared object is modified once between a_i and a_j; (3) $a_i \sim a_j$ means that the shared object remains unchanged between a_i and a_j.

A rule now is of the form $[\,G\,]\,H : M \dashv S : O \mapsto e$ where e is an event. We name such rules as *state consistent rules*. For example, depending on the configuration, the SD replies s_l or s_r in Example 1, and the behavior of replying s_l is modeled as follows:

$$know(\mathsf{enc_a}(\langle m_f, s_l, s_r\rangle, \mathsf{pk}(sksd[])))^① : \{①::a_1\} \dashv \big(SD(init[]), a_0\big),$$
$$\big(SD(\mathsf{h}(m_f, left[])), a_1\big) : \{a_0 \leq a_1\} \mapsto know(s_l) \quad (4)$$

where ① is a reference to the corresponding premise event in H, so that we do not need to repeat the entire event in M, in order to save space and have a clearer presentation. The rule describes that if (1) the SD reads in a ciphertext $\mathsf{enc_a}(\langle m_f, s_l, s_r\rangle, \mathsf{pk}(sksd[]))$ at snapshot a_1, which is denoted by an event $know(\mathsf{enc_a}(\langle m_f, s_l, s_r\rangle, \mathsf{pk}(sksd[])))$, and the mapping between the event and a set of snapshots ① :: $\{a_1\}$ where ① refers to the $know$ event; and (2) snapshot a_1 is reachable, i.e., there should be a valid trace from the initial state $SD(init[])$ to the current state $SD(\mathsf{h}(m_f, left[]))$, which is denoted by the two snapshots $\big(SD(init[]), a_0\big)$, $\big(SD(\mathsf{h}(m_f, left[])), a_1\big)$ and their ordering constraints $\{a_0 \leq a_1\}$, meaning that a_0 needs to appear earlier than a_1 in a trace; then (3) the SD returns s_l, since the current configuration is $\mathsf{h}(m_f, left[])$. Another type of state consistent rule is that the adversary may be able to obtain information from the states, e.g., the reading operation in Example 1 can be modeled as

$$\dashv \big(SD(init[]), a_0\big), \big(SD(m), a_2\big) : \{a_0 \leq a_2\} \mapsto know(m) \quad (5)$$

meaning that if a_2 is reachable (denoted by $\big(SD(init[]), a_0\big), \big(SD(m), a_2\big) : \{a_0 \leq a_2\}$ with a_0 being the initial state), then the adversary can read the current value in the memory, modeled as $know(m)$.

For the second case, we introduce the *state transferring rules* of the form $[\,G\,]\,H : M \dashv S : O \mapsto T$ where T is a set of state transformations (a sequence of two snapshots). For example, the SD can be updated in Example 1, which is modeled as

$$know(x)^② : \{②::a_3\} \dashv \big(SD(init[]), a_0\big), \big(SD(m), a_3\big) : \{a_0 \leq a_3\} \mapsto$$
$$\langle \big(SD(m), a_3\big), \big(SD(\mathsf{h}(m, x)), a_4\big)\rangle \quad (6)$$

meaning that the adversary who has x at state $SD(m)$ can update the SD to be $\mathsf{h}(m, x)$, where $\langle \big(SD(m), a_3\big), \big(SD(\mathsf{h}(m, x)), a_4\big)\rangle$ models the transformation of SD from snapshot a_3 to snapshot a_4.

2.3 Security Properties

We focus on two types of security properties: authentication and secrecy. To formalize authentication properties, we add the following two events: When the protocol initiator starts a protocol run, we add a corresponding *init* event (defined in Table 1) into H; when the protocol responder accepts a protocol run, we add a corresponding *accept* event (defined in Table 1) into C. Then authentication is modeled as correspondence between the *init* and *accept* events (as in most verifiers such as ProVerif and StatVerif).

Definition 1 (Authentication). *In a security protocol, an authentication property holds, i.e., correspondence between an* accept *event and an* init *event with agreed arguments holds, if and only if for every occurrence of event* $accept(m_1, \cdots, m_n)$, *the corresponding* $init(m_1, \cdots, m_n)$ *event must be engaged before, and all the required snapshots form a valid evolving trace, denoted as* $accept(m_1, \cdots, m_n) \Leftarrow init(m_1, \cdots, m_n)$.

The secrecy property specifies that the adversary cannot obtain certain secret messages. It is defined by introducing a rule with the *leak* event (defined in Table 1) as the conclusion. If secrecy is preserved in a protocol, the *leak* event should not be reachable.

Definition 2 (Secrecy). *In a protocol, secrecy holds for a message m if and only if leak(m) is not reachable after adding* $new_1, \cdots, new_n, know(m) \dashv \vdash \mapsto leak(m)$, *where* $new_1, \cdots, new_n$ *are the nonce generation events for all nonces in m.*

Intuitively, if the adversary knows the message $know(m)$, the message m is leaked; and the *new* events are used to accurately specify the nonces in m.

As commonly assumed, we consider an active network attacker who can intercept all communications, compute new messages, generate new nonces and send the messages he obtained. For computation, he can use all the publicly available functions, e.g., encryption, decryption and concatenation. He can also designate honest participants to initiate new protocol runs and to take part in the protocol whenever he needs to.

3   Verification Algorithm

Given a set of rules $\mathcal{B}_{init}$ specifying a protocol (including stateless rules, state consistent rules and state transferring rules) and a property as described in Sect. 2, the verification aims to find the derivations of the target event specified in the property (*accept* event for authentication and *leak* for secrecy) using the rules in $\mathcal{B}_{init}$, and then check whether a derivation contradicts the specified property.

To derive a target event using a set of rules, directly reasoning on the rules would not terminate, e.g., repeatedly applying Rule (1) leads to increasingly complex terms [1,6]. To improve efficiency and help termination, we follow the approach in [1,6] – providing an algorithm to guide the reasoning. Hence, similar to [1], we construct a rule base $\mathcal{B}$, in the first phase, by combining pairs of rules in $\mathcal{B}_{init}$, which may infer new rules. Then we perform query searching in $\mathcal{B}$ to find valid attacks in the second phase. The key idea of our rule-base construction is as follow: If a rule's premise events are trivially satisfiable (events in $\mathcal{N}$), we can use its conclusion to fulfill other rules' complex premises (events not in $\mathcal{N}$). This is called *rule composition*. By applying rule composition repeatedly on existing rules until saturation, we can then safely remove the rules with complex premise events, because whenever the rule with complex premises is used in the reasoning, it can be replaced with an alternative rule (often generated by composition) with all premise events in $\mathcal{N}$. In addition, when a new rule is inferred by rule composition, *rule implication* operation is applied to check whether this rule is necessary to be added to $\mathcal{B}$. If the new rule is implied by existing rules then it is not necessary to add it. These two operations are shown to be efficient in avoiding complex terms and accelerating the verification process in ProVerif.

We generally follow the above procedure as proposed in ProVerif, but we need to add snapshot trace validation in rule composition and rule implication. Intuitively, rule composition applies one rule after another. Thus, regarding states, we ensure that (1) the snapshot ordering constraints in both rules are still preserved and (2) the ordering between the two rules are added to the ordering constraints in the resulting new rule. For rule implication, regarding states, we need to define that the ordering constraints of snapshots in a rule is less than the constraints in another one, i.e., whenever the second rule is applicable, the first rule is also applicable.

In addition, we try to concretize the snapshot traces in a rule if possible, to narrow the possible traces satisfying the ordering constraints in the rule, since it is sufficient as long as one trace exists to reach the conclusion event. To do so, we introduce two additional operations: *state unification* and *state transformation*. The intuition is as follows: Any two snapshots appear in a rule may have three kinds of relations: (1) they are from different objects; (2) they are of the same object, and the object is not modified between two snapshots; (3) they are of the same object, and the object is modified between the two snapshots. In the first case, we do not need to search for a valid trace between the two snapshots. In the second case, we try to unify them to the same value, i.e., *state unification*. In the third case, we try to find the transformations between them, i.e., *state transformation*. Note that these two operations only need to be applied to rules (1) with its premise events in $\mathcal{N}$, since those with premise event not in $\mathcal{N}$ will be eventually removed; and (2) with their conclusion events be *leak* event or *accept* event, since they are the query goals.

3.1 Preliminary Definitions

We first define the set $\mathcal{N}$ as the following three types of events, similar to ProVerif: (1) initializing a new protocol (an *init* event), (2) generating a fresh nonce (a *new* event), (3) knowing an arbitrary value (a *know(x)* event where x is a variable).

Recall that a rule may contain a set of ordering constraints O specified using relation $\mathcal{R}$ defined in Sect. 2, we define O as *closed* if the following properties hold.

$$a_i \lessdot a_j, a_j \sim a_k \in O \Rightarrow a_i \lessdot a_k \in O \qquad a_i \lessdot a_j \in O \Rightarrow a_i \leq a_j \in O$$
$$a_i \lessdot a_j, a_k \sim a_j \in O \Rightarrow a_i \lessdot a_k \in O \qquad a_i \sim a_j \in O \Rightarrow a_i \leq a_j \in O$$
$$a_i \sim a_j, a_j \lessdot a_k \in O \Rightarrow a_i \lessdot a_k \in O \qquad a_i \sim a_j, a_j \sim a_k \in O \Rightarrow a_i \sim a_k \in O$$
$$a_j \sim a_i, a_j \lessdot a_k \in O \Rightarrow a_i \lessdot a_k \in O \qquad a_i \leq a_j, a_j \leq a_k \in O \Rightarrow a_i \leq a_k \in O$$

In verification, we first ensure the O in every rule is closed using the above definition. Given two sets of ordering constraints O and O', we use $O \uplus O'$ to denote their closed union. When all snapshots of the same object are connected by $\prec$ and $\sim$ in an acyclic trace (i.e., no uncertain relation $\leq$), we conclude that a valid evolving trace is found.

Let $[\ G\ ]\ H : M \dashv S : O \mapsto V$ and $R' = [\ G'\ ]\ H' : M' \dashv S' : O' \mapsto V'$ be two rules. (1) 'R having less restricted mappings than R'' means that if some premise events in R are required to be satisfied at a snapshot (s, a_j), the same premise events need to be satisfied at an earlier snapshot (s', a_i) in R' ($a_i \leq a_j$). This indicates that R' has more restrictions on the satisfaction of the premises than R. This requirement can be formally captured by the joint operator '$*$'.

$$M * O = \{\langle e_i, a_j \rangle \mid e_i :: a_k \in M \wedge a_j \leq a_k \in O\}$$

For every event e_i, $M * O$ captures all the snapshots later than the snapshot at which the event should be satisfied. The larger the set $M * O$ is, the earlier the event e_i needs to be satisfied. Hence, $(M * O) \subseteq (M' * O')$ captures that R has less restricted mappings. (2) 'R having more organized ordering than R'' means that for every two snapshots (s_1, a_i) and (s_2, a_j) appearing in both R and R', the ordering of the two snapshots in R is more concrete (less uncertain) than in R'. Since, $a_i \prec a_j$ or $a_i \sim a_j$ is more concrete than $a_i \leq a_j$, given an ordering O, we measure its uncertainty (less concrete) with

$$\delta(O) = \{a_i \leq a_j \mid a_i \leq a_j \in O\} - \{a_t \leq a_k \mid a_t \prec a_k \in O \vee a_t \sim a_k \in O\}.$$

O is more organized than O' if and only if $\delta(O) \subseteq \delta(O')$. $\delta(O)$ captures the uncertain ordering relations between every two snapshots in the snapshot set O. The larger the set $\delta(O')$ is, the more uncertain the ordering O' is, and hence the less organized R' is.

3.2   Rule Operations

Similar to ProVerif, when the premise of a rule contains an event not in $\mathcal{N}$, we try to fulfill/unify the event with a conclusion of other state consistent rules whose premises are in $\mathcal{N}$ by rule composition.

Definition 3 (Rule Composition). *Let* $R[\ G\ ]\ H : M \dashv S : O \mapsto e$ *be a state consistent rule and* $R' = [\ G'\ ]\ H' : M' \dashv S' : O' \mapsto V$ *be either a state consistent rule or a state transferring rule. If there exists* $e_0 \in H'$ *such that* $e =_\sigma e_0$, *then* R *with* R' *can be composed on the event* e_0, *and the newly composed rule is defined as*

$$R \circ_{e_0} R' = ([G \cup G'\ ](H \cup (H' - \{e_0\})) : M \cup M' \cup M_0$$
$$\dashv (S \cup S') : O \uplus O' \uplus O_0 \mapsto V) \cdot \sigma,$$

$M_0 = \{e_i :: a_k \mid e_i \in H, e_0 :: a_k \in M'\}$, $O_0 = \{a_i \leq a_j \mid (s, a_i) \in S, e_0 :: a_j \in M'\}$.

In the resulting rule $R \circ_{e_0} R'$, the guard condition $G \cup G'$, premise events $H \cup (H' - \{e_0\})$ and conclusion event V are straightforward, following the same idea as in ProVerif. Regarding states, $S \cup S'$, $M \cup M'$ and $O \uplus O'$ capture that the snapshots, event-snapshot mapping and ordering constraints in both rules need to be satisfied in the resulting rule. For event-snapshot mapping, we additionally require that any event $e_i \in H$ needs to map to the snapshots of e_0 (i.e. a_k), such that R can be applied at state a_k. Otherwise even if e and e_0 are unifiable, after applying R, R' cannot be applicable, due to that the state of e_0 is not satisfied. This requirement is captured by M_0. For the snapshot ordering, we additionally require that any snapshot in S should appear before the snapshot of e_0, capturing that R is applied before R' in order to obtain e (or e_0), and thus the snapshots of R should appear before the snapshot for e_0, as modeled in O_0.

Given two rules R and R', if R (1) has the same conclusion as R' but requires less guard conditions and less premises (the same as in ProVerif), (2) has less snapshots, less restricted mappings and more organized ordering (additional requirements regarding states), we say that R implies R', denoted as $R \Rightarrow R'$.

Definition 4 (Rule Implication). *Let* $R = [\ G\ ]\ H : M \dashv S : O \mapsto V$ *and* $R' = [\ G'\ ]\ H' : M' \dashv S' : O' \mapsto V'$ *be two rules. We define* R *implies* R' *denoted as* $R \Rightarrow R'$ *if and only if* $\exists \sigma$,

$$(1)\big((V \cdot \sigma = V') \wedge (G \cdot \sigma \subseteq G') \wedge (H \cdot \sigma \subseteq H')\big) \wedge$$
$$(2)\big((S \cdot \sigma \subseteq S') \wedge ((M * O) \cdot \sigma \subseteq (M' * O')) \wedge (\delta(O) \cdot \sigma \subseteq \delta(O'))\big).$$

By now, we updated the rule composition and rule implication with additional requirements on states. Hereafter we introduce operations to concertize a snapshot trace.

Given two snapshots $(s_1, a_i), (s_2, a_j)$ of the same object in a rule, if s_1 and s_2 are unifiable ($s_1 =_\sigma s_2$), the simplest trace between s_1 and s_2 is to unify them as one snapshot, capturing the situation where the object is not modified between the two snapshot (formally $a_i \sim a_j$ or $a_j \sim a_i$).

Definition 5 (State Unification). *Let* $R = [\ G\ ]\ H : M \dashv S : O \mapsto e$ *be a state consistent rule. Assume there exist two distinct snapshots* $(s_1, a_i), (s_2, a_j) \in S$ *such that* $s_1 =_\sigma s_2$, *then we can unify the two snapshots in rule* R; *and the state unification of* s_1 *to* s_2 *on* R *is defined as*

$$R[a_i \sim a_j] = \big([\ G\ ]\ H : M \dashv S : O \uplus \{a_i \sim a_j\} \mapsto e\big) \cdot \sigma.$$

Note that if $s_1 =_\sigma s_2$, both $R[a_i \sim a_j]$ and $R[a_i \sim a_j]$ will be generated.

Given a state consistent rule $R = [\ G\ ]\ H : M \dashv S : O \mapsto e$, if a snapshot $(s, a_i) \in S$ does not have an immediate previous snapshot defined in O, i.e., $\nexists (s', a_j) \in S : a_j \lessdot a_i \in O \vee a_j \sim a_i \in O$, we try to apply a state transferring rule to find an immediate previous snapshot. Given a rule R, we use $\eta(S, O)$ to denote the snapshots in S whose previous snapshots have not been found, i.e.,

$$\eta(S, O) = S - \{(s, a_i) \mid a_j \lessdot a_i \in O \vee a_j \sim a_i \in O\}.$$

Definition 6 (State Transformation). *Let* $R = [\,G\,]\, H : M \dashv S : O \rightarrowtail T$ *be a state transferring rule and* $R'[\,G'\,]\, H' : M' \dashv S' : O' \rightarrowtail e$ *be a state consistent rule. Assume there is an injective function* $f : T \to \eta(S', O')$, *such that* $\forall t = \langle(s, a_i), (s', a_j)\rangle \in T, s' =_\sigma s''$ *if* $f(t) = (s'', a_k)$. *The state transformation of applying* R *to* R' *on* f *is*

$$R \bowtie_f R' = ([G \cup G'](H \cup H') : M \cup M' \dashv (S \cup S') : O \uplus O' \uplus O_0 \uplus O'' \rightarrowtail e) \cdot \sigma,$$

where $O_0 = \{a_i \lessdot a_k \mid \langle(s, a_i), (s', a_j)\rangle \in T, f(t) = (s'', a_k)\}$, *and* $O'' = \{a_t \le a_i \mid a_t \le a_k \in O', t = \langle(s, a_i), (s', a_j)\rangle \in T, f(t) = (s'', a_k)\}$.

O_0 captures that for a state transformation $\langle(s, a_i), (s', a_j)\rangle$ in T and a function $f(t) = (s'', a_k) \in S'$, a_i did exact one transformation to a_k, because the snapshot (s', a_j) will not appear in the new rule, as it is unified with (s'', a_k). O'' enforces the snapshots (e.g., a_t) that appear earlier than a_k in O' to be also earlier than a_i in the new rule. The intuition is that there is an immediate concrete transformation from a_i to a_k ($a_i \lessdot a_k$), but the relation between a_t and a_k is rather uncertain; in this case, we try to align the three snapshots as $a_t \le a_i \lessdot a_k$. Note it is sufficient to find one trace among a_t, a_i and a_k. Applying the above operations leads to new rules, some of which may not be valid.

Definition 7 (Rule Validation). *A rule* $R = [\,G\,]\, H : M \dashv S : O \rightarrowtail V$ *is valid if and only if (1)* $V \notin H$; *(2)* O *is closed and* $\forall\, a_i \le a_j \in O : a_j \le a_i \notin O$; *(3)* $\forall\, know(x), know(y) \in H : x \not\equiv y$, *and* $\forall\, init(x), init(y) \in H : x \not\equiv y$, *and* $\forall\, new([n], l[]), new([n'], l'[]) \in H : n \not\equiv n' \vee l \not\equiv l'$; *(4)* $\forall\, e_i :: a_j \in M : e_i \in H \wedge \exists(s, a_j) \in S$, *and* $\forall\, a_i \mathcal{R} a_j \in O : \exists(s, a_i) \in S \wedge \exists(s', a_j) \in S$. *The rule validation procedure of* R *is denoted as*

$$R \Downarrow = \big(\mathsf{merge}(H) : \mathsf{clear}(M) \dashv S : \mathsf{clear}(O) \rightarrowtail V\big) \cdot \sigma$$

where function merge *removes the duplicated premises, function* clear *removes references of non-existing events and snapshots,* σ *is the most general unifier such that any two redundant events can be merged or unified.*

We use $x \not\equiv y$ to denote that x is not syntactically equal to y. The definition says that a rule $[\,G\,]\, H : M \dashv S : O \rightarrowtail V$ (V is an event e or a set of state transformations T) is valid if and only if it satisfies: (1) If V is an event, V should not be in H; (2) O should be closed and contains no contradictory constraints; (3) there is no redundant events (two events modeling the same thing) in H (redundant events should be unified and merged); and (4) all mappings in M and all orderings in O do not involve non-existing events or snapshots (non-existing events or snapshots should be removed).

Heuristics. If provided with a snapshot pattern, we try to instantiate the snapshots in a rule with the pattern to accelerate the process of finding a concrete snapshot trace. Consider a state consistent rule $R = [\,G\,]\, H : M \dashv S : O \rightarrowtail e$, where $H \subseteq \mathcal{N}$, $e = know(x)$ and x is a variable. This implies that x does not appear in H; otherwise, the rule is not valid. Hence, x must be originated from S, for example the reading operation supported by the security device in Example 1. Since $know(x) \in \mathcal{N}$, we cannot compose R with other rules. To guide the verification, we try to apply the pattern to the states, so that R can be composed with other rules.

Definition 8 (State Instantiation). *Let $R = [\ G\ ]\ H : M \dashv S : O \mapsto e$ be a state consistent rule. Given a snapshot $(s, a_i) \in S$ and its pattern p such that $s =_\sigma p$, we define the state instantiation of the snapshot s with its pattern p as follows*

$$R[s \mapsto p] = ([\ G\ ]\ H : M \dashv S : O \mapsto e) \cdot \sigma.$$

3.3   Rule Base Construction

Using the above rule operations, we develop an algorithm to construct the rule base (Algorithm 1). The algorithm guides the verification by selecting proper rules to perform rule operations. Given an initial set of rules $\mathcal{B}_{init}$ as input, the algorithm returns the rule base $\mathcal{B}$ as output. In the algorithm, we first add the rules in $\mathcal{B}_{init}$ to the set *rules* (line $8 - 11$). During this procedure, redundant rules are removed (line $1 - 6$). Then we apply rule operations on the rules in *rules* and obtain a saturated rule set $\mathcal{B}_v$ (line $13 - 35$). The algorithm defines which operation is applied to which types of rules. Finally, we select those rules in $\mathcal{B}_v$ with premises in $\mathcal{N}$ and conclusion event being *accept* or *leak* to form $\mathcal{B}$. Now we prove the correctness of the algorithm.

Theorem 1. *Any accept or leak event e that is derivable from the initial rules $\mathcal{B}_{init}$ if and only if it is derivable from the knowledge base $\mathcal{B}$ constructed in Algorithm 1.*

The basic idea is as follows: Whenever there is an attack using the rules in $\mathcal{B}_{init}$, there is an attack using the rules in $\mathcal{B}_v$, since there is no rule missing. Then we only need to show that the selected rules (rules in $\mathcal{B}_v$) would not miss an attack. To do so, we first introduce the representation of an attack – the derivation tree for an *leak* or *accept* event from a set of rules as follows:

Definition 9 (Derivation Tree). *A closed rule is a rule with its conclusion initiated by its premises and states. Let $\mathcal{B}_t$ be a set of closed rules and e_t be an event, e_t is derivable from $\mathcal{B}_t$ if and only if there exists a finite derivation tree satisfying the following.*

1. *Every edge in the tree is labeled by an event e, a set of snapshots $S = \{(s_1, a_1), \dots, (s_l, a_l)\}$ and an index i, and $\forall (s_i, a_i), (s_j, a_j) \in S$: $a_i \not\sim a_j$.*
2. *Every node is labeled by a rule in $\mathcal{B}_t$.*
3. *If a node is labeled by a state consistent rule R as in Fig. 1a, then we have $R \Rightarrow H : M \dashv S_0 \cup S : O \mapsto e$ where $H = \{e_1, \cdots, e_n\}$, M is defined as $\forall e \in H : e :: \{a_1, \dots, a_l\}$, $O = \{a_0 \le a_i | (s_0, a_0) \in S_0, (s_i, a_i) \in S\}$ with S_0 being the set of initial snapshot of each object; and the indexes labeled on the outgoing edge and incoming edges (Fig. 1a) are the same.*

Algorithm 1. Rule Base Construction

Input : $\mathcal{B}_{init}$ - initial rules
Output: $\mathcal{B}$ - knowledge base

1 **Procedure** $add(R, \text{rules})$
2   **for** $R_b \in \text{rules}$ **do**
3   **if** $R_b \Rightarrow R$ **then return** rules;
4   **if** $R \Rightarrow R_b$ **then** $\text{rules} = \text{rules} - \{R_b\}$;
5   **end**
6   **return** $\{R\} \cup \text{rules}$;
7 **Algorithm**
8      $\text{rules} = \emptyset$;
9   **for** $R \in \mathcal{B}_{init}$ **do**
10         $\text{rules} = add(R, \text{rules})$;
11   **end**
12   **repeat**
13   **Case 1. Rule Composition**
14   Select a state consistent rule $R = H \dashv\!\!\{\, S : O \,\}\!\!\mapsto e$
15   and a general rule $R' = H' \dashv\!\!\{\, S' : O' \,\}\!\!\mapsto V$ from rules such that
16   1. $H \subseteq \mathcal{N}$; 2. $\exists e_0 \in H' : e_0 \notin \mathcal{N}$;
17         $\text{rules} = add((R \circ_{e_0} R') \Downarrow, \text{rules})$;
18   **Case 2. State Unification**
19   Select a state consistent rule $R = H \dashv\!\!\{\, S : O \,\}\!\!\mapsto e$ from rules such that
20   1. $H \subseteq \mathcal{N}$ and e is an $accept$ event or a $leak$ event;
21   2. $\exists s, s' \in S$, s and s' can be unified;
22         $\text{rules} = add(R[s \sim s'] \Downarrow, \text{rules})$;
23   **Case 3. State Transformation**
24   Select a state transferring rule $R = H \dashv\!\!\{\, S : O \,\}\!\!\mapsto T$
25   and a state consistent rule $R' = H' \dashv\!\!\{\, S' : O' \,\}\!\!\mapsto e$ from rules such that
26   1. $H \cup H' \subseteq \mathcal{N}$ and e is an $accept$ event or a $leak$ event;
27   2. $\exists f, \forall t \in T, f(t) = (s, a_j), \nexists a_i < a_j \in S'$;
28         $\text{rules} = add((R \bowtie_f R') \Downarrow, \text{rules})$;
29   **Case 4. State Instantiation**
30   Select a state consistent rule $R = H \dashv\!\!\{\, S : O \,\}\!\!\mapsto e$ from rules such that
31   1. $H \subseteq \mathcal{N}$, $e \in \mathcal{N}$; 2. $\exists s \in S$, s has pattern p;
32         $\text{rules} = add(R[s \mapsto p] \Downarrow, \text{rules})$;
33   **until** $\text{fix-point is reached}$;
34     $\mathcal{B}_v = \text{rules}$;
35   **return** $\mathcal{B} = \{R = H \dashv\!\!\{\, S : O \,\}\!\!\mapsto e \in \text{rules} \mid \forall p \in H, p \in \mathcal{N} \wedge e$ is an $accept$ event or a $leak$ event$\}$;

---

4. *If a node is labeled by a state transferring rule R as in Fig. 1b, there exists a set of state transformation T such that $R \Rightarrow H : M \dashv\!\!\{\, S_0 \cup S : O \,\}\!\!\mapsto T$ where $H = \{e_1, \cdots, e_n\}$, M is defined as $\forall e \in H : e :: \{a_1, \ldots, a_l\}$, $O = \{a_0 \leq a_i | (s_0, a_0) \in S_0, (s_i, a_i) \in S\}$ with S_0 being the initial snapshots; let $S_{pre} = \{(s_i, a_i) | \langle (s_i, a_i), (s_j, a_j) \rangle \in T\}$ and $S_{post} = \{(s_j, a_j) | \langle (s_i, a_i), (s_j, a_j) \rangle \in T\}$, we have $S_{pre} \subseteq S$; and in Figure 1b, $S' = S - S_{pre} + S_{post}$, e can be any event*

*that is satisfied at S, the indexes labeled on the incoming edges equal to the
index labeled on the outgoing edge plus 1.*
5. *Outgoing edge of the root is labeled by the event e_t and the index 1.*
6. *Incoming edges of the leaves are only labeled by events in $\mathcal{N}$ with the same
index.*
7. *The edges with the same index have the same state.*

(a) State Consistent Rule   (b) State Transferring Rule

Fig. 1. Rule in derivation tree

Then we prove that whenever there is a derivation tree for an *accept* or a
leak event using rules in $\mathcal{B}_v$, there is a derivation for the event using the rule
base $\mathcal{B}$ created using Algorithm 1, and vice versa. The key part in the proof is
the following Lemma which demonstrates how to replace two directly connected
nodes in the derivation tree with one node labeled by a composite rule with the
same state and index. Detailed proofs of the theorem and lemma are available
online [12].

Lemma 1. *If $R_o \circ_{e_0} R'_o$ is valid, $R_t \Rightarrow R_o$ and $R'_t \Rightarrow R'_o$, then either there exists
e' such that $R_t \circ_{e'} R'_t$ is valid and $R_t \circ_{e'} R'_t \Rightarrow R_o \circ_{e_0} R'_o$, or $R'_t \Rightarrow R_o \circ_{e_0} R'_o$.*

3.4 Query Searching

The query of authentication property and secrecy property is to find a rule that
disproves the properties. A rule disproves non-injective authentication if and
only if its conclusion event is an *accept* event, while it does not require the
corresponding *init* event in its premises. A rule disproves secrecy when the *leak*
event is reachable.

Definition 10. *Authentication Counterexample.* *A rule $R = [\,G\,]\,H :
M \dashv S : O \longmapsto e$ disproves authentication property $Q_n := accept \Leftarrow init$ denoted
as $Q_n \nvDash R$ if and only if $G \neq false$, e and accept are unifiable with the most
general unifier σ such that $\forall e' \in H, e' \in \mathcal{N}$ and $\forall \sigma' : (init \cdot \sigma \cdot \sigma' \notin H \cdot \sigma)$.*

Definition 11. *Secrecy Contradiction.* *A rule $R = [\,G\,]\,H : M \dashv S :
O \longmapsto e$ disproves secrecy property $Q_s := leak(m)$ denoted as $Q_s \nvDash R$ if and only
if $\forall e' \in H : e' \in \mathcal{N}$, $G \neq false$, $\exists \sigma, leak(x) \cdot \sigma = e$.*

If we cannot find any counterexample during the verification, when our algorithm terminates, the protocol satisfies the property. For a detailed proof, see [12].

Theorem 2. *Let $\mathcal{B}$ be the rule base generated in Algorithm 1. When Q is a secrecy query or an authentication query, there exists R derivable from $\mathcal{B}_{init}$ such that $Q \not\vdash R$ if and only if there exists $R' \in \mathcal{B}$ such that $Q \not\vdash R'$.*

4   Case Studies

We have implemented the proposed approach in a tool named SSPA (Stateful Security Protocol Analyzer). Using SSPA, we have successfully verified Example 1, three versions of the digital envelope protocols [7,13] and the Bitlocker protocol [14] to show its applicability to stateful protocols. To show that SSPA also works for protocols without global states, we have verified two versions of the Needham-Schroeder public key protocol [15,16]. The tool detected a security flaw in the digital envelope protocol (DEP) when the trusted platform module (TPM) reset is enabled. The tool, all protocol models and their evaluation results are available online at [17]. In the remaining part, we provide more details on the DEP protocol and the detected security flaw.

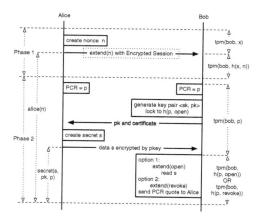

Fig. 2. The DEP protocol

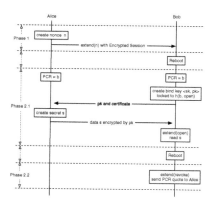

Fig. 3. An attack on DEP

DEP consists of two phases as shown in Fig. 2. In the first phase, *Alice* generates a secret nonce $[n]$ and uses it to extend a given PCR in *Bob*'s TPM with an encrypted session (detailed TPM explanation can be found at [12]). Since the nonce $[n]$ is secret, *Bob* cannot re-enter the current state of the TPM if he makes any changes to the given PCR. In the second phase, *Alice* and *Bob* read the value of the given PCR as p and *Bob* creates a binding key pair $\langle[sk], \mathsf{pk}([sk])\rangle$ locked to the PCR value $\mathsf{h}(p, open[])$ and sends the public binding key together with the key certificate to *Alice*, where *open*[] is an agreed constant in the protocol. This means that the generated binding key can be used only if the value *open*[] is first extended to the PCR of value p. After checking the correctness of the certificate, *Alice* encrypts the data [s] with the public key pk([sk]) and sends it back to *Bob*. Later, *Bob* can either open the digital envelope by extending the PCR with *open*[] or revoke his right to open the envelope by extending another pre-agreed constant *revoke*[]. If *Bob* revokes his right, the quote of PCR value h(p, *revoke*[]) can be used to prove *Bob*'s revoking action.

Using our approach and the implemented tool, we have found a cold-boot attack for this DEP when the TPM rebooting is allowed (see Fig. 3). When the TPM rebooting is allowed, *Bob* can reboot his TPM immediately after the first phase. *Bob* can reset the PCR value, e.g., to b. As a consequence, the secret nonce [n] extended to the PCR is lost. When *Alice* reads the PCR value in the beginning of the second phase, she actually reads a PCR value b that is unrelated to her previous extending action. Later this new PCR value b is used in generating key; and the key is used to encrypt *Alice*'s secret [s]. On receiving *Alice*'s cipher-text, *Bob* can open it and read [s] by extending the PCR value by *open*[]. Since *Bob* is allowed to reboot, he reboots the TPM, resets the PCR value to b, and extends the PCR value by *revoke*[]. Now *Bob* can get a PCR quote proving that he did not open the ciphertext, despite the fact that he has opened it.

The previously DEP verification in [7] fails to detect the above attack, because, in order to use the automatic verification tool ProVerif, which can only handle limited number of TPM steps, the authors made modification to the original DEP protocol – *Bob* always performs the TPM reboot before the first phase; and *Alice* is assumed to have the PCR value h(p, n) without actually reading it, in the beginning of the second phase. As a result, in their model, TPM rebooting can never happen before the second phase. Hence, the modification prevents them from detecting the attack. Since we allow state modeling and unbounded state-evolving, we can remove the assumption made in [7], and thus are able to detect the flaw.

5 Related Works

Formal analysis of security protocols has been an active research area since 1980's. The analysis is with respect to the Dolev-Yao attacker [18], who controls the network by blocking, inserting, eavesdropping messages in the network. Verifying security of protocols with bounded sessions has shown to be decidable [19]; however, the verification of unbounded sessions is, in general, undecidable [20]. Verifiers that do not bound the sessions rely on abstractions that may result in false attacks, e.g., ProVerif [1], and/or allow non-termination, e.g., Maude-NPA [3]. In this work, we focus on protocols with unbounded sessions and in general follow the ProVerif style when no global states are involved. However, our work reduces false attacks when global states are involved.

For verifiers that can handle global states, StatVerif [6] is mostly relevant to our work. As mentioned earlier, StatVerif does not terminate for unbounded involving of global states (see Example 1). In addition, StatVerif still has false attacks due to the monotonicity of Horn clauses, for example, when the security device in [6] (similar protocol to Example 1 which allows the memory to be reset to a value instead of being extended to a value) is first set to either *left* or *right* and then set to *reboot* (the StatVerif code for this scenario and Example 1 can be found at [17]). Our method does not have this problem for the above example protocols. Kremer et al. extended StatVerif with the ability to model unbounded number of global states [4], while our work enables to model and verify unbounded evolving of global states. Hence, our work is orthogonal to the work of Kremer et al. In addition, their work uses Tamarin [11] as its backend verification engine, which is different from the Horn clause based approaches (general comparison is difficult [21]). In general, Tamarin can be used for reasoning on protocols with global states, but its user may need to interact with the verifier [4]. Our verifier, on the other hand, is fully automatic. Furthermore, Mödersheim developed a verification framework that works with global states [22]. The framework extends the IF language with sets and abstracts messages based on its Set-Membership. However its expressivenss and verification applicability is unclear. Guttman extended the strand space with mutable states to deal with stateful protocols [23,24], but without tool support for his approach. Most importantly, none of the above explicitly handles unbounded global state evolving.

6   Conclusions and Future Work

We have presented a new approach for the stateful security protocol verification with unbounded global state evolving. We implemented a tool for our new approach and the verification results of a number of protocols are quite encouraging. For future work, accelerating the redundancy checking would be helpful to improve the tool's performance. In addition, analyzing more stateful protocols, and adapting our approach for protocols with physical properties, e.g., time and space, would be interesting directions.

Acknowledgement. This work is supported by the National Research Foundation, Prime Minister's Office, Singapore under its National Cybersecurity R&D Program (TSUNAMi project, Award No.NRF2014NCR-NCR001-21) and administered by the National Cybersecurity R&D Directorate.

References

1. Blanchet, B.: An efficient cryptographic protocol verifier based on Prolog rules. In: Proceedings 14th IEEE Computer Security Foundations Workshop (CSFW), pp. 82–96. IEEE CS (2001)
2. Viganò, L.: Automated security protocol analysis with the avispa tool. Electron. Notes Theoret. Comput. Sci. (ENTCS) **155**, 61–86 (2006)

3. Escobar, S., Meadows, C., Meseguer, J.: Maude-NPA: cryptographic protocol analysis modulo equational properties. In: Aldini, A., Barthe, G., Gorrieri, R. (eds.) FOSAD 2007-2009. LNCS, vol. 5705, pp. 1–50. Springer, Heidelberg (2009). doi:10.1007/978-3-642-03829-7_1

4. Kremer, S., Künnemann, R.: Automated analysis of security protocols with global state. In: Proceedings 24th IEEE Symposium on Security and Privacy (S & P), pp. 163–178 (2014)

5. Herzog, J.: Applying protocol analysis to security device interfaces. IEEE Secur. Priv. **4**, 84–87 (2006)

6. Arapinis, M., Ritter, E., Ryan, M.D.: StatVerif: verification of stateful processes. In: Proceedings 24th IEEE Computer Security Foundations Symposium (CSF), pp. 33–47. IEEE CS (2011)

7. Delaune, S., Kremer, S., Ryan, M.D., Steel, G.: Formal analysis of protocols based on TPM state registers. In: Proceedings 24th IEEE Computer Security Foundations Symposium (CSF), pp. 66–80. IEEE CS (2011)

8. Dong, N., Jonker, H., Pang, J.: Challenges in eHealth: from enabling to enforcing privacy. In: Liu, Z., Wassyng, A. (eds.) FHIES 2011. LNCS, vol. 7151, pp. 195–206. Springer, Heidelberg (2012). doi:10.1007/978-3-642-32355-3_12

9. Dong, N., Jonker, H., Pang, J.: Formal analysis of privacy in an ehealth protocol. In: Foresti, S., Yung, M., Martinelli, F. (eds.) ESORICS 2012. LNCS, vol. 7459, pp. 325–342. Springer, Heidelberg (2012). doi:10.1007/978-3-642-33167-1_19

10. Dong, N., Jonker, H.L., Pang, J.: Formal modelling and analysis of receipt-free auction protocols in applied PI. Comput. Secur. **65**, 405–432 (2017)

11. Meier, S., Schmidt, B., Cremers, C., Basin, D.: The TAMARIN prover for the symbolic analysis of security protocols. In: Sharygina, N., Veith, H. (eds.) CAV 2013. LNCS, vol. 8044, pp. 696–701. Springer, Heidelberg (2013). doi:10.1007/978-3-642-39799-8_48

12. Li, L., Dong, N., Pang, J., Sun, J., Bai, G., Liu, Y., Dong, J.S.: A verification framework for stateful security protocols - full version (2017). http://www.comp.nus.edu.sg/dongnp/sspa

13. Ables, K., Ryan, M.D.: Escrowed data and the digital envelope. In: Acquisti, A., Smith, S.W., Sadeghi, A.-R. (eds.) Trust 2010. LNCS, vol. 6101, pp. 246–256. Springer, Heidelberg (2010). doi:10.1007/978-3-642-13869-0_16

14. Microsoft: Bitlocker FAQ (2011). http://technet.microsoft.com/en-us/library/hh831507.aspx

15. Needham, R.M., Schroeder, M.D.: Using encryption for authentication in large networks of computers. Commun. ACM **21**, 993–999 (1978)

16. Lowe, G.: An attack on the needham-schroeder public-key authentication protocol. Inf. Process. Lett. **56**, 131–133 (1995)

17. Li, L., Dong, N., Pang, J., Sun, J., Bai, G., Liu, Y., Dong, J.S.: SSPA tool, experiment models and evaluation results (2017). http://lilissun.github.io/r/sspa.html

18. Dolev, D., Yao, A.C.C.: On the security of public key protocols. IEEE Trans. Inf. Theory **29**, 198–207 (1983)

19. Rusinowitch, M., Turuani, M.: Protocol insecurity with a finite number of sessions, composed keys is np-complete. Theoret. Comput. Sci. **299**, 451–475 (2003)

20. Durgin, N.A., Lincoln, P., Mitchell, J.C.: Multiset rewriting and the complexity of bounded security protocols. J. Comput. Secur. **12**, 247–311 (2004)

21. Meier, S.: Advancing automated security protocol verification. Ph.D. thesis, ETH (2013)

22. Mödersheim, S.: Abstraction by set-membership: verifying security protocols and web services with databases. In: Proceedings 17th ACM Conference on Computer and Communications Security (CCS), pp. 351–360. ACM (2010)
23. Guttman, J.D.: Fair exchange in strand spaces. In: Proceedings 7th International Workshop on Security Issues in Concurrency (SECCO), EPTCS, vol. 7, pp. 46–60 (2009)
24. Guttman, J.D.: State and progress in strand spaces: Proving fair exchange. J. Autom. Reasoning **48**, 159–195 (2012)

A Sliding-Window Algorithm for On-The-Fly Interprocedural Program Analysis

Xin Li[1](✉) and Mizuhito Ogawa[2]

[1] East China Normal University, Shanghai, China
xinli@sei.ecnu.edu.cn
[2] Japan Advanced Institute of Science and Technology, Nomi, Japan
mizuhito@jaist.ac.jp

Abstract. Program analysis plays an important role in finding software flaws. Due to dynamic language features like late binding, there are many program analysis problems for which one could not assume a prior program control flow, e.g., Java points-to analysis, the disassembly of binary codes with indirect jumps, etc. In this work, we give a general formalization of such kind of on-the-fly interprocedural program analysis problems, and present a sliding-window algorithm for it in the framework of weighted pushdown systems. Our sliding window algorithm only consists of a series of local static analyses conducted on an arbitrary number of program methods, which does not sacrifice the precision of the whole program analysis at the manageable cost of caching intermediate analysis results during each iteration. We have implemented and evaluated the sliding-window algorithm by instantiating the framework with Java points-to analysis as an application. Our empirical study showed that the analysis based on the sliding-window algorithm always outperforms the whole program analysis on runtime efficiency and scalability.

1 Introduction

Program analysis plays an important role in finding software flaws. An interprocedural (or context-sensitive) program analysis distinguishes and produces analysis results for different calling contexts, whereas an intraprocedural (or context-insensitive) program analysis would confuse them and incur a loss of analysis precision. Precise interprocedural program analyses are crucial to the successful verification of software from the real-world. Due to dynamic language features like late binding, there are many program analysis problems for which one could not assume a prior program control flow, e.g., Java points-to analysis, the disassembly of binary codes with indirect jumps, etc. These analyses are known to be mutually dependent on call graph construction and the underlying system is generated on-the-fly as the analysis proceeds. It is challenging to design precise interprocedural program analyses involving heaps and dynamic language features while being scalable to large-scale software.

In this work, motivated by Java points-to analysis, we are concerned with designing practically more efficient algorithms for solving such kind of *on-the-fly interprocedural program analysis* (OTFIPA) problems. To this end, we first

© Springer International Publishing AG 2017
Z. Duan and L. Ong (Eds.): ICFEM 2017, LNCS 10610, pp. 281–297, 2017.
https://doi.org/10.1007/978-3-319-68690-5_17

give a general formalization of the analysis problem, by mildly extending the classic analysis problem for computing the meet-over-all-valid-path values, and then present a sliding-window algorithm for it that analyzes the program in pieces in isolation. Our approach adapts the powerful framework of weighted pushdown systems (WPDSs) [8], which is known as a generalized framework for interprocedural program analysis (or context-sensitive program analysis) in which method calls and returns are correctly matched with one another. Pushdown systems (PDSs) are natural formalism for modelling the interprocedural control flow of imperative programs, and WPDSs extend PDSs by associating each transition with a weight that is often encoded from a program transformer in classic dataflow analyses. Efficient algorithms have been developed for pushdown model checking by automata-theoretic approach [4], and they are carried over to WPDSs.

The major difficulties of designing an efficient algorithm for OTFIPA are that, the dependency among program parts can be cyclic, and the underlying system for analysis is enlarged on-the-fly by frequently posing dataflow queries on relevant program points. Classic solutions to tackling the first issue include, either building a dependency graph of program parts before the analysis, and analyzing program parts in their topological order after collapsing loops, or breaking such cyclic dependency by providing each program part with summary information of external program parts which it depends upon. The later solution results in modular analysis techniques which is desirable to scalable program analyses. However, it is a long-standing challenge to generate a precise procedure summary for non-trivial dataflow analysis problems. In particular, for the kind of on-the-fly program analysis problems, e.g., higher-order functions in functional programs, dynamic dispatch in Java, it is difficult to adapt classic methods for modular analysis to such occasions, as pointed out in Sect. 8.5 of [3].

Instead of challenging a modular analysis or collapsing loops with sacrificing the precision, we take a mild approach to improving the runtime efficiency for solving the OTFIPA problem without compromising the analysis precision. Our key idea is to generate, cache and reuse two types of intermediate analysis results that implicitly carry procedure summaries when invoking WPDS model checking as the underlying analysis engine. One is for resolving the interdependency among methods, and the other is for locally computing the whole-program analysis results without revisiting the whole program, to answer the on-the-fly dataflow queries that can be overwhelming. Notably, our algorithm is conducted in a sliding-window fashion: the analysis slides over the discovered program coverage so far, and iteratively analyzes a sized subset of methods until the accumulated analysis results from a series of local analyses stablize.

In summary, this paper makes the following contributions:

- We give a general formalization for the kind of OTFIPA problems that are mutually dependent of discovering the program coverage (Sect. 3.1). Such a formal clarification provides us with a basis and framework for reasoning about the correctness of our sliding-window algorithm for tackling the problem. We also show with an example of copy constant propagation that

dataflow analyses with simple conditionals can be instantiated as an instance of the problem (Sect. 3.2).
- We present a sliding-window algorithm for the OTFIPA problem, by adapting the inner algorithmic structures of WPDS model checking based on the $\mathcal{P}$-automata techniques (Sect. 4). Our analysis allows to analyze the program in pieces of an arbitrary size with preserving the precision of the whole-program analysis by caching the minimum intermediate analysis results during the analysis.
- We demonstrate experimentally the effectiveness of our approach with instantiating Java points-to analysis in the algorithmic framework (Sect. 5). Our preliminary empirical study shows that, the sliding-window algorithm brought a 2X speedup over the whole-program analysis for most benchmarks and successfully verify two benchmarks that exceed the time budget when running the whole-program analysis.

Last but not least, we also formally prove the correctness of our approach, for which an interested reader may wish to consult an extended version of the paper.

Related Work. This work is motivated by Japot [6] that is a context-sensitive points-to analyzer for Java designed in the framework of WPDSs. There has been a host of work on points-to analysis. To our knowledge, almost other existing practical points-to analyzer took a cloning-based approach (that resembles inline expansion) to achieving context-sensitivity, which has an inherit limit on analyzing recursive procedural calls. We are concerned with scalable stacking-based points-to analysis algorithms for Java that precisely handles recursive procedure calls by WPDSs. In [6], the authors attempted to carefully interleave the whole program analysis with local ones on small parts of the program in a restricted manner. They used the model checker as a black box, and did not resolve the interdependency among program parts. The whole program analysis is compulsory for ensuring soundness as the final step of the analysis. By adapting the inner algorithmic structures of WPDSs, this work upgrades Japot to a more efficient analyzer which only consists of local static analyses yet preserves the original precision of a whole program analysis.

It is desirable to design a modular analysis by generating procedure summaries for each method and analyzing the program in pieces with instantiating the procedure summaries of callee methods. Many techniques were proposed to achieve a certain degree of modularity. However, it remains a challenge to design a precise modular analysis for context-sensitive heap analysis like Java points-to analysis [12]. Our approach is not modular analysis strictly speaking, because we never generate procedure summaries and the program parts are analyzed iteratively. Yet, the intermediate results that we generate, cache, and reuse in the analysis carry some information that are related to procedure summaries.

Our work can be turned as incremental analyses, since we cache in the analysis necessary information for conducting a local analysis on any part of the program. To our knowledge, [2] is the first work on incremental algorithms for safety analysis of recursive state machines. Lal and Reps presented in [5] a new reachability algorithm of WPDS, and discussed how to derive an incremental algorithm from their new setting. The authors also proposed a technique to improve the running time for (weighted) pushdown model checking. Their technique could be plugged in our tool as a more efficient engine for weighted pushdown systems.

2 Preliminaries

2.1 Weighted Pushdown Model Checking

Definition 1. *A **pushdown system** (PDS) $\mathcal{P}$ is (P, Γ, Δ), where P is a finite set of control locations, Γ is a finite stack alphabet, and $\Delta \subseteq P \times \Gamma \times P \times \Gamma^*$ is a finite set of transition rules. A transition rule $(p, \gamma, q, \omega) \in \Delta$ is written as $\langle p, \gamma \rangle \hookrightarrow \langle q, \omega \rangle$. A **configuration** of P is a pair $\langle p, \omega \rangle$ where $p \in P$ and $\omega \in \Gamma^*$. A set of configurations C is **regular** if $\{\omega \mid \langle p, \omega \rangle \in C\}$ is regular. A transition relation $\Rightarrow$ is defined on configurations of $\mathcal{P}$, such that $\langle p, \gamma\omega' \rangle \Rightarrow \langle q, \omega\omega' \rangle$ for any $\omega' \in \Gamma^*$ if $\langle p, \gamma \rangle \hookrightarrow \langle q, \omega \rangle$. Given a set C of configurations, we define $pre^*(C) = \{c' \mid \exists c \in C : c' \Rightarrow^* c\}$ and $post^*(C) = \{c' \mid \exists c \in C : c \Rightarrow^* c'\}$ which are the sets of pre-images and post-images of C, respectively.*

A pushdown system is a pushdown automaton without the input alphabet. It is known that any pushdown system can be simulated by a pushdown system for which $|\omega| \leq 2$ for each transition rule $\langle p, \gamma \rangle \hookrightarrow \langle q, \omega \rangle$ [10]. In the paper, we assume such a normalized form of pushdown systems.

Definition 2. *A **bounded idempotent semiring** $\mathcal{S}$ is $(D, \oplus, \otimes, \bar{0}, \bar{1})$, where $\bar{0}, \bar{1} \in D$, and*

1. *$(D, \oplus)$ is a commutative monoid with $\bar{0}$ as its unit element, and $\oplus$ is idempotent, i.e., $a \oplus a = a$ for all $a \in D$;*
2. *$(D, \otimes)$ is a monoid with $\bar{1}$ as the unit element;*
3. *$\otimes$ distributes over $\oplus$, i.e., for all $a, b, c \in D$, we have*
   $a \otimes (b \oplus c) = (a \otimes b) \oplus (a \otimes c)$ and $(b \oplus c) \otimes a = (b \otimes a) \oplus (c \otimes a)$;
4. *for all $a \in D, a \otimes \bar{0} = \bar{0} \otimes a = \bar{0}$;*
5. *A partial ordering $\sqsubseteq$ is defined on D such that $a \sqsubseteq b$ iff $a \oplus b = a$ for all $a, b \in D$, and there are no infinite descending chains in D.*

It is not hard to see that $\bar{0}$ is the greatest element in D.

Definition 3. *A **weighted pushdown system** (WPDS) $\mathcal{W}$ is a triplet $(\mathcal{P}, \mathcal{S}, f)$, where $\mathcal{P} = (P, \Gamma, \Delta)$ is a pushdown system, $\mathcal{S} = (D, \oplus, \otimes, \bar{0}, \bar{1})$ is a bounded idempotent semiring, and $f : \Delta \to D$ is a function that assigns a weight in D to each transition rule in Δ.*

Let $\sigma = (r_0, \ldots, r_k)$ be a transition sequence where $r_i \in \Delta$ for each $0 \leq i \leq k$. A value associated with σ is defined by $val(\sigma) = f(r_0) \otimes \cdots \otimes f(r_k)$. Given $c, c' \in Q \times \Gamma^*$, we denote by $path(c, c')$ the set of transition sequences that transform configurations from c into c' for each.

Definition 4. *Given a WPDS $\mathcal{W} = (\mathcal{P}, \mathcal{S}, f)$ where $\mathcal{P} = (P, \Gamma, \Delta)$, and regular sets of configurations $S, T \subseteq P \times \Gamma^*$. The model checking problem for WPDS is to compute the following value:*

$$\mathsf{WPMC}[\mathcal{W}](S, T) = \bigoplus \{val(\sigma) \mid \sigma \in path(c, c'), c \in S, c' \in T\}$$

When applying WPDSs to program analysis, the pushdown system models the interprocedural program control flow with matched calls and returns. The weights in D typically encode program transformers, $\otimes$ models (the reverse of) function composition, and $\oplus$ combines data flows at join points of the program.

2.2   Saturation-Based Algorithm for WPDS Model Checking

PDSs are appealing partly due to having efficient model checking algorithms based on the $\mathcal{P}$-automata techniques. A $\mathcal{P}$-automaton is a NFA (non-deterministic finite automaton) that recognizes a *regular* set of pushdown configurations.

Definition 5. *Given a PDS $\mathcal{P} = (P, \Gamma, \Delta)$. A $\mathcal{P}$-automaton $\mathcal{A} = (Q, \Sigma, \rightarrow, P, F)$ is a NFA, where $Q \supseteq P$ is a finite set of states, $\Sigma = \Gamma \cup \{\varepsilon\}$ is a finite alphabet, $\rightarrow \subseteq Q \times \Sigma \times Q$ is a set of transitions, and P and $F \subseteq Q$ are the sets of initial and final states, respectively. We define $\rightarrow^* \subseteq Q \times \Gamma^* \times Q$ as the smallest relation satisfying that, (i) $p \xrightarrow{\varepsilon}^* p$ for any $p \in Q$; (ii) $p \xrightarrow{\gamma}^* p'$ if $(p, \gamma, p') \in \rightarrow$; (iii) $p \xrightarrow{\omega\gamma}^* p'$ if $p \xrightarrow{\omega}^* p''$ and $p'' \xrightarrow{\gamma}^* p'$ for some $p'' \in Q$. A configuration $\langle p, \omega \rangle$ is accepted by $\mathcal{A}$ if $p \xrightarrow{\omega}^* q$ for some $q \in F$. A set of configurations C is regular if it is accepted by some $\mathcal{P}$-automaton. We denote by $\mathcal{A}_C$ the $\mathcal{P}$-automaton that accepts a regular set C of configurations, and sometime refer to the $\mathcal{P}$-automaton by the set of transitions in it.*

One crucial property of pushdown systems is that, the set of pre-images and post-images of a *regular* set of configurations is also *regular*. Given a $\mathcal{P}$-automaton $\mathcal{A}_C$ that recognizes a regular set C of configurations. The pre-images $pre^*(C)$ and post-images $post^*(C)$ can be computed by augmenting $\mathcal{A}_C$ with new edges and states with applying backward and forward saturation rules until convergence, respectively. In the paper, we limit our focus to forward saturation and illustrate in Fig. 1 the saturation rules for computing $post^*(C)$. In the figure, solid edges and states reside in the current automaton, and dashed edges and states are newly added by saturation rules.

Let l be a mapping from the edges in a $\mathcal{P}$-automaton $\mathcal{A}$ to weights. The model checking problem $\mathsf{WPMC}[\mathcal{W}](S, T)$ in Definition 4 can be solved by first forward saturating $\mathcal{A}_S$ while updating l upon stablization. Initially, $l(t) = \bar{1}$ for each transition t in $\mathcal{A}_S$, and $l(t) = \bar{0}$, otherwise. The rules for updating weights with respect to the saturation rules in Fig. 1 are given as follows:

(a) $l(p', \varepsilon, q) = l(p, \gamma, q) \otimes f(r_{pop})$ (b) $l(p', \gamma', q) = l(p, \gamma, q) \otimes f(r_{normal})$
(c) $l(p', \gamma', q_{p',\gamma'}) = \bar{1}$ and $l(q_{p',\gamma'}, \gamma'', q) = l(p, \gamma, q) \otimes f(r_{push})$
(d) $l(p, \gamma, q') = l(q, \gamma, q') \otimes l(p, \varepsilon, q)$

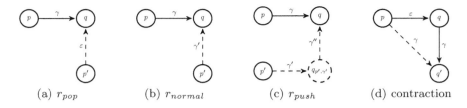

(a) r_{pop} (b) r_{normal} (c) r_{push} (d) contraction

Fig. 1. Saturation rules for computing $post^*(C)$, where r_{pop} is $\langle p, \gamma \rangle \hookrightarrow \langle p', \varepsilon \rangle$, r_{normal} is $\langle p, \gamma \rangle \hookrightarrow \langle p', \gamma' \rangle$, and r_{push} is $\langle p, \gamma \rangle \hookrightarrow \langle p', \gamma'\gamma'' \rangle$. Figure 1(d) shows a contraction rule for taking care of ε-transitions during the saturation.

Next, for any configuration $c = \langle p, \gamma_1 \ldots \gamma_n \rangle$ in C and the saturated automaton $\mathcal{A}_{post^*(C)}$, we define $\mathcal{A}(c) = \bigoplus \{ l(q_{n-1}, \gamma_n, q_n) \otimes \cdots \otimes l(q_1, \gamma_2, q_2) \otimes l(p, \gamma_1, q_1) \mid q_n \in F \}$, and for any set C of configurations, define $\mathcal{A}(C) = \bigoplus \{ \mathcal{A}(c) \mid c \in C \}$. Then we have $\mathsf{WPMC}[\mathcal{W}](S, T) = \mathcal{A}_{post^*(S)}(T)$, and the algorithm for efficiently computing $\mathcal{A}(C)$ will be elaborated in Algorithm 2.

3   On-The-Fly Interprocedural Program Analysis

3.1   A Formal Description of OTFIPA

Assume abstract interpretation has been properly applied to the analysis problem if necessary. Let $((\mathcal{D}, \preceq_{\mathcal{D}}), \sqcap_{\mathcal{D}}, \top_{\mathcal{D}})$ be a meet semi-lattice tailored for the analysis, where $\sqcap_{\mathcal{D}}$ is the binary operator for computing the greatest lower bound, and $\top_{\mathcal{D}}$ is the greatest element in $\mathcal{D}$. Let $\mathcal{V} = \{V_1, \ldots, V_k\}$ be the set of variables in the analysis. An *environment* $\mathcal{E} \in \mathcal{D}^k$ of the program is a k-tuple of values in $\mathcal{D}$, and we denote by $\mathcal{E}(i)$ (or $\mathcal{E}(V_i)$) the value for the variable V_i, and extend $\sqcap_{\mathcal{D}}$ and $\preceq_{\mathcal{D}}$ to environments element-wise. The set of environments is denoted by $\mathcal{E}nv$, and the initial environment $(\top_{\mathcal{D}}, \ldots, \top_{\mathcal{D}}) \in \mathcal{D}^k$ is denoted by $\mathcal{E}_0$ which is the greatest element in $\mathcal{E}nv$. An *environment transformer* $\tau : \mathcal{E}nv \to \mathcal{E}nv$ is a map on environments that is *distributive* (thus monotonic) wrt $\sqcap_{\mathcal{D}}$, i.e., $\tau(\mathcal{E}_1 \sqcap_{\mathcal{D}} \mathcal{E}_2) = \tau(\mathcal{E}_1) \sqcap_{\mathcal{D}} \tau(\mathcal{E}_2)$. The set of environment transformers is denoted by $\mathcal{T}$. Let $(\mathcal{T}, \sqcap, \top)$ be a meet semi-lattice where $\sqcap$ is the greatest lower bound operator on $\mathcal{T}$ defined by $\tau_1 \sqcap \tau_2 = \lambda e.(\tau_1(e) \sqcap_{\mathcal{D}} \tau_2(e))$, and $\top = \lambda e.\mathcal{E}_0$ is the greatest element in $\mathcal{T}$.

Program analysis often first builds an interprocedural control flow graph (ICFG) of the program, and then solves the analysis problem as path problems over it. Here, we explore a so-called *supergraph* of the program for representing an ICFG. A supergraph is a collection of control flow graphs (CFG), where a CFG is constructed for a method as usual, except that each method call is represented by two nodes in the graph: a node for *call site* and a node for *return point*, and CFGs are connected in the graph by *call edges* from call sites to callee' entry points and *return edges* from callees' exits to the corresponding return points.

Let $\mathcal{M}$ be the set of methods in the program. A *supergraph* G is a triplet $(\mathcal{N}, \to_G, l)$ where $\mathcal{N} = \{\mathbf{n}_1, \ldots, \mathbf{n}_m\}$ is a set of nodes, $\to_G \subseteq \mathcal{N} \times \mathcal{N}$ is a set of edges, and $l : (\to_G) \to \mathcal{T}$ is a map that associates each edge with an environment transformer. In particular, we denote by $\mathcal{R} \subseteq \to_G$ the set of call edges, called *call relation*. Given a set of methods $M \subseteq \mathcal{M}$ and a call relation $R \subseteq \mathcal{R}$, one can construct a supergraph, denoted by $G_{\downarrow M,R}$.

A *valid* path in G is a path where call edges and return edges are well-matched with each other, and such valid paths constitutes some context-free language. For any node $\mathbf{n} \in \mathcal{N}$, the (possibly infinite) set of valid paths leading from $\mathbf{e_{main}}$ to $\mathbf{n}$ is denoted by $\mathsf{VPath}(\mathbf{e_{main}}, \mathbf{n})$. Let $\sigma = [t_0, \dots, t_n]$ be a sequence of edges that forms a path in G. We define $\tau_\sigma = l(t_n) \circ l(t_{n-1}) \circ \cdots \circ l(t_0)$. Here, $\circ$ denotes the ordinary function composition. The **meet-over-all-valid-path** (MOVP) problem for G is to compute that, for each $\mathbf{n} \in \mathcal{N}$,

$$\mathsf{MOVP}[G](\mathbf{n}) \stackrel{def}{=} \sqcap_{\mathcal{D}} \{\tau_\sigma(\mathcal{E}_0) \mid \sigma \in \mathsf{VPath}(\mathbf{e_{main}}, \mathbf{n})\}$$
$$= (\sqcap\{\tau_\sigma \mid \sigma \in \mathsf{VPath}(\mathbf{e_{main}}, \mathbf{n})\}) (\mathcal{E}_0) \quad \text{(By definition of } \sqcap)$$

That is, it computes all the valid dataflow values flowing to each node.

We denote by $\overrightarrow{\mathsf{MOVP}[G]} \in \mathcal{E}nv^m$ an m-tuple of environments such that its ith projection, denoted by $\overrightarrow{\mathsf{MOVP}[G]}[i]$ (or $\overrightarrow{\mathsf{MOVP}[G]}[\mathbf{n}_i]$), is the value $\mathsf{MOVP}[G](\mathbf{n}_i)$, for each $i \in [1..m]$. Note that, since $\sqcap_{\mathcal{D}}\emptyset = \mathcal{E}_0$, we have $\overrightarrow{\mathsf{MOVP}[\emptyset]} = \mathcal{E}_0^m$. We introduce a binary relation $\sqsubseteq$ on $\mathcal{E}nv^m$ such that $\overrightarrow{\mathcal{E}}_1 \sqsubseteq \overrightarrow{\mathcal{E}}_2$ iff $\overrightarrow{\mathcal{E}}_1[i] \preceq_{\mathcal{D}} \overrightarrow{\mathcal{E}}_2[i]$ for each $i \in [1..m]$. Then $[\mathcal{E}_0, \dots, \mathcal{E}_0] \in \mathcal{E}nv^m$ is the greatest element.

A function $\phi : \mathcal{E}nv^m \to 2^{\mathcal{M}} \times 2^{\mathcal{R}}$ is a *contract function* for G if ϕ is anti-monotonic. It characterizes dynamic program features, and its semantics is problem-specific. For instance, for Java points-to analysis, ϕ encodes the semantics of dynamic dispatch implemented in Java virtual machine, such that for any $\overrightarrow{\mathcal{E}} \in \mathcal{E}nv^m$, $\phi(\overrightarrow{\mathcal{E}})$ returns the union of methods that can be dispatched at each node $\mathbf{n}_i$ according to the value $\overrightarrow{\mathcal{E}}[\mathbf{n}_i]$, paired with the call relation for those methods. Note that, some program nodes do not matter to the change of the program coverage and may not be considered in the contract function. Provided with ϕ, we define an *enlargement function* $\eta : 2^{\mathcal{M}} \times 2^{\mathcal{R}} \to 2^{\mathcal{M}} \times 2^{\mathcal{R}}$ as follows:

$$\eta = \lambda(x, y).(x, y) \cup \phi\left(\overrightarrow{\mathsf{MOVP}[G_{\downarrow x,y}]}\right)$$

where $\cup$ is extended to a pair of sets element-wise. It characterizes the process of discovering the program coverage. One can conclude with Lemma 1.

Lemma 1. *The function η is monotonic, and the least fixed point of η exists, and it coincides with $\bigcup_{j=0}^{\infty} \eta^j(\emptyset, \emptyset)$.* $\qquad\square$

Definition 6. *Let **gfp** be the greatest fixed point operator, and let **lfp** be the least fixed point operator. An **on-the-fly interprocedural program analysis** (OTFIPA) problem is to compute*[1]

---

[1] There are datalfow analysis problems alternatively formalized over *exploded super-graph* [9], upon which one can similarly define the OTFIPA problem.

(i) the least fixed point of η, i.e., $lfp(\eta)$, which is the set of methods M_r involved in the analysis problem, and a call relation R over them; and

(ii) the tuple $\overrightarrow{MOVP}[G_{\downarrow_{M_r,R}}]$ of environments, which is the dataflow analysis results of solving the $\overline{MOVP}$ problem for $G_{\downarrow_{M_r,R}}$.

3.2 A Running Example

This section describes an example of a *copy constant propagation* (CCP) analysis, partly following [7] and adjusts the example as an instance of OTFIPA. CCP is one of the classic dataflow analysis used for compiler optimization. The analysis is to check whether the value of a variable would remain as a constant along some program execution, so that the constant assigned to the variable can be substituted when the variable is used.

```
n0: int x, y = 0;        void foo(int b) {        void main() {
void bar(int a) {            n9: return b; }          n1: x = 2;
n4: if (x < 3)           void noop() {            n2, n3: bar(x); }
    n5, n6: y = foo(a);      n9: y = x;
else n7, n8: noop (); }      n10: x = 3; }
```

Fig. 2. A code snippet for illustrating copy constant propagation analysis.

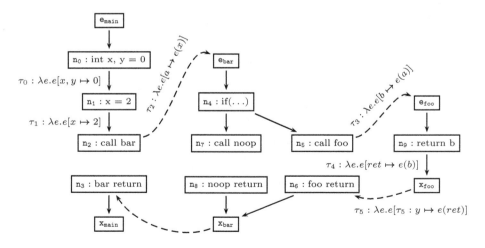

Fig. 3. A supergraph of Fig. 2, where the method **noop** is omitted.

An example code snippet is shown in Fig. 2, where x, y are global variables, a, b are local variables, and each statement in the code is indexed by n_i. Its supergraph is shown in Fig. 3, where solid lines are intraprocedural edges, and dotted lines are call and return edges. Since the method noop is not called, we omit it from the graph. Extra nodes e_f and x_f denote the unique entry and exit point of a method f. Each edge in the graph is labelled with an environment transformer τ. If τ is an identity function $\lambda e.e$, it is omitted in the graph. The abstract domain for the analysis is $\mathcal{D} = \mathbb{Z} \cup \{\bot, \top_\mathcal{D}\}$. Here, $\mathbb{Z}$ denotes integers, $\top_\mathcal{D}$ denotes a value that is irrelevant and is the greatest element, and $\bot$ denotes a value that is not a constant. For all d in $\mathbb{Z}$, $\bot \preceq_\mathcal{D} d$ and $d \preceq_\mathcal{D} \top_\mathcal{D}$, and for any d_1, d_2 in $\mathbb{Z}$ with $d_1 \neq d_2$, d_1 and d_2 are incomparable. In the transformers, ret is a fresh symbol that is introduced to denote the return value of foo.

It is known to be non-trivial (often undecidable) to analyze conditionals in dataflow analysis. Therefore, conditionals are usually abstracted to be non-deterministic choices as an over-approximation of the program branching. Thus whether the method foo and noop are invoked depends on the dataflow reaching at the node n_4, and we know that foo is reachable in this case since $MOVP[G](n) = [x \mapsto 2, y \mapsto 2]$. Then it can be modeled as an OTFIPA problem. For any $\overrightarrow{\mathcal{E}} \in \overrightarrow{\mathcal{D}}$,

$$\phi(\overrightarrow{\mathcal{E}}) = \begin{cases} (\{\texttt{main}, \texttt{bar}, \texttt{foo}\}, R_0) & \text{if } \overrightarrow{\mathcal{E}}[n_4](x) \neq \bot \text{ and } \overrightarrow{\mathcal{E}}[n_4](x) < 3 \\ (\{\texttt{main}, \texttt{bar}, \texttt{noop}\}, R_1) & \text{if } \overrightarrow{\mathcal{E}}[n_4](x) \neq \bot \text{ and } \overrightarrow{\mathcal{E}}[n_4](x) \geq 3 \\ (\{\texttt{main}, \texttt{bar}, \texttt{foo}, \texttt{noop}\}, R_2) & \text{if } \overrightarrow{\mathcal{E}}[n_4](x) = \bot \\ (\emptyset, \emptyset) & \text{if } \overrightarrow{\mathcal{E}}[n_4](x) = \top_\mathcal{D} \end{cases}$$

where $R_0 = \{(\texttt{main}, \texttt{bar}), (\texttt{bar}, \texttt{foo})\}$, $R_1 = \{(\texttt{main}, \texttt{bar}), (\texttt{bar}, \texttt{noop})\}$, $R_2 = R_0 \cup R_1$. It is not hard to see that ϕ is anti-monotonic. In particular, the third case above corresponds to abstracting the conditional as a non-deterministic choice when $\overrightarrow{\mathcal{E}}[n_4](x) = \bot$.

4   Algorithms for the OTFIPA Problem

4.1   A Whole-Program Analysis Algorithm

We can solve the OTFIPA problem by using WPDS as the underlying program analysis engine. Given a supergraph $G = (\mathcal{N}, \to_G, l)$. We can define a WPDS $\mathcal{W}_G = ((P, \Gamma, \Delta), \mathcal{S}, f)$, where there is a unique control location $\star$, i.e., $P = \{\star\}$; the stack alphabet is the set of nodes in G, i.e., $\Gamma = \mathcal{N}$; and Δ is constructed by the follows rules:

- $\langle \star, n \rangle \hookrightarrow \langle \star, n' \rangle \in \Delta$, if there exists an intraprocedural edge $(n, n') \in \to_G$.
- $\langle \star, n \rangle \hookrightarrow \langle \star, e_f\, n' \rangle \in \Delta$, if there exists a call edge $(n, e_f) \in \to_G$, where n' is the return point matching the call site n, and e_f is the entry of the callee f.
- $\langle \star, x_f \rangle \hookrightarrow \langle \star, \epsilon \rangle \in \Delta$, if there exists a return edge $(x_f, n) \in \to_G$ for some n, where x_f is the exit of the callee f.

The environment transformers associated with edges are directly modelled as weights. To form the semiring $\mathcal{S} = (D, \oplus, \otimes, \bar{0}, \bar{1})$, we define the commutative monoid $(D, \oplus)$ to be $(\mathcal{T}, \sqcap, \top)$, $\bar{0}$ is taken as $\top$, $\otimes$ is defined as the reverse of function composition, and $\bar{1}$ is taken as an identity transformer $\lambda e.e$. We denote by $\mathtt{GenWPDS}(G)$ the above procedure that generates a WPDS for G. Given the encoding above, we can conclude with the following fact.

Fact 7. *For each node $n \in \mathcal{N}$, we have that*

$$MOVP[G](n) = WPMC[\mathcal{W}_G](S, T)(\mathcal{E}_0),$$

where $S = \{\langle \star, e_{main} \rangle\}$ and $T = \{\langle \star, n\omega \rangle \mid \omega \in \Gamma^* \}$, respectively.

By Lemma 1 and Fact 7, one may solve the OTFIPA problem as the limit of $\{\eta^j(\emptyset, \emptyset) \mid j \geq 0\}$ by iteratively calling WPDS model checker for solving the MOVP problem on $G_{\downarrow_{\eta^j(\emptyset,\emptyset)}}$ (that is the supergraph for all the methods currently discovered to be involved in the analysis problem up to the jth iteration).

$$
\begin{array}{lll}
\langle \star, e_{main} \rangle \hookrightarrow \langle \star, n_0 \rangle & \langle \star, e_{bar} \rangle \hookrightarrow \langle \star, n_4 \rangle & \\
\langle \star, n_0 \rangle \overset{\tau_0}{\hookrightarrow} \langle \star, n_1 \rangle & \langle \star, n_4 \rangle \overset{\tau_3}{\hookrightarrow} \langle \star, n_5 \rangle & \langle \star, e_{foo} \rangle \hookrightarrow \langle \star, n_9 \rangle \\
\langle \star, n_1 \rangle \overset{\tau_1}{\hookrightarrow} \langle \star, n_2 \rangle & \langle \star, n_5 \rangle \overset{}{\hookrightarrow} \langle \star, e_{foo}\, n_6 \rangle & \langle \star, n_9 \rangle \overset{\tau_4}{\hookrightarrow} \langle \star, x_{foo} \rangle \\
\langle \star, n_2 \rangle \overset{\tau_2}{\hookrightarrow} \langle \star, e_{bar}\, n_3 \rangle & \langle \star, n_6 \rangle \hookrightarrow \langle \star, x_{bar} \rangle & \langle \star, x_{foo} \rangle \overset{\tau_5}{\hookrightarrow} \langle \star, \epsilon \rangle \\
\langle \star, n_3 \rangle \hookrightarrow \langle \star, x_{main} \rangle & \langle \star, x_{bar} \rangle \hookrightarrow \langle \star, \epsilon \rangle &
\end{array}
$$

Fig. 4. WPDS transition rules encoded for the example in Fig. 2 where the transition rules encoded for the method `noop` are omitted.

Example 1. The encoded WPDS transition rules of the code snippet in Fig. 2 is given in Fig. 4 that are grouped method-wise. We denote the system by $\mathcal{W}_{ccp}$. Let $S = \{\langle \star, e_{main} \rangle\}$ and let $T = \{\langle \star, x_{main}\omega \rangle \mid \omega \in \Gamma^* \}$ be the source and target configurations. We have $WPMC[\mathcal{W}_{ccp}](S, T) = \lambda e.e[x \mapsto \bot, y \mapsto 2]$ which computes the dataflow values from the entry to the exit of main, by abstracting the program branchings as non-deterministic choices. By applying the result to the initial environment $\mathcal{E}_0$, we obtain $[x \mapsto \bot, y \mapsto 2]$ which says that x is not a constant and y is a constant at the exit of main. As far as the OTFIPA problem is concerned when the conditional at n_4 is $x < 3$, we obtain a different analysis result $[x \mapsto 2, y \mapsto 2]$ that, both x and y are constants at the exit of main. It is an artificially coined example, yet shows how a OTFIPA problem differs with an ordinary program analysis problem.

4.2   A Sliding-Window Analysis Algorithm

This section presents a sliding-window algorithm for OTFIPA by adapting the inner algorithmic structure of WPDS model checking. As given in Algorithm 1, Line 1 declares those global data structures that are updated through each iteration, where $\overrightarrow{d} \in \mathcal{T}^m$ is the m-tuple of environment transformers for all the program points; M_r is the set of reachable methods and R is the call relation to be discovered by the analysis, respectively, and they are the analysis results of solving the OTFIPA problem upon the algorithm terminates; δ_R records transitions relevant to return values of the callees and δ_S records transitions of summary values propagated from the calling methods, and they are intermediate analysis results cached and reused through the iterations.

Algorithm 1. SwaOTFIPA$(\mathcal{M}, \phi)$: A Sliding Window Algorithm for OTFPA

---

1   $M_r := \emptyset$; $R := \emptyset$; $\overrightarrow{d} := [\overline{0}, \ldots, \overline{0}]$; $\delta_R = \emptyset$; $\delta_S := \emptyset$; $l := \lambda t.\overline{0}$; $iteration := 0$;

2   **foreach** $f \in \mathcal{M}$ **do** $f.checked := 0$;

3   **while** $(not \; \forall f \in M_r. \; f.checked = 1)$ **do**

4     $\overrightarrow{\mathcal{E}} := \overrightarrow{d}(\mathcal{E}_0)$;

5     $(M_r, R) := \phi(\overrightarrow{\mathcal{E}})$;

6     $M_w := \texttt{Schdule}(M_r, iteration + +)$;

7     $(\delta_w, l) := \texttt{SatPost}(\texttt{GenWPDS}(G{\downarrow}_{M_w, R}), \delta_R, l)$;

8     $(\overrightarrow{d}_w, \delta_S, l) := \texttt{GenValue}(\delta_w \cup \delta_S, l)$;

9     $\delta_R := \delta_R \cup \{(q, \epsilon, q') \mid (q, \epsilon, q') \in \delta_w\}$;

10   **foreach** f in M_w **do** $f.checked := 1$;

11     $UpdatedNode := \{\mathbf{n}_i \in \mathcal{N} \mid \exists i \in [1..m]. \overrightarrow{d}[i] \neq \overrightarrow{d}_w[i]\}$;

12   **foreach** $f \in M_r \setminus M_w$ **do**

13   **if** $DepMeth(f) \cap UpdatedNode \neq \emptyset$ **then** $f.checked := 0$;

14     $\overrightarrow{\mathcal{E}}_w := \overrightarrow{d}_w(\mathcal{E}_0)$; $M_r := M_r \cup \phi(\overrightarrow{\mathcal{E}}_w)$;

15     $\overrightarrow{d} := \overrightarrow{d} \oplus \overrightarrow{d}_w$;

16   **return** $(M_r, R, \overrightarrow{d})$;

Definition 8. *Mark variables in Algorithm 1 with superscript iteration numbers to denote their values at the entry of the while loop in that iteration. A function* $Schdule : 2^{\mathcal{M}} \times \mathbb{N} \to 2^F$ *is a* **scheduler** *for Algorithm 1 if, for each* $M \subseteq \mathcal{M}$ *and* $i \in \mathbb{N}$, $Schdule(M, i) \subseteq M_r \cap \{f \in \mathcal{M} \mid \bigcup_{1 \leq j \leq i} f.checked^{(j)} = 0\}$. *A scheduler is* **fair** *if, for each* $i > 0$, *there exists* $f \in M_r^{(i)}$ *with* $f.checked^{(i)} = 0$, *then there exists* $j > i$ *with* $f \in M_w^{(j)}$.

Each method $f \in \mathcal{M}$ is designated with a boolean variable *checked*, and $f.checked = 0$ means that f has to be analyzed in the analysis, and it is not necessarily to be included in the next iteration, otherwise. Initially, each method $f \in \mathcal{M}$ is declared to be unchecked (Line 2). If there remains any method $f \in M_r$ to be analyzed (Line 3), then the while loop will repeat. Line 4 applies $\overrightarrow{d}$ to the initial environment $\mathcal{E}_0$ and returns the current program environments $\overrightarrow{\mathcal{E}}$. Then by applying the contract function to $\overrightarrow{\mathcal{E}}$ at Line 5, the methods and the call relation currently discovered can be obtained. At Line 6, the scheduler (formally given in Definition 8) takes a set of methods M_w from M_r, called a *sliding window*, to be analyzed in the iteration, such that $f.checked = 0$ for each $f \in M_w$.

At Line 7, the algorithm generates a WPDS $\mathcal{W}$ for the supergraph $G_{\downarrow M_w, R}$, and forward saturates δ_R, i.e., to compute $post^*[\mathcal{W}](\delta_R)$ given the mapping l. Here, we denote by `SatPost` the backward saturation procedure conducted on a weighted $\mathcal{P}$-automaton described in Sect. 2.2. After Line 7, we obtain a $\mathcal{P}$-automaton δ_w and the updated mapping l from automata transitions to their weights. Based on the results, we are ready to read out the result $\vec{d}_w$ from the weighted automaton $\delta_w \cup \delta_S$ for solving the MOVP problem for the sliding window, by invoking the subprocedure `GenValue` at Line 8. It also returns the updated summary transitions δ_S along with the updated label l.

At Line 9, δ_R is augmented with those newly-introduced in δ_w that are all resulted from pop transitions. Each method $f \in M_w$ is marked as checked at Line 10. At Line 11, the set $UpdatedNode$ is collected for which the program environments (or environment transformers) are updated by the current analysis. Line 12 to 13 pinpoint the set of methods that would be affected by the new analysis results. Here, $DepMeth(f)$ collects the set of nodes in the super-graph that are source ends of the incoming edges into the nodes in the CFG of f. Line 14 returns the newly-computed environment for the program nodes in the sliding window, returns the updated set of reachable methods, and unify $\vec{d}$ with the newly-updated value $\vec{d}_w$ by extending $\oplus$ to m-tuple element-wise.

Fig. 5. A new forward saturation rule for $r : \langle p, \varepsilon \rangle \hookrightarrow \langle q, \gamma \rangle$ with $l(q, \gamma, p) = f(r)$. Dashed lines and nodes will be added into the automaton in question.

Note that, the program is analyzed method-wise and each sliding window consists of a set of methods. To decouple the interprocedural program analysis into intraprocedural counterparts, we slightly modify the procedure `GenWPDS` such that, for any transition $r : \langle p, \gamma \rangle \hookrightarrow \langle p', \gamma'\gamma'' \rangle$ that encodes some call edge, we split it into two transitions as follows:

$$r_{caller} : \langle p, \gamma \rangle \hookrightarrow \langle q_{p',\gamma'}, \gamma'' \rangle \quad \text{and} \quad r_{callee} : \langle q_{p',\gamma'}, \varepsilon \rangle \hookrightarrow \langle p', \gamma' \rangle$$

and for any transition in the form of $\langle p, \varepsilon \rangle \hookrightarrow \langle q, \gamma \rangle$, we have $\langle p, \omega \rangle \Rightarrow \langle q, \gamma\omega \rangle$ for any $\omega \in \Gamma^*$. The transition r_{caller} belongs to the caller, and r_{callee} belongs to the callee, with $f(r_{caller}) = f(r)$ and $f(r_{callee}) = \bar{1}$. The forward saturation rule for r_{caller} is the same as the one for r_{normal} given in Fig. 1(b), and the new rule for r_{callee} is shown in Fig. 5. Besides, let $\mathcal{A}_S$ be the $\mathcal{P}$-automaton that recognizes the set S of source configurations. We add a set of new transitions into the entry method (i.e., $main$) for encoding the transitions in $\mathcal{A}_S$ in the sliding-window analysis. For each transition (q, γ, q') in $\mathcal{A}_S$, we prepare the new transition $r : \langle q', \varepsilon \rangle \hookrightarrow \langle q, \gamma \rangle$ and add it to the WPDS transitions encoded from the entry method with $f(r) = \bar{1}$.

The subprocedure `GenValue` is given in Fig. 2. It is centered around computing a mapping V from the automata states to weights. Intuitively, $V(q)$ is to store the weight $\mathcal{A}(\mathcal{L}(\mathcal{A}, q))$ (Recall that $\mathcal{A}(C)$ is defined in Sect. 2.2 for a regular set C of configurations). Initially, $V(q_f) = \bar{1}$ for the final state, and $V(q) = \bar{0}$ for any other state q, and the workset ws is set as $\{q_f\}$ (Line 3–4). The while

---

Algorithm 2. GenValue(δ, l): Generating the Analysis Result for OTFIPA

---

1 let $\mathcal{B} = (Q, \Gamma, \delta, P, \{q_f\})$ be the
    $\mathcal{P}$-automaton constructed from δ;
2 let $V : Q \to D$ be a mapping;
3 **foreach** $q \in Q \setminus \{q_f\}$ **do** $V(q) := \bar{0}$;
4 $V(q_f) := \bar{1}; \ ws := \{q_f\}$;
5 **while** $ws \neq \emptyset$ **do**
6   select and remove q from ws;
7   **foreach** $t = (q', \gamma, q) \in \delta$ **do**
8   **if** $q' \notin P$ **then**
9              $new := V(q') \oplus (V(q) \otimes l(t))$;
10   **if** $new \neq V(q')$ **then**
11                 $V(q') := new$;
12                 $ws := ws \cup \{q'\}$;

13 **foreach** $q \in Q \setminus (P \cup \{q_f\})$ **do**
14     $\delta := \delta \cup \{(q, *, q_f)\}$;
15     $l(q, *, q_f) := V(q)$;
16 $\delta_S := \delta \cap (Q \times \{*\} \times \{q_f\})$;
17 $\overrightarrow{d} := [\bar{0}, \ldots, \bar{0}]$;
18 **foreach** $(p, \gamma, q) \in \delta$ $with$ $p \in P$ **do**
19     $\overrightarrow{d}[(p, \gamma)] :=$
        $\overrightarrow{d}[(p, \gamma)] \oplus (V(q) \otimes l(q, \gamma, q'))$
20 **return** $(\overrightarrow{d}, \delta_S, l)$

---

loop (Line 5–12) will repeat if the ws is not empty. For each state in the work-set, the algorithm backward propagates the weights (Line 9) and updates the weights on each state (Line 11) until no more updates are possible. Line 13–14 compute and update the summary transitions. A summary transition $(q, *, q_f)$ can be regarded as an edge for the transitive closure of any path leading from q to q_f in the automaton, and $l(q, *, q_f)$ combines weights along those paths. Line 18–19 finally read out the analysis result for each node in the supergraph. Note that, here we do not assume P is a singleton set, and the algorithm also works for a more general setting when one may take a different encoding of WPDSs.

Theorem 1. *Suppose Algorithm 1 is called with a fair scheduler, and the OTFIPA problem can be encoded into a WPDS model checking problem. Then Algorithm 1 terminates and returns the results of solving the OTFIPA problem.* □

Example 2. In Fig. 6, we illustrate how to conduct a sliding-window analysis for the OTFIPA problem in Fig. 2. The analysis consists in five iterations, and the figures show the weighted $\mathcal{P}$-automaton constructed in each iteration after Line 9 in Algorithm 1, respectively. An edge t in the automaton is labelled with a pair (γ, w) of the alphabet symbol γ and its weight, i.e., $l(t)$. Suppose that a single method is analyzed for each iteration, i.e., the size of a sliding window is set to be $|M_w| = 1$.

    The algorithm starts with analyzing the method *main* (Fig. 6(a)), and generates a summary edge shown in the dashed line. Since $\overrightarrow{d}[\mathbf{n_2}]$ is updated, the method *bar* would be affected. Then it analyzes *bar* in Fig. 6(b). Here, one has to know the program environment at $\mathbf{n_4}$ to judge which conditional branch should be taken. Thanks to caching the summary edge $(q_{*, \mathbf{e}_{bar}}, (*, w_1), q_f)$ that is generated in (a), one can read out the current analysis result $\overrightarrow{d}[\mathbf{n_4}] = [x \mapsto 2, y \mapsto 0]$ in (b), and knows that the method *foo* will be invoked. Since $\overrightarrow{d}[\mathbf{n_5}]$ is updated,

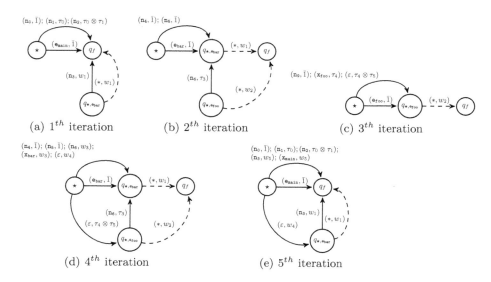

Fig. 6. A sliding-window analysis for the example in Fig. 2, where $w_1 = \tau_0 \otimes \tau_1 \otimes \tau_2$; $w_2 = w_1 \otimes \tau_3$; $w_3 = \tau_3 \otimes \tau_4 \otimes \tau_5$; $w_4 = w_3$; $w_5 = w_1 \otimes w_4$

the method *foo* would be affected and is analyzed in Fig. 6(c). Since $\overrightarrow{d}[\mathbf{x_{foo}}]$ is updated, the calling method *bar* would be affected and is analyzed again in Fig. 6(d), where the pop transition $(\star, (\varepsilon, \tau_4 \otimes \tau_5), q_{\star,\mathbf{e_{foo}}})$ that is newly-generated in (c) is stored into the automaton before the saturation procedure starts. After the analysis at this iteration, $\overrightarrow{d}[\mathbf{x_{bar}}]$ is updated, then its caller *main* would be affected and is analyzed again in Fig. 6(e), where the pop transition $(\star, (\varepsilon, w_4), q_{\star,\mathbf{e_{bar}}})$ that is newly-generated in (d) is stored into the automaton before the saturation procedure starts. Finally, we can read out the analysis result $\overrightarrow{d}[\mathbf{x_{main}}] = [x \mapsto 2, y \mapsto 2]$ at the program exit $\mathbf{x_{main}}$, which tells that both x and y are constants through the program execution.

5   Experiments

We developed a points-to analyser for Java called `mJapot` by instantiating the `SwaOTFIPA` algorithm, following the context-sensitive, field-sensitive, and flow-insensitive Java points-to analysis by WPDS in [6]. In our analysis, we used and extended the WPDS model checker jMoped[2] as the backend analysis engine, for computing forward saturations and reading out analysis results in each sliding window analysis. We use Soot 2.5.0 [11] for preprocessing from Java to Jimple codes which our points-to analyzer was built upon. We evaluate `mJapot` on the Ashes benchmark suite[3] and the DaCapo benchmark suite [1] given in the #App.

---

[2] https://www7.in.tum.de/tools/jmoped/.
[3] http://www.sable.mcgill.ca/ashes.

Table 1. Comparison between the whole-program analysis and the `SwaOTFIPA`-based sliding-window analysis, where _ means time out (>2 h).

# App.	# WPA (s)	# SWA (s)			# Acc.	# Methods		# Stmts
		$k = \infty$	$k = 5000$	$k = 3000$		CHA	mJapot	(mJapot)
soot-c	250	153	140	**139**	1.8	5460	5079	83,936
sablecc-j	616	**194**	209	204	3.2	13,055	9068	144,584
antlr	656	365	390	**348**	1.9	10,728	9133	156,913
pmd	669	**313**	478	332	2.1	12,485	10,406	180,170
hsqldb	350	186	**175**	180	2.0	9983	8394	142,629
xalan	385	**176**	185	193	2.2	9977	8392	141,415
luindex	438	190	**189**	202	2.3	10,596	8961	152,592
lusearch	436	219	**216**	227	2.0	11,190	9580	163,958
eclipse	767	**382**	455	383	2	12,703	10,404	179,539
bloat	_	**4748**	4894	4778	>1.5	12,928	11,090	194,063
jython	_	4633	4857	**2924**	>2.5	14,603	12,033	202,326
chart	_	_	_	_	_	30,831	_	_

column in Table 1. These applications are de facto benchmarks when evaluating Java points-to analysis. We analyze DaCapo benchmark with JDK 1.5, and Ashes benchmarks for which JDK 1.3 suffices. All experiments were performed on a Mac OS X v.10.9.2 with 1.7 GHz Intel Core i7 processor, and 8 GB RAM. A 4 GB RAM is allocated for Java virtual machine.

To measure the performance of points-to analysis, we take *call graph generation* in terms of reachable methods as client analysis. Table 1 shows the preliminary experimental results. The number of reachable methods is given in the "# Methods" column with taking Java libraries into account. The sub-column "CHA" is the result by conducting CHA of Spark in soot-2.5.0. The sub-column "mJapot" gives results computed by our incremental points-to analysis, and the "# Statements" column gives the number of Jimple statements that `mJapot` analyzed. The "# WPA" and "# SWA" columns give the time in seconds of the whole-program analysis and sliding-window analysis, respectively. In the table, k is the size of the sliding window, i.e., the number of the methods analyzed in each iteration.

We set a bound k on the number of methods of each sliding window, shown in the sub-column "$k = \infty$", "$k = 5000$" and "$k = 3000$", respectively, where $k = \infty$ means that we take all methods from the current workset for the analysis. We show the smallest number in bold type. As shown in the "# Acc." column, over all the experiments we performed, `SWA` provided us an average 2X speedup over `WPA`. Note that, it performs almost the same when the size of sliding window changes for most benchmarks expect for "jython", which indicates that the algorithm can be useful for analyses having a limited memory budget. Besides, the number of reachable methods detected by CHA are reduced by 16% using mJapot. Note that mJapot is more efficient than Japot [6] because the backend model checker was changed from the one in C to the one in Java. Since the frontend analyzer is implemented in Java, it reduced the huge disk IO time for exchanging information between the model checker and the analyzer.

6   Conclusion

We studied the OTFIPA problems, for which one could not assume a prior interprocedural control flow of the program, and therefore, the discovery of the program coverage is often mutually dependent on the analysis problem, such as Java points-to analysis. We give a general formalization of the OTFIPA problem, and present a sliding-window algorithm for it. Our algorithm is conducted in a sliding window fashion that iteratively analyzes the program in an arbitrary set of methods, which can be useful for analysis having a tight memory budget. We implemented the algorithm and evaluated it with a context-sensitive points-to analysis for Java. The preliminary empirical study confirmed the effectiveness of our approach.

Acknowledgment. We would like to thank anonymous referees for useful comments. The work has been partially supported by Shanghai Pujiang Program (No. 17PJ1402200), the JSPS KAKENHI Grant-in-Aid for Scientific Research(B) (15H02684) and the JSPS Core-to-Core Program (A. Advanced Research Networks).

References

1. Blackburn, S.M., et al.: The DaCapo benchmarks: Java benchmarking development and analysis. In: Proceedings of the 21st Annual ACM SIGPLAN Conference on Object-Oriented Programing, Systems, Languages, and Applications, OOPSLA 2006, pp. 169–190. ACM, New York (2006)
2. Conway, C.L., Namjoshi, K.S., Dams, D., Edwards, S.A.: Incremental algorithms for inter-procedural analysis of safety properties. In: Etessami, K., Rajamani, S.K. (eds.) CAV 2005. LNCS, vol. 3576, pp. 449–461. Springer, Heidelberg (2005). doi:10.1007/11513988_45
3. Cousot, P., Cousot, R.: Modular static program analysis. In: Horspool, R.N. (ed.) CC 2002. LNCS, vol. 2304, pp. 159–179. Springer, Heidelberg (2002). doi:10.1007/3-540-45937-5_13
4. Esparza, J., Hansel, D., Rossmanith, P., Schwoon, S.: Efficient algorithms for model checking pushdown systems. In: Emerson, E.A., Sistla, A.P. (eds.) CAV 2000. LNCS, vol. 1855, pp. 232–247. Springer, Heidelberg (2000). doi:10.1007/10722167_20. http://dl.acm.org/citation.cfm?id=647769.734087
5. Lal, A., Reps, T.: Improving pushdown system model checking. In: Ball, T., Jones, R.B. (eds.) CAV 2006. LNCS, vol. 4144, pp. 343–357. Springer, Heidelberg (2006). doi:10.1007/11817963_32
6. Li, X., Ogawa, M.: Stacking-based context-sensitive points-to analysis for Java. In: Namjoshi, K., Zeller, A., Ziv, A. (eds.) HVC 2009. LNCS, vol. 6405, pp. 133–149. Springer, Heidelberg (2011). doi:10.1007/978-3-642-19237-1_14

7. Reps, T., Lal, A., Kidd, N.: Program analysis using weighted pushdown systems. In: Arvind, V., Prasad, S. (eds.) FSTTCS 2007. LNCS, vol. 4855, pp. 23–51. Springer, Heidelberg (2007). doi:10.1007/978-3-540-77050-3_4

8. Reps, T., Schwoon, S., Jha, S., Melski, D.: Weighted pushdown systems and their application to interprocedural dataflow analysis. Sci. Comput. Program. **58**(1–2), 206–263 (2005)

9. Sagiv, M., Reps, T., Horwitz, S.: Precise interprocedural dataflow analysis with applications to constant propagation. Theor. Comput. Sci. **167**(1–2), 131–170 (1996). http://dx.doi.org/10.1016/0304-3975(96)00072-2

10. Schwoon, S.: Model-checking pushdown systems. Ph.D. thesis (2002)

11. Vallée-Rai, R., Gagnon, E., Hendren, L., Lam, P., Pominville, P., Sundaresan, V.: Optimizing Java bytecode using the soot framework: is it feasible? In: Watt, D.A. (ed.) CC 2000. LNCS, vol. 1781, pp. 18–34. Springer, Heidelberg (2000). doi:10. 1007/3-540-46423-9_2

12. Yorsh, G., Yahav, E., Chandra, S.: Generating precise and concise procedure summaries. In: Proceedings of the 35th Annual ACM SIGPLAN-SIGACT Symposium on Principles of Programming Languages, POPL 2008, pp. 221–234. ACM, New York (2008). http://doi.acm.org/10.1145/1328438.1328467

Exploring Design Alternatives for RAMP Transactions Through Statistical Model Checking

Si Liu[1], Peter Csaba Ölveczky[1,2]($\boxtimes$), Jatin Ganhotra[3], Indranil Gupta[1], and José Meseguer[1]

[1] University of Illinois, Urbana-Champaign, USA
[2] University of Oslo, Oslo, Norway
peterol@ifi.uio.no
[3] IBM Research, New York, USA

Abstract. Arriving at a mature distributed system design through implementation and experimental validation is a labor-intensive task. This limits the number of design alternatives that can be explored in practice. In this work we use formal modeling with probabilistic rewrite rules and statistical model checking to explore and extend the design space of the RAMP (Read Atomic Multi-Partition) transaction system for large-scale partitioned data stores. Specifically, we formally model in Maude eight RAMP designs, only two of which were previously implemented and evaluated by the RAMP developers; and we analyze their key consistency and performance properties by statistical model checking. Our results: (i) are consistent with the experimental evaluations of the two implemented designs; (ii) are also consistent with conjectures made by the RAMP developers for other unimplemented designs; and (iii) uncover some promising new designs that seem attractive for some applications.

1 Introduction

The Problem. Distributed systems are remarkably hard to get right, both in terms of their correctness and in meeting desired performance requirements. Furthermore, in cloud-based storage systems, correctness and performance properties are intimately intertwined: designers must choose between stronger consistency guarantees and better performance. In this paper we systematically explore the design space of the RAMP (Read Atomic Multi-Partition) transaction system for large-scale partitioned data stores [5,6], which offers high performance but a fairly weak consistency guarantee: read atomicity (RA).

Arriving at a good design of a cloud storage system with both performance and correctness requirements is highly non-trivial. Building such a system is challenging. To improve its performance the only available option is making changes to a large source code base. This is labor-intensive, has a high risk of introducing new bugs, and is not repeatable. In practice, very few design

© Springer International Publishing AG 2017
Z. Duan and L. Ong (Eds.): ICFEM 2017, LNCS 10610, pp. 298–314, 2017.
https://doi.org/10.1007/978-3-319-68690-5_18

alternatives can be explored in this way. In the case of RAMP, three designs were explored in detail, and three more were sketched out but not implemented. Even for the implemented designs, only a limited number of performance parameters were actually evaluated, due to the effort involved in experimental evaluation.

Our Proposed Solution. Since design errors can be orders of magnitude more costly than coding errors, the most cost-effective application of formal methods is during the system design, to maximize the chances of arriving at a good design *before* the system is implemented. In this way, formal methods can bring the power of the *Gedankenexperiment* to system design, greatly increasing the capacity of designers to explore design alternatives and subject them to rigorous analysis before implementation. For cloud storage systems, where correctness and performance are intertwined, the formal method should support: (i) *executability*, so that specifications can serve as *system prototypes*; (ii) *qualitative analysis* of correctness properties with a Yes/Counterexample answer; and (iii) *quantitative analysis* of performance properties.

In previous work [15], we used Maude [9] to develop formal, executable specifications of several RAMP designs, some proposed by the RAMP designers and some by us; and model checked such specifications in Maude to analyze consistency properties, thus meeting above requirements (i)–(ii). In this work we meet requirement (iii) by extending our previous specifications of RAMP designs to *probabilistic rewrite theories* [3] and exploring in depth various performance and consistency properties for eight RAMP designs, six of them never implemented before, through statistical model checking [18,20] using PVESTA [4].

Main Contributions. Our first main contribution is *methodological*. It applies not just to RAMP designs, but more broadly to the design of complex distributed systems with non-trivial correctness and performance requirements. Using RAMP as a case study, we illustrate in detail a formal method by which: (i) designers can easily and quickly develop formal executable models of alternative designs for a system; (ii) system behavior can be specified with *probabilistic rewrite rules*; (iii) alternative system designs can then be thoroughly analyzed through *statistical model checking* to measure and compare them against each other along various performance and correctness dimensions; and, as we show, (iv) a thorough analysis, widely ranging in properties and parameter choices, can be easily achieved, whereas a similar experimental evaluation would require prior implementation and a large effort.

A second key contribution is the uncovering by the above method of *several unimplemented RAMP designs* that seem promising alternatives to the three already implemented. Specifically: (1) the RAMP-F+1PW design sketched in [5] outperforms all others if read atomicity must be guaranteed; and (2) our new RAMP-Faster design provides the best performance in terms of throughput, latency, and strong consistency for workloads with 25%–75% write transactions, while still providing read atomicity for more than 93% of the transactions. Modeling analyses do not provide as much assurance as experimental evaluations; however, our evaluations: (i) are consistent with those in [5,6] for the properties measured experimentally for the implemented designs; (ii) are also consistent with the conjectures by the RAMP designers for their unimplemented designs; and (iii) subject the eight designs to a wider range of properties—and parameter variations for each property—than previous experimental evaluation, thus providing further insights about both the implemented and unimplemented designs.

The rest of the paper is organized as follows. Section 2 gives some background on RAMP, Maude, and statistical model checking with PVESTA. Section 3 presents our new RAMP design alternative, RAMP-Faster. Section 4 shows how we can specify our RAMP designs as probabilistic rewrite theories. Section 5 explains how we can evaluate the performance of the designs for different performance parameters and workloads, and shows the results of these evaluations. Section 6 discusses related work, and Sect. 7 gives some concluding remarks.

2   Preliminaries

2.1   Read-Atomic Multi-Partition (RAMP) Transactions

To deal with ever-increasing amounts of data, distributed databases *partition* their data across multiple servers. Unfortunately, many real-world systems do not provide useful semantics for transactions accessing multiple partitions, since the latency needed to ensure correct multi-partition transactional access is often high. In [5,6], Bailis *et al.* propose a new isolation model, *read atomic* (RA) isolation, and *Read Atomic Multi-Partition* (RAMP) transactions, that together provide efficient multi-partition operations with the following guarantee: either all or none of a transaction's updates are visible to other transactions.

RAMP transactions use metadata and multi-versioning. Metadata is attached to each write, and the reads use this metadata to get the correct version. There are three versions of RAMP, which offer different trade-offs between the size of the metadata and performance: RAMP-Fast, RAMP-Small, and RAMP-Hybrid. This paper focuses on RAMP-Fast and RAMP-Small, which lie at the end points. To guarantee that all partitions perform a transaction successfully or that none do, RAMP performs two-phase writes using the two-phase commit protocol (2PC). 2PC involves two phases: In the *prepare* phase, each timestamped write is sent to its partition, which adds the write to its local database. In the *commit* phase, each such partition updates an index which contains the highest-timestamped committed version of each item stored at the partition. The RAMP algorithms in [5] only deal with read-only and write-only transactions.

RAMP-Fast (abbreviated RAMP-F). In RAMP-Fast, read operations require one round trip time delay (RTT) in the race-free case, and two RTTs in the worst case; writes require two RTTs. Read transactions first fetch the highest-timestamped committed *version* of each requested data item from the corresponding partition, and then decide if they have missed any version that has been prepared but not yet committed. The timestamp and the metadata from each version read induce a mapping from items to timestamps that records the highest-timestamped write for each transaction, appearing in the first-round read set. If the reader has a lower timestamp version than indicated in the mapping for that item, a second-round read will be issued to fetch the missing version. Once all the missing versions have been fetched, the client can return the resulting set of versions, which includes both the first-round reads as well as any missing versions fetched in the second round of reads.

RAMP-Small (abbreviated RAMP-S). RAMP-Small read transactions proceed by first fetching the highest committed *timestamp* of each requested data item; the readers then send the entire set of those timestamps in a second message. The highest-timestamped version that also exists in the received set will be returned to the reader by the corresponding partition. RAMP-Small transactions require two RTTs for reads and writes. RAMP-Small writes only store the transaction timestamp, instead of attaching the entire write set to each write.

Extensions of RAMP. The paper [5] briefly discusses the following extensions and optimizations of the basic RAMP algorithms, but without giving any details:

- *RAMP with one-phase writes* (RAMP-F+1PW and RAMP-S+1PW), where writes only require one *prepare* phase, as the client can execute the *commit* phase asynchronously.
- *RAMP with faster commit detection* (RAMP-F+FC). If a server returns a version with the timestamp fresher than the highest committed version of the item, then the server can mark the version as committed.

In [15] we formalized these extensions in Maude and used Maude model checking to analyze their correctness properties. In [15] we also developed two new RAMP-like designs on our own, where RAMP-F and RAMP-S are executed *without two-phase commit* (denoted RAMP-F¬2PC and RAMP-S¬2PC). This allows interleaving the prepare phase and the commit phase (unlike RAMP where those two phases are strictly ordered).

2.2   Rewriting Logic and Maude

In rewriting logic [17] a concurrent system is specified as a *rewrite theory* $(\Sigma, E \cup A, R)$, where $(\Sigma, E \cup A)$ is a *membership equational logic theory* [9], with Σ an algebraic signature declaring sorts, subsorts, and function symbols, E a set of conditional equations, and A a set of equational axioms. It specifies the system's state space as an algebraic data type. R is a set of *labeled conditional rewrite rules*, specifying the system's local transitions, of the form $[l] : t \longrightarrow t'$ if $cond$, where $cond$ is a condition and l is a label. Such a rule specifies a transition from an instance of t to the corresponding instance of t', provided the condition holds.

Maude [9] is a language and tool for specifying, simulating, and model checking rewrite theories. The distributed state of an object-oriented system is formalized as a *multiset* of objects and messages. An object of class C is modeled as a term $< o : C \mid att_1 : v_1,\ att_2 : v_2,\ \ldots,\ att_n : v_n >$, where o is its object identifier, and where the attributes att_1 to att_n have the current values v_1 to v_n, respectively. Upon receiving a message, an object can change its state and/or send messages to other objects. For example, the rewrite rule (with label 1)

```
rl [1]  :  m(O,z)     < O : C | a1 : x, a2 : O' >
        =>            < O : C | a1 : x + z, a2 : O' >  m'(O',x + z) .
```

defines a transition where an incoming message m, with parameters O and z, is consumed by the target object O of class C, the attribute a1 is updated to x + z, and an outgoing message m'(O',x + z) is generated.

2.3   Statistical Model Checking and PVESTA

Probabilistic distributed systems can be modeled as *probabilistic rewrite theories* [3] with rules of the form

$$[l] : t(\overrightarrow{x}) \longrightarrow t'(\overrightarrow{x}, \overrightarrow{y}) \ \textbf{if} \ cond(\overrightarrow{x}) \ with \ probability \ \overrightarrow{y} := \pi(\overrightarrow{x})$$

where the term t' has additional new variables $\overrightarrow{y}$ disjoint from the variables $\overrightarrow{x}$ in the term t. For a given matching instance of the variables $\overrightarrow{x}$ there can be many ways to instantiate the extra variables $\overrightarrow{y}$. The values of these variables $\overrightarrow{y}$ are drawn/sampled according to the probability distribution $\pi(\overrightarrow{x})$, which depends on the matching instance of $\overrightarrow{x}$.

Statistical model checking [18,20] is an attractive formal approach to analyzing probabilistic systems against temporal logic properties. Instead of offering a yes/no answer, it can verify a property up to a user-specified level of confidence by running Monte-Carlo simulations of the system model. Existing statistical verification techniques assume that the system is purely probabilistic. Using the methodology in [3] we can eliminate nondeterminism in the choice of firing rules. We then use PVESTA [4], a parallelization of the tool VESTA [19], to statistically model check purely probabilistic systems against properties expressed by QUATEX probabilistic temporal logic [3]. The expected value of a QUATEX expression is iteratively evaluated w.r.t. two parameters α and δ provided as input by sampling until the size of $(1-\alpha)100\%$ confidence interval is bounded by δ, where the result of evaluating a formula is a real number.

3   The RAMP-Faster Design

We developed two new RAMP-like designs already in [15]. More recently, we have developed a third design, called RAMP-Faster, which also decouples two-phase commitment. It commits a write transaction in one RTT instead of the two RTTs required by writes in RAMP and RAMP without two-phase commit.

In RAMP-F, upon receiving a **prepare** message, the partition adds the timestamped write to its local database, and upon receiving the **commit** message, updates an index containing the highest-timestamped committed version of each item. Instead, in RAMP-Faster, a partition performs both operations upon receiving the **prepare** message, and hence requires only one RTT. Note that all information required to complete the two operations is provided by the **prepare** message: RAMP-Faster does not need to store more data than RAMP-F.

Since each write in RAMP-Faster needs only one RTT, it should incur lower latency per transaction and provide higher throughput. Since writes are faster, it also seems reasonable to conjecture that there is a higher chance that reads fetch the latest write; this means that RAMP-Faster should provide better consistency[1] than other RAMP designs. Even though RAMP-Faster does not guarantee read atomicity, as the client does not ensure that each partition has received the `prepare` message before issuing the `commit` message, it would be interesting to check whether RAMP-Faster indeed provides better performance, and a high degree of read atomicity, for classes of transactions encountered in practice. If so, RAMP-Faster would be an attractive option for multi-partition transactions where read atomicity, good consistency properties, and low latency are desired.

4   Probabilistic Modeling of RAMP Designs

In [15] we describe how RAMP and its variations can be modeled in Maude for correctness analysis purposes. The state consists of a number of objects modeling partitions $< p_i :$ `Partition` | `versions` : ver, `latestCommit` : $lc >$, with ver the versions of the items in the partition, and lc the timestamp of the latest commit of each item; and objects modeling clients $< c_j :$ `Client` | `transac` : $txns$, `sqn` : n, `pendingOps` : ops, `pendingPrep` : pw, `1stGets` : $1st$, `latest` : $latest >$, with $txns$ a list of transactions the client wants to issue, n the sequence number used to determine timestamps, ops the pending reads/writes, pw the pending writes in the prepare phase, $1st$ the pending first-round reads, and $latest$ a map from each item to its latest committed timestamp.

The models in [15] are untimed, non-probabilistic, and nondeterministic, so that Maude LTL model checking analyzes all possible interleavings. In this paper we are interested in estimating the *performance* (expected latency, percentage of transactions satisfying certain properties, etc.) of our designs. We therefore need to: (i) include time and probabilities in our models, and (ii) eliminate any nondeterminism, so that our models become purely probabilistic and can be subjected to statistical model checking.

To address both of these issues, following [3], we *probabilistically* assign to each message a *delay*. If each rewrite rule is triggered by the arrival of a message, and the delay is sampled probabilistically from a dense/continuous time interval, then the probability that two messages have the same delay is 0. Hence no two actions could happen at the same time, eliminating nondeterminism.

Nodes send messages of the form $[\Delta, rcvr$ `<-` $msg]$, where Δ is the message delay, $rcvr$ the recipient, and msg the message content. When time Δ has elapsed, this message becomes a *ripe* message $\{T, rcvr$ `<-` $msg\}$, where T is the "current global time" (used for analysis purposes only). Such a ripe message must then be consumed by the receiver $rcvr$ before time advances.

---

[1] "Consistency" in such a non-replicated setting is understood as reads reading the "latest writes."

We show an example of how we have transformed the untimed non-proba-bilistic rewrite rules in [15] to the timed and probabilistic setting. All our models are available at https://sites.google.com/site/siliunobi/ramp-smc.

The following rewrites rules describe how a partition reacts when it receives a `commit` message from the client O' with transaction ID `TID`, operation ID `ID`, and timestamp `ts(O',SQN')`. The partition O invokes the function `cmt` to update the latest commit timestamp in the set `latestCommit` with the fresher timestamp of the incoming one and the local one; it then notifies the client to commit the write by sending the message `committed`. The difference between the untimed version (`[...-untimed]`) and the probabilistic version (`[...-prob]`) is that in the latter, the outgoing message `committed` is equipped with a delay D sampled from the probability distribution `distr(...)`.[2]

```
rl [on-receive-commit-untimed] :
   commit(TID, ID, ts(O', SQN')) from O' to O
   < O : Partition | versions : VS, latestCommit : LC >
=>
   < O : Partition | versions : VS, latestCommit : cmt(LC, VS, ts(O', SQN')) >
   committed(TID, ID) from O to O' .

crl [on-receive-commit-prob] :
   {T, O <- commit(TID, ID, ts(O', SQN'), O')}
   < O : Partition | versions: VS, latestCommit: LC, AS >
=>
   < O : Partition | versions: VS, latestCommit: cmt(...), AS >
   [D, O' <- committed(TID, ID, O)]
   with probability D := distr(...) .
```

We next illustrate how easily we can specify different RAMP designs.

The main difference between the different versions of RAMP is how writes are committed; i.e., what happens when a node receives a `prepared` message. In the original RAMP, a client needs to check if all `prepared` messages are received (by checking if `IDS'` is empty) before starting to commit each write operation (using the function `startCommit` to generate all `commit` messages):[3]

```
crl [receive-prepared-with-2PC] :
   {T, O <- prepared(TID, ID, O')}
   < O : Client | pendingPrep: IDS, pendingOps: OI, sqn: SQN, AS >
=>
   < O : Client | pendingPrep: IDS', pendingOps: OI, sqn: SQN, AS >
   (if IDS' == empty then startCommit(TID, OI, SQN, O) else null fi)
if IDS' := delete(ID, IDS) .
```

RAMP-Faster integrates the two phases in writes: upon receiving a `prepare` message, the partition adds the incoming version to its local database VS, and

---

[2] We do not show the variable declarations, but follow the Maude convention that variables are written with (all) capital letters.

[3] The variable AS of sort `AttributeSet` denotes the "other attributes" of the object.

also updates the index containing the highest-timestamped committed version of the item by invoking the function `cmt`:

```
crl [receive-prepare-faster] :
    {T, O <- prepare(TID, ID, X, V, ts(O', SQN), MD, O')}
    < O : Partition | versions: VS,  latestCommit: LC, AS >
 =>
    < O : Partition | versions: VS',
                      latestCommit: cmt(LC, VS', ts(O', SQN)), AS >
    [D, O' <- committed(TID, ID, O)]
 if VS' := (v(X, V, ts(O', SQN), MD), VS)  with probability D := distr(...) .
```

5   Quantitative Analysis of RAMP Designs

The main difference between the RAMP designs in [5] and the three new designs we have proposed is that those in [5] guarantee read atomicity whereas ours do not. On the other hand, we conjecture that (at least) RAMP-Faster may provide not only better performance (throughput, average latency, etc.) but also better "consistency," in the sense of reads more often reading the latest value written.

In this section we compare the performance—along a number of performance parameters, including throughput, average latency, percentage of strongly consistent reads[4]—of the different RAMP designs using statistical model checking.

5.1   Extracting Performance Measures from Executions

For analysis purposes we add an object `< record : Monitor | log:` *log* `>`, which stores crucial information about each transaction, to the state. The *log* is a list of items `record(`*tid, issueTime, commitTime, client, result, 2RoundReads*`)`, with *tid* the transaction's ID, *issueTime* its issue time, *commitTime* its commit time, *client* the identifier of the client issuing the transaction, *result* the values read/written by the transaction, and *2RoundReads* a flag that is `true` if the transaction required second-round reads.

We refine our models by updating the `Monitor` when needed. For example, when a client has received all `committed` messages (`allOpsCommitted(...)`), the monitor records the commit time (`T`) for that transaction. The client then also issues its next transaction, if any:

```
crl [receive-committed] :
    {T, O <- committed(TID, ID, O')}
    < M : Monitor | log: (LOG record(TID, T4, T', O, R, F) LOG') >
    < O : Client | transac: TRS,  sqn: SQN,  pendingOps: OI, AS >
  =>
    if allOpsCommitted(TID, OI')    *** commit a write txn ***
    then < M : Monitor | log: (LOG record(TID, T4, T, O, R, F) LOG') >
```

---

[4] Strong consistency is not evaluated in [5].

```
             < O : Client | transac: TRS, sqn: s SQN, pendingOps: OI', AS >
             (if TRS =/= nil then [0.0, O <- next] else null fi)
   else < M : Monitor | log: (LOG record(TID, T4, T', O, R, F) LOG') >
             < O : Client | transac: TRS, sqn: SQN, pendingOps: OI', AS >   fi
  if OI' := remove(ID,OI) .
```

We can now define a number of functions on (states with) such a monitor that extract different performance parameters from the "system execution log."

Throughput. The function `throughput` computes the number of committed transactions per time unit. `size` computes the length of `LOG`, and `totalRunTime` the time when all transactions are committed (the largest *commitTime* in `LOG`):

```
var C : Config .
op throughput : Config -> Float [frozen] .
eq throughput(< M : Monitor | log: LOG > C) = size(LOG) / totalRunTime(LOG) .
```

Average Latency. The function `avgLatency` computes the average transaction latency by dividing the sum of all transaction latencies by the number of transactions. The first argument of the function `$avgLatency` computes the sum of all transaction latencies (time between the issue time and the commit time of a transaction), and the second argument computes the number of transactions:

```
op avgLatency : Config -> Float [frozen] .
op $avgLatency : Float Float Records -> Float .

eq avgLatency(< M : Monitor | log: LOG > C) = $avgLatency(0.0, 0.0, LOG) .
eq $avgLatency(N1, N2, (record(TID1, T1, T1', O1, R, F) LOG))
 = $avgLatency(N1 + (T1' - T1), N2 + 1.0, LOG) .
eq $avgLatency(N1, N2, nil) = N1 / N2 .
```

Strong Consistency. Strong consistency means that each read transaction returns the value of the last write transaction that occurred before that read transaction. As all transactions from different clients can be totally ordered by their issuing times (stored in `Monitor`), we can define a function that computes the fraction of read-only transactions which satisfy strong consistency: For each read transaction in *log*, it checks if the values read match those of the last write transaction. We refer to our report [14] for the specification of this function.

Read Atomicity. A system provides *read atomic* isolation if it prevents fractured reads, and also prevents transactions from reading uncommitted, aborted, or intermediate data. A transaction T_j exhibits *fractured reads* if transaction T_i writes version x_m and y_n, T_j reads version x_m and version y_k, and $k < n$ [5].

The function `ra` computes the fraction of read transactions which satisfy read atomic isolation. For each read transaction in *log*, it checks if its stored values match those of any write transaction (see [14] for the definition of `ra`).

5.2   Generating Initial States

Statistical model checking verifies a property up to a user-specified level of confidence by running Monte-Carlo simulations from a given initial state. We use an operator `init` to probabilistically generate initial states. init(rtx, wtx, $clients$) generates an initial state with rtx number of read-only transactions, wtx number of write-only transactions, and $clients$ number of clients. We use two partitions and two data items x and y, with each partition storing one data item. The following parts of the initial states are chosen probabilistically by uniform sampling from the given distribution: (i) whether a read-only or write-only transaction is generated next, and (ii) which client is the issuer of the generated transaction. Each transaction consists of two operations, on different data items.

Each PVESTA simulation starts from init(rtx,wtx,$clients$), which rewrites to a *different* initial state in each simulation. `init` is defined as follows:

```
op init : NzNat NzNat NzNat -> Config .
eq init(RTX, WTX, CLIENTS)
 = {0 | nil}  < record : Monitor | log: nil >
   < x : Partition | versions: (v(x, 0, null, empty)),
                     latestCommit: (x |-> ts(0,0)) >
   < y : Partition | versions: (v(y, 0, null, empty)),
                     latestCommit: (y |-> ts(0,0)) >
   generateClientsAndTranses(RTX, WTX, CLIENTS) .
```

When generating clients and transactions, we first generate the clients; then we generate the next transaction and assign it probabilistically to some client:

```
op generateClientsAndTranses : NzNat NzNat NzNat -> Config .
op genCT : Nat Nat Nat NzNat Config -> Config .

eq generateClientsAndTranses(RTX, WTX, CLIENTS)
 = genCT(RTX, WTX, CLIENTS, CLIENTS, null) .

*** first generate clients and add then to the last parameter:
eq genCT(RTX, WTX, s CLIENTS, CLIENTS2, C)
 = genCT(RTX, WTX, CLIENTS, CLIENTS2, C
       < s CLIENTS : Client | transac: nil, sqn: 1, pendingOps: empty,
                     pendingPrep: empty, 1stGets: empty,
                     latest: empty, result: nil > {d,s CLIENTS <- start}) .
```

When all clients have been generated, we generate transactions one by one, and assign each one to a client. The following probabilistic rule treats the case when the number of clients left to generate is 0, and the number of read (s RTX ($=$ RTX $+1$)) and write (s WTX) transactions to generate both are greater than 0:

```
crl [genTrans] :
   genCT(s RTX, s WTX, 0, CLIENTS, C)
```

```
=>
    if R-OR-W < s RTX      *** new read transaction
    then genCT(RTX, s WTX, O, CLIENTS, addReadTrans(CLIENT + 1, C))
    else genCT(s RTX, WTX, O, CLIENTS, addWriteTrans(CLIENT + 1, C)) fi
    with probability R-OR-W := sampleUniWithInt(s RTX + s WTX) /\
                      CLIENT := sampleUniWithInt(CLIENTS) .
```

This rule first probabilistically decides whether the next transaction is a read or a write transaction. Since the probability of picking a read transaction should be $\frac{\#readsLeft}{\#txnLeft}$, it uniformly picks a value R-OR-W from $[0, \ldots, \#txnLeft - 1]$ (the number of transactions left to generate is s RTX + s WTX) using the expression sampleUniWithInt(s RTX + s WTX). If the value picked is in $[0, \ldots, \#readsLeft - 1]$ (< s RTX), we generate a new read transaction next (then branch); otherwise we generate a new write transaction (else branch). But which client should issue the transaction? The clients have identities 1, 2, $\ldots$, n, where n is the number of clients (CLIENTS). The expression sampleUniWithInt(CLIENTS) + 1 (i.e., CLIENT + 1) gives us the client, sampled uniformly from $[1, \ldots, n]$.

When there are no more transactions or clients left to generate, genCT returns the generated client objects (each with a list of transactions to issue):

```
eq genCT(O, O, O, CLIENTS, C) = C .
```

We refer to the technical report [14] for the full definition of genCT.

5.3   Statistical Model Checking Results

This section shows the result of the PVESTA statistical model checking from the initial states in Sect. 5.2 to compare all eight RAMP versions w.r.t. the performance and consistency measures defined in Sect. 5.1.

We use the lognormal distribution for message delay with mean $\mu = 0.0$ and standard deviation $\sigma = 1.0$ [8]. All properties are computed with a 99% confidence level of size at most 0.01 (Sect. 2.3). We could not find the distribution used in [5] for message delays, so we use those in [13]. Due to the large number of simulations needed to obtain 99% statistical confidence, our analyses consider a limited number of data items (2), operations per transaction (2), clients (up to 50), and transactions (up to 400). We consider not only the 95%/5% read/write proportion workloads in [5], but also explore how the RAMP designs behave for different read/write proportions (with 25 clients).

Throughput. Figure 1 shows the results of analyzing throughput against the number of concurrent clients (left) and percentage of read transactions (right).[5]

For the original RAMP designs, under a 95% read proportion, as the number of clients increases, both RAMP-F and RAMP-S's throughput increases, and RAMP-F provides higher throughput than RAMP-S. As the read proportion increases, RAMP-F's throughput increases, while RAMP-S's throughput keeps

---

[5] Larger versions of our figures can be found in the report [14].

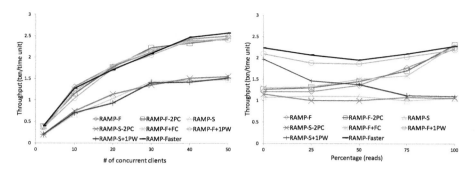

Fig. 1. Throughput under varying client and read load.

nearly constant; and RAMP-F also outperforms RAMP-S in throughput. These observations are consistent with the experimental results in [5].

There are no conjectures in [5] about the throughput of the designs that were only sketched there. We observe that, unlike other RAMP-F-like algorithms, whose throughput increases as read activities increase, RAMP-F+1PW's throughput keeps high with all reads/writes. As the right plot shows, when there are more writes, RAMP-F+1PW and RAMP-Faster perform better than other RAMP-F-like designs. This happens because RAMP-F requires two RTTs for a write, RAMP-F+1PW needs only one RTT and RAMP-Faster, our proposed design, performs commit when the `prepare` message is received.

RAMP-F¬2PC and RAMP-S¬2PC are not competitive with RAMP-F and RAMP-S, respectively. The reason is that, although they sacrifice 2PC, they still need to commit each write operation before committing the write transaction, which brings no apparent improvement in throughput.

Average Latency. Figure 2 shows the average transaction latency as the number of concurrent clients (left) and the proportion of read transactions (right) increases. Under a 95% read proportion, as the number of clients increases, the

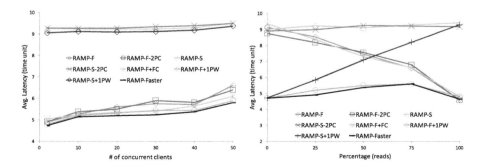

Fig. 2. Average transaction latency under varying client and read load.

RAMP-F versions' average latency increases slightly, and the RAMP-S versions are almost twice as slow as the RAMP-F versions. And although RAMP-F+1PW and RAMP-S+1PW as expected have lower latencies than RAMP-F and RAMP-S, respectively, the differences are surprisingly small. In the same way, removing 2PC does not seem to help much. Although the differences are small, RAMP-Faster is the fastest, followed by RAMP-F with one-phase writes.

Figure 2(right) shows that RAMP-F+1PW and RAMP-Faster significantly outperform the other algorithms when the read proportion is between 25% and 75%.

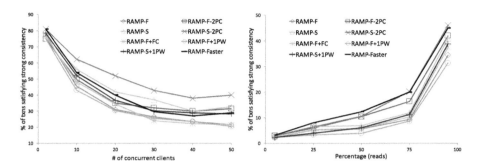

Fig. 3. Probability of satisfying strong consistency under varying client and read load.

Strong Consistency. Figure 3 shows the percentage of transactions satisfying strong consistency under varying number of clients and read/write proportions.

In all RAMP designs, the probability of satisfying strong consistency decreases as the number of clients increases, since there are more races between reads and writes, which decreases the probability of reading the preceding write.

It is natural that the percentage of transactions satisfying strong consistency increases as the reads increase: the chance of reading the latest preceding write should increase when writes are few and far between.

RAMP-S-like designs provide stronger consistency than their RAMP-F counterparts, since they always use second-round reads, which can increase the chance of reading the latest write. The only exception seems to be that RAMP-Faster outperforms all the other RAMP designs for 25–75% read workloads. The reason is that RAMP-Faster only requires one RTT for a write to commit, which increases a read transaction's chance to fetch the latest write.

Read Atomicity. Figure 4 shows the percentage of transactions satisfying read atomicity. As it should be, all designs in [5] satisfy read atomic isolation. Our own design alternatives provide 92–100% read atomicity under all scenarios.

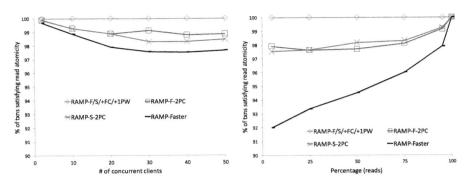

Fig. 4. Probability of satisfying read atomicity under varying client and read load.

Summary. Our results are consistent with the experimental evaluations in [5]. For example: the throughput of both RAMP-F and RAMP-S increases with the number of concurrent clients, and RAMP-F provides higher throughput than RAMP-S; the latency also increases with the number of concurrent clients (minimally for RAMP-S). Our results are also consistent with the conjectures about the sketched designs in [5], which were never experimentally validated. For example: RAMP-F+FC and RAMP-F+1PW have lower latency than RAMP-F. We also see that RAMP-F+1PW provides better performance than RAMP-F+FC.

We can also evaluate our own designs. It seems that RAMP without 2PC does not improve the performance of RAMP. On the other hand, our new design RAMP-Faster provides the smallest average latency, strongest consistency, and highest throughput among all RAMP designs for 25%–75% read transactions, while providing more than 92% read atomicity even for write-heavy workloads. RAMP-Faster could therefore be useful for, e.g., recommender systems (products on Amazon, etc.), where read atomicity is not an absolute requirement (if a user recommends 3 products, the system can do useful things even if a transaction only sees two recommendations), and which tend to be somewhat write-heavy.

The actual values might differ between the experiments in [5] and our statistical analysis, due to factors like hard-to-match experimental configurations, processing delay at client/partition side, and different distributions of item accesses. The important observation is that the *relative performance* measured between design alternatives is similar in both methods.

It is also worth remarking we only use two data items, while the experiments in [5] use up to thousands. This implies that we "stress" the algorithms much more, since there are much fewer potential clashes between small transactions (typically with four operations) in a 1000-data-object setting than between our two-operation transactions on two data objects.

All RAMP models in this paper consist of around 4000 lines of code *altogether*. Computing the probabilities for strong consistency took around 15 hours (worst-case), and for other metrics around 8 hours (worst-case) on a 2.7 GHz Intel Core i5 CPU with 8 GB memory. Each point in the plots represents the average of three statistical model checking results.

6 Related Work

Maude for Distributed Storage Systems. In [15] we formalized RAMP and some extensions, and used Maude model checking to analyze their correctness properties. In contrast, this paper focuses on analyzing the performance of RAMP and its variations using statistical model checking with PVESTA. In addition, this paper also introduces our most promising RAMP design: RAMP-Faster. The papers [11,12] use Maude to formalize and analyze Google's Megastore and a proposed extension. Those papers also focus on correctness analysis, although they present some *ad hoc* performance estimation using randomized Real-Time Maude simulations. In contrast to the methodology in this paper, such ad hoc simulations cannot give any measure of statistical confidence in the results. The papers [13,16] describe how the Cassandra key/value store has been analyzed both for correctness and performance using Maude and PVESTA. The main differences between [13,16] and this paper are: Cassandra only supports single read and write operations, whereas RAMP supports transactions, which also implies that the consistency levels to analyze in RAMP are more complex; in this paper we also propose a promising variation of the system (RAMP-Faster).

Model-Based Performance Estimation of Distributed Storage Systems. Despite the importance of distributed transactional databases, we are not aware of work on (formal) model-based performance analysis of such systems. One reason might be that the most popular formal tools supporting probabilistic/statistical model checking are mainly based on automata (e.g., Uppaal SMC [2] and Prism [1]), and it is probably very hard, or impossible, to model state-of-the-art distributed transactional systems using timed/probabilistic automata. Another reason might be that NoSQL stores became mainstream earlier than globally-distributed transactional databases and gathered attention from the research community to work on model-based performance analysis of NoSQL stores [7,10].

7 Concluding Remarks

We have explored eight design alternatives for RAMP transactions following a general methodology based on formal modeling with probabilistic rewrite rules and analyzing performance using statistical model checking. Substantial knowledge about both implemented and unimplemented RAMP designs has thus been gained. This knowledge can help find the best match between a given RAMP version and a class of applications. For example, we now know how the different designs behave not just for read-intensive workloads, but understand their behavior across the entire spectrum from read-intensive to write-intensive tasks.

   Our work has also shown that it is possible to use this methodology to identify promising new design alternatives for given classes of applications relatively easily *before* they are implemented. This of course does not replace the need for implementation and experimental validation, but it allows us to focus implementation and validation efforts where they are most likely to pay off.

Much work remains ahead. A natural next step is to confirm experimentally our findings about some of the RAMP unimplemented designs by implementing and evaluating them to demonstrate their practical advantages. On the other hand, since our methodology can be applied not just to RAMP, but to many other distributed systems, more case studies like the one presented here should be developed to both improve the methodology, and to demonstrate its effectiveness.

Acknowledgments. We thank the anonymous reviewers for helpful comments on a previous version of this paper. This work was partially supported by NSF CNS 1409416, AFOSR/AFRL FA8750-11-2-0084, and NSF CNS 1319527.

References

1. PRISM. http://www.prismmodelchecker.org/
2. Uppaal SMC. http://people.cs.aau.dk/adavid/smc/
3. Agha, G.A., Meseguer, J., Sen, K.: PMaude: rewrite-based specification language for probabilistic object systems. Electr. Notes Theor. Comput. Sci. **153**(2), 213–239 (2006)
4. AlTurki, M., Meseguer, J.: PVESTA: a parallel statistical model checking and quantitative analysis tool. In: Corradini, A., Klin, B., Cîrstea, C. (eds.) CALCO 2011. LNCS, vol. 6859, pp. 386–392. Springer, Heidelberg (2011). doi:10.1007/978-3-642-22944-2_28
5. Bailis, P., Fekete, A., Ghodsi, A., Hellerstein, J.M., Stoica, I.: Scalable atomic visibility with RAMP transactions. ACM Trans. Database Syst. **41**(3) (2016)
6. Bailis, P., Fekete, A., Hellerstein, J.M., Ghodsi, A., Stoica, I.: Scalable atomic visibility with RAMP transactions. In: Proceedings SIGMOD 2014. ACM (2014)
7. Barbierato, E., Gribaudo, M., Iacono, M.: Performance evaluation of NoSQL big-data applications using multi-formalism models. Future Gen. Comp. Syst. **37**, 345–353 (2014)
8. Benson, T., Akella, A., Maltz, D.A.: Network traffic characteristics of data centers in the wild. In: IMC, pp. 267–280 (2010)
9. Clavel, M., Durán, F., Eker, S., Lincoln, P., Martí-Oliet, N., Meseguer, J., Talcott, C.L.: All About Maude. LNCS, vol. 4350. Springer, Heidelberg (2007)
10. Gandini, A., Gribaudo, M., Knottenbelt, W.J., Osman, R., Piazzolla, P.: Performance evaluation of NoSQL databases. In: Horváth, A., Wolter, K. (eds.) EPEW 2014. LNCS, vol. 8721, pp. 16–29. Springer, Cham (2014). doi:10.1007/978-3-319-10885-8_2
11. Grov, J., Ölveczky, P.C.: Formal modeling and analysis of Google's Megastore in Real-Time Maude. In: Iida, S., Meseguer, J., Ogata, K. (eds.) Specification, Algebra, and Software. LNCS, vol. 8373, pp. 494–519. Springer, Heidelberg (2014). doi:10.1007/978-3-642-54624-2_25
12. Grov, J., Ölveczky, P.C.: Increasing consistency in multi-site data stores: Megastore-CGC and its formal analysis. In: Giannakopoulou, D., Salaün, G. (eds.) SEFM 2014. LNCS, vol. 8702, pp. 159–174. Springer, Cham (2014). doi:10.1007/978-3-319-10431-7_12
13. Liu, S., Ganhotra, J., Rahman, M., Nguyen, S., Gupta, I., Meseguer, J.: Quantitative analysis of consistency in NoSQL key-value stores. Leibniz Trans. Embed. Syst. **4**(1), 031–0326 (2017)

14. Liu, S., Ölveczky, P.C., Ganhotra, J., Gupta, I., Meseguer, J.: Exploring design alternatives for RAMP transactions through statistical model checking. Technical report (2017). https://sites.google.com/site/siliunobi/ramp-smc
15. Liu, S., Ölveczky, P.C., Rahman, M.R., Ganhotra, J., Gupta, I., Meseguer, J.: Formal modeling and analysis of RAMP transaction systems. In: SAC. ACM (2016)
16. Liu, S., Rahman, M.R., Skeirik, S., Gupta, I., Meseguer, J.: Formal modeling and analysis of Cassandra in Maude. In: Merz, S., Pang, J. (eds.) ICFEM 2014. LNCS, vol. 8829, pp. 332–347. Springer, Cham (2014). doi:10.1007/978-3-319-11737-9_22
17. Meseguer, J.: Conditional rewriting logic as a unified model of concurrency. Theoret. Comput. Sci. **96**(1), 73–155 (1992)
18. Sen, K., Viswanathan, M., Agha, G.: On statistical model checking of stochastic systems. In: Etessami, K., Rajamani, S.K. (eds.) CAV 2005. LNCS, vol. 3576, pp. 266–280. Springer, Heidelberg (2005). doi:10.1007/11513988_26
19. Sen, K., Viswanathan, M., Agha, G.A.: VESTA: a statistical model-checker and analyzer for probabilistic systems. In: QEST 2005. IEEE Computer Society (2005)
20. Younes, H.L.S., Simmons, R.G.: Statistical probabilistic model checking with a focus on time-bounded properties. Inf. Comput. **204**(9), 1368–1409 (2006)

An Improved Android Collusion Attack Detection Method Based on Program Slicing

Yunhao Liu[1,3], Xiaohong Li[1,3(✉)], Zhiyong Feng[2], and Jianye Hao[2]

[1] School of Computer Science and Technology,
Tianjin University, Tianjin 300350, China
{yunhaoliu,xiaohongli}@tju.edu.cn
[2] School of Computer Software, Tianjin University, Tianjin 300350, China
{zyfeng,jianye.hao}@tju.edu.cn
[3] Tianjin Key Laboratory of Advanced Networking (TANK),
School of Computer Science and Technology,
Tianjin University, Tianjin 300350, China

Abstract. Android applications can leak sensitive information through collusion, which gives the smartphone users a great security risk. We propose an Android collusion attack detection method based on control flow and data flow analysis. This method gives analysis of data propagation between different applications firstly. And then, a multi-apps program slice model based on both data and control flow are given. Last, the privacy data leakage paths of multi-apps are computed by reaching-definition analysis. Meanwhile, the criterions of mobile device information leakage edge are redefined according to the correlation of mobile devices. Based on the above principle, we implemented an Android collusion attack sensitive information leakage detection tools called CollusionDetector. Case study is carried out for typical collusion attack scenarios and it can obtain better results than existing tools and methods. Experiments show that the analysis of control flow can more accurately find the path of privacy propagation, and more effectively to identify collusion attacks.

Keywords: Android Collusion Attack · Privacy leakage · Taint analysis · Program slicing

1 Introduction

Many privacy leak attacks are accomplished by multi-apps collaboration [7,18], and these kinds of attacks are called "Android Collusion Attack" [25]. Different from traditional privacy leak attack which rely on single app, Android Collusion Attack often lunched by at least two apps, called *source app* and *sink app*. *Source app* often responsible for acquiring sensitive data and passing it to the *sink app* while the *sink app* sends the sensitive data out of the device. Each collusion app has different task and corresponding required permissions, this can easily circumvent those detection methods which focus on single app [3,9,12].

© Springer International Publishing AG 2017
Z. Duan and L. Ong (Eds.): ICFEM 2017, LNCS 10610, pp. 315–331, 2017.
https://doi.org/10.1007/978-3-319-68690-5_19

To address this problem, Android Collusion Attack [1, 26] are widely studied. A complete survey on those topics can be found in [19]. In particular, Epicc [18] and IccTA [17] makes precisely static taint analysis on single app and it can find propagation of privacy cross apps with the help of ApkCombiner [16]. Amandroid [23] and SCanDroid [11] can do static taint analysis for a group of app and detect the privacy leak caused by multi-apps.

Nevertheless, the propagation of sensitive information depends not only on the assignment between variables, but also on the control statements such as branch and loop. According to [4], most exist methods and tools ignore the detection of taint propagation based on control flow and this can cause some malicious app could not be found. Moreover, to prevent missing report, current approaches regard the privacy has leaked when they are sent out of an app. But actually, when sensitive information is sent out of an application does not mean it is certain to be sent out of the device. In other words, existing rules can cause false positives. Therefore, detecting Android Collusion Attack accurately and protecting the smartphone users' privacy data have become urgent needs.

In this paper, we design and build CollusionDetector – an improved detection framework for Android Collusion Attack. Static taint analysis method is adopted to build the taint propagation path between multi-apps and find the app group which can leak privacy. In order to solve the above problems, an improved taint checking algorithm both focus on control flow and data flow taint analysis is proposed. Meanwhile, Android APIs are re-classified to re-define the boundaries of sensitive information. For a set of Apk file to be detected, the interaction information between apps from resource and manifest files of apps are extracted. Together with each app's control flow graph, an inter-app control flow graph (IACFG) can be built. Last, privacy leakage and the collusion app groups can be detected by the improved taint analysis. CollusionDetector can detect the collusion attack which use the control flow to propagate sensitive information and improve the accuracy of detection.

Challenges also exist. The real-world applications may have complex business logic, which can lead to a large control flow graph. When building an inter-app control flow graph and perform taint analysis over it, the efficiency will be low. To this end, we extract *suspicious paths* from each Apk's control flow graph and build *inter-app suspicious paths* according to interaction information between apps before doing taint analysis. *Suspicious path* is a statement path in control flow graph which has the ability to send any information out of device whether the information is sensitive. Obviously, the size of *inter-app suspicious paths* is much smaller than IACFG and it narrowed the scope of our taint analysis.

To verify our approach, we implement three groups of Android Collusion Attack examples as test cases. Each group includes several Android apps that can collaborate to leak privacy and these three groups stands for different kinds of Android Collusion Attack. CollusionDetector perform analysis on test cases with other existing tool at the same time and our methods can detect all test cases successfully. Moreover, CollusionDetector is used to detect real-world privacy leak and the result is as good as other tools. These illustrate that our work has improvement on the detection of Android Collusion Attack.

The rest of the paper is organized as follow. Section 2 describe the attack scenario of Android Collusion Attack. Section 3 shows each step of our work. Case study and results are presented in Sect. 4 and the limitations of this work are presented in Sect. 5. We conclude the paper in Sect. 6.

2 Attack Scenario

According to the Android security report [15] published by Nokia Threat Intelligence Laboratories in 2016, Android Collusion Attack is widely found in real-world Android apps. As Fig. 1 shows, the attacker repackage malicious code into an benign app's Apk. Because Android allow user to install app from any source, these repackaged apps are easily installed by users from some insecure third party sources. After the user install these collusion apps, malicious programs execute in the background, and the functionality of these apps do not appear abnormal, so it is hard for users to find that privacy information has been leaked.

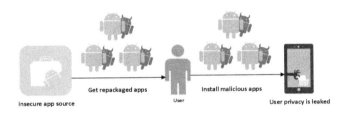

Fig. 1. Android Collusion Attack in real-world

When collusion apps are installed on the device, they begin to work together to leak the user privacy. Figure 2 shows an example of two apps that cooperate to leak user privacy. First, *ContactReader* obtains the contacts information and send it to *InfoSender*. And then, *InfoSender* send these sensitive data to attackers server.

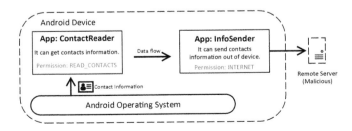

Fig. 2. Mechanism of Android Collusion Attack

Actually, the above-mentioned attack scenario can be easily detect out by current approaches. To circumvent current approaches, attackers change the way of data propagation. Many prior works [5,6,10,13,21] have mentioned the limitation of detecting control dependence attack and the threat of these attack is large. In [4], there are two types of control flow based data propagation, called *Simple Encoding* and *File Length*.

2.1   Simple Encoding

Simple Encoding is an effective way to spoof current taint checking mechanisms for Android app. In Fig. 3, *ASCII_Table* is the string which contains all character in ASCII table and *Tainted* is the privacy data. Attackers often build a new string called *unTainted* to save the sensitive data. Secondly, they traverse each character (called *taintedChar*) in *Tainted* and compare *taintedChar* with every character in *ASCII_Table*. And *curValue* is used to store the current character when traverse the *ASCII_Table*. Lastly, if the two variables, *taintedChar* and *curValue*, are equal in this matching process, the *curValue* will be appended to *unTainted*.

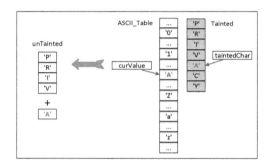

Fig. 3. If the values in *curValue* and *taintedChar* are equal, copy *curValue* to *unTainted*

Simple Encoding prevent direct assignments from *Tainted* to *unTainted*, thus *unTainted* will not regarded as an tainted object according to current taint checking mechanisms. Figure 4 shows Simple Encoding can spoof these tradition mechanisms successfully and send the privacy out of device. The red variables and lines are taint propagation path detected by traditional taint checking mechanism.

2.2   File Length

Traditional taint checking mechanisms can be circumvented by File Length with ease. A file should be regarded as an untainted object only if there is no sensitive data is written into it. And the metadata of the file can store information such as length of file. In Fig. 5, attackers encode the taint data firstly, because file

```
String Tainted = source(); //sensitive data
String ASCII_Table;
String unTainted = new String();

for(int i = 0; i < Tainted.length(); ++i)
{
    char taintedChar = Tainted.charAt(i);
    for(int j = 0; j < ASCII_Table.length(); ++j)
    {
        char curValue = ASCII_Table.charAt(j);
        if(taintedChar == curValue)
        {
            unTainted += curValue;
        }
    }
}
SendToRemoteServer(unTainted);
```

Fig. 4. Current taint checking mechanisms track taints according to assignments

length can only store integer types of information. The sensitive data code is an integer and its value is N. Secondly, random data is written, one byte at the time, to a file until its size equals N. Last, attackers get the file length N and decode the number into a string.

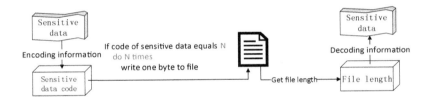

Fig. 5. File length example

In this way, the file is not a tainted object and its size can be read as an untainted variable. As shown in Fig. 6, the sensitive data can circumvents traditional taint checking mechanism and successfully leaked by using File Length.

```
String Sensitive_data = source();
int Sensitive_data_code = Encode(Sensitive_data);
File file = new File();
for(int i = 0; i < Sensitive_data_code; ++i)
{
    writeOneByte(file);
}
int fileLength = file.length();
String Untainted_Sensitive_data = Decode(fileLength);
SendToRemoteServer(Untainted_Sensitive_data);
```

Fig. 6. Taint tracking is ended at the condition statement and privacy is leaked

Traditional taint checking mechanism neglect to analysis the control flow based taint propagation. This can cause huge security risks to the users' privacy. While one could extend the prior works to address this limitation, we use a different approach (outlined in Sect. 1) which we describe in more details in the following sections.

3   CollusionDetector

As Fig. 7 shows, CollusionDetector contains four phases. First, the control flow graph (CFG) for each Apk will be built and the IAC information will be extracted from each Apk's manifest file. On this basis, the *suspicious paths* for each Apk can be sliced out from corresponding CFG. In the third step, *inter-app suspicious paths* can be made up of several *suspicious paths* according to the IAC information in Phase 1. Last, the privacy propagation can be detected on *inter-app suspicious paths* by doing improved taint analysis thus the collusion apps can be found.

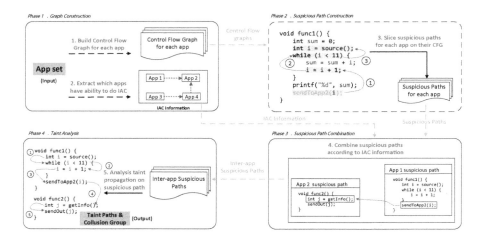

Fig. 7. Overview of CollusionDetector

3.1   Analysing Each APK

According to the Phase 1 in Fig. 7, there are two tasks in this step, one is obtaining each input APK's CFG. Another task is parsing each APK's manifest file to find out the IAC information which determine the destination of data flow.

The CFG for each app can be obtained with the help of a static analysis framework for Android app, called FlowDroid. This framework can analyze Android app accurately and provides a series of API to allow user to obtain each Apk's CFG by programming. The IAC information need to be extracted

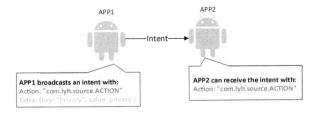

Fig. 8. Inter-app communication with specific attribute value

by analysing *AndroidManifest.xml*. This file lists all components which an app owned and the configuration of these components. One of the configuration for components is *Intent-Filter*, which can determine the component can receive Intent objects with specific attribute. In addition, We need to extract the attribute values for each of the Intent objects being sent. As shown in Fig. 8, Attackers predefined same *Action* attribute values to ensure two collusion app can communicate.

An IAC information is defined as a 5-tuple $I = (\sigma, \alpha, \delta, \rho)$ and IAC information for an app set is a collection of I. For one IAC information, σ stands for an app and α is the *Action* property of the Intent object to which the application is sent. If the app can not send any Intent object, the element α can be null. δ represents the property value of the Intent object that the application can receive and ρ means which applications can receive Intent objects whose property value is α. If the app can not receive any Intent object, its δ can be null.

Algorithm 1. IAC Matching Algorithm

   Input : Initial collection: $InfoSet_I$
   Output: Complete $InfoSet_I$
1 some description;
2 $Size \leftarrow The\ number\ of\ I\ in\ InfoSet_I$;
3 **for** $i = 0$ to $Size$ **do**
4 | $tmp_1 \leftarrow the\ ith\ element\ of\ InfoSet_I$;
5 | **for** $j = i$ to $Size$ **do**
6 | | $tmp_2 \leftarrow the\ jth\ element\ of\ InfoSet_I$;
7 | | **if** $tmp_1 \cdot \alpha == tmp_2 \cdot \delta$ **then**
8 | | | $tmp_2 \cdot \rho \leftarrow tmp_1 \cdot \alpha$;
9 | | **end**
10 | **end**
11 **end**

To compute IAC information for an app set, we use $InfoSet_I$ to express all I for each app. In the initial state, the value of σ, α and δ for each I should be determined because the analysis for every app. The last element ρ should be calculate by Algorithm 1.

3.2   Computing Suspicious Paths

To reduce the scope of taint analysis, *Suspicious Paths* should be built firstly. It is a code execution path that can cause information leakage, whether or not the information is sensitive. In this step, static program slicing is used to obtain each Apk's suspicious paths. There has been a numbers of approaches about program slicing [14,20,24] and computing dependency graph is used in this work. Next subsections describe the process of computing suspicious paths.

Slicing Criterion. To slice *Suspicious Paths* for each APK, the first challenge is to define slicing criterion. *Suspicious Paths* focus on sending data out an app, therefore, only those functions which can send information out should be defined as slicing criterion. In Android, there are many APIs can be points of interest such as *sendBrodcast()*, *sendTextMessage()*, *Log.i()* and the objects or variables sent by them.

Computing Dependency Graph. In order to compute program slice, Data Dependency Graph (DDG) and Control Dependency Graph (CDG) are necessary. CDG can be built according to CFG easily. In a CFG, statements a and b has a control dependency if the outcome of a determines whether b should be executed or not. Meanwhile, Reaching-Definition analysis is used for the calculation of DDG. In a program, a variable's value depends on its definition and it can be used to define other variables. A definition of variable is defined as a two tuple, $Def = (S, V)$. In Def, V is the variable and S is the statement where V is defined lately. During the execution of the program, the value of each variable may be change, new definitions can be generated, old definitions can be killed, and some definitions may remain unchanged. Therefore, we use collection Gen_S to save the $Defs$ are newly created in statement S. Meanwhile, collection $Kill_S$ is defined for storing the $Defs$ which are redefined. For each statement S, there are two set, called $InSet_S$ and $OutSet_S$, to describe the definitions of status before and after the execution of statement S. Equation (1) shows that $InSet_S$ is the union set of definitions after execute all predecessors of S, $pred[S]$. While Eq. (2) shows that $OutSet_S$ adds the newly created definitions and delete the killed definitions after execute S.

$$InSet_S = \bigcup_{p \in pred[S]} OutSet_p \tag{1}$$

$$OutSet_S = Gen_S \cup (InSet_S - Kill_S) \tag{2}$$

Reaching Definition Analysis is to compute each statement's $InSet$ and $OutSet$, Algorithm 2 shows a worklist algorithm. The input of this algorithm is each Apk's CFG with all $InSet_S$ and $OutSet_S$ are initialized to empty. When Algorithm start running, it loads all statements V into worklist and repeats the calculation shown by Eqs. (1) and (2), until $InSet_S$ and $OutSet_S$ for all elements are no longer changed. During the calculation, if the $OutSet_S$ is different from the old one after analyzed the statement S, it means that the $InSet$ of successors of S ($succ[S]$) is change. Hence, the successors of S should be recalculated and $succ[S]$ are send back to worklist again.

Algorithm 2. Reaching Definition Analysis WorkList Algorithm

    Input   : control flow graph $G = (V, E)$
    Output: $\forall S \in V, InSet_S$
1 some description;
2 **foreach** S *in* V **do**
3     $InSet_S \leftarrow \emptyset$;
4     $OutSet_S \leftarrow \emptyset$;
5 **end**
6 $WorkList \leftarrow V$;
7 **while** $WorkList \neq \emptyset$ **do**
8     $S \leftarrow$ Pop one basic block from WorkList;
9     $OldOutSet_S \leftarrow OutSet_S$;
10    $InSet_S \leftarrow \bigcup\limits_{p \in pred[S]} OutSet_p$;
11    $OutSet_S = Gen_S \cup (InSet_S - Kill_S)$;
12   **if** $OutSet_S \neq OldOutSet_S$ **then**
13       $WorkList \leftarrow WorkList \cup succ[S]$;
14   **end**
15 **end**

After getting the reaching definitions for each statement (e.g., $InSet_S$), which statements have data dependency relationship with slicing criterion is clear. Moreover, the data dependency graph (DDG) can be worked out and we can obtain the program slice by performing union operation on DDG and CDG.

3.3 Combination of Suspicious Paths

When we do inter-app static analysis, the cross app dataflow should be considered. In previous step, we obtain each APK's suspicious paths and these statements sequences are probably send data to another app. That is to say, suspicious belongs to different APKs can be combine.

In the first section, we get the connection points between dataflow through the analyze for AndroidManifest.xml and source files. Here, we combine cross app suspicious paths according to IAC information. Like the example in Sect. 3.1, Fig. 9 shows that two suspicious paths can be combined into an inter-app suspicious path.

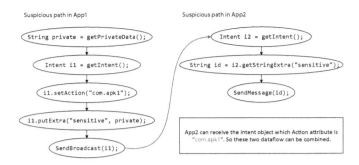

Fig. 9. The Combination of Dataflow

3.4   Improved Inter-App Taint Analysis

This step consists doing taint analysis on inter-app suspicious paths. In other words, we need to determine whether these suspicious paths will leak sensitive information. Firstly, the *source* and *sink* functions should be ascertained. In this work, *source* is the method which can get the private data (e.g., getLatitude(), getDeviceId()) or receive information from other apps (e.g., getIntent()). Different from prior works, the definition of *sink* is the method which can send the sensitive information out of the device (e.g., sendTextMessage(), Log.i()). In most current approaches, the method which can send data out of an app is also regarded as *sink*. However, the privacy data is safe until it flow out of device.

Meanwhile, to address the problem in Sect. 2, we propose a new static taint checking mechanism for Android app. To be able to explain our taint propagation rules in detail we declare the following formalization descriptions and helper functions.

To describe the whole program, we use 2-tuple $P =< B, E >$. B is the set of all basic blocks in the program and E is the edge between basic blocks. B is defined as 3-tuple $B =< R, L, V >$. R is the variable in stack area and it can be a basic type variable or a reference of an object. L is the memory location of object in heap area. V is the value of variable.

Besides the descriptions above, there are several helper functions to ensure our precise model for program.

$arrayElem(x)$ can determines whether a variable belongs to an array. The parameter x is the input variable and the return value will be true when x is an array's element.

$source()$ returns sensitive data and the variable which is assigned by this function is tainted variable.

A tainted path T is defined for the basic blocks which contain tainted variables and at the beginning it holds that $T \leftarrow \emptyset$. Tainted access paths are added to the set whenever the analysis reaches a call to a source, or when processing a statement that propagates an existing taint to a new memory location. Algorithm 3 shows the taint checking for each basic block in a program.

Algorithm 3. Improved Taint Analysis Algorithm

Input   : One *BasicBlock*, Current tainted variable set T
Output: Tainted variable set T
1 some description;
2 **if** *BasicBlock is like* $Var_x = Var_y$ **then**
3 | **if** $\forall Var_y \in T$ **then**
4 | | $T \cup \{Var_x\}$;
5 | **end**
6 | **if** $Var_y \notin T \wedge \neg arrayElem(Var_x$ **then**
7 | | $T \setminus \{Var_x\}$;
8 | **end**
9 | **if** $x \in source()$ **then**
10 | | $T \cup \{Var_x\}$;
11 | **end**
12 | **if** $\forall Var_y \in T$ **then**
13 | | $T \cup \{Var_x\}$;
14 | **end**
15 **end**
16 **if** *The type of BasicBlock is* $Var_x = new\, Object()$ **then**
17 | **if** $Var_x \in T | \neg arrayElem(Var_x)$ **then**
18 | | $T \setminus \{Var_x\}$;
19 | **end**
20 **end**
21 **if** *The type of BasicBlock is branch structure* **then**
22 | **if** $Var_y \in condition \wedge Var_y \in T$ **then**
23 | | $T \cup \{Var_x\}$;
24 | **end**
25 **end**

For an assignment basic block with the structure $Var_x = Var_y$, we should consider that whether variable Var_x is an element of an array first. To ensure the accuracy of analysis if any element in the array is tainted, the array is polluted. According to this rule, if Var_x is a polluted variable, the array is tainted. Even if Var_x is assigned a new *ObjectLocation*, as long as it belongs to the array, it must be contaminated.

Another case is the *new* basic block which creates a fresh object (e.g., $Var_x = new\,\,\, Object()$), whether the Var_x was tainted before, the variable Var_x should be removed from T.

When the basic block is a branch structure like *if(condition) then statements* or *loop(condition) do statements*, the principle of this rule is that the variable Var_x are tainted if its condition expression contains tainted variables.

According to the above algorithm, the implementation of taint analysis on inter-app suspicious paths by doing Reaching Definition analysis. The difference is that the point of interest is the *source*, because the inter-app suspicious paths have the ability to send any information out. When a variable defined by *source()* can reach the *sink()* and can be send by sink method, this path is a taint path.

4   Case Study

In this section, we firstly introduce the implementation of CollusionDetector and some examples of Android collusion attack. Then, we use our approach to analysis these attack examples to show the effectiveness of this work. Third, in order to show the improvement of this work in the Android collusion attack detection, we use three other different tools to detect the above attack examples and compare all results.

4.1   Implementation

There are already many outstanding static analysis tools for Android application, such as SCanDroid, FlowDroid and Amandroid. Although most of these tools are open source software, there is a lack of interface specification and programming guide. Only FlowDroid provides detailed develop guidance, therefore, our approach is implemented based on it. FlowDroid can be deployed in a development environment as several java projects and it provides us a lot of useful programming interfaces and a dataflow analysis framework. To prove the effectiveness of our approach, we implement several groups of Android Collusion Attack examples and these examples will be analyzed by CollusionDetector and other tools as test cases.

Implementation of CollusionDetector. Because we need programming interfaces offered by FlowDroid, the related FlowDroid projects should be imported into our IDE. We finished this work under the guidance of the Wiki of FlowDroid [2] and build the programming framework successfully according to the guide book [8]. The input of CollusionDetector is am APK file set and the out put is:

- Whether there is collusion attack in the input APK file set?
- If collusion attack exists, which apps are collaborated to leak privacy?
- The conjunction point of each collusion group.
- The control flow graph which can identifies taint paths.

Implementation of Android Collusion Attack Example. We implement three groups of Android Collusion Attack examples, including one group of traditional collusion attack and two groups of collusion attack based on control flow (Simple Encoding and File Length). As shown in Table 1, the example of traditional collusion attack has two applications, one application called "ContactReader" is responsible for obtaining the contacts information which stored in the mobile phone and send them to another application. Another one called "InfoSender" is responsible for receiving contacts information and transmitting the information through the network to attackers remote server. The difference between examples of collusion attack based on control flow and traditional collusion attack is that they exploit the vulnerabilities of prior works to ensure the tainted data to be "washed up".

Table 1. Different kinds of Android Collusion Attack examples

Type	Name	Permission
Traditional collusion attack	ContactReader.apk	CONTACT_INFO
	InfoSender.apk	INTERNET
Simple encoding	SEContactReader.apk	CONTACT_INFO
	SEInfoSender.apk	INTERNET
File length	FLContactReader.apk	CONTACT_INFO
	FLInfoSender.apk	INTERNET

4.2   Evaluation

After the implementation, we use CollusionDetector to analysis test cases to demonstrate the effectiveness of our approach. And then, in order to compare the results of different methods, we use four existing Android privacy leak detection methods and CollusionDetector to analysis the above three groups of test cases. Our evaluation addresses the following research questions:

RQ1. Can CollusionDetector find Android Collusion Attack?
RQ2. How does CollusionDetector compare with existing tools?
RQ3. Can CollusionDetector detect real-world leak?

All the experiments discussed in this subsection are performed on a Core i5 CPU running with Java8.

RQ1: Experimental Results on Test Cases. We use CollusionDetector to analysis three groups of test cases separately and the results of detection are shown in command line. If there exist collusion attack in the test case, we will map out the taint propagation path in the form of dot graph. FlowDroid provides programming interfaces which can draw dot graph according to control flow graph and we make further development to show taint path as dot graph.

RQ2: Comparison with Existing Tools. In this research question, we compare CollusionDetector with four existing tools: FlowDroid, IccTA and Scan-Droid. There are three issues we focus on:

– Can each tool or method find privacy leak in single app?
– Can each tool or method find traditional collusion attack in Android?
– Can each tool or method find File Length and Simple Encoding?

In Table 2, ⊙ means that this tool can detect privacy leak in a test case and ⊕ has the opposite meaning. ✓ stands for the tool can detect the inter-app taint propagation and find out the collusion apps. We can find that FlowDroid and IccTA can not analysis multiple APK files. They can detect the privacy

Table 2. All methods and tools detection results

Test cases		Methods			
Type	Name	FlowDroid	IccTA	SCanDroid	Collusion- detector
Traditional android	ContactReader	⊙	⊙	⊙ ✓	⊙ ✓
collusion attack	InfoSender	⊙	⊙	⊙ ✓	⊙ ✓
Simple	SEContactReader	⊗	⊙	⊗	⊙ ✓
encoding	SEInfoSender	⊗	⊙	⊗	⊙ ✓
File length	FLContactReader	⊗	⊙	⊗	⊙ ✓
	FLInfoSender	⊗	⊙	⊗	⊙ ✓

leak in single app without control flow based taint propagation successfully. Furthermore, IccTA can detect the taint propagation with Simple Encoding and File Length. ScanDroid can successfully find out the traditional collusion attack but it is failed in File Length and Simple Encoding.

According to the results, the reason why ScanDroid is failed in detect test case group "Simple Encoding" and "File Length" is same with FlowDroid: it can not detect the privacy leak in single app without control flow based taint propagation. We find a defect through the analysis of taint checking mechanism in FlowDroid: they only focus on taint propagation like $Y \leftarrow X_{tainted}$ but ignore the taint propagation based on control flow. Because it is difficult to analyze the source code for all existing tools, we hypothesized that SCanDroid use similar taint propagation rules as FlowDroid but IccTA use a different one. And that is why they can not track taint data propagate with Simple Encoding and File Length methods.

RQ3: Can CollusionDetector Detect Real-World Leak? We use CollusionDetector and tools which have been used in RQ3 to detect real-world leak. The test cases are apps which downloaded from Google Play and we found several apps have privacy leakage behavior.

In Table 3, the ⊙, ⊗ and has the same meaning in Table 2. According to the result, all methods can detect privacy leak except a failure caused by SCanDroid. Limited by the size of the app collection, none of the tools found the collusion

Table 3. My caption

Test cases	Methods and tools				
Package name	FlowDroid	Epicc	IccTA	SCanDroid	Collusion-detector
com.zsdevapp.renyu	⊙	⊙	⊙	⊙	⊙
com.y.lovefamily	⊙	⊙	⊙	⊙	⊙
com.gotonyu.android.PhotoShare	⊙	⊙ ✓	⊙ ✓	⊙	⊙ ✓
com.liars.lineLearn	⊙	⊙	⊙	⊗	⊙

app group based on control flow. While it still prove that CollusionDetector can detect privacy leak in real-world.

5   Limitations

At the moment, CollusionDetector resolves traditional collusion attack and two kinds of collusion attack depend on control flow. Currently, our approach still can not do taint analysis for native code, web applications (e.g., applications developed using PhoneGap [22]) and dynamic linking library in Android. Although CollusionDetector can avoid the false negative caused by control flow based taint propagation, however, we neglect the false positive cause by analyzing conditional statements. The principle of taint checking mechanism is simple and some complicated situations are overlooked.

6   Conclusion

It is proved that this method can detect the Android Collusion Attacks which contain the control flow based pollution, and we also use this method to detect the general privacy leakage applications. Compared with the detection accuracy of existing Android privacy leak detection methods, the result of the proposed method is approximately the same as them. It can be proved that this method can effectively detect the privacy leakage behavior of Android applications, and can also detect collusion attacks that have control flow based pollution. Limited by the size of the application set to be detected, we haven't found privacy leaks based on control flow. We will detect more real-world apps; Moreover, we are prepared to repackage malicious code which can leak privacy data based on control flow into some real-world apps, and then use our tools to detect them.

Acknowledgments. The authors are grateful to the anonymous reviews for their insightful comments, and that will have a great significance to our future work. This work is supported by Tianjin Key Laboratory of Advanced Networking (TANK), School of Computer Science and Technology, Tianjin University, Tianjin China300350. This work has partially been sponsored by the National Science Foundation of China (No. 61572349, 61272106).

References

1. Davi, L., Dmitrienko, A., Sadeghi, A.-R., Winandy, M.: Privilege escalation attacks on android. In: Burmester, M., Tsudik, G., Magliveras, S., Ilić, I. (eds.) ISC 2010. LNCS, vol. 6531, pp. 346–360. Springer, Heidelberg (2011). doi:10.1007/978-3-642-18178-8_30
2. Arzt, S., Rasthofer, S., Fritz, C., Bodden, E., Bartel, A., Klein, J., Traon, Y.L., Octeau, D., Mcdaniel, P.: How to run flowdroid. https://github.com/secure-software-engineering/soot-infoflow-android/wiki

3. Arzt, S., Rasthofer, S., Fritz, C., Bodden, E., Bartel, A., Klein, J., Traon, Y.L., Octeau, D., Mcdaniel, P.: Flowdroid: precise context, flow, field, object-sensitive and lifecycle-aware taint analysis for android apps. ACM Sigplan Not. **49**(6), 259–269 (2014)

4. Babil, G.S., Mehani, O., Boreli, R., Kaafar, M.A.: On the effectiveness of dynamic taint analysis for protecting against private information leaks on android-based devices. In: International Conference on Security and Cryptography, pp. 1–8 (2013)

5. Cavallaro, L., Saxena, P., Sekar, R.: Anti-taint-analysis: practical evasion techniques against information flow based malware defense. Stony Brook University (2007)

6. Cavallaro, L., Saxena, P., Sekar, R.: On the limits of information flow techniques for malware analysis and containment. In: Zamboni, D. (ed.) DIMVA 2008. LNCS, vol. 5137, pp. 143–163. Springer, Heidelberg (2008). doi:10.1007/978-3-540-70542-0_8

7. Chin, E., Felt, A.P., Greenwood, K., Wagner, D.: Analyzing inter-application communication in android. Plant Soil **269**(1–2), 309–320 (2011)

8. Einarsson, A., Nielsen, J.D.: A survivor's guide to java program analysis with soot. Notes from Department of Computer Science (2008)

9. Enck, W., Ongtang, M., McDaniel, P.: On lightweight mobile phone application certification (2009)

10. Enck, W., Gilbert, P., Chun, B.G., Cox, L.P., Jung, J., Mcdaniel, P., Sheth, A.N.: Taintdroid: an information-flow tracking system for realtime privacy monitoring on smartphones. In: USENIX Conference on Operating Systems Design and Implementation, pp. 99–106 (2010)

11. Fuchs, A.P., Chaudhuri, A., Foster, J.S.: Scandroid: automated security certification of android applications (2009)

12. Gibler, C., Crussell, J., Erickson, J., Chen, H.: AndroidLeaks: automatically detecting potential privacy leaks in android applications on a large scale. In: Katzenbeisser, S., Weippl, E., Camp, L.J., Volkamer, M., Reiter, M., Zhang, X. (eds.) Trust 2012. LNCS, vol. 7344, pp. 291–307. Springer, Heidelberg (2012). doi:10.1007/978-3-642-30921-2_17

13. Graa, M., Cuppens-Boulahia, N., Cuppens, F., Cavalli, A.: Detecting control flow in smarphones: combining static and dynamic analyses. In: Xiang, Y., Lopez, J., Kuo, C.-C.J., Zhou, W. (eds.) CSS 2012. LNCS, vol. 7672, pp. 33–47. Springer, Heidelberg (2012). doi:10.1007/978-3-642-35362-8_4

14. Horwitz, S., Reps, T., Binkley, D.: Interprocedural slicing using dependence graphs. In: ACM Sigplan 1988 Conference on Programming Language Design and Implementation, pp. 35–46 (1988)

15. Nokia Threat Intelligence Laboratories: Nokia threat intelligence report. http://resources.alcatel-lucent.com/asset/200492

16. Li, L., Bartel, A., Bissyandé, T.F., Klein, J., Traon, Y.L.: ApkCombiner: combining multiple android apps to support inter-app analysis. In: Federrath, H., Gollmann, D. (eds.) SEC 2015. IAICT, vol. 455, pp. 513–527. Springer, Cham (2015). doi:10.1007/978-3-319-18467-8_34

17. Li, L., Bartel, A., Klein, J., Traon, Y.L., Arzt, S., Rasthofer, S., Bodden, E., Octeau, D., Mcdaniel, P.: IccTA: detecting inter-component privacy leaks in android apps. In: IEEE/ACM IEEE International Conference on Software Engineering, pp. 280–291 (2015)

18. Octeau, D., Mcdaniel, P., Jha, S., Bartel, A., Bodden, E., Klein, J., Traon, Y.L.: Effective inter-component communication mapping in android with epicc: an essential step towards holistic security analysis. In: USENIX Conference on Security, pp. 543–558 (2013)

19. Rashidi, B., Fung, C.: A survey of android security threats and defenses. J. Wirel. Mob. Netw. Ubiquitous Comput. Dependable Appl. **6**, 3–35 (2015)
20. Reps, T., Horwitz, S., Sagiv, M.: Precise interprocedural dataflow analysis via graph reachability. In: POPL 1995, vol. 167(96), pp. 49–61 (1995). Lecture Notes in Computer Science
21. Schwartz, E.J., Avgerinos, T., Brumley, D.: All you ever wanted to know about dynamic taint analysis and forward symbolic execution (but might have been afraid to ask). In: Security and Privacy, pp. 317–331 (2010)
22. Wargo, J.M.: Phonegap Essentials: Building Cross-platform Mobile Apps. Pearson Schweiz AG, Zug (2012)
23. Wei, F., Roy, S., Ou, X., Robby.: Amandroid: a precise and general inter-component data flow analysis framework for security vetting of android apps. In: ACM SIGSAC Conference on Computer and Communications Security, pp. 1329–1341 (2014)
24. Weiser, M.: Program slicing. In: International Conference on Software Engineering, pp. 439–449 (1981)
25. Wu, L., Grace, M., Zhou, Y., Wu, C., Jiang, X.: The impact of vendor customizations on android security. In: ACM SIGSAC Conference on Computer and Communications Security, pp. 623–634 (2013)
26. Xing, L., Pan, X., Wang, R., Yuan, K., Wang, X.F.: Upgrading your android, elevating my malware: privilege escalation through mobile OS updating. In: IEEE Symposium on Security and Privacy, pp. 393–408 (2014)

Parameterized Complexity of Resilience Decision for Database Debugging

Dongjing Miao[1(✉)] and Zhipeng Cai[1,2]

[1] Department of Computer Science, Georgia State University,
Atlanta, GA 30303, USA
dmiao1@student.gsu.edu
[2] College of Computer Science and Technology, Harbin Engineering University,
Harbin 150001, China

Abstract. Resilience decision problem plays a fundamental and important role in database debugging, query explanation and error tracing. Resilience decision problem is defined on a database d, given a boolean query q which is *true* initially, and a constant $k > 0$, it is to decide if there is a fact set *res* of size no more than k such that query q becomes false after deleting all facts in *res*. Previous results showed it is NP-hard in many cases. However, we revisit this decision problem, in the light of the recent parametric refinement of complexity theory, provide some new results including negative and positive ones. We show that, there are still some cases intractable if only consider the query size or variable numbers as the parameter.

Keywords: Resilience · Database · Parameterized complexity

1 Introduction

Resilience of a given query q with respect to a database d is defined as a set *res* of facts in d, whose deletion will result in a boolean query getting *false* which initially is *true*. Formally, its decision problem can be defined as follow,

Definition 1 (RES decision problem [1]). *Given a database d, a fixed natural constant k^{res}, and a boolean query q where $q(d)$ is true, it is to decide if there is subset res of d such that (i) $|res| < k^{res}$;(ii) $q(d - res)$ is false.*

This is a fundamental decision problem in the study of database debugging, cleansing, error tracing, query result explanation and many other applications, since the most important and common task in these applications is to answer the question that given some partial result T of a query q on a database d, why the result T happens here (*why-provenance*), by means of different definitions on *why*, so that we can locate these witnesses of T inside d if we found it.

This work is partly supported by the National Science Foundation (NSF) under grant NOs 1252292, 1741277 and 1704287, and the NSF of China under contract 61502116 and 61370084.

Z. Duan and L. Ong (Eds.): ICFEM 2017, LNCS 10610, pp. 332–344, 2017.
https://doi.org/10.1007/978-3-319-68690-5_20

Typically, there are two ways to define '*why*', as identified in [2], way of source side effect free (ssef) and way of view side effect free (vsef). Intuitively, given a source database d, a query q, its materialized view $q(d)$ and a testing result $t \subseteq q(d)$, the former is to find an r of size k such that $q(d-r) \subseteq q(d) - t$, while the later is to find an r such that $q(d-r) = q(d) - t$.

Example 1. Let's visit an example of resilience in tracing error in *database debugging process.* Consider a file management database of a company including two relations, Dept(dept, user) records department each user belongs to, and Author(dept, file) records files that each group has the authority to access. There is also a view defined as a conjunctive query (Selection-Projection-Join) "show the file and users have authority to access it"

$$q(x, z) :- dept(y, x), author(y, z)$$

Dept :	dept	user		Author :	dept	file		$q(x, z):$	user	file
	d1	u1			d1	f1			u1	f1
	d2	u2			d2	f2			u2	f2
	d2	u3			d2	f3			u2	f3
									u3	f2
									u3	f3

First, we want to check if there is a single fact in the database whose absence will result in the query result $q(u2, z)$ becoming *false*, that are two alternative set of facts in source data d,

(*a*) fact '(d1, u1)' in Dept,
(*b*) fact '(d1, f1)' in Author,

In this case, either of the two facts is the *res* for query $q(u2, z)$.
But consider another suspicious query result '$q(u2, z)$', we also want to check if there is a single fact whose absence will make it *false*, then potential candidates are

(*a*) fact '(d2, u2)' in Dept,
(*b*) fact '(d2, f2)' in Author.
(*b*) fact '(d2, f3)' in Author.

Here, '(*a*)' is the resilience we want, because it will make the query *false*. However, either of '(d2, f2)' and '(d2, f3)' is not able to make the query *false*.

Therefore, we regard the resilience '(d2, u2)' as a suspicious error or explanation candidate of the query result $q(u2, z)$.

As shown by Freire et al. 2015 [1], RES can be reduced polynomially to the two above decision problems (ssef and vsef). This is to say that, RES is a more fundamental part of the two problems, the lower bound of RES will also

Table 1. Polynomial tractable cases of source side effect free decision problem

Complexity	Citations	Query fragment
PTime	Buneman et al. 2002 [2]	Conjunctive query without *projection* and *self-join*
	Cong et al. 2012 [3]	Conjunctive query with *key-preserving*
	Freire et al. 2015 [1]	Conjunctive query without *triad* and *self-join*
		Conjunctive query without *fd-induced triad* and *self-join*

Table 2. Hard cases of source side effect free decision problem

Complexity	Citations	Query fragment
NP-complete	Buneman et al. 2002 [2]	Conjunctive query without *selection*
	Cong et al. 2012 [3]	Conjunctive query without *key-preserving*
	Freire et al. 2015 [1]	Conjunctive query containing *triad*
		Conjunctive query containing *fd-induced triad*
co-W[1]-complete	**This paper**	Conjunctive query parameterized by query size or #variables
		Positive query parameterized by query size
co-W[SAT]-hard		Positive query parameterized by #variables
co-W[t]-hard		First-order query parameterized by query size
co-W[P]-hard		First-order query parameterized by #variables

dominate the lower bound of the two problems. Therefore, we want to revisit the complexity of RES in this paper.

The previous studies provides the pictures of the classical complexity results of these two ways, we summary these as Tables 1, 2, 3 and 4. In total, the previous results is mainly on the classical computational complexity. In this case, the complexity of query languages proposed by Chandra and Merlin has been next to expressibility one of the main preoccupations of database theory ever since two four decades ago. It has been noted rather early that, when considering the complexity of evaluating a query on an instance, one has to distinguish between two kinds of complexity metric: *Data complexity* is the complexity of evaluating a query on a database instance, when the query is fixed, and we express the complexity as a function of the size of the database. The other one is

Table 3. Polynomial tractable cases of view side effect free decision problem

Complexity	Citations	query fragment
PTime	Buneman et al. 2002 [2]	Conjunctive query without *projection* and *self-join*
	Cong et al.2012 [3]	Conjunctive query with *key-preserving*
	Kimefeld et al. 2012 [4]	Conjunctive query with *head-domination* and without *self-join*
		Conjunctive query with *fd-head-domination* and without *self-join*
FPT	Kimefeld et al. 2013 [5]	Conjunctive query with *level-k head-domination* and without *self-join* under k view deletions
		Conjunctive query with *head-domination* and without *self-join* under c view deletions

called combined complexity, considers both the query and the database instance as input variables; The *combined complexity* of a query language is typically one exponential higher than data complexity. Of the two, data complexity is somehow regarded as more meaningful and relevant to database if only consider query evaluation.

There have been some complexity results on the view side effect free problem [2–7]. On the data complexity of deletion propagation, Kimelfeld et al. [6] showed the dichotomy '*head domination*' for every conjunctive query without self-join, deletion propagation is either APX-hard or solvable (in polynomial time) by the unidimensional algorithm. For functional dependency restricted version, it is radically different from the case without functional dependency (FD), they also showed the dichotomy '*fd-head domination*' [4]. For multiple or group deletion [5], they especially showed the trichotomy for group deletion a more general case including *level-k head domination* and so on; On the combined complexity of deletion propagation, [3,7] showed the variety results for different combination of relational algebraic operators. At the same time, [8] studied the functional dependency restricted version deletion propagation problem and showed the tractable and intractable results on both data and combined complexity aspects.

Besides research on view side effect, there are previous works on source side effect decision problem [1–3,7], they show some complexity results on the source side-effect problem on both data and combined complexity. Basically, Freire et al. show that for RES studied in this paper is PTime if q is a conjunctive query without structure of *triad*, NP-complete otherwise. They also extend the dichotomy condition '*triad*' into a more general one '*fd-induced triad*' for case with presence of functional dependencies. All the previous results in Tables 1, 2, 3 and 4 showed that, for most cases, the deletion propagation is hard due to the huge searching space.

Table 4. Hard cases of view side effect free decision problem

Complexity	Citations	query fragment
NPcomplete	Buneman et al. 2002 [2]	Conjunctive query without *selection*
	Cong et al. 2012 [3]	Conjunctive query *non-key-preserving*
	Kimefeld et al. 2012 [4]	Conjunctive query without *head-domination*
		Conjunctive query without *fd-head-domination*
	Kimefeld et al. 2013 [5]	Optimal version of Conjunctive query with *level k head-domination* under *k* view deletions
NP(k)-complete	Miao et al. 2016 [8]	Conjunctive query under *bounded source deletions*
Σ_2^P-complete	Miao et al. 2016 [8]	Conjunctive query

Additionally, a related topic the view update problem in database has been extensively investigated for more than three decades in the database community, which is stated as follows: given a desired update to a database view, what update should be performed towards the source tables to reflect this update to the view [9–13]. Generally, previous works mainly focus on identifying the condition to make the update unique, and studying under the identified condition how to carry out the update. These works are only effective for very restricted circumstances where there is a unique update Δd to a source database d that will cause a specified update to the view $q(d)$. In practice, an update to d is not always unique. Therefore, an alternative is to find a minimum update to d resulting in the specified update to $q(d)$, which is a more practical task of view propagation.

However, two metrics of complexity seem to be not completely reasonable and appropriate. To the hard one, combined complexity is so restrictive that it takes both input queries and databases in account equally, no matter the relation between the size of query q and the size of database d. Generally, the query size is always much smaller than the size of database, say $q \sim o(d)$. Due to this usual case, study of the complexity of query languages mostly concentrates on data complexity. But as argued in [14], "*polynomial time in the context of data* *complexity means time $O(d^q)$, and in fact the known algorithms that place the above-mentioned languages in PTime have precisely such a running time. Besides this, in the case of fix-point logic, this is known to be inherently unavoidable. Even if $q < n$, it is not reasonable to consider q fixed, because even for small values of q, a running time of n^q hardly qualifies as tractable, especially in view of the fact that n is typically huge."*

Therefore, in this paper, we want to re-examine the parameterized complexity of RES decision problem, since the running time in which n is not raised to a power that depends on q, that is, the dependence on n is only permitted as the n^c where c is a constant independent of the query, and this is the typical paradigm of the parameterized complexity theory.

2   Preparation

We first give a necessary introduction of the *Parameterized complexity theory* [15]. The concerns of parameterized complexity theory are (decision) problems with two or more inputs. Formally, considering languages $L \subseteq \Sigma^* \times \Sigma^*$. We refer to such languages as parameterized languages. If (x, k) is in a parameterized language L, we call k the parameter. Usually the parameter will be provided as a positive integer, no matter it is a graph or algebraic structure, the domain of the parameter is usually identified as the natural numbers $\mathbb{N}$ and hence consider languages $L \subseteq \Sigma^* \times \mathbb{N}$. For a fixed k, we call $L_k = \{(x, k) | (x, k) \in L\}$ as the k-th slice of L. Such as in this paper, input of the RES is

$$\left(\langle q, d \rangle, \langle k^{res}, k^{q/v} \rangle \right)$$

where the parameter k is the size of query q or the number of variables in the query q.

Fixed parameter tractable (f.p.t). The main idea of the parameterized complexity theory is to study languages that are tractable "by the slice." A problem is said to be tractable by the slice meant that there is a constant c, independent of parameter k, such that for all k, membership of L_k can be determined in time polynomial of the size of input x. Formally speaking, let P be a parameterized problem, P is fixed-parameter tractable if there is an algorithm A, a constant c, and an arbitrary computable function $f : \mathbb{N} \to \mathbb{N}$ such that A outputs *yes* on input (x, k) within a running time of $f(k) \times |x|^c$ iff '(x, k)' is *yes*.

W-hierarchy. In parameterized complexity theory, for the problems probably not in f.p.t, W-hierarchy was introduced by Downey and Fellows, which is analogous to the polynomial hierarchy in the classical complexity theory. It contains a series of complexity classes of parametrized problems. They are jointly called the W-hierarchy, which classifies the problems under the parameterized perspective [15]. Concretely, classes in W-hierarchy beyond FPT (in which, every problem can be solved in time of $f(k) \cdot n^c$) are W[i] where $i = 1, 2, \ldots$, and limits to two classes W[P] and W[SAT]. It means that problem in W[i] is at least harder than W[j] if $i \geq j$.

Database. A database schema is a finite set $\{R_1, \ldots, R_m\}$ of distinct relations. Each relation R_i has r_i attributes, say $\{A_1, \ldots, A_{r_i}\}$, where r_i is the arity of R_i. Each attribute A_j has a corresponding domain $dom(A_j)$ which is a set of valid values. A domain $dom(R_i)$ of a relation R_i is a set $dom(A_1) \times \cdots \times dom(A_{r_i})$. Any element of $dom(R_i)$ is called a fact. A database d can be written as $\{D; R_1, \ldots, R_m\}$, representing a schema over certain domain D, where D is a set $dom(R_1) \times \cdots \times dom(R_m)$.

Boolean database queries. A boolean query q is a function mapping database d to $\{true, false\}$. We limit our study inside the first order query language, so that queries can be written by a certain fragment of the first order query language. We consider three important query fragments, in descending order of expressive capability, first-order, positive and conjunctive query.

Conjunctive query. By *datalog*-style notation, a boolean conjunctive query can be written as following

$$q :- R_{i_1}(\bar{x}_1), R_{i_2}(\bar{x}_2), \ldots, R_{i_k}(\bar{x}_k)$$

where each $\bar{x}_i$ has an arity of r_{i_1} consisting of constants and variables. Query result $q(d)$ is *true* if there exists facts $\{t_1, t_2, \ldots, t_k\}$ in d can be mapped to build-in variables $\bar{x}_1, \bar{x}_2, \ldots, \bar{x}_k$ consistently, say consistent with constants in each $\bar{x}_1$; Otherwise, $q(d)$ is *false*. Intuitively, the $\{t_1, t_2, \ldots, t_k\}$ is a witness such that q is true. From the perspective of relational algebra, conjunctive query written as a paradigm with combination of selection, projection and join operation equivalently.

In the example above, we have a conjunctive query with two atoms(or relations),

$$q(x, z) :- dept(y, x), author(y, z)$$

Positive query. Positive query can be written as a disjunction of conjunctive queries. That is also equivalence to a paradigm written with union, selection, projection and join operations. In this paper, we denote a boolean positive query as following

$$q :- q_1 \wedge q_2 \wedge \cdots \wedge q_s$$

where each q_i is a conjunctive query. Due to the semantic of disjunction, $q(d)$ is *true* if there exists at least one q_i is *true*; Otherwise, it is *false*.

First-order query. First-order query can be written as positive query with negation, that is also equivalence to an arbitrary first-order formula by only using the predicates $R_1, \ldots, R_m$.

We follow the metric using in [14], where the two parameters are, separately, the number of variables x appearing in the query q, and the size of query q which is the number of atoms in the query. The relationship between both parameters is that the query size is no more than the number variables.

Therefore, if the complexity class of the latter case should belong to the class of the former case for our decision problem. However, both are between the data and combined complexity.

3   Results of Query Fragments

In this section, we examine the parameterized complexity of different fragments of first-order query on number of variables and query size.

Complement of classes in the W-hierarchy. A parameterized problem is in co-W$[i]$, $i \in \mathbb{N}$, if its complement is in W$[i]$, where the *complement* of a parameterized problem is the parameterized problem resulting from reversing the YES and NO answers. If any co-W$[i]$-complete problem is fixed-parameter tractable, then co-W$[i]$ = FPT = co-FPT = W$[i]$ follows, but this will cause the Exponential Time Hypothesis to fail [15]. Hence co-W$[i]$-completeness provides strong theoretical evidence that a problem is not fixed-parameter tractable.

Theorem 1. *The parametric complexity of* RES *over conjunctive query is* co-W$[1]$-complete, *for cases with parameter of both query size and number of variables in the input query.*

Proof. To the *upper bound*, we can transform RES for conjunctive queries to the *weighted satisfiability problem* for boolean formulas in 2-CNF. The complementary of RES should be stated to decide if there is no tuple deletion of size less or equal than k. Let q and d be the conjunctive query and database given in RES. Without loss of generality, let

$$q :- p_1(\bar{x}_1), \ldots, p_k(\bar{x}_k)$$

It is to decide if there is an instantiation of the variables in q such that every atom of q maps to at least $k^{\mathsf{RES}} + 1$ different tuples in the database d, due to the following lemma.

Lemma 1. *The answer of the complementary of* RES *for constant* k^{RES} *is yes iff for the given* q, *there are at least* $k^{\mathsf{RES}} + 1$ *disjoint join paths can be taken from the input database* d.

Proof. Here, we say a fact t is '*consistent*' with an atom p if (1) the i-th entry of fact t is the constant c whenever the i-th entry of atom p is some constant c; (2) the i-th and j-th entries of fact t are the same constant whenever the i-th and j-th entries of atom p are the same variables.

For each atom p_i in the given query q, and each fact t of the same relation p_i in the database d which is consistent with atom p_i, we introduce $k^{\mathsf{RES}} + 1$ boolean variables, $z_{i,t}^{(j)}$ where $0 \leq j \leq k^{\mathsf{RES}}$. Intuitively, it means that

$$z_{i,t}^{(j)} := \begin{cases} 1, & \text{if atom } p_i \text{ is mapped to fact } t; \qquad (1) \\ 0, & \text{otherwise.} \qquad\qquad\qquad\qquad\quad (2) \end{cases}$$

Now we build the 2-CNF as follows by using only the variables introduced above,

– For each fact t, build a 2-CNF expression "E_t" as follow

$$\bigwedge_{0 \leq j_1 \neq j_2 \leq k^{\mathsf{RES}}, 1 \leq i \leq k} (\neg z_{i,t}^{(j_1)} \vee \neg z_{i,t}^{(j_2)})$$

- For each atom p_i and two different facts t, t' consistent with it, build a 2-CNF expression "E_i"

$$\bigwedge_{0 \leq j \leq k^{\mathsf{RES}}} (\neg z_{i,t}^{(j)} \vee \neg z_{i,t'}^{(j)})$$

- For two joining atoms $p_i, p_{i'}$ and corresponding pair of facts t, t', that is, p_i and $p_{i'}$ has the same joining variable v, but facts t and t' have different constants on position of v, (i.e., t and t' will not occur in the same join path), we build a 2-CNF expression "$E_{(i,t),(i',t')}$"

$$\bigwedge_{0 \leq j \leq k^{\mathsf{RES}}} (\neg z_{i,t}^{(j)} \vee \neg z_{i',t'}^{(j)})$$

- Using three kinds of 2-CNF above to build the complete 2-CNF F as follow

$$\bigwedge_{1 \leq i \neq i' \leq k, t \neq t' \in d} E_{(i,t),(i',t')} \bigwedge_{1 \leq i \leq k, t \in d} E_i \bigwedge_{t \in d} E_t$$

- Finally, the parameter of 2-CNF is $(k^{\mathsf{RES}} + 1) \cdot k$, where k is the parameter of RES, i.e., number of atom in given query q.

Note that such construction can be done in

$$O\left((k^{\mathsf{RES}} + 1)^2 k \cdot n + (k^{\mathsf{RES}} + 1)k \cdot n^2 + k^2(k^{\mathsf{RES}} + 1) \cdot n^2\right)$$

Consider some instantiation of variables in given query q, it guarantees that $z_{i,t}^{(j)}$ is *true* if atom p_i in q is mapped to tuple t; the assignment has exactly "$(k^{\mathsf{RES}} + 1)k$" true variables and make all the clauses *true*. Meanwhile, an assignment with "$(k^{\mathsf{RES}} + 1)k$" true variables making all clauses *true*, should have exactly one set of true variable $z_{i,t}^{(j)}$ for each of the k atoms due to the expression E_i. It will also induce an assignment for the variables of q that maps each atom p to a tuple t due to expression $E_{(i,t),(i',t')}$. And E_t guarantees the $k + 1$ disjoint joining paths. Therefore, it is easy to see that 2-CNF boolean formula constructed by this reduction has a satisfying assignment with k true variables, iff the answer of RES is no for constant k^{RES}, that is, there exist k^{RES} initiations of the variables in q that maps all the atoms to tuples of the database d, and these initiations are totally disjoint.

To the *lower bound*, we build a simple reduction from the clique problem to the complement of RES (q, k'). Clique problem is W[1]-complete, so that RES is co-W[1]-hard.

- For any instance (G, k) of clique we construct a database consisting of one binary relation $G(\cdot, \cdot)$ (the graph), i.e., $G(x_i, x_j)$ if $(v_i, v_j) \in E$.
- Then insert a unique dummy tuple (x, x).
- Let $k' = 1$.

The boolean query for parameter k is simply

$$q :- \bigwedge_{1 \leq i < j \leq k} G(x_i, x_j).$$

One can verify that (a) the query size is bounded by $O(k^2)$; (b) the boolean query q is $true$ at first; (c) since (x, x) must be deleted in order to guarantee q is $false$, therefore, deletion of any k' tuple makes query still $true$ iff G has a clique of size k. □

Theorem 2. *The parametric complexity of* RES *over positive query is* co-W[1]-complete, *for case with parameter of query size.*

Proof. To the *lower bound*, conjunctive query is a special case of positive query, therefore, we can simply reduce the case of conjunctive query to this case of positive query, and we can know it is co-W[1]-hard.

To the *upper bound*, case of positive query is also co-W[1]. This is really because that we can rewrite any positive query q into a disjunction of several conjunctive queries, and the number of conjunctive queries introduced is at most exponential to the size of q. Therefore, this rewriting is fixed parameter tractable. However, it is not naive to build the new dummy element and the corresponding parameter k. Therefore, we show the detailed reduction. Concretely, first we know that "*there is no solution deletion of size k in d for query q iff for each conjunctive query q_i in the transformed disjunction expression of q, there is no deletion of size k in d making q_i false.*" Then, we can transform each (q_i, k) into the corresponding clique instance (G_i, k_i) by f.p.t reduction, such that "*there is no solution deletion of size k in d for query q_i iff G_i has a clique of size k_i.*"

To the correctness, we should uniform all the different k_i. Pick the $k^{clique} = \max_i\{k_i\}$. Then in each G_i, add $k^{clique} - k_i$ new nodes adjacent to each other, and link them to all the other nodes in G_i. Finally, one can verify that "*RES has a solution of size k for a positive query iff G (disjoint set of all the G_i) has a clique of size k^{clique}*". □

Theorem 3. *The parametric complexity of* RES *over positive query is* co-W[SAT]-hard, *for case with parameter of number of variables.*

Proof. We now give a proof that for RES in the condition of exactly k deletions. Here we reduce the k-Weighted SAT to RES. In k-weighted SAT problem, given a Boolean formula F (with no restriction on depth) and integer k, it is to decide if F has a satisfying assignment of Hamming weight exactly k.

We can also use dummy element to construct the reduction by combining the technique in [14].

- Build a database d with three relations, say

$$Pos(x, y), \ Neg(x, y), \ Dummy(x)$$

For each variables $x_1, \ldots, x_n$ in the given boolean formula F, fill in the $Pos(X, Y)$ with facts $(1, 1), \ldots, (n, n)$, fill in the $Neg(x, y)$ with (i, j) for each pair $1 \leq i \neq j \leq n$, and let unary relation $Dummy(x)$ includes a fact (a).

- Build query q as follows. First, to simulate the k weighted solution, introduce a sentence

$$P :- (\exists z_1, \ldots, z_k) \bigwedge_{1 \leq i \neq j \leq k} Neg(z_i, z_j)$$

Then, for each literal l_i of variable x_i in the given boolean formula F, define a transform as

$$\tau(l_i) := \begin{cases} \bigwedge_{1 \leq j \leq k} Neg(i, z_j), & \text{if } l_i \text{ is negative literal;} & (3) \\ \bigvee_{1 \leq j \leq k} Pos(i, z_j), & \text{if } l_i \text{ is positive literal.} & (4) \end{cases}$$

We denote the proposition transformed by τ as F_τ. At last, build query as

$$q :- (P \wedge F_\tau) \vee Dummy(a)$$

- let $k' = 1$.

Clearly, one can verify that (a) the number of variables is bounded by k; (b) the boolean query q is *true* initially due to the dummy elements; (c) since unary fact (a) must be deleted in order to guarantee q is *false*, therefore, deletion of any k' tuple makes query still *true* iff F has no satisfying assignment of Hamming weight exactly k. □

Theorem 4. *The parametric complexity of* RES *over first-order query is*

- co-W[P]-hard, for case with parameter of the number of variables.
- co-W[t]-hard, for case with parameter of query size.

The proof is basically established by reductions from *"weighted circuit satisfiability"* and *"depth-t weighted circuit satisfiability"* separately, which are the typical problem in W[P]-hard and W[t]-hard [16]. For simplicity, we omit the detail of the reduction here.

4   Conclusion

We study the complexity of the RES problem by means of parameterized complexity, and provide the results of conjunctive query, positive query and first-order query. The results are summarized in Table 2. In the future work, We plan to investigate the tractable condition and approximation algorithms for intractable cases. Furthermore, we plan to study another objective of this problem which is the side effect on source database. The cases considering other types of dependency constraints on database, such as independent dependencies, also need to be further explored.

References

1. Freire, C., Gatterbauer, W., Immerman, N., Meliou, A.: The complexity of resilience and responsibility for self-join-free conjunctive queries. Proc. VLDB Endow. **9**(3), 180–191 (2015). doi:10.14778/2850583.2850592

2. Buneman, P., Khanna, S., Tan, W.-C.: On propagation of deletions and annotations through views. In: Proceedings of the Twenty-first ACM SIGMOD-SIGACT-SIGART Symposium on Principles of Database Systems, PODS 2002, pp. 150–158. ACM, New York (2002). doi:10.1145/543613.543633

3. Cong, G., Fan, W., Geerts, F., Li, J., Luo, J.: On the complexity of view update analysis and its application to annotation propagation. IEEE Trans. Knowl. Data Eng. **24**(3), 506–519 (2012). doi:10.1109/TKDE.2011.27

4. Kimelfeld, B.: A dichotomy in the complexity of deletion propagation with functional dependencies. In: Proceedings of the 31st Symposium on Principles of Database Systems, PODS 2012, pp. 191–202. ACM, New York (2012). doi:10.1145/2213556.2213584

5. Kimelfeld, B., Vondrák, J., Woodruff, D.P.: Multi-tuple deletion propagation: approximations and complexity. Proc. VLDB Endow. **6**(13), 1558–1569 (2013). doi:10.14778/2536258.2536267

6. Kimelfeld, B., Vondrák, J., Williams, R.: Maximizing conjunctive views in deletion propagation. ACM Trans. Database Syst. **37**(4), 1–237 (2012). doi:10.1145/2389241.2389243

7. Cong, G., Fan, W., Geerts, F.: Annotation propagation revisited for key preserving views. In: Proceedings of the 15th ACM International Conference on Information and Knowledge Management, CIKM 2006, pp. 632–641. ACM, New (2006). doi:10.1145/1183614.1183705

8. Miao, D., Liu, X., Li, J.: On the complexity of sampling query feedback restricted database repair of functional dependency violations. Theor. Comput. Sci. **609**, 594–605 (2016)

9. Dayal, U., Bernstein, P.A.: On the correct translation of update operations on relational views. ACM Trans. Database Syst. **7**(3), 381–416 (1982). doi:10.1145/319732.319740

10. Bancilhon, F., Spyratos, N.: Update semantics of relational views. ACM Trans. Database Syst. **6**(4), 557–575 (1981). doi:10.1145/319628.319634

11. Cosmadakis, S., Papadimitriou, C.H.: Updates of relational views. J. ACM **31**(4), 742–760 (1984). doi:10.1145/1634.1887

12. Bohannon, A., Pierce, B.C., Vaughan, J.A.: Relational lenses: a language for updatable views. In: Proceedings of the Twenty-Fifth ACM SIGMOD-SIGACT-SIGART Symposium on Principles of Database Systems, PODS 2006, pp. 338–347. ACM, New York (2006). doi:10.1145/1142351.1142399

13. Keller, A.M.: Algorithms for translating view updates to database updates for views involving selections, projections, and joins. In: Proceedings of the Fourth ACM SIGACT-SIGMOD Symposium on Principles of Database Systems, PODS 1985, pp. 154–163. ACM, New York (1985). doi:10.1145/325405.325423

14. Papadimitriou, C.H., Yannakakis, M.: On the complexity of database queries (extended abstract). In: Proceedings of the Sixteenth ACM SIGACT-SIGMOD-SIGART Symposium on Principles of Database Systems, PODS 1997, pp. 12–19. ACM, New York (1997). doi:10.1145/263661.263664

15. Downey, R.G., Fellows, M.R.: Parameterized Complexity. Springer Publishing Company Incorporated, New York (2012)
16. Grohe, M.: The parameterized complexity of database queries. In: Proceedings of the Twentieth ACM SIGMOD-SIGACT-SIGART Symposium on Principles of Database Systems, PODS 2001, pp. 82–92. ACM, New York (2001). doi:10.1145/375551.375564

Formal Analysis of Linear Control Systems Using Theorem Proving

Adnan Rashid[(✉)] and Osman Hasan

School of Electrical Engineering and Computer Science (SEECS)
National University of Sciences and Technology (NUST), Islamabad, Pakistan
{adnan.rashid,osman.hasan}@seecs.nust.edu.pk

Abstract. Control systems are an integral part of almost every engineering and physical system and thus their accurate analysis is of utmost importance. Traditionally, control systems are analyzed using paper-and-pencil proof and computer simulation methods, however, both of these methods cannot provide accurate analysis due to their inherent limitations. Model checking has been widely used to analyze control systems but the continuous nature of their environment and physical components cannot be truly captured by a state-transition system in this technique. To overcome these limitations, we propose to use higher-order-logic theorem proving for analyzing linear control systems based on a formalized theory of the Laplace transform method. For this purpose, we have formalized the foundations of linear control system analysis in higher-order logic so that a linear control system can be readily modeled and analyzed. The paper presents a new formalization of the Laplace transform and the formal verification of its properties that are frequently used in the transfer function based analysis to judge the frequency response, gain margin and phase margin, and stability of a linear control system. We also formalize the active realizations of various controllers, like Proportional-Integral-Derivative (PID), Proportional-Integral (PI), Proportional-Derivative (PD), and various active and passive compensators, like lead, lag and lag-lead. For illustration, we present a formal analysis of an unmanned free-swimming submersible vehicle using the HOL Light theorem prover.

Keywords: Control systems · Higher-order logic · Theorem proving

1 Introduction

Linear control systems are widely used to regulate the behavior of many safety-critical applications, such as process control, aerospace, robotics and transportation. The first step in the analysis of a linear control system is the construction of its equivalent mathematical model by using the physical and engineering laws. For example, in the case of electrical systems, we need to model the currents and voltages passing through the electrical components and their interactions in the corresponding electrical circuit using the system governing laws, such as

© Springer International Publishing AG 2017
Z. Duan and L. Ong (Eds.): ICFEM 2017, LNCS 10610, pp. 345–361, 2017.
https://doi.org/10.1007/978-3-319-68690-5_21

Kirchhoff's current law (KCL) and Kirchhoff's voltage law (KVL). The mathematical model is then used to derive differential equations describing the relationship between the inputs and outputs of the underlying system. The next step in the analysis of a linear control system is to solve these equations to obtain a transfer function, which is in turn used to assess many interesting control system characteristics, such as frequency response, phase margin and gain margin. However, solving these equations in the time domain is not so straightforward as they usually involve the integral and differential operators. The Laplace transform, which is an integral based transform method, is thus often used to convert these differential equations to their equivalent algebraic equations in s-domain by converting the differential and integral operations into multiplication and division operators, respectively. This algebraic equation can be quite easily solved to obtain the corresponding transfer function, frequency response, gain margin and the phase margin and perform the stability analysis of the given control system.

Traditionally, the linear control system analysis is performed using paper-and-pencil proof methods. However, these methods are human-error prone and cannot be relied upon for the analysis of safety-critical applications. Moreover, there is always a risk of misusing an existing mathematical result as this manual analysis method does not provide the assurance that a mathematical law would be used only if all of its required assumptions are valid. Computer simulation and numerical methods are also frequently used to analyze linear control systems. However, they also compromise the accuracy of the results due to the involvement of computer arithmetic and the associated round-off errors. Computer algebra systems (CAS), such as Mathematica [14], are also used for the Laplace transform based analysis of linear control systems. However, CAS are primarily based on unverified symbolic algorithms and thus there is no formal proof to ascertain the accuracy of their analysis results. Given the inaccurate nature of all the above-mentioned analysis techniques, they are not very suitable to analyze control systems used in safety-critical domains, where even a slight error in analysis may lead to disastrous consequences, including the loss of human lives.

To overcome the above-mentioned limitations, model checking [11] has been also used to analyze control systems [12,22] but the continuous nature of their environment and physical components cannot be truly captured by a state-transition system in this technique. Similarly, a Hoare logic based framework [6] and the KeYmaera tool [2] have been used for the formal frequency domain analysis and verification of the safety properties of control systems with sampled-time controllers, respectively. However, the former is limited to the analysis of systems that can be expressed using a block diagram with a tree structure, whereas in the later, the continuous nature of the models is abstracted in the formal modeling process and hence the completeness of the analysis is compromised in both cases.

Recently, the HOL Light theorem prover has been used for the formal analysis of control systems. *Hasan et al.* presented a formalization of the block diagrams in HOL Light and used it to reason about the transfer function and the steady-state error analysis of a feedback control system [10]. *Ahmed et al.* used this formalization of block diagrams to verify the steady-state error of a unity feed-back control system [1]. Similarly, *Beillahi et al.* formalized the signal flow graphs in HOL Light, which can be used to formally verify transfer functions of linear control systems [5]. However, all these existing works focus on the verification of the transfer functions for a control system and, to the best of our knowledge, no prior work dealing with the formal analysis of dynamics of a linear control system exists in the literature of higher-order-logic theorem proving.

In this paper, we present a framework to conduct the formal analysis of dynamical characteristics of a linear control system using higher-order-logic theorem proving. The main idea behind the proposed framework, depicted in Fig. 1, is to formalize all the foundational components of a linear control system to facilitate formal modeling and reasoning about linear control systems within the sound core of a theorem prover. For this purpose, we built upon the higher-order-logic formalizations of Multivariable calculus [9] and a library of analog components, like resistor, capacitor and inductor [21]. We present a *new formalization of Laplace transform*, which includes the formal verification of some of its frequently used properties in reasoning about the transfer function of an n-order system. We also formalized some widely used *characteristics of linear control systems*, such as frequency response, gain margin and phase margin, which can be used for the stability analysis of a linear control system. Moreover, we formalize the *active realizations of various controllers*, such as Proportional-Integral-Derivative (PID), Proportional-Integral (PI), Proportional-Derivative (PD), Proportional (P), Integral (I) and Derivative (D) and various *active and passive compensators*, such as lag, lead and lag-lead.

The proposed framework, depicted in Fig. 1, allows us to build a formal model of the given linear control system, based on the active realizations of its controllers and compensators, the passive realizations of compensators and differential equations. Moreover, it also allows to formalize the behavior of the given linear control system in terms of its differential equation, transfer function specification and its properties, such as phase margin, frequency response and gain

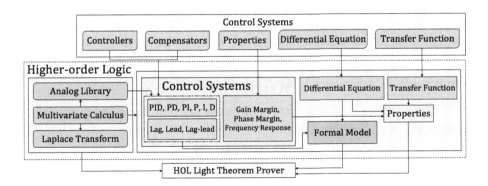

Fig. 1. Proposed framework

margin. We can then use these formalized models and properties to verify an implication relationship between them, i.e., model implies its specification. In order to demonstrate the effectiveness of our proposed formalization, we formalize the control system of an unmanned free-swimming submersible vehicle [15]. We have used the HOL Light theorem prover [8] for the proposed formalization in order to build upon its multivariable calculus theories. We have also developed a tactic that can be used to automatically verify the transfer function of any control system up to $20^{th} order$. This tactic was found to be very handy in the formal analysis of the unmanned submersible vehicle.

2   Multivariable Calculus Theories in HOL Light

An N-dimensional vector is formalized in the multivariable theory of HOL Light as a $\mathbb{R}^N$ column matrix of real numbers [9]. All of the multivariable calculus theorems are verified for functions with an arbitrary data-type $\mathbb{R}^N \to \mathbb{R}^M$.

A complex number is defined as a 2-dimensional vector, i.e., a $\mathbb{R}^2$ matrix.

Definition 1. $\vdash \forall$ a. Cx a = complex (a, &0)
$\vdash$ ii = complex (&0, &1)

Cx : $\mathbb{R} \to \mathbb{R}^2$ is a type casting function that accepts a real number and returns its corresponding complex number with the imaginary part equal to zero, where the & operator type casts a natural number to its corresponding real number. Similarly, ii (iota) represents a complex number having the real part equal to zero and the magnitude of the imaginary part equal to 1.

Definition 2. $\vdash \forall$ z. Re z = z\$1
$\vdash \forall$ z. Im z = z\$2
$\vdash \forall$ x. lift x = (lambda i. x)
$\vdash \forall$ x. drop x = x\$1

The function Re accepts a complex number (2-dimensional vector) and returns its real part. Here, the notation z\$i represents the ith component of vector z. Similarly, Im takes a complex number and returns its imaginary part. The function lift accepts a variable of type $\mathbb{R}$ and maps it to a 1-dimensional vector with the input variable as its single component. Similarly, drop takes a 1-dimensional vector and returns its single element as a real number.

Definition 3. $\vdash \forall$ x. exp x = Re (cexp (Cx x))

The complex exponential and real exponentials are represented as cexp : $\mathbb{R}^2 \to \mathbb{R}^2$ and exp : $\mathbb{R} \to \mathbb{R}$ in HOL Light, respectively.

Definition 4. $\vdash \forall$ f i. integral i f = (@y. (f has_integral y) i)
$\vdash \forall$ f i. real_integral i f = (@y. (f has_real_integral y) i)

The function `integral` represents the vector integral and is defined using the Hilbert choice operator @ in the functional form. It takes the integrand function `f`, having an arbitrary type $\mathbb{R}^N \to \mathbb{R}^M$, and a vector-space `i` : $\mathbb{R}^N \to \mathbb{B}$, which defines the region of convergence as $\mathbb{B}$ represents the boolean data type, and returns a vector $\mathbb{R}^M$, which is the integral of `f` on `i`. The function `has_integral` represents the same relationship in the relational form. Similarly, the function `real_integral` accepts the integrand function `f` : $\mathbb{R} \to \mathbb{R}$ and a set of real numbers `i` : $\mathbb{R} \to \mathbb{B}$ and returns the real-valued integral of function `f` over `i`. The region of integration, for both of the above integrals can be defined to be bounded by a vector interval $[a, b]$ or real interval $[a, b]$ using the HOL Light functions `interval` $[\mathsf{a}, \mathsf{b}]$ and `real_interval` $[\mathsf{a}, \mathsf{b}]$, respectively.

Definition 5. $\vdash \forall$ `f net. vector_derivative f net =`
$$(\mathsf{@f'.(f\ has\_vector\_derivative\ f')\ net)}$$

The function `vector_derivative` takes a function `f` : $\mathbb{R}^1 \to \mathbb{R}^M$ and a `net` : $\mathbb{R}^1 \to \mathbb{B}$, which defines the point at which `f` has to be differentiated, and returns a vector of data-type $\mathbb{R}^M$, which represents the differential of `f` at `net`. The function `has_vector_derivative` defines this relationship in the relational form.

Definition 6. $\vdash \forall$ `f net. lim net f = (@l. (f → l) net)`

The function `lim` accepts a `net` with elements of arbitrary data-type $\mathbb{A}$ and a function `f` : $\mathbb{A} \to \mathbb{R}^M$ and returns `l` of data-type $\mathbb{R}^M$, i.e., the value to which `f` converges at the given `net`.

3   Formalization of Laplace Transform

Mathematically, Laplace transform is defined for a function $f : \mathbb{R}^1 \to \mathbb{R}^2$ as [4]:

$$\mathcal{L}[f(t)] = F(s) = \int_0^\infty f(t)e^{-st}dt, \ s \ \epsilon \ \mathbb{C} \tag{1}$$

We formalize Eq. 1 in HOL Light as follows:

Definition 7. $\vdash \forall$ `s f. laplace_transform f s =`
      `integral {t| &0 <= drop t} (λt. cexp (--(s * Cx (drop t))) * f t)`

The function `laplace_transform` accepts a complex-valued function `f` : $\mathbb{R}^1 \to \mathbb{R}^2$ and a complex number `s` and returns the Laplace transform of `f` as represented by Eq. 1. In the above definition, we used the complex exponential function `cexp` : $\mathbb{R}^2 \to \mathbb{R}^2$ because the return data-type of the function `f` is $\mathbb{R}^2$. Here, the data-type of `t` is $\mathbb{R}^1$ and to multiply it with the complex number `s`, it is first converted into a real number by using `drop` and then it is converted to data-type $\mathbb{R}^2$ using `Cx`. Next, we use the vector function `integral` (Definition 4) to integrate the expression $f(t)e^{-i\omega t}$ over the positive real line since the data-type of this expression is $\mathbb{R}^2$. The region of integration is {t | &0 <= drop t}, which represents the positive real line. Laplace transform was earlier formalized using a limiting process as [20]:

⊢ ∀ s f. laplace f s = lim at_posinfinity (λb. integral
    (interval [lift (&0), lift b]) (λt. cexp (--(s * Cx (drop t))) * f t))

However, the HOL Light definition of the integral function implicitly encompasses infinite limits of integration. So, our definition covers the region of integration, i.e., $[0, \infty)$, as {t | &0 <= drop t} and is equivalent to the definition given in [20]. However, our definition considerably simplifies the reasoning process in the verification of Laplace transform properties since it does not involve the notion of limit.

The Laplace transform of a function f exists, if f is piecewise smooth and is of exponential order on the positive real line [4, 19]. A function is said to be piecewise smooth on an interval if it is piecewise differentiable on that interval.

Definition 8. ⊢ ∀ s f. laplace exists f s ⇔
    (∀ b. f piecewise_differentiable_on interval [lift (&0),lift b]) ∧
    (∃ M a. Re s > drop a ∧ exp_order_cond f M a)

The function exp_order_cond in the above definition represents the exponential order condition necessary for the existence of the Laplace transform [4, 20]:

Definition 9. ⊢ ∀ f M a. exp_order_cond f M a ⇔ &0 < M ∧
    (∀ t. &0 <= t ⇒ norm (f (lift t)) <= M * exp (drop a * t))

We used Definitions 7, 8 and 9 to formally verify some of the classical properties of Laplace transform, given in Table 1. The properties namely linearity, frequency shifting, differentiation and integration were already verified using the formal definition of the Laplace transform [20]. We formally verified these using our new definition of the Laplace transform. Moreover, we formally verified some new properties, such as, time shifting, time scaling, cosine and sine-based modulations and the Laplace transform of a n-order differential equation. The assumptions of these theorems describe the existence of the corresponding Laplace transforms. For example, the predicate laplace_exists_higher_deriv in the theorem corresponding to the n-order differential equation ensures that the Laplace of all the derivatives up to the nth order of the function f exist. Similarly, the predicate differentiable_higher_derivative provides the differentiability of the function f and its higher derivatives up to the nth order. The verification of these properties not only ensures the correctness of our definitions but also plays a vital role in minimizing the user effort in reasoning about Laplace transform based analysis of systems, as will be depicted in Sects. 4 and 5 of this paper.

The generalized linear differential equation describes the input-output relationship for a generic n-order linear control system [15]:

$$\sum_{k=0}^{n} \alpha_k \frac{d^k}{dt^k} y(t) = \sum_{k=0}^{m} \beta_k \frac{d^k}{dt^k} x(t), \quad m \leq n \tag{2}$$

where $y(t)$ is the output and $x(t)$ is the input to the system. The constants α_k and β_k are the coefficients of the output and input differentials with order k, respectively. The greatest index n of the non-zero coefficient α_n determines the order of the underlying system. The corresponding transfer function is obtained

Table 1. Properties of Laplace transform

Property	Formalized Form
Integrability $e^{-st}f(t)$ *integrable* *on* $[0,\infty)$	⊢ ∀ f s. laplace_exists f s ⇒ (λt. cexp (--(s * Cx (drop t))) * f t) integrable_on {t | &0 <= drop t}
Linearity $\mathcal{L}[\alpha f(t) + \beta g(t)] =$ $\alpha F(s) + \beta G(s)$	⊢ ∀ f g s a b. laplace_exists f s ∧ laplace_exists g s ⇒ laplace_transform (λt. a * f t + b * g t) s = a * laplace_transform f s + b * laplace_transform g s
Frequency Shifting $\mathcal{L}[e^{s_0 t}f(t)] =$ $F(s - s_0)$	⊢ ∀ f s s0. laplace_exists f s ⇒ laplace_transform (λt. cexp (s0 * Cx (drop t)) * f t) s = laplace_transform f (s - s0)
First-order Differentiation in Time Domain $\mathcal{L}\left[\frac{d}{dt}f(t)\right] =$ $sF(s) - f(0)$	⊢ ∀ f s. laplace_exists f s ∧ (∀ t. f differentiable at t) ∧ laplace_exists (λt. vector_derivative f (at t)) s ⇒ laplace_transform (λt. vector_derivative f (at t)) s = s * laplace_transform f s - f (lift (&0))
Higher-order Differentiation in Time Domain $\mathcal{L}[\frac{d^n}{dt^n}f(t)] = s^n F(s)$ $-\sum_{k=1}^{n} s^{k-1}\frac{d^{n-k}f(0)}{dx^{n-k}}$	⊢ ∀ f s n. laplace_exists_higher_deriv n f s ∧ (∀ t. differentiable_higher_derivative n f t) ⇒ laplace_transform (λt. higher_vector_derivative n f t) s = s pow n * laplace_transform f s - vsum (1..n) (λx. s pow (x - 1) * higher_vector_derivative (n - x) f (lift (&0)))
Integration in Time Domain $\mathcal{L}\left[\int_0^t f(\tau)d\tau\right] = \frac{1}{s}F(s)$	⊢ ∀ f s. &0 < Re s ∧ laplace_exists f s ∧ laplace_exists (λx. integral (interval [lift (&0),x]) f) s ∧ (∀ x. f continuous_on interval [lift (&0),x]) ⇒ laplace_transform (λx. integral (interval [lift (&0),x]) f) s = $\frac{\text{Cx(\&1)}}{\text{s}}$ * laplace_transform f s

(*continued*)

Table 1. (*continued*)

Time Shifting $\mathcal{L}[f(t - t_0)u(t - t_0)] = e^{-t_0 s}F(s)$	⊢ ∀ f s t0. &0 < drop t0 ∧ laplace_exists f s ⇒ laplace_transform (shifted_fun f t0) s = cexp (--(s * Cx (drop t0))) * laplace_transform f s
Time Scaling $\mathcal{L}[f(ct)] = \dfrac{1}{c}F\left(\dfrac{s}{c}\right),$ $0 < c$	⊢ ∀ f s c. &0 < c ∧ laplace_exists f s ∧ laplace_exists f$\left(\dfrac{s}{Cx\ c}\right)$ ⇒ laplace_transform (λt. f(c % t)) s = $\dfrac{Cx(\&1)}{Cx\ c}$ * laplace_transform f$\left(\dfrac{s}{Cx\ c}\right)$
Cosine Based Modulation $\mathcal{L}[f(t)cos(\omega_0 t)] = \dfrac{F(s - i\omega_0)}{2} + \dfrac{F(s + i\omega_0)}{2}$	⊢ ∀ f s w0. laplace_exists f s ⇒ laplace_transform (λt. ccos (Cx w0 * Cx (drop t)) * f t) s = $\dfrac{\text{laplace\_transform f (s - ii * Cx w0)}}{Cx(\&2)}$ + $\dfrac{\text{laplace\_transform f (s + ii * Cx w0)}}{Cx(\&2)}$
Sine Based Modulation $\mathcal{L}[f(t)cos(\omega_0 t)] = \dfrac{F(s - i\omega_0)}{2i} - \dfrac{F(s + i\omega_0)}{2i}$	⊢ ∀ f s w0. laplace_exists f s ⇒ laplace_transform (λt. csin (Cx w0 * Cx (drop t)) * f t) s = $\dfrac{\text{laplace\_transform f (s - ii * Cx w0)}}{Cx(\&2) * ii}$ - $\dfrac{\text{laplace\_transform f (s + ii * Cx w0)}}{Cx(\&2) * ii}$
n-order Differential Equation $\mathcal{L}\left(\sum_{k=0}^{n} \alpha_k \dfrac{d^k y}{dt^k}\right) = F(s)\sum_{k=0}^{n} \alpha_k s^k$ $-\sum_{k=0}^{n}\sum_{i=1}^{k} s^{i-1}\dfrac{d^{k-i}f(0)}{dt^{k-i}}$	⊢ ∀ f lst s n. laplace_exists_higher_deriv n f s ∧ (∀ t. differentiable_higher_derivative n f t) ⇒ laplace_transform (λt. diff_eq_n_order n lst f t) s = laplace_transform f s * vsum (0..n) (λk. EL k lst * s pow k) - vsum (0..n) (λk. EL k lst * vsum (1..k) (λi. s pow (i - 1) * higher_vector_derivative (k - i) f (lift (&0))))

by setting the initial conditions equal to zero [15]:

$$\frac{Y(s)}{X(s)} = \frac{\sum_{k=0}^{m} \beta_k s^k}{\sum_{k=0}^{n} \alpha_k s^k} \tag{3}$$

We verified the transfer function, given in Eq. 3, for the generic n-order linear control system as the following HOL Light theorem.

Theorem 1. ⊢ ∀ y x m n inlst outlst s.
(∀ t. differentiable_higher_deriv m n x y t) ∧
laplace_exists_of_higher_deriv m n x y s ∧ zero_init_conditions m n x y ∧
diff_eq_n_order_sys m n inlst outlst y x ∧
~(laplace_transform x s = Cx (&0)) ∧

$$\sim(\text{vsum } (0..n) \ (\lambda t. \ \text{EL } t \ \text{outlst } * \ s \ \text{pow } t) = Cx \ (\&0))$$
$$\Rightarrow \frac{\text{laplace\_transform } y \ s}{\text{laplace\_transform } x \ s} = \frac{\text{vsum } (0..m) \ (\lambda t. \ \text{EL } t \ \text{inlst } * \ s \ \text{pow } t)}{\text{vsum } (0..n) \ (\lambda t. \ \text{EL } t \ \text{outlst } * \ s \ \text{pow } t)}$$

The first assumption ensures that the functions y and x are differentiable up to the nth and m^{th} order, respectively. The next assumption represents the Laplace transform existence condition up to the nth order derivative of function y and m^{th} order derivative of the function x. The next assumption models the zero initial conditions for both of the functions y and x, respectively. The next assumption represents the formalization of Eq. 2 and the last two assumptions provide the conditions for the design of a reliable linear control system. Finally, the conclusion of the above theorem represents the transfer function given by Eq. 3. The verification of this theorem is very useful as it allows to automate the verification of the transfer function of any linear control system as described in Sects. 4 and 5 of the paper. The formalization, described in this section, took around 2000 lines of HOL Light code [17] and around 130 man-hours.

4   Formalization of Linear Control Systems Foundations

A general closed-loop control system is depicted in Fig. 2a. Here, $X(s)$ and $Y(s)$ represent the Laplace transforms of the time domain input $x(t)$ and the output $y(t)$, respectively. $G(s)$ and $H(s)$ represent the forward path and the feedback path transfer functions, respectively. Similarly, $G(s)H(s)$ is the open loop transfer function of the system and $Y(s)/X(s)$ is the closed loop transfer function [7]. Table 2 presents the formalization of the frequency response, phase margin and gain margin of this control system. These properties are used to study the dynamics of a linear control system in the frequency domain and to perform its stability analysis.

The frequency response is used to analyze the dynamics of the system by studying the impact of different frequency components on the intended behaviour of the given linear control system. We also formally verified the frequency response of a generic n-order system based on assumptions that are very similar to the ones used for Theorem 1.

Phase margin and gain margin provide useful information about controlling the stability of the system [7]. Phase margin represents 180° shifted phase angle of the open loop transfer function evaluated at the gain crossover frequency (ω_{gc}), which is the frequency at which the magnitude of the open loop transfer function is equal to 0 dB. The gain margin represents the magnitude of the open loop transfer function evaluated at the phase crossover frequency (ω_{pc}), which is the frequency at which the resultant phase curve of the open loop gain has a phase of 180°. In our formal definitions of these notions, the function $\text{Arg}(z)$ represents the argument of a complex number z.

The controllers form the most vital part of any control system as they are mainly responsible for the correct operation of every component of the underlying system. Controllers are modeled using their active realizations based on

Table 2. Properties of linear control systems

Property	Formalized Form
Frequency Response $M(j\omega) = M(s)\|_{(j\omega)} =$ $\left.\dfrac{Y(s)}{X(s)}\right\|_{(j\omega)} = \dfrac{Y(j\omega)}{X(j\omega)}$	$\vdash \forall$ y x w. frequency_response x y w = $\dfrac{\texttt{laplace\_transform y (ii } * \texttt{ Cx w)}}{\texttt{laplace\_transform x (ii } * \texttt{ Cx w)}}$
Frequency Response of an n-order System $\dfrac{Y(j\omega)}{X(j\omega)} = \dfrac{\sum_{k=0}^{m}\beta_k(j\omega)^k}{\sum_{k=0}^{n}\alpha_k(j\omega)^k}$	$\vdash \forall$ y x m n inlst outlst s. ($\forall$ t. differentiable_higher_deriv m n x y t) $\wedge$ laplace_exists_of_higher_deriv m n x y w $\wedge$ zero_init_conditions m n x y $\wedge$ diff_eq_n_order_sys m n inlst outlst y x $\wedge$ non_zero_denom_cond n x w outlst $\Rightarrow$ frequency_response x y w = $\dfrac{\texttt{vsum (0..m) (}\lambda\texttt{t. EL t inlst } * \texttt{ (ii} * \texttt{Cx w) pow t)}}{\texttt{vsum (0..n) (}\lambda\texttt{t. EL t outlst } * \texttt{ (ii} * \texttt{Cx w) pow t)}}$
Phase Margin $[\angle G(j\omega)H(j\omega)]_{\omega=\omega_{gc}}$ $+ 180^{\circ}$	$\vdash \forall$ g h wgc. phase_margin g h wgc = pi + Arg (g (ii $*$ Cx wgc) $*$ h (ii $*$ Cx wgc))
Gain Margin $\left[20log_{10}\left\|G(j\omega)\right.\right.$ $\left.\left.H(j\omega)\right\|_{\omega=\omega_{pc}}\right]dB$	$\vdash \forall$ g h wpc. gain_margin_db g h wpc = &20 $*$ $\dfrac{\texttt{log (norm (g (ii } * \texttt{ Cx wpc) } * \texttt{ h (ii } * \texttt{ Cx wpc)))}}{\texttt{log (\&10)}}$

an electrical circuit, which comprises of an inverting operational amplifier (op-amp) with unity gain, and two components, i.e., C_A and C_B, which are shown as rectangular boxes in Fig. 2b. The boxes C_A and C_B contain different configurations of the passive components, i.e., resistors and capacitors [16]. By making an appropriate choice of these passive components, we obtain various controllers, such as P, I, D, PI, PD, PID [15]. For the analysis of these controllers, we first need to formalize them in higher-order logic. This step requires a formal library of analog components [17,21], describing the voltage-current relationships of resistor, capacitors and inductors, and the KCL and KVL, which model the currents and voltages in an electrical circuit.

The PID controller, depicted in Fig. 2c, can be formalized as follows:

Definition 10. $\vdash \forall$ C1 R1 Vi R2 C2 Vo Vb Va.
  pid_controller_implem Vi Vo Va Vb C1 C2 R1 R2 $\Leftrightarrow$
  ($\forall$ t. &0 < drop t $\Rightarrow$ kcl [λt. capacitor_current C1 (λt. Vi t - Va t) t;
                          λt. resistor_current R1 (λt. Vi t - Va t) t;
                          λt. resistor_current R2 (λt. Vb t - Va t) t] t $\wedge$
  ($\forall$ t. &0 < drop t $\Rightarrow$ kcl [λt. resistor_current R2 (λt. Va t - Vb t) t;
                          λt. capacitor_current C2 (λt. Vo t - Vb t) t] t $\wedge$
  ($\forall$ t. &0 < drop t $\Rightarrow$ Va t = Cx (&0))

where Vi and Vo are the input and the output voltages, respectively, having data type $\mathbb{R}^1 \to \mathbb{R}^2$, and Va and Vb are the voltages at nodes a and b, respectively. The

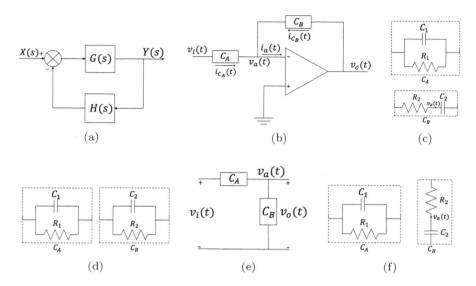

Fig. 2. Control Systems Foundations (a) Closed Loop Control System (b) Generic Active Realization of Controller (c) PID Configuration (d) Lag/lead Compensator Configuration (e) Generic Passive Realization of Compensator (f) Lag-lead Compensator Configuration

functions `resistor_current` and `capcitor_current` are the currents across the resistor and capacitor, respectively. The function `kcl` accepts a list of currents across the components of the circuit and a time variable `t` and returns the predicate that guarantees that the sum of all the currents leaving a particular node at time `t` is zero. The first conjunct of the above definition represents the application of KCL across node a. Similarly, the second conjunct models the KCL at node b, whereas the last conjunct provides the voltage across the non-inverting input of the op-amp using the virtual ground condition, as shown in Fig. 2b. We also develop a simplification tactic `KCL_SIMP_TAC`, which simplifies the implementations of the PID controller as well as other controllers and compensators. The details can be found in [17].

Next, we model the dynamical behaviour of the PID controller using the n-order differential equation:

Definition 11. ⊢ ∀ R1 R2 C1 C2. inlst_pid_contr R1 R2 C1 C2 =
      [--Cx (&1); --Cx (R2 * C2 + R1 * C1); --Cx (R1 * R2 * C1 * C2)]
⊢ ∀ R1 C2. outlst_pid_contr R1 C2 = [Cx (&0); Cx (R1 * C2)]
⊢ ∀ Vo R1 R2 C1 C2 Vi t. pid_controller_behav_spec R1 R2 C1 C2 Vi Vo t ⇔
                diff_eq_n_order 1 (outlst_pid_contr R1 C2) Vo t =
                diff_eq_n_order 2 (inlst_pid_contr R1 R2 C1 C2) Vi t

We verified the behavioural specification based on the implementation of the PID controller as the following theorem:

Theorem 2. ⊢ ∀ R1 R2 C1 C2 Vi Va Vb Vo t. &0 < R1 ∧ &0 < R2 ∧
&0 < C1 ∧ &0 < C2 ∧ (∀ t. differentiable_higher_derivative Vi Vo Vb t) ∧
  pid_controller_implem Vi Vo Va Vb C1 C2 R1 R2
    ⇒ (&0 < drop t ⇒ pid_controller_behav_spec R1 R2 C1 C2 Vi Vo t)

The first four assumptions model the design requirement for the underlying system. The next assumption provides the differentiability of the higher-order derivatives of Vi, Vo and Vb up to the order 1, 2 and 2, respectively. The last assumption presents the implementation for the PID controller. Finally, the conclusion presents its behavioral specification. We also develop a simplification tactic DIFF_SIMP_TAC, which simplifies the behavioural specifications of the PID controller as well as the other controllers and compensators [17].

Next, we verified the transfer function of the PID controller as follows:

Theorem 3. ⊢ ∀ R1 R2 C1 C2 Vi Vo s t. &0 < R1 ∧ &0 < R2 ∧ &0 < C1 ∧
  ~(laplace_transform Vi s = Cx (&0)) ∧ ~(Cx R1 * Cx C2 * s = Cx (&0)) ∧
  &0 < C2 ∧ (∀ t. differentiable_higher_derivative Vi Vo t) ∧
  laplace_exists_higher_deriv Vi Vo s ∧ zero_initial_conditions Vi Vo ∧
  (∀ t. pid_controller_behav_spec R1 R2 C1 C2 Vi Vo t)
    ⇒ $\dfrac{\texttt{laplace\_transform Vo s}}{\texttt{laplace\_transform Vi s}} =$
$$\dfrac{--\big(\mathrm{Cx}(R1*C1*R2*C2)*\mathtt{s}\ \mathtt{pow}\ 2 + (\mathrm{Cx}(R2*C2) + \mathrm{Cx}(C1*R1))*\mathtt{s} + \mathrm{Cx}(\&1)\big)}{\mathrm{Cx}(R1*C2)*\mathtt{s}}$$

The first six assumptions present the design requirements for the underlying system. The next two assumptions provide the differentiability and the Laplace existence condition for the higher-order derivatives of Vi and Vo up to the order 2 and 1, respectively. The next assumption models the *zero initial conditions* for the voltage functions Vi and Vo. The last assumption presents the behavioural specification of the PID controller. Finally, the conclusion of Theorem 3 presents its required transfer function. By judicious selection of the configuration of passive components, we obtain various controllers, such as P, I, D, PI, PD and perform the above-mentioned analysis for all of them.

Compensators are widely used in control systems, to improve their frequency response, steady-state error and the stability and hence, act as a fundamental block of a control system. Like controllers, the compensators are also modeled using their active realizations. A compensator uses the same analog circuit, which is used for the controllers, presented in Fig. 2b, by making an appropriate choice of the passive components C_A and C_B, as shown in Fig. 2d. It acts as a lag-compensator under the condition $R_2C_2 > R_1C_1$, whereas for the case of $R_1C_1 > R_2C_2$, it acts as a lead-compensator. The configurations of the passive components for the controllers and compensators, and their formalization is presented in [17].

Compensators are also modeled using their passive realizations based on an electrical circuit, which comprises of two components, i.e., C_A and C_B, which are shown as rectangular boxes in Fig. 2e. The boxes C_A and C_B contain different configurations of the passive components, i.e., resistors and capacitors. By making an appropriate choice of these passive components, we obtain various compensators, such as lag, lead and lag-lead [15]. The configuration of the lag-lead compensator is shown in Fig. 2f. Moreover, the configurations of the passive components for the compensators and their formalization in HOL Light is presented in [17].

The formalization of this section took around 300 lines of HOL Light code and around 14 man-hours. This clearly illustrates the effectiveness of our foundational formalization, presented in the previous section.

5   Unmanned Free-Swimming Submersible Vehicle

Unmanned Free-Swimming Submersible (UFSS) vehicles are a kind of autonomous underwater vehicles (AUVs) that are used to perform different tasks and operations in the submerged areas of the water. These vehicles have their own power and control systems, which are autonomously operated and controlled by the onboard computer system without any involvement of human assistance as it is difficult for humans to work in an underwater environment. UFSS vehicles are used in many safety-critical domains to perform different tasks, such as underwater navigation and object detection [13], performing deep sea rescue and salvage operations [23], searching for sea mines [24] and securing sea harbour [24]. Due to their wider usage in the above-mentioned safety-critical applications, an accurate analysis of their control system is of utmost importance.

We present a formal analysis of the pitch control system of a UFSS vehicle. The pitch control system is responsible for the uninterrupted operation and functionality of the UFSS vehicle by manipulating different parameters, such as, elevator surface, pitch angle [15]. Figure 3 depicts its block diagram.

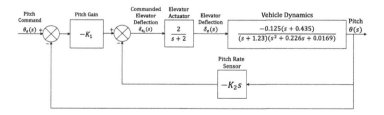

Fig. 3. Pitch control model for unmanned free-swimming submersible vehicle

The dynamics of the UFSS vehicle are represented by its corresponding differential equation, which presents the relationship between the pitch command angle $\theta_e(t)$ and the pitch angle $\theta(t)$, and is given as follows:

$$\frac{d^4\theta}{dt^4} + 3.456\frac{d^3\theta}{dt^3} + (3.207 + 0.25K_2)\frac{d^2\theta}{dt^2} + (0.616 + 0.1088K_2 + 0.25K_1)\frac{d\theta}{dt} +$$

$$(0.1088K_1 + 0.0416) = 0.25K_1\frac{d\theta_e}{dt} + 0.1088K_1 \tag{4}$$

We formalize the above differential equation as follows [18]:

Definition 12. ⊢ ∀ K1. inlst_ufsv K1 = [Cx (#0.1088) * Cx K1; Cx (#0.25) * Cx K1]
⊢ ∀ K1 K2. outlst_ufsv K1 K2 =
[Cx (#0.1088) * Cx K1 + Cx (#0.0416) ; Cx (#0.25) * Cx K1 + Cx (#0.1088) * Cx K2
+ Cx (#0.6106) ; Cx (#0.25) * Cx K2 + Cx (#3.207) ; Cx (#3.456) ; Cx (&1)]
⊢ diff_eq_ufsv inlst_ufsv outlst_ufsv theta thetae K1 K2 ⇔
           (∀t. diff_eq_n_order 4 (outlst_ufsv K1 K2) theta t =
                    diff_eq_n_order 1 (inlst_ufsv K1) thetae t)

where **thetae** and **theta** represent the input and the output of the pitch control system and K1 and K2 are the pitch gain and pitch rate sensor gain, respectively. The symbol # is used to represent a decimal number of data type $\mathbb{R}$ in HOL Light and is same as symbol & for the integer literal of data type $\mathbb{R}$.

The transfer function of the pitch control of the UFSS vehicle is as follows:

$$\frac{\theta(s)}{\theta_e(s)} = \frac{0.25K_1s + 0.1088K_1}{s^4 + 3.456s^3 + (3.207 + 0.25K_2)s^2 + (0.6106 + 0.1088K_2 + 0.25K_1)s + (0.1088K_1 + 0.0416)} \tag{5}$$

We verified the above transfer function as the following HOL Light theorem:

Theorem 4. ⊢ ∀ thetae theta s K1 K2.
(∀ t. differentiable_higher_deriv theta thetae t) ∧
laplace_exists_of_higher_deriv theta thetae s ∧
zero_init_conditions theta thetae ∧
diff_eq_ufsv inlst_ufsv outlst_ufsv theta thetae K1 K2 ∧
non_zero_denominator_condition theta s

⇒ $\dfrac{\text{laplace\_transform theta s}}{\text{laplace\_transform thetae s}}$ =

$$\frac{(\text{Cx}\,(\#0.25) * \text{Cx K1}) * \text{s} + \text{Cx}\,(\#0.1088) * \text{Cx K1}}{\text{s pow } 4 + \text{Cx}\,(\#3.456) * \text{s pow } 3 + \Big(\text{Cx}\,(\#0.25) * \text{Cx K2} + \text{Cx}\,(\#3.207)\Big)}$$

$$* \text{ s pow } 2 + \Big(\text{Cx}\,(\#0.25) * \text{Cx K1} + \text{Cx}\,(\#0.1088) * \text{Cx K2} + \text{Cx}\,(\#0.6106)\Big)$$

$$* \text{s } + \text{Cx}\,(\#0.1088) * \text{Cx K1} + \text{Cx}\,(\#0.0416)$$

The first two assumptions present the differentiability and the Laplace existence condition of the higher-order derivatives of **thetae** and **theta** up to order

1 and 4, respectively. The next assumption provides the *zero initial conditions* for `thetae` and `theta`. The next assumption presents the differential equation specification for the pitch control system of UFSS vehicle. The final assumption models the non-negativity of the denominator of the transfer function presented in the conclusion of the above theorem. We also verified the open loop transfer function $\theta(\mathbf{s})/\delta_{\mathbf{e}}(\mathbf{s})$, frequency response (open and closed loop) and gain margin, for the UFSS vehicle and the details can be found in [17].

The distinguishing feature of Theorem 4 and the other properties, compared to traditional analysis methods is their generic nature, i.e., all of the variables and functions are universally quantified and can thus be specialized in order to obtain the results for some given values. Moreover, all of the required assumptions are guaranteed to be explicitly mentioned along with the theorems due to the inherent soundness of the theorem proving approach. The high expressiveness of the higher-order logic enables us to model the differential equation and the corresponding transfer function in their true continuous form, whereas, in model checking they are mostly discretized and modeled using a state-transition system, which compromises the accuracy of the analysis.

To facilitate control engineers in using our formalization, we developed an automatic tactic `TRANSFER_FUN_TAC`, which automatically verifies the transfer function of the systems up to 20th-order. This tactic was successfully used for the automatic verification of the transfer functions of the controllers, compensators and the pitch control system of the UFSS vehicle. This automatic verification tactic only requires the differential equation and the transfer function of the underlying system and automatically verifies the transfer function. Thus, the formal analysis of the UFSS vehicle took only 25 lines of code and about half an hour, thanks to our automatic tactic and the foundational formalization of Sect. 3.

6 Conclusion

This paper presented a higher-order-logic theorem proving based approach for the formal analysis of the dynamical aspects of linear control systems using theorem proving. The main idea behind the proposed framework is to use a formalization of Laplace transform theory in higher-order logic to formally analyze the dynamic aspects of linear control systems. For this purpose, we develop a new formalization of Laplace transform theory, which includes its formal definition and verification of its properties, such as linearity, frequency shifting, differentiation and integration in time domain, time shifting, time scaling, cosine and sine-based modulation and the Laplace transform of an n-order differential equation, which are used for the verification of the transfer function of a generic n-order linear control system. Moreover, the paper also presents the formal verification of some widely used linear control system characteristics, such as frequency response, phase margin and the gain margin, using the verified transfer function, which can be used for the stability analysis of a linear control system. We also formalize the active realization of various controllers, such as PID, PD,

PI, P, I, D, and various compensators, such as lag and lead. Finally, we formalize the passive realization of the various compensators, such as lag, lead and lag-lead and verified the corresponding behavioral (differential equation) and the transfer function specifications. To facilitate the usage of these formalizations in analyzing real-world linear control systems, we developed some simplification and automatic verification tactics, in particular the tactic TRANSFER_FUN_TAC, which automatically verifies the transfer function of any real-world linear control system based on its differential equation. These foundations can be used to analyze a wide range of linear control systems and for illustration purposes, the paper presents the formal analysis of an unmanned free-swimming submersible vehicle.

In future, we plan to link the proposed formalization with Simulink so that the users can provide the system model as a block diagram. This diagram can be used to extract the corresponding transfer function [3], which can in turn be formally verified, almost automatically, to be equivalent to the corresponding block diagram based on the reported formalization and reasoning support.

Acknowledgements. This work was supported by the National Research Program for Universities grant (number 1543) of Higher Education Commission (HEC), Pakistan.

References

1. Ahmad, M., Hasan, O.: Formal verification of steady-state errors in unity-feedback control systems. In: Lang, F., Flammini, F. (eds.) FMICS 2014. LNCS, vol. 8718, pp. 1–15. Springer, Cham (2014). doi:10.1007/978-3-319-10702-8_1
2. Aréchiga, N., Loos, S.M., Platzer, A., Krogh, B.H.: Using theorem provers to guarantee closed-loop system properties. In: American Control Conference (ACC), 2012, pp. 3573–3580. IEEE (2012)
3. Babuska, R., Stramigioli, S.: Matlab and Simulink for Modeling and Control. Delft University of Technology (1999)
4. Beerends, R.J., Morsche, H.G., Van den Berg, J.C., Van de Vrie, E.M.: Fourier and Laplace Transforms. Cambridge University Press, Cambridge (2003)
5. Beillahi, S.M., Siddique, U., Tahar, S.: Formal analysis of power electronic systems. In: Butler, M., Conchon, S., Zaïdi, F. (eds.) ICFEM 2015. LNCS, vol. 9407, pp. 270–286. Springer, Cham (2015). doi:10.1007/978-3-319-25423-4_17
6. Boulton, R.J., Hardy, R., Martin, U.: A hoare logic for single-input single-output continuous-time control systems. In: Maler, O., Pnueli, A. (eds.) HSCC 2003. LNCS, vol. 2623, pp. 113–125. Springer, Heidelberg (2003). doi:10.1007/3-540-36580-X_11
7. Ghosh, S.: Control Systems, vol. 1000. Pearson Education, New Delhi (2010)
8. Harrison, J.: HOL light: a tutorial introduction. In: Srivas, M., Camilleri, A. (eds.) FMCAD 1996. LNCS, vol. 1166, pp. 265–269. Springer, Heidelberg (1996). doi:10.1007/BFb0031814
9. Harrison, J.: The HOL light theory of euclidean space. J. Autom. Reason. **50**(2), 173–190 (2013)
10. Hasan, O., Ahmad, M.: Formal analysis of steady state errors in feedback control systems using HOL-light. In: Design, Automation and Test in Europe, pp. 1423–1426 (2013)

11. Hasan, O., Tahar, S.: Formal verification methods. In: Khosrow-Pour, M. (ed.) Encyclopedia of Information Science and Technology, pp. 7162–7170. IGI Global Pub, Hershey (2015)
12. Johnson, M.E.: Model checking safety properties of servo-loop control systems. In: Dependable Systems and Networks, pp. 45–50. IEEE (2002)
13. Kondo, H., Ura, T.: Navigation of an AUV for investigation of underwater structures. Control Eng. Pract. **12**(12), 1551–1559 (2004)
14. Lutovac, M., Tošić, D.: Symbolic analysis and design of control systems using mathematica. Int. J. Control **79**(11), 1368–1381 (2006)
15. Nise, N.S.: Control Systems Engineering. Wiley, New York (2007)
16. Ogata, K., Yang, Y.: Modern Control Engineering. Prentice-Hall, Englewood Cliffs (1970)
17. Rashid, A.: Formal Analysis of Linear Control Systems using Theorem Proving (2017). http://save.seecs.nust.edu.pk/projects/falcstp
18. Rashid, A., Hasan, O.: On the formalization of fourier transform in higher-order logic. In: Blanchette, J.C., Merz, S. (eds.) ITP 2016. LNCS, vol. 9807, pp. 483–490. Springer, Cham (2016). doi:10.1007/978-3-319-43144-4_31
19. Rashid, A., Hasan, O.: Formalization of transform methods using HOL light. In: Geuvers, H., England, M., Hasan, O., Rabe, F., Teschke, O. (eds.) CICM 2017. LNCS(LNAI), vol. 10383, pp. 319–332. Springer, Cham (2017)
20. Taqdees, S.H., Hasan, O.: Formalization of laplace transform using the multivariable calculus theory of HOL-light. In: McMillan, K., Middeldorp, A., Voronkov, A. (eds.) LPAR 2013. LNCS, vol. 8312, pp. 744–758. Springer, Heidelberg (2013). doi:10.1007/978-3-642-45221-5_50
21. Taqdees, S.H., Hasan, O.: Formally verifying transfer functions of linear analog circuits. IEEE Des. Test **5**(99), 1–7 (2017)
22. Tiwari, A., Khanna, G.: Series of abstractions for hybrid automata. In: Tomlin, C.J., Greenstreet, M.R. (eds.) HSCC 2002. LNCS, vol. 2289, pp. 465–478. Springer, Heidelberg (2002). doi:10.1007/3-540-45873-5_36
23. Wernli, R.L.: Low cost UUV's for military applications: is the technology ready? In: Pacific Congress on Marine Science and Technology (2001)
24. Willcox, S., Vaganay, J., Grieve, R., Rish, J.: The Bluefin BPAUV: An Organic Widearea Bottom Mapping and Mine-hunting Vehicle. Unmanned Untethered Submersible Technology (2001)

Policy Dependent and Independent Information Flow Analyses

Manuel Töws[⊠] and Heike Wehrheim

Department of Computer Science, Paderborn University, Paderborn, Germany
mtoews@mail.uni-paderborn.de

Abstract. Information Flow Analysis (IFA) aims at detecting illegal flows of information between program entities. "Legality" is therein specified in terms of various *security policies*. For the analysis, this opens up two possibilities: building generic, policy independent and building specific, policy dependent IFAs. While the former needs to track all dependencies between program entities, the latter allows for a reduced and thus more efficient analysis.

In this paper, we start out by formally defining a policy independent information flow analysis. Next, we show how to specialize this IFA via policy specific variable tracking, and prove soundness of the specialization. We furthermore investigate *refinement relationships* between policies, allowing an IFA for one policy to be employed for its refinements. As policy refinement depends on concrete program entities, we additionally propose a precomputation of policy refinement conditions, enabling an efficient refinement check for concrete programs.

1 Introduction

Information Flow Analysis (IFA) is concerned with the detection of illegal flows of information between program entities. The most prominent application for IFA today is the analysis of apps, answering questions like "is my contact data being sent to a third party via the internet?". Consequently, a number of information flow analyses specialize to this area [2, 9, 14, 24, 25].

In an information flow analysis, illegal flows can be specified in various ways: while some analyses aim at simply detecting flows from specific sources (e.g., my contact data) to specific sinks (e.g., internet) [2], others need to find flows violating complex *security policies* [6, 7, 11, 17, 19]. A security policy specifies the allowed flows of information between security classes, and the analysis of a program requires a mapping of program entities (e.g., variables) onto these classes. The source-to-sink analysis can be seen as a specific instance of a policy dependent analysis, classifying sources as secret (or *high*), sinks as public (*low*), all other program entities as internal, and disallowing direct or indirect flows from high to low entities.

Today, the majority of approaches for information flow analysis follows this high-low policy, implicitly specified via sources and sinks (e.g., [1, 8, 15, 22]). More complicated policies often just confine to lattices that specify multiple layers (e.g., confidential,

This work was partially supported by the German Research Foundation (DFG) within the Collaborative Research Centre "On-The-Fly Computing" (SFB 901).

© Springer International Publishing AG 2017
Z. Duan and L. Ong (Eds.): ICFEM 2017, LNCS 10610, pp. 362–378, 2017.
https://doi.org/10.1007/978-3-319-68690-5_22

secret and top-secret) [11]. Analysis frameworks for arbitrary policies are rather uncommon but exist. Our comprehension of security policies is based on Foley's framework [6,7] (slightly differing in notation). However, even the approaches with more complicated policies always carry out a *policy dependent analysis*: the analysis results are just valid for the specific policy, and once the policy is changed, the analysis has to be repeated.

To get around policy dependency, some techniques propose *refinement relations* between policies. In Foley's work [6,7], a refinement relation on policies is contained in the policy algebra operations. However, the relationship is coarse and considers only policies where the security classes of one policy form a subset of another. The concrete program scenario with its mapping to security classes is not considered in this definition. Hunt and Sands [11] consider policy dependent as well as independent IFAs. Their policy dependent analysis information is, however, more abstract than ours: instead of keeping flow information between program entities, they keep flow information between entities and security classes, thereby maintaining even less information than our policy dependent analysis. Mantel et al. [17–19] studies re-use of analyses checking for specific security *concerns* (such as generalized non-interference or separability properties). In this re-use, the security policy is always kept the same.

In this paper, we investigate the usefulness of policy independent as well as dependent information flow analyses. Our policy independent analysis tracks all dependencies among program entities. While this opens up the possibility of checking the program against arbitrary policies, this naturally enlarges the complexity of the analysis. We consequently introduce a specialization of this policy independent IFA to a policy dependent one via a policy specific variable tracking, and furthermore prove its soundness.

Our major contribution is the investigation of conditions under which an information flow analysis for policy P_1 can be used to check security with respect to policy P_2. This allows for a *re-use* of policy dependent flow information, and helps to avoid several analysis runs on the same program for different policies. To this end, we define two sorts of *refinement* (or coverage) relationships between policies, and prove flow information valid for one policy to be valid for refined policies as well. For the second relationship we generalize similar scenarios by abstracting away program dependent information and describe precomputations that can be carried out for efficiently checking the second refinement relationship.

Finally, we report on some experimental evaluation, showing the gain in going from policy independent to dependent IFAs, and the runtime-complexity in checking refinement relationships among policies compared to running a completely new analysis.

The paper is structured as follows. Next, we introduce in Sect. 2 some background notation on programs and policies. In Sect. 3 we formally specify the policy independent variant. We continue in Sect. 4 by extending the analysis to be policy dependent with respect to the security policy and security mapping, and prove soundness of the analysis as well as preservation of violation detection between both analyses. In Sect. 5 we investigate re-use of policy specific flow information. We present two refinement relations there. For the second one, we continue to show how prior precomputations can help in an efficient refinement check at runtime. We finally present our experimental results in Sect. 6.

2 Background

In this section, we formalize the basics we use later. We start by defining the programs which we consider in this paper. A program is given in the form of a control-flow automaton (CFA) $G = (L, flow, cd)$, where L stands for a set of program locations, $flow : L \times L$ stands for a set of control flow edges and the mapping $cd : L \to 2^L$ is an extension of the control-flow graph that represents *control dependencies*. Control dependencies are not standardly included in control flow graphs. A control dependency states that the execution of a statement in a program depends on another, typically a conditional statement in an IF or WHILE: $\ell' \in cd(\ell)$ denotes that ℓ' controls whether ℓ can be executed or not. We require a pre-computation of control dependencies, e.g. like proposed in [10, 16].

Each location $\ell \in L$ represents an operation from a set *Ops* given by a total mapping $\Theta : L \to Ops$. Therein,

$$Ops ::= skip \mid b \mid x := e$$

describes three kind of operations: *skip* an empty operation, *b* a boolean condition (of an IF or WHILE) and $x := e$ an assignment. We let *Var* be the set of variables. From the CFA of a program S, we derive a set of starting locations $init(S) \subseteq L$, which are locations without predecessors in the control flow relation. Furthermore, we write $vars(e)$ for the set $W \subseteq Var$ that contains all variables occurring in the expression e.

Our technique aims at the enforcement of a general specification of non-interference wrt. arbitrary security policies via a data flow analysis that overapproximates the dependencies of entities. Therefore, we first give a specification of what we understand by a security policy. We base our definition of *security policies* on a generalization similar to the one used by Foley [6,7]. Let *Sec* denote a set of *security classes*. A security policy specifies the allowed flow of information for each individual security class. A security-policy P is technical a collection of pairs of the form $Sec \times 2^{Sec}$. We call an element $(a, A) \in P$ a *secure state*. It describes that an element $a \in Sec$ is allowed to depend on information equal to the security classes $A \in 2^{Sec}$.

Definition 1. *Let Sec be a set of security classes. A security policy P is an element of $2^{Sec \times 2^{Sec}}$. The set of all security-policies is defined as $Pol(Sec) := 2^{Sec \times 2^{Sec}}$.*

We continue with our definition of a violation. For each set of security classes *Sec*, we introduce the *non-violating policy* $\top \in Pol(Sec)$: $\top(Sec) := Sec \times 2^{Sec}$. In $\top(Sec)$, every possible single pair is allowed. With this at hand we can define the *non-secure states* of a policy $P \in Pol(Sec)$.

Definition 2. *Let Sec be a set of security classes. An element $(a, A) \in \top(Sec)$ is a non-secure state of a policy $P \in Pol(Sec)$ iff $(a, A) \in \top(Sec) \setminus P$ holds.*

In this paper, we focus on *aggregation policies* [6,7] where removing some security classes from the right-hand side cannot turn a secure state into an non-secure state.

Definition 3. *Let Sec be a set of security classes. A security-policy $P \in Pol(Sec)$ is an aggregation policy iff for all $a \in Sec$ and $A \subseteq B \subseteq Sec$*

$$(a, B) \in P \Rightarrow (a, A) \in P \tag{1}$$

holds.

A connection between a program and a policy is given by a *security class mapping* $SC: Var \rightarrow Sec$. A security class mapping defines a static mapping of program entities onto security classes. We call a security class mapping together with a policy a *configuration*.

Here, we use two policies as recurring examples. For defining them, we use the following auxiliary operation according to Foley [6,7] (with $d \in Sec$ and $D \in 2^{Sec}$):

$$d \rightsquigarrow D := \bigcup_{A \in 2^D} \{(d, A)\}$$

The first policy is the most often used one consisting of three security classes: l *(low)*, h *(high)* and i *(internal)*. We denote this policy as *LHI*.

Definition 4. *Let $Sec_{LHI} = \{l, h, i\}$ be a set of security classes. The LHI-policy is defined as*

$$LHI := \left(l \rightsquigarrow \{l, i\}\right) \cup \left(i \rightsquigarrow \{l, h, i\}\right) \cup \left(h \rightsquigarrow \{l, h, i\}\right).$$

The security class h is used for entities that initially contain secret information. The class l declares entities that could be observed at several program states (i.e., public entities) whereas the class i is used for entities that are initially uninteresting. However, we do not want that information of security class h can flow transitively via i entities into l entities.

As second policy, we use a Chinese-wall policy [5] consisting of three security classes: c, b_1 and b_2. Thereby, an entity with security class c (consultant) is allowed to know information of at most one of the two banks b_1, b_2, but not of both of them.

Definition 5. *Let $Sec_{CW} = \{c, b_1, b_2\}$ be a set of security classes. The two-bank Chinese-Wall policy (CW-policy) is defined as*

$$CW := \left(c \rightsquigarrow \{c, b_1\}\right) \cup \left(c \rightsquigarrow \{c, b_2\}\right) \cup \left(b_1 \rightsquigarrow \{b_1\}\right) \cup \left(b_2 \rightsquigarrow \{b_2\}\right).$$

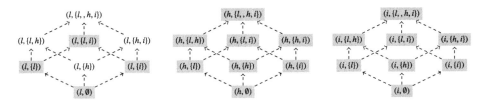

Fig. 1. The secure states (gray) of the *LHI*-policy ordered according to $\sqsubseteq$. Non-secure states are not highlighted.

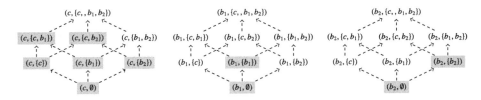

Fig. 2. The secure states (gray) of the *CW*-policy ordered according to ⊑. Non-secure states are not highlighted.

In this notation the security states define a partial order $\sqsubseteq : (Sec \times 2^{Sec}) \times (Sec \times 2^{Sec})$ with $((a, A) \sqsubseteq (b, B))$ iff $(a = b) \wedge A \subseteq B$. By this relation we can display the secure states of policies graphical. The *LHI*-policy is displayed in ⊑-order in Fig. 1. Therein, secure states are highlighted in gray. Analogously, the *CW*-policy is displayed in Fig. 2.

3 Policy Independent Information Flow Analysis

Resting upon the idea of our previous work [23], we define an information flow analysis in form of a data flow analysis to overapproximate the actual dependencies. Technically, this is below formulated in the style of static analyses [21], in our case a forward analysis. The analysis determines for each location $\ell \in L$ two sorts of information: *Dependencies* $D = Var \rightarrow 2^{Var}$ and *contexts* $C = L \rightarrow 2^{Var}$, i.e. the flow information for a location $\ell \in L$ is $IF_\ell \in D \times C$. An entry $(v, V) \in D$ states that at location ℓ the entity v depends at most on the initial values of V. An entry $(\ell', V) \in C$ serves as a pending additional information that tell us that a control dependency of ℓ to ℓ' will result in additional implicit dependencies to $V \in 2^{Var}$.

Data flow analyses define the computation of analysis information by equations, and use fixpoint computations to compute solutions to these equation systems. The equations state how analysis information for a program location is computed from given analysis information of its predecessors (in case of a forward analysis). To this end, they define a *transfer function* which states how program statements change analysis information.

We use the following transfer function $\varphi : L \times (D \times C) \rightarrow (D \times C)$ for our forward analysis. In this, $[op]^\ell$ denotes a statement (or block) in our program at location ℓ with $\Theta(\ell) = op$, and ℓ is the first parameter to φ.

- Empty statement: $\varphi([skip]^\ell)(d, c) = (d, c)$,
- boolean conditions: $\varphi([b]^\ell)(d, c) = (d, c')$ with

$$c'(\ell') = \begin{cases} c(\ell') \cup d(vars(b)) & \ell' = \ell \\ c(\ell') & \text{else ,} \end{cases}$$

- assignment: $\varphi([x := e]^\ell)(d, c) = (d', c)$ with

$$d'(v) = \begin{cases} d(vars(e)) \cup \bigcup_{\ell' \in cd(\ell)} c(\ell') & v = x \\ d(v) & \text{else .} \end{cases}$$

Note that the control dependencies are used here to determine implicit information flows. When a location ℓ has more than one predecessor in the flow relation, the analysis information coming from the predecessors needs to be joined in an appropriate way. A natural join operation for two information pairs (d, c) and (d', c') is given by

$$(d, c) \uplus (d', c') = (d \cup d', c \cup c') \text{ with}$$
$$\forall v \in Var : (d \cup d')(v) = d(v) \cup d'(v)$$
$$\forall \ell \in L : (c \cup c')(\ell) = c(\ell') \cup c'(\ell)$$

With this at hand, we define the equation system for the policy independent information flow analysis of a program S as

$$IF_\ell = \begin{cases} (\{v \mapsto \{v\} \mid v \in Var\}, \{\ell \mapsto \emptyset \mid \ell \in L\}) & \text{if } \ell \in init(S) \\ \uplus \{\varphi_{\ell'}(IF_{\ell'}) \mid (\ell', \ell) \in flow(S)\} & \text{else} \end{cases}$$

The solution to this equation system will be computed by a fixpoint computation.

We call this analysis a *policy independent analysis* since policy and security mapping have no influence on the computations of the analysis itself, and changing the policy and/or security mapping would still lead to the same results. However, the conclusion we draw from the analysis, i.e., whether a violation is occurring, has the policy and security mapping involved.

Definition 6. *Let S be a program, $P \in Pol(Sec)$ a policy and SC a security mapping. S violates (P, SC) iff*

$$\exists \ell \in L, \exists v \in Var : IF_\ell = (d, c) \wedge (SC(v), SC(d(v))) \notin P,$$

i.e. a non-secure state is occurring.

We do not state soundness of this data flow analysis here, for this see e.g. [23]. Because we statically compute dependencies, the analysis is overapproximating the actual flows of information in program executions. The analysis might thus detect violations which are not in the program (false positives). For a technique to increase the precision of the analysis see also [23]. In the following, we will nevertheless use the prior definition of violation as a concept for comparing the soundness of policy dependent analyses. Being a sound overapproximation, programs tagged as "secure" by the analysis (i.e., no violation) will indeed be secure.

As an example for such an analysis, let us consider the following small program snippet in Listing 3. The associated graph $G = (L, flow, cd)$ contains the set $L = \{1, 2, 3, 5, 6\}$ as locations and the *flow* relation according to the Listing. The control dependencies are $cd := \{3 \mapsto \{2\}\}$. For this example, the fixpoint computation for location 6 yields the result $IF_6 = (d, c)$ with $d = \{v \mapsto \emptyset; w \mapsto \{w\}; x \mapsto \{x\}; y \mapsto \{w, x\}; z \mapsto \{w, x\}\}, c = \{2 \mapsto \{x\}\}$. Using the policy-mapping-configuration (LHI, SC_{LHI}) with $SC_{LHI} = \{v \mapsto i; w \mapsto i; x \mapsto h; y \mapsto i; z \mapsto l\}$, we conclude that there is a violation since $(SC_{LHI}(z), SC_{LHI}(\{w, x\})) = (l, \{i, h\}) \notin LHI$. With the same result, we can conclude that also for another configuration (CW, SC_{CW}) with $SC_{CW} = \{v \mapsto b_2; w \mapsto b_1; x \mapsto b_2; y \mapsto c; z \mapsto c\}$ we have a violation since for $(SC_{CW}(y), SC_{CW}(\{w, x\})) = (c, \{b_1, b_2\}), (SC_{CW}(z), SC_{CW}(\{w, x\})) = (c, \{b_1, b_2\}) \notin CW$ holds.

4   Policy Dependent Information Flow Analysis

The drawback of a policy independent analysis is its space-complexity which is $\mathcal{O}(|L| \cdot (|Var|^2 + |L| \cdot |Var|))$. In the following we improve on this by just tracking the necessary policy dependent information needed to take the right conclusion.

Let us first introduce the set of *critical security classes* $Crit(P)$ of a policy P. These are those security classes that can cause a violation:

$$Crit(P) := \{s \in Sec \mid \exists s' \in Sec, S' \in 2^{Sec} : (s', S') \in P \wedge (s', S' \cup \{s\}) \notin P\}$$

In addition, the *critical entities* $V_t^{(P,SC)}$ are those entities whose initial contents are mapped to a security class of $Crit(P)$: $V_t^{(P,SC)} := \{v \in Var \mid SC(v) \in Crit(P)\}$. The critical entities are those which need to be tracked during the analysis. To this end, we slightly change our equation system by adapting the initialization of the information flow analysis to $IF_{\ell}^{(P,SC)}$ such that only this set $V_t^{(P,SC)}$ is tracked:

$$IF_{\ell}^{(P,SC)} =$$
$$\begin{cases} (\{v \mapsto \{v\} \mid v \in V_t^{(P,SC)}\} \cup \{v \mapsto \emptyset \mid v \in Var \setminus V_t^{(P,SC)}\}, \{\ell \mapsto \emptyset \mid \ell \in L\}) & \text{if } \ell \in init(S) \\ \biguplus\{\varphi_{\ell'}(IF_{\ell'}^{(P,SC)}) \mid (\ell', \ell) \in flow(S)\} & \text{else} \end{cases}$$

We leave the transfer relation and join operation untouched in comparison to Sect. 3, since it is not necessary to intersect each state change with $V_t^{(P,SC)}$ as this happens implicitly. This is shown in the following Theorem 1:

Theorem 1. *Let* $IF_{\ell} = (d_{\ell}, c_{\ell})$ *and* $IF_{\ell}^{(P,SC)} = (d'_{\ell}, c'_{\ell})$ *be the analysis results for the policy independent and policy dependent analyses, respectively. Then:*

$$\forall \ell \in L : (d_{\ell}^P, c_{\ell}^P) = (d_{\ell} \cap V_t^{(P,SC)}, c_{\ell} \cap V_t^{(P,SC)})$$

Proof. We proof this by induction.
We show first that this relation holds for all initial locations $\ell_0 \in init(S)$:

$$\forall \ell \in L : c_{\ell_0}^P(\ell) = \emptyset = c_{\ell_0}(\ell) = c_{\ell_0}(\ell) \cap V_t^{(P,SC)}$$
$$v \in V_t^{(P,SC)} : d_{\ell_0}^P(v) = v = d_{\ell_0}(v) = d_{\ell_0}(v) \cap V_t^{(P,SC)}$$
$$v \notin V_t^{(P,SC)} : d_{\ell_0}^P(v) = \emptyset = \{v\} \cap V_t^{(P,SC)} = d_{\ell_0}(v) \cap V_t^{(P,SC)}$$

We show that each transfer relation will maintain the following induction hypothesis on the result:

$$\forall \ell \in L : (d_{\ell}^P, c_{\ell}^P) = (d_{\ell} \cap V_t^{(P,SC)}, c_{\ell} \cap V_t^{(P,SC)}) \tag{2}$$

For lack of space, the proof of join and skip preserving the hypothesis is elided.

- boolean conditions:

$$\varphi([b]^{\ell'})(d_{\ell}^P, c_{\ell}^P) = (d_{\ell}^P, c_{\ell}'^P) \wedge \varphi([b]^{\ell'})(d_{\ell}, c_{\ell}) = (d_{\ell}, c_{\ell}') \overset{2}{\Rightarrow} d_{\ell}^P = d_{\ell} \cap V_t^{(P,SC)}$$

Case $\ell^* \neq \ell'$: $c_{\ell}'^P(\ell^*) = c_{\ell}^P(\ell^*) \overset{2}{=} c_{\ell}(\ell^*) \cap V_t^{(P,SC)} = c_{\ell}'(\ell^*) \cap V_t^{(P,SC)}$

Case $\ell^* = \ell'$: $c_{\ell}'^P(\ell^*) = c_{\ell}^P(\ell^*) \cup \bigcup_{b' \in vars(b)} d_{\ell}^P(b') \overset{2}{=} (c_{\ell}(\ell^*) \cap V_t^{(P,SC)}) \cup \bigcup_{b' \in vars(b)} (d_{\ell}(b') \cap V_t^{(P,SC)})$

$$= (c_{\ell}(\ell^*) \cup \bigcup_{b' \in vars(b)} d_{\ell}(b')) \cap V_t^{(P,SC)} = c_{\ell}'(\ell^*) \cap V_t^{(P,SC)}$$

– assignments:

$$\varphi([x := e]^{\ell'})(d_\ell^P, c_\ell^P) = (d_\ell'^P, c_\ell^P) \wedge \varphi([x := e]^{\ell'})(d_\ell, c_\ell) = (d_\ell', c_\ell) \stackrel{2}{\Rightarrow} c_\ell^P = c_\ell \cap V_t^{(P,SC)}$$

Case $v \neq x : d_\ell'^P(v) = d_\ell^P(v) \stackrel{2}{=} d_\ell(v) = d_\ell'(v)$

Case $v = x : d_\ell'^P(v) = \bigcup_{e' \in vars(e)} d_\ell^P(e') \cup \bigcup_{\ell^* \in cd(\ell')} c_\ell^P(\ell^*)$

$$\stackrel{2}{=} \bigcup_{e' \in vars(e)} (d_\ell(e') \cap V_t^{(P,SC)}) \cup \bigcup_{\ell^* \in cd(\ell')} (c_\ell(\ell^*) \cap V_t^{(P,SC)})$$

$$= (\bigcup_{e' \in vars(e)} d_\ell(e') \cup \bigcup_{\ell^* \in cd(\ell')} c_\ell(\ell^*)) \cap V_t^{(P,SC)} = d_\ell'(v) \cap V_t^{(P,SC)}$$

□

A direct conclusion of this theorem is that a policy dependent analysis result can be generated from a policy independent analysis result just by intersecting each computed information with $V_t^{(P,SC)}$. We assume that this improves space-complexity which is $\mathcal{O}(|L| \cdot (|Var| \cdot |V_t^{(P,SC)}| + |L| \cdot |V_t^{(P,SC)}|))$ since $V_t^{(P,SC)} \subseteq Var$.

We continue by showing in Theorem 2 that we will not miss any violation of the original analysis by computing an analysis result of $IF^{(P,SC)}$ instead of IF.

Theorem 2. *Let S be a program. Let $P \in Pol(Sec)$ be an aggregation policy and $SC : Var \to Sec$ be a security mapping. Then*

$$S \text{ violates } (P, SC) \text{ in } IF \text{ iff } S \text{ violates } (P, SC) \text{ in } IF^{(P,SC)}$$

holds.

Proof. From Theorem 1 we can conclude that $d_\ell^{(P,SC)} \subseteq d_\ell$ and hence for the images of SC

$$SC(d_\ell^{(P,SC)}(v)) \subseteq SC(d_\ell(v)) \tag{3}$$

holds as an auxiliary statement. We use this for both proof directions.
" $\Leftarrow$ " : Suppose S violates (P, SC) in $IF^{(P,SC)}$. Then there exist $\ell \in L, v \in Var$ s.t. $(SC(v), SC(d_\ell^{(P,SC)}(v))) \notin P$. Combing Statement 3 with the contra-position of the Definition 3 of aggregation policies we can therefore conclude that additionally $(SC(v), SC(d_\ell(v))) \notin P$ holds. In other words, S violates (P, SC) in IF.
" $\Rightarrow$ " : We take the contra-position. Suppose S does not violate (P, SC) in $IF^{(P,SC)}$. We show now that additionally assuming S violates (P, SC) in IF leads to a contradiction. Assuming this means there are $\ell \in L, v \in Var$ s.t. $(SC(v), SC(d_\ell(v))) \notin P \wedge (SC(v), SC(d_\ell^{(P,SC)}(v))) \in P$. Combing auxiliary Statement 3 with the Definition 3 we can conclude that there has to be a set $S' \in 2^{Sec}$ that lies in the interval $SC(d_\ell^{(P,SC)}(v)) \subseteq S' \subset SC(d_\ell(v))$ s.t. for all $T \subseteq S' (SC(v), T) \in P$ and there exist a $s' \in SC(d_\ell(v)) \setminus S'$ s.t. $(SC(v), S' \cup \{s'\}) \notin P$. But this means $s' \in Crit(P)$ by definition and so $s' \in SC(d_\ell^{(P,SC)}(v))$ ⨍. Therefore, S does not violate (P, SC) in IF. □

For an example, we go back to the program of Fig. 3. Considering again the configuration (LHI, SC_{LHI}) with $SC_{LHI} = \{v \mapsto i; w \mapsto i; x \mapsto h; y \mapsto i; z \mapsto l\}$, we conclude that

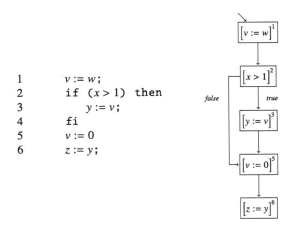

```
1       v := w;
2       if (x > 1) then
3           y := v;
4       fi
5       v := 0
6       z := y;
```

Fig. 3. A small program and its control flow automaton

$V_t^{(LHI,SC_{LHI})} = \{x\}$. The result for location 6 computed by a policy dependent analysis is $IF_6 = (d, c)$ with

$$d = \{v \mapsto \emptyset; w \mapsto \emptyset; x \mapsto \{x\}; y \mapsto \{x\}; z \mapsto \{x\}\}$$
$$c = \{2 \mapsto \{x\}\}.$$

Note that this is different from the policy independent result. Nevertheless, we can still conclude that we have a violation of the *LHI*-policy since $(SC_{LHI}(z), SC_{LHI}(\{x\})) = (l, \{h\}) \notin LHI$. Note also that – though we do preserve the violation – the state pair used for justifying the violation differs as the policy independent result used the state pair $(l, \{h, i\}) \notin LHI$. However, application of a different policy and security mapping configuration to the same analysis result is not possible anymore. For example, when applying $SC_{CW} = \{v \mapsto b_2; w \mapsto b_1; x \mapsto b_2; y \mapsto c; z \mapsto c\}$ to this analysis result, we would miss both the violations in y and z since we removed the necessary information about w. In both cases this would lead to the false conclusion of a secure analysis result with $(c, \{b_2\}) \in CW$.

5   Re-Use of Analysis Results

With the improvement in Sect. 4, we loose the property of checking violations of *arbitrary policies* and security mappings on a computed analysis result. In this section, we investigate under which circumstances we can *re-use* a policy dependent analysis result computed for a first configuration (P_1, SC_1) with $P_1 \in Pol(Sec_1)$ and $SC_1 : Var \rightarrow Sec_1$ for a second configuration (P_2, SC_2) with $P_2 \in Pol(Sec_2)$ and $SC_2 : Var \rightarrow Sec_2$.

Complete Re-Usability of Analysis Results. An intuitively easy case are the configurations where the critical variables $V_t^{(P_2,SC_2)}$ form a subset of $V_t^{(P_1,SC_1)}$.

Definition 7. *A configuration* (P_2, SC_2) *is a* relaxation *of a configuration* (P_1, SC_1) *(or* (P_1, SC_1) *is* stricter *as* (SC_2, P_2)*),* $(P_2, SC_2) \geq (P_1, SC_1)$, *iff* $V_t^{(P_2, SC_2)} \subseteq V_t^{(P_1, SC_1)}$.

In this scenario – regardless of the analysis result – all information which is needed for detecting a violation in the relaxed configuration was already tracked. So no relevant information needed for applying the second configuration on the analysis result is lost.

Proposition 1. *Let* $(P_2, SC_2) \geq (P_1, SC_1)$. *Then* S *violates* (P_2, SC_2) *in* $IF^{(P_1, SC_1)}$ *iff* S *violates* (P_2, SC_2) *in IF.*

Proof. Analogously to the proof of Theorem 2 but with

$$SC_2(d_\ell^{(P_2, SC_2)}(v)) \subseteq SC_2(d_\ell^{(P_1, SC_1)}(v)) \subseteq SC_2(d_\ell(v))$$

as auxiliary statement instead. □

Re-Use of Analysis Conclusion. Next, we investigate under which circumstances we can transfer the non-violation conclusion from one configuration to another. Contrary to the previous re-use, we do not want to check the analysis result again – against a different configuration – but simply want to transfer the ultimate result of non-violation. This requires a different kind of relationship between configurations.

Definition 8. *A configuration* (P_1, SC_1) covers (P_2, SC_2), $(P_2, SC_2) \sqsubseteq (P_1, SC_1)$ *iff*

$$\forall v \in Var, V \in 2^{Var} : (SC_2(v), SC_2(V)) \notin P_2 \Rightarrow (SC_1(v), SC_1(V)) \notin P_1 .$$

A covering allows us to directly transfer analysis conclusions.

Theorem 3. *Let* (P_1, SC_1) *and* (P_2, SC_2) *be configurations with* $(P_2, SC_2) \sqsubseteq (P_1, SC_1)$. *If* S *does not violate* (P_1, SC_1) *in* $IF^{(P_1, SC_1)}$, *then* S *does not violate* (P_2, SC_2) *in* $IF^{(P_2, SC_2)}$.

Proof. We take the contra-position. When S violates (P_2, SC_2) in $IF^{(P_2, SC_2)}$ than there exist $\ell \in L, v \in Var$ s.t. $(SC_2(v), SC_2(d_\ell(v))) \notin P_2$. By using Definition 8 for $(P_1, SC_1) \sqsupseteq (P_2, SC_2)$ we know that this additionally implies $(SC_1(v), SC_1(d_\ell(v))) \notin P_1$ holds. But this means S violates (P_1, SC_1) in IF. Using Theorem 2 we conclude that S violates (P_1, SC_1) in $IF^{(P_1, SC_1)}$. □

The two relationships between configurations are generally incomparable. First case: $(P_1, SC_1) \leq (P_2, SC_2) \Rightarrow (P_1, SC_1) \sqsupseteq (P_2, SC_2)$ does not hold for example for the following small program snippet $[v = w;]$ with $P_2 = LHI$ and $SC_2 = \{v \mapsto l; w \mapsto h\}$ and $P_1 = CW$ and $SC_1 = \{v \mapsto c; w \mapsto b_1\}$ since $(P_1, SC_1) \leq (P_2, SC_2)$ but $(P_1, SC_1) \not\sqsupseteq (P_2, SC_2)$. Second case: $(P_1, SC_1) \sqsupseteq (P_2, SC_2) \Rightarrow (P_1, SC_1) \leq (P_2, SC_2)$ does not hold for the same program with $P_2 = CW$, $SC_2 = \{v \mapsto b_1; w \mapsto c\}$ and $P_1 = LHI$ and $SC_1 = \{v \mapsto l; w \mapsto h\}$ since $(P_1, SC_1) \sqsupseteq (P_2, SC_2)$ but $(P_1, SC_1) \not\leq (P_2, SC_2)$. The reason is that our definition of $Crit(P)$ used in the definition of $V_t^{(P, SC)}$ is too coarse. For example the entry $SC(v) = b_1$ in the security-mapping function causes us to consider pairs that cannot occur. All violations that involve b_1 are either not possible or would still be violations even by removing b_1: $((c, \{c, b_1, b_2\}), (c, \{b_1, b_2\}), (b_2, \{c, b_1, b_2\}), (b_2, \{b_1, b_2\}),$ $(b_2, \{c, b_1\}), (b_2, \{b_1\}), (b_1, \{c, b_1, b_2\}), (b_1, \{b_1, b_2\}))$. All pairs that contain b_2 are not possible simple for the reason that there are no b_2-mapped entities. In the remaining violation $(b_1, \{c, b_1\})$, b_1 is not the critical variable but c.

Program Independent Re-Usability Precomputations. In the previous paragraph, we stated when we can re-use a conclusion of security from one analysis result for another configuration. This relation is not solely dependent on the policy but also on the concrete program S and security mappings SC_1, SC_2 that connect the program to the policy. Next, we want to abstract from the concrete program and security mapping, and group similar scenarios (i.e., programs and security mappings). The idea is to *precompute* certain relationships just by considering the policies $P_1 \in Pol(Sec_1), P_2 \in Pol(Sec_2)$, and later – when supplied with programs and security mappings – simply check whether these fit into one of the precomputed relationships. An analysis result for P_1 could then be used for P_2 whenever the concrete security mappings fit into one of the precomputed relationships.

Such relationships will be captured by *constellations*: A constellation F is a relation $F \subseteq Sec_1 \times Sec_2$ grouping similar scenarios. Intuitively, a *concrete constellation* $F_{(S,SC_1 \to SC_2)}$ for a program S and two different mappings SC_1 and SC_2 states that whenever $(s_1, s_2) \in F$, then there is at least one entity v in S with $SC_1(v) = s_1$ and $SC_2(v) = s_2$. If $(s_1, s_2) \notin F$ such a v does not exist:

$$F_{(S,SC_1 \to SC_2)} := \{(s_1, s_2) \in Sec_1 \times Sec_2 \mid \exists v \in Var : SC_1(v) = s_1 \text{ and } SC_2(v) = s_2\} \quad (4)$$

Concrete constellations require knowledge about security mappings. The precomputation should now derive all those constellations (i.e., relations between security classes) which would potentially allow for a P_1 analysis result to be re-usable for a policy P_2.

Definition 9. *Let $P_1 \in Pol(Sec_1)$ and $P_2 \in Pol(Sec_2)$ be security policies. An (abstract) constellation $F \subseteq Sec_1 \times Sec_2$ is* valid *for a P_1 to P_2 transfer* iff

$$\forall s_2 \in F(Sec_1); \forall S_2 \subseteq F(Sec_1); \forall s_1 \in F^{-1}(s_2); \forall S_1 : S_1 = \bigcup_{s_2' \in S_2} R_{s_2'} \text{ s.t. } \emptyset \subset R_{s_2'} \subseteq F^{-1}(s_2')$$

$$(s_2, S_2) \notin P_2 \Rightarrow (s_1, S_1) \notin P_1$$

holds. Here, F and F^{-1} are the image and reverse image of the relation F.

For the precomputation, we are not interested in all, but just in the maximal abstract constellations. Constellations can simply be ordered by subset inclusion and validity of transfer is closed under this ordering.

Proposition 2. *Let $F \subseteq Sec_1 \times Sec_2$ be a constellation valid for a P_1 to P_2 transfer. Then all $F' \subseteq F$ are constellations valid for a P_1 to P_2 transfer as well.*

We let $\mathscr{F}_{P_1,P_2}^{max}$ be the set of maximal constellations for P_1 to P_2 transfers. Whenever we have a concrete constellation at hand (i.e., we have one program and two different security mappings), we now just need to check the concrete constellation against all the precomputed maximal abstract constellations.

Definition 10. *A concrete constellation $F_{(S,SC_1 \to SC_2)}$ derived for a program S and the two configurations $(P_1, SC_1), (P_2, SC_2)$* fits *the maximal constellations for P_1 to P_2 transfers iff $\exists F_{max} \in \mathscr{F}_{P_1,P_2}^{max}$ s.t. $F_{(S,SC_1 \to SC_2)} \subseteq F_{max}$.*

Table 1. Maximal constellations for CW to LHI transfers

	c	b_1	b_2
l	√	√	√
h			
i	√	√	√

	c	b_1	b_2
l		√	√
h	√		
i	√	√	√

	c	b_1	b_2
l		√	
h	√		√
i	√	√	√

	c	b_1	b_2
l			√
h	√	√	
i	√	√	√

	c	b_1	b_2
l			
h	√	√	√
i	√	√	√

This finally gives us the intended result: Whenever a concrete constellation fits a maximal abstract one, then we obtain a covering relationship between the configurations and, hence, the analysis result for one policy can be transfered to the other policy by virtue of Theorem 3.

Proposition 3. *If a constellation $F_{(S,SC_1 \to SC_2)}$ derived for a program S and the two configurations (P_1, SC_1), (P_2, SC_2) fits the maximal constellations for P_1 to P_2 transfers, then $(P_2, SC_2) \sqsubseteq (P_1, SC_1)$ holds.*

As an example consider the constellations in Table 1. A pair (s_1, s_2) is in such a constellation whenever there is a √ in the table. Table 1 gives the maximal constellations for CW to LHI transfers. This now provides us with the following re-use possibility: Assume that we are given a program S, the CW policy and a security mapping SC_1 and our policy dependent analysis for CW has stated that the program does not violate the CW policy. Next, we are interested in security wrt. the LHI policy and a different mapping SC_2. We now compute $F_{(S,SC_1 \to SC_2)}$ and check whether it fits to one of the five maximal constellations in Table 1. If yes, we are done and can safely conclude the program also not violating the LHI policy under mapping SC_2.

6 Experimental Results

We have integrated our approach into the configurable program analysis framework CPACHECKER [3,4] and carried out a number of experiments to see in particular whether our re-use techniques pay off. Our experiments were performed on a Intel(R) Core(TM)i7 4600U @ 2.10GHz running a 64 bit Ubuntu 16.04 LTS[1] with 4096 MB RAM. The installed Java version was JDK 1.8.0.91.

For the evaluation we used a number of handcrafted programs (including our example program here called example1) plus some benchmarks from the CPACHECKER repository. The programs have up to 64 variables and up to 132 lines of code. We studied the following research questions:

RQ1 Are policy dependent analyses faster than policy independent ones?
RQ2 How many maximal constellations do we get for policy transfers, and how long does it take to compute them?
RQ3 How long does it take to determine whether a re-use of analysis results is possible?

---

[1] Actually, Ubuntu was executed in the Oracle VM Virtual Box version 4.3.28 running on a 64 bit Windows with 8192.

Table 2. Runtimes and memory consumption of policy independent and dependent analyses

File			IF	[s]	[MB]	$IF^{(P,SC)}$	[s]	[MB]
Example1	LHI	×		0.042	60	×	0.052	51
	CW	×		0.061	52	×	0.047	52
Assignchain	LHI	√		0.200	60	√	0.143	57
	CW	√		0.209	57	√	0.190	60
Loops2	LHI	√		0.046	51	√	0.046	49
	CW	√		0.054	60	√	0.064	61
Assign0	LHI	√		0.032	49	√	0.031	51
	CW	√		0.036	52	√	0.028	48
CallstackSize5	LHI	×		0.056	56	×	0.056	55
	CW	×		0.058	52	×	0.064	54
Double	LHI	√		0.082	55	√	0.078	63
	CW	×		0.044	59	×	0.047	63
Float	LHI	√		0.095	54	√	0.080	53
	CW	×		0.048	59	×	0.052	60
Float_inaccuracy_error	LHI	×		0.044	53	×	0.036	51
	CW	×		0.048	62	×	0.039	51
Implicit	LHI	×		0.051	51	×	0.047	58
	CW	×		0.075	53	×	0.042	63
Int	LHI	×		0.131	63	×	0.072	54
	CW	×		0.084	53	×	0.054	53
Large-64bit-constant	LHI	×		0.038	54	×	0.033	63
	CW	×		0.050	62	×	0.049	60
Mixed	LHI	×		0.064	53	×	0.051	54
	CW	×		0.050	59	×	0.076	53
Random	LHI	√		0.073	63	√	0.051	62
	CW	×		0.050	52	×	0.055	59
Test-multiplefuntions	LHI	×		0.081	63	×	0.066	54
	CW	×		0.092	57	×	0.075	62

Table 3. Maximal constellation computation

Policy transfer	$|\mathscr{F}^{max}|$	Max pairs	Runtime [ms]
$LHI \rightarrow LHI$	3	6	4.746
$LHI \rightarrow CW$	5	3	0.783
$CW \rightarrow LHI$	5	6	4.012
$CW \rightarrow CW$	11	3	1.956

Table 4. Runtimes of re-use checks

Example		≤	Runtime [ms]	⊒	Runtime [ms]
Example1	$LHI \rightarrow CW$	×	0.836	×	0.522
	$CW \rightarrow LHI$	√	0.288	×	0.203
Assignchain	$LHI \rightarrow CW$	×	0.659	√	0.610
	$CW \rightarrow LHI$	√	0.606	√	0.512
Loops2	$LHI \rightarrow CW$	×	0.154	×	0.100
	$CW \rightarrow LHI$	√	0.179	√	0.113
Assign0	$LHI \rightarrow CW$	×	0.178	√	0.117
	$CW \rightarrow LHI$	√	0.161	√	0.109
Callstacksize5	$LHI \rightarrow CW$	√	0.229	√	0.185
	$CW \rightarrow LHI$	√	0.189	√	0.131
Double	$LHI \rightarrow CW$	×	0.150	×	0.102
	$CW \rightarrow LHI$	√	0.139	×	0.090
Float	$LHI \rightarrow CW$	×	0.120	×	0.082
	$CW \rightarrow LHI$	√	0.128	×	0.093
Float_inaccuracy_error	$LHI \rightarrow CW$	×	0.085	×	0.072
	$CW \rightarrow LHI$	√	0.124	×	0.090
Implicit	$LHI \rightarrow CW$	×	0.113	×	0.080
	$CW \rightarrow LHI$	√	0.114	×	0.079
Int	$LHI \rightarrow CW$	×	0.155	×	0.104
	$CW \rightarrow LHI$	√	0.165	×	0.126
Large-64bit-constant	$LHI \rightarrow CW$	×	0.084	×	0.083
	$CW \rightarrow LHI$	√	0.098	×	0.070
Mixed	$LHI \rightarrow CW$	×	0.147	×	0.138
	$CW \rightarrow LHI$	√	0.130	×	0.092
Random	$LHI \rightarrow CW$	×	0.140	×	0.080
	$CW \rightarrow LHI$	√	0.123	√	0.079
Test-multiplefuntions	$LHI \rightarrow CW$	×	0.118	×	0.105
	$CW \rightarrow LHI$	√	0.138	×	0.097

Table 2 presents runtimes (in seconds) and memory consumption (in MB) for policy independent (IF) and policy dependent ($IF^{(P,SC)}$) analyses and their outcomes (× or √). In this, the security mappings were chosen randomly. We see that – as expected – the policy dependent analysis is faster in almost all cases. However, the difference in runtimes is not that big. Note, that the runtime of $IF^{(P,SC)}$ includes computation of $Crit(P)$ and $V_t^{(P,SC)}$. We conjecture that policy dependency will pay off for larger programs, but for this we need to make more experiments.

We also measured how many maximal constellations we get for policy transfers. Table 3 shows the number of maximal constellations, the maximal number of entries in these constellations (i.e., number of √s in a maximal constellation) plus the runtime for computing them (given in milliseconds). Note that it also makes sense to precompute constellations for P to P transfers, as we might be interested in checking a program wrt. the same policy but with a different security mapping. We see that precomputation of constellations is generally fast.

Finally, Table 4 gives the runtimes for checking relaxation and covering relationships. For determining covering, we have used the precomputed maximal constellations. Note that runtimes are again given in milliseconds. In summary, our experiments show that policy dependent analyses plus re-use definitely pays off: precomputation of constellations just has to be done once and is fast, the checking of covering is also fast and – once it succeeds – can save us from doing another complete policy dependent analysis.

7 Conclusion

In this paper, we presented two techniques for information flow analysis of arbitrary aggregation policies. The first analysis computes policy independent information on which a policy of interest can then be applied. The second analysis is goal-oriented and computes reduced analysis information tailored to a specific configurations – at the cost of loosing the property of policy independency.

We then focused on re-use of previously computed policy dependent results for different configurations. To this end, we studied two refinement relations between policies: Starting with a policy dependent analysis result of a first configuration, the relaxation relation tells us that the computed information can be used for checking violations for a second configuration. The covering relation on the other hand allows to directly transfer results of non-violation from one to another configuration, without further checking. We furthermore introduced precomputations easing covering checks.

We performed experiments showing that the runtime of policy dependent analyses can justify its usage. The experiments further showed that re-use can pay off as refinement checking is very fast.

Future Work. As future work, building up on the techniques of Jakobs and Wehrheim [12, 13] we plan the development of proof-carrying-code techniques [20] (PCC) for information flow analysis. We intend to expand the analysis information of our policy dependent and independent analyses described in this paper together with the ideas from goal-oriented refinement of false positives from our previous paper [23] to PCC-techniques.

With respect to refinement relations, we plan to investigate whether we can enhance the definition of ≤-relation in such a way that a ⊒-relation implies a ≤-relation (at least for aggregation policies). Also, we intend to remove our current restriction to aggregation policies (whose purpose is to guarantee sound joining in data-flow analyses) and investigate refinement relations between unrestricted configurations.

References

1. Amtoft, T., Banerjee, A.: Information flow analysis in logical form. In: Giacobazzi, R. (ed.) SAS 2004. LNCS, vol. 3148, pp. 100–115. Springer, Heidelberg (2004). doi:10.1007/978-3-540-27864-1_10
2. Arzt, S., Rasthofer, S., Fritz, C., Bodden, E., Bartel, A., Klein, J., Le Traon, Y., Octeau, D., McDaniel, P.: FlowDroid: precise context, flow, field, object-sensitive and lifecycle-aware taint analysis for android apps. In: PLDI, pp. 259–269. ACM (2014)
3. Beyer, D., Henzinger, T.A., Théoduloz, G.: Configurable software verification: concretizing the convergence of model checking and program analysis. In: Damm, W., Hermanns, H. (eds.) CAV 2007. LNCS, vol. 4590, pp. 504–518. Springer, Heidelberg (2007). doi:10.1007/978-3-540-73368-3_51
4. Beyer, D., Keremoglu, M.E., Wendler, P.: Predicate abstraction with adjustable-block encoding. In: Bloem, R., Sharygina, N. (eds.) FMCAD 2010, pp. 189–197. IEEE (2010)
5. Brewer, D.F.C., Nash, M.J.: The chinese wall security policy. In: IEEE Symposium on Security and Privacy, 1989, pp. 206–214. IEEE Computer Society (1989)
6. Foley, S.N.: Unifying Information Flow Policies. Technical report, DTIC Document (1990)
7. Foley, S.N.: Aggregation and separation as noninterference properties. J. Comput. Secur. 1(2), 159–188 (1992)
8. Hammer, C., Krinke, J., Snelting, G.: Information flow control for java based on path conditions in dependence graphs. In: IEEE International Symposium on Secure Software Engineering 2006 (2006)
9. Holavanalli, S., Manuel, D., Nanjundaswamy, V., Rosenberg, B., Shen, F., Ko, S.Y., Ziarek, L.: Flow permissions for android. In: ASE, pp. 652–657 (2013)
10. Horwitz, S., Reps, T.W.: The use of program dependence graphs in software engineering. In: Montgomery, T., Clarke, L.A., Ghezzi, C. (eds.) ICSE 1992, pp. 392–411. ACM Press (1992)
11. Hunt, S., Sands, D.: On flow-sensitive security types. In: POPL 2006 (2006)
12. Jakobs, M., Wehrheim, H.: Certification for configurable program analysis. In: Rungta, N., Tkachuk, O. (eds.) SPIN 2014, pp. 30–39. ACM (2014)
13. Jakobs, M., Wehrheim, H.: Programs from proofs of predicated dataflow analyses. In: Wainwright, R.L., Corchado, J.M., Bechini, A., Hong, J. (eds.) SAC 2015, pp. 1729–1736. ACM (2015)
14. Klieber, W., Flynn, L., Bhosale, A., Jia, L., Bauer, L.: Android taint flow analysis for app sets. In: SOAP, pp. 1–6 (2014)
15. Rustan, K., Leino, M., Joshi, R.: A semantic approach to secure information flow. In: Jeuring, J. (ed.) MPC 1998. LNCS, vol. 1422, pp. 254–271. Springer, Heidelberg (1998). doi:10.1007/BFb0054294
16. Lengauer, T., Tarjan, R.E.: A fast algorithm for finding dominators in a flowgraph. ACM Trans. Program. Lang. Syst. 1(1), 121–141 (1979)
17. Mantel, H.: Possibilistic definitions of security - an assembly kit. In: IEEE Computer Security Foundations Workshop, CSFW 2000. IEEE Computer Society (2000)
18. Mantel, H.: Preserving information flow properties under refinement. In: IEEE Symposium on Security and Privacy 2001, pp. 78–91. IEEE Computer Society (2001)
19. Mantel, H.: On the composition of secure systems. In: IEEE Symposium on Security and Privacy 2002 (2002)
20. Necula, G.C.: Proof-carrying code. In: Lee, P., Henglein, F., Jones, N.D. (eds.) POPL 1997, pp. 106–119. ACM Press (1997)
21. Nielson, F., Nielson, H.R., Hankin, C.: Principles of Program Analysis. Springer, New York (1999)

22. Taghdiri, M., Snelting, G., Sinz, C.: Information flow analysis via path condition refinement. In: Degano, P., Etalle, S., Guttman, J. (eds.) FAST 2010. LNCS, vol. 6561, pp. 65–79. Springer, Heidelberg (2011). doi:10.1007/978-3-642-19751-2_5

23. Töws, M., Wehrheim, H.: A CEGAR scheme for information flow analysis. In: Ogata, K., Lawford, M., Liu, S. (eds.) ICFEM 2016. LNCS, vol. 10009, pp. 466–483. Springer, Cham (2016). doi:10.1007/978-3-319-47846-3_29

24. Wei, F., Roy, S., Ou, X., Robby: amandroid: a precise and general inter-component data flow analysis framework for security vetting of android apps. In: CCS, pp. 1329–1341. ACM, New York (2014)

25. Yang, Z., Yang, M.: LeakMiner: detect information leakage on android with static taint analysis. In: WCSE, pp. 101–104 (2012)

Improving Probability Estimation Through Active Probabilistic Model Learning

Jingyi Wang[1](✉), Xiaohong Chen[1,2], Jun Sun[1], and Shengchao Qin[3]

[1] Singapore University of Technology and Design, Singapore, Singapore
wangjyee@gmail.com, jingyi_wang@mymail.sutd.edu.sg
[2] The University of Illinois at Urbana-Champaign, Champaign, USA
[3] Teesside University, Middlesbrough, UK

Abstract. It is often necessary to estimate the probability of certain events occurring in a system. For instance, knowing the probability of events triggering a shutdown sequence allows us to estimate the availability of the system. One approach is to run the system multiple times and then construct a probabilistic model to estimate the probability. When the probability of the event to be estimated is low, many system runs are necessary in order to generate an accurate estimation. For complex cyber-physical systems, each system run is costly and time-consuming, and thus it is important to reduce the number of system runs while providing accurate estimation. In this work, we assume that the user can actively tune the initial configuration of the system before the system runs and answer the following research question: how should the user set the initial configuration so that a better estimation can be learned with fewer system runs. The proposed approach has been implemented and evaluated with a set of benchmark models, random generated models, and a real-world water treatment system.

1 Introduction

It is often necessary to estimate the probability of certain events occurring in a given system. In the following, we describe a real-world scenario where such a task arises. The SWaT testbed[1] at Singapore University of Technology and Design is a complex water treatment system that consists of multiple phases including filtering and chemical dosing, etc. The system is safety critical and has built-in monitors that check violation of safety requirements. For instance, water-level monitors are put in place to check whether the level of water in tanks is too low or too high. Whenever a monitor issues a safety alarm, a shutdown sequence is triggered so that the system halts and expert engineers are called upon to inspect the system. Such a design guarantees that safety violation is detected at runtime, at the cost of potentially shutting the system down occasionally. To show that the system satisfies certain availability requirements, we would like

---

This work was supported by project RG101NR0114A.
[1] http://itrust.sutd.edu.sg/research/testbeds/secure-water-treatment-swat/.

Z. Duan and L. Ong (Eds.): ICFEM 2017, LNCS 10610, pp. 379–395, 2017.
https://doi.org/10.1007/978-3-319-68690-5_23

to show that the likelihood of triggering the shutdown sequence is low, i.e., the probability of shutdown triggering events occurring is below a certain threshold.

One way to solve the problem is to run the system multiple times, observe how the system evolves through time, construct a probabilistic model of the system (i.e., a discrete-time Markov Chain [5]) and estimate the probability of the interesting events based on the model. To observe how the system evolves at runtime, we can introduce a logger in the system to record the system state, e.g., to log the sensor readings of the water level and the status of the valves and pumps in the system. To construct the Markov Chain model, we can apply an estimation function to estimate the transition probability between system states. Commonly used estimators include empirical frequency, Laplace estimator [9] and Good-Turing estimator [10]. To estimate the probability of the interesting events occurring, we additionally need an initial probability distribution, i.e., the probability of having certain initial configuration of the system (e.g., the initial water level of the tanks and the status of the actuators), which we can often obtain either through historical data or expert experience. When we run the system multiple times, the same initial distribution is applied to configure the system accordingly.

Such a method however may not be effective if the interesting events have low probability. For instance, some events may only be triggered under certain particular initial configurations. For instance, the event of water underflow may only occur when the initial water level is set to be near the boundary and the water valve is set to drain the water. If there are a large number of possible initial configurations and these particular initial configurations have low probability according to the initial distribution, it would take many system runs so that we can trigger the events for a sufficient number of times and estimate their probability accurately. However, conducting an experiment to run a system like the water treatment system (or other real-world cyber-physical systems) often has non-negligible cost. Thus, it is desirable to reduce the number of system runs while being able to accurately estimate the transition probability based on which we compute the probability of the interesting events.

In this work, we propose to smartly configure the system initially so that during the system runs, "interesting" system transitions are more likely to be triggered (than configuring the system according to the originally given initial distribution). Our idea is to first get an initial estimation of the transition probabilities, based on which we calculate an 'optimal' initial distribution which we should follow to conduct further experiments. Intuitively, an initial distribution is considered optimal if the estimation of the transition probabilities based on the experiment results according to the initial distribution is more accurate than other initial distributions. Afterwards, we run the system multiple times according to the optimal initial distribution and update the estimation of the transition probabilities accordingly. We repeat the process until a stopping criteria is satisfied.

Our method can be viewed as an active learning method for Markov Chain models [5], which are useful in modeling and analyzing a wide range of systems [20]. The method is designed to learn a Markov Chain model actively in a particular setting. That is, we assume that a prior initial distribution is given, and we are allowed to tune the initial probability distribution but not the transition probability distributions, which yields a weaker and more realistic requirement than other distribution manipulation techniques for rare event analysis like importance sampling [12]. In addition, our method is not restricted to one particular way of estimating transition probability. We show that our method works for common estimation techniques like empirical frequency, Laplace estimator and Good-Turing estimator. In order to evaluate the effectiveness of our approach, we implemented a prototype tool in Java called IDO (short for Initial Distribution Optimizer). We set up experiments to compare IDO with alternative approaches. The experiment results show that IDO always estimates more accurately with the same number of system runs, or requires fewer system runs to achieve the same level of accuracy. Our test subjects include several benchmark systems, a set of randomly generated models, and the SWaT testbed mentioned above.

2 Problem Definition

We will formally state the problem that we consider in this paper upon discrete-time Markov chains (DTMCs), a widely-used formalization that models probabilistic transition system with a finite number of states [20]. Before that, we will present a succinct review of DTMCs and introduce our notations.

2.1 The Model

Definition 1. *A discrete-time Markov chain (DTMC) is a tuple $\mathcal{M} = (S, S_0, P, \mu)$ with a finite nonempty set of states S, a nonempty set of initial states $S_0 \subseteq S$, a transition matrix $P : S \times S \to [0,1]$, and an initial probability distribution μ over initial states. A path is a nonempty sequence of states starting with an initial state.*

Note that different from the standard definition, we distinguish a set of initial states from the rest and constrain that the initial distribution μ only assign probabilities to initial states. The value $P(s, s')$ (where $s, s' \in S$) is the conditional probability of visiting s' given the current state is s. When the set of states S is indexed or enumerated in order (which is often the case), we denote the ith state of S as s_i, and $P(s_i, s_j)$ as p_{ij}. Given a path $s_{i_1} \dots s_{i_k}$, the probability of observing that path is $\mu_{i_1} p_{i_1 i_2} \dots p_{i_{k-1} i_k}$, denoted[2]

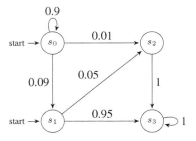

Fig. 1. An example DTMC

---

[2] We use P to denote transition matrices and $\mathscr{P}$ to denote the probability measure defined by P.

by $\mathscr{P}(i_1 \ldots i_k)$. Which depends not only on the transition matrix P but also on the initial distribution μ. Figure 1 shows an example DTMC with four states and two initial states. Transition probabilities are labeled upon arrows, and the initial states are attached by the label "start". Not drawing an arrow means a zero transition probability.

2.2   The Problem

The problem we investigate in this work can be defined as follows. Given a system that is modeled as a DTMC with a fixed set of states and an initial distribution, how to estimate (1) its transition matrix, and (2) the probability of reaching certain states (a.k.a. the *reachability probability*)? In this paper, we assume the transition matrix is fixed, but we can try different initial configurations when running the system. In our SWaT testbed [1], for example, we can set different levels of water in tanks (and/or other configurations such as the initial pH value of the water) when we initialize the system, and once the system is turned on, we can only observe how the system evolves through time, but not affect how it goes.

Contrary to our approach, a *passive* approach to solve the problem is to set the initial configuration of the system as the given initial distribution μ and run the system multiple times. After a couple times of experiments, the actual transition matrix P can be estimated based on the experiment results (and subsequently the reachability probability can be estimated, too). In the beginning of every experiment, an initial state s is randomly generated according to the initial distribution μ. Starting from s, the system transits to the next state according to the transition matrix P, and then transits the third state, and so on, until a certain number of steps are taken and a path is obtained. Such a random path, often denoted as π, is a random variable whose distribution is fully decided by the initial distribution μ and the transition matrix P. We denote that as $\pi \sim (P, \mu)$. By abuse use of notation, we write $\Pi \sim (P, \mu)$ if Π is a set of paths that are independently generated from P and μ. Once a sample set $\Pi \sim (P, \mu)$ is obtained, an estimation function (a.k.a. an estimator) is applied on Π to generate an estimation $\widehat{P}$ of the transition matrix P. In practice, there are three commonly used estimators, which we introduce in the next definition.

Definition 2. *Let $\Pi \sim (P, \mu)$ be a set of path samples. For any states s and t, let $\#_{s,t}$ be the number of times that the one-step transition from s to t occurs in Π, and $\#_s = \Sigma_t \#_{s,t}$. We provide three commonly-used estimators $\widehat{P}$'s that are purely based on $\#_{s,t}$'s. They are*

- *The empirical frequency estimator: $\widehat{P}_E(s,t) = \#_{s,t}/\#_s$;*
- *The Laplace estimator [9]: $\widehat{P}_L(s,t) = (1 + \#_{s,t})/(n + \#_s)$, where n is the total number of states in $\mathcal{M}$;*
- *The Good-Turing estimator [10]: $\widehat{P}_G(s,t) = \frac{(\#_{s,t}+1) \times N_{\#_{s,t}+1}}{\#_s \times N_{\#_{s,t}}}$ where $N_r = |\{t \in S | \#_{s,t} = r\}|$ is the number of states which are visited after s exactly r times in Π.*

The empirical frequency estimator estimates the transition probability based on the frequency. It may be problematic if the system contains transitions with low probability. That is, if a transition from s to t is not observed in Π because the actual $P(s,t)$ is small, $\widehat{P}_E(s,t)$ is zero by the empirical frequency estimator. The Laplace estimator overcomes this problem by adding a constant 1 to the numerator and the number of state to the denominator of the estimated transition probability. In other words, if state t is never visited after state s, the probability $\widehat{P}_L(s,t) = 1/(n + \#_s)$. The Good-Turing estimator is widely used when the amount of samples is relatively small compared to the number of states. We skip the discussion on how the Good-Turing estimator works intuitively and refer the readers to [10] for comprehensive discussion on when different estimators are effective. Once an estimation of P is obtained, we can calculate the probability of reaching certain state straightforwardly using methods like probabilistic model checking [5].

All the above-mentioned estimators guarantee that they converge to an accurate estimate of P with an unbounded number of samples. It might however take a large number of samples in order to obtain an accurate estimate of P. In practice, we may not be able to run a complex system (like the SWaT tested) for many times since each run has non-negligible cost in terms of money and time. *In this work, we aim to develop a method which allows us to reduce the number of samples required to generate an accurate estimate of P by actively choosing the initial state to sample from.* Ideally, it should work with any of the above-mentioned estimators. In particular, the question is: if a user is only allowed to tune the initial distribution (e.g., by initializing the system using a probability distribution of initial configuration/inputs different from μ_0), how should she/he tune the initial distribution so that we can estimate P more effectively? We believe this is a realistic assumption. Consider the above-mentioned SWaT test bed for example. The user can only choose a set of initial configurations following certain distribution to perform experiments and simply observe how the system evolves afterwards.

3   Our Approach

Our approach is inspired and built on the idea of *active learning*, one that has been studied extensively in automaton learning (e.g., [4]) and classifier learning (e.g., [7]). The basic idea is to sample smartly, based on the current estimation $\widehat{P}$ of the transition matrix, so as to obtain informative samples that effectively improve the estimation.

The overall algorithm is shown in Algorithm 1. Initially, since we do not have any knowledge of P, we obtain samples of the system with the user-provided initial distribution μ. After obtaining some number of samples, we apply an estimator to obtain an estimate $\widehat{P}$ at line 4. Based on $\widehat{P}$ and the current samples Π, we compute an "optimal" initial distribution μ_0 with respect to our objective at line 5. Then, we repeat from line 3, i.e., acquire more samples Π' based on μ_0, add them to Π and apply the estimator on the updated Π to obtain an updated estimation of $\widehat{P}$. The process continues until a stopping criterion is satisfied. This approach is inspired by the expectation-maximization (EM) algorithm from statistics [16].

Algorithm 1. Sampling based on active learning

1: Let μ_0 be μ, Π be empty;
2: **while** stopping criteria unsatisfied **do**
3:    Sample the system N times to obtain $\Pi' \sim (\mathcal{M}, \mu_0)$;
4:    Update $\Pi = \Pi \cup \Pi'$;
5:    Apply an estimator to obtain $\widehat{P}$ based on Π;
6:    Set μ_0 to be the optimal initial distribution computed based on $\widehat{P}$ and Π;
7: **end while**
8: Output $\widehat{P}$;

3.1 Estimating Transition Probability

In order to identify the "optimal" initial distribution, we must firstly identify our analysis objective. In this work, our overall objective is to estimate the transition probability and reachability probability. In the following, we first focus on estimating the transition matrix P. The accuracy of an estimation $\widehat{P}$ of P can be measured using measurements such as the *mean squared error* (MSE), the standard deviation, or bias [3]. As an example, the MSE of an estimation $\widehat{P}$ is defined as

$$\mathrm{MSE}(\widehat{P}, P) = \frac{1}{(|S|)^2} \sum_{s,t \in S} (\widehat{P}(s,t) - P(s,t))^2. \qquad (3.1)$$

Ideally, we would like to identify an initial distribution μ_0 such that the estimation would be most accurate. However, since the actual transition matrix P is unknown, we cannot directly compare the estimation $\widehat{P}$ and P (e.g., in term of MSE). Thus, we need to define an alternative optimization objective. The optimization objective is important as it should guarantee that not only will we eventually learn P accurately, but also we will do it in a more effective way than sampling according to μ. Intuitively, a sample is most useful in improving our estimation if it can help eliminate most uncertainty in our current learning result. In general, if a state is rarely visited by the training samples, the estimation of the transition probability from this state is likely to be inaccurate, whereas transition probabilities from a state which is often visited is likely to be estimated more accurately. For instance, given the DTMC in Fig. 1, it is hard to estimate the probability of transitioning from state s_1 to s_2 if a limited number of samples are available and s_1 is visited only a few times. Based on this observation, the following optimization objective is adopted.

$$\max_{\mu_0 \in \mathcal{D}} \min_{s \in S} E(s, \mu_0, \widehat{P}, N, k) \qquad (3.2)$$

where $\mathcal{D}$ is the set of all initial distributions that only assigns non-zero probability to initial states; and $E(s, \mu_0, \widehat{P}, N, k)$ is the expected number of times a state s is visited if we sample N paths (each of which with k transitions) according to the initial distribution μ_0 and the transition matrix $\widehat{P}$. It is defined as follows.

$$E(s, \mu_0, \widehat{P}, N, k) = N\left(\mu_0(s) + \mu_0\widehat{P}(s) + \mu_0\widehat{P}^2(s) + \cdots + \mu_0\widehat{P}^k(s)\right) \quad (3.3)$$

where $\mu_0\widehat{P}^l(s)$ is the probability of visiting state s after l transitions. Intuitively, we would like to identify an initial distribution μ_0 so as to maximize the probability of visiting the least likely state to be visited within k steps.

Optimization. In each iteration, given current sample set Π, let $\gamma = \min_{s \in S} \#_s$ and $i = \mathrm{argmin}_{s \in S} \#_s$. The optimization objective of Eq. 3.2 turns to the following.

$$\max_{\mu_0 \in \mathcal{D}} E(i, \mu_0, \widehat{P}, N, k) = \max_{\mu_0 \in \mathcal{D}} N\left(\mu_0(i) + \mu_0\widehat{P}(i) + \mu_0\widehat{P}^2(i) + \cdots + \mu_0\widehat{P}^k(i)\right) \quad (3.4)$$

The initial distribution μ_0 has two constraints: (1) every element of μ_0 is between 0 and 1; (2) the sum of the elements are equal to 1. This forms a standard linear optimization problem [2] which can be solved by applying a linear optimization solver like Gurobi [11]. We then generate the 'optimal' initial distribution μ_0 by solving the optimization problem stated in Eq. 3.4 over the constraints.

Convergence. In this section, we discuss why the above objective works. In particular, we show that it guarantees we would always converge to an accurate estimation of P and our estimation $\widehat{P}$ monotonically improves, no matter which of the three above-mentioned estimators are used.

The following notations are frequently used. We define $\|\cdot\|$ as the max norm $\|A\| = \max_{ij}|a_{ij}|$. Notice that the estimator $\widehat{P}$ is a random variable that is fully determined by the path samples, whose distribution is given by $\mathscr{P}$, so we simply use the same notation $\mathscr{P}(\phi)$ with ϕ being a predicate to denote the probability of ϕ being true. The choice of matrix normality in this paper is mainly a taste of flavor. Different norms will result in different actual bounds of the inequalities that will be presented later, but since our goal here is to establish that the estimation $\widehat{P}$ getting closer and closer to the actual value P, i.e., $\|\widehat{P} - P\| \to 0$, using different norms will not make a difference, thanks to the next proposition, whose proof we omit.

Proposition 1. *Suppose $\|\cdot\|_1$ and $\|\cdot\|_2$ are two matrix norms, and $A_1, A_2, \ldots$ is a sequence of $m \times n$ matrices. Then*

$$\|A_n\|_1 \to 0 \quad \text{iff} \quad \|A_n\|_2 \to 0.$$

Definition 3. *An estimator is strongly-consistent, if $\mathscr{P}(\|\widehat{P} - P\| < \epsilon) \to 1$ as $\gamma = \min_{s \in S} \#_s \to \infty$. It is stable, if $\mathscr{P}(\|\widehat{P} - P\| < \epsilon) > 1 - \delta(\epsilon, \gamma)$, where for any $\epsilon > 0$, $\delta(\epsilon, \gamma)$ is a non-increasing function as γ increases.*

Estimators defined as above guarantee that, by optimizing our optimization objective, $\widehat{P}$ will converge to P (strongly-consistency), and $\widehat{P}$ will improve monotonically (stability). This is stated in the following Lemma.

Lemma 1. *The return value of Algorithm 1 converges to the exact transition matrix P if an estimator is strongly-consistent and stable.*

Proof. Recall that our algorithm samples according to an initial distribution which maximizes $\min_{s \in S} E(s, \mu_0, \widehat{P}, N, k)$ during each iteration. As it goes to ∞, by the definition of a strongly-consistent and stable estimator, the maximum difference between two entries of P and $\widehat{P}$ converges to 0. Thus, for every entry (i, j), we have $|p_{ij} - \widehat{p}_{ij}| \leq \|P - \widehat{P}\| \to 0$, i.e., the estimation $\widehat{P}$ converges to P.   □

Next, we establish all above-mentioned estimators are strongly-consistent and stable.

Lemma 2. *The empirical frequency estimator, Laplace estimator and Good-Turing estimator are all strongly-consistent and stable.*

Proof. Let n be the number of states in the DTMC, $\#_s$ be the number that state s is visited, and $\gamma = \min_s \#_s$. For each $1 \leq k \leq n$, we have $\#_k \geq \gamma$. Let (i, j) be the index pair such that $p_{ij} - \widehat{p}_{ij} = \|P - \widehat{P}\|$. By Chebyshev inequality, we have

$$\mathscr{P}(\|\widehat{P} - P\| < \epsilon) = \mathscr{P}(|\widehat{p}_{ij} - p_{ij}| < \epsilon) \geq 1 - \frac{1}{\epsilon^2} \operatorname{Var} \widehat{p}_{ij}$$

For strong-consistency, we only need to show that for each estimator we have $\operatorname{Var} \widehat{p}_{ij} \to 0$ as $\gamma = \min_s \#_s \to \infty$. For stability, we only need to show that for each estimator we have $\operatorname{Var} \widehat{p}_{ij}$ is a non-increasing function as γ increases. Respectively,

Empirical Frequency Estimator. It is easy to prove

$$\operatorname{Var} \widehat{p}_{ij} \leq \frac{p_{ij}(1 - p_{ij})}{\gamma} \to 0 \quad \text{as} \quad \gamma \to \infty \text{ and is non-increasing as } \gamma \text{ increases.}$$

Laplace Estimator. It is easy to prove

$$\operatorname{Var} \widehat{p}_{ij} \leq \frac{\gamma}{4(\gamma + n)^2} \to 0 \quad \text{as} \quad \gamma \to \infty \text{ and is non-increasing as } \gamma \text{ increases.}$$

Good-Turing Estimator. Assume state j occurs λ times after state i, i.e., $\#_{ij} = \lambda$. From the results of [15], for $\forall \sigma > 0$, the approximate bound is:

$$\|\widehat{P}_G - P\| = |\widehat{p}_{ij} - p_{ij}| \leq \begin{cases} 2\ln(3\gamma/\sigma)\sqrt{\frac{2\ln 3/\sigma}{\gamma}} & \text{if } \lambda \text{ small compared to } \ln \frac{3\gamma}{\sigma} \\ \\ 2\lambda\sqrt{\frac{2\ln 3/\sigma}{\gamma}} & \text{if } \lambda \text{ large compared to } \ln \frac{3\gamma}{\sigma} \end{cases} .$$

In both cases, the bounds go to 0 as $\gamma \to \infty$ and is monotonically decreasing as γ increases. $\qquad\square$

Thus, we have the following Theorem on the correctness of Algorithm 1.

Theorem 1. *The estimation $\widehat{P}$ returned by Algorithm 1 eventually converges to P for the empirical frequency estimator, Laplace estimator and Good-Turing estimator.*

Proof. By Lemmas 1 and 2. $\qquad\square$

Stopping Criteria of Algorithm 1. We provide two stopping criteria for two common scenarios when the algorithm is used in practice. The first is when we have a limited sampling budget, which is a very common case in reality. For instance, we can run the system only for a bounded number of times, in which case Algorithm 1 terminates when we run out of budget. The other scenario is when we require our estimation $\widehat{P}$ be as close as possible to the actual P with a high probability. That is, $\mathscr{P}(|p_{ij} - \hat{p}_{ij}| < \epsilon) > 1 - \alpha$ for all i and j, where the *sampling parameters* ϵ and α are positive numbers close to 0. Given ϵ and α, we calculate a threshold ξ on the minimum number of $\#_i$ to satisfy the requirement based on the bounds described in the proof of Lemma 2. Then we run Algorithm 1 until $\gamma = \min_{s \in S} \#_s \geq \xi$. Note that the latter scenario often results in a larger sample size given a small ϵ and α, as we observed from our experiments described in Sect. 4.2.

Approximation of Optimization. In Algorithm 1, the optimal initial distribution is calculated based on the estimation $\widehat{P}$, instead of the actual P. In the following, we aim to show that sampling according to the optimal initial distributions calculated based on $\widehat{P}$ approximates sampling according to the actual optimal initial distribution in terms of the numbers that states are visited.

Assume $\widehat{P}$ and P are $n \times n$ square matrices and their difference is bounded by ϵ. Define $\widehat{A} = I + \widehat{P} + \widehat{P}^2 + \cdots + \widehat{P}^{l-1}$ and $A = I + P + P^2 + \cdots + P^{l-1}$ be the l-step accumulation matrices of $\widehat{P}$ and P respectively for $l > 0$. The next proposition shows the difference between $\widehat{A}$ and A is bounded by $O(l^2)\epsilon$.

Proposition 2. $\|\widehat{A} - A\| \leq l(l-1)n\epsilon/2$.

Proof. Let $\tau_k = \|\widehat{P}^k - P^k\|$ for any $k \geq 0$, then

$$
\begin{aligned}
\|\widehat{A} - A\| &\leq \|(I - I) + (\widehat{P} - P) + \cdots + (\widehat{P}^{l-1} - P^{l-1})\| \\
&\leq \|I - I\| + \|\widehat{P} - P\| + \cdots + \|\widehat{P}^{l-1} - P^{l-1}\| \\
&= \tau_0 + \tau_1 + \cdots + \tau_{l-1}.
\end{aligned}
$$

Recall that $\widehat{P}$ and P are transition matrices. We have $\tau_0 = 0$, and for any $k > 0$,

$$
\begin{aligned}
\tau_k &= \|\widehat{P}^k - P^k\| = \|\widehat{P}^k - \widehat{P}^{k-1}P + \widehat{P}^{k-1}P - P^k\| \\
&\leq \|\widehat{P}^{k-1}(\widehat{P} - P)\| + \|(\widehat{P}^{k-1} - P^{k-1})P\| \\
&\leq n\|\widehat{P} - P\| + \|\widehat{P}^{k-1} - P^{k-1}\| \\
&\leq n\epsilon + \tau_{k-1} \leq 2n\epsilon + \tau_{k-2} \leq \cdots \leq kn\epsilon + \tau_0 = kn\epsilon.
\end{aligned}
$$

Therefore $\|\widehat{A} - A\| \leq (0 + 1 + 2 + \cdots + l)n\epsilon = l(l-1)n\epsilon/2$. $\qquad\square$

Next, we take the initial distribution μ into consideration. We use subscript i to denote the ith projection of vectors.

Proposition 3. *For any μ and i, $|(\mu A)_i - (\mu \widehat{A})_i| \le l(l-1)n\epsilon/2$.*

Proof. Assume $\mu = (\mu_1, \ldots, \mu_n)$, $A = (a_{ij})_{n \times n}$, and $\widehat{A} = (\hat{a}_{ij})_{n \times n}$. Notice that μ is a distribution, so $\mu_1 + \cdots + \mu_n = 1$ and $0 \le \mu_i \le 1$, for each $i = 1, \ldots, n$, and

$$|(\mu \widehat{A})_i - (\mu A)_i| \le \mu_1 |\hat{a}_{1i} - a_{1i}| + \cdots + \mu_n |\hat{a}_{ni} - a_{ni}|$$
$$\le \max(|\hat{a}_{1i} - a_{1i}|, \ldots, |\hat{a}_{ni} - a_{ni}|)$$
$$\le \|\widehat{A} - A\| \le l(l-1)n\epsilon/2. \qquad \square$$

Recall that our optimization goal is formula (3.2), in which the estimation $\widehat{P}$ is used as an approximation of the actual transition matrix P, and as a result, the optimal initial distribution $\hat{\mu}_{opt} = \arg\max_\mu \min_i(\mu\widehat{A})_i$ is in general not the actual (unknown) optimal initial distribution $\mu_{opt} = \arg\max_\mu \min_i(\mu A)_i$. The next proposition shows that even so, it makes little difference whether we do sampling according to $\hat{\mu}_{opt}$ or μ_{opt}, as long as our estimation $\widehat{P}$ gets close enough to the actual P.

Proposition 4. *Under previous notations and conditions, $|\min_i(\hat{\mu}_{opt}A)_i - \min_i(\mu_{opt}A)_i| \le l(l-1)n\epsilon$.*

Proof.

$$|\min_i(\hat{\mu}_{opt}A)_i - \min_i(\mu_{opt}A)_i| = |\min_i(\hat{\mu}_{opt}A)_i - \max_\mu\min_i(\mu A)_i|$$
$$\le |\min_i(\hat{\mu}_{opt}A)_i - \max_\mu\min_i(\mu\widehat{A})_i| + |\max_\mu\min_i(\mu\widehat{A})_i - \max_\mu\min_i(\mu A)_i|$$
$$\le |\min_i(\hat{\mu}_{opt}A)_i - \min_i(\hat{\mu}_{opt}\widehat{A})_i| + l(l-1)n\epsilon/2 \le l(l-1)n\epsilon. \qquad \square$$

Recall that $\#_s$ is the expected number of times we visit a state s when sampling according to (P, μ). In particular, we write $\widehat{\#}_s$ if paths are sampled from the optimal initial distribution obtained by solving the optimization problem (3.2), i.e., from $(P, \hat{\mu}_{opt})$. Then Proposition 4 directly leads to the next main theorem, which guarantees that solving the approximate optimization problem gives us an approximate solution to the original optimization problem, and thus justifies our approach.

Theorem 2. *Using previous notations, $|\max_\mu\min_i \#_s - \min_i \widehat{\#}_s| \le l(l-1)n\epsilon$ if $\|\widehat{P} - P\| < \epsilon$, where l is the length of each path sample and n is the dimension of the transition matrix P and its estimation $\widehat{P}$.*

3.2   Estimating Reachability Probability

In previous sections, we have shown how to obtain an approximation $\widehat{P}$ of the actual transition matrix P. From now on we will assume such an approximation exists, and will use $\widehat{\mathscr{P}}$ to denote the probability measure that it defines. In this section, we will show one important application of such approximation $\widehat{\mathscr{P}}$, which is estimating the *reachability probability*, the probability of reaching certain states or observing certain events occurring. Given a DTMC $\mathcal{M} = (S, S_0, P, \mu)$, the probability of reaching state t from state s within l steps is defined as follows.

$$\mathscr{P}(Reach_l(s,t)) = \begin{cases} 1 & \text{if } s = t \wedge l \geq 0, \\ 0 & \text{if } s \neq t \wedge l = 0, \\ \sum_{x \in S} P(s,x)\mathscr{P}(Reach_{l-1}(x,t)) & \text{otherwise.} \end{cases}$$

We aim to prove that estimating reachability probability using the estimation returned by Algorithm 1 also converges to the actual reachability probability and improves monotonically, no matter which estimator is used.

To facilitate discussion, let us fix a target state $s_i \in S$. We will show that

$$\widehat{\mathscr{P}}(Reach_l(s_i)) \to \mathscr{P}(Reach_l(s_i)) \quad \text{as} \quad \widehat{P} \to P.$$

Notice that $\mathscr{P}(Reach_l(s_i))$ (and similarly $\widehat{\mathscr{P}}(Reach_l(s_i))$) can be computed by

$$\mathscr{P}(Reach_l(s_i)) = \left(\mu \cdot \underbrace{P_a \cdot P_a \cdots P_a}_{l \ times} \right)_i = (\mu P_a^l)_i, \tag{3.5}$$

where P_a is the amended transition matrix in which we make the state s *absorbing*, i.e., all outgoing transitions from s are replaced by a single self-loop at s.

The next proposition provides an $O(l)\epsilon$ bound on the difference between $\widehat{P}_a^l$ and P_a^l. We omit the proofs of Propositions 5 and 6 because they use the same tricks that we have seen in proving Propositions 2 and 3.

Proposition 5. $\|\widehat{P}_a^l - P_a^l\| \leq nl\epsilon$ if $\|\widehat{P} - P\| < \epsilon$, where n is the dimension of P.

Now let us take the initial distribution μ into consideration.

Proposition 6. For any μ and i, if $\|\widehat{P} - P\| < \epsilon$, then $|(\mu\widehat{P}_a^l)_i - (\mu P_a^l)_i| \leq nl\epsilon$.

This leads to the following theorem on the bound of reachability probability.

Theorem 3. $|\widehat{\mathscr{P}}(Reach_l(s_i)) - \mathscr{P}(Reach_l(s_i))| \leq nl\epsilon$ for any state $s_i \in S$ and a bounded number of steps l.

Proof. By Eq. (3.5) and Proposition 6.   □

4   Evaluation

We have developed a prototype implementation of our approach called IDO in 4k lines of Java code. To evaluate the effectiveness of IDO, we compare it with the passive approach (i.e., random sampling, referred to as PA) using the following metrics. *Firstly, we count the minimum number of times that a state is visited among all the reachable states (referred to as MV).* Note that this is precisely our optimization objective. By measuring MV, we aim to check whether the optimization technique we adopt has worked as expected. The larger the MV value is, the better. *Secondly, we compare the estimated probability of reaching a state of interest.* We use the relative difference from the estimated reachability probability to the actual reachability probability (RRD) as a measure, which is defined as

$$\frac{|\widehat{\mathscr{P}}(Reach_k(s)) - \mathscr{P}(Reach_k(s))|}{\mathscr{P}(Reach_k(s))}.$$

A smaller RRD indicates a more precise estimation of reachability probability. If there are more than one state of interest, we calculate the average RRD. *Thirdly, we compare the estimated transition matrix $\widehat{P}$ using the standard notion MSE (defined by Eq. 3.1).* A smaller MSE indicates a more precise estimation. For a fair comparison, the experiments are designed such that the number of samples used are the same for IDO and PA, i.e., using the first stopping criteria.

4.1   Test Subjects

Three groups of systems are used for our evaluation. The first set contains three benchmark systems, i.e., the small example shown in Fig. 1 and two systems from the literature [6]. One is the *queuing model*. In a queuing model, customers arrive at a station for service. States represent the number of persons in the queue. We consider a scenario where the only possible transitions are the arrival or departure of someone. The number of transitions between two consecutive observations are assumed to be independent and identically distributed (i.i.d.). For convenience, we assume a maximum number of persons in the queue to be 10. Thus, the Markov chain has 11 possible states and a transition matrix as follows:

$$M = \begin{bmatrix}
0 & 1 & 0 & 0 & 0 & 0 & 0 & 0 & 0 & 0 & 0 \\
0.53 & 0 & 0.47 & 0 & 0 & 0 & 0 & 0 & 0 & 0 & 0 \\
0 & 0.65 & 0 & 0.35 & 0 & 0 & 0 & 0 & 0 & 0 & 0 \\
0 & 0 & 0.45 & 0 & 0.55 & 0 & 0 & 0 & 0 & 0 & 0 \\
0 & 0 & 0 & 0.30 & 0 & 0.70 & 0 & 0 & 0 & 0 & 0 \\
0 & 0 & 0 & 0 & 0.62 & 0 & 0.38 & 0 & 0 & 0 & 0 \\
0 & 0 & 0 & 0 & 0 & 0.68 & 0 & 0.32 & 0 & 0 & 0 \\
0 & 0 & 0 & 0 & 0 & 0 & 0.64 & 0 & 0.36 & 0 & 0 \\
0 & 0 & 0 & 0 & 0 & 0 & 0 & 0.52 & 0 & 0.48 & 0 \\
0 & 0 & 0 & 0 & 0 & 0 & 0 & 0 & 0.61 & 0 & 0.39 \\
0 & 0 & 0 & 0 & 0 & 0 & 0 & 0 & 0 & 1 & 0
\end{bmatrix} \quad (4.1)$$

We set the first 6 states as initial states and assume an initial uniform distribution over the 6 states. The reachability probability of interest is the probability of reaching the last 3 states in 11 (which is the number of states) steps. Based on the above model, the precise reachability probability can be calculated as: 0.0444, 0.0194 and 0.0075 respectively. The other model is the *hollow matrix*. This case study deals with Markov chains that changes state at each transition. The transition matrix is as follows.

$$P = \begin{bmatrix} 0 & 0.992 & 0.0003 & 0.0005 \\ 0.98 & 0 & 0.01 & 0.01 \\ 0.40 & 0.13 & 0 & 0.47 \\ 0.42 & 0.20 & 0.38 & 0 \end{bmatrix} \tag{4.2}$$

We set the first 2 states as initial states and assume a distribution $(0.99, 0.01)$ over them. The reachability probabilities of interests are reaching the last 2 states in 4 (number of states) steps, which are 0.0147 and 0.0159 respectively.

The second group is a set of randomly generated models (referred to as *rmc*). These models are generated with different numbers of states and transition densities using an approach similar to the approach in [17]. For reachability analysis, we choose first half of the states to be the initial states and assume a uniform initial distribution over them. We select those states with reachability probability less than 0.05 as states of interest, since we are interested in improving reachability probability of low probability states.

The last group contains the SWaT testbed [1]. SWaT is a real world complex system which involves a series of water treatments process from raw water like ultra-filtration, chemical dosing, dechlorination through an ultraviolet system, etc. The system is safety critical and ideally we want to accurately estimate the probability of reaching some *bad* states, like tank overflow or underflow, abnormal water pH level, etc. Modeling SWaT is challenging and thus we would like to have a way of estimating the transition probability as well as some reachability probability. SWaT has many configurable parameters which can be set before the system starts and it can be restarted if necessary. However, restarting SWaT is non-trivial as we have to follow a predefined shutdown sequence and thus we would like to obtain some precise estimation with as few restarts as possible. In our experiment, we focus on tank overflow or underflow. We select states with normal tank levels as initial states and assume a uniform initial distribution over them. Furthermore, we select states with abnormal tank level as states of interest.

4.2   Experiment Results

We first show the experiment results on the benchmark systems. Figure 2 presents the comparison of IDO and PA in terms of MV, RRD, and MSE respectively for the three benchmark systems. The first row shows the results of the first example. It can be observed that MV of IDO improves linearly as we increase the number of samples, whereas MV of PA remains almost zero due to the low

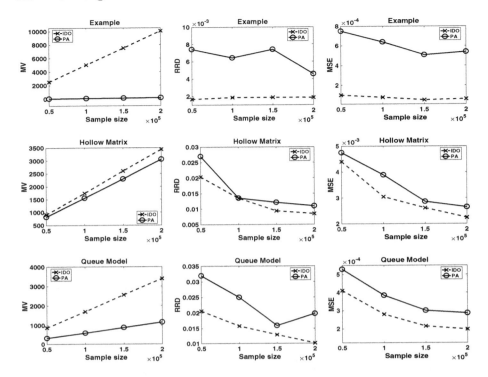

Fig. 2. Experiment results of benchmark systems.

probability of reaching some states according to the original initial distribution. IDO has significantly better estimation of both the reachability probability (in terms of RRD) as well as the transition probability (in terms of MSE). The second row shows the results of the hollow matrix. It can be observed that the improvement of MV and the probability estimation are not as significant as for the first example. A closer investigation shows that the reason is that its two initial states have very high probability of transitioning to each other. As a result, adjusting the initial distribution does not effectively change how the other states are visited. The third row shows the results of the queuing model. We observe a noticeable improvement in terms of MV, RRD ad MSE. This is because that a state of the queuing model can only be transit from its neighboring states. Since the states of interests here are the states in the last (e.g. state 9, 10, 11), an initial distribution which favors the latter part of the initial states (e.g. state 5, 6) is more likely to reach the target states. IDO successfully identifies such an initial distribution, which subsequently leads to more visits of the target states.

Next, we present the experiment results on the random models. The results are shown in Fig. 3. We consider random models with 8 states or 16 states. We randomly generate a set of 20 models of 8 states and 20 models of 16 states and present the average results, to avoid the influence of randomness. It can

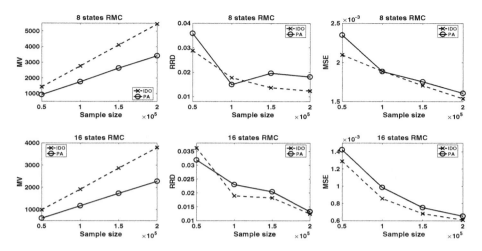

Fig. 3. Experiment results of *rmc*.

be observed that IDO improves MV, RRD and MSE in almost all the cases. On one hand, we observe from the results that as the state number increases, IDO's improvement over PA in terms of MSE goes down. The reason is that IDO targets to improve the worst estimated transitions, while MSE is computed in terms of all transitions. Consequently, the improvement is flattened with a large number of transitions. On the other hand, we observe a more and more significant improvement in terms of reachability estimation when the number of states increases. This is due to the fact that IDO actively selects an initial distribution which is likely to visit the target state most often, which effectively improves the estimation. In comparison, random sampling using a uniform initial distribution may visit the target states much less. We remark this is an important advantage of IDO since for complex systems, there are often many states and we are often interested in estimating the probability of certain unlikely states (e.g., unsafe states). Considering the extreme case when only one initial state s_0 would lead to visit of some target state s_t. If the number of initial states is large, there is a very low probability to sample s_0 through uniform random sampling. As a result, s_t is rarely visited. In comparison, IDO optimizes the initial distribution and samples from s_0 with probability 1.

Lastly, we report the results on the SWaT testbed. One difficulty we face in evaluating the effectiveness of our approach for SWaT is that we do not have the actual DTMC model. To overcome this problem, we run a large number of simulations (120 k traces, each trace is a simulation of half an hour of real world system with uniform initial distribution), and then apply empirical frequency to estimate the transition probability, which we regard as an approximation of the actual transition matrix. We remark that all the traces of SWaT are generated using a simulator which fully mimics the testbed, and for each trace the running time of the simulator is scaled less than the running time of the actual system.

Note that we define a state of SWaT as a combination of sensor values. Since the target states that we are looking into are overflow and underflow of water tanks, we collect those sensors that indicate water levels to encode states. In other words, we abstract away the internal states for simplicity. We further abstract the sensor values (which are continuous float variables) into discrete states. Two different abstraction are experimented, one with 64 states and the other with 216 states. In our experiment, we generate the first estimation $\widehat{P}$ based on 5000 traces (randomly selected from the 120 K traces). Afterwards, we iteratively refine the estimation using IDO by adding and learning from additional 5000 traces each time. The total number of traces used by IDO and PA are the same. Similarly, we compare the MV, MSE and RRD of a set of target states, whose reachability probabilities are less than 0.01, for IDO and PA respectively. The results are shown in Table 1. It can be observed that the MSE is expectedly not improving as we have many states to take average on. However, we can see from the results of RRD that IDO effectively improves our estimation of probability of water tank overflow or underflow which interests us. Furthermore, we observe almost negligible overhead of IDO over PA in terms of running time.

Table 1. Results of SWaT.

#state	MV		RRD		MSE		Time cost(s)	
	IDO	PA	IDO	PA	IDO	PA	IDO	PA
64	19	8	6.31	7.13	4.58E-4	3.93E-4	12553	12601
216	3	1	43	59.7	5.49E-4	4.86E-4	13700	12785

5   Conclusion and Related Work

In this paper, we proposed an active learning approach to "smartly" tune the system configurations so as to generate traces that can effectively improve our current probability estimation. We prove that our algorithm converges under three existing common estimators. Our experiment results show that our approach effectively improves random sampling in terms of probability estimation and reachability analysis (especially).

This work is mainly related to the following three lines of work. Firstly, it is a further effort in the recent trend of learning probabilistic models for model checking [14,18,19]. Instead of learning from fixed data, we propose to actively sample the system for more informative traces to make learning more effective for reachability analysis [13]. Such an active learning idea is applied in [8] to learn Markov decision process actively by choosing optimal actions in each step. Secondly, importance sampling [12] is another approach of smart sampling, but it may require us to change the probability distribution in the process of system operation, which is sometimes unrealistic for cyber-physical systems. Our work differs in that we only require to tune the initial distribution by adjusting the initial configuration of the system. Lastly, this work relies and works on a variety of estimators [9,10,15], which are designed for different applications.

References

1. http://itrust.sutd.edu.sg/research/testbeds/secure-water-treatment-swat/
2. Linear programming – Wikipedia, the free encyclopedia (2016). Accessed 24 Nov 2016
3. Mean squared error – Wikipedia, the free encyclopedia (2016). Accessed 7 Dec 2016
4. Angluin, D.: Learning regular sets from queries and counterexamples. Inf. Comput. **75**(2), 87–106 (1987)
5. Baier, C., Katoen, J.-P., et al.: Principles of Model Checking, vol. 26202649. MIT Press, Cambridge (2008)
6. Barsotti, F., De Castro, Y., Espinasse, T., Rochet, P.: Estimating the transition matrix of a markov chain observed at random times. Stat. Probab. Lett. **94**, 98–105 (2014)
7. Brinker, K.: Incorporating diversity in active learning with support vector machines. In: Machine Learning, Proceedings of the Twentieth International Conference (ICML 2003), 21–24 August 2003, Washington, DC, USA, pp. 59–66 (2003)
8. Chen, Y., Nielsen, T.D.: Active learning of markov decision processes for system verification. In: 2012 11th International Conference on Machine Learning and Applications (ICMLA), vol. 2, pp. 289–294. IEEE (2012)
9. Cochran, G.: Laplace's ratio estimator. In: David, H.A. (ed.) Contributions to Survey Sampling and Applied Statistics, pp. 3–10. Academic Press, New York (1978)
10. Gale, W.A., Sampson, G.: Good-turing frequency estimation without tears*. J. Quant. Linguist. **2**(3), 217–237 (1995)
11. Gurobi Optimization Incorporation: Gurobi optimizer reference manual (2016)
12. Heidelberger, P.: Fast simulation of rare events in queueing and reliability models. ACM Trans. Model. Comput. Simul. (TOMACS) **5**(1), 43–85 (1995)
13. Lesser, K., Oishi, M.: Reachability for partially observable discrete time stochastic hybrid systems. Automatica **50**(8), 1989–1998 (2014)
14. Mao, H., Chen, Y., Jaeger, M., Nielsen, T.D., Larsen, K.G., Nielsen, B.: Learning probabilistic automata for model checking. In: Eighth International Conference on Quantitative Evaluation of Systems (QEST), pp. 111–120. IEEE (2011)
15. McAllester, D.A., Schapire, R.E.: On the convergence rate of good-turing estimators. In: COLT, pp. 1–6 (2000)
16. Moon, T.K.: The expectation-maximization algorithm. IEEE Sig. Proces. Mag. **13**(6), 47–60 (1996)
17. Tabakov, D., Vardi, M.Y.: Experimental evaluation of classical automata constructions. In: Sutcliffe, G., Voronkov, A. (eds.) LPAR 2005. LNCS (LNAI), vol. 3835, pp. 396–411. Springer, Heidelberg (2005). doi:10.1007/11591191_28
18. Wang, J., Sun, J., Qin, S.: Verifying complex systems probabilistically through learning, abstraction and refinement. arXiv preprint arXiv:1610.06371 (2016)
19. Wang, J., Sun, J., Yuan, Q., Pang, J.: Should we learn probabilistic models for model checking? a new approach and an empirical study. In: Huisman, M., Rubin, J. (eds.) FASE 2017. LNCS, vol. 10202, pp. 3–21. Springer, Heidelberg (2017). doi:10.1007/978-3-662-54494-5_1
20. Whittaker, J.A., Thomason, M.G.: A markov chain model for statistical software testing. IEEE Trans. Softw. Eng. **20**(10), 812–824 (1994)

Nested Timed Automata with Diagonal Constraints

Yuwei Wang[1], Yunqing Wen[1], Guoqiang Li[1(✉)], and Shoji Yuen[2]

[1] School of Software, Shanghai Jiao Tong University, Shanghai, China
{wangywgg,wyqwyq,li.g}@sjtu.edu.cn
[2] Graduate School of Information Science, Nagoya University, Nagoya, Japan
yuen@is.nagoya-u.ac.jp

Abstract. Time constraints are usually used in timed systems to rule on discrete behaviours based on the valuations of clocks. They are categorized into *diagonal-free constraints* and *diagonal constraints*. In timed automata, it is well-known that diagonal constraints are just a useful syntax sugar since each diagonal constraint can be encoded into diagonal-free constraints. However, it is yet unknown when recursion is taken into consideration. This paper investigates the decidability results of these systems with diagonal constraints, under the model of *nested timed automata (NeTAs)*. We show that the NeTAs containing a singleton global clock with diagonal constraints are Turing complete, even when the *clock assignment* is restricted to the *clock reset*. In comparison, the reachability problem for a subclass, NeTAs without frozen clocks, is decidable under diagonal constraints.

1 Introduction

For decades, lots of formal models [1], such as *timed automata* [2,3], have been proposed and widely used for modelling and analysis of real-time systems. Time constraints are usually used in these models to rule on discrete behaviours based on the valuations of clocks. A time constraint that checks whether the value of a clock belongs to a given interval is named a *diagonal-free constraint*, while checks whether the difference between two clocks belongs to an interval is a *diagonal constraint*. Diagonal constraints usually play an important role in applications of modelling and verification [4]. It is well-known that timed automata with two kinds of constraints have the same expressiveness [2]. When recursions are taken into account, researchers usually believe the same result [5].

A *nested timed automaton (NeTA)* [6,7] is a pushdown system whose stack symbols are TAs. In such a system clocks are naturally classified into *global clocks*, which can be updated and observed by all TAs, *local clocks*, which belong to a TA and will be stored in the stack when the TA is interrupted. A special type of local clocks are *frozen clocks*, whose values are not updated while their context is preempted and restart update when resumed. Other local clocks are *proceeding*. This hierarchical design captures the dynamic feature of event-driven timed systems and programs, such as real-time embedded systems, interrupts

© Springer International Publishing AG 2017
Z. Duan and L. Ong (Eds.): ICFEM 2017, LNCS 10610, pp. 396–412, 2017.
https://doi.org/10.1007/978-3-319-68690-5_24

and asynchronous programs, which are suitable to be modeled by NeTAs. For example, in interrupts each time-aware interrupt handler is described as an independent TA, and preemptions and resumptions are depicted as push and pop operations. Different types of clocks are flexible to describe the different time requirement of each interrupt handler. Recently, NeTAs are used as a backbone for the schedulability analysis of complex task systems without the information of a worst-case execution time [8].

This paper investigates the decidability result of NeTAs with diagonal constraints. The expressiveness of such a system is one of the main contributions of this paper. The reachability problem of a NeTA with one global clock under diagonal-free constraints is known to be decidable [7]. In comparison, in this paper we prove that a general NeTA with one global clock under diagonal constraints is Turing complete even for a subclass, where the *clock assignment*, through which the value of a clock is adjusted to an arbitrary value in an interval, is restricted to *clock reset*, through which the value of a clock can only be reset to zero. This difference in decidability implies that the diagonal constraints strictly increases the expressiveness of a subclass of NeTAs, NeTAs with one global clock. We further show that the reachability of another subclass, NeTAs without frozen clocks [6] and with bounded assignment and diagonal constraints is decidable.

Paper Organization. The rest of the paper is organized as follows: Sect. 2 introduces time constraints and assignments, and timed automata (TAs). Section 3 gives an introduction of general NeTAs. Section 4 shows the undecidability results of general NeTAs, when the clock assignments, through which arbitrary value in an interval is restricted to clock reset. Section 5 introduces Extended Dense Timed Pushdown Automata (EDTPDAs) and proves their decidability results. Section 6 shows the decidable reachability of NeTAs without frozen clocks by encoding them to EDTPDAs. Section 7 introduces related work and Sect. 8 concludes the paper.

2   Preliminaries

For two sets A and B, we denote the set difference of set B from set A, $A \setminus B = \{e \mid e \in A \wedge e \notin B\}$.

For finite words $w = aw'$, we denote $a = head(w)$ and $w' = tail(w)$. The concatenation of two words w, v is denoted by $w.v$, and ϵ is the empty word.

Let $\mathbb{R}$, $\mathbb{R}^{\geq 0}$ and $\mathbb{Z}$ denote the sets of real, non-negative real and integer numbers respectively. Let ω denote the first limit ordinal. Let $\mathcal{I}$ denote the set of *intervals* over $\mathbb{Z}^{\omega}$. An interval can be written as a pair of a lower limit and an upper limit in the form of either $(a, b), [a', b), [a', b'], (a, b']$, where $a \in \mathbb{Z} \cup \{-\omega\}$, $a' \in \mathbb{Z}$, $b \in \mathbb{Z} \cup \{\omega\}$, $b' \in \mathbb{Z}$, '(' and ')' denote open limits, and '[' and ']' denote closed limits. Let $\mathcal{I}^{\geq 0}$ denote the sets of intervals that do not cover any negative number. Given a natural number n, we define the bounded intervals $\mathcal{I}^{\geq 0}_{\leq n}$ as $\{I \setminus (n, \omega) \mid I \in \mathcal{I}^{\geq 0}\}$.

Let $X = \{x_1, \ldots, x_n\}$ be a finite set of *clocks*. A *clock valuation* $\nu : X \to \mathbb{R}^{\geq 0}$, assigns a value to each clock $x \in X$. ν_0 represents all clocks in X assigned to zero. Given a clock valuation ν and a time $t \in \mathbb{R}^{\geq 0}$, $(\nu + t)(x) = \nu(x) + t$, for $x \in X$. A clock assignment function $\nu[y \leftarrow b]$ is defined by $\nu[y \leftarrow b](x) = b$ if $x = y$, and $\nu(x)$ otherwise. We also define a clock valuation ν over X by $\{t_1, \ldots, t_n\}$, which means $\nu(x_i) = t_i$ for $1 \leq i \leq n$, where $\forall i \in [1..k]$, $t_i \in \mathbb{R}^{\geq 0}$. $Val(X)$ is used to denote the set of clock valuations of X.

2.1 Time Constraints and Assignments

Definition 1 (Time Constraint). *Given a finite set of clocks X, we define diagonal-free constraints con_{df} and diagonal constraints con as follows:*

$$con_{df} ::= x \in I? \qquad con ::= x \in I? \mid x - x' \in I'?$$

where, $x, x' \in X$, $I \in \mathcal{I}^{\geq 0}$ and $I' \in \mathcal{I}$.

Definition 2 (Clock Assignment). *Given a finite set of clocks X, we define unbounded assignments $assgn^\omega$, bounded assignments $assign^n$ and resets $reset$ as follows:*

$$assgn^\omega ::= x \leftarrow I \quad assign^n ::= x \leftarrow I' \quad reset ::= x \leftarrow I_0$$

where $x \in X$, n is the maximum integer to which a clock is allowed to be assigned, $I \in \mathcal{I}^{\geq 0}$, $I' \in \mathcal{I}^{\geq 0}_{\leq n}$ and $I_0 = [0, 0]$.

2.2 Timed Automata

Definition 3 (Timed Automata). *A timed automaton (TA) is a tuple $\mathcal{A} = (Q, q_0, F, X, \Delta) \in \mathscr{A}$, where*

- *Q is a finite set of control locations, with the initial location $q_0 \in Q$,*
- *$F \subseteq Q$ is the set of final locations,*
- *X is a finite set of clocks,*
- *$\Delta \subseteq Q \times \mathcal{O} \times Q$, where $\mathcal{O}$ is a set of operations. A transition $\delta \in \Delta$ is a triplet (q_1, ϕ, q_2), written as $q_1 \xrightarrow{\phi} q_2$, in which ϕ is either of*
  - **Local** *ϵ, an empty operation,*
  - **Test** *con_{df} or con on X,*
  - **Assignment** *$assign$ on X, where $assign \in \{assign^\omega, assign^n, reset\}$, and*
  - **Value passing** *$x \leftarrow x'$, where $x, x' \in X$.*

Given a TA $\mathcal{A} \in \mathscr{A}$, we use $Q(\mathcal{A})$, $q_0(\mathcal{A})$, $F(\mathcal{A})$, $X(\mathcal{A})$ and $\Delta(\mathcal{A})$ to represent its set of control locations, initial location, set of final locations, set of clocks and set of transitions, respectively. We will use similar notations for other models.

Definition 4 (Semantics of TAs). *Given a TA $\mathcal{A} = (Q, q_0, F, X, \Delta)$, a configuration is a pair (q, ν) of a control location $q \in Q$, and a clock valuation ν on X. The transition relation of the TA is represented as follows,*

– Progress transition: $(q, \nu) \xrightarrow{t}_{\mathscr{A}} (q, \nu + t)$, where $t \in \mathbb{R}^{\geq 0}$.

– Discrete transition: $(q_1, \nu_1) \xrightarrow{\phi}_{\mathscr{A}} (q_2, \nu_2)$, if $q_1 \xrightarrow{\phi} q_2 \in \Delta$, and one of the following holds,

- **Local** $\phi = \epsilon$, then $\nu_1 = \nu_2$.
- **Test** $\phi = x \in I?$ or $x - x' \in I'$, then $\nu_1 = \nu_2$ and $\nu_2(x) \in I$ or $\nu_2(x) - \nu(x') \in I'$ holds respectively.
- **Assignment** $\phi = x \leftarrow I$, $\nu_2 = \nu_1[x \leftarrow r]$, where $r \in I$.
- **Value passing** $\varphi = x \leftarrow x'$, $\nu_2 = \nu_1[x \leftarrow \nu_1(x')]$.

The initial configuration is (q_0, ν_0). The transition relation is $\rightarrow$ and we define $\rightarrow = \xrightarrow{t}_{\mathscr{A}} \cup \xrightarrow{\phi}_{\mathscr{A}}$, and define $\rightarrow^*$ to be the reflexive and transitive closure of $\rightarrow$.

Definition 3 involves choices of **Test** and **Assignment**. In the following, we will specify the type of time constraint and clock assignment when a TA is mentioned.

3   General Nested Timed Automata

Definition 5 (Nested Timed Automata). *A general nested timed automaton (NeTA) is a quadruplet $\mathcal{N} = (T, \mathcal{A}_0, X, C, \Delta)$, where*

– *T is a finite set $\{\mathcal{A}_0, \mathcal{A}_1, \cdots, \mathcal{A}_k\}$ of TAs, with the initial TA $\mathcal{A}_0 \in T$. We assume the sets of control locations of $\mathcal{A}_i$, $Q(\mathcal{A}_i)$, are mutually disjoint, i.e., $Q(\mathcal{A}_i) \cap Q(\mathcal{A}_j) = \emptyset$ for $i \neq j$.*
– *C is a finite set of global clocks, and X is a finite set of k local clocks.*
– *$\Delta \subseteq Q \times (Q \cup \{\varepsilon\}) \times Actions^+ \times Q \times (Q \cup \{\varepsilon\})$ describes transition rules below, where $Q = \cup_{\mathcal{A}_i \in T} Q(\mathcal{A}_i)$.*

*A transition rule is described by a sequence of $Actions^+ = \{internal, push, fpush, pop, c \in I?, c - c' \in I'?, c \leftarrow I, x \leftarrow c, c \leftarrow x\}$ for $c \in C$, $x \in \bigcup_{\mathcal{A}_i \in T} X(\mathcal{A}_i)$, $I \in \mathcal{I}^{\geq 0}$ and $I' \in \mathcal{I}$. The internal actions are **Local**, **Test**, **Assignment**, and **Value-passing** in Definition 3.*

– **Internal** *$(q, \varepsilon, internal, q', \varepsilon)$, which describes an internal transition in the working TA (placed at a control location) with $q, q' \in \mathcal{A}_i$.*
– **Push** *$(q, \varepsilon, push, q_0(\mathcal{A}_{i'}), q)$, which interrupts the currently working TA $\mathcal{A}_i$ at $q \in Q(\mathcal{A}_i)$ and pushes it to the stack with all local clocks of $\mathcal{A}_i$. The local clocks in the stack generated by **Push** operation still evolve as time elapses. Then, a TA $\mathcal{A}_{i'}$ newly starts.*
– **F-Push** *$(q, \varepsilon, fpush, q_0(\mathcal{A}_{i'}), q)$, which is similar to **Push** except that all local clocks in the stack generated by **F-Push** are frozen (i.e. stay the same as time elapses).*
– **Pop** *$(q, q', pop, q', \varepsilon)$, which restarts $\mathcal{A}_{i'}$ in the stack from $q' \in Q(\mathcal{A}_{i'})$ after $\mathcal{A}_i$ has finished at $q \in Q(\mathcal{A}_i)$.*
– **Global-test**$_{df}$ *$(q, \varepsilon, c \in I?, q', \varepsilon)$, which tests whether the value of a global clock c is in I.*

- **Global-test** $(q, \varepsilon, c - c' \in I?, q', \varepsilon)$, *which tests whether the difference of two clocks c and c' is in I, where $c, c' \in C$.*
- **Global-assign** $(q, \varepsilon, c \leftarrow I, q', \varepsilon)$, *which assigns a value in $r \in I$ to a global clock c.*
- **Global-load** $(q, \varepsilon, x \leftarrow c, q', \varepsilon)$, *which assign the value of a global clock c to a local clock $x \in X$ in the working TA.*
- **Global-store** $(q, \varepsilon, c \leftarrow x, q', \varepsilon)$, *which assign the value of a local clock $x \in X$ of the working TA to a global clock c.*

Definition 6 (Semantics of general NeTAs). *Given a general NeTA $(T, \mathcal{A}_0, X, C, \Delta)$, the current control state is referred by q. Let $Val_X = \{\nu : X \to \mathbb{R}^{\geq 0}\}$ and $Val_C = \{\mu : C \to \mathbb{R}^{\geq 0}\}$. A configuration of a general NeTA is an element in $Q \times Val_X \times Val_C \times (Q \times \{0,1\} \times Val_X)^*$. For $w = (q_1, flag_1, \nu_1). \cdots .(q_n, flag_n, \nu_n) \in (Q \times \{0,1\} \times Val_X)^*$, t-time passage on the stack, written as $w + t$, is $(q_1, flag_1, progress(\nu_1, t, flag_1)). \cdots .(q_n, flag_n, progress(\nu_n, t, flag_n))$, where*

$$progress(\nu, t, flag) = \begin{cases} \{\nu(x_1) + t, \cdots, \nu(x_k) + t\} & flag = 1 \\ \nu & flag = 0 \end{cases}$$

- *Time progress transitions: $(\langle q, \nu, \mu \rangle, v) \xrightarrow{t} (\langle q, \nu + t, \mu + t \rangle, v + t)$ for $t \in \mathbb{R}^{\geq 0}$, where $v + t$ set $\nu' := progress(\nu', t, flag)$ of each $\langle q', flag, \nu' \rangle$ in the stack.*
- *Discrete transitions: $\kappa \xrightarrow{\varphi} \kappa'$ is defined as follows.*
  - **Internal** $(\langle q, \nu, \mu \rangle, v) \xrightarrow{\varphi} (\langle q', \nu', \mu \rangle, v)$, *if $\langle q, \nu \rangle \xrightarrow{\varphi} \langle q', \nu' \rangle$ is in Definition 4.*
  - **Push** $(\langle q, \nu, \mu \rangle, v) \xrightarrow{push} (\langle q_0(\mathcal{A}_{i'}), \nu_0, \mu \rangle, \langle q, 1, \nu \rangle .v)$.
  - **F-Push** $(\langle q, \nu, \mu \rangle, v) \xrightarrow{f\text{-}push} (\langle q_0(\mathcal{A}_{i'}), \nu_0, \mu \rangle, \langle q, 0, \nu \rangle .v)$.
  - **Pop** $(\langle q, \nu, \mu \rangle, \langle q', flag, \nu' \rangle .w) \xrightarrow{pop} (\langle q', \nu', \mu \rangle, w)$.
  - **Global-test** $(\langle q, \nu, \mu \rangle, v) \xrightarrow{c \in I?} (\langle q', \nu, \mu \rangle, v)$, *if $\mu(c) \in I$.*
  - **Global-test** $(\langle q, \nu, \mu \rangle, v) \xrightarrow{c-c' \in I?} (\langle q', \nu, \mu \rangle, v)$, *if $\mu(c) - \mu(c') \in I$ holds.*
  - **Global-assign** $(\langle q, \nu, \mu \rangle, v) \xrightarrow{c \leftarrow I} (\langle q', \nu, \mu[c \leftarrow r] \rangle, v)$ *for $r \in I$.*
  - **Global-load** $(\langle q, \nu, \mu \rangle, v) \xrightarrow{x \leftarrow c} (\langle q', \nu[x \leftarrow \mu(c)], \mu \rangle, v)$.
  - **Global-store** $(\langle q, \nu, \mu \rangle, v) \xrightarrow{c \leftarrow x} (\langle q', \nu, \mu[c \leftarrow \nu(x)] \rangle, v)$.

The initial configuration of a general NeTA is $(\langle q_0(\mathcal{A}_0), \nu_0, \mu_0 \rangle, \varepsilon)$, where $\nu_0(x) = 0$ for $x \in X$ and $\mu_0(c) = 0$ for $c \in C$. We use $\longrightarrow$ to range over these transitions.

Definition 5 for general NeTAs extends Definition 12 in [7] with *diagonal constraints*. We already have the following result for general NeTAs with diagonal-free constraints [7].

Theorem 1 (Theorem 2 in [7]). *The reachability of NeTAs $(T, \mathcal{A}_0, X, C, \Delta)$ with diagonal-free constraints is undecidable, if $|C| > 1$.*

Theorem 2 (Theorem 3 in [7]). *The reachability of NeTAs $(T, \mathcal{A}_0, X, C, \Delta)$ with diagonal-free constraints is decidable, if $|C| = 1$.*

From the above result, obviously general NeTAs with multiple global clocks are undecidable. We will focus on some subclasses to expand the frontier between decidable and undecidable classes of NeTAs with diagonal constraints.

4 Undecidability Result of NeTAs

Note that a TA with **diagonal constraints** and **unbounded assignments** is already Turing-complete. In this section we show the undecidability of NeTAs with a single global clock variable, even when global-assign is restricted to clock **reset**.

For showing the undecidability, we encode the halting problem of Minsky machines [11] in a general NeTA with a single global clock and reset assignment.

Definition 7 (Minsky machine). *A Minsky machine $\mathcal{M}$ is a tuple (L, C, D) where:*

- *L is a finite set of states, and $l_0, l_f \in L$ are the initial state and terminal state respectively,*
- *$C = \{ct_1, ct_2\}$ is the set of two counters, and*
- *D is the finite set of transition rules of the following types,*
  - **increment counter** *$d_i : ct := ct + 1$, goto l_k,*
  - **test-and-decrement counter** *$d_i : if (ct > 0)$ then $(ct := ct - 1$, goto $l_k)$ else goto l_m,*

  where $ct \in C$, $d_i \in D$ and $l_k, l_m \in L$.

A Minsky machine $\mathcal{M} = (L, C, D)$ can be encoded into a general NeTA with a single global clock and reset assignment $\mathcal{N} = (T, \mathcal{A}_0, X, C, \Delta)$, with $T = \{\mathcal{A}_0, \mathcal{A}_1\}$ where

- $C = \{c\}$ and $Q(\mathcal{A}_0) = \{q_l \mid l \in L(\mathcal{M})\} \bigcup \{q_l^i \mid l \in L(\mathcal{M}), 3 \le i \le 4\}$ and $Q(\mathcal{A}_1) = \{q_l^i \mid l \in L(\mathcal{M}), 1 \le i \le 2\}$.
- $X = \{x_1, x_2, x_3\}$, where for $i = 1, 2$, x_i is a local clock to encode the value of counter ct_i and x_3 is introduced to ensure no time passage in $\mathcal{A}_0$. Here x_1, x_2 and x_3 are all local clocks of $\mathcal{A}_0$, which is critical in the encoding.

Zero-test of a counter ct_i for $i = 1, 2$, in the form of $l \xrightarrow{ct_i = 0?} l_m$, where $l, l_m \in L(\mathcal{M})$ is simply simulated by $q_l \xrightarrow{x_i \in [0,0]?} q_{l_m}$.

Increment of a counter ct_i for $i = 1, 2$, in the form of $l \xrightarrow{ct_i := ct_i + 1} l_k$, where $l, l_k \in L(\mathcal{M})$ is simulated by the following transitions: $q_l \xrightarrow{fpush} q_l^1 \xrightarrow{c \leftarrow [0,0]} q_l^2 \xrightarrow{pop} q_l \xrightarrow{c - x_i \in [1,1]?} q_{l_k}^3 \xrightarrow{x_i \leftarrow c} q_{l_k}^4 \xrightarrow{x_3 \in [0,0]?} q_{l_k}$ Intuitively, we frozen-push the *initial* TA $\mathcal{A}_0$, reset the global clock c, wait for some time, later pop back to $\mathcal{A}_0$. Only when $c - x_i = 1$ holds, the execution can continue. Then the value of c is passed to x_i, which is equivalent to increasing x_i by one. Note that, if q_{l_k} is reachable, then time does not elapse in $\mathcal{A}_0$ in this execution. Firstly, a local clock of $\mathcal{A}_0$, x_3, is initialized to 0 and afterwards never changes the value during the simulation. The zero-test for x_3 at the tail of the simulation ensures this. Secondly, thanks to the frozen push, when the global clock c elapses, local clocks of $\mathcal{A}_0$ are frozen.

Decrement of a counter ct_i for $i = 1, 2$, in the form of $l \xrightarrow{ct_i := ct_i - 1} l_k$, is simulated in a way similar to the increment of a counter ct_i, except for testing $x_i - c \in [1, 1]$? instead of $c - x_i \in [1, 1]$?

By the above encoding, we have the following results.

Theorem 3. *The reachability of NeTAs with one global clock, diagonal constraints, and resets is undecidable.*

5   Extended Dense Timed Pushdown Automata

In this section, we introduce extended dense timed pushdown automata (EDT-PDAs) and prove their decidability results. Later in Sect. 6 the decidability of the reachability on NeTAs without frozen clocks is shown by encoding them to EDTPDAs. We extend DTPDAs from Definition 1 in [7] with global clocks for which the value is not affected by push and pop actions.

Definition 8 (Extended Dense Timed Pushdown Automata). *An extended dense timed pushdown automaton (EDTPDA) is a tuple $\mathcal{D} = \langle S, s_0, \Gamma, X, C, \Delta \rangle \in \mathscr{D}$, where*

- *S is a finite set of states with the initial state $s_0 \in S$,*
- *Γ is finite stack alphabet,*
- *X is a finite set of local clocks (with $|X| = k$),*
- *C is a finite set of global clocks (with $|C| = k'$) and,*
- *$\Delta \subseteq S \times Actions \times S$ is a finite set of actions.*

A (discrete) transition $\delta \in \Delta$ is a sequence of actions $(s_1, \varphi_1, s_2), \cdots, (s_i, \varphi_i, s_{i+1})$ written as $s_1 \xrightarrow{\varphi_1; \cdots; \varphi_i} s_{i+1}$, in which φ_j (for $1 \leq j \leq i$) is one of the followings,

- **Local** *ϵ, an empty operation,*
- **Test** *con on $X \cup C$,*
- **Assign** *$assign^n$ on $X \cup C$, where n is the maximum integer appearing in Δ,*
- **Value passing** *$x \leftarrow y$ where $x, y \in X \cup C$.*
- **Push** *$push(\gamma)$, where $\gamma \in \Gamma$, and*
- **Pop** *$pop(\gamma)$, where $\gamma \in \Gamma$.*

Definition 9 (Semantics of EDTPDA). *For an EDTPDA $\langle S, s_0, \Gamma, X, C, \Delta \rangle$, a configuration is a triplet (s, w, ν) with $s \in S$, $w \in (\Gamma \times (\mathbb{R}^{\geq 0})^k)^*$, and a clock valuation ν on $X \cup C$. For $t \in \mathbb{R}^{\geq 0}$ and $\bar{t} = (t_1, t_2, \ldots, t_k) \in (\mathbb{R}^{\geq 0})^k$, $\bar{t} + t = (t_1 + t, t_2 + t, \ldots, t_k + t)$. For $w = (\gamma_1, \bar{t}_1). \cdots .(\gamma_n, \bar{t}_n)$, $w + t = (\gamma_1, \bar{t}_1 + t). \cdots .(\gamma_n, \bar{t}_n + t)$.*

The transition relation consists of time progress and a discrete transition.

- *Time progress: $(s, w, \nu) \xrightarrow{t}_{\mathscr{D}} (s, w + t, \nu + t)$, where $t \in \mathbb{R}^{\geq 0}$.*
- *Discrete transition: $(s_1, w_1, \nu_1) \xrightarrow{\varphi}_{\mathscr{D}} (s_2, w_2, \nu_2)$, if $s_1 \xrightarrow{\varphi} s_2$, and one of the following holds,*

- **Local** $\varphi = \epsilon$, then $w_1 = w_2$, and $\nu_1 = \nu_2$.
- **Test** $\varphi = x \in I$? or $x - y \in I'$?, then $w_1 = w_2$, $\nu_1 = \nu_2$, and $\nu_1(x) \in I$ holds or $\nu_1(x) - \nu_1(y) \in I'$ holds respectively.
- **Assign** $\varphi = x \leftarrow I$, then $w_1 = w_2$, $\nu_2 = \nu_1[x \leftarrow r]$, where $r \in I$.
- **Value passing** $\varphi = x \leftarrow x'$, then $w_1 = w_2$, $\nu_2 = \nu_1[x \leftarrow \nu_1(x')]$.
- **Push** $\varphi = push(\gamma)$, then $\nu_2 = \nu_1[\bar{x} \leftarrow (0, \cdots, 0)]$, $w_2 = (\gamma, (\nu_1(x_1), \cdots, \nu_1(x_k))).w_1$, where $\bar{x} = (x_1, \cdots, x_k)$.
- **Pop** $\varphi = pop(\gamma)$, then $\nu_2 = \nu_1[\bar{x} \leftarrow (t_1, \cdots, t_k)]$, $w_1 = (\gamma, (t_1, \cdots, t_k)).w_2$, where $\bar{x} = (x_1, \cdots, x_k)$.

The initial configuration $\varrho_0 = (s_0, \epsilon, \nu_0)$.

Example 1. Figure 1 shows transitions of an EDTPDA with $S = \{\bullet\}$ (omitted in the figure), $X = \{x_1, x_2\}$, $C = \{c_1\}$ and $\Gamma = \{a, b, d\}$. At $\varrho_1 \hookrightarrow \varrho_2$, the values of x_1 and x_2 (0.5 and 3.9) are pushed with d. After pushing, value of x_1 and x_2 will be reset to zero, Then, x_2 is set a value in $(1, 2]$, say 1.7. At $\varrho_2 \hookrightarrow \varrho_3$, time elapses 2.6, and both clocks and ages in the stack (in **bold**) proceed. At $\varrho_3 \hookrightarrow \varrho_4$, test whether the difference between the value of x_2 and the value of x_1 is in $(1, 2)$. Yes, then pop the stack and x_1, x_2 are set to the popped ages.

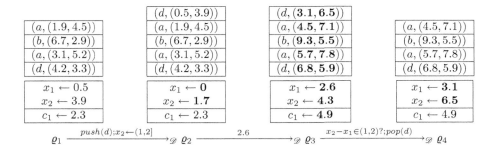

Fig. 1. An example of EDTPDA

In the following subsections, we prove the decidability result of EDTPDAs.

We denote the set of finite multisets over D by $\mathcal{MP}(D)$, and the union of two multisets M, M' by $M \uplus M'$. We regard a finite set as a multiset with the multiplicity 1, and a finite word as a multiset by ignoring the ordering.

5.1 Digiword and Operations

Let $\langle S, s_0, \Gamma, X, C, \Delta \rangle$ be an EDTPDA and let n be the largest integer (except for ω) appearing in Δ. For $v \in \mathbb{R}$, $proj(v) = \mathbf{r}_i$ if $v \in \mathbf{r}_i \in Intv(n)$, where $Intv(n) = \{\mathbf{r}_{2i} = [i, i] \mid -n \leq i \leq n\} \cup \{\mathbf{r}_{2i+1} = (i, i+1) \mid -n \leq i < n\} \cup \{\mathbf{r}_{2n+1} = (n, \omega)\} \cup \{\mathbf{r}_{-2n-1} = (-\omega, -n)\}$.

For a set of clocks $X = \{x_1, \cdots, x_k\} \cup C = \{c_1, \cdots, c_{k'}\}$, an *index* function $idx(x)$ over $X \cup C$ is defined by i if $x = x_i \in X$ otherwise $i+k$ for $x = c_i \in C$. Also, we denote its inverse function by $ridx(i)$ (i.e., if $idx(x) = i$, then $ridx(i) = x$ for $x \in X \cup C$).

Definition 10 (Difference Bound Matrix). *A difference bound matrix (DBM) D is a $(k + k') - by - (k + k')$ matrix, where D_{ij} (i.e., element (i, j) in the matrix) is an interval* $\mathbf{r} \in Intv(n)$, *which represents the $\nu(ridx(i)) - \nu(ridx(j)) \in \mathbf{r}$. $\mathcal{D}bm(X \cup C)$ is used to denote the set of DBMs over $X \cup C$.*

Note that the indexes for the first row and first column are 1. We say a clock valuation ν over $X \cup C$ is *compatible* with a DBM $D \in \mathcal{D}bm(X \cup C)$ if $\forall x, y \in X \cup C$, $\nu(x) - \nu(y) \in D_{idx(x), idx(y)}$. We also denote $DBM(\nu) = D$ if a clock valuation ν is compatible with a DBM D.

The idea of the next digitization is inspired by [12–14].

Definition 11. *Let $frac(x, t) = t - floor(t)$ for $(x, t) \in (X \cup C \cup \Gamma) \times \mathbb{R}^{\geq 0}$, and $\Phi \subset \mathcal{MP}((X \cup C \cup \Gamma) \times \mathbb{R}^{\geq 0})$ be the set whose element has exactly one occurrence of (x, t), for each $x \in X \cup C$, where $t \in \mathbb{R}^{\geq 0}$. A digitization* digi : $\Phi \to \mathcal{MP}((X \cup C \cup \Gamma) \times Intv(n))^* \times \mathcal{D}bm(X \cup C)$ *is defined as follows.*

For $\bar{y} \in \Phi$, let $Y_0, Y_1, \cdots, Y_m$ be multisets that collect $(x, proj(t))$'s having the same $frac(x, t)$ for $(x, t) \in \bar{y}$ and D be the corresponding DBM in which D_{ij} is an interval $\mathbf{r} \in Intv(n)$ satisfying $t - t' \in \mathbf{r}$, where $(ridx(i), t), (ridx(j), t') \in \bar{y}$. Among $Y_0, Y_1, \cdots, Y_m$, Y_0 (which is possibly empty) is reserved for the collection of $(x, proj(t))$ with $frac(t) = 0$. We assume that Y_i's except for Y_0 is non-empty (i.e., $Y_i = \emptyset$ with $i > 0$ is omitted), and Y_i's are sorted by the increasing order of $frac(x, t)$ (i.e., $frac(x, t) < frac(x', t')$ for $(x, proj(t)) \in Y_i$ and $(x', proj(t')) \in Y_{i+1}$).

For a stack frame $v = (\gamma, (t_1, \cdots, t_k))$ of an EDTPDA, we denote a word $(\gamma, t_1) \cdots (\gamma, t_k)$ by $dist(v)$. Given a clock valuation ν, we denote a clock word $(x_1, \nu(x_1)) \ldots (x_n, \nu(x_n))$ by $time(\nu)$, where $x_1 \ldots x_n \in X \cup C$.

Example 2. If $n = 6$, we have 25 intervals illustrated in Fig. 2.

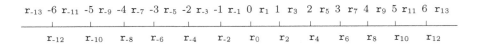

Fig. 2. An interval with $n = 6$

For the configuration $\varrho_1 = (\bullet, v_4 \cdots v_1, \nu)$, let $\bar{\mathcal{Y}} = dist(v_4) \uplus \ldots \uplus dist(v_1) \uplus time(\nu)$ be a word, and $U = \text{digi}(\bar{\mathcal{Y}})$, i.e.,

$$\bar{\mathcal{Y}} = \{(a, 1.9), (a, 4.5), (b, 6.7), (b, 2.9), (a, 3.1), (a, 5.2),$$
$$(d, 4.2), (d, 3.3), (x_1, 0.5), (x_2, 3.9), (c_1, 2.3)\}$$
$$\bar{Y} = \{(a, \mathbf{r}_7)\}\{(a, \mathbf{r}_{11}), (d, \mathbf{r}_9)\}\{(c_1, \mathbf{r}_5), (d, \mathbf{r}_7)\}\{(x_1, \mathbf{r}_1),$$
$$(a, \mathbf{r}_9)\}\{(b, \mathbf{r}_{13})\}\{(x_2, \mathbf{r}_7), (a, \mathbf{r}_3), (b, \mathbf{r}_5)\}$$
$$D = \begin{bmatrix} \mathbf{r}_0 & \mathbf{r}_{-7} & \mathbf{r}_{-3} \\ \mathbf{r}_7 & \mathbf{r}_0 & \mathbf{r}_3 \\ \mathbf{r}_3 & \mathbf{r}_{-3} & \mathbf{r}_0 \end{bmatrix}$$
$$U = (\bar{Y}, D)$$

A word in $(\mathcal{MP}((X \cup C \cup \Gamma) \times Intv(n)))^* \times \mathcal{D}bm(X \cup C)$ is called a *digiword*. Let $U = (\bar{Y}, D)$ be a digiword, where $\bar{Y}$ is a word of multisets and D is a DBM. We denote $Y|_\Lambda$ for $\Lambda \subseteq X \cup C \cup \Gamma$, by removing $(x, \mathbf{r}_i)$ with $x \notin \Lambda$ in $\bar{Y}$. We also denote $U|_\Lambda = (Y|_\Lambda, D)$. A *k-pointer* $\bar{\rho}$ of a digiword U is a tuple of k pointers to mutually different k elements in $\bar{Y}$ of $U|_\Gamma$, where k is the number of local clocks. We refer to the element pointed by the i-th pointer by $\bar{\rho}[i]$. From now on, we assume that a digiword has one pair of k-pointers $(\bar{\rho}_1, \bar{\rho}_2)$. We also assume that they do not overlap each other, i.e., there are no i, j, such that $\bar{\rho}_1[i] = \bar{\rho}_2[j]$.

$\bar{\rho}_1$ and $\bar{\rho}_2$ intend the store of values of the local clocks at the last and one before the last **Push**, respectively.

Definition 12. *For $\bar{Y} = Y_0, Y_1, \cdots, Y_m \in (\mathcal{MP}((X \cup C \cup \Gamma) \times Intv(n)))^*$, $[\bar{Y}]$ is defined by $\{\nu \mid \mathtt{digi}(time(\nu)) = (\bar{Z}, D) \wedge \bar{Y}|_{X \cup C} = \bar{Z}\}$, and $\overline{DBM}(\bar{Y})$ defined by $\{D \mid \nu \in [\bar{Y}] \wedge DBM(\nu) = D\}$.*

Remark 1. For $\bar{Y} = Y_0, Y_1, \cdots, Y_m \in (\mathcal{MP}((X \cup C \cup \Gamma) \times Intv(n)))^*$, $\overline{DBM}(\bar{Y})$ is computable, since there are fixed number of DBMs over $X \cup C$ and for $D \in \mathcal{D}bm(X \cup C)$, we can easily check if it is *compatible* with $\bar{Y}$ (i.e. check if there exists at least one feasible solution when combining all constraints represented by $\bar{Y}$ and D).

Definition 13. *For digiwords $U = (Y_1 \cdots Y_m, D)$ and $V = (Z_1 \cdots Z_{m'}, D')$ with pairs of k-pointers $(\bar{\rho}_1, \bar{\rho}_2)$, and $(\bar{\rho}'_1, \bar{\rho}'_2)$, respectively. We define an embedding $U \sqsubseteq V$, if $D = D'$ and there exists a monotonic injection $f : [1..m] \to [1..m']$ such that $Y_i \subseteq Z_{f(i)}$ for each $i \in [1..m]$, and $\bar{\rho}_i = \bar{\rho}'_i \circ f$, for $i = 1, 2$.*

Definition 14. *Let $U = (\bar{Y}, D), U' = (\bar{Y}', D') \in (\mathcal{MP}((X \cup C \cup \Gamma) \times Intv(n)))^* \times \mathcal{D}bm(X \cup C)$ such that U (resp. U') has a pair of k-pointers $(\bar{\rho}_1, \bar{\rho}_2)$ (resp. $(\bar{\rho}'_1, \bar{\rho}'_2)$), where $\bar{Y} = Y_0 \cdots Y_m$ and $\bar{Y}' = Y'_0 \cdots Y'_{m'}$. We define digiword operations as follows. Note that except for **Map$^\to$**, **Map$^\leftarrow$**, and **Permutation**, k-pointers do not change.*

- **Insert$_I$** *$insert_I(U, (x, \mathbf{r}_i))$ for $x \in X \cup C$ and $\mathbf{r}_i \subset [0, n]$ inserts $(x, \mathbf{r}_i)$ to $\bar{Y}$ at*

$$\begin{cases} \text{either put into } Y_j \text{ for } j > 0, \text{ or put the singleton set } \{(x, \mathbf{r}_i)\} \\ \quad \text{at any place after } Y_0 & \text{if } i \text{ is odd} \\ \text{put into } Y_0 & \text{if } i \text{ is even} \end{cases}$$

and then replaces the DBM D with D_{new}, where $D_{new} \in \{D'' \mid D'' \in \overline{DBM}(\bar{Y}'') \wedge \forall i, j \in [1..(k+k')] \setminus \{idx(x)\}, D_{ij} = D''_{ij}\}$, and $\bar{Y}''$ is the resulting multisets after insertion.

- **Insert**$_x$ $insert_x(U, x, y)$ *adds* $(x, \mathbf{r}_i)$ *to* Y_j *for* $(y, \mathbf{r}_i) \in Y_j \in \bar{Y}$, $x, y \in X \cup C$ *and updates DBM* D *in the following way: replace* $D_{idx(x), idx(y)}$ *and* $D_{idx(y), idx(x)}$ *with* $\mathbf{r}_0$, *and then for* $1 \leq i' \leq k + k'$, *replace* $D_{i', idx(x)}$ *and* $D_{idx(x), i'}$ *with* $D_{i', idx(y)}$ *and* $D_{idx(y), i'}$ *respectively.*
- **Init** $init(U)$ *is obtained by removing all elements* $(x, \mathbf{r})$ *for* $x \in X$, *updating* Y_0 *with* $Y_0 \uplus \{(x, \mathbf{r}_0) \mid x \in X\}$ *and updating DBM* D *in the following way: replace* D_{ij} *for* $\forall i, j \in [1..k]$ *with* $\mathbf{r}_0$, *and for* $\forall i \in [1..k]$ *and* $\forall j \in [(k+1)..(k+k')]$, *replace* D_{ij} *and* D_{ji} *with* $\mathbf{r}_{-t}$ *and* $\mathbf{r}_t$ *respectively, where* $(ridx(j), \mathbf{r}_t) \in Y \in \bar{Y}$.
- **Delete** $delete(U, x)$ *for* $x \in X \cup C$ *is obtained from* $\bar{Y}$ *by deleting the element* $(x, \mathbf{r})$ *indexed by* x.
- **Shift.** *A one-step shift* $U = (\bar{Y}, D) \Rightarrow U' = (\bar{Y}', D')$ *if and only if* $\bar{Y} \Rightarrow \bar{Y}'$ *and* $D = D'$, *where a one-step shift* $\bar{Y} = Y_0 Y_1 \cdots Y_m \Rightarrow \bar{Y}' = Y_0' Y_1' \cdots Y_{m'}'$ *is defined in the following.*

$$
\begin{cases}
\bar{Y}' = Y_0', Y_1', \cdots, Y_{m+1}' & \text{if } Y_0 \neq \emptyset, \text{ then } Y_0' = \emptyset, \\
\quad Y_1' = \{(x, \mathbf{r}_{min\{i+1, 2n+1\}}) \mid (x, \mathbf{r}_i) \in Y_0\} \text{ and} \\
\quad Y_j' = Y_{j-1} \text{ for } j \in [2..m+1]. \\
\bar{Y}' = Y_0', Y_1', \cdots, Y_{m-1}' & \text{otherwise, then } Y_0' = \\
\quad \{(x, \mathbf{r}_{min\{i+1, 2n+1\}}) \mid (x, \mathbf{r}_i) \in Y_m\} \text{ and} \\
\quad Y_j' = Y_j \text{ for } j \in [1..m-1].
\end{cases}
$$

$(\bar{\rho}_1, \bar{\rho}_2)$ *is updated to correspond to the shift accordingly. As convention, we define* $\Rightarrow^*$ *as reflexive transitive closure of* $\Rightarrow$.
- **Rotate.** *For* k-*pointers* $(\bar{\rho}_1, \bar{\rho}_2)$ *of* U *and* $\bar{\rho}'$ *of* V, *let* $U|_\Gamma \Rightarrow^* V|_\Gamma$ *such that the permutation makes* $\bar{\rho}_1$ *match with* $\bar{\rho}$. *Then,* $rotate_{\bar{\rho}_1 \mapsto \bar{\rho}}(\bar{\rho}_2)$ *is the corresponding* k-*pointer of* V *to* $\bar{\rho}_2$.
- **Map**$^\rightarrow$ $map^\rightarrow(U, \gamma)$ *for* $\gamma \in \Gamma$ *is obtained from* U *by, for each* $x_i \in X$, *replacing* $(x_i, \mathbf{r}_j)$ *with* $(\gamma, \mathbf{r}_j)$. *Accordingly,* $\bar{\rho}_1[i]$ *is updated to point to the replacement* $(\gamma, \mathbf{r}_j)$, *and* $\bar{\rho}_2$ *is set to the original* $\bar{\rho}_1$.
- **Map**$^\leftarrow$ $map^\leftarrow(U, U', \gamma)$ *for* $\gamma \in \Gamma$ *is obtained from* U, *by removing* $(x_i, \mathbf{r}_j)$ *for* $x_i \in X$, *and replacing each* $\bar{\rho}_1[i] = (\gamma, \mathbf{r}_j)$ *in* $U|_\Gamma$ *with* $(x_i, \mathbf{r}_j)$ *for* $x_i \in X$ *and DBM* D *by* $D_{new} \in \overline{DBM}(\bar{Y}'')$, *where* $\bar{Y}''$ *is the resulting multisets after replacement. Accordingly, new* $\bar{\rho}_1$ *is set to the original* $\bar{\rho}_2$, *and new* $\bar{\rho}_2$ *is set to* $rotate_{\bar{\rho}_1' \mapsto \bar{\rho}_2}(\bar{\rho}_2')$.

5.2   Snapshot PDS

A *snapshot pushdown system* (snapshot PDS) keeps the digitization of all values of clocks and ages and the difference between all pairs of two clocks in the top stack frame, as a *digiword*.

We show that an EDTPDA can be encoded into its digitization, called a *snapshot PDS*. The key of the encoding is that when a pop occurs, the time progress recorded at the top stack symbol is propagated to the next stack symbol after finding some shifts by matching between k-pointers $\bar{\rho}_2$ and $\bar{\rho}_1'$.

Definition 15. *Let* $\pi : \varrho_0 = (q_0, \epsilon, \nu_0) \hookrightarrow^* \varrho = (s, w, \nu)$ *be a transition sequence of an EDTPDA from the initial configuration. If* π *is not empty, we refer the last step as* $\lambda : \varrho' \hookrightarrow \varrho$, *and the preceding sequence by* $\pi' : \varrho_0 \hookrightarrow^* \varrho'$. *Let* $w = v_m \cdots v_1$. *A snapshot is* $snap(\pi) = U$, *where*

$$U = \mathtt{digi}(\uplus_i dist(v_i) \uplus \{(x, \nu(x)) \mid x \in X \cup C\})$$

Let a k-*pointer* $\bar{\xi}(\pi)$ *be* $\bar{\xi}(\pi)[i] = (\gamma, proj(t_i))$ *for* $(\gamma, t_i) \in dist(v_m)$. *A snapshot configuration* $Snap(\pi)$ *is inductively defined from* $Snap(\pi')$.

$$
\begin{cases}
(q_0, snap(\epsilon)) & if\ \pi = \epsilon.\ (\bar{\rho}_1, \bar{\rho}_2)\ are\ \text{undefined}. \\
(s', snap(\pi)\ tail(Snap(\pi'))) & if\ \lambda\ is\ \textbf{Time progress}\ with\ U' \Rightarrow^* U. \\
\quad Then,\ the\ permutation\ U' \Rightarrow^* U\ updates\ (\bar{\rho}_1', \bar{\rho}_2')\ to\ (\bar{\rho}_1, \bar{\rho}_2). \\
(s', snap(\pi)\ tail(Snap(\pi'))) & if\ \lambda\ is\ \textbf{Local}, \textbf{Test}, \textbf{Assign}, \textbf{Value-passing}. \\
(s, snap(\pi)\ Snap(\pi')) & if\ \lambda\ is\ \textbf{Push}.\ Then,\ (\bar{\rho}_1, \bar{\rho}_2) = (\bar{\xi}(\pi), \bar{\rho}_1'). \\
(s, snap(\pi)\ tail(tail(Snap(\pi')))) & if\ \lambda\ is\ \textbf{Pop}. \\
\quad Then,\ (\bar{\rho}_1, \bar{\rho}_2) = (\bar{\rho}_2', rotate_{\bar{\rho}_1'' \mapsto \bar{\rho}_2'}(\bar{\rho}_2'')).
\end{cases}
$$

We refer $head(Snap(\pi'))$ *by* U', $head(tail(Snap(\pi'))$ *by* U''. *Pairs of* k-*pointers of* U, U', *and* U'' *are denoted by* $(\bar{\rho}_1, \bar{\rho}_2)$, $(\bar{\rho}_1', \bar{\rho}_2')$, *and* $(\bar{\rho}_1'', \bar{\rho}_2'')$, *respectively. If not mentioned,* k-*pointers are kept as is.*

Definition 16. *For an EDTPDA* $\langle S, s_0, \Gamma, X, C, \Delta \rangle$, *a snapshot PDS* $\mathcal{S}$ *is a PDS (with possibly infinite stack alphabet)* $\langle S, s_0, \mathcal{MP}((X \cup C \cup \Gamma) \times Intv(n))^* \times \mathcal{D}bm(X \cup C), \Delta_d \rangle$, *with the initial configuration* $\langle s_{init}, \{(x, \mathbf{r}_0) \mid x \in X \cup C\} \rangle$. *Then* Δ_d *consists of:*

- **Time progress** $\quad \langle s, U \rangle \hookrightarrow_{\mathcal{S}} \langle s, U' \rangle$ *for* $U \Rightarrow^* U'$.
- **Local** $(s \xrightarrow{\epsilon} s' \in \Delta)$ $\quad \langle s, U \rangle \hookrightarrow_{\mathcal{S}} \langle s', U \rangle$.
- **Test** $(s \xrightarrow{x \in I?} s' \in \Delta)$ $\quad$ *If* $U = (\bar{Y}, D)$, $(x, \mathbf{r}_i) \in Y \in \bar{Y}$ *and* $\mathbf{r}_i \subseteq I$,
  $\langle s, U \rangle \hookrightarrow_{\mathcal{S}} \langle s', U \rangle$.
- **Test** $(s \xrightarrow{x - y \in I?} s' \in \Delta)$ $\quad$ *If* $U = (\bar{Y}, D)$, $D_{idx(x), idx(y)} = \mathbf{r}_i$ *and* $\mathbf{r}_i \subseteq I$,
  $\langle s, U \rangle \hookrightarrow_{\mathcal{S}} \langle s', U \rangle$.
- **Assign** $(s \xrightarrow{x \leftarrow I} s' \in \Delta$ *with* $x \in X)$ $\quad$ *for* $\forall \mathbf{r} \subseteq I$,
  $\langle s, U \rangle \hookrightarrow_{\mathcal{S}} \langle s', insert_I(delete(U, x), (x, \mathbf{r})) \rangle$.
- **Value-passing** $(s \xrightarrow{x \leftarrow y} s' \in \Delta$ *with* $x, y \in X \cup C)$
  $\langle s, U \rangle \hookrightarrow_{\mathcal{S}} \langle s', insert_x(delete(U, x), x, y) \rangle$.
- **Push** $(s \xrightarrow{push(\gamma)} s' \in \Delta)$
  $\langle s, U \rangle \hookrightarrow_{\mathcal{S}} \langle s', init(map^{\rightarrow}(U, \gamma))U \rangle$.
- **Pop** $(s \xrightarrow{pop(\gamma)} s' \in \Delta)$
  $\langle s, UU' \rangle \hookrightarrow_{\mathcal{S}} \langle s', map^{\leftarrow}(U, U', \gamma) \rangle$.

By induction on the number of steps of transitions, the encoding relation between an EDTPDA and a snapshot PDS is observed. Note that the initial clock valuation of the DTPDA to be set ν_0 is essential.

Lemma 1. *Let us denote ϱ_0 and ϱ (resp. $\langle q_0, \tilde{w}_0 \rangle$ and $\langle s, \tilde{w} \rangle$) for the initial configuration and a configuration of an EDTPDA (resp. its snapshot PDS $\mathcal{S}$).*

(Preservation).   *If $\pi : \varrho_0 \hookrightarrow^* \varrho$, there exists $\langle s, \tilde{w} \rangle$ such that $\langle q_0, \tilde{w}_0 \rangle \hookrightarrow_{\mathcal{S}}^* \langle s, \tilde{w} \rangle$ and $Snap(\pi) = \langle s, \tilde{w} \rangle$.*
(Reflection).   *If $\langle q_0, \tilde{w}_0 \rangle \hookrightarrow_{\mathcal{S}}^* \langle s, \tilde{w} \rangle$, there exists $\pi : \varrho_0 \hookrightarrow^* \varrho$ with $Snap(\pi) = \langle s, \tilde{w} \rangle$.*

5.3   Well-Formed Constraints

A snapshot PDS is *a growing WSPDS* (Definition 6 in [15]) and $\Downarrow_\Upsilon$ gives a *well-formed constraint* (Definition 8 in [15]). Let us recall the definitions.

Let P be a set of control locations and let Γ be a stack alphabet. Different from an ordinary definition of PDSs, we do not assume that P and Γ are finite, but associated with well-quasi-orderings (WQOs) $\preceq$ and $\leq$, respectively. Note that the embedding $\sqsubseteq$ over digiwords is a WQO by Higman's lemma.

For $w = \alpha_1 \alpha_2 \cdots \alpha_n, v = \beta_1 \beta_2 \cdots \beta_m \in \Gamma^*$, let $w \ll v$ if $m = n$ and $\forall i \in [1..n].\alpha_i \leq \beta_i$. We extend $\ll$ on configurations such that $(p, w) \ll (q, v)$ if $p \preceq q$ and $w \ll v$ for $p, q \in P$ and $w, v \in \Gamma^*$. A partial function $\psi \in \mathcal{P}Fun(X, Y)$ is *monotonic* if $\gamma \leq \gamma'$ with $\gamma \in dom(\psi)$ implies $\psi(\gamma) \ll \psi(\gamma')$ and $\gamma' \in dom(\psi)$.

A *well-structured PDS* (WSPDS) is a triplet $\langle (P, \preceq), (\Gamma, \leq), \Delta \rangle$ of a set $(P, \preceq)$ of WQO states, a WQO stack alphabet $(\Gamma, \leq)$, and a finite set $\Delta \subseteq \mathcal{P}Fun(P \times \Gamma, P \times \Gamma^{\leq 2})$ of monotonic partial functions. A WSPDS is *growing* if, for each $\psi(p, \gamma) = (q, w)$ with $\psi \in \Delta$ and $(q', w') \geqq (q, w)$, there exists (p', γ') with $(p', \gamma') \geqq (p, \gamma)$ such that $\psi(p', \gamma') \geqq (q', w')$.

A well-formed constraint describes a syntactical feature that is preserved under transitions. Theorem 3 in [15] ensures the decidability the quasi-coverability of a growing WSPDS, and Theorem 5 in [15] lifts it to reachability when a growing WSPDS has a well-formed constraint. Theorem 4 in [15] shows the finite convergence of a P-automaton for the quasi-coverability, which concludes that a WSPDS with a well-formed constraint holds the decidability of the reachability.

Definition 17. *Let $(s, \tilde{w})$ be a configuration of a snapshot PDS $\mathcal{S}$. An element in a stack frame of $\tilde{w}$ has a* parent *if it has a corresponding element in the next stack frame. The transitive closure of the parent relation is an ancestor. An element in $\tilde{w}$ is* marked, *if its ancestor is pointed by a k-pointer in some stack frame. We define a projection $\Downarrow_\Upsilon (\tilde{w})$ by removing unmarked elements in $\tilde{w}$. We say that $\tilde{w}$ is* well-formed *if $\Downarrow_\Upsilon (\tilde{w}) = \tilde{w}$.*

The idea of $\Downarrow_\Upsilon$ is to remove unnecessary elements (i.e., elements not related to previous actions) from the stack content. Note that a configuration reachable from the initial configuration by $\hookrightarrow_{\mathcal{S}}^*$ is always well-formed. Since a snapshot PDS is a growing WSPDS with $\Downarrow_\Upsilon$, we conclude the following theorem from Lemma 1.

Theorem 4. *The reachability of an EDTPDA $\langle S, s_0, \Gamma, X, C, \Delta \rangle$ is decidable.*

6   Decidability Results of NeTAs Without Frozen Clocks

In this section, for clarity we will introduce a subclass of general NeTAs, NeTAs with **diagonal constraints** and **bounded assignment** and without **frozen clocks**, and then prove that the decidability results by encoding them to EDT-PDAs.

Note that such a model is just the Definition 5 by removing **F-Push** rules, and choosing bounded assignment in **Assignment** rules.

6.1   Encoding

Let $\mathcal{N} = (T, \mathcal{A}_0, X, C, \Delta)$ be a NeTA without frozen clocks. We define a corresponding EDTPDA $\mathcal{E}(\mathcal{N}) = \langle S, s_0, \Gamma, X, C, \nabla \rangle$, such that

- $S = \Gamma = \bigcup_{\mathcal{A}_i \in T} Q(\mathcal{A}_i)$ is the set of all locations of TAs in T, with
- $s_0 = q_0(\mathcal{A}_0)$ is the initial location of the initial TA $\mathcal{A}_0$ of $\mathcal{N}$.
- $X = \{x_1, \ldots, x_k\}$ is the set of k local clocks, and $C = \{c_1, \ldots, c_{k'}\}$ is the set of k' global clocks.
- ∇ is the union $\bigcup_{\mathcal{A}_i \in T} \Delta(\mathcal{A}_i) \bigcup \mathcal{G}(\mathcal{N}) \bigcup \mathcal{H}(\mathcal{N})$ where

$$\begin{cases} \Delta(\mathcal{A}_i) = \{\textbf{Local}, \textbf{Test}, \textbf{Assignment}, \textbf{Value-passing}\}, \\ \mathcal{G}(\mathcal{N}) = \{\textbf{Global-test}, \textbf{Global-assign}, \textbf{Global-load}, \textbf{Global-store}\}, \\ \mathcal{H}(\mathcal{N}) \text{ consists of rules below.} \end{cases}$$

$$\textbf{Push} \quad q \xrightarrow{push(q)} q_0(\mathcal{A}_{i'}) \text{ if } (q, \varepsilon, push, q_0(\mathcal{A}_{i'}), q) \in \Delta(\mathcal{N})$$
$$\textbf{Pop} \quad q \xrightarrow{pop(q')} q' \qquad \text{if } (q, q', pop, q', \varepsilon) \in \Delta(\mathcal{N})$$

Definition 18. *Let $\mathcal{N}$ be a NeTA without frozen clocks $(T, \mathcal{A}_0, X, C, \Delta)$ and let $\mathcal{E}(\mathcal{N})$ be an EDTPDA $\langle S, s_0, \Gamma, X, C, \nabla \rangle$. For a configuration $\kappa = (\langle \mathcal{A}, q, \nu, \mu \rangle, v)$ of $\mathcal{N}$ such that $v = (q_1, \nu_1) \ldots (q_n, \nu_n)$, $[\![\kappa]\!]$ denotes a configuration $(q, \overline{w}(\kappa), \nu \cup \mu)$ of $\mathcal{E}(\mathcal{N})$ where $\overline{w}(\kappa) = w_1 \cdots w_n$ with $w_i = (q_i, \nu_i)$.*

Lemma 2. *For a NeTA without frozen clocks $\mathcal{N}$, an EDTPDA $\mathcal{E}(\mathcal{N})$, and configurations κ, κ' of $\mathcal{N}$,*

(Preservation) *if $\kappa \longrightarrow_{\mathcal{N}} \kappa'$, then $[\![\kappa]\!] \hookrightarrow^*_{\mathcal{E}(\mathcal{N})} [\![\kappa']\!]$, and*

(Reflection) *if $[\![\kappa]\!] \hookrightarrow^*_{\mathcal{N}} \varrho$, there exists κ' with $\varrho \hookrightarrow^*_{\mathcal{E}(\mathcal{N})} [\![\kappa']\!]$ and $\kappa \longrightarrow^*_{\mathcal{N}} \kappa'$.*

By this encoding, we have our main result.

Theorem 5. *The reachability of a NeTA without frozen clocks is decidable.*

7   Related Work

Timed automata (TAs) proposed in [2] are finite automata with a finite set of clocks and only allow reset assignment. Reachability of TAs is proved to be decidable based on the construction of region automata, which finitely abstracts timed behaviors of TA. It is also shown that diagonal constraints does not effect the decidability and thus only a syntax sugar.

Dense timed pushdown automata (DTPDAs) [5,16] provided a backbone of our technologies In original DTPDAs, local clocks must be dealt within some proper bookkeeping process, which was not an essential part of the analysis. In [17], a discrete version of DTPDAs, named *discrete timed pushdown automata*, was introduced, where time was incremented in discrete steps and thus the ages of clocks and stack symbols are in the natural numbers. This made the reachability problem much simpler, and easier for efficient implementation.

Based on *recursive state machines* [18], two similar timed extensions, *timed recursive state machines (TRSMs)* [19] and *recursive timed automata (RTAs)* [10], were given independently. A finite number of clocks was distinguished into two categories, call-by-reference and call-by-value. When entering a fresh context, clock values were stored in the stack. After popping, the values of call-by-reference clocks were unaltered, while the values of call-by-value ones restored to the previous value from the stack. When either all of clocks or none of them were call-by-reference, the state reachability problem was decidable.

Interrupt timed automata (ITAs) [9], which are well suited to the description of multi-task systems with interruptions in a single processor environment, is a subclass of hybrid automata. It is shown that in ITA the reachability problem is in 2-EXPSPACE and in PSPACE when the number of clocks is fixed. *Recursive timed automata (RTAs)* [10] is an extension of TAs with recursive structure. It has clocks by the mechanism of "pass-by-value". When the condition of "glitch-freeness", i.e. all the clocks of components are uniformly either by "pass-by-value" or by "pass-by-reference", the reachability is shown to be decidable.

Nested timed automata (NeTAs) [6,7,20] extend TAs with recursive structure in another way. They allowed clocks of some TAs in the stack elapse simultaneously with the current running clocks during time passage. Those clocks are named *local clocks*, while clocks in other TAs kept unaltered clocks during time passage are named *frozen clocks*. It is shown that the reachability of NeTAs with both types of clocks and a singleton *global clock* that can be observed by all TAs is decidable, while that with two or more global clocks is undecidable [7].

8   Conclusion

This paper investigates the decidability results of nested timed automata with diagonal constraints. We show that the general NeTAs with diagonal constraints are Turing complete, even when the clock assignment, say, arbitrary value in an interval, is restricted to clock reset. In comparison, reachability problem of a subclass, NeTAs with bounded assignment and without frozen clocks are decidable, which is shown by encoding them to snapshot PDSs. They are WSPDSs with a well-formed constraint [15]. The future work includes to efficiently implement the general NeTA by adopting data structure BDD as backbones, and CEGAR [21,22] as the verification technique, and to investigate more model checking problem on the model [23].

Acknowledgements. This work is supported by National Natural Science Foundation of China with grant No. 61472240, 61672340, 61472238, and the NSFC-JSPS bilateral joint research project with grant No. 61511140100.

References

1. Mattai, J.: Real-Time Systems: Specification, Verification, and Analysis. Prentice Hall, Englewood Cliffs (1995)
2. Alur, R., Dill, D.L.: A theory of timed automata. Theoret. Comput. Sci. **126**, 183–235 (1994)
3. Henzinger, T.A., Nicollin, X., Sifakis, J., Yovine, S.: Symbolic model checking for real-time systems. Inf. Comput. **111**, 193–244 (1994)
4. Bengtsson, J., Yi, W.: Timed automata: semantics, algorithms and tools. In: Desel, J., Reisig, W., Rozenberg, G. (eds.) ACPN 2003. LNCS, vol. 3098, pp. 87–124. Springer, Heidelberg (2004). doi:10.1007/978-3-540-27755-2_3
5. Clemente, L., Lasota, S.: Timed pushdown automata, revisited. In: Proceedings of LICS 2015, pp. 738–749
6. Li, G., Cai, X., Ogawa, M., Yuen, S.: Nested timed automata. In: Braberman, V., Fribourg, L. (eds.) FORMATS 2013. LNCS, vol. 8053, pp. 168–182. Springer, Heidelberg (2013). doi:10.1007/978-3-642-40229-6_12
7. Li, G., Ogawa, M., Yuen, S.: Nested timed automata with frozen clocks. In: Sankaranarayanan, S., Vicario, E. (eds.) FORMATS 2015. LNCS, vol. 9268, pp. 189–205. Springer, Cham (2015). doi:10.1007/978-3-319-22975-1_13
8. Fang, B., Li, G., Sun, D., Cai, H.: Schedulability analysis of timed regular tasks by under-approximation on WCET. In: Fränzle, M., Kapur, D., Zhan, N. (eds.) SETTA 2016. LNCS, vol. 9984, pp. 147–162. Springer, Cham (2016). doi:10.1007/978-3-319-47677-3_10
9. Berard, B., Haddad, S., Sassolas, M.: Real time properties for interrupt timed automata. In: Proceedings of TIME 2010, pp. 69–76. IEEE Computer Society (2010)
10. Trivedi, A., Wojtczak, D.: Recursive timed automata. In: Bouajjani, A., Chin, W.-N. (eds.) ATVA 2010. LNCS, vol. 6252, pp. 306–324. Springer, Heidelberg (2010). doi:10.1007/978-3-642-15643-4_23
11. Minsky, M.: Computation: Finite and Infinite Machines. Prentice-Hall, Englewood Cliffs (1967)
12. Ouaknine, J., Worrell, J.: On the language inclusion problem for timed automata: closing a decidability gap. In: Proceedings of LICS 2004, pp. 54–63. IEEE Computer Society (2004)
13. Abdulla, P.A., Jonsson, B.: Verifying networks of timed processes. In: Steffen, B. (ed.) TACAS 1998. LNCS, vol. 1384, pp. 298–312. Springer, Heidelberg (1998). doi:10.1007/BFb0054179
14. Abdulla, P., Jonsson, B.: Model checking of systems with many identical time processes. Theoret. Comput. Sci. **290**, 241–264 (2003)

15. Cai, X., Ogawa, M.: Well-structured pushdown system: case of dense timed pushdown automata. In: Codish, M., Sumii, E. (eds.) FLOPS 2014. LNCS, vol. 8475, pp. 336–352. Springer, Cham (2014). doi:10.1007/978-3-319-07151-0_21

16. Abdulla, P.A., Atig, M.F., Stenman, J.: Dense-timed pushdown automata. In: Proceedings of LICS 2012, pp. 35–44. IEEE Computer Society (2012)

17. Abdulla, P.A., Atig, M.F., Stenman, J.: The minimal cost reachability problem in priced timed pushdown systems. In: Dediu, A.-H., Martín-Vide, C. (eds.) LATA 2012. LNCS, vol. 7183, pp. 58–69. Springer, Heidelberg (2012). doi:10.1007/978-3-642-28332-1_6

18. Alur, R., Etessami, K., Yannakakis, M.: Analysis of recursive state machines. In: Berry, G., Comon, H., Finkel, A. (eds.) CAV 2001. LNCS, vol. 2102, pp. 207–220. Springer, Heidelberg (2001). doi:10.1007/3-540-44585-4_18

19. Benerecetti, M., Minopoli, S., Peron, A.: Analysis of timed recursive state machines, pp. 61–68. In: Proceedings of the TIME 2010. IEEE Computer Society (2010)

20. Wang, Y., Li, G., Yuen, S.: Nested timed automata with various clocks. Sci. Found. Chin. **24**, 51–68 (2016)

21. Tian, C., Duan, Z.: Detecting spurious counterexamples efficiently in abstract model checking. In: Proceedings of the ICSE 2013, pp. 202–211. IEEE/ACM (2013)

22. Tian, C., Duan, Z., Duan, Z.: Making CEGAR more efficient in software model checking. IEEE Trans. Softw. Eng. **40**, 1206–1223 (2014)

23. Liu, Y., Duan, Z., Tian, C.: A decision procedure for a fragment of linear time Mu-calculus. In: Proceedings of the IJCAI 2016, pp. 1195–1201. IJCAI/AAAI Press (2016)

Integration of Metamorphic Testing with Program Repair Methods Based on Adaptive Search Strategies and Program Equivalence

Tingting Wu[1,2]([✉]), Yunwei Dong[1], Tsong Yueh Chen[2], Mingyue Jiang[3],
Man Lau[2], Fei-Ching Kuo[2], and Sebastian Ng[2]

[1] School of Computer Science and Engineering,
Northwestern Polytechnical University,
Xi'an 710072, People's Republic of China
[2] Department of Computer Science and Software Engineering,
Swinburne University of Technology, Hawthorn, VIC 3122, Australia
tingtingwu@swin.edu.au
[3] School of Information Science, Zhejiang Sci-Tech University,
Hangzhou 310018, People's Republic of China

Abstract. Automated program repair (APR) is a promising approach to localize faults and generate patches for program under repair. One of the test suite based APR techniques, a method leveraging Adaptive search strategies and program Equivalence (AE), has been commonly used for program repair. AE assumes the availability of test oracles, which brings the oracle problem to AE repair procedure. Metamorphic Testing (MT) has been introduced to alleviate the test oracle problem, and it tests the correctness of programs through metamorphic relations (MRs) which are relations among multiple inputs and outputs. This paper presents an integration of AE with MT (referred to as AE-MT) to extend the applicability of AE to those applications with oracle problems. To evaluate the repair effectiveness of AE-MT, an empirical study is conducted against *IntroClass* benchmark. We conclude that AE-MT outperforms AE in terms of success rate, but is of lower repair quality than AE.

Keywords: Automated program repair · Metamorphic testing · Metamorphic relation · Test oracle problem

1 Introduction

After testing reveals a program having errors, a software developer debugs the buggy version, hoping to fix the mistakes so that the revised version passes the original test cases that reveal the mistakes. The developer also needs to ensure that this revised version also passes the original test suite. By doing so, the developer can then be sure that no new mistakes are introduced to the revised

Z. Duan and L. Ong (Eds.): ICFEM 2017, LNCS 10610, pp. 413–429, 2017.
https://doi.org/10.1007/978-3-319-68690-5_25

version during the repair process. During the manual debugging process, software developers rely on a given test suite to determine whether the program succeeds or fails by comparing the actual result to the expected result.

Automated Program Repair (APR) aims at automating this manual and labour-intensive repair process. There are mainly two kinds of APR approaches, namely *program specifications based APR* and *test suite based APR*. Program specification based APR such as ABF [1] uses information from the program specifications to guide the APR process whereas test suite based APR such as GenProg [8, 25] uses test suite to guide the APR process. We focus on test suite based APR approach in this paper.

Many different test suite based APR techniques have been proposed. They fall roughly into two main categories, namely the *Generate-and-Validate (GaV)* techniques and *Correct-by-Construction (CbC)* techniques [14]. The *GaV* techniques, search based techniques, generate multiple revised versions, referred to as *candidate repairs*, and then validate them with selected test cases (e.g., GenProg [25], AE [24], TrpAutoRepair [20], Kali [21]). On the other hand, the *CbC* techniques, semantics based techniques, fix programs by program synthesis or constraint solving to generate patches (e.g., CETI [19], SemFix [18], Angelix [16]).

The generic APR process accepts two inputs: (1) a buggy program P_{buggy} and (2) a test suite T containing at least some test cases that can reveal the bugs in P_{buggy}. It then applies a specific APR technique to find a fixed version, which is referred to as a *repair* P_{repair}. If it can find one, it will return the repair that passes the original test suite T. Otherwise, it reports that no repair could be found. As T is only a partial subset of the entire input domain, it may not reveal any other faults in P_{repair} and hence, P_{repair} may not be "correct." The original test suite is referred to as the *input test suite* because the APR process uses this test suite as one of its inputs. In order to determine whether P_{repair} is of good quality, we need to evaluate it using an independent test suite. Such a test suite is called the *evaluation test suite* (ET) because it is used for evaluating the quality of the repair.

Researchers have been using three different metrics to measure and compare the performance of individual APR technique, namely *success rate*, *repair quality* and *repair time*. First, the success rate is defined as the number of repairs successfully found over the total number of trails to find a repair. Second, the repair quality is defined as the number of test cases in the evaluation test suite ET that can be passed by the repair returned by the APR process over the total number of test cases in ET. Finally, the repair time is defined as the time required to find a repair.

Test suite based APR approach relies heavily on the existence of a *test oracle* of the program under repair [12]. A test oracle of a program is a mechanism to determine whether the input-output relationship holds for the program. In software testing, there are programs that (1) do not have a test oracle or (2) are too time consuming to verify the input-output relationship. This problem is usually referred to as *the test oracle problem* of software testing [2]. In the repairing procedure of APR, it relies on the test oracles to determine whether the candidate program can pass the test cases in the input test suite or test cases in the evaluation test suite when assessing the repair quality. We would then ask the question: For programs having test oracle problems, how could we perform APR on such programs?

Metamorphic Testing (MT) has long been used in software testing to alleviate the test oracle problem [4,5]. Assume we have a program P without test oracles. After executing P with a test case t, we obtained an output o. MT uses certain property of the algorithm to be implemented by the program P, the source test case t and its output o to generate a follow-up test case t'. Such a property is usually referred to as the *metamorphic relation* (MR) of the algorithm. After executing P with the follow-up test case t', the corresponding output o' is obtained. MT then verifies whether t, o, t' and o' satisfy the relevant MR. If they do not satisfy the MR, the program P is incorrect. If they satisfy the MR, we have more confidence on P. For example, assume P_{sp} is a program that computes the shortest path (SP) between two nodes x and y in an undirected graph G (that is, P_{sp} implements $SP(G, x, y)$). Since "$length(SP(G, a, b)) = length(SP(G, a, h))$ $+ length(SP(G, h, b))$" where h is a node in the shortest path from a to b in G, MT uses this MR to generate and execute two follow-up test cases, (G, a, h) and (G, h, b). If this MR does not hold, P_{sp} is incorrect. If this MR holds, P_{sp} passes the metamorphic test cases generated based on this MR. As illustrated in this example, depending on the actual MR being used, a source test case t may give rise to multiple follow-up test cases t'_1, t'_2, ... Hence, the source test case and its follow-up test cases (that is, $\{t, t'_1, t'_2, \dots\}$) forms a *metamorphic testing group* (MTG), used to test the correctness of program P.

Recent research proposed a framework APR-MT to integrate test suite based APR techniques with MT. This framework was applied to form two integrated techniques GenProg-MT [12] and CETI-MT [11] to demonstrate the feasibility and effectiveness of APR-MT. It seems that MT can also be integrated with other APR techniques. However, after the integration, it is still not known about the effectiveness and efficiency of the integrated technique. Hence, more in-depth research is needed.

In this paper, we investigate the possibility of integrating MT with another *GaV* technique, known as *Adaptive search strategies and program Equivalance* (AE) [24], denoted as AE-MT. We choose AE rather than other APR techniques because AE not only delivers a repair for a faulty program, but also reduces search spaces significantly through adaptive search strategies. We also compare the performance of AE-MT with AE against the same benchmark *IntroClass* [14] and the same metamorphic relations in [12], using three metrics mentioned earlier (that is, success rate, repair quality, and repair time). In addition, we proposed to use one more MR to investigate the repair capability of AE-MT using different metamorphic relations.

The remainder of this paper is organized as follows. Section 2 presents the background information of AE and MT. In Sect. 3, we discuss how to integrate AE and MT. Sections 4 and 5 discuss our empirical study and the results. Section 6 briefly discusses the related work of APR-MT. Section 7 concludes the paper and discusses the future work.

2   Background

2.1   Adaptive Search Strategies and Program Equivalence

AE [24] is a typical GaV APR technique, and the whole repair procedure is based on the existence of test oracles of program under repair. AE has been commonly used as a comparison object in APR researches [14,21]. AE leverages two adaptive search strategies and program equivalence to conduct program repair and reduce repair cost and search spaces more significantly than other APR techniques [14,23,24].

AE first generates a candidate repair set CR by operator Edits for the given faulty program P, such as *delete* a possible faulty statement or *insert* a statement from elsewhere of the program after a possible faulty statement. Then, AE reduces the number of candidate repairs through program equivalence relation ($\sim$). For instance, given two candidate repairs A and A' of P, if A and A' are semantically equivalent and have the same test case behavior, A' is regarded as an equivalent program of A, denoted as $A \sim A'$. When $A \sim A'$, AE algorithm will only take one of them as a candidate repair. After determining the set of candidate repairs, AE iterates the **adaptive repair strategy** and **adaptive test strategy** nested in the former one. It then repeats the process that selects a candidate program P' from the set CR not tried before, and selects test cases that satisfy the input restriction of P' from the input test suite T. Then, it validates P' on these test cases. The repair iteration stops only if (1) a repair program is found that passes all test cases in T, or (2) when no repair can be found in a candidate repair set. AE prioritizes the candidate repairs in CR so as to choose one that is most likely to pass all test cases according to the repair strategy. Similarly, the test iteration terminates only when a failed test is found, or the entire test set T is tried. It favours the test case that is most likely to fail as early as possible according to the test strategy.

Although these strategies are quite effective, test oracle is still an indispensable element to evaluate the execution result of individual test case, pass or fail, through the whole repair process. Therefore, it is necessary to solve the oracle problem of AE process.

2.2   Metamorphic Testing

MT is a testing approach widely used to alleviate the test oracle problem [5,15, 22]. MT verifies a program using the source and follow-up test cases based on the MRs. MT involves the following steps:

(1) Identify effective MRs for the program;
(2) Select source test cases that satisfy restrictions in MRs according to some test case selection strategies;
(3) Construct follow-up test cases based on the source test cases and MRs;
(4) Construct MTG sets according to source, follow-up test cases and MRs;
(5) Verify the correctness of program by evaluating whether MRs are satisfied or not by MTGs.

Algorithm 1. AE-MT algorithm

Input: faulty program P
Input: a set of metamorphic testing groups $MTGs$ with at least one violated MTG
Output: Program repair P' satisfying all $MTGs$ or no repair.
1: $EC \leftarrow \emptyset$ // EC is a set of equivalent class of candidate repairs
2: $CR \leftarrow GenerateCandidateRepair(P)$ // CR is a set of candidate repairs
3: **while** $CR \neq \emptyset$ **do**
4:     $P' \leftarrow RepairStrat(CR)$ // select a repair that is most likely to pass
5:     $CR \leftarrow CR \setminus \{P'\}$
6:     //Is P' equal to any candidate repair previously tried?
7:     **if** $\neg(\exists Previous \in EC$ **and** $P' \sim Previous)$ **then**
8:         $EC \leftarrow EC \cup \{P'\}$
9:         $TR \leftarrow MTGs$ // TR is the remaining $mtgs$ in the set of MTGs
10:        $r \leftarrow non\text{-}violated$
11:        **while** $TR \neq \emptyset$ **and** $r = non\text{-}violated$ **do**
12:            $mtg \leftarrow TestStrat(TR)$ // select a mtg that is most likely to fail
13:            $TR \leftarrow TR \setminus \{mtg\}$
14:            $r \leftarrow Perform(P', mtg)$ // perform MT with P' using test cases in mtg
15:        **end while**
16:        **if** $r = non\text{-}violated$ **then**
17:            **return** P'
18:        **end if**
19:     **end if**
20: **end while**
21: **if** $CR = \emptyset$ **and** $r = violated$ **then**
22:     **return** "no repair"
23: **end if**

Metamorphic testing has been integrated with many other application domains, such as model driven engineering [13], APR [12], machine learning [17], constraint logic programming [9], fault localization [27] and symbolic execution [7]. Furthermore, it is essential to investigate more systematic and automatic approaches for MR identification [15] and study the detection capability of different MRs [3,6,15].

3   Integration of Adaptive Search Strategies and Program Equivalence (AE) with Metamorphic Testing (MT)

As previously discussed, AE strongly relies on a test oracle to verify the "correctness" of the actual outputs of the test cases. Therefore, our key steps of integrating MT with AE are (1) using a set of MTGs instead of an input test suite and (2) the satisfaction or violation of MR by the relevant MTG set instead of the pass or fail of the candidate repair with respect to the individual test case. When all MTGs are satisfied, a program is said to be repaired by AE-MT.

AE-MT is an integration of AE with MT to deliver a repair in the absence of test oracles. Algorithm 1 presents the pseudocode of AE-MT. Given a faulty program P and a set of $MTGs$, with at least one $violated$. This denotes that the relevant MR is not satisfied.

AE-MT first generates a set of candidate repairs CR. AE-MT iteratively checks the candidate repair P' that is not in the equivalent class set EC (line 3 $\sim$ line 20). Then, AE-MT repeatedly tests P' on each mtg from the set of MTGs and returns execution result r (line 11 $\sim$ line 15). If P' satisfies the entire set of MTGs, P' is a repair of the faulty program P. If each candidate repair in CR violates its corresponding MTG set, no repair can be found for program P.

The main difference between AE-MT and AE is the procedure of candidate program validation. AE deals with a candidate program based on outcomes of test suite, while AE-MT tests each candidate program against MTGs and execution result of each mtg. Once an mtg is violated, that is, its relevant MR is not satisfied, validation procedure for this candidate program will stop immediately. When the set of MTGs is satisfied, this candidate will be output and considered as a repair for the input faulty program.

4   Experimental Design

In previous two studies [11,12], the effectiveness of APR-MT techniques is found to be comparable to the original APR techniques. It is not sufficient to achieve this conclusion by only two experiments. Therefore, we investigate a further APR-MT technique, AE-MT. An empirical study is conducted to study the effectiveness of AE-MT against the same benchmark and two MRs [12], namely MR1 and MR2. Interested readers may refer to [12] for details of MR1 and MR2. Moreover, one more metamorphic relation, referred to as MR3, for each target program is applied to investigate the detection capability of different MRs in order to have a more thorough analysis.

4.1   Subject Programs

The *IntroClass* benchmark [14] includes 6 small C programs and 1143 faulty versions altogether. This benchmark was designed for assessing the effectiveness of APR techniques. Two kinds of test suites, black-box and white-box, for each subject program were also designed to reveal various types of faults. The information of *IntroClass* and test suites are listed in Table 1.

Checksum. Program checksum takes as input a line of string. It computes the sum of all characters, and outputs the relative character after the sum modulo 64 and pluses the ASCII value of space character.

Table 1. Subject programs and test data

Program	LOC	Version	Test data								Description
			T_b	T_w	M_b^1	M_w^1	M_b^2	M_w^2	M_b^3	M_w^3	
Checksum	13	69	6	10	6	10	6	10	6	10	Computing the sum of a string
Digits	15	236	6	10	6	10	6	10	6	10	Listing all digits of an integer
Grade	19	268	9	9	9	9	7	7	9	9	Computing the grade of a score
Median	24	232	7	6	7	6	7	6	7	6	Computing the median of three integers
Smallest	20	177	8	8	8	8	8	8	8	8	Computing the smallest of four integers
Syllables	23	161	6	10	6	10	6	10	6	10	Counting vowels of a string

Input: $c_1 c_2 ... c_i ... c_n$, in which $1 \leqslant i \leqslant n$.

Output: "Check sum is X", where $\text{ASCII}(X) = (int)(c_1 + c_2 + ... + c_i + ... + c_n)\%64 + 32$.

Take t_s and t_f as source and follow-up test cases, o_s and o_f as the ASCII value of source and follow-up output characters.

MR3: Construct t_f by permutating any two characters in t_s (that is, $t_f = c_{s_1}...c_{s_j}...c_{s_i}...c_{s_n}$). Then $o_f = o_s$.

Digits. Program digits takes as input an integer. It outputs each base-10 digit on a single line from the least significant to the most significant. For example, if input is -6789, the output is an integer array $\{9,8,7,-6\}$.

Input: $N = n_1 n_2 ... n_i ... n_m$, in which $1 \leqslant i \leqslant m$, and n_i indicates a base-10 digit.

Output: $\{n_m, n_{m-1}, \ ... \ , n_i, n_{i-1}, \ ... \ , n_1\}$

Take $N_s = n_{s_1} n_{s_2} ... n_{s_i} ... n_{s_m}$ $(1 \leqslant i \leqslant m)$ and $N_f = n_{f_1} n_{f_2} ... n_{f_j} ... n_{f_p}$ $(1 \leqslant j \leqslant p)$ as source and follow-up test cases, two integer arrays $o_s = \{o_{s_1}, o_{s_2}, ..., o_{s_m}\}$ and $o_f = \{o_{f_1}, o_{f_2}, ..., o_{f_j}, ..., o_{f_p}\}$ as source and follow-up outputs.

MR3: Construct N_f by reversing the digits in N_s except the sign, then we have the following cases:

(1) N_s does not have trailing zeros (that is, $n_{s_m} \neq 0$):- we have (a) $o_f.size = o_s.size$ $(p = m)$, (b) $o_f[0] = |o_s[m-1]|$, (c) $o_f[j] = o_s[m-j-1]$, for all j where $0 < j < p - 1$, (d) $|o_f[p-1]| = o_s[0]$, and (e) both $o_f[p-1]$ and $o_s[m-1]$ are of the same sign (either both positive or both negative).

(2) N_s has k trailing zeros where $1 \leq k \leq m$ (that is, $n_{s_{m-k+1}} = 0$, $n_{s_{m-k+2}} = 0,..., n_{s_m} = 0$):- we have (a) $o_f.size = o_s.size - k$ $(p = m - k)$, (b) $o_f[0] = |o_s[m-1]|$, (c) $o_f[j] = o_s[m-j-1]$, for all j where $0 < j < p - 1$, (d) $|o_f[p-1]| = o_s[k]$, and (e) both $o_f[p-1]$ and $o_s[m-1]$ are of the same sign when $k < m$ or both are '0' when $k = m$.

Grade. Program grade takes as input five double values. The first four represent the thresholds for grade level A, B, C and D separately. The last one represents a score of a student. Program grade outputs the corresponding grade level by comparing score with four thresholds. For example, the first four values are 90.0, 80.0, 70.0, 60.0, and the student's score is 75.0. Then the student gets a grade level of B.

Input: a double array $T = \{t_1, t_2, t_3, t_4, t_5\}$, in which t_1, t_2, t_3, t_4 denote the thresholds for grade level A, B, C and D, and t_5 is a student's score.

Output: "Student has an X grade" when $t_i \leqslant t_5 < t_{i-1}$ $(1 \leqslant i \leqslant 4)$, where X is the grade level corresponded to t_i; or "Student has failed the course".

Take $T_s = \{t_{s_1}, t_{s_2}, t_{s_3}, t_{s_4}, t_{s_5}\}$ and $T_f = \{t_{f_1}, t_{f_2}, t_{f_3}, t_{f_4}, t_{f_5}\}$ as source and follow-up test cases, o_s, o_f as source and follow-up outputs. To identify the relationship between o_s and o_f, the first four thresholds in two double arrays are the same respectively.

MR3: Construct $t_{f_5} = t_{s_5} + 1$ when $t_{s_5} = t_{s_i}, 1 \leqslant i \leqslant 4$, then $o_f = o_s$; constructing $t_{f_5} = t_{s_5} + x$ when $t_{s_5} \notin \{t_{s_1}, t_{s_2}, t_{s_3}, t_{s_4}\}$, and x is a random positive value, then o_f is not lower than o_s.

Median. Program median takes as input three integer values and outputs their median.

   Input: int array $T = \{t_1, t_2, t_3\}$

   Output: "X is the median"

   Take $T_s = \{t_{s_1}, t_{s_2}, t_{s_3}\}$ and $T_f = \{t_{f_1}, t_{f_2}, t_{f_3}\}$ as source and follow-up test cases, o_s, o_f as source and follow-up outputs.

   MR3: Construct T_f by permutating any two integers in T_s, then $o_f = o_s$.

Smallest. Program smallest takes as input four integer values and outputs the smallest one.

   Input: int array $T = \{t_1, t_2, t_3, t_4\}$

   Output: "X is the smallest"

   Take $T_s = \{t_{s_1}, t_{s_2}, t_{s_3}, t_{s_4}\}$ and $T_f = \{t_{f_1}, t_{f_2}, t_{f_3}, t_{f_4}\}$ as source and follow-up test cases, and and o_s, o_f as source and follow-up outputs.

   MR3: Construct T_f by permutating any two integers in T_s, then $o_f = o_s$.

Syllables. Program syllables takes as input a line of string with maximum length 20, counts the number of vowels ('a', 'e', 'i', 'o', 'u' and 'y') in this string.

   Input: string $t = c_1 c_2 ... c_i ... c_n$, in which $n \leqslant 20$.

   Output: "The number of syllables is N".

   Take $t_s = c_{s_1} c_{s_2} ... c_{s_i} ... c_{s_j} ... c_{s_n}$ and $t_f = c_{f_1} c_{f_2} ... c_{f_k} ... c_{f_l} ... c_{f_m}$ as source and follow-up test cases, o_s and o_f as source and follow-up outputs.

   MR3: Construct t_f by permutating any two characters in t_s, that is, $t_f = c_{s_1} c_{s_2} ... c_{s_j} ... c_{s_i} ... c_{s_n}$, then $o_f = o_s$.

4.2   Test Data

Table 1 also shows the sizes of individual black-box and white-box test suite for subject programs. T_b and T_w are used as black-box and white-box test suites for AE and to construct source test cases for M_b^i, M_w^i $(1 \leqslant i \leqslant 3)$ respectively. M_b^i and M_w^i denote the black-box and white-box MTG sets of MRi $(1 \leqslant i \leqslant 3)$ for each subject program. As shown in Table 1, some sizes of MTG sets are smaller than T_b or T_w, e.g. $|M_b^2| < |T_b|$ for program $grade$. It is because there exist some restrictions in MRs, and only those MTG sets satisfying restrictions are used.

   Since AE and AE-MT use different test suites and MTG sets, we present the following scenarios.

(1) AE$_b$: AE with input test suite T_b;
(2) AE$_w$: AE with input test suite T_w;
(3) AE-MT$_b^1$: AE-MT with input MTG set M_b^1;

(4) AE-MT$_w^1$: AE-MT with input MTG set M_w^1;
(5) AE-MT$_b^2$: AE-MT with input MTG set M_b^2;
(6) AE-MT$_w^2$: AE-MT with input MTG set M_w^2;
(7) AE-MT$_b^3$: AE-MT with input MTG set M_b^3;
(8) AE-MT$_w^3$: AE-MT with input MTG set M_w^3;

All the experiments ran on Ubuntu 10.04 virtual machine with one processor and memory of size 4 GB, and got the experimental results about the success rate, repair quality and average repair time for each program. Since AE is deterministic [24], we ran AE and AE-MT with a single time on related test suites and MTG sets for each faulty version.

5   Experimental Results

5.1   Success Rates

The success rate, a ratio of the number of programs successfully repaired to the total number of faulty programs being applied in relative scenarios, is used to measure the repair capability of an APR tool. Note that, only if the input test suite and MTG set contain at least one fail test case or one violated MTG, the scenario could be applied to start the repair procedure. The number of programs repaired by AE and AE-MT are listed in Table 2.

Table 2. Success rates for AE and AE-MT

(a) Success rates for black-box scenarios

Program	AE_b	$AE-MT_b^1$	$AE-MT_b^2$	$AE-MT_b^3$
Checksum	$\frac{1}{30} = 0.033$	$\frac{11}{31} = 0.355$	$\frac{2}{31} = 0.067$	$\frac{27}{27} = 1.000$
Digits	$\frac{14}{93} = 0.151$	$\frac{65}{80} = 0.813$	$\frac{1}{236} = 0.004$	$\frac{26}{79} = 0.329$
Grade	$\frac{2}{228} = 0.009$	$\frac{0}{226} = 0.000$	$\frac{0}{226} = 0.000$	$\frac{147}{148} = 0.993$
Median	$\frac{77}{167} = 0.461$	$\frac{111}{120} = 0.925$	$\frac{109}{154} = 0.708$	$\frac{132}{166} = 0.795$
Smallest	$\frac{124}{148} = 0.838$	$\frac{89}{91} = 0.978$	$\frac{86}{101} = 0.851$	$\frac{97}{113} = 0.858$
Syllables	$\frac{20}{116} = 0.172$	$\frac{92}{98} = 0.939$	$\frac{11}{102} = 0.108$	$\frac{4}{4} = 1.000$

(b) Success rates for white-box scenarios

Program	AE_w	$AE-MT_w^1$	$AE-MT_w^2$	$AE-MT_w^3$
Checksum	$\frac{1}{53} = 0.019$	$\frac{1}{30} = 0.033$	$\frac{12}{52} = 0.231$	$\frac{29}{30} = 0.967$
Digits	$\frac{47}{170} = 0.276$	$\frac{117}{145} = 0.807$	$\frac{0}{236} = 0.000$	$\frac{4}{236} = 0.017$
Grade	$\frac{2}{224} = 0.009$	$\frac{0}{168} = 0.000$	$\frac{0}{168} = 0.000$	$\frac{145}{146} = 0.993$
Median	$\frac{17}{151} = 0.113$	$\frac{103}{103} = 1.000$	$\frac{75}{137} = 0.547$	$\frac{149}{198} = 0.793$
Smallest	$\frac{118}{121} = 0.975$	$\frac{86}{91} = 0.945$	$\frac{133}{141} = 0.943$	$\frac{127}{152} = 0.836$
Syllables	$\frac{6}{118} = 0.051$	$\frac{103}{109} = 0.945$	$\frac{1}{160} = 0.006$	$\frac{79}{79} = 1.000$

According to Table 2(a), AE-MT$_b^1$ achieves a higher success rate than AE$_b$ for five of six subject programs and lower rate for one. While AE-MT$_b^2$ has a higher success rate than AE$_b$ for three of six and lower for three. And AE-MT$_b^3$ has a higher success rate than AE$_b$ for six programs. Similarly, as shown in Table 2(b), AE-MT$_w^1$ achieves a higher success rate than AE$_w$ for four of six, and lower for two. AE-MT$_w^2$ performs higher for two, and lower for four. And AE-MT$_w^3$ performs higher for four, and lower for two. We can conclude that AE-MT is not only comparable to AE in terms of success rate, but also outperforms AE, sometimes quite higher.

The success rates also vary with different MRs. According to Table 2, AE-MT$_b^1$ has a higher success rate than AE-MT$_b^2$ for five of six, and equal for one, while it has a higher success rate for three programs than AE-MT$_b^3$ and lower for three respectively. And AE-MT$_b^2$ even has no higher success rate than AE-MT$_b^3$. On the other hand, AE-MT$_w^1$ achieves a higher success rate than AE-MT$_w^2$ for four of six, equal for one and lower for one, while compared to AE-MT$_w^3$ it has a higher and lower success rate for three programs and three programs respectively. And AE-MT$_w^2$ has a higher success rate than AE-MT$_w^3$ for only one program while worse for five programs. Therefore, MR1 performs best while MR2 performs worst in terms of success rate.

5.2   Repair Quality

We would like to investigate that whether AE-MT produces repairs are of similar quality to those produced by AE. In our empirical study, each repair is evaluated by four test sets, that is, a test suite with test oracles and three MTGs sets. For instance, a repair generated by scenario AE$_b$ is evaluated by T$_w$ and M$_w^i$ ($1 \leqslant i \leqslant 3$). A repair produced by AE-MT$_b^j$ ($1 \leqslant j \leqslant 3$) is measured by T$_w$ and M$_w^i$ ($1 \leqslant i \leqslant 3$). Note that, the passing rates of test suite and non-violating rate of MTG set are used as the measurement criterion of repair quality and a higher rate indicates higher quality of a repair.

Statistical Analysis. To measure the repair quality of AE and AE-MT, we conduct a statistical analysis for repairs produced from black-box and white-box scenarios. Repair comparison between AE$_b$ and AE-MT$_b^i$ ($1 \leqslant i \leqslant 3$) and between AE$_w$ and AE-MT$_w^i$ with one test suite and three MTGs sets requires totally 24 comparison pairs for each subject program.

Because the size of two groups of data may be different, and data distribution may not be normal, we applied the Mann-Whitney U Test [26] to verify the null hypothesis H_0 that the distribution of repair quality is the same across AE and AE-MT with the significance level 0.05.

Then, we applied the Vargha and Delaney $\hat{A}_{12}$ [10] statistics to measure the effect size of repairs produced by AE and AE-MT. The $\hat{A}_{12}$ statistics measures the probability that the first technique (AE) is superior to the second technique (AE-MT). $\hat{A}_{12} < 0.44$ suggests that repairs generated from AE-MT are superior to AE; $\hat{A}_{12} > 0.56$ suggests that repairs by AE are of higher quality; $0.44 < \hat{A}_{12} < 0.56$ indicates that repairs produced by two techniques are of similar quality.

Table 3. Statistical analysis of AE and AE-MT repair quality

(a) Checksum

Pairwise comparison	Evaluation data			
	T_w	M_w^1	M_w^2	M_w^3
AE_b vs. $AE\text{-}MT_b^1$	p=0.167, $\hat{A}_{12}$=0.955	p=0.333, $\hat{A}_{12}$=0.909	p=0.333, $\hat{A}_{12}$=0.909	p=0.333, $\hat{A}_{12}$=0.909
	AE_b is better	AE_b is better	AE_b is better	AE_b is better
AE_b vs. $AE\text{-}MT_b^2$	p=0.667, $\hat{A}_{12}$=0.750	p=0.667, $\hat{A}_{12}$=0.750	p=1.000, $\hat{A}_{12}$=0.500	p=1.000, $\hat{A}_{12}$=0.500
	AE_b is better	AE_b is better	Similar	Similar
AE_b vs. $AE\text{-}MT_b^3$	p=0.071, $\hat{A}_{12}$=0.981	p=0.071, $\hat{A}_{12}$=0.981	p=0.143, $\hat{A}_{12}$=0.944	p=1.000, $\hat{A}_{12}$=0.519
	AE_b is better	AE_b is better	AE_b is better	Similar

Pairwise comparison	Evaluation data			
	T_b	M_b^1	M_b^2	M_b^3
AE_w vs. $AE\text{-}MT_w^1$	p=1.000, $\hat{A}_{12}$=1.000	p=1.000, $\hat{A}_{12}$=0.500	p=1.000, $\hat{A}_{12}$=0.500	p=1.000, $\hat{A}_{12}$=0.500
	AE_w is better	Similar	Similar	Similar
AE_w vs. $AE\text{-}MT_w^2$	p=0.154, $\hat{A}_{12}$=0.958	p=0.923, $\hat{A}_{12}$=0.542	p=1.000, $\hat{A}_{12}$=0.500	p=1.000, $\hat{A}_{12}$=0.500
	AE_w is better	Similar	Similar	Similar
AE_w vs. $AE\text{-}MT_w^3$	p=0.067, $\hat{A}_{12}$=0.983	p=0.067, $\hat{A}_{12}$=0.983	p=0.133, $\hat{A}_{12}$=0.948	p=1.000, $\hat{A}_{12}$=0.500
	AE_w is better	AE_w is better	AE_w is better	Similar

(b) Digits

Pairwise comparison	Evaluation data			
	T_w	M_w^1	M_w^2	M_w^3
AE_b vs. $AE\text{-}MT_b^1$	p=0.000, $\hat{A}_{12}$=0.888	p=0.020, $\hat{A}_{12}$=0.698	p=0.004, $\hat{A}_{12}$=0.738	p=0.000, $\hat{A}_{12}$=0.785
	AE_b is better	AE_b is better	AE_b is better	AE_b is better
AE_b vs. $AE\text{-}MT_b^2$	p=0.133, $\hat{A}_{12}$=1.000	p=0.133, $\hat{A}_{12}$=1.000	p=0.533, $\hat{A}_{12}$=0.210	p=0.133, $\hat{A}_{12}$=0.000
	AE_b is better	AE_b is better	$AE\text{-}MT_b^2$ is better	$AE\text{-}MT_b^3$ is better
AE_b vs. $AE\text{-}MT_b^3$	p=0.585, $\hat{A}_{12}$=0.555	p=0.726, $\hat{A}_{12}$=0.464	p=0.664, $\hat{A}_{12}$=0.544	p=0.000, $\hat{A}_{12}$=0.077
	Similar	Similar	Similar	$AE\text{-}MT_b^3$ is better

Pairwise comparison	Evaluation data			
	T_b	M_b^1	M_b^2	M_b^3
AE_w vs. $AE\text{-}MT_w^1$	p=0.000, $\hat{A}_{12}$=0.898	p=0.182, $\hat{A}_{12}$=0.550	p=0.000, $\hat{A}_{12}$=0.705	p=0.000, $\hat{A}_{12}$=0.881
	AE_w is better	Similar	AE_w is better	AE_w is better
AE_w vs. $AE\text{-}MT_w^2$	-	-	-	-
	AE_w is better	AE_w is better	AE_w is better	AE_w is better
AE_w vs. $AE\text{-}MT_w^3$	p=0.000, $\hat{A}_{12}$=1.000	p=0.332, $\hat{A}_{12}$=0.655	p=0.000, $\hat{A}_{12}$=1.000	p=0.298, $\hat{A}_{12}$=0.665
	AE_w is better	AE_w is better	AE_w is better	AE_w is better

(c) Grade

Pairwise comparison	Evaluation data			
	T_w	M_w^1	M_w^2	M_w^3
AE_b vs. $AE\text{-}MT_b^1$	-	-	-	-
	AE_b is better	AE_b is better	AE_b is better	AE_b is better
AE_b vs. $AE\text{-}MT_b^2$	-	-	-	-
	AE_b is better	AE_b is better	AE_b is better	AE_b is better
AE_b vs. $AE\text{-}MT_b^3$	p=0.000, $\hat{A}_{12}$=1.000	p=0.011, $\hat{A}_{12}$=0.953	p=0.000, $\hat{A}_{12}$=1.000	p=0.000, $\hat{A}_{12}$=0.000
	AE_b is better	AE_b is better	AE_b is better	$AE\text{-}MT_b^3$ is better

Pairwise comparison	Evaluation data			
	T_b	M_b^1	M_b^2	M_b^3
AE_w vs. $AE\text{-}MT_w^1$	-	-	-	-
	AE_w is better	AE_w is better	AE_w is better	AE_w is better
AE_w vs. $AE\text{-}MT_w^2$	-	-	-	-
	AE_w is better	AE_w is better	AE_w is better	AE_w is better
AE_w vs. $AE\text{-}MT_w^3$	p=0.001, $\hat{A}_{12}$=0.993	p=0.015, $\hat{A}_{12}$=0.945	p=0.000, $\hat{A}_{12}$=0.996	p=0.000, $\hat{A}_{12}$=0.000
	AE_w is better	AE_w is better	AE_w is better	$AE\text{-}MT_w^3$ is better

(*continued*)

Table 3. (continued)

(d) Median

Pairwise comparison	Evaluation data			
	T_w	M_w^1	M_w^2	M_w^3
AE_b vs. $AE\text{-}MT_b^1$	p=0.000, $\hat{A}_{12}$=0.648	p=0.332, $\hat{A}_{12}$=0.465	p=0.667, $\hat{A}_{12}$=0.517	p=0.000, $\hat{A}_{12}$=0.699
	AE_b is better	Similar	Similar	AE_b is better
AE_b vs. $AE\text{-}MT_b^2$	p=0.000, $\hat{A}_{12}$=0.679	p=0.203, $\hat{A}_{12}$=0.455	p=0.000, $\hat{A}_{12}$=0.349	p=0.000, $\hat{A}_{12}$=0.683
	AE_b is better	Similar	$AE\text{-}MT_b^2$ is better	AE_b is better
AE_b vs. $AE\text{-}MT_b^3$	p=0.000, $\hat{A}_{12}$=0.639	p=0.174, $\hat{A}_{12}$=0.550	p=0.082, $\hat{A}_{12}$=0.570	p=0.546, $\hat{A}_{12}$=0.478
	AE_b is better	Similar	AE_b is better	Similar

Pairwise comparison	Evaluation data			
	T_b	M_b^1	M_b^2	M_b^3
AE_w vs. $AE\text{-}MT_w^1$	p=0.040, $\hat{A}_{12}$=0.363	p=1.000, $\hat{A}_{12}$=0.500	p=0.940, $\hat{A}_{12}$=0.505	p=0.002, $\hat{A}_{12}$=0.296
	$AE\text{-}MT_w^1$ is better	Similar	Similar	$AE\text{-}MT_w^1$ is better
AE_w vs. $AE\text{-}MT_w^2$	p=0.000, $\hat{A}_{12}$=0.786	p=1.000, $\hat{A}_{12}$=0.500	p=0.000, $\hat{A}_{12}$=0.152	p=0.063, $\hat{A}_{12}$=0.638
	AE_w is better	Similar	$AE\text{-}MT_w^2$ is better	AE_w is better
AE_w vs. $AE\text{-}MT_w^3$	p=0.930, $\hat{A}_{12}$=0.494	p=0.020, $\hat{A}_{12}$=0.624	p=0.132, $\hat{A}_{12}$=0.607	p=0.000, $\hat{A}_{12}$=0.171
	Similar	AE_w is better	AE_w is better	$AE\text{-}MT_w^3$ is better

(e) Smallest

Pairwise comparison	Evaluation data			
	T_w	M_w^1	M_w^2	M_w^3
AE_b vs. $AE\text{-}MT_b^1$	p=0.000, $\hat{A}_{12}$=0.804	p=0.359, $\hat{A}_{12}$=0.521	p=0.000, $\hat{A}_{12}$=0.816	p=0.361, $\hat{A}_{12}$=0.465
	AE_b is better	Similar	AE_b is better	Similar
AE_b vs. $AE\text{-}MT_b^2$	p=0.000, $\hat{A}_{12}$=0.752	p=0.005, $\hat{A}_{12}$=0.449	p=0.000, $\hat{A}_{12}$=0.693	p=0.404, $\hat{A}_{12}$=0.533
	AE_b is better	Similar	AE_b is better	Similar
AE_b vs. $AE\text{-}MT_b^3$	p=0.000, $\hat{A}_{12}$=0.619	p=0.163, $\hat{A}_{12}$=0.533	p=0.000, $\hat{A}_{12}$=0.744	p=0.027, $\hat{A}_{12}$=0.416
	AE_b is better	Similar	AE_b is better	$AE\text{-}MT_b^3$ is better

Pairwise comparison	Evaluation data			
	T_b	M_b^1	M_b^2	M_b^3
AE_w vs. $AE\text{-}MT_w^1$	p=0.008, $\hat{A}_{12}$=0.401	p=0.022, $\hat{A}_{12}$=0.341	p=0.455, $\hat{A}_{12}$=0.475	p=0.115, $\hat{A}_{12}$=0.447
	$AE\text{-}MT_w^1$ is better	$AE\text{-}MT_w^1$ is better	Similar	Similar
AE_w vs. $AE\text{-}MT_w^2$	p=0.046, $\hat{A}_{12}$=0.432	p=0.042, $\hat{A}_{12}$=0.539	p=0.000, $\hat{A}_{12}$=0.328	p=0.009, $\hat{A}_{12}$=0.586
	$AE\text{-}MT_w^2$ is better	Similar	$AE\text{-}MT_w^2$ is better	AE_w is better
AE_w vs. $AE\text{-}MT_w^3$	p=0.000, $\hat{A}_{12}$=0.688	p=0.000, $\hat{A}_{12}$=0.808	p=0.000, $\hat{A}_{12}$=0.768	p=0.000, $\hat{A}_{12}$=0.394
	AE_w is better	AE_w is better	AE_w is better	$AE\text{-}MT_w^3$ is better

(f) Syllables

Pairwise comparison	Evaluation data			
	T_w	M_w^1	M_w^2	M_w^3
AE_b vs. $AE\text{-}MT_b^1$	p=0.000, $\hat{A}_{12}$=0.959	p=0.000, $\hat{A}_{12}$=0.864	p=0.000, $\hat{A}_{12}$=0.983	p=0.000, $\hat{A}_{12}$=0.913
	AE_b is better	AE_b is better	AE_b is better	AE_b is better
AE_b vs. $AE\text{-}MT_b^2$	p=0.451, $\hat{A}_{12}$=0.584	p=0.008, $\hat{A}_{12}$=0.784	p=0.555, $\hat{A}_{12}$=0.569	p=0.699, $\hat{A}_{12}$=0.554
	AE_b is better	AE_b is better	AE_b is better	AE_b is better
AE_b vs. $AE\text{-}MT_b^3$	p=0.000, $\hat{A}_{12}$=1.000	p=0.000, $\hat{A}_{12}$=1.000	p=0.682, $\hat{A}_{12}$=0.425	p=1.000, $\hat{A}_{12}$=0.500
	AE_b is better	AE_b is better	$AE\text{-}MT_b^3$ is better	Similar

Pairwise comparison	Evaluation data			
	T_b	M_b^1	M_b^2	M_b^3
AE_w vs. $AE\text{-}MT_w^1$	p=0.000, $\hat{A}_{12}$=0.995	p=0.010, $\hat{A}_{12}$=0.743	p=0.000, $\hat{A}_{12}$=0.995	p=0.509, $\hat{A}_{12}$=0.534
	AE_w is better	AE_w is better	AE_w is better	Similar
AE_w vs. $AE\text{-}MT_w^2$	p=0.286, $\hat{A}_{12}$=1.000	p=1.000, $\hat{A}_{12}$=0.420	p=0.286, $\hat{A}_{12}$=1.000	p=1.000, $\hat{A}_{12}$=0.500
	AE_w is better	$AE\text{-}MT_w^2$ is better	AE_w is better	Similar
AE_w vs. $AE\text{-}MT_w^3$	p=0.000, $\hat{A}_{12}$=1.000	p=0.000, $\hat{A}_{12}$=0.831	p=0.000, $\hat{A}_{12}$=0.962	p=1.000, $\hat{A}_{12}$=0.500
	AE_w is better	AE_w is better	AE_w is better	Similar

The statistical analysis of AE and AE-MT repair quality is listed in Table 3, and the comparison results are summarized in Table 4 with the number of repair quality between AE-MT and AE in terms of *better, similar* and *worse*.

According to Tables 3 and 4, AE outperforms AE-MT in terms of repair quality. Among all of the 144 comparison pairs, AE-MT only has 18 better and 35 similar results, while there are 91 lower cases than AE. Therefore, we conclude that repairs generated by AE-MT are of lower quality than those from AE. This is expected that AE produces a better repair than AE-MT because MR is a property weaker than test oracle.

Table 4. Summary of repair quality comparison

(a) Black-box scenarios

Comparison	ET	Better	Similar	Worse
AE$_b$ vs. AE-MT$_b^1$	T_w	6	0	0
	M_w^1	4	2	0
	M_w^2	5	1	0
	M_w^3	5	1	0
AE$_b$ vs. AE-MT$_b^2$	T_w	6	0	0
	M_w^1	4	2	0
	M_w^2	3	1	2
	M_w^3	3	2	1
AE$_b$ vs. AE-MT$_b^3$	T_w	5	1	0
	M_w^1	3	3	0
	M_w^2	4	1	1
	M_w^3	0	3	3

(b) White-box scenarios

Comparison	ET	Better	Similar	Worse
AE$_w$ vs. AE-MT$_w^1$	T_b	4	0	2
	M_b^1	2	3	1
	M_b^2	3	3	0
	M_b^3	2	3	1
AE$_w$ vs. AE-MT$_w^2$	T_b	5	0	1
	M_b^1	2	3	1
	M_b^2	3	1	2
	M_b^3	4	2	0
AE$_w$ vs. AE-MT$_w^3$	T_b	5	1	0
	M_b^1	6	0	0
	M_b^2	6	0	0
	M_b^3	1	2	3

5.3 Repair Time

The average repair time for a successful repair is listed in Table 5. According to Table 5, AE-MT uses more time to produce a repair than AE in most cases. The reason is that AE only needs to execute test suite and verify it at each single time, while AE-MT executes source and follow-up test cases respectively, and verifies whether the input MTGs sets are satisfied or not.

5.4 Discussion

Impact of Source Test Case on the Effectiveness for AE-MT. Since each subject program has two test suites of T_b and T_w, we constructed two MTG sets for each MR from T_b and T_w, referred to as M_b^i and M_w^i for MRi ($1 \leqslant i \leqslant 3$). These two different MTG sets can cause different repair results for AE-MT. For example, M_b^1 and M_w^1 of MR1 used for *checksum* generate quite different repair results. While AE-MT produces several repairs using M_b^1, only one repair is generated by M_w^1. M_b^1 for *checksum* performs more effectively than M_w^1 in this experiment. Thus, selection of good source test cases will undoubtedly improve AE-MT performance.

Table 5. Average repair time (s)

(a) Black-box scenarios

program	AE_b	AE-MT$_b^1$	AE-MT$_b^2$	AE-MT$_b^3$
checksum	3.629	25.952	0.986	3.023
digits	4.225	6.562	1.251	3.318
grade	42.627	-	-	6.804
median	6.639	14.103	17.945	6.551
smallest	16.183	13.284	14.813	18.918
syllables	35.799	4.640	21.344	13.447

(b) White-box scenarios

program	AE_w	AE-MT$_w^1$	AE-MT$_w^2$	AE-MT$_w^3$
checksum	2.398	3.144	9.321	3.715
digits	10.111	16.771	-	3.485
grade	40.369	-	-	6.844
median	2.829	24.523	31.319	5.752
smallest	11.081	21.211	27.820	61.286
syllables	19.316	5.122	245.900	3.890

Impact of MRs on the Effectiveness of AE-MT. Considering the scenarios related to MR1 and MR2 showed in Table 2, while both scenarios $AE-MT_b^1$ and $AE-MT_w^1$ produces success rate up to 80%, $AE-MT_b^2$ and $AE-MT_w^2$ yield only one repair and none repair for *digits*. Similar results are observed for program *median* and *syllables*. When compared to the success rate of MR1, MR3 performs better on *checksum*, *grade* and *syllables*, but worse on other three programs. When compared to MR2, MR3 is always inferior to MR2. Therefore, it will be worthwhile to identify sufficient diverse MRs for AE-MT.

6   Related Work

GenProg-MT [12] applies a genetic algorithm to repair a faulty program. It first constructs an initial set of candidate repairs, and then selects a candidate program with higher fitness through the fitness function by leveraging the input MTGs set. GenProg-MT stops if a candidate repair is found to satisfy the entire input MTGs set; otherwise no repair is found within the maximum number of generations.

CETI-MT [11] constructs a reachability instance program from a faulty program by replacing a suspicious statement with a parameterized statement encoding all the requirements of MTGs set. Then CETI-MT checks the reachability by an independent MR checking function. Once the relevant MR on all input MTGs is satisfied, this instance program is considered reachable and a repair for the given faulty program is found as well.

Based on our experimental results of AE-MT and those of GenProg-MT reported in [12], GenProg-MT is more effective than AE-MT in terms of success rate and repair quality, even though AE-MT requires much less time on the same MRs. Compared to the empirical results on MR1 and MR2 of CETI-MT reported in [11], AE-MT performs comparably to CETI-MT in terms of success rate but worse in terms of repair quality. By comparing with GenProg-MT, CETI-MT has a higher success rate and higher repair quality than GenProg-MT. In summary, among the existing APR-MT techniques, CETI-MT performs better than another two techniques.

7 Conclusion and Future Work

To alleviate test oracle problem in APR, the integrated framework APR-MT was proposed and applied to implement GenProg-MT and CETI-MT respectively. However, it is necessary to distinguish the effectiveness of different APR-MT techniques. Therefore, we propose one more APR-MT, AE-MT. According to the empirical results and discussion, AE-MT can achieve a much higher success rate but a lower repair quality than AE. Based on the individual experimental results reported so far, among the three APR-MT techniques, CETI-MT is the most effective so that researchers can make use of CETI-MT to alleviate test oracle problem of APR and get comparable performance as well.

In this paper, we investigate the effectiveness of APR-MT techniques against different MRs separately. Intuitively speaking, a repair satisfying all of the MRs must be of higher repair quality than the one satisfying some MRs but not all MRs. Therefore, our future work will investigate the repair capability of APR-MT against a set of MTGs which is constructed from a group of diverse metamorphic relations.

Acknowledgments. This work is supported by the National Key Research and Development Program of China under Grant No. 2017YFB0903000, and the program of China Scholarship Council (CSC).

References

1. Arcuri, A.: On the automation of fixing software bugs. In: Companion of the 30th International Conference on Software Engineering, pp. 1003–1006. ACM (2008)
2. Barr, E.T., Harman, M., McMinn, P., Shahbaz, M., Yoo, S.: The oracle problem in software testing: a survey. IEEE Trans. Softw. Eng. **41**(5), 507–525 (2015)
3. Cao, Y., Zhou, Z.Q., Chen, T.Y.: On the correlation between the effectiveness of metamorphic relations and dissimilarities of test case executions. In: 2013 13th International Conference on Quality Software (QSIC), pp. 153–162. IEEE (2013)
4. Chan, F., Chen, T., Cheung, S.C., Lau, M., Yiu, S.: Application of metamorphic testing in numerical analysis. In: Proceedings of the IASTED International Conference on Software Engineering (SE98) (1998)
5. Chen, T.Y., Cheung, S.C., Yiu, S.M.: Metamorphic testing: a new approach for generating next test cases. Department of Computer Science, Hong Kong University of Science and Technology, Technical report HKUST-CS98-01 (1998)
6. Chen, T.Y., Huang, D., Tse, T., Zhou, Z.Q.: Case studies on the selection of useful relations in metamorphic testing. In: Proceedings of the 4th Ibero-American Symposium on Software Engineering and Knowledge Engineering (JIISIC 2004), pp. 569–583. Polytechnic University of Madrid (2004)
7. Chen, T.Y., Tse, T., Zhou, Z.Q.: Semi-proving: an integrated method for program proving, testing, and debugging. IEEE Trans. Softw. Eng. **37**(1), 109–125 (2011)
8. Forrest, S., Nguyen, T., Weimer, W., Le Goues, C.: A genetic programming approach to automated software repair. In: Proceedings of the 11th Annual conference on Genetic and evolutionary computation, pp. 947–954. ACM (2009)

9. Gotlieb, A., Botella, B.: Automated metamorphic testing. In: 2003 27th Annual International Computer Software and Applications Conference (COMPSAC), pp. 34–40. IEEE (2003)

10. Arcuri, A., Briand, L.: A practical guide for using statistical tests to assess randomized algorithms in software engineering. In: 2011 33rd International Conference on Software Engineering (ICSE), pp. 1–10. IEEE (2011)

11. Jiang, M., Chen, T.Y., Kuo, F.C., Ding, Z., Choi, E.H., Mizuno, O.: A revisit of the integration of metamorphic testing and test suite based automated program repair. In: The 2nd International Workshop on Metamorphic Testing, pp. 14–20. IEEE (2017)

12. Jiang, M., Chen, T.Y., Kuo, F.C., Towey, D., Ding, Z.: A metamorphic testing approach for supporting program repair without the need for a test oracle. J. Syst. Softw. **126**, 127–140 (2016)

13. Jiang, M., Chen, T.Y., Kuo, F.C., Zhou, Z., Ding, Z.: Testing model transformation programs using metamorphic testing. In: The 26th International Conference on Software Engineering and Knowledge Engineering (SEKE), pp. 94–99 (2014)

14. Le Goues, C., Holtschulte, N., Smith, E.K., Brun, Y., Devanbu, P., Forrest, S., Weimer, W.: The manybugs and introclass benchmarks for automated repair of c programs. IEEE Trans. Softw. Eng. **41**(12), 1236–1256 (2015)

15. Liu, H., Kuo, F.C., Towey, D., Chen, T.Y.: How effectively does metamorphic testing alleviate the oracle problem? IEEE Trans. Softw. Eng. **40**(1), 4–22 (2014)

16. Mechtaev, S., Yi, J., Roychoudhury, A.: Angelix: scalable multiline program patch synthesis via symbolic analysis. In: Proceedings of the 38th International Conference on Software Engineering, pp. 691–701. ACM (2016)

17. Murphy, C., Shen, K., Kaiser, G.: Automatic system testing of programs without test oracles. In: Proceedings of the Eighteenth International Symposium on Software Testing and Analysis, pp. 189–200. ACM (2009)

18. Nguyen, H.D.T., Qi, D., Roychoudhury, A., Chandra, S.: Semfix: program repair via semantic analysis. In: Proceedings of the 2013 International Conference on Software Engineering, pp. 772–781. IEEE Press (2013)

19. Nguyen, T.: Automating program verification and repair using invariant analysis and test input generation. Ph.D. thesis (2014)

20. Qi, Y., Mao, X., Lei, Y.: Efficient automated program repair through fault-recorded testing prioritization. In: 2013 29th IEEE International Conference on Software Maintenance (ICSM), pp. 180–189. IEEE (2013)

21. Qi, Z., Long, F., Achour, S., Rinard, M.: An analysis of patch plausibility and correctness for generate-and-validate patch generation systems. In: Proceedings of the 2015 International Symposium on Software Testing and Analysis, pp. 24–36. ACM (2015)

22. Segura, S., Fraser, G., Sanchez, A.B., Ruiz-Cortés, A.: A survey on metamorphic testing. IEEE Trans. Softw. Eng. **42**(9), 805–824 (2016)

23. Sidiroglou-Douskos, S., Lahtinen, E., Long, F., Rinard, M.: Automatic error elimination by horizontal code transfer across multiple applications. ACM SIGPLAN Not. **50**, 43–54 (2015). ACM

24. Weimer, W., Fry, Z.P., Forrest, S.: Leveraging program equivalence for adaptive program repair: models and first results. In: 2013 IEEE/ACM 28th International Conference on Automated Software Engineering (ASE), pp. 356–366. IEEE (2013)

25. Weimer, W., Nguyen, T., Le Goues, C., Forrest, S.: Automatically finding patches using genetic programming. In: Proceedings of the 31st International Conference on Software Engineering, pp. 364–374. IEEE Computer Society (2009)
26. Wilcoxon, F.: Individual comparisons by ranking methods. Biometrics Bull. **1**(6), 80–83 (1945)
27. Xie, X., Wong, W.E., Chen, T.Y., Xu, B.: Metamorphic slice: an application in spectrum-based fault localization. Inf. Softw. Technol. **55**(5), 866–879 (2013)

Learning Types for Binaries

Zhiwu Xu[1]([✉]), Cheng Wen[1], and Shengchao Qin[1,2]

[1] College of Computer Science and Software Engineering, Shenzhen University,
Shenzhen, China
`xuzhiwu@szu.edu.cn`, `2150230509@email.szu.edu.cn`
[2] School of Computing, Teesside University, Middlesbrough, UK
`shengchao.qin@gmail.com`

Abstract. Type inference for Binary codes is a challenging problem due partly to the fact that much type-related information has been lost during the compilation from high-level source code. Most of the existing research on binary code type inference tend to resort to program analysis techniques, which can be too conservative to infer types with high accuracy or too heavy-weight to be viable in practice. In this paper, we propose a new approach to learning types for recovered variables from their related representative instructions. Our idea is motivated by "duck typing", where the type of a variable is determined by its features and properties. Our approach first learns a classifier from existing binaries with debug information and then uses this classifier to predict types for new, unseen binaries. We have implemented our approach in a tool called *BITY* and used it to conduct some experiments on a well-known benchmark *coreutils* (v8.4). The results show that our tool is more precise than the commercial tool Hey-Rays, both in terms of correct types and compatible types.

1 Introduction

Binary code type inference aims to infer a high-level typed variables from executables, which is required for, or significantly benefits, many applications such as decompilation, binary code rewriting, vulnerability detection and analysis, binary code reuse, protocol reverse engineering, virtual machine introspection, game hacking, hooking, malware analysis, and so on. However, unlike high-level source codes, binary code type inference is challenging because, during compilation, much program information is lost, particularly, the variables that store the data, and their types, which constrain how the data are stored, manipulated, and interpreted.

A significant amount of research has been carried out on binary code type inference, such as REWORD [1], TIE [2], SmartDec [3], SecondWrite [4], Retypd [5] and Hex-Rays [6]. Most of them resort to program analysis techniques, which are often too conservative to infer types with high accuracy. For example, for a memory byte (*i.e.*, a variable) that is only used to store 0 and 1, most existing tools, such as SmartDec and Hex-Rays, recover the type *char* or *byte_t* (*i.e.*, a type for bytes), which is clearly either incorrect or too conservative.

© Springer International Publishing AG 2017
Z. Duan and L. Ong (Eds.): ICFEM 2017, LNCS 10610, pp. 430–446, 2017.
https://doi.org/10.1007/978-3-319-68690-5_26

Moreover, some of them are too heavy-weight to use in practice, for example, in the sense that they may generate too many constraints to solve for large-scale programs.

In this paper, we propose a new approach to learning types for binaries. Our idea is motivated by "duck typing", where the type of a variable is determined by its features and properties. Our approach first learns a classifier from existing binaries with debug information and then uses this classifier to predict types for new, unseen binaries. In detail, we first recover variables from binary codes using Value-Set Analysis (VSA) [7], then extract the related representative instructions of the variables as well as some other useful information as their features. Based on binaries with debug information collected from programs that are used in teaching materials and from commonly used algorithms and real-world programs, we learn a classifier using Support Vector Machine (SVM) [8,9]. Using this classifier, we then predict the most possible types for recovered variables.

We implement our approach as a prototype called BITY in Python. Using BITY, we conduct some experiments on a benchmark *coreutils* (v8.4). Compared with the commercial tool Hey-Rays, our tool is more precise, both in terms of correct types and compatible types. We also perform BITY on binaries of different sizes. The results show that our tool is scalable and suitable in practice.

Our main contributions are summarised as follows. We have proposed a new approach to learning types for binaries, and implemented it in a tool BITY, which is scalable and suitable in practice. Through experiments we have also demonstrated that our approach can predict types with high accuracy and has reasonable performance.

The rest of the paper is constructed as follows. Sect. 2 illustrates some motivating examples. Sect. 3 presents our approach to learning types for binaries, followed by the implementation in Sect. 4 and experimental results in Sect. 5. Related work is given in Sect. 6 and Sect. 7 concludes.

2   Motivation

In this section, we illustrate some examples that are not easy to recover the precise types by existing methods and explain our motivation.

The first example, shown in Fig. 1, comes from an encode and decode program *base64.c* of C runtime Library. The program uses a variable *decode* with type *bool* to record users' options. Nevertheless, after compiling, the variable *decode* is simply represented as a *byte* in stack (*i.e.*, [*ebp-1*]) and the type *bool* is lost. Due to the over-conservative program analysis they adopt, most existing tools, such as SmartDec and Hex-Rays, recover for the variable [*ebp-1*] the type *char* or *byte_t*, which is clearly either incorrect or conservative.

To make matters worse, programs with fewer instructions are more difficult to recover types correctly. Let us consider three simple assignments for three variables with different types, shown in Fig. 2. SmartDec recovers the same type *int32_t* for all these three variables, while Hex-Rays infers the type *Dword** for *i* and *f* and the type *Qword** for *d*. Again, most of these results are either incorrect or conservative.

Listing 1.1. C Source Code

```
int main ( )
{
    bool decode = false ;
    int opt = getopt ;
    switch (opt) {
        case 'd':
            decode = true ;
            break ;
        default :
            break ;
    }
    if (decode)    do_decode ;
}
```

Listing 1.2. Pseudo ASM Code

```
mov        byte ptr [ebp−1], 0
cmp        dword ptr [ebp−8], 64h
jz         short loc_40101B
jmp        short loc_40101F
loc_40101B :
mov        byte ptr [ebp−1], 1
loc_40101F :
movzx      eax, byte ptr [ebp−1]
test       eax, eax
jz         short loc_401035
call       do_decode
loc_401035 :
retn
```

Fig. 1. Snippet code from base64.c

Listing 1.3. C Source Code

```
func1(int* i){
    *i = 10;
}
func2(float* f){
    *f = 10.0;
}
func3(double* d){
    *d = 10.0;
}
```

Listing 1.4. Pseudo ASM Code

```
mov      [i], 0Ah

movss    xmm0, ds:XX
movss    [f], xmm0

movsd    xmm0, ds:XX
movsd    [d], xmm0
```

Fig. 2. Assignments of different types

One may note that the variables of different types are compiled with different instructions, that is, *mov*, *movss* and *movsd*. Hence, a simple solution is to enhance the program analysis techniques with three new rules to infer these three different types corresponding to these three different instructions. However, it is pity that *mov* (*movsd* resp.) is not only used for *int* (*double* resp.). Even if it works, there are too many instructions and types to figure out the reasonable rules. For example, there are more than 30 kinds of *mov* instructions in the x86 instruction set and the source operand and the destination operand may have different meanings.

Generally, the set of the related instructions of a variable reflects how the variable is stored, manipulated, and interpreted. So our solution is to take the related instruction set as a feature of a variable, and then to learn for the variable the most possible type from the feature. This is motivated by "duck typing", where the type of a variable is determined by its features and properties instead of being explicitly defined. Let us consider *base64.c* again. The related instruction set of [ebp-1] is {mov _, 0; mov _, 1; movzx eax, _}, which is most likely to be a feature of *bool*, where _ denotes the concerning variable. Accordingly, we recover *bool* as the type of [ebp-1]. Similarly to the variables of the second example. Note that *movsd* may be a feature of *double*, but not all of them belong to *double*.

3   Approach

In this section, we present our approach to learning the most possible type for a recovered variable.

As mentioned in Sect. 2, we try to learn the most possible type for a variable from its related instruction set. Our approach first learns a classifier from existing binaries with debug information and then uses this classifier to predict types for new, unseen binaries. Figure 3 shows the main idea of our approach. In detail, our approach consists of the following steps: (1) target variable recovery; (2) related instruction extraction; (3) feature selection and representation; (4) classifier training; (5) type predicting. In the following, we describe each of them, using another program *memchr* from C runtime Library as an illustrative example, which is shown in Fig. 4.

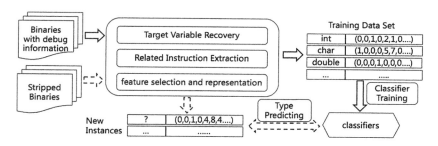

Fig. 3. Approach

3.1   Target Variable Recovery

During compilation, variables of the source program and their type information are not included in the resulting binary. So the first step is to identify the target variables in binaries. Indeed, variables are abstractions of memory blocks, which are accessed by data registers or specifying absolute address directly or indirectly through address expressions of the form "$[base+index \times scale + offset]$" in binaries, where *base* and *index* are registers, and *scale* and *offset* are integer constants. Take the variables in stack frame for example. Parameters[1] are always accessed by the form "$[ebp+offset]$", while local variables are by "$[ebp-offset]$", where *ebp* is the stack base pointer register. We recover the possible variables in binaries using Value-Set Analysis (VSA) [7], which is widely used in many binary analysis platforms. Note that, due to compiler optimization, a stack location may be used to represent multiple different local variables in the same function, which is not considered here.

---

[1] In FASTCALL convention, the first two parameters are passed in ECX and EDX.

```
%%  C Code
char *memchr (char *buf,int chr,int cnt) {
    while (cnt && *buf++ != chr) cnt--;
    return (cnt ? --buf : NULL);
}
%%  ASM Code Snippet
sub_401000          proc  near
......
loc_401009:
07                  cmp     dword ptr [ebp+10h], 0
08                  jz      short loc_40103A
09                  mov     eax, [ebp+8]
10                  movsx   ecx, byte ptr [eax]
11                  mov     [ebp-44h], ecx
12                  mov     edx, [ebp+0Ch]
13                  mov     [ebp-48h], edx
14                  mov     eax, [ebp+8]
15                  add     eax, 1
16                  mov     [ebp+8], eax
17                  mov     ecx, [ebp-44h]
18                  cmp     ecx, [ebp-48h]
19                  jz      short loc_40103A
20                  mov     eax, [ebp+10h]
21                  sub     eax, 1
22                  mov     [ebp+10h], eax
23                  jmp     short loc_401009
loc_40103A:
24                  cmp     dword ptr [ebp+10h], 0
25                  jz      short loc_401051
26                  mov     eax, [ebp+8]
27                  sub     eax, 1
28                  mov     [ebp+8], eax
29                  mov     ecx, [ebp+8]
30                  mov     [ebp-44h], ecx
31                  jmp     short loc_401058
loc_401051:
32                  mov     dword ptr [ebp-44h], 0
loc_401058:
......
sub_401000          endp
```

Fig. 4. Snippet code of *memchr*

Considering the illustrated example *memchr* in Fig. 4, the variables we recovered in stack frame are listed in Table 1. There are three parameters, which conform to the declarations in the C code. Due to the low-level instructions, there are two more local variables, which are used respectively to store the values of *buf* and *chr* temporarily.

Table 1. Target variables in *memchr*

Variable	Offset	Variable	Offset	Variable	Offset
Parameter1	[ebp+8]	Parameter2	[ebp+0Ch]	Parameter3	[ebp+10h]
LocalVar1	[ebp-48h]	LocalVar2	[ebp-44h]		

3.2 Related Instruction Extraction

Next, we want to extract the related instructions for the recovered target variables, which reflect how the variables are used and will be used as a feature to learn the types.

The instructions using a variable directly are extracted for the variable. However, an instruction of a variable in high-level codes may be compiled into several instructions in low-level codes, some of which may not use the corresponding variable directly. For example, the statement *if (decode)* in *base64* is complied into two instructions in ASM codes (see Fig. 1), one of which uses the corresponding variable directly (*i.e.*, "movzx eax, byte ptr [ebp-1]"), while the other does not (*i.e.*, "test eax, eax"). Clearly, the second one is more representative for *bool*. On the other hand, the data registers like *eax*, *ebx*, *ecx* and *edx* are usually used as an intermediary to store data temporarily and they may store different data (*i.e.*, have different types) in different time. Therefore, we make use of use-defined chains on the data registers to extract the indirect usage instructions: if a data register is defined by a variable, then all the uses of the register are considered as the uses of the variable as well. Consequently, the instruction "test eax, eax" belongs to the variable [ebp-1] in *base64*, since it is a use of *eax*, which is defined by [epb-1].

Let us consider the target variable [epb+8] in the *memchr* example. The instructions related with [epb+8] are shown in Fig. 5. There are 10 instructions in total, 6 of which use [epb+8] directly and 4 are collected due to the use-defined chain (denoted by "use of" followed by a data register).

```
09      mov       eax, [ebp+8]          //def of eax by epb+8
10      movsx     ecx, byte ptr [eax]   //use of eax
14      mov       eax, [ebp+8]          //def of eax by epb+8
15      add       eax, 1                //use of eax
16      mov       [ebp+8], eax
26      mov       eax, [ebp+8]          //def of eax by epb+8
27      sub       eax, 1                //use of eax
28      mov       [ebp+8], eax
29      mov       ecx, [ebp+8]          //def of ecx by epb+8
30      mov       [ebp-44h], ecx        //use of ecx
```

Fig. 5. Related instructions of [ebp+8] in *memchr*

3.3 Feature Selection and Representation

In this paper, we focus on the x86 instruction set on Intel platforms. The others are similar.

According to the official document of the x86 instruction set [10], different instructions have different usages. So we perform some pre-processing on these instructions based on their usages. Firstly, we note that not all the instructions are interesting for type inference. For example, *pop* and *push* are usually used by the stack, rather than variables. Secondly, as different operands may have different meanings, we differentiate between two operands in a dyadic instruction, for example, the operands of *mov* respectively represent the source and the destination, which are clearly not the same. Thirdly, some instructions need further processing, since using them in different circumstances may have different meanings. For instance, using *mov* with registers of different sizes offers us different meaningful information. Table 2 lists the typical usage patterns of *mov* we use, where _ denotes a variable, *regn* denotes a register with size n, *imm* denotes an immediate number which is neither 0 nor 1, and *addr* denotes a memory address (*i.e.*, another variable).

Table 2. Usage patterns of *mov*

mov _, reg32	mov reg32, _	mov _, reg16	mov reg16, _	mov _, reg8	mov reg8, _
mov _, addr	mov addr, _	mov _, 0	mov _, 1	mov _, imm	

Moreover, not all the instructions are widely used or representative. For that we do a statistical analysis on our dataset, which consists of real-world programs and source codes from some course books, using the well-known scheme Term Frequency Inverse Document Frequency (TF-IDF) weighting [11]. Based on the result, we select the N most frequently used and representative instructions as the feature indicators. Theoretically, the more instructions, the better. While in practice, we found 100 instructions are enough.

In addition, we also take into account some other useful information as features, namely, the memory size and being an argument of a function.

Finally, we represent the selected features of variables using a vector space model [12], which is an algebraic model for representing any objects as vectors of identifiers. We only concern that how many times an interesting instruction are performed on a variable, leaving the order out of consideration. So a representation of a variable is a vector consisting of the frequency of each selected instruction and the extra useful information. Formally, a variable is represented as the following vector v:

$$v = [f_1 : t_1, \ f_2 : t_2, \ \ldots, \ f_n : t_n]$$

where f_i is a feature term, t_i is the value of feature f_i, and n is the number of features. For example, Table 3 shows the vector of the variable [ebp+8] in the illustrated example *memchr*, where only the nonzero features are listed. Note that "mov eax, _" and "mov ecx, _" are merged together, since both *eax* and *ecx* are registers of 32 bits. To be more precise, one can also take into account the IDF that have been computed for each selected instruction or some other correlation functions.

Table 3. Representation of *epb+8*

Before proceeding		After proceeding	
Feature	Value	Feature	Value
size	32	size32	1
mov eax, _	3	mov reg32, _	4
movsx ecx, [_]	1	movsx reg32, [_]	1
add _, imm	1	add _, imm	1
mov _,eax	2	mov _, reg32	2
sub _, imm	1	sub _, imm	1
mov ecx, _	1	Merged to mov reg32, _	
mov [ebp-44h], _	1	mov addr, _	1

3.4   Classifier Training and Type Predicting

For now, we only consider the base types without type quantifiers, that is, the set L of labels we are learning in this paper are

$$L = \{bool, char, short, float, int, pointer, longlongint, double, longdouble\}$$

The reason is that (1) the other types, such as structs, can be composed from the base types; (2) too many levels may make against the classifier.

We use supervised learning to train our classifier, so a labeled dataset is needed. For that, we compile a dataset of C programs with debugging and then extract type information from the compiled binaries. Generally, our training problem can be expressed as:

Given a labeled dataset $D = \{(v_1, l_1), (v_2, l_2), \ldots, (v_m, l_m)\}$, the goal is to learn a classifier C such that $C(v_i) = l_i$ for all $i = 1, 2, \ldots, m$, where v_i is the feature vector of a variable, $l_i \in L$ is the corresponding type, m is the number of variables.

We use Support Vector Machine (SVM) [8,9] to learn the classifier. Clearly, our training problem is a multi-class one. By using the "one-against-one" approach [13], we first reduce the multi-class problem into a *binary* classifier learning one: for every two different types, a classifier is trained from the labeled dataset. Some size information of variables may be unknown, so for simplicity, we do not distinguish between types of different sizes. That is to say, assume there are k types, we will train $k \times (k-1)/2$ binary classifiers.

As mentioned in Sect. 3.3, a variable is represented as a vector, namely, is regarded as a point in the feature vector space. SVM tries to construct an n-dimensional hyperplanes that optimally separates the variables into categories, which is achieved by a linear or nonlinear separating surface in the input vector space of the labeled dataset. Its main idea is to transform the original input set to a high-dimensional feature space by using a kernel function, and then achieve optimum classification in this new feature space.

After the binary classifiers are trained, we then can use them to predict the most possible type for each variable that have been recovered from new or unseen binaries. This proceeds as follows: we use each binary classifier to vote a type for a variable, and then select the one that gets the most votes as the most possible type. Let us consider the variable [epb+8] in the illustrative example again. Note that its feature instructions contain "mov reg32, _; movsx reg32, [_]" (to read from an address), "mov reg32, _; add _,imm" (to increase the address), and "mov reg32, _; sub _,imm" (to decrease the address), which are the typical usages of *pointer*. Most classifiers involved *pointers* will vote for the type *pointer* for [epb+8], and thus the most possible type we learn is *pointer*. Another example is the variable *decode* in the program *base64* presented in Sect. 2. According to its feature instructions (*i.e.*, "mov _, 0; mov _, 1; movzx reg32, _; test _, _"), most of the classifiers will vote for the type *bool*.

3.5   Type Lattice

Finally, we present the lattice of our types we are learning, which gives the hierarchy of types and will be used to measure the precision of our approach as TIE does [2] (see Sect. 5).

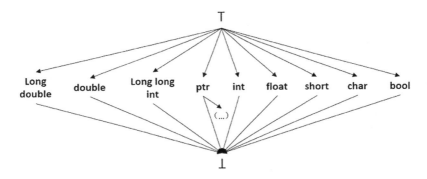

Fig. 6. Type lattice

The lattice is given in Fig. 6, where ⊤ and ⊥ respectively denote that a variable can or cannot be any type and there is a "pointer" to the lattice itself for the type *pointer*, that is, the lattice is level-by-level. In other words, our approach handles *pointer* level-by-level, which proceeds as follows:

1. once a variable v is predicted to have type *pointer* by the classifier, our approach first tries to recover another variable that the *pointer* variable points to;
2. if such an indirect variable v' exists, the approach then extracts related features for this newly recovered variable v' and continues to learn a (next-level) type t for it;
3. finally, the type for v is a *pointer* to t if v' exists, otherwise a *pointer* (to any type).

This enables us to predict *pointer* more precise (see Sect. 5) and to handle multi-level *pointers* considered in [4]. Theoretically, our approach can handle a *pointer* with any levels (and thus may not terminate). While in practice, we found only 3 levels are enough.

Let us go on with [epb+8] in the illustrative example. In Sect. 3.4, we have learnt that the most possible type for [epb+8] is *pointer*. So our approach carries on to recover an indirect variable, which is "byte ptr [eax]", and then to extract its feature vector [size8: 1; movsx reg32, _: 1; mov addr, _: 1], which covers the data move with sign extension. There are two types with 8 bits, namely, *bool* and *char*. Compared with *bool*, it is more like to have type *char* according to the known binaries. Thus the final type for [epb+8] is *pointer* to *char*.

4   Implementation

We have implemented our approach as a prototype called BITY in 3k lines of Python codes. We use IDA Pro [6] as a front end to disassemble binaries, since it supports a variety of executable formats for different processors and operating systems, and use LIBSVM [14], a Library for Support Vector Machines, to implement our classifiers. Moreover, as mentioned before, we select 100 most frequently used and representative instructions as features and consider 3 levels for *pointer* types.

For a high precision, we consider a training dataset that should contain different possible usages of different types. For that, we collect binaries with debug information obtained from programs that are used in teaching materials and from commonly used algorithms and real-world programs. Programs of the first kind always cover all the types and their possible usages, in particular, they demonstrate how types and their corresponding operations are used for beginners. While programs of the second kind reflect how (often) different types or usages are used in practice, which help us to select the most possible type. In detail, our training dataset consists of the binaries obtained from the following programs:

- Source codes of the C programming language (K&R);
- Source codes of basic algorithms in C programming language [15];
- Source codes of commonly used algorithms [16];
- C Runtime Library;
- Some C programs from github.

Any other valuable data will be added into our data set in the future.

5   Experiments

In this section, we present the experiments.

5.1   Results on Benchmark *coreutils*

To evaluate our approach, we perform our tool BITY on programs from *coreutils* (v8.4), a benchmark used by several existing work [1,2,17]. We first compile the test programs into (stripped) binaries, and then use BITY to predict types for the recovered variables. To measure the accuracy of our approach, we compare the types that BITY predicts with the type information extracted from the binaries that are obtained by compiling the test programs with debug support. We also compare our tool BITY against Hex-Rays decompiler-v2.2.0.15[2], a plug-in of the commercial tool IDA Pro [6]. All the experiments are run on a machine with 3.30 GHz i5-4590 and 8 GB RAM.

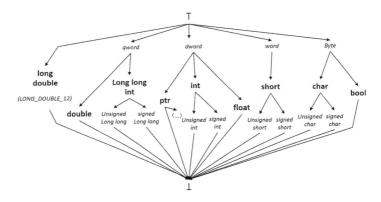

Fig. 7. Type lattice for Hex-Rays and BITY

To measure between types, we borrow the notation *distance* from TIE [2]. For that, we extend our type lattice with the types recovered by Hex-Rays, which is shown in Fig. 7, where our tool consider only the types in bold, while Hex-Rays considers all the types except $\top$ and $\bot$. We say that two types are compatible if one of them is a subtype of the other one following the top-level lattice. Given two types t_1, t_2, the distance between them, denoted as $|t_1 - t_2|$, is defined as follows: (1) at most one of them is a *pointer*: the distance $|t_1 - t_2|$ is the number of hierarchies between them in the top-level lattice if they are compatible, otherwise the maximum hierarchies' height (*i.e.*, 4); (2) both of them are *pointer*, namely, *pointer* to t_1' and t_2' respectively: the distance $|t_1 - t_2|$ is the half[3] of the maximum hierarchies height (*i.e.*, 2) multiplied by 0, 0.5

---

[2] Hex-Rays makes use of debug information, so we perform both our tool and Hex-Rays on stripped binaries.

[3] Theoretically, we can use the radio of the number of common levels among the number of maximum levels between t_1 and t_2 [4]. Since we consider 3 levels in practice, we use the half here.

and 1, according to whether t_1' and t_2' are the same, compatible or incompatible respectively. For example, $|int - dword| = 1$ and $|*int - *dword| = 1$, while $|int - *dword| = 4$.

The selected results of our tool BITY and Hex-Rays on the benchmark *coreutils* are given in Table 4, where **Vars** denotes the number of recovered variables in stack, **Corr** denotes the number of variables, whose types are recovered correctly, **Comp** denotes the number of variables, whose types are recovered compatibly, **Fail** denotes the number of variables, whose types are recovered incorrectly, and **Dist** denotes the average distance of each program.

The results show that our tool predicts correct types for 58.15% (1356) variables and compatible types for 31.22% (728) variables (most are due to the lack of the type quantifier *signed* and *unsigned*), in total proper types for 89.37% (2084) variables; while Hex-Rays recovers correct types for 54.80% (1278) variables and compatible types for 25.26% (589) variables (most are due to the consideration of the conservative types), in total proper types for 80.06% (1876) variables. This indicates that our tool is (11.63%) more precise than Hex-Rays, both in terms of correct types and compatible types.

Moreover, we found 43.8% (1021 among 2332) of the recovered variables are *pointer* ones. For these *pointer* types of the variables, our tool can recover 43.39% (443) correct types and 38.98% (398) compatible types, in total 82.37% (841) proper types; while Hex-Rays recovers 38.30% (391) correct types and 21.74% (222) compatible types, in total 60.03% (613) proper types. Consequently, our tool is also (37.21%) more precise than Hex-Rays in terms of *pointer* types.

Concerning the failures, most of them are due to *pointer*: 72.58% (180 among 248) for our tool and 87.74% (408 among 465) for Hex-Rays. We perform manual analysis on some failure cases. There are two main reasons: (1) there are too few representative instructions to predict the right types for some variables, especially for *pointer* variables; (2) some variables are of composed types such as *struct* and *array*, which are not considered by our tool yet.

Finally, let us consider the distance. For most programs, our tool predict types with a shorter distance than Hex-Rays. While in several other cases (*e.g.*, *chroot* and *pinky*), Hex-Rays recovers types better. One main reason is that Hex-Rays can reconstruct some *pointer* to *struct* such as FILE*, FTSENT* and FTS*. On average, our tool predicts more precise types.

5.2   Performance

To evaluate the scalability of our tool, we conduct experiments on binaries of different sizes. Table 5 shows the experimental results, where **ALOC** denotes the lines of the assemble codes, **Vars** denotes the number of recovered variables in stack, **ProT** denotes the preprocessing time excluding the disassembling time by IDA Pro and **PreT** denotes the predicting time. The results show that (1) the preprocessing time accounts for a great proportion and is linear on LOC and variable numbers; (2) the predicting time does not cost too much and is linear on variable numbers; (3) our tool predicts types for binaries of sizes ranging from 7 KB to 1341.44 MB in just a few seconds, which indicates our tool is scalable and viable in practice.

Table 4. Selected results of BITY and Hex-Rays on *coreutils* (v8.4)

Program	Vars	BITY				Hex-Rays			
		Corr	Comp	Fail	Dist	Corr	Comp	Fail	Dist
base64	41	20	19	2	0.66	29	7	5	0.80
basename	22	17	4	1	0.55	12	4	6	1.32
cat	50	29	19	2	0.60	18	19	13	1.52
chcon	55	39	8	8	0.73	32	7	16	1.36
chgrp	31	21	4	6	0.90	17	4	10	1.42
chmod	42	19	20	3	0.71	20	13	19	1.23
chown	42	19	4	3	0.94	5	6	5	1.65
chroot	23	12	9	2	0.74	18	4	10	0.39
cksum	14	7	6	1	0.71	7	6	1	0.79
comm	20	10	4	6	1.40	11	1	8	1.65
copy	135	69	48	18	0.92	53	42	40	1.60
cp	78	46	26	6	0.78	45	23	10	0.94
csplit	66	27	32	7	1.02	26	25	15	1.38
cut	47	32	14	1	0.47	31	15	1	0.64
date	30	18	8	4	0.77	15	8	7	1.37
dd	128	81	35	12	0.72	78	30	20	0.88
df	92	51	32	9	0.89	45	25	22	1.27
dircolors	55	31	23	1	0.62	26	23	6	0.98
du	68	27	28	13	1.19	26	15	27	1.90
echo	11	8	3	0	0.55	5	6	0	0.82
expand	25	16	8	1	0.48	16	9	0	0.48
expr	85	29	39	17	1.36	28	35	22	1.47
factor	30	20	9	1	0.43	22	4	4	0.73
fmt	62	40	15	7	0.71	40	7	15	1.12
fold	25	17	8	0	0.36	20	5	0	0.28
getlimits	20	17	3	0	0.15	17	2	1	0.30
groups	9	5	4	0	0.44	5	4	0	0.55
head	111	63	41	7	0.65	52	42	17	1.14
id	20	13	5	2	0.65	12	5	3	0.90
join	106	48	52	6	0.79	54	24	28	1.33
kill	27	18	6	3	0.70	15	9	3	0.89
ln	29	23	3	3	0.62	21	5	3	0.76
ls	352	189	105	58	1.04	186	73	93	1.32
mkdir	22	15	4	3	0.91	10	5	7	1.55
mkfifo	10	7	2	1	1.11	7	0	3	1.78
mktemp	35	23	9	3	0.60	16	15	4	1.09
mv	35	20	8	7	1.14	15	8	12	1.74
nice	16	15	1	0	0.13	15	1	0	0.13
nl	18	11	4	3	1.06	12	3	3	0.94
nohup	22	20	1	1	0.27	19	1	2	0.41
od	120	88	23	9	0.53	86	25	9	0.58
operand2sig	13	11	0	2	0.62	9	2	2	0.77
paste	35	26	7	2	0.54	24	9	2	0.71
pathchk	19	15	3	1	0.37	14	4	1	0.53
pinky	62	34	22	6	0.74	44	9	9	0.71
Total	2332	1356	728	248	-	1278	589	465	-
Avg	–	–	–	–	0.72	–	–	–	1.02
pointers	1021	443	398	180	-	391	222	408	-

Table 5. Results on different sizes of binaries

Program	Size	ALOC	Vars	ProT	PreT
strcat	7 KB	508	8	0.187	0.011
Notepad++ 7.3.3_Installer.exe	2.80 MB	12032	113	0.807	0.229
SmartPPTSetup_1.11.0.7.exe	4.76 MB	128381	166	1.156	0.365
DoroPDFWriter_2.0.9.exe	16.30 MB	25910	71	0.692	0.068
QuickTime_51.1052.0.0.exe	18.30 MB	61240	247	2.132	0.607
Firefox Portable.exe	110.79 MB	12068	113	0.906	0.254
VMware workstation v12.0.exe	282.00 MB	39857	352	3.739	0.911
opencv-2.4.9.exe	348.00 MB	61636	287	4.130	0.722
VSX6_pro_TBYB.exe	1341.44 MB	129803	450	4.762	1.921

6 Related Work

There have been many works about type inference on binaries. In this section we briefly discuss a number of more recent related work. Interested readers can refer to [18] for more details.

TIE [2] is a static tool for inferring primitive types for variables in a binary, where the inferred type is limited to integer and pointer type. Moreover, the output of TIE is the upper bound or the lower bound rather than the specific type, which may not be accurate enough for it to be useful for a binary engineer. PointerScope [19] uses type inference on binary execution to detect the pointer misuses induced by an exploit. Aiming for scalability, SecondWrite [4] combines a best-effort VSA variant for points-to analysis with a unification-based type inference engine. But accurate types depend on high-quality points-to data. The work of Robbins *et al.* [17] reduces the type recovery to a rational-tree constraint problem and solve it using an SMT solver. Yan and McCamant [20] propose a graph-based algorithm to determine whether each integer variable is declared as signed or unsigned. Retypd [5] is a novel static type-inference algorithm for machine code that supports recursive types, polymorphism, and subtyping. Hex-Rays [6] is a popular commercial tool for binary code analysis and its exact algorithm is proprietary. However, these tools resort to static program analysis approaches, which are either too conservative to infer types with high accuracy or too heavy-weight for practical use.

REWARDS [1] and Howard [21] both take a dynamic approach, generating type constraints from execution traces, to detect data structures. ARTISTE [22] is another tool to detect data structures using a dynamic approach. ARTISTE generates hybrid signatures that minimize false positives during scanning by combining points-to relationships, value invariants, and cycle invariants. While MemPick [23] is a tool that detects and classifies high-level data structures such as singly- or doubly-linked lists, many types of trees (*e.g.*, AVL, red-black trees, B-trees), and graphs. But as dynamic analysis-based approaches, they cannot achieve full coverage of variables defined in a program.

Some tools focus on recovering object oriented features from C++ binaries [3, 24–26]. Most of them adopt program analysis, while the work of Katz *et al.* [26] uses object tracelets to capture potential runtime behaviors of objects and use the behaviors to generate a ranking of their most likely types. Similar to Katz et. al.'s work, we use the instructions set, leaving the order out of consideration, to capture potential behaviours of variables. Thus our solution is simper.

In addition, Raychev *et al.* [27] present a new approach for predicting program properties, including types, from big code based on conditional random fields. Their approach leverages program structures to create dependencies and constraints used for probabilistic reasoning. Their approach works well at high-level source code since lots of program structures are easy to discover. While for stripped binaries, less program structures can be recovered.

7   Conclusion

Recovering type information from binaries is valuable for binary analysis. In this paper, we have proposed a new approach to predicting the most possible types for recovered variables. Different with existing work, our approach bases on classifiers, without resorting to program analysis like constraint solving techniques. To demonstrate the viability of the approach, we have implemented our approach in a prototype tool and carried out some interesting experiments. The results show that our tool is more precise than the commercial tool Hey-Rays.

As for future work, we may consider the binary classifiers of different types of the same size to improve the approach or try other classifiers. We can perform a points-to analysis to improve our analysis on multi-level *pointers*. We can take type quantifiers (*e.g.*, signed) or the composite types (*e.g.*, *struct*) into account. We can also conduct more experiments on more real world programs to compare BITY with other tools.

Acknowledgements. The authors would like to thank the anonymous reviewers for their helpful comments. This work was partially supported by the National Natural Science Foundation of China under Grants No. 61502308 and 61373033, Science and Technology Foundation of Shenzhen City under Grant No. JCYJ20170302153712968.

References

1. Lin, Z., Zhang, X., Xu, D.: Automatic reverse engineering of data structures from binary execution. In: Network and Distributed System Security Symposium (2010)
2. Lee, J.H., Avgerinos, T., Brumley, D.: Tie: principled reverse engineering of types in binary programs. In: Network and Distributed System Security Symposium (2011)
3. Fokin, A., Derevenetc, E., Chernov, A., Troshina, K.: SmartDec: approaching C++ decompilation. In: Reverse Engineering, pp. 347–356 (2011)
4. Elwazeer, K., Anand, K., Kotha, A., Smithson, M., Barua, R.: Scalable variable and data type detection in a binary rewriter. In: ACM Sigplan Conference on Programming Language Design and Implementation, pp. 51–60 (2013)

5. Noonan, M., Loginov, A., Cok, D.: Polymorphic type inference for machine code. In: ACM Sigplan Conference on Programming Language Design and Implementation, pp. 27–41 (2016)
6. The IDA Pro and Hex-Rays. http://www.hex-rays.com/idapro/
7. Balakrishnan, G., Reps, T.: Analyzing memory accesses in x86 binary executables. University of Wisconsin-Madison Department of Computer Sciences (2012)
8. Burges, C.J.C.: A tutorial on support vector machines for pattern recognition. Data Min. Knowl. Disc. **2**(2), 121–167 (1998)
9. Smola, A.J., Schlkopf, B.: On a kernel-based method for pattern recognition, regression, approximation, and operator inversion. Algorithmica **22**(1), 211–231 (1998)
10. IntelCorporation: Intel 64 and IA-32 Architectures Software Developer Manuals, December 2016
11. Crnic, J.: Introduction to Modern Information Retrieval. McGraw-Hill, New York (1983)
12. Salton, G.: A vector space model for automatic indexing. Commun. ACM **18**(11), 613–620 (1975)
13. Kang, S., Cho, S., Kang, P.: Constructing a multi-class classifier using one-against-one approach with different binary classifiers. Neurocomputing **149**(PB), 677–682 (2015)
14. LIBSVM. http://www.csie.ntu.edu.tw/~cjlin/libsvm/
15. 178 Algorithm C language source code. http://www.codeforge.com/article/220463
16. Xu, S.: Commonly Used Algorithm Assembly (C Language Description). Tsinghua University Press, Beijing (2004). (in Chinese)
17. Robbins, E., Howe, J.M., King, A.: Theory propagation and rational-trees. In: Symposium on Principles and Practice of Declarative Programming, pp. 193–204 (2013)
18. Caballero, J., Lin, Z.: Type inference on executables. ACM Comput. Surv. **48**(4), 65 (2016)
19. Zhang, M., Prakash, A., Li, X., Liang, Z., Yin, H.: Identifying and analyzing pointer misuses for sophisticated memory-corruption exploit diagnosis. Proc. West. Pharmacol. Soc. **47**(47), 46–49 (2013)
20. Yan, Q., McCamant, S.: Conservative signed/unsigned type inference for binaries using minimum cut. Technical report, University of Minnesota (2014)
21. Slowinska, A., Stancescu, T., Bos, H.: Howard: a dynamic excavator for reverse engineering data structures. In: Network and Distributed System Security Symposium (2011)
22. Elwazeer, K., Anand, K., Kotha, A., Smithson, M., Barua, R.: Artiste: automatic generation of hybrid data structure signatures from binary code executions. Technical report TRIMDEA-SW-2012-001, IMDEA Software Institute (2012)
23. Haller, I., Slowinska, A., Bos, H.: MemPick: high-level data structure detection in C/C++ binaries. In: Reverse Engineering, pp. 32–41 (2013)
24. Jin, W., Cohen, C., Gennari, J., Hines, C., Chaki, S., Gurfinkel, A., Havrilla, J., Narasimhan, P.: Recovering C++ objects from binaries using inter-procedural data-flow analysis. In: ACM Sigplan on Program Protection and Reverse Engineering Workshop, p. 1 (2014)
25. Yoo, K., Barua, R.: Recovery of object oriented features from C++ binaries. In: Asia-Pacific Software Engineering Conference, pp. 231–238 (2014)

26. Katz, O., El-Yaniv, R., Yahav, E.: Estimating types in binaries using predictive modeling. In: ACM SIGPLAN-SIGACT Symposium on Principles of Programming Languages, pp. 313–326 (2016)
27. Raychev, V., Vechev, M., Krause, A.: Predicting program properties from "big code". In: The ACM SIGPLAN-SIGACT Symposium on Principles of Programming Languages, pp. 111–124 (2015)

Inconsistency Analysis of Time-Based Security Policy and Firewall Policy

Yi Yin[1,2(✉)], Yuichiro Tateiwa[3], Yun Wang[1], Yoshiaki Katayama[3],
and Naohisa Takahashi[3]

[1] School of Computer Science and Engineering,
Southeast University, Nanjing, China
yi837@hotmail.com, 101004974@seu.edu.cn
[2] School of Computer Science and Technology,
Nanjing Normal University, Nanjing, China
[3] Department of Computer Science and Engineering, Graduate School
of Engineering, Nagoya Institute of Technology, Nagoya, Japan
{tateiwa,katayama,naohisa}@nitech.ac.jp

Abstract. Packet filtering in firewall either accepts or denies packets based upon a set of predefined rules called firewall policy. In recent years, time-based firewall policies are widely used in many firewalls such as CISCO ACLs. Firewall policy is always designed under the instruction of security policy, which is a generic document that outlines the needs for network access permissions. It is difficult to maintain the consistency of normal firewall policy and security policy, not to mention time-based firewall policy and security policy. Even though there are many analysis methods for security policy and firewall policy, they cannot deal with time constraint. To resolve this problem, we firstly represent time-based security policy and firewall policy as logical formulas, and then use satisfiability modulo theories (SMT) solver *Z3* to verify them and analyze inconsistency. We have implemented a prototype system to verify our proposed method, experimental results showed the effectiveness.

Keywords: Security policy · Firewall policy · Time-based rules · Satisfiability modulo theories

1 Introduction

Firewall is a traditional and very important component for network security. When packets come to firewall, they are accepted or denied based on a set of predefined rules called **firewall policy** (represented as **FP**). FP is usually designed under the instruction of some generic rules for network access permissions, which is called **security policy** (represented as **SP**). SP is an essential directory document in an organization, it defines the broad boundaries of information security. In recent years, time-based rules are widely used by firewall vendors to control network traffics, such as Cisco ACLs [1], Linux iptables [2], and so on. Time-based rules are very useful when a service is required to be

© Springer International Publishing AG 2017
Z. Duan and L. Ong (Eds.): ICFEM 2017, LNCS 10610, pp. 447–463, 2017.
https://doi.org/10.1007/978-3-319-68690-5_27

available only at certain times. For example, a bank will close WEB Server for the maintenance during 24:00 to 8:00 in the next morning. A firewall policy and a security policy with a time constraint are called **time-based firewall policy** (represented as *TFP*) and **time-based security policy** (represented as *TSP*) respectively. The design of *TFP* should be consistent with *TSP*, the inconsistencies of *TSP* and *TFP* may bring about security hole and even lead to irreparable consequences. Therefore, it is very important to detect and resolve the inconsistencies of *TSP* and *TFP*. However, *TSP* and *TFP* are described in different forms and abstractions, correctly verifying whether they are consistent and detect their inconsistencies is by no means easy.

We have proposed some methods to verify whether *SP* and *FP* are consistent [3,4]. In previous work [3], we developed a geometric analysis method and interpreted *SP* and *FP* as a set of packets, and then we compared the two sets of packets to decide whether *SP* and *FP* are consistent. In previous work [4], we represented *SP* and *FP* as Constraint Satisfaction Problem, then used CSP solver *Sugar* [5] to verify the consistency of *SP* and *FP*. Two previous works could only verify whether *SP* and *FP* are consistent, if *SP* and *FP* are not consistent, two previous works could not detect and deal with their inconsistencies. In addition, previous two works did not consider time constraint of rules. Related work [6] proposed a system to detect conflict rules of *TFP* by using bit-vectors. Although this work could deal with time-based rules, its aim was conflict rules detection of *TFP* rather than the inconsistencies detection of *TSP* and *TFP*. To resolve the above problems, in this paper, by using SMT solver *Z3* [7], we propose a method that can detect and deal with the inconsistencies of *TSP* and *TFP*. The major contributions of this paper are stated as follows:

(1) We propose an inconsistency detection method of *TSP* and *TFP*, that is, we construct some logical formulas and use SMT solver *Z3* to verify them, the inconsistencies of *TSP* and *TFP* could be decided based on the verification results of *Z3*. There is no need to interpret the meanings of *TSP* and *TFP* rules by means of additional complex analysis technology.

(2) Since the SMT solver *Z3* supports equality reasoning, and arithmetic, which let the description of abstract *TSP* rules become more intuitively. For example, to represent *TSP* rule, we introduce set operators of "*not*", "*and*", etc.

(3) We have developed a prototype system and evaluated the feasibility of our proposed method. Experimental results show the effectiveness.

This paper is organized as follows. Section 2 introduces the specification of *TSP* and *TFP*. Section 3 describes SMT solver and internal form of *TSP* and *TFP*. Section 4 presents the inconsistency detection method of *TSP* and *TFP*. Section 5 introduces our prototype system and experiments. Section 6 discusses relevant works. Finally, Sect. 7 draws the conclusions and future works.

2   Specification of *TSP* and *TFP*

2.1   *TFP* Specification

We define a time-based firewall policy *TFP* usually consists of an ordered set of n rules $\{f_1, f_2, ..., f_n\}$. Each rule f_i is shown as follows:

$$f_i :\ p_{i1}, p_{i2}, ..., p_{it}, time_i, action_i,$$

where $p_{i1} \sim p_{it}$ are **predicates** for the values of key fields of header used in packet filtering. The commonly used header fields are: protocol, source IP (**SrcIP**), destination IP (**DesIP**), source port (**SrcPort**) and destination port (**DesPort**). Possible values of $action_i$ are *accept* and *deny*. We define the time constraint $time_i$ has the following **periodic** or **non-periodic** formats.

(1) Type1: The periodic time constraint is represented as $(T,\ W,\ M)$, where subfield T is a range of start and end time. T is represented as 24-h format of $hh{:}mm$, such as [18:00, 24:00). Subfield W is a subset of week days {**Sun**, **Mon**, $\cdots$, **Sat**}, for example, W = {Mon, Fri}. Subfield M is a set of designated months with the format of $yyyy/mm$, such as M = {2017/06, 2017/11}.
(2) Type2: The non-periodic time constraint is represented as $(T,\ D)$, where subfield T is the same as the format of the periodic time constraint. Subfield D is a set of designated days with the format of $yyyy/mm/dd$, for example, D = {2017/06/17, 2017/09/20, 2017/11/30}.

A packet P matches a time-based rule if and only if the arrival time of P satisfies the rule's time constraint, and the values of P's key fields satisfy all the predicates of the rule. For example, Fig. 1 shows periodic and non-periodic time-based rules respectively. From 8:00 to 12:00 on every Monday and Friday in June and November, 2017, when a packet P arrives and the header of P satisfies all the predicates of rule f_1, the packet P matches rule f_1. From 12:00 to 24:00 on July 31, 2017 and December 31, 2017, when a packet P arrives and the header of P satisfies all the predicates of rule f_2, the packet P matches rule f_2.

	Protocol	SrcIP	SrcPort	DesIP	DesPort	Time	Action
f_1	tcp	129.8.50.200	≥1023	123.4.5.*	25	[8:00-12:00) {Mon, Fri} {2017/06, 2017/11}	*accept*
f_2	tcp	*	≥ 1023	129.8.50.200	80	[12:00-24:00) {2017/07/31, 2017/12/31}	*deny*

Fig. 1. Time-based rules example

2.2 *TSP* Specification

TSP is a generic instruction scenario for network access permissions, it is a specification for *TFP* rules design. In our previous work [3], we have designed a model to represent *SP*. To represent *TSP* rules, we add the time constraint based on our previous *SP* representation model. We design the *TSP* representation model includes specification of **network**, **network services** and **rules**.

To represent network, we divided the target network into several disjoint sub-networks(called **regions**). Each region is a range of IP addresses or an address. For example, the region "DMZ" shown in Fig. 2 is represented as 166.68.13.0/28. We use **Host List** (shown in Table 1) to show all the available hosts and use a Region Definition Table (**RDT**, shown in Table 4) to represent all the divided regions of the network. In addition, we permit to use set operators to represent *TSP* rule, such as "! (*not*)", "*and*", and so on. For example, "! (*not*)" represents other than a certain subnet or a region, "*and*" connects two different regions or subnets.

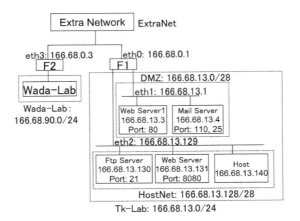

Fig. 2. Network example

Table 1. Host list

Host list
166.68.90.0/24
166.68.13.0/24

Table 2. Service definition table

Service name	Protocol	Des port	Src port
WEBserver	tcp	80	*
FTPserver	tcp	21	*

To represent network services, we use a Service Definition Table (**SDT**, shown in Table 2) and a Protocol Definition Table (**PDT**, shown in Table 3) to represent

Table 4. Region definition table

Table 3. Protocol definition table

Protocol	Protocol number
tcp	6
udp	17
any	0−255

Region name	IP address of region
DMZ	166.68.13.0/28
HostNet	166.68.13.128/28
Tk-Lab	166.68.13.0/24
ExtraNet	!166.68.13.0/24
	and !166.68.90.0/24

all the services provided in the network. SDT includes services name, protocol, destination and source port number, PDT includes the protocol name and protocol number.

To represent *TSP* rules, we suppose that *TSP* consists of m rules $\{s_1, s_2, ..., s_m\}$ and each rule s_i ($i \in [1, m]$) is described as follows:

$$s_i : \text{ if } S_i \text{ in } R_{i1} \text{ from } R_{i2} \text{ at } W_i \text{ then } A_i$$

Each *TSP* rule s_i represents that firewall takes the action A_i (*accept* or *deny*) to the access, which comes from the region of R_{i2} to the service S_i in the region of R_{i1} at the time W_i. The time constraint W_i uses the same two formats as *TFP* rule. For example, the meaning of the following *TSP* rule s_1 is that the access from external network (represented as "ExtraNet") to the FTP server in "TK-Lab" is denied from 8:00 to 12:00 at November 30, 2017.

s_1: if *FTPserver* in *Tk-Lab* from *ExtraNet* at [8:00, 12:00) 2017/11/30 then *deny*

3   SMT Solver and Internal Form of *TSP* and *TFP*

3.1   SMT Solver and Internal Form of *TSP* and *TFP*

Satisfiability Modulo Theories (SMT) problem is a decision problem for logical first order formulas with respect to combinations of background theories such as: arithmetic, bit vectors, arrays, and so on. An SMT solver is a tool for deciding the satisfiability of formulas in these theories. *Z3* is a new SMT solver freely available from Microsoft Research [8]. In this paper, we call *Z3* solver procedurally by using ANSI C API [9]. To construct logical formulas that could be verified by using *Z3*, we transform *TSP* and *TFP* to the unified format.

Each predicate p_{ij} ($i \in [1, n]$, $j \in [1, t]$) in a rule, is a matching condition for a packet header field, and it commonly allows four kinds of matchings: exact matching, prefix matching, range matching, and list matching. However, in this work, for the simplicity, each predicate p_{ij} in a rule is represented as a uniform range value, $[a_{ij}, b_{ij}]$. Predicates in other forms can be easily converted into one or multiple rules with range values. Time constraint is represented as a uniform

UTC time range value. A rule where each predicate and time constraint are represented as range values is called an **internal form rule**. An internal form rule, f_i ($i \in [1, n]$), is represented as follows:

$$f_i : [a_{i1}, b_{i1}], [a_{i2}, b_{i2}], \ldots\ldots [a_{it}, b_{it}], [t_{si}, t_{ei}), action_i.$$

The range values $[a_{ij}, b_{ij}]$ ($i \in [1, n]$, $j \in [1, t]$) represent commonly used header fields: protocol, SrcIP, SrcPort, DesIP and DesPort. $[t_{si}, t_{ei})$ represents the time constraint. Assume a packet P comes within the time t_{si} to t_{ei}, and the header values of P are (x_1, x_2, ..., x_t), if and only if $(a_{i1} \leq x_1 \leq b_{i1}) \wedge (a_{i2} \leq x_2 \leq b_{i2}) \wedge \ldots\ldots \wedge (a_{it} \leq x_t \leq b_{it})$, packet P matches the f_i, and the action of rule f_i is performed on the packet P.

3.2   Transformation of *TSP* and *TFP* to Internal Form Rules

To detect the inconsistencies of *TSP* and *TFP* by using *Z3* solver, we need to transform *TSP* and *TFP* rules into internal form rules. We divide the transformation procedures into two phases, the first phase is the transformation of rule's predicates, and the second phase is the transformation of time constraint.

In the first phase, for *TFP* rule's predicates transformation, the protocol is transformed to integer protocol number. IP addresses are changed to long integers. Port number could be transformed as integer range value. For example, when the protocol is "tcp", the range value in internal form rule is equal to $[6, 6]$. IP address 129.8.50.200 is transformed as long integer range value of $[2164798152, 2164798152]$. Transformation of *TSP* rules is the procedure that replace service name, port number and region name by using their corresponding values shown in Tables 1, 2, 3 and 4. For example, the service in *TSP* rule s_1 shown in Sect. 2.2 is "*FTPserver*", according to Tables 2 and 3, the source and destination port are "*" and "21" respectively. Therefore, the corresponding range values in internal form rule are equal to $[0, 65535]$ and $[21, 21]$.

In the second phase, we divided the transformation of time constraint into two steps. The first step is changing periodic or non-periodic time constraint into individual $yyyy/mm/dd$, $hh{:}mm$ format time range values. In the second step, we change the $yyyy/mm/dd$, $hh{:}mm$ format values into UTC format time range values.

For example, if the time constraint is non-periodic, such as $(T, D) = ([12{:}00{-}24{:}00), \{2017/07/31, 2017/12/31\})$, in the first phase, we represent (T, D) as ranges with $yyyy/mm/dd$, $hh{:}mm$ format shown in Fig. 3. In the second phase, the results in Fig. 3 are changed to UTC time ranges shown as in Fig. 4.

For another example, if the time constraint is periodic, such as, $(T, W, M) = ([08{:}00{-}12{:}00), \{Mon\}, \{2017/04, 2017/05\})$, which means that there exist 8 Mondays in April and May. Therefore, in the first phase, we split (T, W, M) into 8 $yyyy/mm/dd$, $hh{:}mm$ format ranges shown as in Fig. 5. In the second phase, we change 8 time ranges into UTC time ranges shown as in Fig. 6.

The internal form transformation of *TSP* and *TFP* rules are the composition of transformation results of predicates and time constraints. For example, rule f_2 shown in Fig. 1 is transformed into two internal form rules shown in Fig. 7.

2017/07/31, 12:00 → 2017/07/31, 24:00
2017/12/31, 12:00 → 2017/12/31, 24:00

Fig. 3. $yyyy/mm/dd$, $hh:mm$ format range

[1501470000, 1501513200)
[1514689200, 1514732400)

Fig. 4. UTC time ranges of Fig. 3

2017/04/03 08:00:00-->2017/04/03 12:00:00
2017/04/10 08:00:00-->2017/04/10 12:00:00
2017/04/17 08:00:00-->2017/04/17 12:00:00
2017/04/24 08:00:00-->2017/04/24 12:00:00
2017/05/01 08:00:00-->2017/05/01 12:00:00
2017/05/08 08:00:00-->2017/05/08 12:00:00
2017/05/15 08:00:00-->2017/05/15 12:00:00
2017/05/22 08:00:00-->2017/05/22 12:00:00

Fig. 5. Periodic time constraint split example

[1491174000, 1491188400)
[1491778800, 1491793200)
[1492383600, 1492398000)
[1492988400, 1493002800)
[1493593200, 1493607600)
[1494198000, 1494212400)
[1494802800, 1494817200)
[1495407600, 1495422000)

Fig. 6. UTC time ranges of Fig. 5

	Protocol	SrcIP	SrcPort	DesIP	DesPort	Time	Action
f_{21}	[6, 6]	[0, 4294967295]	[1023, 65535]	[2164798152, 2164798152]	[80, 80]	[1501470000, 1501513200)	*deny*
f_{22}	[6, 6]	[0, 4294967295]	[1023, 65535]	[2164798152, 2164798152]	[80, 80]	[1514689200, 1514732400)	*deny*

Fig. 7. Internal rules example

4   Inconsistency Detection of *TSP* and *TFP*

4.1   Inclusion Relations Between *TSP* and *TFP*

We define S to represent a set of rules and $\mathbf{P}(S)$ to represent the set of packets that match S. Despite the description forms of *TSP* and *TFP* are different, they both stipulate some conditions for filtering packets. Therefore, *TSP* and *TFP* could be viewed as sets of packets that satisfy some conditions. We use $\mathbf{P}(TSP)$ to represent the set of packets that matches *TSP*, and use $\mathbf{P}(TFP)$ to represent the set of packets that matches *TFP*. We also define $\mathbf{R}(TSP, TFP)$ to represent inclusion relations between P(*TSP*) and P(*TFP*). According to set theory, R(*TSP*, *TFP*) could be classified into five kinds shown as in formula (1).

$$R(TSP, TFP) = \begin{cases} Equal & \text{when } P(TSP) = P(TFP) \\ Inside & \text{when } P(TSP) \subseteq P(TFP) \\ Cover & \text{when } P(TSP) \supseteq P(TFP) \\ Disjoint & \text{when } P(TSP) \cap P(TFP) = \varnothing \\ Overlap & \text{Otherwise} \end{cases} \quad (1)$$

4.2   Consistency Decision of *TSP* and *TFP*

According to the set theory, two sets A and B are equal if and only if they have the same elements, which could be represented as in formula (2). Suppose *TSP* consists of m rules $\{s_1, s_2, ..., s_m\}$ and *TFP* consists of n rules $\{f_1, f_2, ..., f_n\}$. To verify the consistency of *TSP* and *TFP*, we constructed P_1 and P_2 shown as in formulas (3)(4). We can use *"not"* operator to unify the actions of rules, for the simplicity, we suppose the actions of *TSP* or *TFP* rules are all *accept*.

$$A = B \quad \text{if and only if} \quad A \subseteq B \quad \text{and} \quad B \subseteq A \tag{2}$$

$$P_1 = (\neg s_1) \wedge (\neg s_2) \wedge ... \wedge (\neg s_m) \wedge (f_1 \vee f_2 \vee ... \vee f_n) \tag{3}$$

$$P_2 = (\neg f_1) \wedge (\neg f_2) \wedge ... \wedge (\neg f_n) \wedge (s_1 \vee s_2 \vee ... \vee s_m) \tag{4}$$

The formula P_1 wants to check whether the set of packets denied by *TSP* rules have intersection with the set of packets accepted by the *TFP* rules. Similarly, the formula P_2 wants to check whether the set of packets denied by *TFP* rules have intersection with the set of packets accepted by the *TSP* rules.

Then we use SMT solver *Z3* to verify P_1 and P_2. If the *Z3*'s output of P_1 is *UNSATISFIABLE*, which means that the set of packets denied by *TSP* have no intersection with the packets accepted by *TFP*. So, conversely, we can think that the set of packets accepted by *TSP* includes or equals to the set of packets accepted by *TFP*, that is, P(*TSP*)⊇P(*TFP*). Similarly, if *Z3*'s output of P_2 is *UNSATISFIABLE*, which means P(*TFP*)⊇P(*TSP*), or P(*TSP*)⊆P(*TFP*). According to the formula (2), when *Z3*'s outputs of P_1 and P_2 are both *UNSAT-ISFIABLE*, we can decided that P(*TFP*) = P(*TSP*).

4.3   Classification of Inconsistency of TSP and TFP

Other than R(*TSP*, *TFP*) is *Equal*, we say that there exist **inconsistencies** of *TSP* and *TFP*. We considered that *TSP* is an abstract demands outline for firewall design, once *TSP* is constructed, it does not change frequently. For this reason, we take the *TSP* as the standard, the inconsistencies are viewed as the differences of *TFP* compared with *TSP*. To resolve the inconsistencies, we should add rules in *TFP* or delete rules from *TFP*, and let *TFP* to be the same as *TSP*. We also suppose that there have no anomalies in individual *TSP* or *TFP*. We classify the inconsistencies of *TFP* and *TSP* as the following three kinds.

1. **Redundancy**: If we take the *TSP* as the standard, *TFP* have redundant rules that should be deleted.
2. **Insufficiency**: If we take the *TSP* as the standard, there exist some rules that should be added in *TFP*.
3. **Warning**: If we take the *TSP* as the standard, *TFP* have some special rules, which are not completely redundant rules. Especially if we delete them from *TFP*, which may affect the original intentions of *TSP*. To resolve this kind of inconsistency, we detect and show them to the administrator. For example, if *TFP* and *TSP* only consist one rule f and s respectively, and they are transformed into internal form rules shown as in Fig. 8, rule f is a warning rule to s.

	Protocol	SrcIP	SrcPort	DesIP	DesPort	Time	Action
f	[6, 6]	[0, 4294967295]	[0, 65535]	[0, 4294967295]	[137, 139]	[1501470000, 1501513200]	*accept*
s	[6, 6]	[2164798152, 2164798152]	[0, 65535]	[0, 4294967295]	[0, 65535]	[1514689200, 1514732400]	*accept*

Fig. 8. Warning rule example

4.4 Inconsistency Decision Analysis

We think that *TSP* and *TFP* have inconsistencies when R(*TSP*, *TFP*) are *Cover*, *Inside*, *Overlap*, and *Disjoint* relations. We explain how to detect the corresponding inconsistency of each inclusion relation as follows.

When R(*TSP*, *TFP*) is *Cover*, that is, P(*TSP*)⊇P(*TFP*), which means that *TFP* has insufficient rules compared with *TSP*. We should check each *TSP* rule $s_i (i \in [1, m])$ to decide whether it should be added in *TFP*. To make further detection, we define $\mathbf{P}(s_i)$ to represent the set of packets that matches rule s_i, we also define $\mathbf{R}(s_i, \mathbf{TFP})$ to represent the inclusion relations between P(s_i) and P(*TFP*). Similar as formula (1), R(s_i, *TFP*) also have five inclusion relations shown in formula (5), the corresponding inconsistency of each relation and resolving method are summarized as in Table 5.

$$R(s_i, TFP) = \begin{cases} Equal & \text{when } P(s_i) = P(TFP) \\ Inside & \text{when } P(s_i) \subseteq P(TFP) \\ Cover & \text{when } P(s_i) \supseteq P(TFP) \\ Disjoint & \text{when } P(s_i) \cap P(TFP) = \varnothing \\ Overlap & \text{Otherwise} \end{cases} \tag{5}$$

Table 5. Insufficiency analysis

R(s_i, *TFP*)	Inconsistency	Resolving inconsistency
Disjoint	Insufficiency	Add s_i in *TFP*
Inside	No inconsistency	—
Cover	Insufficiency	Add s_i in *TFP*
Overlap	Insufficiency	Add s_i in *TFP*
Equal	No inconsistency	—

When R(*TSP*, *TFP*) is *Inside*, that is, P(*TSP*)⊆P(*TFP*), which means that there exist warning or redundant rules in *TFP*. We should check each *TFP* rule $f_i (i \in [1, n])$ and decide whether it is a redundant or warning rule. To make further detection, we define $\mathbf{P}(f_i)$ to represent the set of packets that matches rule f_i, we also define $\mathbf{R}(f_i, \mathbf{TSP})$ to represent the inclusion relations between P(f_i) and P(*TSP*). R(f_i, *TSP*) also have five inclusion relations shown as in formula (6), the corresponding inconsistency of each relation and resolving method are summarized as in Table 6.

$$R(f_i, TSP) = \begin{cases} Equal & \text{when } P(f_i) = P(TSP) \\ Inside & \text{when } P(f_i) \subseteq P(TSP) \\ Cover & \text{when } P(f_i) \supseteq P(TSP) \\ Disjoint & \text{when } P(f_i) \cap P(TSP) = \varnothing \\ Overlap & \text{Otherwise} \end{cases} \qquad (6)$$

Table 6. Redundancy or warning analysis

R(f_i, TSP)	Inconsistency	Resolving inconsistency
Disjoint	Redundancy	Delete f_i from TFP
Inside	No inconsistency	—
Cover	Warning	Show f_i to administrator
Overlap	Warning	Show f_i to administrator
Equal	No inconsistency	—

When R(TSP, TFP) are Overlap and Disjoint relations, the inconsistency detection could be divided into insufficiency analysis and redundancy or warning analysis, that is, we can firstly check whether exist insufficient rules, and then check whether exist redundant or warning rules.

4.5   Algorithms for Inconsistency Decision

From the above analysis, if we know R(s_i, TFP) and R(f_i, TSP), we can decide which rules caused the inconsistencies. The following pseudo-code algorithm describes the whole procedures of inconsistency detection. According to Sect. 4.2, we firstly constructed formulas P_1 and P_2, then used Z3 to verify whether they are SATISFIABLE(SAT) or UNSATISFIABLE(UNSAT). If Z3's output of P_1 and P_2 are both UNSAT, which means that TSP is equal to TFP and then exit. If only Z3's output of P_1 is UNSAT, which means that TSP $\supseteq$ TFP. In line 11, we call Insufficiency function to detect insufficient rules. If only Z3's output of P_2 is UNSAT, which means that TSP $\subseteq$ TFP. In line 13, we call Redundancy_Warning function to detect redundant or warning rules. Otherwise, we call Insufficiency function and Redundancy_Warning function in turn.

```
1: Input: TSP, TFP     Output: NewTFP
2: Algorithm RuleSet Inconsistency_Detection(TSP, TFP)
3: { RuleSet NewTFP, TFP_Temp;
4:    NewTFP=TFP; TFP_Temp=TFP;
```

```
 5:     Construct  P₁=(¬s₁)∧(¬s₂)∧...∧(¬sₘ)∧(f₁ ∨ f₂ ∨ ... ∨ fₙ),
 6:                P₂=(¬f₁)∧(¬f₂)∧...∧(¬fₙ)∧(s₁ ∨ s₂ ∨ ... ∨ sₘ),
 7:     Use Z3 to verify P₁ and P₂;
 8:     if((Z3(P₁)==UNSAT)&&((Z3(P₂)==UNSAT))
 9:        TSP=TFP, then exit;
10:     else if(Z3(P₁)==UNSAT)
11:          NewTFP=Insufficiency(TSP, TFP);
12:     else if(Z3(P₂)==UNSAT)
13:          NewTFP=Redundancy_Warning(TSP, TFP);
14:     else
15:     {   TFP_Temp=Insufficiency(TSP, TFP);
16:          NewTFP=Redundancy_Warning(TSP, TFP_Temp); }
17:     Return NewTFP;
18: }
19: End of Algorithm
```

The following pseudo-code is *Insufficiency* detection algorithm, we firstly constructed T_1 shown as in formula (7), then used *Z3* to verify it. If *Z3*'s output of T_1 is *UNSAT*, which means that P(s_i) and P(*TFP*) have no intersections, R(s_i, *TFP*) is *disjoint*. According to Table 5, s_i is an insufficient rule to *TFP*, it should be added in *TFP*. If *Z3*'s output of T_1 is *SAT*, which means that s_i and *TFP* have intersections, that is, R(s_i, *TFP*) is one of the *Overlap, Inside, Cover* or *Equal* relations. To implement further detection, we constructed T_2 and T_3 shown as in formulas (8)(9), then we used *Z3* to verify them. R(s_i, *TFP*) can be decided by *Z3*'s outputs of $T_1 \sim T_3$, which are summarized in Table 7. Then, we can deal with rule s_i according to Table 5.

```
 1: Input: TSP, TFP     Output: NewTFP
 2: Algorithm RuleSet Insufficiency(TSP, TFP)
 3: { RuleSet NewTFP;
 4:    NewTFP=TFP;
 5:    for each sᵢ in TSP do
 6:    { Construct T₁=(sᵢ)∧(f₁ ∨ f₂ ∨ ... ∨ fₙ),
 7:                T₂=(¬sᵢ)∧(f₁ ∨ f₂ ∨ ... ∨ fₙ),
 8:                T₃=(¬f₁)∧(¬f₂)∧...∧(¬fₙ)∧(sᵢ);
 9:       if(Z₃(T₁)==UNSAT)
10:            Add sᵢ in NewTFP;
11:       if(Z₃(T₁)==SAT)
12:       { if( (Z₃(T₂)==UNSAT)&&(Z₃(T₃)==UNSAT) )
13:            Continue;
14:         else if(Z₃(T₂)==UNSAT)
15:            Add sᵢ into NewTFP;
16:         else if(Z₃(T₃)==UNSAT)
17:            Continue;
18:         else
19:            Add sᵢ into NewTFP;
```

```
20:      }
21:  }
22:    Return NewTFP;
23: }
24: End of Insufficiency Algorithm
```

$$T_1 = (s_i) \wedge (f_1 \vee f_2 \vee ... \vee f_n) \tag{7}$$

$$T_2 = (\neg s_i) \wedge (f_1 \vee f_2 \vee ... \vee f_n) \tag{8}$$

$$T_3 = (\neg f_1) \wedge (\neg f_2) \wedge ... \wedge (\neg f_n) \wedge (s_i) \tag{9}$$

Table 7. $Z3$'s outputs of $T_1 \sim T_3$ and $\mathrm{R}(s_i, TFP)$

T_1	T_2	T_3	$\mathrm{R}(s_i, TFP)$
UNSAT	SAT	SAT	*Disjoint* when $\mathrm{P}(s_i) \cap \mathrm{P}(TFP) = \varnothing$
SAT	UNSAT	SAT	*Cover* when $\mathrm{P}(s_i) \supseteq \mathrm{P}(TFP)$
SAT	SAT	UNSAT	*Inside* when $\mathrm{P}(s_i) \subseteq \mathrm{P}(TFP)$
SAT	UNSAT	UNSAT	*Equal* when $\mathrm{P}(s_i) = \mathrm{P}(TFP)$
SAT	SAT	SAT	*Overlap* when $\mathrm{P}(s_i) \cap \mathrm{P}(TFP) \neq \varnothing$

Similarly, in *Redundancy_Warning* algorithm, we firstly constructed T_4 shown as in formula (10) to verify whether $\mathrm{R}(f_i, TSP)$ is *disjoint*. If $Z3$'s output of T_4 is *UNSAT*, which means that $\mathrm{R}(f_i, TSP)$ is *disjoint*. According to Table 6, f_i is a redundant rule to TSP, it should be deleted from TFP. If $Z3$'s output of T_4 is *SAT*, we constructed T_5 and T_6 shown as in formulas (11)(12) to implement further detection. Then, we used $Z3$ to verify them. $\mathrm{R}(f_i, TSP)$ can be decided by $Z3$'s outputs of $T_4 \sim T_6$, which are summarized as in Table 8. Then, we can deal with each f_i according to Table 6.

```
1: Input: TSP, TFP     Output: NewTFP
2: Algorithm RuleSet Redundancy_Warning(TSP, TFP)
3: { RuleSet NewTFP;
4:    NewTFP=TFP;
5:    for each f_i in TFP do
6:    {Construct T_4=(f_i)∧(s_1 ∨ s_2 ∨ ... ∨ s_m),
7:               T_5=(¬f_i)∧(s_1 ∨ s_2 ∨ ... ∨ s_m),
8:               T_6=(¬s_1)∧(¬s_2)∧ ... ∧(¬s_m)∧(f_i);
9:       if (Z3(T_4)==UNSAT)
10:           Delete f_i from NewTFP;
11:       if (Z3(T_4)==SAT)
12:       { if ((Z3(T_5)==UNSAT)&&(Z3(T_6)==UNSAT))
13:             Continue;
14:         else if(Z3(T_5)==UNSAT)
```

```
15:              Show fi to Administrator;
16:         else if(Z3(T6)==UNSAT)
17:            Continue;
18:         else
19:            Show fi to Administrator;
20:      }
21:    }
22:    Return NewTFP;
23: }
24: End of Redundancy_Warning Algorithm
```

$$T_4 = (f_i) \wedge (s_1 \vee s_2 \vee ... \vee s_m) \tag{10}$$

$$T_5 = (\neg f_i) \wedge (s_1 \vee s_2 \vee ... \vee s_m) \tag{11}$$

$$T_6 = (\neg s_1) \wedge (\neg s_2) \wedge ... \wedge (\neg s_m) \wedge (f_i) \tag{12}$$

Table 8. $Z3$'s outputs of $T_4 \sim T_6$ and $R(f_i, TSP)$

T_4	T_5	T_6	$R(f_i, TSP)$
UNSAT	SAT	SAT	*Disjoint* when $P(f_i) \cap P(TSP) = \varnothing$
SAT	UNSAT	SAT	*Cover* when $P(f_i) \supseteq P(TSP)$
SAT	SAT	UNSAT	*Inside* when $P(f_i) \subseteq P(TSP)$
SAT	UNSAT	UNSAT	*Equal* when $P(f_i) = P(TSP)$
SAT	SAT	SAT	*Overlap* when $P(f_i) \cap P(TSP) \neq \varnothing$

5 Implementation and Experiments

5.1 Prototype System

We have implemented a prototype system. Figure 9 shows the architecture of the prototype system. The inputs are: abstract *TSP* rules, network topology information, and *TFP* rules. According to network topology, *TSP* rules are represented as the same internal form with *TFP* rules. Then the prototype system constructs formulas P_1 and P_2 and uses $Z3$ to verify them. According to $Z3$'s results of P_1 and P_2, insufficiency detection and redundancy or warning detection functions are used to detect and deal with inconsistencies. The dashed line rectangle in Fig. 9 is our proposed inconsistency detection procedures.

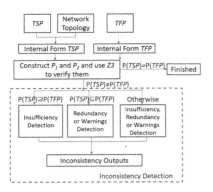

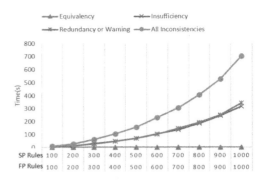

Fig. 9. Architecture of prototype system

Fig. 10. Experimental results

5.2 Experiments and Considerations

The prototype system implemented in C language. Experiments were performed using a computer equipped with an Intel Core i5 (3.2 GHz) and 8 GB RAM. To evaluate the feasibility of our proposed method, we manually designed *TSP* and *TFP* rules ranged from $100 \sim 1000$ respectively, then we did the following four experiments. The experimental results are shown in Fig. 10.

1. Measure the execution time for verifying whether *TSP* is equal to *TFP*.
2. Measure the execution time for only detecting insufficiency of *TFP*.
3. Measure the execution time for only detecting redundancy or warning of *TFP*.
4. Measure the execution time for detecting insufficiency, redundancy or warning of *TFP*.

The execution time of each experiment includes: the time of making formulas of P_1, P_2, and $T_1 \sim T_6$ in each loop; the time of using *Z3* to verify P_1, P_2, and $T_1 \sim T_6$ in each loop; the time of inconsistency detection and resolving. The results in Fig. 10 show that when *TSP* and *TFP* have 1000 rules respectively, in the worst case, that is, when R(*TSP, TFP*) are *Disjoint* and *Overlap* relations, it took about 700 s to detect and resolve all inconsistencies. When we only detect and resolve insufficiencies, or when we only detect and resolve redundancies or warnings, the prototype system took similar times, it took about 320 and 350 s respectively. If we only verify whether *TSP* and *TFP* are consistent, it took about 0.35 second. In average, the prototype system needs about 0.35 s to check whether each rule should be added in *TFP* or deleted from *TFP*.

6 Related Works

The anomalies classification and discovery of *FP* have gained a lot of attention. Wool [10] recently inspected *FP*s collected from different organizations and indicated that all examined *FP*s have security flaws. Al-Shaer and Hamed [11] reported comprehensive and in-depth study of automated *FP* analysis for designing, configuring and managing distributed firewalls. It also provided methodologies, techniques, tools and case studies. Work [12] proposed a novel anomaly management framework that facilitates systematic detection and resolution of *FP* anomalies. A rule-based segmentation mechanism and a grid-based representation technique were introduced to achieve the goal of effective and efficient anomaly analysis. This work also provided an effective redundancy elimination mechanism. Research [13] presented a *FP* checking model, then used SAT solver to analyze reachability of policy definition. It also did some experiments and compared the proposed model with BDD-based configuration analysis approaches. The aims of the above works were anomalies detection methods only in *FP*, but not the goal of inconsistency detection of *SP* and *FP*, not to mention inconsistency detection of *TSP* and *TFP*.

Some similar works use formal representation to model *FP* and *SP* [14–16]. Work [14] presented a Firewall Policy Query Engine (FPQE) that renders the whole process of anomaly resolution in a fully automated one, and no need to any human intervention. FPQE used *MiniSat* solver to check whether *FP* rules are correct and complete with respect to a *SP*. Work [15] defined Boolean formula representation of *SP* and *FP*, and formulated the condition that ensures correctness of firewall configuration. Then, it also used *MiniSat* solver to check the validity of the condition. If the configuration is not correct, this work produced an example of packet to help users to correct the configuration. Work [16] proposed a formal method and used SMT solver *Yices* [17] to certify automatically that a *FP* is sound and complete with *SP*. The above works only considered how to verify *FP* with *SP* by using formal methods, but these methods could not be used to detect inconsistencies of *TSP* and *TFP*.

Work [18] provided the methods automatically perform comparisons algebraically of two *FP*s. It used algebraic structure to determine the semantics required of a policy language, and to make comparisons rule-order and firewall implementation independent. It also provided a formalism to compute the composition of rule sets. However, this work only took two *FP*s comparison as a goal. Because *SP* and *FP* have different descriptions, the proposed method could not be directly used to detect inconsistency of *TSP* and *TFP*. In works [19,20], the authors address the problem of automatic verification by providing automatic translation tool of the *SP* and *FP*. These methods can handle the whole problem of conformance of *FP* to *SP*, but the validity of the compilation itself has not been proved. In particular, the *FP* rules obtained may be in conflict. In addition, these works also did not consider the time constraint of *SP* and *FP*.

7   Conclusion and Future Work

In this paper, we have proposed a method to detect the inconsistency of *TSP* and *TFP*. We firstly construct consistency decision model and use SMT solver *Z3* to verify whether *TSP* and *TFP* are consistent. If *TSP* and *TFP* are not consistent, to implement the inconsistency detection, we constructed some logical formulas and used *Z3* to verify them and analyze inconsistency. We also implemented a prototype system and did some experiments to show the effectiveness of our proposed method. Our future work includes optimization of our proposed method and results visualization.

Acknowledgments. This research was partially supported by National scholarship for studying abroad of China Scholarship Council (CSC); National Natural Science Foundation of China (No. 60973122, 61572256).

References

1. Cisco PIX Firewall Release Notes. https://www.cisco.com/en/US/docs/security/pix/pix63/release/notes/pixrn634.html
2. Linux man page. http://linux.die.net/man/8/iptables
3. Yin, Y., Xu, X., Katayama, Y., Takahashi, N.: Inconsistency detection system for security policy and rewall policy. In: 2010 First International Conference on Networking and Computing, pp. 294–297. IEEE (2011)
4. Yin, Y., Xu, J., Takahashi, N.: Verifying consistency between security policy and firewall policy by using a constraint satisfaction problem server. In: Zhang, Y. (ed.) Future Wireless Networks and Information Systems. LNEE, vol. 144, pp. 135–145. Springer, Heidelberg (2012). doi:10.1007/978-3-642-27326-1_18
5. Sugar: a SAT-based Constraint Solver. http://bach.istc.kobe-u.ac.jp/sugar/
6. Thanasegaran, S., Tateiwa, Y., Katayama, Y., Takahashi, N.: Design and implementation of conflict detection system for time-based firewall policies. J. Next Gener. Inf. Technol. **2**(4), 24–39 (2011)
7. Z3 Theorem Prover. https://github.com/Z3Prover/z3/wiki
8. Moura, L.D., Bjørner, N.: Z3: an efficient SMT solver. In: Proceedings of the Theory and practice of software, 14th International Conference on Tools and Algorithms for the Construction and Analysis of Systems, pp. 337–340 (2008)
9. Z3 C API. https://z3prover.github.io/api/html/group__capi.html
10. Wool, A.: Trends in firewall configuration errors: measuring the holes in swiss cheese. IEEE Internet Comput. **14**(4), 58–65 (2010)
11. Al-Shaer, E.: Automated Firewall Analytics Design, Configuration and Optimization. Springer, Heidelberg (2014)
12. Hu, H., Ahn, G., Kulkarni, K.: Detecting and resolving firewall policy anomalies. IEEE Trans. Secure Comput. **9**(3), 318–331 (2012)
13. Jeffrey, A., Samak, T.: Model checking firewall policy configurations. In: IEEE International Symposium on Policies for Distributed Systems and Networks, pp. 60–67 (2009)
14. Bouhoula, A., Yazidi, A.: A security policy query engine for fully automated resolution of anomalies in firewall configurations. In: IEEE 15th International Symposium on Network Computing and Applications, pp. 76–80 (2016)
15. Matsumoto, S., Bouhoula, A.: Automatic verification of firewall configuration with respect to security policy requirements. In: Proceedings of the International Workshop on Computational Intelligence in Security for Information Systems, pp. 123–130 (2008)
16. Youssef, N.B., Bouhoula, A., Jacquemard, F.: Automatic verification of conformance of firewall configurations to security policies. In: IEEE Symposium on Computers and Communications, pp. 526–531 (2009)

17. Dutertre, B., Moura, L.D.: The YICES SMT solver. http://gauss.ececs.uc.edu/Courses/c626/lectures/SMT/tool-paper.pdf
18. Ranathunga, D., Roughan, M., Kernick, P., Falkner, N.: Malachite: firewall policy comparison. In: IEEE Symposium on Computers and Communication, pp. 310–317 (2016)
19. Cupens, F., Cuppens-Boulahia, N., Sans, T., Miege, A.: A formal approach to specify and deploy a network security policy. In: Second Workshop on Formal Aspects in Security and Trust, pp. 203–218 (2004)
20. Bartal, Y., Mayer, A.J., Nissim, K., Wool, A.: Firmato: a novel firewall management toolkit. ACM Trans. Comput. Syst. **22**(4), 381–420 (2004)

An Algebraic Approach to Automatic Reasoning for NetKAT Based on Its Operational Semantics

Yuxin Deng, Min Zhang$^{(\boxtimes)}$, and Guoqing Lei$^{(\boxtimes)}$

Shanghai Key Laboratory of Trustworthy Computing,
MOE International Joint Lab of Trustworthy Software,
and International Research Center of Trustworthy Software,
East China Normal University, Shanghai, China
zhangmin@sei.ecnu.edu.cn, 51151500022@ecnu.cn

Abstract. NetKAT is a network programming language with a solid mathematical foundation. In this paper, we present an operational semantics and show that it is sound and complete with respect to its original axiomatic semantics. We achieve automatic reasoning for NetKAT such as reachability analysis and model checking of temporal properties, by formalizing the operational semantics in an algebraic executable specification language called Maude. In addition, as NetKAT policies are normalizable, two policies are operationally equivalent if and only if they can be converted into the same normal form. We provide a formal way of reasoning about network properties by turning the equivalence checking problem of NetKAT policies into the normalization problem that can be automated in Maude.

Keywords: NetKAT · Operational semantics · Model checking · LTL · Maude

1 Introduction

In recent years, there has been exciting development in the area of *software-defined networking* (SDN), where physically distributed switches are programmable and managed in a logically centralized way so as to effectively implement many applications such as traffic monitoring, access control, and intrusion detection. Several domain-specific languages for SDN have been proposed, e.g. [3,6,9,11,14,15], in order to have a high-level abstraction of network programs where it is more effective to specify, program and reason about the behaviour of networks. Among them, NetKAT [3] is a network programming language based on Kleene algebra with tests (KAT) [10]. The design of NetKAT was influenced by NetCore [10] and Pyretic [12], both of which originate from Frenetic [6]. Different from other languages, NetKAT has a solid mathematical foundation

---

Partially supported by the National Natural Science Foundation of China (Grant No. 61672229, 61261130589, 61502171), Shanghai Municipal Natural Science Foundation (16ZR1409100), and ANR 12IS02001 PACE.

Z. Duan and L. Ong (Eds.): ICFEM 2017, LNCS 10610, pp. 464–480, 2017.
https://doi.org/10.1007/978-3-319-68690-5_28

with a denotational semantics and an axiomatic semantics based on KAT. It has also been extended to the probabilistic setting [7].

In this paper we present an operational semantics for NetKAT. The basic idea is to view the (global) state of a network as the set of all packets currently available in the network. Transitions between states are enabled by the execution of policies: the behaviour of a policy is to transform a given packet into a (possibly empty) set of packets, which leads to the change of state for the whole network. The operational semantics induces a natural equivalence on policies. Intuitively, two policies p and q are equivalent, if starting from any state Π, both policies can change Π into the same state Π'. We show that two policies are operationally equivalent if and only if they are provably equal according to the equational theory defined in [3]. In other words, our operational semantics is sound and complete with respect to the original axiomatic semantics of NetKAT.

In order to facilitate the reasoning about NetKAT programs, we formalize the operational semantics and the normalization theory of NetKAT in an algebraic formal reasoning system Maude [5]. The operational semantics is executable in Maude so we can search if a desired state is reachable from a starting state. The normalization theory of NetKAT tells us that all policies are normalizable, and two policies are operationally equivalent if and only if they can be converted into the same normal form. This gives rise to a formal way of reasoning about network properties by turning the equivalence checking problem of NetKAT policies into the normalization problem. More specifically, to check if two policies are equivalent, we first normalize them and check if their normal forms are the same. Both steps can be automated in Maude. For instance, in order to check the reachability from one switch to another in a network, we first define a high-level specification that is independent of the underlying network topology and a low-level implementation that describes a hop-by-hop routing from the source to the destination. Both the specification and the implementation are written as NetKAT policies. We then exploit our rewriting-based reasoning to check the (in)equivalence of the two policies. If Maude produces a positive answer, meaning that the two policies are equivalent, we know that the implementation conforms to the specification, thus the destination switch is indeed reachable from the source switch. Equivalence checking of policies are also useful for other applications such as proving compilation correctness and non-interference property of programs [3]. In addition, we combine the formalized operational semantics with Maude LTL model checker to verify temporal properties of packets traveling in a network. This differs from [4], which enriches the original NetKAT language with temporal predicates to specify properties of a packet's history. The current work considers a lightweight NetKAT that does not record any packet history, but we still achieve automatic reasoning about packet histories by using Maude.

The rest of this paper is structured as follows. In Sect. 2 we recall the syntax and the axiomatic semantics of NetKAT as given in [3]. In Sect. 3 we present an operational semantics and show that it is sound and complete with respect to its axiomatic semantics. In Sect. 4 we formalize the operational and axiomatic semantics of NetKAT in Maude. In Sect. 5 we use Maude to do reachability analysis, model checking of LTL properties, and equivalence checking of policies. In Sect. 6 we discuss our experiments. Finally, we conclude in Sect. 7.

2   NetKAT

We briefly review the syntax and the axiomatic semantics of NetKAT; see [3] for a more detailed exposition.

NetKAT is based on Kleene algebra with tests (KAT) [10], an algebra for reasoning about partial correctness of programs. KAT is Kleene algebra (KA), the algebra of regular expressions, augmented with Boolean tests. Formally, a KAT is a two-sorted structure $(K, B, +, \cdot, *, \neg, 0, 1)$ such that

- $(K, +, \cdot, *, 0, 1)$ is a Kleene algebra
- $(B, +, \cdot, \neg, 0, 1)$ is a Boolean algebra
- $(B, +, \cdot, 0, 1)$ is a subalgebra of $(K, +, \cdot, 0, 1)$.

Elements of B and K are called *tests* and *actions* respectively; they are called predicates and policies in NetKAT.

A packet π is a record with fields $f_1, ..., f_k$ mapping to fixed-width integers $n_1, ..., n_k$, respectively. We assume that every packet contains the same fields, including two special fields for the switch (sw) and the port (pt) that identify the position of a packet in a global network. We write $\pi.f$ for the value in field f of π, and $\pi[n/f]$ for the packet obtained by updating field f of π by value n.

Table 1. Syntax of NetKAT

Fields	$f ::= f_1 \mid \cdots \mid f_k$			
Packets	$\pi ::= \{f_1 = n_1, \cdots, f_k = n_k\}$			
Predicates $a, b, c ::=$	1	*Identity*	Policies	
	0	*Drop*	$p, q, r ::= a$	*Filter*
	$f = n$	*Match*	$\mid f \leftarrow n$	*Modification*
	$a + b$	*Disjunction*	$\mid p + q$	*Parallel composition*
	$a \cdot b$	*Conjunction*	$\mid p \cdot q$	*Sequential composition*
	$\neg a$	*Negation*	$\mid p^*$	*Kleene star*

The syntax of NetKAT is given in Table 1. There are two categories of expressions: predicates (a, b, c) and policies (p, q, r). Predicates include true (1) and false (0), matches $(f = n)$, negation $(\neg a)$, disjunction $(a + b)$, and conjunction $(a \cdot b)$ operators. Policies include predicates, modifications $(f \leftarrow n)$, parallel $(p + q)$ and sequential $(p \cdot q)$ composition, and iteration (p^*). By convention, $(*)$ binds tighter than $(\cdot)$, which binds tighter than $(+)$. The only and key difference from the original NetKAT presented in [3] is the absence of the dup operator. This operator is hardly used in practical network programming and is introduced mainly to facilitate the completeness proof of an axiomatic semantics with respect to a denotational semantics [3]. For easy formalization and reasoning in Maude, it seems more reasonable to drop this operator than to keep it.

The axiomatic semantics of NetKAT is displayed in Table 2, where $p \leq q$ is an abbreviation for $p + q \equiv q$. We write $\vdash p \equiv q$ if the equality $p \equiv q$ is derivable by using the axioms in Table 2. A denotational semantics based on packet histories is shown to be sound and complete with respect to the axiomatic semantics in [3].

Table 2. Axioms of NetKAT

Kleene Algebra Axioms

$p + (q + r) \equiv (p + q) + r$	KA-Plus-Assoc	$(p + q) \cdot r \equiv p \cdot r + q \cdot r$	KA-Seq-Dist-R
$p + q \equiv q + p$	KA-Plus-Comm	$0 \cdot p \equiv 0$	KA-Zero-Seq
$p + 0 \equiv p$	KA-Plus-Zero	$p \cdot 0 \equiv 0$	KA-Seq-Zero
$p + p \equiv p$	KA-Plus-Idem	$1 + p \cdot p^* \equiv p^*$	KA-Unroll-L
$p \cdot (q \cdot r) \equiv (p \cdot q) \cdot r$	KA-Seq-Assoc	$q + p \cdot r \leq r \Rightarrow p^* \cdot q \leq r$	KA-Lfp-L
$1 \cdot p \equiv p$	KA-One-Seq	$1 + p^* \cdot p \equiv p^*$	KA-Unroll-R
$p \cdot 1 \equiv p$	KA-Seq-One	$q + r \cdot p \leq r \Rightarrow q \cdot p^* \leq r$	KA-Lfp-R
$p \cdot (q + r) \equiv p \cdot q + p \cdot r$	KA-Seq-Dist-L		

Additional Boolean Algebra Axioms

$a + (b \cdot c) \equiv (a + b) \cdot (a + c)$	BA-Plus-Dist	$a \cdot b \equiv b \cdot a$	BA-Seq-Comm
$a + 1 \equiv 1$	BA-Plus-One	$a \cdot \neg a \equiv 0$	BA-Contra
$a + \neg a \equiv 1$	BA-Excl-Mid	$a \cdot a \equiv a$	BA-Seq-Idem

Packet Algebra Axioms

$f \leftarrow n \cdot f' \leftarrow n' \equiv f' \leftarrow n' \cdot f \leftarrow n$, if $f \neq f'$	PA-Mod-Mod-Comm
$f \leftarrow n \cdot f' = n' \equiv f' = n' \cdot f \leftarrow n$, if $f \neq f'$	PA-Mod-Filter-Comm
$f \leftarrow n \cdot f = n \equiv f \leftarrow n$	PA-Mod-Filter
$f = n \cdot f \leftarrow n \equiv f = n$	PA-Filter-Mod
$f \leftarrow n \cdot f \leftarrow n' \equiv f \leftarrow n'$	PA-Mod-Mod
$f = n \cdot f = n' \equiv 0$, if $n \neq n'$	PA-Contra
$\sum_i f = i \equiv 1$	PA-Match-All

3   Operational Semantics

Below we give an operational semantics for NetKAT. We assume a global network that consists of a finite number of switches. Each switch has a finite number of ports. A *state* of the network is the set of all packets in the network. We denote by **S** the set of all possible states in the network, ranged over by Π.

Intuitively, the behaviour of a policy is to transform a given packet into a (possibly empty) set of packets. This can be described by an evaluation relation of the form $\langle p, \pi \rangle \rightarrow \Pi$, where p is a policy, π is a packet to be processed and Π is the set of packets obtained by applying p to π, as defined in Table 3. The evaluation relation can be lifted to the form $\langle p, \Pi \rangle \rightarrow \Pi'$, where both Π and Π' are sets of packets, according to the last rule in Table 3.

Table 3. Operational semantics of NetKAT

$$\frac{}{\langle 1, \pi \rangle \rightarrow \{\pi\}} \text{[Identity]} \qquad \frac{}{\langle 0, \pi \rangle \rightarrow \emptyset} \text{[Drop]} \qquad \frac{}{\langle f \leftarrow n, \pi \rangle \rightarrow \{\pi[n/f]\}} \text{[Modification]}$$

$$\frac{\pi.f = n}{\langle f = n, \pi \rangle \rightarrow \{\pi\}} \text{[Match-I]} \qquad \frac{\pi.f \neq n}{\langle f = n, \pi \rangle \rightarrow \emptyset} \text{[Match-II]} \qquad \frac{\langle a, \pi \rangle \rightarrow \Pi}{\langle \neg a, \pi \rangle \rightarrow \{\pi\} \setminus \Pi} \text{[Negation]}$$

$$\frac{\langle p, \pi \rangle \rightarrow \Pi_p \quad \langle q, \pi \rangle \rightarrow \Pi_q}{\langle p + q, \pi \rangle \rightarrow \Pi_p \cup \Pi_q} \text{[Parallel composition]} \qquad \frac{\forall i \in I : \langle p, \pi_i \rangle \rightarrow \Pi_i}{\langle p, \{\pi_i\}_{i \in I} \rangle \rightarrow \cup_{i \in I} \Pi_i} \text{[Packet set]}$$

$$\frac{\langle p, \pi \rangle \rightarrow \{\pi_i \mid i \in I\} \quad \forall i \in I : \langle q, \pi_i \rangle \rightarrow \Pi_i}{\langle p \cdot q, \pi \rangle \rightarrow \cup_{i \in I} \Pi_i} \text{[Sequential composition]}$$

$$\frac{\langle p^0, \pi \rangle \rightarrow \Pi_0 = \{\pi\} \quad \forall i \geq 0 : \langle p^{i+1}, \pi \rangle = \langle p \cdot p^i, \pi \rangle \rightarrow \Pi_{i+1}}{\langle p^*, \pi \rangle \rightarrow \cup_{i \geq 0} \Pi_i} \text{[Kleene star]}$$

A pair of the form $\langle p, \Pi \rangle$ represents a configuration from which it remains to execute by applying policy p to state Π. The execution may terminate in a final state, or may diverge and never yield a final state, because the rule for p^* potentially requires infinite computations. However, in practical applications, we often specify p in such a way that after finitely many iterations, the set Π_i will stabilize to be empty, thus we can terminate the computation when a sufficiently large bound is reached. We will see in Sect. 6 a concrete example where the length of the selected path between two nodes in a network actually gives a bound for the number of iterations.

The operational semantics immediately induces an equivalence on policies.

Definition 1. *Two policies are* operationally equivalent, *written $p \sim q$, if*

$$\forall \Pi, \Pi' \in S : \langle p, \Pi \rangle \rightarrow \Pi' \Leftrightarrow \langle q, \Pi \rangle \rightarrow \Pi'.$$

If two policies p and q are provably equal by using the axioms in Table 2, then they are operationally equivalent.

Theorem 2 (Completeness). *If $\vdash p \equiv q$ then $p \sim q$.*

Proof. Let us first define a denotational semantics as follows.

$$\llbracket p \rrbracket \in \Pi \to \mathcal{P}(\Pi) \qquad\qquad \llbracket \neg a \rrbracket \pi := \{\pi\} \backslash (\llbracket a \rrbracket \pi)$$
$$\llbracket 1 \rrbracket \pi := \{\pi\} \qquad\qquad \llbracket f \leftarrow n \rrbracket \pi := \{\pi[n/f]\}$$
$$\llbracket 0 \rrbracket \pi := \emptyset \qquad\qquad \llbracket p + q \rrbracket \pi := \llbracket p \rrbracket \pi \cup \llbracket q \rrbracket \pi$$
$$\llbracket p \cdot q \rrbracket \pi := (\llbracket p \rrbracket \bullet \llbracket q \rrbracket) \pi \qquad\qquad \llbracket p^* \rrbracket \pi := \bigcup_{i \in \mathbb{N}} F^i \pi$$
$$\llbracket f = n \rrbracket \pi := \begin{cases} \{\pi\} & \text{if } \pi.f = n \\ \emptyset & \text{otherwise} \end{cases},$$

where $F^0 \pi := \{\pi\}$ and $F^{i+1} \pi := (\llbracket p \rrbracket \bullet F^i) \pi$, and $\bullet$ is the Kleisli composition of functions of type $\Pi \to \mathcal{P}(\Pi)$ defined as:

$$(f \bullet g)(x) := \bigcup \{g(y) \mid y \in f(x)\}.$$

This is essentially the standard packet-history semantics for NetKAT [3] without the dup operator. In the absence of this operator, only the current packet is recorded and all its history is forgotten. By the soundness of the packet-history semantics, we know that

$$\text{if } \vdash p \equiv q \text{ then } \llbracket p \rrbracket = \llbracket q \rrbracket. \tag{1}$$

By a simple induction on the structure of policies, it is not difficult to show that $\llbracket p \rrbracket \pi = \Pi$ iff $\langle p, \pi \rangle \to \Pi$. It follows that

$$\llbracket p \rrbracket = \llbracket q \rrbracket \text{ iff } p \sim q. \tag{2}$$

Combining (1) and (2), we obtain that $\vdash p \equiv q$ implies $p \sim q$. $\qquad\square$

The inverse of the above theorem also holds, and the rest of this section is devoted to proving it. Inspired by [3] we first introduce a notion of reduced NetKAT in order to define normal forms of policies.

Let $f_1, ..., f_k$ be a list of all fields of a packet in some fixed order. For each tuple $\bar{n} = n_1, ..., n_k$ of values, let $\bar{f} = \bar{n}$ and $\bar{f} \leftarrow \bar{n}$ denote the expressions

$$f_1 = n_1 \cdot ... \cdot f_k = n_k \qquad\qquad f_1 \leftarrow n_1 \cdot ... \cdot f_k \leftarrow n_k,$$

respectively. The former is a predicate called an *atom* and the latter a policy called a *complete assignment*. The atoms and the complete assignments are in one-to-one correspondence according to the values $\bar{n}$. If α is an atom, we denote by σ_α the corresponding complete assignment, and if σ is a complete assignment, we denote by α_σ the corresponding atom. We write At and P for the sets of atoms and complete assignments, respectively. Note that all matches can be replaced by atoms and all modifications by complete assignments. Hence, any NetKAT policy may be viewed as a regular expression over the alphabet $At \cup P$.

Definition 3. *A policy is in* normal form *if it is in the form* $\sum_{i \in I} \alpha_i \cdot \sigma_i$, *where I is a finite set, $\alpha_i \in At$ and $\sigma_i \in P$. It degenerates into 0 if I is empty. A policy p is* normalizable *if $\vdash p \equiv p'$ for some p' in normal form. A normal form p is* uniform *if all the summands have the same atom α, that is $p = \sum_{i \in I} \alpha \cdot \sigma_i$.*

Lemma 4. *Every policy is normalizable.*

Proof. Similar to the normalization proof in [3]. The most difficult case is Kleene star. In order to obtain the normal form of p^*, we first need to consider the case that p is a uniform normal form, based on which we consider the general form and make use of an important KAT theorem called `KAT-Denesting` in [10]:

$$(p + q)^* \equiv p^* \cdot (q \cdot p^*)^*. \qquad \square$$

Theorem 5 (Soundness). *If $p \sim q$ then $\vdash p \equiv q$.*

Proof. By Lemma 4, we know that there are normal forms $\hat{p}$ and $\hat{q}$ such that $\vdash p \equiv \hat{p}$ and $\vdash q \equiv \hat{q}$. By completeness we have $p \sim \hat{p}$ and $q \sim \hat{q}$, which implies $\hat{p} \sim \hat{q}$ by transitivity. Let $\hat{p} = \sum_{i \in I} \alpha_i \cdot \sigma_i$ and $\hat{q} = \sum_{j \in J} \beta_j \cdot \rho_j$. Note that for each atom α there is a unique packet that satisfies it (if α is $\bar{f} = \bar{n}$, then the packet has fields $f_i = n_i$ for each $1 \le i \le k$). Let us denote this packet by π_α. The behaviour of any summand $\alpha_i \cdot \sigma_i$ is to block all packets that do not satisfy α_i and transform the packet π_{α_i} into $\pi_{\alpha_{\sigma_i}}$. In view of `KA-Plus-Idem`, we may assume that no two summands in $\hat{p}$ are the same; similarly for $\hat{q}$.

Below we infer from

$$\sum_{i \in I} \alpha_i \cdot \sigma_i \ \sim \ \sum_{j \in J} \beta_j \cdot \rho_j \tag{3}$$

that I is in one-to-one correspondence with J and

$$\forall i \in I, \exists j \in J : \ \alpha_i \cdot \sigma_i = \beta_j \cdot \rho_j. \tag{4}$$

To see this, take any packet π. By the operational semantics of NetKAT, we know that

$$\langle \sum_{i \in I} \alpha_i \cdot \sigma_i, \ \pi \rangle \to \bigcup_{i \in I} \Pi_i,$$

where $\Pi_i = \{\pi_{\alpha_{\sigma_i}}\}$ if $\pi = \pi_{\alpha_i}$, and $\emptyset$ otherwise. Similarly,

$$\langle \sum_{j \in J} \beta_j \cdot \rho_j, \ \pi \rangle \to \bigcup_{j \in J} \Pi'_j,$$

where $\Pi'_j = \{\pi_{\alpha_{\rho_j}}\}$ if $\pi = \pi_{\beta_j}$, and $\emptyset$ otherwise. We know from (3) that

$$\bigcup_{i \in I} \Pi_i = \bigcup_{j \in J} \Pi'_j. \tag{5}$$

If indeed $\pi = \pi_{\alpha_k}$ for some $k \in I$, we let $[k]_1$ be the set $\{i \in I \mid \alpha_k = \alpha_i\}$ and $[k]_2$ be the set $\{j \in J \mid \alpha_k = \beta_j\}$. We have that

$$\bigcup_{i \in I} \Pi_i = \bigcup_{i \in [k]_1} \Pi_i = \bigcup_{i \in [k]_1} \{\pi_{\alpha_{\sigma_i}}\}$$
$$\bigcup_{j \in J} \Pi'_i = \bigcup_{j \in [k]_2} \Pi'_i = \bigcup_{j \in [k]_2} \{\pi_{\alpha_{\rho_j}}\}.$$

Combining them with (5), we obtain that

$$\bigcup_{i\in[k]_1} \{\pi_{\alpha_{\sigma_i}}\} = \bigcup_{j\in[k]_2} \{\pi_{\alpha_{\rho_j}}\}.$$

Note that the elements in the left union are pair-wise different and similarly for the elements in the right union. Therefore, $[k]_1$ is in one-to-one correspondence with $[k]_2$, that is, for each $i \in [k]_1$ there is a unique $j \in [k]_2$ such that $\pi_{\alpha_{\sigma_i}} = \pi_{\alpha_{\rho_j}}$. Observe that $\{[k]_1 \mid k \in I\}$ is actually a partition of I, and so is $\{[k]_2 \mid k \in I\}$ for J (there is no $j \in J$ with $\beta_j \neq \alpha_i$ for all $i \in I$, otherwise the packet π_{β_j} would be blocked by $\hat{p}$ but not by $\hat{q}$). This means that I is in one-to-one correspondence with J and for each $i \in I$ there is a corresponding $j \in J$ with $\alpha_i = \beta_j$ and $\pi_{\alpha_{\sigma_i}} = \pi_{\alpha_{\rho_j}}$. Note that the only complete assignment (a string in P) that produces $\pi_{\alpha_{\sigma_i}}$ is σ_i. So we must have $\sigma_i = \rho_j$ and hence $\alpha_i \cdot \sigma_i = \beta_j \cdot \rho_j$. Therefore, we have completed the proof of (4).

As a consequence, we can derive $\vdash \sum_{i\in I} \alpha_i \cdot \sigma_i \equiv \sum_{j\in J} \beta_j \cdot \rho_j$ by using KA-Plus-Comm, and hence $\vdash p \equiv q$ by transitivity.   □

The proof of Lemma 4 is largely influenced by [3]. However, due to the absence of the dup operator, our proof of Theorem 5 is much simpler and more elementary than its counterpart [3, Theorem 2]; the latter is based on a reduction to the completeness of Kleene algebra, which is not needed any more in our proof.

4   Formalization of NetKAT in Maude

4.1   Maude in a Nutshell

Maude is a state-of-the-art algebraic specification language and an efficient rewrite engine [5], which can be used to formally define semantics of programming languages. One main feature of Maude is that formal definitions in Maude are executable [13], which allows us to *execute* programs with the defined semantics and perform formal analysis for the programs.

Maude specifies both equational theories and rewrite theories. An equational theory is a pair $(\Sigma, E \cup A)$, where Σ is a signature specifying the sorts and operators, E is a set of equations, and A is a set of equational attributes. An equation is an unoriented pair of two terms t_1, t_2 of the same sort. In Maude, it is defined in the form of (eq t_1 = t_2.). An equation can be conditional, and it is defined in the form of (ceq t_1 = t_2 if c.), where c can be an ordinary equation $t = t'$, a matching equation $t := t'$, or a conjunction of such equations. A matching equation, e.g., $t := t'$, is mathematically treated as an ordinary equation, but operationally t is matched against the canonical form of t' and the new variables in t are instantiated by the matching. Although an equation is unoriented mathematically, they are used only from left to right by Maude for computation. Equations must be guaranteed terminating and confluent when they are used as simplification rules. Intuitively, terminating means that there must not exist an infinite sequence of applying these equations, and confluence means that the final result after applying these equations must be unique.

A rewrite theory $\mathcal{R} = (\Sigma, E \cup A, R)$ consists of an underlying equational theory $(\Sigma, E \cup A)$ and a set of (possibly conditional) rewrite rules R. A rewrite rule is an oriented pair (from left to right), which is defined in the form of (rl t_1 => t_2.) for the case of unconditional rules or (crl t_1 => t_2 if c'.) for the case of conditional rules, where c' is a more general condition than that in conditional equations by allowing rewrite condition in the form of t => t'. A rewrite condition t => t' holds if and only if there exists a finite rewrite sequence from t to t' by applying the rewrite rules in R. Computationally, both equations and rewrite rules are used from left to right to *rewrite* target terms. Mathematically, equations are interpreted as the definition of functions, while rewrite rules are interpreted as transitions or inference rules. Unlike equations, rewrite rules are not necessarily terminating and confluent.

Rewrite theories can be used to naturally specify transition systems or logical frameworks. The underlying equational theory is used to specify the statics of systems such as data types, state structures, and R specifies the dynamics, i.e., the transitions among states. System states are specified as elements of an algebraic data type, namely, the initial algebra of the equational theory (Σ, E). In Σ state constructors are declared to build up distributed states out of simpler state components. The equations in E specify the algebraic identities that such distributed states enjoy. The rewrite rules in R specify the local concurrent transitions of transition systems.

4.2   Formalization of the Operational Semantics of NetKAT

Before formalizing the operational semantics of NetKAT, we need first formalize the basic concepts such as fields, packets, policies and configuration in NetKAT. Maude allows for user-defined data types. We explain the definition of some important data types such as `Field`, `Packet`, `Policy` and `Configuration`.

```
1 sorts    FieldId , Field , Policy , Predicate , Configuration .
2 subsort Field < Packet .
3 ops src typ dst vlan ip−src ip−dst tcp−src tcp−dst udp−src
      udp−dst sw pt : −> FieldId [ ctor ]  .
4 op ( _:_ )    : FieldId Int    −> Field   [ ctor ]  .
5 op nil        :                −> Packet  [ ctor ]  .
6 op __         : Packet Packet −> Packet  [ assoc ctor id: nil ]  .
7 op _←_        : FieldId Int   −> Policy  [ ctor ]  .
8 op _+_        : Policy Policy −> Policy  [ ctor assoc comm]  .
9 op _·_        : Policy Policy −> Policy  [ ctor assoc]  .
10 op _*        : Policy        −> Policy  [ ctor ]  .
11 ops 1 o      :               −> Predicate [ ctor ]  .
12 op _=_       : FieldId Int   −> Predicate [ ctor ]  .
13 op _+_ : Predicate Predicate −> Predicate [ ctor assoc comm].
14 op _#_ : Predicate Predicate −> Predicate [ ctor assoc comm].
15 op ~_  : Predicate           −> Predicate [ ctor ]  .
16 op <_,_>  : Policy PackSet   −> Configuration .
```

The Maude keyword **sorts** is used to declare sorts to represent sets of data elements, and **subsort** declares a partial order relation of two sorts. By declaring that **Field** is a subsort of **Packet**, it formalizes the fact that a field is also regarded as a packet, but not vice versa. Keyword **op** (resp. **ops**) is used to declare an operator (resp. multiple operators). Maude allows infix operators, in which the underbars indicate the place where arguments should be located. Operator (_:_) is used to construct fields with field identifiers and integer numbers. Operator **nil** is called a constant because it does not take any arguments, and it represents an empty packet. The union of two packets constitute a new one, as formalized by the operator _ _. The operators declared for policies and predicates have clear correspondence to the syntax defined in Table 1, and thus we omit more detailed explanations about them. It is worth mentioning that **ctor**, **assoc** and **comm** are attributions of operators, declaring that an operator is a constructor, associative and commutative, respectively. We use o to represent *Drop* and 1 for *Identity*. We declare a new operator # instead of · to represent conjunction of predicates because · is used for sequential composition of policies and is not commutative, while conjunction of predicates is commutative.

We declare a sort **Configration** to represent the sets of the pairs of the form $\langle p, \Pi \rangle$. An element of sort **Configuration** is called a *configuration*, written in the form of <p,PI> with a policy p and a set PI of packets.

The operational semantics of NetKAT is formalized by the transformation of a configuration into another. As defined in Table 3, the *execution* of a policy $p \cdot q$ can be viewed as a sequential execution of p and q. We define the following set of rewrite rules with each formalizing one case for the structure of p.

```
1  rl   [o]     : < o, PI > => < 1, empty > .
2  rl   [MAT]   : < (F = N) · P, PI > => < P, filter(PI,F,N)> .
3  crl  [NEG]   : < (˜ Q) · P, PI > => < P, PI \ PI' >
4          if < Q, PI > => < 1, PI' > .
5  rl   [ASG]   : < (F ← N) · P, PI > => < P, update(PI,F,N)> .
6  crl  [COM]   : < (P + Q) · R, PI > => < R, (PI1, PI2) >
7          if < P, PI > => < 1, PI1 > /\ < Q, PI > => < 1, PI2 > .
8  rl   [KLE-0] : < (P *) · R, PI > => < R, PI >
9  rl   [KLE-1] : < (P *) · R, PI > => < P · R, PI1 > .
10 rl   [KLE-n] : < (P *) · R, PI > => < P · (P *) · R, PI > .
```

The first rule specifies the semantics of *Drop*, i.e., 0 in NetKAT. The rule in Line 2 formalizes the operational semantics of *match*. In the rule, F, N, P and PI are Maude variables of sort **Field**, **Nat**, **Policy** and **PackSet**. These variables are universally quantified. Thus, (F = N) represents an arbitrary match, P an arbitrary policy, and PI an arbitrary set of packets. After the execution of (F = N), those packets whose value of the field F is not N are removed from PI. The rule in Line 3 formalizes the case of negation. It is worth mentioning that the condition in the rule is a *rewrite condition*, meaning that the rule takes place if there is a transition from <Q, PI> to <1, PI'>. The transition means that after executing Q on a set PI of packets, we obtain a new set PI' of packets. According to the operational semantics of negation, the packets that are in both PI' and PI must be removed from PI after ˜ Q is executed, as defined by the body of the rule. The last three rules formalize the operational semantics of Kleene star for the cases of executing policy P by zero, one or more times, respectively.

5 Automatic Reasoning for NetKAT

By the executable operational semantics we can perform various formal analysis on NetKAT policies using Maude's built-in functionalities such as simulation, state space exploration and LTL model checking.

5.1 Reachability Analysis by State Exploration

Given a policy p and a set PI of packets, one fundamental analysis is to verify if the packets in PI will eventually reach their destination. Because all the rules except for those about Kleene star are deterministic, there is one and only one result if in p there is no Kleene star. We can check the reachability problem by calculating the execution result using Maude's `rewrite` command, i.e., `rew <p, PI>`, which *simulates* the execution of the policy on PI using the rewrite rules defined for the operational semantics of NetKAT.

If there are Kleene stars in p, the results after applying p on PI may be multiple. If that is the case, it is important to verify if some desired result can be obtained by applying p to PI. It is equivalent to checking the reachability from the initial configuration <p, PI> to some desired destination <p', PI'>, where p' is the remaining policy to execute when PI' is reached after applying p to PI. The reachability verification can be achieved by Maude's state exploration function using `search` command as follows:

```
1 search [m,n] < p, PI > =>* < p', PI' > [such that condition] .
```

In the square brackets are optional arguments of the command, where m and n are natural numbers specifying the expected number of solutions and the maximal rewriting steps, and *condition* is a Boolean term specifying the condition that target configurations must satisfy.

5.2 Model Checking of LTL Properties of NetKAT

Using Maude LTL model checker, we can verify not only the reachability of packets with respect to a policy, but also some temporal properties that the policy needs to satisfy. Temporal properties of a policy are used to describe the behavior that the policy should have when packets are transmitted in the network. By model checking the temporal properties, we study the process of packet transmission as well as the transmission result.

The usage of Maude LTL model checker follows the conventional methodology for model checking, i.e., we need first define state propositions, then define LTL formulas with the state propositions and logical as well as temporal connectors, and finally do model checking with a fixed initial state and an LTL formula.

```
1 mod NETKAT-LTL-MODELCHECKING is
2   including OPERATIONAL-SEMANTICS + MODEL-CHECKER .
3   subsort Configuration < State .
4   ops hasPS hasDS : Int Int -> Prop . vars SW PR DS : Int .
5   var P : Policy . var PS : PackSet . var PK : Packet .
6   eq < P , PS > |= hasDS(SW,PR) = checkHasDS(PS,DS,PR) .
7   eq < P , PS > |= hasPS(SW,PR) = checkHasPS(PS,SW,PR) .
8   eq C:Configuration |= PP:Prop = false [owise] .
9 endm
```

As an example, we show model checking of forwarding traces of packets in
Maude. In the above Maude module two state propositions hasDS and hasPS
are defined. Given a packet PR, a switch DS and a configuration <p,PS>, hasDS
returns true if there is a packet PR in PS whose destination is DS. The other one
i.e., hasPS, returns true if there is a packet PR at SW in PS. They are defined by
two equations at Lines 6 and 7, where two auxiliary predicates are needed. We
omit the detailed definition of the two predicates due to space limitation.

With predefined state propositions we can define and model check LTL properties that are composed by the propositions and LTL operators. For instance,
the first command below is used to model check whether a packet X whose destination is switch Y eventually reaches the switch Y with respect to policy p.

```
1 red modelCheck(< p, PI >, [](hasDS(X,Y) -> <> hasPS(X,Y))) .
2 red modelCheck(< p, PI >, [](hasPS(X,Y1)/\hasDS(X,Y2) -> <>
    hasPS(X,Y2))) .
```

The second command above is used to verify the property that wherever a
packet X is, e.g., Y1, it must be eventually delivered to switch Y2 if its destination
is Y2. This verification is more general than the first one in that we can verify the
reachability of two arbitrary switches in a topology w.r.t. to a forwarding policy.

5.3   Equivalence Proving by Normalization

By Theorem 5 we can verify the equivalence of two policies p, q by reducing them
to their normal forms and checking if they are syntactically equal. To automate
the process, we formalize the normalization of policies based on the proof of
Lemma 4 in Maude.

We declare a function **norm** which takes two arguments, i.e., a policy in
NetKAT and a set of field information, and returns the normal form of the
policy. Part of the declaration and the definition of **norm** is listed as follows:

```
1 op   norm : Policy FieldRangeSet -> NormalForm .
2 ceq norm(F = N, FS) = (if PS =/= empty then normPred(F = N ·
    PS) else normPred(F = N) fi) if PS := com(rm(FS,F)) .
3 eq   norm(~(F = N), FS) = normPred((~(F = N)) · com(FS)) .
4 eq   norm(F <- N, FS) = normPoli(com(FS),(F <- N)) .
5 eq   norm(PL1 + PL2, FS) = norm(PL1, FS) + norm(PL2, FS) .
6 eq   norm(PD · PD1, FS) = product(norm(PD, FS),norm(PD1,FS)) .
7 ...
```

```
 8 ceq  norm((PL) *, FS) = normPred(com(FS)) + NF
 9       if NF := norm(PL,FS) /\ uniform(NF) .
10 ceq  norm((PL) *, FS) = product(NF2, normPred(com(FS)) + NF3)
11       if NF := norm(PL,FS) /\ not uniform(NF) /\
12          (AT,PL1)+NF1 := NF /\ NF2 := norm( nf2pol(NF1)*,FS) /\
13          NF3 := product((AT,PL1),NF2) .
```

We take the formalization of the normalization of match and Kleene star for examples. The equation in Line 2 formalizes the normalization of match F = N with respect to a set FS of field information. In the equation, com is a function which takes a set of field information such as $\{(f_1, m_1), (f_2, m_2), \ldots, (f_k, m_k)\}$ with each $m_i \in \mathbb{N}$ ($1 \leq i \leq k$), and returns a predicate

$$\sum_{x_1 \leq m_1, x_2 \leq m_2, \ldots, x_n \leq m_n} (f_1 = x_1) \cdot (f_2 = x_2) \cdot \ldots \cdot (f_k = x_k). \tag{6}$$

Each summand of the predicate and the match forms an atom α. The customized function normPred returns a parallel composition of all $\alpha \cdot \sigma_\alpha$.

The last two equations define the normalization of the Kleene star of a policy, e.g., PL *, where PL is a policy. The equation in Line 9 defines the case where the normal form of PL is uniform. The last equation recursively defines the non-uniform case. If the normal form NF of the policy PL is not uniform, it can be rewritten in the form of (AT, PL1) + NF1 where AT is an atom, PL1 is the complete assignment of AT, and (AT, PL1) is a Maude representation of $AT \cdot PL1$. We then compute the normal form of NF1 and denote it by NF2. Using KAT-Denesting we obtain the normal form of PL, as defined by the right-hand term in the body of the equation. The equation formalizes the normalization of Kleene star when the summands in PL are not uniform, as described in the proof of Lemma 4.

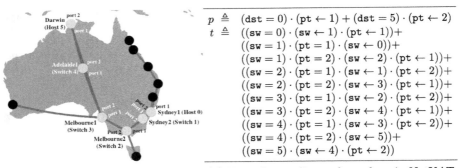

$$p \triangleq (\texttt{dst} = 0) \cdot (\texttt{pt} \leftarrow 1) + (\texttt{dst} = 5) \cdot (\texttt{pt} \leftarrow 2)$$
$$t \triangleq ((\texttt{sw} = 0) \cdot (\texttt{sw} \leftarrow 1) \cdot (\texttt{pt} \leftarrow 1))+$$
$$((\texttt{sw} = 1) \cdot (\texttt{pt} = 1) \cdot (\texttt{sw} \leftarrow 0))+$$
$$((\texttt{sw} = 1) \cdot (\texttt{pt} = 2) \cdot (\texttt{sw} \leftarrow 2) \cdot (\texttt{pt} \leftarrow 1))+$$
$$((\texttt{sw} = 2) \cdot (\texttt{pt} = 1) \cdot (\texttt{sw} \leftarrow 1) \cdot (\texttt{pt} \leftarrow 2))+$$
$$((\texttt{sw} = 2) \cdot (\texttt{pt} = 2) \cdot (\texttt{sw} \leftarrow 3) \cdot (\texttt{pt} \leftarrow 1))+$$
$$((\texttt{sw} = 3) \cdot (\texttt{pt} = 1) \cdot (\texttt{sw} \leftarrow 2) \cdot (\texttt{pt} \leftarrow 2))+$$
$$((\texttt{sw} = 3) \cdot (\texttt{pt} = 2) \cdot (\texttt{sw} \leftarrow 4) \cdot (\texttt{pt} \leftarrow 1))+$$
$$((\texttt{sw} = 4) \cdot (\texttt{pt} = 1) \cdot (\texttt{sw} \leftarrow 3) \cdot (\texttt{pt} \leftarrow 2))+$$
$$((\texttt{sw} = 4) \cdot (\texttt{pt} = 2) \cdot (\texttt{sw} \leftarrow 5))+$$
$$((\texttt{sw} = 5) \cdot (\texttt{sw} \leftarrow 4) \cdot (\texttt{pt} \leftarrow 2))$$

(a) The graphical network topology   (b) Forwading policy and topology in NetKAT

Fig. 1. An example of Australia network named aarnet

6   Experiments and Evaluation

In this section, we evaluate the proposed approach by formally verifying the reachability of nodes in the network topologies defined in the website named Internet Topology Zoo [1].

As a concrete example, we consider the network topology highlighting the connection between Sydney and Darwin which is depicted in Fig. 1(a). There is a path between Sydney1 and Darwin. It is marked by yellow nodes in the network. The path can be formalized as t that specifies all the bi-directional links along the path. We declare a forwarding policy p for the switches in that path, which are defined in NetKAT as shown in Fig. 1(b).

The following **search** command verifies the reachability between Sydney1 and Darwin:

```
1 search [1] < (p·t)*, | (dst : 5) (sw : 0) (pt : X:Nat) > =>!
2             < 1 | (dst : 5) (sw : 5) (pt : Y:Nat) > .
```

Maude returns one solution with Y being instantiated to be 2. It means that there indeed exists a path, along which packets can reach node 5 from port 2 of node 0 after applying the policy $(p \cdot t)^*$.

Searching only shows the reachability of two nodes but cannot guarantee a packet sent from node 0 must eventually reach node 5 based on the result. Such property can be verified by Maude LTL model checking as explained in Sect. 5.2. The following command is used to verify the property.

```
1 red modelCheck(< (p·t)*, (dst : 5)(sw : 0)(pk : 1) >,
2       [](hasPS(1,0) /\ hasDS(1,5) -> <> hasPS(1,5))) .
```

Maude returns true with the above command, which means that if there is a packet in Host 0 (Sydney1) with destination being Host 5 (Darwin), the packet must eventually reach Darwin.

Another alternative of verifying the reachability between two nodes in a network is to prove the equivalence of a specification and an implementation by normalization, as explained in Sect. 5.3. In this example, we define a specification policy s which only specifies the effect, but ignores the concrete implementation. For instance, the first summand specifies that all the packets sent from node 0 to node 5 must arrive node 5. The policy i formalizes the implementation of sending/receiving packets along the path described by t between nodes 0 and 5.

$$s \triangleq ((\mathtt{sw} = 0) \cdot (\mathtt{dst} = 5) \cdot (\mathtt{sw} \leftarrow 5) \cdot (\mathtt{pt} \leftarrow 2))$$
$$+ ((\mathtt{sw} = 5) \cdot (\mathtt{dst} = 0) \cdot (\mathtt{sw} \leftarrow 0) \cdot (\mathtt{pt} \leftarrow 1)) \qquad \text{(SPECIFICATION)}$$
$$i \triangleq ((\mathtt{sw} = 0) \cdot (\mathtt{dst} = 5)) \cdot ((p \cdot t)^*) \cdot ((\mathtt{sw} = 5) \cdot (\mathtt{pt} = 2))$$
$$+ ((\mathtt{sw} = 5) \cdot (\mathtt{dst} = 0)) \cdot ((p \cdot t)^*) \cdot ((\mathtt{sw} = 0) \cdot (\mathtt{pt} = 1)) \quad \text{(IMPLEMENTATION)}$$

We prove that the specification and the implementation are equal by checking their normal forms are the same with the following command:

```
1 red norm(i,(sw,5)(pt,2)(dst,5))==norm(s,(sw,5)(pt,2)(dst,5)) .
```

Maude returns true, meaning that the specification and the implementation are operationally equivalent. Therefore, packets can be routed from node 0 to node 5, and vice versa.

Table 4. Reachability verification of the network topologies in Internet Topology Zoo using searching, model checking and normalization

Network name	Nodes	By searching		By model checking		By normalization	
		Result	Time	Result	Time	Result	Time
Aarnet	3	✓	1 ms	✓	0 ms	✓	2.12 min
Bellsouth	4	✓	0 ms	✓	1 ms	✓	9.53 min
Bellsouth	5	✓	0 ms	✓	1 ms	✓	38.47 min
Aarnet	6	✓	4 ms	✓	2 ms	✓	1.92 h
Aarnet	7	✓	6 ms	✓	3 ms	✓	5.84 h
Aarnet	8	✓	5 ms	✓	3 ms	✓	10.52 h
Aarnet	9	✓	8 ms	✓	3 ms	✓	21.89 h
Aarnet	10	✓	8 ms	✓	3 ms	✓	23.13 h

We verify the reachability property of eight network topologies in Internet Topology Zoo. For each we use three different approaches i.e., searching, model checking, and normalization, as we explained above. Table 4 shows the verification results. All the experiments are conducted on a desktop running Ubuntu 15.10 with an Intel(R) Core(TM) i5-4590 @ 3.30 GHz CPU and 2.00 GB memory. The data shows that as far as reachability properties are concerned, it is faster to search a desired path by executing the operational semantics than to check the equivalence of two policies by normalization. The inefficiency of normalization can be explained as follows. As we can see from (6), to obtain the normal form of a policy we need to do the Cartesian product of terms. When the number of nodes in a network increases, the size of the normal form of the term that describes the network topology will grow exponentially. Maude expands terms according to our definition of normal form without any optimization, which makes normalization a very time-consuming process. However, equivalence checking can be used for verifying other network properties such as loop-freedom and translation validation [8]. It also shows that model checking has a better performance than searching with the increment of node numbers.

7   Concluding Remarks

We have proposed an operational semantics for NetKAT and shown that it is sound and complete with respect to the axiomatic semantics given by Anderson et al. in their seminal paper. We have also formalized the operational semantics and the equational theory of NetKAT in Maude, which allows us to normalize

NetKAT expressions and to check if two expressions are equivalent. In addition, we have investigated other verification techniques including searching and model checking. They constitute a formal approach of reasoning about NetKAT expressions with applications such as checking reachability properties in networks. The full Maude code is available online [2]. To our knowledge, the current work is the first to employ a rewrite engine for manipulating NetKAT expressions so as to verify network properties.

As mentioned in Sect. 1, NetKAT is proposed in [3], with its axiomatic and denotational semantics carefully defined by building upon previous work on Kleene algebra and earlier network programming languages; see the references in the aforementioned work. In order to verify network properties, it is crucial to develop highly efficient algorithms for checking the equivalence of NetKAT expressions. An attempt in this direction is the coalgebraic decision procedure proposed in [8]. It first converts two NetKAT expressions into two automata by Brzozowski derivatives, and then tests if the automata are bisimilar. On the other hand, our approach heavily relies on the rewriting of NetKAT expressions into normal forms. In terms of time efficiency, unfortunately, both the coalgebraic decision procedure in [8] and our rewriting-based approach are not satisfactory when handling large networks. Therefore, an interesting future work is to pursue faster algorithms for checking the equivalence of NetKAT expressions.

References

1. The Internet Topology Zoo Website. http://www.topology-zoo.org
2. The Maude Code. https://github.com/zhmtechie/NetKAT-Maude
3. Anderson, C.J., Foster, N., Guha, A., Jeannin, J., Kozen, D., Schlesinger, C., Walker, D.: NetKAT: semantic foundations for networks. In: Proceedings of the POPL 2014, pp. 113–126. ACM (2014)
4. Beckett, R., Greenberg, M., Walker, D.: Temporal NetKAT. In: Proceedings of the PLDI 2016, pp. 386–401. ACM (2016)
5. Clavel, M., Durán, F., Eker, S. (eds.): All About Maude - A High-Performance Logical Framework, How to Specify, Program and Verify Systems in Rewriting Logic. LNCS, vol. 4350. Springer, Heidelberg (2007)
6. Foster, N., Harrison, R., Freedman, M.J., Monsanto, C., Rexford, J., Story, A., Walker, D.: Frenetic: a network programming language. In: Proceedings of the ICFP 2011, pp. 279–291. ACM (2011)
7. Foster, N., Kozen, D., Mamouras, K., Reitblatt, M., Silva, A.: Probabilistic NetKAT. In: Thiemann, P. (ed.) ESOP 2016. LNCS, vol. 9632, pp. 282–309. Springer, Heidelberg (2016). doi:10.1007/978-3-662-49498-1_12
8. Foster, N., Kozen, D., Milano, M., Silva, A., Thompson, L.: A coalgebraic decision procedure for NetKAT. In: Proceedings of the POPL 2015, pp. 343–355. ACM (2015)
9. Guha, A., Reitblatt, M., Foster, N.: Machine-verified network controllers. In: Proceedings of the PLDI 2013, pp. 483–494. ACM (2013)
10. Kozen, D.: Kleene algebra with tests. ACM Trans. Program. Lang. Syst. **19**(3), 427–443 (1997)

11. Monsanto, C., Foster, N., Harrison, R., Walker, D.: A compiler and run-time system for network programming languages. In: Proceedings of the POPL 2012, pp. 217–230. ACM (2012)

12. Monsanto, C., Reich, J., Foster, N., Rexford, J., Walker, D.: Composing software defined networks. In: Proceedings of the NSDI 2013, pp. 1–13. USENIX Association (2013)

13. Verdejo, A., Martí-Oliet, N.: Executable structural operational semantics in Maude. J. Log. Algebr. Program. **67**(1–2), 226–293 (2006)

14. Voellmy, A., Hudak, P.: Nettle: taking the sting out of programming network routers. In: Rocha, R., Launchbury, J. (eds.) PADL 2011. LNCS, vol. 6539, pp. 235–249. Springer, Heidelberg (2011). doi:10.1007/978-3-642-18378-2_19

15. Voellmy, A., Wang, J., Yang, Y.R., Ford, B., Hudak, P.: Maple: simplifying SDN programming using algorithmic policies. In: Proceedings of the SIGCOMM 2013, pp. 87–98. ACM (2013)

Pareto Optimal Reachability Analysis for Simple Priced Timed Automata

Zhengkui Zhang[1(✉)], Brian Nielsen[1], Kim Guldstrand Larsen[1], Gilles Nies[2],
Marvin Stenger[2], and Holger Hermanns[2]

[1] Department of Computer Science, Aalborg University, Aalborg, Denmark
{zhzhang,bnielsen,kgl}@cs.aau.dk
[2] Department of Computer Science, Saarland University, Saarbrücken, Germany
{nies,s9mnsten,hermanns}@cs.uni-saarland.de

Abstract. We propose Pareto optimal reachability analysis to solve multi-objective scheduling and planing problems using real-time model checking techniques. Not only the makespan of a schedule, but also other objectives involving quantities like performance, energy, risk, cost etc., can be optimized simultaneously in balance. We develop the Pareto optimal reachability algorithm for UPPAAL to explore the state-space and compute the goal states on which all objectives will reach a Pareto optimum. After that diagnostic traces are generated from the initial state to the goal states, and Pareto optimal schedules are obtainable from those traces. We demonstrate the usefulness of this new feature by two case studies.

1 Introduction

In reactive system design, engineers face the challenge of optimizing schedules regarding a variety of quantitative objectives like the makespan of a schedule, performance, energy consumption, resource intensiveness, risk assessment etc. Because in most cases a subset of these objectives are conflicting, there may not always exist any single solution that can simultaneously optimize all objectives, but advisable trade-offs ought to be made by human decision makers. This problem is generally called *multi-objective optimization* (MOO), which has been studied extensively in the areas such as economics, operation research, game theory, and control theory. Vilfredo Pareto (1848–1923) proposed the well-known concept of *Pareto optimality* as "the state of allocating resources where it is impossible to make any one individual better off without making at least one individual worse off." A solution is called *Pareto optimal* if none of the objectives can be improved in value without degrading some of the other objective values. Without additional preference information, all Pareto optimal solutions are considered equally good.

One of the most popular formalisms to model stimuli and behaviors of real-time reactive systems is *timed automata* (TA) [1], which was introduced by Alur and Dill in 1994 for the purpose of verification. It is capable of modeling guards,

---

This work has been supported by Danish National Research Foundation – Center for Foundations of Cyber-Physical Systems, a Sino-Danish research center.

Z. Duan and L. Ong (Eds.): ICFEM 2017, LNCS 10610, pp. 481–495, 2017.
https://doi.org/10.1007/978-3-319-68690-5_29

time constraints, instantaneous actions and time elapsing in a natural way. Real-time model checkers such as UPPAAL [4] and KRONOS [11] based on the network of timed automata were developed. They have been successfully applied to solve enormous industrial verification case studies including but not limited to control protocols [7,20], schedulability analysis [10,13,19], etc.

Related Work. Pareto optimality concept is widely applied to solve many multi-objective scheduling problems [3,15,16]. In real-time system design, mature model checkers like UPPAAL and KRONOS have been successfully extended to do quantitative analysis. In particular, CORA aims at solving optimal scheduling and planning problems modeled by *priced timed automata* (PTA) [2,6]. PTA uses an additional observer clock to accumulate cost according to either discrete price annotations on transitions or price rates on locations. The scheduling problem boils down to a cost-optimal reachability problem. The reachability algorithm is also enhanced by *branch and bound* (B&B), which can effectively prune parts of the state-space that for sure will not to lead to an optimal solution, avoiding exploring the entire state-space. In [18] the optimal reachability analysis on the *multi-priced timed automata* (MPTA) was proved decidable. However, the model checking problem on MPTA was proven undecidable [12]. In [14], efficient algorithms for multi-objective probabilisitic model checking of a stochastic system were proposed and implemented in PRISM.

Contributions. Firstly we introduce *simple priced timed automata* (SPTA) – a priced extension of TA – to model a subset of multi-objective scheduling problems. Particularly we only allow discrete prices on transitions for multiple cost variables. There exist more general multi-priced timed automata (MPTA) which allow price rates on locations. However, data structures and reachability algorithms on MPTA are difficult to implement, because multiple cost variables with respect to price rates entail constructing high-dimensional priced zones and complex operations on priced zones. In contrast, SPTA only need a vector of integer variables to maintain different accumulated costs. Although price rate on locations are not supported, SPTA may also suffice for a number of classical scheduling cases, where the tasks' spans are pre-determined thus the energy consumption of every task can be approximated in advance, or the resources required by every task are not affected by the task's span at all. **Secondly** we provide the *Pareto optimal reachability* (POR) algorithms to compute Pareto optimal costs when reaching target goal states. Diagnostic traces are obtainable from the initial state to the goal states, and Pareto optimal schedules are obtainable from those traces. **Thirdly** we implement the semantics of SPTA and POR algorithms as a new feature in UPPAAL. **Fourthly** we demonstrate the usage of this feature using two case studies: (1) time-optimal and power-aware scheduling of a task graph; (2) power-aware scheduling of the GOMX-3 nano satellite.

Outline. The rest of the paper is organized as follows. Section 2 defines simple priced automata and Pareto optimality. Section 3 explains the Pareto optimal reachability algorithms and implementation. Section 4 gives the experiment results of two case studies. Section 5 concludes.

2   Preliminaries

This section gives the formal definitions for simple priced timed automata (SPTA), and recalls the notion of Pareto optimality.

2.1   Simple Priced Timed Automata

Let $X = \{x, y, \dots\}$ be a finite set of *clocks*. We define $\mathcal{B}(X)$ as the set of *clock constraints* over X generated by grammar: $g, g_1, g_2 :: = x \bowtie n \mid x - y \bowtie n \mid g_1 \wedge g_2$, where $x, y \in X$ are clocks, $n \in \mathbb{N}$ and $\bowtie \in \{\leq, <, =, >, \geq\}$.

Definition 1. *A* Timed Automaton (TA) [1] *is a 6-tuple* $\mathcal{A} = (L, \ell_0, X, \Sigma, E, Inv)$, *where: L is a finite set of locations; $\ell_0 \in L$ is the initial location; X is a finite set of non-negative real-valued clocks; Σ is a finite set of actions; $E \subseteq L \times \mathcal{B}(X) \times \Sigma \times 2^X \times L$ is a finite set of edges, each of which contains a source location, a guard, an action, a set of clocks to be reset and a target location; $Inv : L \to \mathcal{B}(X)$ sets an invariant for each location. For simplicity an edge $(\ell, g, a, r, \ell') \in E$ is written as $\ell \xrightarrow{g, a, r} \ell'$.*

Let $\bar{p} = [p_1, p_2, \dots, p_k]$ denote a finite vector of k prices, where $p_i \in \mathbb{N}$.

Definition 2. *A* Simple Priced Timed Automaton (SPTA) *extends TA as a 7-tuple* $\mathcal{S} = (\mathcal{A}, P)$, *where: $\mathcal{A}$ is timed automaton, $P : E \to \mathbb{N}^k$ assigns vectors of prices $\bar{p}$ to edges.*

Definition 3. *The semantics of a simple priced timed automaton $\mathcal{S}$ is a priced timed transition system $S_{\mathcal{S}} = (Q, Q_0, \Sigma, \to)$, where: $Q = \{(\ell, v) \mid (\ell, v) \in L \times \mathbb{R}_{\geq 0}^X$ and $v \models Inv(\ell)\}$ are states, $Q_0 = (\ell_0, 0)$ is the initial state, Σ is the finite set of actions, $\to \subseteq Q \times (\Sigma \cup \mathbb{R}_{\geq 0}) \times Q$ is the transition relation defined separately for action $a \in \Sigma$ and delay $d \in \mathbb{R}_{\geq 0}$ as:*

(1) $(\ell, v) \xrightarrow{a}_{\bar{p}} (\ell', v')$ if there is an edge $(\ell \xrightarrow{g, a, r} \ell') \in E$ such that $v \models g$, $v' = v[r \mapsto 0]$, $v' \models Inv(\ell')$, and $\bar{p} = P(\ell \xrightarrow{g, a, r} \ell')$ is the vector of prices for this edge;
(2) $(\ell, v) \xrightarrow{d}_{\bar{0}} (\ell, v + d)$ such that $v \models Inv(\ell)$, $v + d \models Inv(\ell)$, and $\bar{0}$ denotes the zero-price vector for delay.

Definition 4. *A* trace (or run) *ρ of $\mathcal{S}$ can be expressed in $S_{\mathcal{S}}$ as a sequence of alternative delay and action transitions starting from the initial state: $\rho = q_0 \xrightarrow{d_1}_{\bar{0}} q_0' \xrightarrow{a_1}_{\bar{p}_1} q_1 \xrightarrow{d_2}_{\bar{0}} q_1' \xrightarrow{a_2}_{\bar{p}_2} \cdots \xrightarrow{d_n}_{\bar{0}} q_{n-1}' \xrightarrow{a_n}_{\bar{p}_n} q_n \cdots$, where $a_i \in \Sigma$, $d_i \in \mathbb{R}_{\geq 0}$, q_i is state (ℓ_i, v_i), and q_i' is reached from q_i after delay d_{i+1}. State q is reachable if there exists a finite trace with the final state of q.*

Definition 5. *The* cost (or cost vector) *of a finite trace ρ is defined as the finite sum of all the prices along the trace $\mathsf{Cost}(\rho) = \Sigma_{i=1}^n \bar{p}_i$. For a given location ℓ, multi-objective scheduling on SPTA is to minimize $\mathsf{Cost}(\rho)$, where finite traces ρ end in (ℓ, v) for all possible v.*

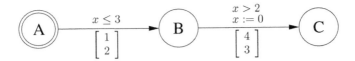

Fig. 1. An example of SPTA

An example SPTA (in Fig. 1) has a single clock x, and each transition is decorated with a vector of two prices. A sample run[1] of this SPTA is for instance:

$$(A,0) \xrightarrow{\ \epsilon(2),\ \begin{bmatrix} 0 \\ 0 \end{bmatrix}\ } (A,2) \xrightarrow{\ \tau,\ \begin{bmatrix} 1 \\ 2 \end{bmatrix}\ } (B,2) \xrightarrow{\ \epsilon(0.5),\ \begin{bmatrix} 0 \\ 0 \end{bmatrix}\ } (B,2.5) \xrightarrow{\ \tau,\ \begin{bmatrix} 4 \\ 3 \end{bmatrix}\ } (C,2.5)$$

The runtime of this trace to reach location C is 2.5 time units. The cost of this trace, which is $[5,5]^T$, is the summary of all price vectors along the transitions. It is worth noting that only discrete prices on the transitions contribute to the final cost, while prices at locations during the delay stay at $\bar{0}$ constantly and never accumulating with time elapsing.

2.2   Pareto Optimality

Multi-objective scheduling (MOS) tries to minimize a vector of costs. We resort to the concept of Pareto optimality to compute a set of Pareto optimal result cost vectors that are mutually incomparable. Then human decision makers can choose the most appropriate results that best fit and balance the problem objectives.

Definition 6. *Let* $\bar{c} = [c_1, c_2, \ldots, c_k]$, $\bar{b} = [b_1, b_2, \ldots, b_k]$ *denote two cost vectors.* $\bar{c}$ Pareto dominates $\bar{b}$ *(written as* $\bar{c} \prec \bar{b}$*), iff both the following conditions are true:*

(1) $\forall i \in \{1, \ldots, k\}\ c_i \leq b_i$;
(2) $\exists j \in \{1, \ldots, k\}\ c_j < b_j$.

Definition 7. *A result cost vector* $\bar{c}$ *is* Pareto optimal *if there does not exist another cost vector* $\bar{b}$ *such that* $\bar{b} \prec \bar{c}$. *The set of Pareto optimal results is called the* Pareto frontier.

3   Pareto Optimal Reachability

The real-time model-checker UPPAAL works by exploring a finite *symbolic reachability graph*, where the nodes are *symbolic states*. A symbolic state of TA is a pair (ℓ, Z), where $\ell \in L$ is a location, and $Z = \{v \mid v \models g_z, g_z \in \mathcal{B}(X)\}$ is a convex set of clock valuations called *zone* [17], which is normally efficiently represented and stored in memory as *difference bound matrices* (DBM) [8].

---

[1] ϵ denotes a delay at locations; τ denotes an inner transition between locations.

The symbolic state of SPTA extends that of TA as $(\ell, \langle Z, \bar{c} \rangle)$, where $\bar{c}$ is the cost (or cost vector) of a finite trace ρ that ends in (ℓ, v) and $v \in Z$. Therefore, symbolic states in SPTA with the same ℓ and Z are discriminated by $\bar{c}$. We call $\langle Z, \bar{c} \rangle$ the *discrete priced zone* of a symbolic state in SPTA. We further define Pareto dominance between discrete priced zones as: $\langle G, \bar{u} \rangle \preceq \langle Z, \bar{c} \rangle$ iff $Z \subseteq G \wedge (\bar{u} = \bar{c} \vee \bar{u} \prec \bar{c})$.

3.1   Pareto Optimum on Prices

Algorithm 1 shows the Pareto optimal reachability algorithm that computes the Pareto optimal cost vector at goal states satisfying the proposition Goal. WAIT-ING and PASSED keep unexplored and explored symbolic states respectively; and WAITING has the initial state. FRONT maintains the Pareto frontier consisting of current Pareto optimal costs at goal states. Inside procedure Main, whenever WAITING is not empty, an unexplored state is popped from WAITING in a loop. If the state is a goal state, the current cost $\bar{c}$ is passed into procedure Update to check for Pareto dominance with the existing solutions inside FRONT, and update FRONT if necessary. At line 10 all elements in FRONT that are Pareto dominated by $\bar{c}$ are discarded. At line 12 $\bar{c}$ is added into FRONT, if existing elements in FRONT do not Pareto dominate it.

If the state is not goal state, it is subject to both inclusion checking and B&B elimination at line 5, and discarded if either test satisfies. Procedure Included determines that a state is included, if a previously explored state in PASSED with the same location has its discrete priced zone dominate that of the current state (as $\langle Z', \bar{c}' \rangle \preceq \langle Z, \bar{c} \rangle$). A state is eligible for pruning in procedure Prune, if $\bar{c}$ is Pareto dominated by an element in FRONT. If the state endures the two tests at line 5, it is added to PASSED as already explored, and then its successor states are generated and added to WAITING. For simplicity we denote the action and delay transitions between symbolic states uniformly as $\rightsquigarrow$.

Let TS be the zone-based transition system of SPTA with V symbolic states and E transitions. Let n be the number of clocks and k be the number of price variables. The time complexity of Algorithm 1 is in $\mathcal{O}((V + E) \cdot (n^3 + k + k^2))$, where the first factor is the complexity for state-space exploration, the second factor is the complexity for Pareto inclusion checking as well as pruning.

3.2   Implementation Issues

Algorithm 1 resembles the normal reachability algorithm [8] for TA. The implementation extensions into existing UPPAAL are four folded as follows.

1. The symbolic state of SPTA is a pair of location and discrete prized zone as $(\ell, \langle Z, \bar{c} \rangle)$. A UPPAAL model may contain both cost variables (associated with $\bar{c}$) and normal variables (nothing to do with $\bar{c}$). Therefore UPPAAL should be able to identify cost variables automatically by analyzing pareto objectives in the query, because only cost variables will contribute to the objectives.

Algorithm 1. Pareto Optimal Reachability

WAITING $\longleftarrow \{(\ell_0, \langle Z_0, \bar{0} \rangle)\}$, PASSED $\longleftarrow \emptyset$, FRONT $\longleftarrow \emptyset$

Procedure Main()

1   **while** WAITING $\neq \emptyset$ **do**
2   select $(\ell, \langle Z, \bar{c} \rangle)$ from WAITING
3   **if** $(\ell, \langle Z, \bar{c} \rangle) \models$ Goal **then**
4   Update$(\bar{c})$
5   **else if** $\neg$Included$((\ell, \langle Z, \bar{c} \rangle))$ *and* $\neg$Prune$(\bar{c})$ **then**
6   add $(\ell, \langle Z, \bar{c} \rangle)$ to PASSED
7   **forall** $(\ell', \langle Z', \bar{c}' \rangle)$ *such that* $(\ell, \langle Z, \bar{c} \rangle) \rightsquigarrow (\ell', \langle Z', \bar{c}' \rangle)$ **do**
8   add $(\ell', \langle Z', \bar{c}' \rangle)$ to WAITING

9   **return** FRONT

Procedure Update($\bar{c}$)

10   FRONT $\longleftarrow$ FRONT $\setminus \{\varphi \in$ FRONT $\mid \bar{c} \prec \varphi\}$
11   **if** $\forall \varphi \in$ FRONT $s.t.$ $\bar{c} \not\prec \varphi$ **then**
12   FRONT $\longleftarrow$ FRONT $\cup \{\bar{c}\}$

Procedure Included($(\ell, \langle Z, \bar{c} \rangle)$)

13   **if** $\exists (\ell, \langle Z', \bar{c}' \rangle) \in$ PASSED $s.t.$ $Z \subseteq Z' \wedge (\bar{c}' = \bar{c} \vee \bar{c}' \prec \bar{c})$ **then return** TRUE
14   **return** FALSE

Procedure Prune($\bar{c}$)

15   **if** $\exists \varphi \in$ FRONT, $\varphi \prec \bar{c}$ **then return** TRUE
16   **return** FALSE

---

2. UPPAAL should apply Pareto dominance between discrete priced zones as: $\langle G, \bar{u} \rangle \preceq \langle Z, \bar{c} \rangle$ iff $Z \subseteq G \wedge (\bar{u} = \bar{c} \vee \bar{u} \prec \bar{c})$. That is, $\langle G, \bar{u} \rangle$ dominates $\langle Z, \bar{c} \rangle$, if zone Z is included by or equal to zone G, and cost vector $\bar{u}$ is equal to or Pareto dominates cost vector $\bar{c}$. During *Pareto inclusion checking*, for every new waiting state $(\ell, \langle Z, \bar{c} \rangle)$, if $\exists (\ell, \langle G, \bar{u} \rangle) \in$ PASSED s.t. $\langle G, \bar{u} \rangle \preceq \langle Z, \bar{c} \rangle$, then $(\ell, \langle Z, \bar{c} \rangle)$ is discarded for further exploration.

3. A global container named frontier maintains the Pareto optimal cost vectors at goal states. When a goal state is reached, the current cost at goal is checked for Pareto dominance with the solutions in the frontier, and the frontier is updated if necessary. In the pruning process, a state is discarded if its cost is dominated by a solution in the frontier.

4. The algorithm only returns the frontier. In UPPAAL, multiple traces, each of which corresponding to a Pareto optimal solution inside the frontier, are also computed and stored into different files.

3.3 Pareto Optimum on Objective Functions

We propose three extensions to make Algorithm 1 more powerful and flexible: (1) support formatting multi-objectives as a vector of objective functions $F(\bar{c}) = [f_1(\bar{c}), f_2(\bar{c}), \ldots, f_n(\bar{c})]$ parameterized by the cost vector $\bar{c}$; (2) support a global clock (let us call it now) as a singular objective function to measure the makespan (accumulated delay on a finite trace); (3) support negative prices on action transitions. The first extension requires procedures Update and Prune to evaluate $F(\bar{c})$, and Front to contain Pareto optimal outcomes of $F(\bar{c})$ on goal states. We define *monotonically increasing* for $f \in F(\bar{c})$ as: $\bar{c} \prec \bar{c}' \Rightarrow f(\bar{c}) < f(\bar{c}')$. These three extensions however, are applied under specific additional conditions:

Cond 1. For extension 1, if $\exists f \in F(\bar{c})$ is not monotonically increasing, Prune must be disabled, and the Pareto check of cost vectors $\bar{c}' \prec \bar{c}$ at line 13 in Included must be skipped.

Cond 2. For extension 2, clock now must not be reset nor tested in guards or invariants.

Cond 3. For extension 3, (1) the state-space graph of the model must be acyclic; (2) if $\forall f \in F(\bar{c})$ are monotonically increasing, Prune must be disabled; (3) if $\exists f \in F(\bar{c})$ is not monotonically increasing, do as in **Cond 1**.

B&B pruning and Pareto inclusion checking are valid only if the costs and evaluation results of objective functions are monotonically increasing. Conditions 1 & 3 are of utmost importance to notice, otherwise there is a risk to have incomplete results due to discarding some intermediate states prematurely that may lead to better results on goal states. The consequence of applying these two conditions is to explore the full state-space. Because the Pareto inclusion checking decays to normal inclusion checking as in the standard reachability algorithm, and the state-space is not pruned.

We extended UPPAAL to compute Pareto optimum on prices and objective functions of SPTA. The query to enable this new feature inside the verifier follows the syntax of:

$$\text{PO } (f_1, f_2, \ldots, f_k) \; [-(\text{L1}|\text{L2})] : \text{E} <> \text{Goal},$$

where PO is the keywords for Pareto optimum, f_i ($i \in [1, k]$) are objective functions or cost variables. Next comes the optional switch: $[-\text{L1}]$ disables pruning only, or $[-\text{L2}]$ disables both pruning and Pareto inclusion checking as in **Cond 1**. Following the colon is the normal reachability query. Goal is the proposition to specify the target goal states. If an objective is to be maximized, it is equivalent to put it in negative. But this typically turns a monotonically increasing objective function into decreasing, then $[-\text{L2}]$ is necessary.

4   Experiment Results

4.1   Case Study 1: Task Graph Scheduling

A task graph consists of a number of computation tasks with precedence constraints (predecessor tasks) such that a task can start only if all its predecessor tasks have completed. In this case study (Task-Graph-16), an embedded system has 16 tasks, whose precedence constraints are within $[0, 3]$ and processing time are predictable and within the range of $[1, 66]$ clock cycles. Those jobs can be scheduled on four processors with the speeds of [1, 1, 2, 2] clock cycles per time unit and the power consumptions at busy state of [10, 10, 40, 40] micro watts per time unit. We neglect the power for processors at idle state. The objective is to synthesize a non-preemptive schedule that can minimize the time for all tasks to terminate as well as the total power consumption by four processors.

Figure 2 depicts the dependency graph of 16 tasks. These precedence constraints are coded as a dependency matrix in the UPPAAL model. Figure 3 shows the templates for task and processor. Task is scheduled if the guard "dependsDone()" approves that all its predecessor tasks are completed. Once a processor is available, the task is bound to that processor. The predefined clock cycles for this task is also passed to that processor. Then the task starts executing until it is notified for termination by signal "done[p]". Processor transforms from Free to InUse once it is scheduled to handle a task, meanwhile "CPUTime()" calculates the expected execution time D in time units from clock cycles of a task and current processor speed. After delaying at InUse for D time units, Processor moves back to Free and notifies the binding task. R_T[pid], which keeps the accumulated elapsing time at InUse for each processor and acts as cost variables, is also increased by D.

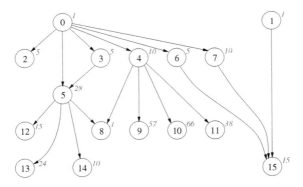

Fig. 2. Task dependency graph. Task Ids are in the center of nodes. Predicted clock cycles of tasks are in blue italic font on the top right corner of nodes. (Color figure online)

```
PO  (10*(R_T[0]+R_T[1]) +40*(R_T[2]+R_T[3]) , now)  :
E<>  forall  (i:TaskID)  Task(i).Done && now<=65
```

The original goal to minimize makespan and energy consumption is expressed as the query above. The Pareto optimality section contains two objective functions: the total energy consumption expressed as the linear combination of power and processor in-use time, and a global clock now measuring the makespan. The reachability proposition section specifies all tasks are to complete and the makespan is equal to or less than 65 time units. UPPAAL reports seven Pareto

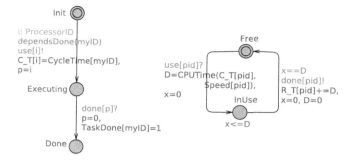

Fig. 3. Templates for Task (left) and Processor (right)

optimal outcomes as follows with the corresponding traces. Assuming we prefer the 3rd outcome (4700, 59) with the energy consumption of 4700 micro joules and makespan of 59 time units, we can parse the trace into a visualizable schedule as shown in Fig. 4.

1. (4600, 63)	3. (4700, 59)	5. (4800, 54)	7. (4560, 65)
2. (4770, 55)	4. (4850, 51)	6. (4590, 64)	

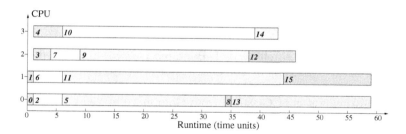

Fig. 4. Schedule for the 3rd outcome (4700, 59). Horizontal bar denotes tasks scheduled on a processor. The segments inside each bar denote individual tasks with the task ids in the front of each segment.

We experimented this model on a Ubuntu 14.04 PC with 6 GB memory and Intel Core i3 CPU at the frequency of 2.53 GHz. We made five runs for each search order: *breadth-first search* (BFS), *depth-first search* (DFS) and *random depth-first search* (RDFS). We measured the average runtime (RT) in seconds and the average maximum residence memory (RSS) in GB as in Table 1. BFS terminates the fastest, although the runtime of all three search orders are very close. The empirical explanation is that BFS is good at making large zones, while DFS/RDFS will cause higher degree of fragmentation of the underlying symbolic state-space requiring exploring more symbolic states [5].

Table 1. Runtime (sec) and memory (GB) of Task-Graph-16

	BFS	DFS	RDFS
RT	77.22	80.21	81.05
RSS	1.17	1.16	1.16

The bad news is that the UPPAAL engine cannot terminate on larger task graph with more than 16 tasks. BFS on an example task graph with 17 tasks consumed 5.22 GB memory, then the operating system started swapping, essentially blocking the exploration process. For fully exploring larger models, one may resort to parallel and distributed computing, or apply better guiding and heuristics. Sometimes the absolute optimal results may not be necessary, but near optimal results may suffice. In this case, random-depth-first search or swarm strategy may be promising options.

4.2 Case Study 2: Nano Satellite Scheduling

The GOMX-3 CubeSat is a 3 L 3 kg nano satellite commissioned by the European Space Agency (ESA). It was designed, delivered, and operated by GomSpace in Aalborg Denmark, and was launched from Japan aboard the HTV-5 cargo spacecraft on August 19th 2015. GOMX-3 was successfully deployed on October 5 2015. The satellite supports precise 3-axis rotation by gyroscopes and magnetorquers which enable the following main payloads: (1) in-flight tracking of ADS-B beacons emitted by commercial aircrafts, (2) monitoring signals from geostationary INMARSAT satellites by L-Band receiver, (3) high-speed downlinking collected data to stations in Toulouse (France) or Kourou (French Guiana) by X-Band transmitter and UHF radio module, (4) uplinking new instructions to and monitoring status of GOMX-3 from GomSpace by the UHF module.

The purposes of GOMX-3 are tracking commercial aircrafts, testing X-Band transmitters, and monitoring INMARSAT satellites. ESA and GomSpace want to maximize the amount of *jobs* (operations of payloads) without depleting the onboard battery. Power is the most critical sparse resource for a satellite in orbit. In particular when GOMX-3 passes into eclipse, the battery is the only source for it to draw power from. If battery voltage drops below 14.4 V, the satellite switches to the safe mode, where all non-essential hardware components are switched off, preventing the satellite from being productive. Since GOMX-3 follows an equatorial orbit, insolation periods and possible operation windows for different payloads are predictable over the time horizon of a few days, hence the power budget of jobs can be predicted.

In [9] a PTA model of GOMX-3 was analyzed by CORA to generate productive and power-aware schedules for GOMX-3 to carry out jobs over 20 orbits (about 31 h) around the earth. Three types of jobs were scheduled in the model: data collection by payloads (2), data downlink by payload (3), and satellite control by payload (4). The principle idea was to assign a penalty price rate R_i to each skipped job J_i ($i \in [0, 6]$). The satellite control jobs should always be scheduled whenever possible, and data downlink jobs are given the highest penalty price rate. If a job J_k is skipped, the integral of the R_k over the operation window W_k of this skipped job (equal $R_k \times W_k$) contributes to the global penalty cost (or weighted sum of skipped jobs). Then CORA searches the entire state-space and finds the cost optimal trace which has the smallest penalty cost.

In this paper we adapt the original PTA model in [9] into a SPTA model, and use Pareto optimal reachability analysis to generate schedules that optimize the productivity of payloads and energy consumption simultaneously in a natural way. Instead of using penalty price rates, we directly record the number of operated jobs for data collection, data downlink and satellite control. Not only to maximize the different kinds of operated jobs, but also the data collection and downlink jobs are important to be kept in balance. We wish the remaining battery level is high enough too.

There are six template automata in the model (detailed description in [9]). Figure 5 shows the three principle ones. (1) Provider takes care of initiating and terminating jobs on each payload repeatedly. It waits at location Idle for every predicted operation window to come, notifies Experiment to start preheating and to start actual operation after preheating is completed, then moves back to Idle. (2) Battery represents a linear battery model with capacity. It can be charged/discharged with piecewise constant energy gain from solar panels or energy drain by payloads. If the battery level is below a threshold lb which is 40% of the maximum capacity, a deadlock state is reached via the transition Check → Depletion. (3) Experiment models two possible outcomes when it is

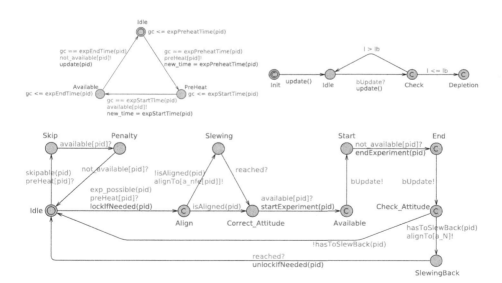

Fig. 5. Templates for Provider (top left), Battery (top right) and Experiment (bottom)

notified of a job opportunity. A job can be skipped because of low priority or resource constrains. Otherwise, the job can execute by slewing to the predefined attitude, performing actual operation and slewing back to the normal attitude. We count the number of fully executed jobs on each individual payloads as cost variables. The remaining three templates are: (4) `AttitudeControl` for slewing GOMX-3 to the predetermined attitude of each job, (5) `Sun` for switching on (off) energy harvesting from solar panels based on the predicted insolation and eclipse time, and (6) `OrbitCounter` for monitoring and counting the completed orbits of GOMX-3.

```
PO (-getAllJobs(), -getCollectJobs(), -getDownlinkJobs(), -l)
[-L2]  : E<> n==20 && l>89856000 && ac_lock==0 && lastXband
```

Our goal to maximize the number of all executed jobs, data collection and downlink jobs, and remaining battery level over 20 orbits is expressed as the query above. Functions `getAllJobs`, `getCollectJobs` and `getDownlinkJobs` count the number of executions for all jobs and data collection jobs and data downlink jobs respectively, and `l` is the battery level. They are put in negative form because we want to get their maximum values. Realizing that prices on battery level `l` are negative[2] when discharging, and the former three objective functions are monotonically decreasing, switch [−L2] is turned on (Sect. 3.3). The reachability proposition section specifies that the orbit count is to reach 20, the battery level[3] is above 55% of capacity, and two additional conditions proposed by GomSpace engineers.

```
1.  (-11, -4, -1, -124833863)     9.  (-14, -3, -5, -118593763)
2.  (-11, -3, -2, -138544388)    10.  (-14, -4, -4, -104763388)
3.  (-12, -3, -3, -133181973)    11.  (-14, -2, -6, -131801398)
4.  (-12, -4, -2, -118645643)    12.  (-15, -4, -5,  -97648603)
5.  (-12, -5, -1, -100905253)    13.  (-15, -3, -6, -110989688)
6.  (-13, -4, -3, -112367463)    14.  (-15, -2, -7, -123752127)
7.  (-13, -3, -4, -126078388)    15.  (-16, -3, -7, -102940417)
8.  (-13, -5, -2,  -96406878)
```

UPPAAL reports 15 Pareto optimal outcomes as follows with the corresponding traces. Assuming we prefer the 12th outcome (-15, -4, -5, -97648603) with 15 jobs in total, 4 data collection and 5 data downlink jobs, and remaining battery level at 97648603 milli joules. We can parse the trace and obtain the visualizable schedule as shown in Fig. 6.

We tested this model under the same experiment setting as in the 1st case study. All search orders behaved equally well as shown in Table 2.

---

[2] If negative prices are present, the state-space graph must be acyclic. This is guaranteed by the finite time horizon over 20 orbits (about 31 h).

[3] This level is larger than the threshold of 40% in the linear battery model so as to make the satellite on-board battery that is non-linear work safer in the real situation.

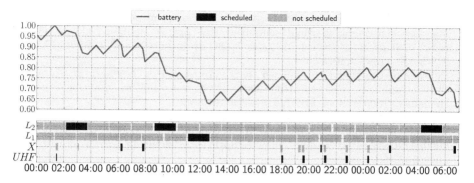

Fig. 6. Schedule for the 12th outcome (-15, -4, -5, -97648603) consisting of battery level plot (top) and payload operation plot (bottom). In the payload operation plot, L_1 and L_2 show 4 data collection jobs, X shows 5 data downlink jobs, and UHF shows 6 satellite control jobs. Data collection and downlink jobs are maximized and kept in balance.

Table 2. Runtime (sec) and memory (GB) of GomX-3

	BFS	DFS	RDFS
RT	69.23	69.17	69.73
RSS	1.18	1.18	1.18

5 Conclusions

Pareto optimality is about optimizing conflicting quantitative objectives simultaneously in balance for multi-objective optimization problems. We proposed the Pareto optimal reachability analysis to solve a subset of multi-objective scheduling and planing problems modeled by simple priced timed automata (SPTA). We developed the algorithms for UPPAAL and performed two case studies.

SPTA can only support discrete prices on transitions, not price rate on locations. So this is a start work of Pareto optimality analysis of multi-priced timed automata (MPTA) models. Future directions include: (1) support price rate on locations by construction multi-priced zones in UPPAAL; (2) develop efficient data structures for Pareto inclusion checking and pruning; (3) support larger models using parallel and distributed computing.

References

1. Alur, R., Dill, D.L.: A theory of timed automata. Theor. Comput. Sci. **126**(2), 183–235 (1994)
2. Alur, R., La Torre, S., Pappas, G.J.: Optimal paths in weighted timed automata. Theor. Comput. Sci. **318**(3), 297–322 (2004)

3. Beegom, A.S.A., Rajasree, M.S.: A particle swarm optimization based pareto optimal task scheduling in cloud computing. In: Tan, Y., Shi, Y., Coello, C.A.C. (eds.) ICSI 2014. LNCS, vol. 8795, pp. 79–86. Springer, Cham (2014). doi:10.1007/978-3-319-11897-0_10

4. Behrmann, G., David, A., Larsen, K.G.: A tutorial on UPPAAL. In: Bernardo, M., Corradini, F. (eds.) SFM-RT 2004. LNCS, vol. 3185, pp. 200–236. Springer, Heidelberg (2004). doi:10.1007/978-3-540-30080-9_7

5. Behrmann, G., Hune, T., Vaandrager, F.: Distributing timed model checking — how the search order matters. In: Emerson, E.A., Sistla, A.P. (eds.) CAV 2000. LNCS, vol. 1855, pp. 216–231. Springer, Heidelberg (2000). doi:10.1007/10722167_19

6. Behrmann, G., Larsen, K.G., Rasmussen, J.I.: Priced timed automata: algorithms and applications. In: de Boer, F.S., Bonsangue, M.M., Graf, S., de Roever, W.-P. (eds.) FMCO 2004. LNCS, vol. 3657, pp. 162–182. Springer, Heidelberg (2005). doi:10.1007/11561163_8

7. Bengtsson, J., Griffioen, W.O.D., Kristoffersen, K.J., Larsen, K.G., Larsson, F., Pettersson, P., Yi, W.: Automated verification of an audio-control protocol using UPPAAL. J. Logic Algebraic Program. **52–53**, 163–181 (2002)

8. Bengtsson, J., Yi, W.: Timed automata: semantics, algorithms and tools. In: Desel, J., Reisig, W., Rozenberg, G. (eds.) ACPN 2003. LNCS, vol. 3098, pp. 87–124. Springer, Heidelberg (2004). doi:10.1007/978-3-540-27755-2_3

9. Bisgaard, M., Gerhardt, D., Hermanns, H., Krčál, J., Nies, G., Stenger, M.: Battery-aware scheduling in low orbit: the GoMX–3 case. In: Fitzgerald, J., Heitmeyer, C., Gnesi, S., Philippou, A. (eds.) FM 2016. LNCS, vol. 9995, pp. 559–576. Springer, Cham (2016). doi:10.1007/978-3-319-48989-6_34

10. Boudjadar, A., Kim, J.H., Larsen, K.G., Nyman, U.: Compositional schedulability analysis of an avionics system using UPPAAL. In: ICAASE, CEUR Workshop Proceedings, vol. 1294, pp. 140–147. CEUR-WS.org (2014)

11. Bozga, M., Daws, C., Maler, O., Olivero, A., Tripakis, S., Yovine, S.: Kronos: a model-checking tool for real-time systems. In: CAV, pp. 546–550 (1998)

12. Brihaye, T., Bruyère, V., Raskin, J.-F.: Model-checking for weighted timed automata. In: Lakhnech, Y., Yovine, S. (eds.) FORMATS/FTRTFT -2004. LNCS, vol. 3253, pp. 277–292. Springer, Heidelberg (2004). doi:10.1007/978-3-540-30206-3_20

13. Fehnker, A.: Scheduling a steel plant with timed automata. In: RTCSA, pp. 280–286. IEEE Computer Society (1999)

14. Forejt, V., Kwiatkowska, M., Parker, D.: Pareto curves for probabilistic model checking. In: Chakraborty, S., Mukund, M. (eds.) ATVA 2012. LNCS, pp. 317–332. Springer, Heidelberg (2012). doi:10.1007/978-3-642-33386-6_25

15. Kacem, I., Hammadi, S., Borne, P.: Pareto-optimality approach for flexible job-shop scheduling problems: hybridization of evolutionary algorithms and fuzzy logic. Math. Comput. Simul. **60**(3–5), 245–276 (2002)

16. Khalesian, M., Delavar, M.R.: Wireless sensors deployment optimization using a constrained pareto-based multi-objective evolutionary approach. Eng. Appl. AI **53**, 126–139 (2016)

17. Larsen, K.G., Pettersson, P., Yi, W.: Model-checking for real-time systems. In: Reichel, H. (ed.) FCT 1995. LNCS, vol. 965, pp. 62–88. Springer, Heidelberg (1995). doi:10.1007/3-540-60249-6_41

18. Larsen, K.G., Rasmussen, J.I.: Optimal reachability for multi-priced timed automata. Theor. Comput. Sci. **390**(2–3), 197–213 (2008)

19. Mikučionis, M., Larsen, K.G., Rasmussen, J.I., Nielsen, B., Skou, A., Palm, S.U., Pedersen, J.S., Hougaard, P.: Schedulability analysis using Uppaal: Herschel-Planck case study. In: Margaria, T., Steffen, B. (eds.) ISoLA 2010. LNCS, vol. 6416, pp. 175–190. Springer, Heidelberg (2010). doi:10.1007/978-3-642-16561-0_21
20. Schuts, M., Zhu, F., Heidarian, F., Vaandrager, F.W.: Modelling clock synchronization in the chess gmac WSN protocol. QFM. EPTCS **13**, 41–54 (2009)

Author Index

Printed in the United States
By Bookmasters